1

ZHdK A Future for the Arts

Zurich University of the Arts Inaugural Publication

£10

GK

Scheidegger & Spiess

ZHdK. A Future for the Arts
Zurich University of the Arts Inaugural Publication

Editor: Hans-Peter Schwarz

Idea, concept development, editing, text/image coordination:
Urs Fanger, Peter Köppel, Janine Schiller, Hans-Peter Schwarz

Design concept:
Jonas Voegeli & Kurt Eckert
Design and typesetting: Benjamin Roffler, Vinzenz Blaas, Kurt Eckert, Jonas Voegeli

Organization chart: Martin Woodtli
Videograms: Hannes Rickli

Image research: Claudia Hürlimann, Kurt Eckert, Urs Fanger

Translation: Tradukas GbR

Lithography by: Hürlimann Medien AG
Printed by: Druckerei Odermatt
Bound by: BUBU, Buchbinderei Burkhardt AG

CD/DVD
Concept and realization:
Nicole Biermaier/Media Studio LIFT
General coordination: Janine Schiller
Music selection: Patrick Müller
Material for the DVD:
Nils Röller, Christian Hübler (New Media), Hartmut Wickert, Ursula Rey (Drama), Bernhard Lehner (Film), Oliver Matz, Steffi Schwerzer (Dance), Judith Albert, Daniel Schibli (Art/Performance), Ulrich Götz (Interaction & Game Design)

ISBN 978-3-85881-709-9

A more extensive German edition is available under the title ZHdK: *Den Künsten eine Zukunft,* also published by Verlag Scheidegger & Spiess
ISBN 978-3-85881-200-1

www.scheidegger-spiess.ch

Hans-Peter Schwarz

The Zurich School of Music, Drama and Dance and the School of Art and Design Zurich are conjoining at a time in which universities are facing unprecedented challenges. Old certainties are being questioned, while new situations demand new solutions.

University-level training in the arts is no longer regarded without question as a social necessity and therefore sacrosanct. Educational systems, resting on a foundation of fine traditions, have to be reviewed. The need for them to have a multicultural, global direction has been proclaimed ad nauseam, but it is no less imperative for all that. Confusion and uncertainty characterize the process of change at the very institution which has, like no other, dedicated itself to creative innovation. Therefore it is especially important to secure the origins, the roots, of the new kind of institution represented by the Zurich University of the Arts (ZHdK), just as it is essential to be sure of the shared vision which inspired it. In this age of fundamental changes, it is our most urgent and most noble task to lay the foundations of a new self-awareness, a new self-confidence within our shared home of the arts.

In today's academic landscape, a university of the arts with the comprehensiveness of the new institution in Zurich has become a rare thing. Most art schools insist on the divisions between their disciplines of dance, theater, music, the fine arts, film, and architecture; or they have followed the Anglo-Saxon model and, as a college, department, or school, have been swallowed by an often leviathan university apparatus.

Between these two opposites, a small number of universities of the arts still survive: for instance, the Kunsthøgscholen in Oslo, which is also Norway's national academy, and the Hochschule für Künste in Bremen, which is smaller but all the more renowned. Then there is the Bern University of the Arts, which is a department of the Bern University of Applied Sciences, and last but not least—a preferred partner of the Zurich University of the Arts—the Berlin University of the Arts (UdK). The UdK is, as far as enrolments go, more than twice the size of the Zurich University of the Arts, and its offerings even extend to architecture, which is a distant future project for Zurich, but its infrastructure and its stature as an academic institution teaching the arts, bringing together (almost) all the arts and the corresponding academic disciplines that reflect them and nurture their innovations, create an important link between it and our Zurich institution.

The founding of an academic institution for the arts is not just an administrative act. The collected essays and visual statements in this volume arose from the need to lay a theoretical foundation stone, too, for our university of the arts.

The relationship with tradition so specific to the Zurich University of the Arts is reflected, for example, in the visual main part of this book, which Urs Fanger designed in his highly subjective but very impressive way to give context to the works and artistic biographies of the teachers and graduates of the institutions which go to make up the university.[1]

1 The German-language edition of this book expands upon the specific relationship with tradition with essays on the institutional history of the branches of study which go to make up the departments of the Zurich University of the Arts: art and design (Hans-Peter Schwarz), music (Dominik Sackmann), drama (Peter Danzeisen), dance (Ursula Pellaton), and film (Thomas Schärer).

These traditions in the various artistic and academic disciplines form the foundations for the cross-disciplinary visions which will determine the future of research and teaching in the university's departments.

In the Design Department, which will particularly distinguish itself in an environment encompassing the full breadth of the arts, great care will be taken to "uncover differences, engage in communication, and provide material and non-material blueprints for the future" (Jacqueline Otten).

The Department of Cultural Analysis will develop consistent thinking "outside of the box," with the aim of becoming the university's "center of transdisciplinarity" (Christoph Weckerle).

The Music Department will increasingly turn its attention to cross-border experiments (Daniel Fueter).

In the drama program of the Department of Performing Arts, "artistic performance will no longer mean the representation of a different world, but rather the creation of a special, possibly unique, relationship between actor(s) and audience" (Hartmut Wickert).

In the dance program, training will emphasize "individuality, learning the skills of the trade, and an artistic creativity that is not arbitrary" (Oliver Matz), while in the film program, "students and lecturers are confronted with the contradictions of the film world, in which uniqueness and universality are equally required" (Bernhard Lehner); at the Department of Art & Media, the "art school without conditions" is being developed, a space of endless possibilities for creative and performative activities (Giaco Schiesser).

Above and beyond its designated task as an institute of higher education, the Zurich University of the Arts will gain importance through its production centers, its exhibitions, its museum collections, its dance and dramatic performances, its film presentations, and its series of concerts, because "in the beginning was not the word, nor even the lesson; in the beginning was the deed." (Michael Eidenbenz).

Cross-discipline research—which is what really makes the Zurich University of the Arts into an institution worthy of its position in the academic landscape mentioned above—will have to take place as "adisciplinary research," "between the arts" (Corina Caduff).

A profound and well-grounded tour of the architecture of art schools—which is a particularly good indicator of the social significance of the arts as well as reflecting the curricular concepts the institutions nurture—ends, not surprisingly, with the presentation of the real house of the arts in which the Zurich University of the Arts will set up its home at the end of the first decade of the twenty-first century (Andrea Gleiniger).

And finally, the introductory essay is meant to contribute toward "making memory more precise"—which could be the best way of giving an historical framework to the visions of the future (Hans-Peter Schwarz).

All the essays and visual interventions collected in this book show that the Zurich University of the Arts makes time and space available to a free community of teachers and learners so that they are able to study, research, and experiment within, between, and beyond the traditional academic disciplines. They show that the Zurich University of the Arts is an innovative institution par excellence, where vision is just as much at home as tradition is, a school which reflects the past, re-creates the present, and discovers the future.

For their fine work on this book, the publishers and authors would like to thank the editorial team, Peter Köppel, who edited many texts, Urs Fanger, who edited the pictures, and above all Janine Schiller, who coordinated all the elements and who took great care in putting them together. We would like to thank Jonas Voegeli and Kurt Eckert for the book's congenial design and layout—for once one would not be wrong in judging a book by its cover. And we thank Thomas Kramer and Robert Züblin of the publishers Scheidegger & Spiess for having the courage to include this book among their titles.

Horizons of Art. Against the
history, our understanding of the
the near future is explored. Art e
brings to society are at the focu
more precise. We consider comp
the total work of art to gain insi
the differences and common gro

horizon of art and cultural
arts today, in the past, and in
ucation and the benefits it
of our project to make memory
ition between the arts and
t into the history and future,
d of art education.

Hans-Peter Schwarz

> Everything continues,
> Turning from the old position
> To a new.
> Everything retains its basic behavior
> But you?
> *Gottfried Benn*

Though times have changed and despite all the divergent notions of what in this age of globalization we all now call higher education in the arts, the main issues have remained to a remarkable extent identical or similar. They are, and will continue to be, concerned with grounding; the relationship between theory and practice; what Susan Sontag has called the venerable antinomy of liberal and applied arts; the debate around inductive, deductive, and open forms of curricula; problems of research in and by the arts (which go back further than those in scientific research); efforts to professionalize training and improve the status of the arts in society; and, finally, whether a formal training in the arts is even possible.

These problems have always been solved in different ways in different places at different times, and different answers have been found to the questions. Yet the fact that they are posed over and over again proves that no linear relationship exists between tradition and innovation in the arts nor, consequently, in art education. Positions that seem to have been transcended are not obsolete per se, as most of our scientific or techno-scientific concepts of the future suggest. Ever since Johann Gottfried Herder proclaimed the basic equivalence of all cultural groups and epochs in his *Ideas for a Philosophy of the History of Mankind,* this claim has had to be defended time and again against chauvinistic champions of culture or fundamentalist modernizers. fig. 1–3

It is also necessary to defend, in this connection, the luxury commodity time. Art education institutions now have to organize themselves in a society that is still geared to ideas of work that are based on a tightly organized and rigorously apportioned time structure, one that has not changed substantially even in the postindustrial, post-Taylorist, and post-Fordist phase of reflexive modernity. Indeed, the adoption of genuinely artistic work structures in the context of the New Economy and its ideologies of creativity has led to even more rigorous time management in the world of work.

1 Johann Heiss, *Life-Drawing Class with Models,* 1687
2 Johann Jacobé, *Life-Drawing Class at the Vienna Academy,* 1790

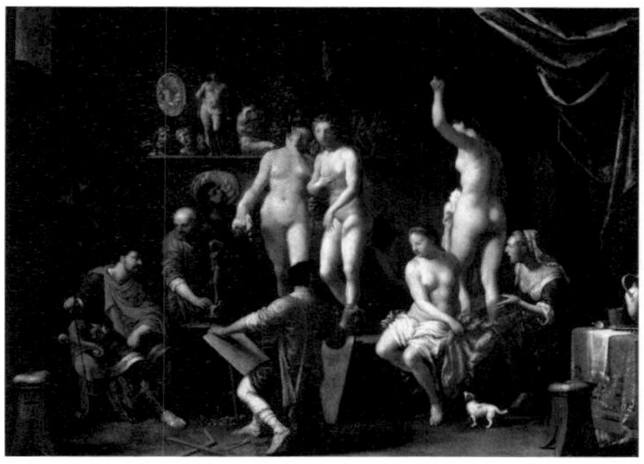

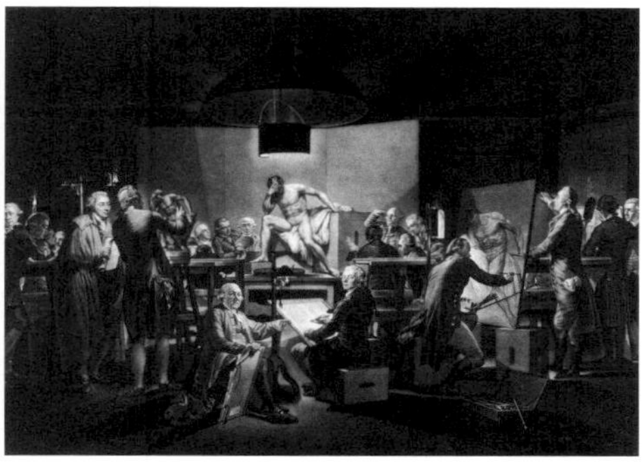

3 Life-drawing class with model at the Zurich School of Art and Design, 2003

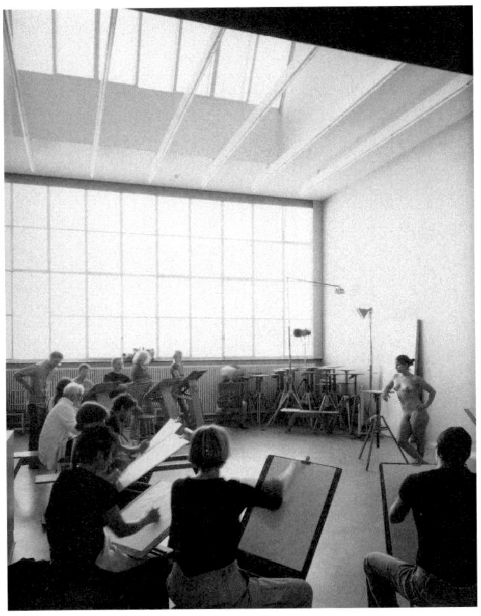

Yet the luxury commodity time is in several respects a basic component of the curriculum at a school of the arts. First, the currently fashionable concepts of art do not necessarily provide orientations to which budding artists relate, and the currently prevailing concepts of art certainly do not do so. Time, both past and present, is subject matter for artistic transformation. Second, study of the arts is not geared merely to efficient acquisition of knowledge or swift acquisition of skills. Rather, the point is to engender attitudes that cannot be learned from role models or the curriculum alone, but require independent-minded experiment. Failure is a necessary intermediate step in training for artistic professionalism, starting anew over and over and again an indispensable experience. All this requires time. Third, the time spent on producing art must not be apparent in the result. For all the layperson's admiration of the virtuosity of a musician, a dancer, or an actor, despite the star status of some artist celebrities, despite the almost cult-like reverence for some media authors, the results of their time-intensive labor must not reflect that effort, nor even allow it to show through.

In a chapter headed "Interrupting Time" of an essay setting out his thoughts on the use of (traditional) art academies, the German art historian Walter Grasskamp mentioned a fourth time paradigm: "Considering the new circumstances required by the media, art is threatened with becoming the victim of its own greatest privilege. If artists have an unusually large amount of time to work on their products, art must also require a large amount of time from the observer, whose perception, however, has begun to alter under the hectic dictates of advertising aesthetics and the challenge of new media."[1]

This comment, written shortly before the turn of the millennium, that is, in the heat of the communication society's start-up phase, may appear curiously non-synchronous or belated, and we cannot fail to hear the nostalgic undertone in the Festschrift of one of the most traditional art education institutions in the German-speaking countries. Yet Grasskamp's lament for lost time points to the central question that all arts

1 Walter Grasskamp, "Why Art Academies?" in *190 Years Academy of Fine Arts Munich,* trans. Allison Plath-Moseley (Munich, 1999), n. p.

have in common, one that the highly precarious coexistence of the arts in a college organism that is meant to include all arts, such as the Zurich University of the Arts, must take into account. What is it that allows the arts the necessary independence of spirit while still enabling them to offer joint resistance in the highly complex arena of the global communication society?

This does not mean offering resistance in the backward-looking way in which monodisciplinary academies of the diverse arts excluded innovative media concepts in their respective fields for so long, and so systematically, until the latter created their own, more successful institutions for education, research, and presentation.

The differences between traditional and technology-based arts were especially fierce and protracted in Germany. Thus not until 2007 did the standing conference of German ministers with responsibility for the arts include a film section in its program. Even in Germany, however, most schools of the arts—music, drama, and design rather more enthusiastically than visual arts institutions—have now reconciled themselves with the media arts.

Yet we are still a long way away from genuine integration, as Ute Vorkoeper points out in her 2005 study on art education in the media culture, published under the telling title *Hybride Dialoge:* "Instead of relying on reconciliation between the fields [of media art and traditional art], or of laying differences to rest by introducing new media courses or outsourcing to media colleges, the conflicts should be described and ... fought out. Amid the jungle of traditions and in view of the separating worlds of art and media art and art and design, the need is not so much to establish targeted media courses at schools of the arts as to create an enduring dialogue between art forms and disciplines. This ultimately became evident in all pilot projects."[2]

It is certainly right not simply to relinquish some of the achievements that schools of art have worked or struggled to secure during the course of their history. One achievement I have in mind is the indisputably useful social mission of being able to seek out especially gifted young people to train, in comparatively small units and with as much support and supervision as possible, as artists in both the narrower and broader sense. Colleges and universities of science and technology, in many parts of Europe at least, have included this type of elite student sponsorship in their plans only recently.

Of course, this type of selection can be unfair. It is very rarely "objective." Sometimes it proves to have been justified only at a much later date. There are good reasons for this. In modern times, at least, we have seen often enough that visual, aural, or performance innovations in the arts that contemporaries found incomprehensible or uncomfortable proved indispensable for the next generation.[3]

A further advantage of art education in general lies in the privilege that teachers as a rule do not need to have been raised within the confines of academe. Consequently they need not necessarily have had to slog along the strictly regimented path that leads to a professorship

2 Ute Vorkoeper, *Hybride Dialoge: Kunstausbildung in der Medienkultur; Rückschau auf die Modellversuche zur künstlerischen Ausbildung an Hochschulen im BLK [= Bund-Länder-Kommission]-Programm Kulturelle Bildung im Medienzeitalter* (Hamburg, 2005), available online at http://www.blk-info.de/fileadmin/BLK-Materialien/heft125.pdf.

3 See Grasskamp, "Why Art Academies?" (see note 1).

in universities, but along whose wayside delight in innovation and experimental curiosity all too often fall. Art school teachers and researchers and their works must stand the test of audiences and observers in opera houses, theaters, concert halls, galleries, or museums before they can even think of a career in teaching. The criteria for measuring the quality of artistic work and the standing of an artist have long since ceased to come from an internal "academic" system of values and norms.

Incidentally, the fact that the criteria for evaluating the quality of teachers at schools of art are mainly set extramurally does not make it any easier to objectify the required proofs of achievement the way they are in the evaluation systems of the (internal) university science community.

The controversies over recruitment procedures that flare up regularly at schools of art in particular speak a clear language in this context. After all, the arts, and even more so artists, lay a common claim to a high degree of autonomy extending beyond the Humboldtian guiding principle of freedom to teach and research.

Nonetheless, views differ over the concept of autonomy, or rather over what each means by autonomy, in general rather than in detail, and transdisciplinary discourses degenerate into monodisciplinary disputations.

This relates to the self-image of stakeholders, by which I mean both teachers and students, the structure of curricula and, in some cases, the content of research in individual fields of art.

The visual arts, especially where they define themselves by the term "liberal art," are in many cases still governed by what Beat Wyss described as "dilettante magic of shamanistic laying on of hands," H. U. Reck as curricular "botching," and Ute Vorkoeper as "tinkering, with reference to Claude Lévi-Strauss," whose exponents derive their self-image from the first phase of art that was critical of institutions in the early 1960s, or from the idea of *nullo doctore nobilis fuit,* i.e. (self-) doubt as to whether art can be taught at all. This idea runs as a kind of leitmotif through the self-justifying writings of eccentric and self-educated avant-gardes from the start of modernity to the present day. In terms of the program, the resulting marginality (only a fraction of students at art schools are enrolled on traditional visual arts courses) is related to the opposition of monomedial art to mass-media culture. Curricula are, to put it mildly, very open. Those of master classes, where they still exist, are designed in a quasi-Darwinian fashion. The self-image of media artists, who are still excluded from most traditional academies, is expressed in their preference for the term "author" as opposed to the antiquated "artist." And the fields of art that work on public and private commissions and that therefore used to be called applied arts are distinguished by very hierarchical, deductive curricula, as are courses in music and dance, at least where young people train for the concert platform or ballet company. Meanwhile, curricula in the performing arts and drama, and in film and photography, are genuinely almost transdisciplinary in design, since what Susan Sontag called the venerable antinomy between liberal and applied arts is less relevant there than in other disciplines. If in addition one considers the in part diametrically opposed relationships that image producers and music interpreters have with the tradition of their respective art, one could doubt (or despair at) the need to have, indeed the justification for having, a joint house of all the arts.

Still, the arts are unique. The people who practice those arts are unique, as are those who desire to learn them. Finally, the institutions that teach these arts to people are unique.

Every art institution must remove within itself the obstacle of uniqueness of components that genuinely tend toward the centrifugal, especially an institution that plans to bring all the arts under one roof. Making memory more precise—the motto I set at the outset—is intended to help people not to despair of this mission. I was referring to something Thomas Koebner wrote in the introduction to his book on Laocoön. Koebner surmises that "a more precise memory of past circumstances can heighten our sensitivity to present conditions" and encourages us in our attempt to find models for cross-fertilization by the arts in the past by saying that "the path to the artistic present is paved with examples where the interweaving of the arts was seen and accepted as a special challenge."[4] The Zurich University of the Arts will meet this challenge.

The Order of the Arts

Let me begin by saying that there has never been widespread consensus on what Goethe's Faust might have called "what holds the arts together in their innermost essence," or even a generally accepted system of arts (parallel to the system of sciences). Attempts to devise one, by d'Alembert (in the *Encylopédie*), Sulzer (in his *General Theory of the Fine Arts*) or in Baumgarten's *Aesthetics* immediately provoked opposition, or were even ridiculed as bizarre. True, the erudite specialist on humanism P. O. Kristeller states in his essay "The Modern System of the Arts" that a canon of five "authoritative" arts—painting, sculpture, architecture, music, and poetry—was accepted during the course of the eighteenth century. However, the only principal witness he can pin down to testify to this is d'Alembert's "Discours préliminaire" of the 1751 *Encyclopédie,* though he cites the popularity and wide distribution of the *Encyclopédie* as an argument for the normative status of this "canon."

Nonetheless, artists, art theoreticians, and philosophers have tried time and again to discern common features, hierarchies, mutual dependencies, and reciprocal dissent between individual arts. Moreover, although the arts included fluctuated greatly from system to system, we can synthesize from these attempts some common features of a visionary order of the arts along the lines Foucault aspired to in *The Order of Things.*

For many years, attempts at systematization concentrated primarily on exploring the system of *artes liberales,* the seven liberal arts, as popularized in the Middle Ages mainly through a didactic poem by Martianus Capella. In this poem Grammar, Rhetoric, and Dialectics (later known as the trivium), and Arithmetic, Geometry, Music, and

4 Thomas Koebner (ed.), *Laokoon und kein Ende: Der Wettstreit der Künste* (Munich, 1989), p. 8.

Astronomy (the quadrivium) appeared, as it were, as "bridesmaids" at the wedding of Mercury and Philologia. In our understanding of art, of these only music (albeit more in the form of musical theory) and literature (as implied by the language-oriented trivium) are liberal arts, that is, arts worthy of higher social recognition. The visual arts, insofar as they were deemed worthy of mention at all, were included in the canon of *artes mechanicae* and relegated to the socially inferior sphere of production. fig. 4

In the early twelfth century, Hugh of Saint Victor constructed a system of seven mechanical arts, presumably for the sake of symmetry. They were fabric-making, armament (including the building of walls), commerce, agriculture, hunting, medicine, and theatrics.[5] Later, painting and sculpture were added to the instruments of building. Arts and therefore artists were separated into two vastly different social spheres, into free and not free, and these categories were not just academic, like Susan Sontag's venerable antinomy between liberal and applied arts, which still creates differences in some schools of the arts. Moreover, apart from some examples in the evolution of the profession of architect and the species of court artists, this social difference persisted well into the early modern age.

Unsurprisingly, visual artists who had attained a certain confident autonomy, usually in a court environment, made claims that were recited more and more loudly, including in public, from the Renaissance onward, resorting to increasingly imaginative speculation in order to prove that their profession should be counted as one of the liberal arts, and as such no longer subject to guild norms.

In occasionally violent confrontations with guild masters, these artists built and furnished houses that vividly demonstrated these claims, which they also sought to underpin in the academic discourse of the *paragone.* This contest between the arts was used in attempts to establish and publicize a new systematization to satisfy the claims of the visual arts. Leonardo's famous *paragone* probably contains the first system of arts in this context, since he allows writers and musicians to appear alongside painters, sculptors, and architects. What P. O. Kristeller called "the modern system of the arts" did not, therefore, begin with formal recognition of specific principles, but with antagonistic and agonistic

4 Artes liberales

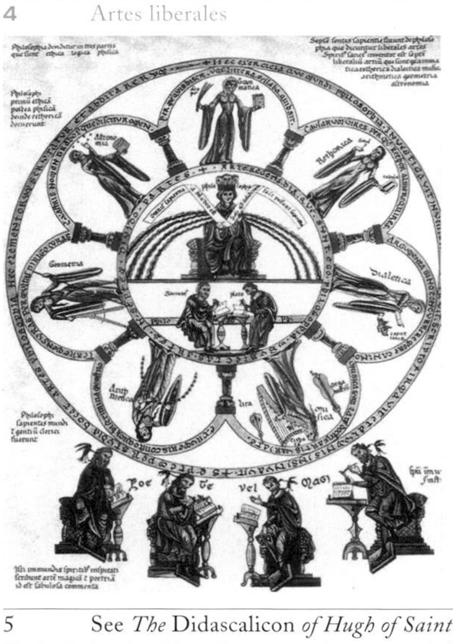

5 See *The* Didascalicon *of Hugh of Saint Victor: A Medieval Guide to the Arts,* trans. Jerome Taylor (New York: Columbia Univ. Press, 1961), p. 74 and Appendix A, p.153.

distinction as a means of self-organization. Of course, the agonistic principle requires a common basis, too.

The Italian (art) academies attempted rapprochement with the *artes liberales* mainly for status reasons, and people like Vasari, Zuccari, and later Lomazzo, developed a sophisticated system of *disegno* in the process. They related art education to the concept of genius (Michelangelo's slaves for the tomb of Pope Julius II that were never completed were repeatedly cited as examples), dematerializing and thereby laying the shaky foundation stone for the academic art education of the *ancien régime.* Meanwhile, in absolutist France the arts were instrumentalized systematically as luxury goods for the expropriation of provincial power elites. While used to raise the profile of courtly society, they were integrated into the mercantilist system. The hierarchical system laid down in the statutes of the academies of fine arts, dance, music, literature, architecture, etc., which the French leaders Richelieu, Mazarin, and above all Colbert established with all possible speed in the last third of the seventeenth century, was specifically designed to meet the needs of a courtly style that was intended to make the court of the Sun King Louis XIV a domestic and foreign policy model for the whole of Europe, and was highly successful in doing so.

In fact, the next serious theoretical thoughts on a system of the arts did not appear until the *querelle des Anciens et des Modernes,* especially in the writings of Charles Perrault. In his *cabinet des beaux arts* Perrault included eight disciplines, including optics and mechanics, which he called "fine" (or beautiful) arts, distinguishing them expressly from the "liberal" arts. The reference to the *artes liberales* as a common denominator of the arts, aimed at enhancing the artist's social status, was thus replaced by the concept of the beautiful which, along with that of mimesis, now became the key term in art-theoretical systematization concepts. This lasted until the appearance of the sublime, "a sudden, irresistible, terrifying power and force that can be overcome in nature by reason or in visual art by sympathy."[6]

Charles Batteux developed the first comprehensive attempt at systematization, the first elaborated system of fine arts, in the mid-eighteenth century. Kristeller asserts that Batteux in *Les beaux arts réduits à un même principe,* published in 1746, "codified the modern system of the fine arts almost in its final form, whereas all previous authors had merely prepared it."[7] Batteux, basing his ideas loosely on Aristotle, relates what Kristeller called the five authoritative arts—painting, sculpture, architecture, and, with a certain amount of rhetorical sophistry, music and literature—to mimesis, the imitation of nature. Following the number of *artes liberales,* he lists seven arts in all, divided into two categories. In addition to the "actual" fine arts of music, poetry, painting, sculpture, and dance, which are geared to pleasure as the main occupation of courtly society, he lists rhetoric and architecture as arts that give both pleasure and satisfaction.[8]

6 Quoted after Julia Benthien, "Rezension von Corina Caduff, *Die Literarisierung von Musik und Bildender Kunst um 1800, München 2003,*" *Sehepunkte* 4, no. 2 (2004).

7 Paul Oskar Kristeller, "The Modern System of the Arts: A Study in the History of Aesthetics," *Journal of the History of Ideas* 13, no. 1 (January 1952), pp. 17–46.

8 Charles Batteux, *Les beaux arts réduits à un même principe* (Paris, 1746), pp. 6–7. Quoted after Wolfgang Ullrich, "System der Künste," in *Ästhetische Grundbegriffe: Historisches Wörterbuch in sieben Bänden,* ed. Karlheinz Barck et al., 7 vols., vol. 3 (Stuttgart: J. B. Metzler, 2001), pp. 556–93, at p. 578.

Both Moses Mendelssohn and August Wilhelm Schlegel subsequently adopted the Batteux classification of seven *beaux arts,* though they rejected its inner mechanics in line with their own philosophical systems. Mendelssohn based his system on his theory of sentiment, while Schlegel postulated that dance was the *Urkunst* (original art) and that the "three natural arts," that is visual art, music, and poetry, had evolved from it. This formed the basis of the Romantic systems of art.

Therefore, at the end of the eighteenth century, contrary to P. O. Kristeller's much-repeated view, there was no system of five authoritative arts, but as the lowest common denominator the triad of poetry, visual arts, and music. Distinguished individuals opposed even this, including Johann Jacob Winckelmann and Gotthold Ephraim Lessing, who in their respective essays on Laocoön dismantled the concept *ut pictura poesis,* each in his own way. Among the dissenters was also Johann Gottfried Herder, who in his 1778 treatise *Plastik* (Sculpture), in remarks that may have been aimed at Lessing, opposed the view of painting as being on a par with sculpture, arguing that "no single law, no effect of the one [art applies] without difference and qualification to the other."[9] fig. 5

It is therefore unsurprising that probably the most elaborate attempt at systematization of the arts, the *General Theory of Fine Arts* by the Swiss national Johann Georg Sulzer, though arousing distinguished opposition (from no less a personage than Johann Wolfgang Goethe, then still motivated by *Sturm und Drang*), developed no major impact and met with no response in the philosophical systems of the late eighteenth century. This was despite the fact that, as Kristeller notes, Sulzer's system may have represented "the first attempt to carry out on a large scale the program [of an order of the arts] formulated by Baumgarten [the 'inventor' of aesthetics] and Mendelssohn."[10]

As the nineteenth century progressed, the claim to autonomy of the arts that Winckelmann and Schiller had initiated and the Romantics elevated to a principle was accompanied by the emergence of the dichotomy that Adorno meant when he diagnosed the dominance of a concept of art that induces the abolition of differences between individual branches of art (admittedly in connection with what he called "fraying" of genres, which we prefer to see as a crossover).[11]

Philosophical aesthetics is usually based on a concept of art whose definition is derived from a single genre, commonly literature or sometimes music. This is true of Hegel, in whose system of arts "architecture, sculpture, and painting represent the steps up to the throne of all art, which Queen Poetry had now occupied."[12] In academic or secessionist artists' theories, the respective arts' claims to autonomy evolve into a universal claim to validity of fine differentiations between art and non-art. To some extent, in the heated discussions about the inclusion of new genres such as photography, film, and digital art, this claim to validity even now leads to an atomistic canon of arts.

9 Ibid, p. 581.

10 Kristeller, "The Modern System" (see note 7).

11 See Theodor W. Adorno, "Die Kunst und die Künste (1866)," in *Parva Aesthetica* (Frankfurt a. M.: Suhrkamp, 1967), pp. 169–92, at p. 169.

12 Quoted after Dietrich Scheunemann, "Die Schriftzeichen der Maler—Die Stillleben der Dichter: Grenzwahrnehmungen zwischen den Künsten um 1910," in Koebner, *Laokoon und kein Ende* (see note 4), p. 61.

The early-twentieth-century avant-gardes wanted to, and did, counter the paragonal differentiation and separation of the arts by system, which at the end of the nineteenth century was experienced as a fundamental fragmentation, with a movement toward unity and a penchant for the gesamtkunstwerk. And indeed, the new openness of the arts toward one another that is evident from so many manifestations during the period from 1905 to 1920 was certainly a, if not the prime, mover in the renewal of the arts—of all arts—in the first third of the twentieth century. Avant-garde movements such as the futurists and the Bauhaus that subscribed to ideas of a synthesis of the arts interpreted the crisis of art as a crisis of society, and expected the overcoming of the crisis of art to end the social crises, too. In manifestations that sought to (re)unite all the arts, they attempted to erect a great cathedral to unity, such as the Bauhaus or, in the case of the futurists, to proclaim a total mobilization against the antiquated art institutions and art concepts of the past. Still, when one considers the development of these two avant-garde movements, which we will take here as being paradigmatic of nearly all the others, one is struck by the fact that nearly every genre had its own futuristic manifesto that was clearly different from the rest. Moreover, by the time Hannes Meyer and Mies van der Rohe succeeded its founder Walter Gropius, if not before, the Bauhaus was clearly dominated by architecture, as is demonstrated by the impacts it had after World War II.

The avant-gardes had resorted to the Romantic idea that art would exert a healing influence on society. After World War II, the idea of a radical autonomization of art, an idea practiced on art for art's sake and early abstraction, crossed over from the United States. Theoreticians such as Clement Greenberg and painters such as Ad Reinhardt, protagonists of abstract expressionism, suggested that the arts should definitely not intermingle, but must maintain their freedom, since their sole legitimacy lay in their autonomy.

5 The Laocoön Group, ca. 156 BC, Vatican, Rome

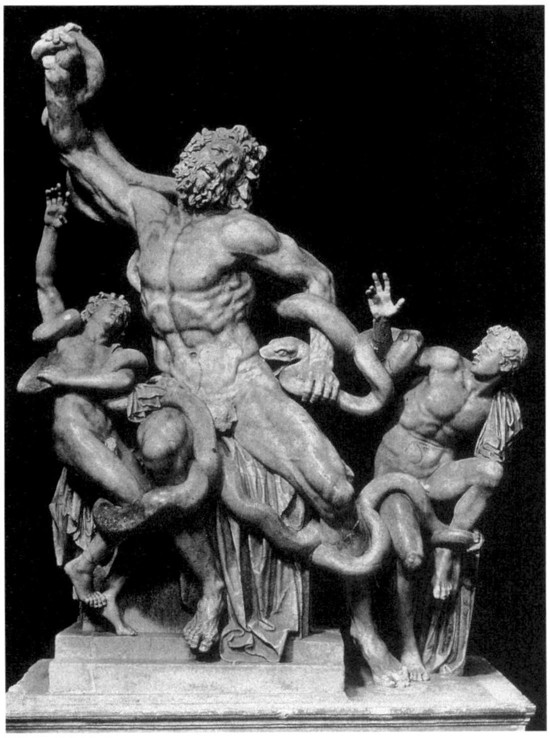

In a way, Martin Warnke put this thesis the right way around when he wrote: "The arts became autonomous, not so much because that was what they always wanted and with many sacrifices finally achieved, but probably because they were no longer needed in their traditional roles, as other media that are more effective in modern mass society were taking their place." He concluded that art had only succeeded in securing a new right to exist and in surviving its own end by adhering strictly to a "duty of defense."[13]

Obviously, the purity law that Greenberg supports with such proverbial power, inter alia in his essay "Toward a Newer Laocoön," could not tolerate a systematic relationship between the arts. Equally obviously, it did not remain unopposed. In the name of intermedia, Flux, and conceptual art, under the rubric of postmodernism in manifestations of critique of institutions and big digital media arts events, an orgiastic crossover ensued of all the arts, of the arts and sciences, a crossover of art and society. These orgiastic boundary crossings were accompanied by a revival of the *paragone* in the sciences as well as the arts, in the form of countless cultural "turns," ranging from the linguistic turn via the iconic and pictorial turn to the universal cultural turn.

With the triumphal progress of pop art in the late 1960s, if not before, the purity law of abstraction was declared obsolete. Now, boundary crossing, rather than exclusive autonomy, became the trademark of artistic freedom. The boundaries between the arts, and the boundary between art and life, became so fluid as to lead cultural critics such as the American Arthur C. Danto to diagnose self-disenfranchisement. In *The Philosophical Disenfranchisement of Art* he argued that it was now hardly possible to distinguish between non-art and art, especially given the omnipresent flood of mass-media images. Art historians such as Hans Belting proclaimed the "end of art history," arguing that the volume of images that were not art was so much greater than the volume of artistic images that the latter were being compressed into (what visual media science would deem) a negligible entity. fig. 6

Once again the end of art was diagnosed and attempts at systematization in the field of the arts increasingly took refuge in the abstract. The arts were declared a text, so that they could be compared and deconstructed in a condensed form, as it were. The Luhmann style of systems theory drew a distinction between the work of art as a "marked space" and the "unmarked spaces" of the undefined world. In doing so, it explained to some extent what non-art is while once more casting fundamental doubt on the definability of art as such.[14] And that is the complicated state of the order of the arts to this day.

Art Education

Attempts to fit the fine arts into a more or less concise system also guided education in the arts.

Music and literature were among the seven liberal arts (*septem artes liberales*) borrowed from the scientific theory of late antiquity and were therefore taught in monasteries, cathedrals, universities, and other institutions. Visual art, in contrast, was taught and learned within the

13 Quoted after Ullrich, "System der Künste" (see note 8), p. 558.

14 Cf. Boris Groys, "Die dunkle Seite der Kunst; Rezension von Niklas Luhman: *Die Kunst der Gesellschaft,*" *Soziale Systeme* 2, no. 1 (1996), p. 172.

context and following the rules of the craft guild system as one of the more lowly *artes mechanicae.* It was only when scientific methods were introduced and when court artists became established at the princely courts that the visual arts became a fit subject for academic training.

In the year 1400, the French architect Jean Mignot challenged the company of master builders of Milan Cathedral with the dictum *ars sine scientia nihil est* (art without science is nothing). This is often cited as evidence of early interaction between art and science.

However, Alessandro Conti recently demonstrated persuasively that the concept of science in those days had nothing in common with our science, or more precisely, scientific engineering. He concluded that "it [science] is articulated essentially in the—a priori—selection of some schemata into which the entire building must fit both in terms of design and of aesthetic aspects."[15]

Ackermann, who first published this dispute, emphasizes the geometric and speculative, as it were "painterly," way in which Mignot improved the very precarious design of the cathedral pillars. The first documented use of scientific method thus relates one of the key *artes mechanicae,* architecture, to the many attempts made in the early modern age to equate the visual arts with the *artes liberales,* that is, to ennoble them, as it were, by making them more scientific or literary.

From the Accademia de Disegno to the Accademia di San Luca

The first "academies" dedicated to the visual arts must be seen as part of this process. A century after the establishment of literary and scientific academies, and after several precursors in Florence under the first Medici dynasty, the first proper academies of art emerged in the late sixteenth century. They were Giorgio Vasari's Accademia dell'Arte de Disegno in Florence, founded in 1563, and Federico Zuccari's Accademia di San Luca in Rome, which was founded in 1593 and is still in existence. fig. 7

The link between art and science, as advocated by no less a personage than Leonardo da Vinci, the archetypal Renaissance Man, was of prime importance in the founding of these academies. Leonardo wrote, "Quelli che s'inamorano di pratica senza scientia sono come li

6 Richard Hamilton, *Just what is it that makes today's homes so different, so appealing?* Collage, 1956

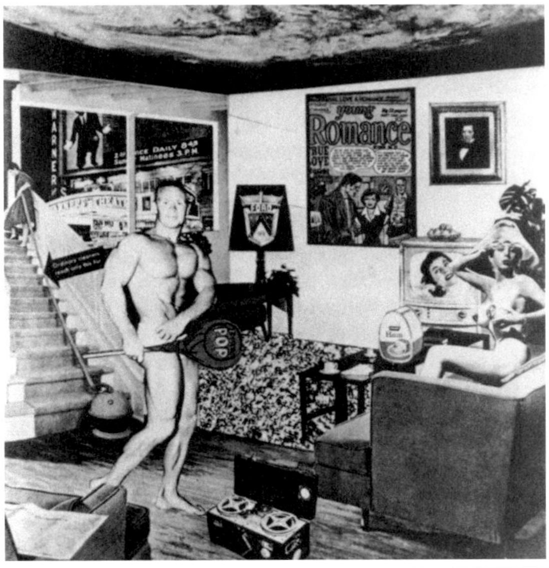

15 Quoted after Alessandro Conti, *Der Weg des Künstlers: Vom Handwerker zum Virtuosen* (Berlin, 1998), p. 87; also see J. S. Ackermann, "Ars sine scientia nihil est," *Art Bulletin* XXI (1949), pp. 84–111.

nocchieri che entran in naviglio senza timone o bussola" (Those who fall in love with practice without science are like helmsmen who board a ship without a rudder or compass).[16]

Numerous private academies existed alongside these two public "art academies." The earliest, of which a picture exists, was the academy of Baccio Bandinelli in Rome. Though no pictures of Vasari's or Zuccari's academies have survived, we do have impressive portrayals of their systematic theories of art. These are found in a type of architecture that Jacob Burckhardt, the doyen of Renaissance research, described as one of the finest chapters in art history—the houses of the artists themselves. Those built by Giorgio Vasari in Florence and Arezzo and by Federico Zuccari in Florence and Rome provide eloquent testimony to the sense of entitlement with which artists could, and desired to, show themselves (off) to the egalitarian-minded urban oligarchies, and of how they integrated their theories as artists into these strategies. In particular, the *stanza del disegno* in Vasari's house in Florence and the *camera del disegno* in Zuccari's Roman palace are both pretentious and precise reflections of art as an operating system in the early modern era. One of the earliest guides to Florence describes the main room in Giorgio Vasari's house as the *stanza del disegno,* thereby alluding to the concept that more than any other describes how artistic work was distinguished from the lowly realms of craft. The central illustration in the room depicts the famous story, taken from legends of the artists in antiquity, about how Zeuxis painted his picture of Helen of Troy. This legend had become a constituent element of the entire High Renaissance ideal of art, based on Raphael, with its specific relationship between nature (the model) and art. The great fresco which covers almost the entire north wall of the room is divided into two halves by an illusionistic partition, creating two barrel-vaulted pictorial rooms. The right-hand room is conceived as an entrance loggia with a balustrade separating it from the expansive landscape in the background. On it stands a statue of Diana of Ephesus, the many-breasted natural deity, who marks this section of the picture as a reference field of nature. Here, accompanied by torch-bearing serving maids, we are introduced to the models that are, for the painter, "nature in the sense of the subject, of the materials to

7 Agostino Veneziano, *The Academy of Baccio Bandinelli,* 1531

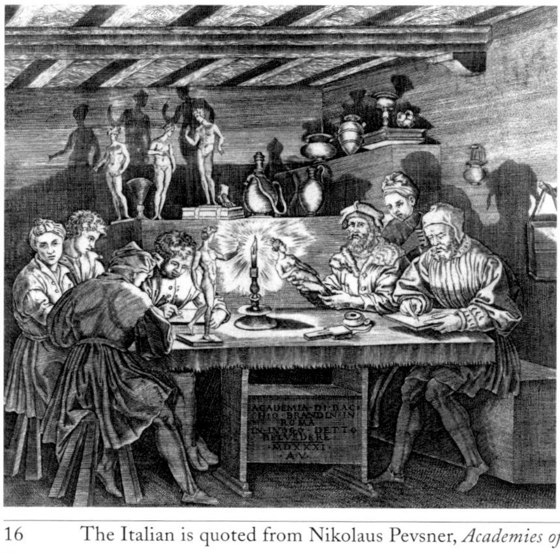

16 The Italian is quoted from Nikolaus Pevsner, *Academies of Art, Past and Present* (Cambridge: Cambridge Univ. Press, 1940), p. 35, whom we owe what is still the best summary on the subject, despite the undifferentiated skepticism with regard to the nineteenth century that is typical for the avant-gardes.

be created," according to Wolfgang Kemp's perceptive analysis of the *stanza del disegno.*[17] fig. 8

The painter himself stands on the left-hand side of the picture in an enclosed space. In the background, an open door reveals two assistants preparing materials in what, despite the imposing interior design, is thus recognizable as a studio. This is where the artist chooses from the models the one that is suitable for transforming the imperfect natural subject into an ideal work of art.

In an architectural niche at the intersection of the partition is a figurative composition that represents the concept in art theory that mediates between *natura* and *ars*—the personification of *disegno.* This masculine figure has three faces, thus identifying itself as the "father of the arts," that is of painting, architecture, and sculpture, the instruments of which it holds in its hands.

Disegno had already featured in the works of Petrarch and Cennini, and later of Ghiberti and Filarete, as a synonym for that aspect of artistic design that extends beyond mere delineation, that is beyond the purely practical dimension. None of the countless subsequent "theoreticians" of the *cinquecento* failed to provide a more or less systematic representation of *disegno.* The fundamental intention of these theories was to declare that *disegno* as the basis of artistic work was largely an intellectual activity, without denying its propensity to generate real works. Considering the constant fluctuations in the esteem in which theory and practice are held in our present-day schools of art, this is a very modern problem.

8 Giorgio Vasari, *Zeuxis and the Maidens of Croton,* after 1569

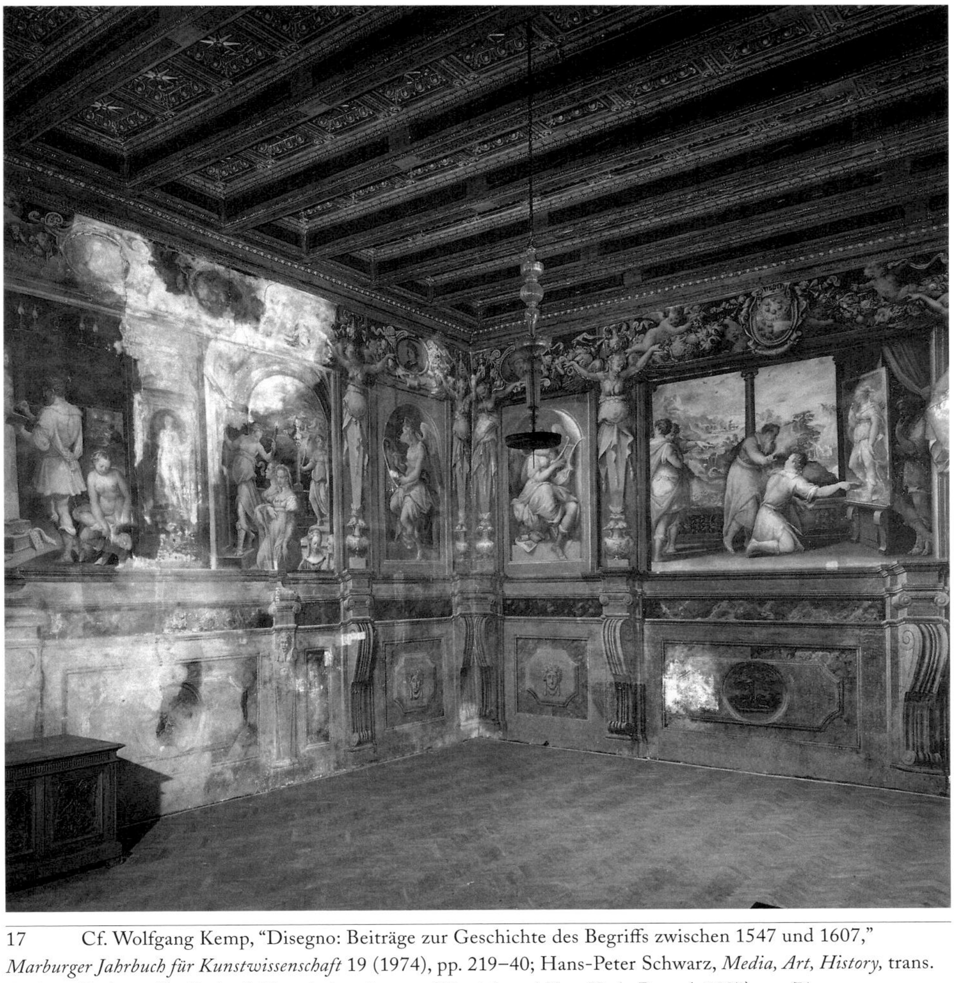

17 Cf. Wolfgang Kemp, "Disegno: Beiträge zur Geschichte des Begriffs zwischen 1547 und 1607," *Marburger Jahrbuch für Kunstwissenschaft* 19 (1974), pp. 219–40; Hans-Peter Schwarz, *Media, Art, History,* trans. Freiherr Karl von Teuffenbach Translation Agency (Munich and New York: Prestel, 1997), pp. 71.

I do not plan to go into detail about the development of theoretical speculations as to the function and effect of *disegno*. What is of interest to us here is the effect that the concept of *disegno* had on the design of art education, into which it introduced a clear separation between ennobled, intellectually inspired design activity and technically oriented execution.

Vasari uses the narrative depiction of *disegno* in connection with a modified version of the legend of the Virgins of Croton in order to define the relationship between *natura* and *ars* as vividly as possible. His position on this is clear from the arguments he puts forward in the prefaces to the two editions of his *Lives of the Artists,* the first history of art, which had been published shortly before work started at his house in Florence.

To demonstrate the *nobilitas* of the arts, in the preface to the first edition he still makes a somewhat vague reference to the Creation story, writing, "Almighty God ... at the same time as He freely invented all things fashioned the first forms of sculpture and painting."[18]

In the second edition of the *Lives,* Vasari restores to *disegno* its dual meaning as both an intellectual and a practical activity, thereby transcending the Neoplatonist idea of art that "the idea, the plainly given and preexistent, [was] not a derivative of natural reality that had first to be created by election."[19]

Thus both the intellectual and practical aspects of the artist's work are conceived as having been ennobled. The *belle arti* have sufficient autonomy from the other, previously recognized, liberal arts to lay claim to a higher status and therefore a higher education in both the practical and the theoretical aspects.

The significance of the artist's intellectual accomplishment is also emphasized in a Neoplatonist style in the capricious, ambitious *palazzo* that the second eminent artist-theoretician of the late sixteenth century built in Rome. Simultaneously, *disegno* is transcended and becomes demiurgic, that is, it is propagated as a general creation myth, in a way that resembles avant-garde fantasies of omnipotence in the early twentieth century.

The two-part *palazzo*, the original layout of which was dominated by the studio building, was widely known as a *caprice* on account of the mask gate through which one entered the garden, a reference to Dante's *Inferno.* Zuccari decorated the palace with a cycle of frescoes with a complex interfusion of themes from his family history, moral-philosophical allegories of virtue, and apotheoses of artists. This was intended to express the predominance that the principal of the Accademia di San Luca wished to see accorded to *disegno* as a maxim of art theory and practice. fig. 9/10

The painted theory of art and society culminates, in a sense, in the *camera del disegno,* a comparatively small room that the artist may have used as a *studiolo.* Here, he represents the highest principle governing both the artistic and the other social activities of human beings—*disegno.* In his theoretical writings, indulging in metaphysical speculation,

18 Giorgio Vasari, "Preface" in *Lives of the Artists: A Selection,* trans. George Bull (London: Folio Society, 1993), p. 3.

19 Quoted after Kemp, "Disegno" (see note 17), p. 227.

Zuccari interpreted it as a *segno di dio in noi,* a sign of God in us. In the central field of the vaulted ceiling that spans the relatively small room, the personification of this principle, an approximation of God the Father, equipped with the instruments of the arts and crowned by three interwoven wreaths, is enthroned. Unlike in Vasari's s*tanza del disegno,* where the concept of *disegno* appears in the context of a narrative pictorial parable of nature and art, for Zuccari it plays a central role in the metaphysics of his conception of the world. At the heart of his palace complex, at the nucleus of the entire estate, in the *studiolo* of the master of the house, *disegno,* accompanied by personifications of the visual arts, dominates the entire field of nature in its natural and socialized form. This is depicted in four oval fields by extremely complex allegories. Just beneath *disegno,* called *scintilla divinitatis,* is the allegorical figure of *scientia,* labeled by a slogan-like inscription as *vera nobilitas.* In it, philosophy, theology, and jurisprudence are united by means of codices and genre pictures placed in the background as adjuncts. They illustrate teaching and research, that is, theory and practice. In this combination, the allegory appears simultaneously to personify a cardinal virtue, *justitia.* Other areas of social life are identified with cardinal virtues in a similar manner. The second allegory, assigned to the *vita contemplativa,* functions as *temperantia.* In connection with this allegory, Apollo and the Muses personify social harmony. The allegories of *medicina* and *militia* are shown as fields of *vita activa,* and *prudentia* and *fortitudo* can be assigned to them as cardinal virtues.

Thus Zuccari seeks to portray the entire field of human activity systematically and to ground it in moral philosophy by assigning it to *virtutes* developed from Aristotle's Nichomachean Ethics.

In doing so, unlike Vasari, he also tries to define the evidence for the *nobilitas* of art not so much by reference to the specific relationship between art and nature as to the relationship between art and society.

It is not very surprising, therefore, that this very Federico Zuccari, whose main written work, *L'Idea de' pittori, scultori, ed architetti* (The Concept of Sculptors, Painters, and Architects), made him known as a proven speculative mannerist, may have drawn up the first concrete teaching and research plans for an actually existing academy. This is not counting, because they had few immediate consequences, Leonardo's notes on the training of a young artist, which he composed for his fictitious private academy and which were also based on the separation of theory and practice and the primacy of theory.

In a letter written between 1575 and 1578 that Nikolaus Pevsner discovered in the National Library in Florence while conducting research

9 Gate to the garden of Federico Zuccari's house in Rome, built after 1590
10 Federico Zuccari, *The Triumph of Disegno,* Rome, after 1590

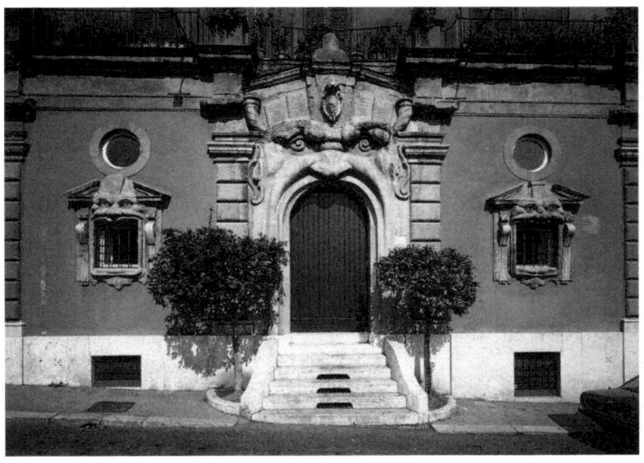

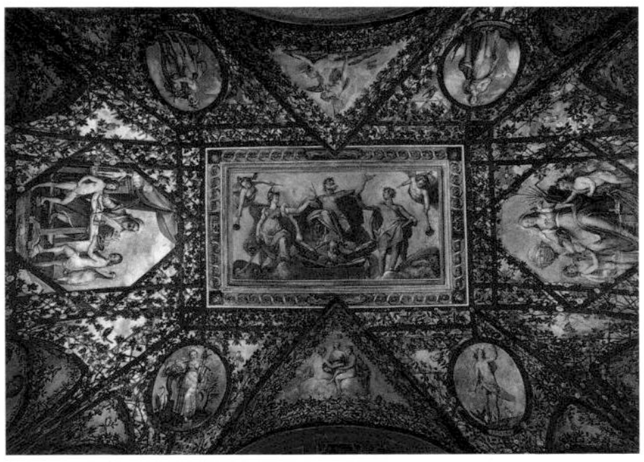

for his *Academies of Art, Past and Present,* Zuccari drew up proposals for reforming the Accademia del Disegno in Florence. Pevsner refers to Zuccari's proposal for a life-drawing class and a mentorate for sculpture. Of importance are Zuccari's proposals for theoretical instruction in mathematics and physics, subjects he considered indispensable to proficiency in the fine arts. He was prescribing a kind of modular course that now seems strangely modern. As far as we know, his suggestions elicited no response in Florence. The Accademia del Disegno was and remained an academy of peers analogous to the classical academies. Nonetheless, Zuccari was very soon able to put his ideas into practice in Rome.

With the support of his patron, Cardinal Federigo Borromeo, on November 14, 1593, Zuccari opened the Accademia di San Luca—named after St. Luke, the patron saint of artists—and became the academy's first principal.

In addition to detailed stipulations concerning the theoretical discourse that was to be conducted, the academy statutes contain clear indications that the Accademia di San Luca was in fact to be dedicated primarily to teaching and learning. Twelve *accademici* were appointed (from 1607 they were called *professori*) to supervise teaching. Great emphasis was placed on drawing, as Leonardo had suggested. Students drew copies of originals by the masters and went on to copy ancient sculptures, landscapes, or animals. The highest level of basic training was life-drawing of nude subjects. Only then, on the Master's course as it were, were students permitted to practice a profession, for example as a painter or sculpture. The sixteenth-century concept of academic education in the visual arts progressed from the general to the specialist, in sharp contrast to the training in technical workshops.

The Académie Royale and Its Consequences

Along with the development of culture as a whole, the center of development of educational institutions now shifted from Rome to Paris. After lengthy arguments with the guilds, who were influential in France as well, the Académie Royale de Peinture et de Sculpture was established on February 1, 1648. Its chief initiators were court artists, many of them foreigners. Also involved was a then very young painter, Charles Le Brun, who had just returned from Italy.

As in Rome, twelve professors (known as *anciens)* were to lecture students on the theoretical foundations of art and to teach them to draw from nature.

Faced with stubborn opposition from the guilds and a lack of public funds, the Académie was under continuous pressure from the guilds' educational principles. It even saw itself compelled to join forces with a rival institution set up by the guilds. Not until the end of 1654 were the courtly academicians able to push through new statutes giving the Académie Royale a monopoly in art education.

After Jean-Baptiste Colbert became vice-protector of the Académie in 1661, he forged ahead with establishing its monopoly position. All court painters were required to join the Académie or risked losing their privileges.

Colbert also adapted the Académie concept to further his comprehensive efforts at mercantilist centralization. In quick succession he founded the Académie de Danse, the Académie des Sciences, the Académie de Musique, and finally, in 1671, the Académie d'Architecture. The absolutist system could communicate its wishes and intentions to a body of royal academicians much more directly than to a private society, a guild, or a university.

For at least as long as the influence of Colbert and Le Brun (the Académie's first real director and a kind of chief architect of the entire kingdom) endured, the Académie remained an educational institution with the mission to develop the courtly style that was to spread throughout Europe within a short time. The curriculum was divided into the three areas designed by Leonardo, that is, copying drawings, drawing from casts, and life drawing. Pevsner rightly draws attention to the fact that academic training at the time did not include practical specialist training in the diverse visual arts. "He neither painted nor carved nor modeled figures or reliefs during his working hours at the academy. All this he had to learn in the studio, or, as one may safely say, the workshop of his master, with whom he still lived and under whom he still worked, in a way almost identical with that of the Middle Ages."[20] fig. 11–14a

11 Gérard Audran, details of the physical Apollo, from *Les proportions des corps humains*, Paris 1683
12 Charles Le Brun, sketchbook leaf with head of the Medici Venus
13 William Hogarth, *Analysis of Beauty*, 1753
14a Eugène Buland, *Nude Study*, 1873

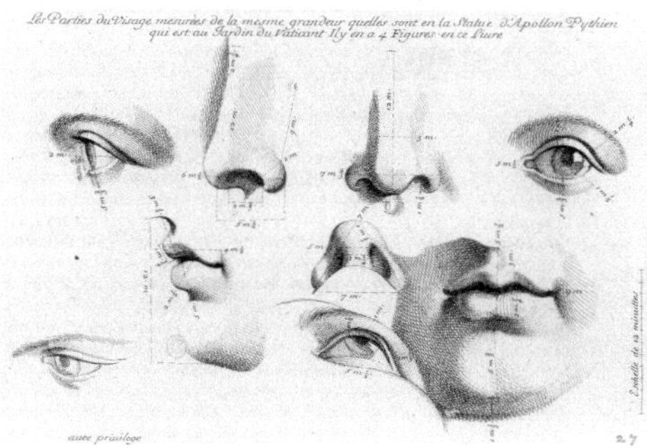

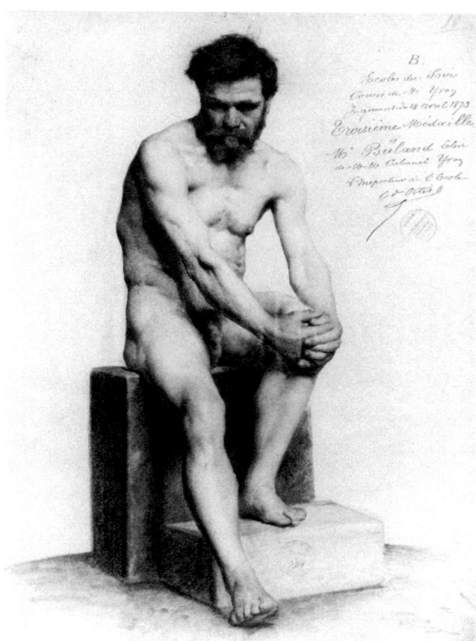

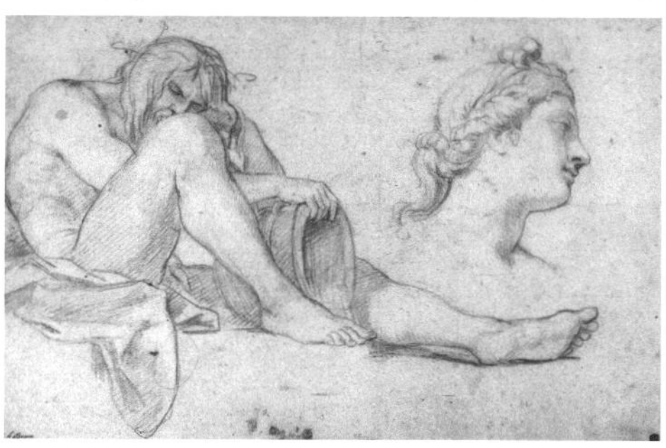

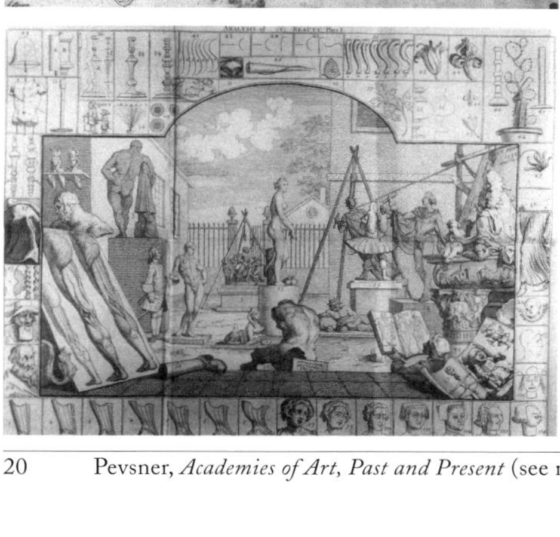

20 Pevsner, *Academies of Art, Past and Present* (see note 16), p. 92.

The central instrument for promulgating the courtly style of the Académie were lectures designed, as it were, to supply receptors of "good style." This formalization of art analysis culminated in Roger de Piles's "notorious book"[21] *Balance des Peintres,* in which he gave marks from zero to eighty to all famous artists according to the value of their composition, expression, drawing, and color.[22]

The recent publication of the *Conférences de l'Académie Royale* from 1648 until 1681, when its first secretary Henry Testelin retired from office, reveals that discourse at the Académie Royale was by no means entirely dominated by that dry, academic doctrine that Pevsner and indiscriminate critics of the Académie's development identified. Thomas Gaethgers, who titles his preface to the first two volumes "La doctrine académique: Histoire d'une fiction," states that "Contrary to popular belief ... no academic canon following state directives was obeyed. Rather, a heterogeneous discourse prevailed, one that took an interest in practical questions of art."[23]

By the 1670s, the structures of the Académie Royale had grown so influential that the Accademia di San Luca in Rome adapted to it to some extent and elected Le Brun as its principal.

The numerous new academies that sprang up all over Europe after the second half of the eighteenth century also followed the Paris model. By now, however, the Académie had tried to regenerate itself, as it were, by conducting the *querelles des Anciens et des Modernes,* the dispute between the "Poussinists," the guardians of ancient standards, and the "Rubenists," who as revolutionaries felt committed to the present. Thus even the early phase of institutionalized art education witnessed the first of those secessions that were to define the rhythmics of the institutional history of art academies throughout the epoch when their influence was widespread.

That first secession was terminated in a manner that, more than three hundred years later, was to be described as repressive tolerance. The two sides were accepted as equals and the "Rubenist" leader Roger de Piles was even made an honorary academy member. The Académie Royale relinquished its claim to monopoly. Subsequently, *procès verbaux* and curricula that adhered largely to the principles of Colbert and Le Brun were felt to be no longer in keeping with the times. Academic life increasingly descended into nostalgic representation.

The Rococo protagonists of skepticism toward antiquity were almost without exception academy members, though they cared little for academic tradition. Only after that skepticism had subsided, in the mid-eighteenth century, did some reform of academic teaching take place, including at the Académie Royale. This was in the context of a reactivation of art theory and practice that culminated in the Neopalladianism of Winckelmann or Burlington.

Pevsner pointed out that the establishing of academies during the Enlightenment was not motivated solely by neoclassical theory, but by something that was actually diametrically opposed to the ideas of Winckelmann, Mengs, Oeser, and the artists they influenced—commer-

21 Ibid.

22 It is perhaps not too far-fetched to compare this to today's ECTS evaluations.

23 Quoted after Franz Zelger, "Revidiertes Bild der Académie Royale," *Neue Zürcher Zeitung,* no. 62, March 15, 2007, p. 62.

cial utility. It is interesting to read that the dialectics that continue to shape institutionalized art education now were relevant even in the very early days of art schools of the modern era. They are the dialectics of freedom and necessity, as still expressed in differences over the postulated vocational relevance of modular courses of study under the Bologna Process.

Perhaps the most influential of these "new" academies, that in Vienna, was to be reorganized "in special recognition of the arts and likewise to promote trade." Moreover, the statement of reasons for reintroducing the Dresden academy in 1763 turned into an out-and-out eulogy of mercantilism. Art, it said, must also be looked at from the commercial point of view. With reference to the successful production of luxury goods in France, the activities of the Dresden academy were to concentrate on supervising industrial vocational schools, whose mission was to train young people to work in the Meissen porcelain manufactory and the Leipzig printing and publishing industry. In fact, all teaching of drawing in Saxony's schools was to be managed from Dresden, by remote control as it were.

The relaunch of the Berlin academy was introduced as follows: "We pursue no other aim than to enhance national industry. Just as France and England in the Western and Italy in the Southern provinces of Europe have made art an important source of income, so we intend to make Berlin and the Prussian state fit to become a store-house of art for the Northerly parts of our Continent."[24]

Moreover, the stated aim of probably the earliest public institution of art education in Switzerland, the municipal drawing school in Geneva, opened in 1748 or 1751, was to improve production methods of importance to trade and daily life.[25]

Certainly Pevsner, whom we have to thank for these examples, and who cites many more from smaller European countries, wrote *Academies of Art, Past and Present* to some extent teleologically with reference to the Bauhaus and applied arts schools movement. It is nonetheless remarkable that the art academies were oriented toward business in this way—the manufactories, after all, were the model for the national economy—considering their subsequent retreat into the ivory tower of academe.

Major tension developed between theory, as expressed in Winckelmann's "noble simplicity and quiet grandeur," and practice, as exemplified by Hagedorn's axiom that "art may be looked at from the commercial point of view."[26]

The curricula of the new schools that were meant to unite art and craft were written down in detail, following the Paris model. As a result, they were extraordinarily similar. There was no need for a European Credit Transfer System (ECTS) because comparable material was taught in a similar way everywhere. The Swiss national Johann Georg Sulzer, whose system of the arts we have discussed, described the customary model as follows: "The academy must be well supplied with objects necessary for learning the art of drawing. These consist chiefly of the following in sufficient variety: Books of drawings showing firstly separate

24 Quoted after Pevsner, *Academies of Art, Past and Present* (see note 16), p. 145.
25 See ibid.
26 Quoted after ibid., p. 153.

parts of figures, form and proportion of heads, of noses, ears, lips, eyes; then larger parts of figures and complete figures. To copy these is the first task to be set to the beginner. They are to be followed by drawings of figures taken from the most outstanding works of art, correct drawings of classical sculpture, selected figures by the greatest masters, by Raphael, Michael Angelo, the Carracci, etc. In copying these the student receives a first insight into the higher spheres of art. Besides the stock of drawings, a stock of plaster casts is necessary, representing the noblest works of Antiquity and some more recent works, in parts as well as in complete figures and groups. Students will have to draw from these assiduously, because this not only helps them to develop a just eye and an appreciation of beautiful forms, but also a knowledge of light and shade, of variations of attitudes and of foreshortenings. Furthermore, the academy must have models, men of beautiful form, to pose on a raised platform or table in different attitudes as instructed by of the leading teachers ... This will enable the teachers to explain almost everything that refers to the observation of light and shade on single figures. For the equipment of the room where life drawing is to be held must be so that it can be used both by day-light and by artificial light."[27]

Of Secessionists and Reformers

"O ye heralds of universal rules! How little you understand Art and how little do you possess of the genius that created the pattern on which you want to build art."[28] This cry was uttered by Johann Georg Hamann, whom Goethe dubbed the "Magnus of the North" and who was much admired by the German *Sturm und Drang* movement and the early Romantics. It was not aimed at the academies, but highlights the counter-movement that emerged—mainly, but not exclusively, in the German-speaking countries of Europe—at almost the same time as academies were being reorganized along neoclassical lines. "Genius is the magic word of the young generation,"[29] and genius cannot be learned, least of all by following academic rules.

In France, the ideas of the *ancien régime* were renewed, as it were. This followed a brief anti-academy intermezzo, spearheaded inter alia by Jacques-Louis David, during the course of which the academies were dissolved and replaced by David's *commune des arts.* Meanwhile, the anti-academy revolution that took place in the Germany of *Sturm und Drang* and Romanticism led first to reform and then to secession, or rather to an institutionalized counter-reformation. The Nazarene artist Peter Cornelius spoke of "pernicious academies and their desiccated directors." On being appointed to the art academy in Düsseldorf he developed a program that to some extent introduced into the institution the pre-academic ideal of the workshop with apprentices, the system of master classes. Yet it was not Cornelius's but his successor Wilhelm von Schadow's reforms that were to become an essential element at the majority of European (and, insofar as they existed, American) art academies in the nineteenth century. In addition to introducing master classes, Schadow's main innovation was to include painting classes in the academic curriculum. This idea was adopted from the successful

27 Quoted after ibid., p. 172.
28 Quoted after ibid., p. 90.
29 Ibid., p. 190.

private academies such as Jacques-Louis David had built up in Paris and Schadow himself in Berlin. Only now did academies take responsibility for the entire education of artists, from twelve-year-old beginners in elementary classes who were still being made to copy plaster parts of figures, via preparatory classes where paintings were copied, through to the "class of practitioner students" who were allowed to execute their own designs. Students could then attend master classes, a postgraduate course during which master students were even allotted their own studios in the academy building.

This "academization" of education was fully implemented after the last guild and craft institutions had been liberalized, that is, dissolved, around the mid-nineteenth century. Finally, in the last third of that century, it led to a split between the academy of peers on the one hand and the actual teaching institutions, the *écoles des beaux arts,* on the other. The key experience leading to further development of art education was gained in large private academies that were established in the palatial private homes of prominent artists such as David, Delacroix, Courbet, and Makart, whose studio became a model for the interior decor of grand bourgeois showcases, or Franz von Stuck, whose studio-cum-villa was an idiosyncratic gesamtkunstwerk. Even the secessionists had their private academies, as a glance into the studio of Henri Matisse reveals. fig. 14b–d

Alternatively, this further development took place among the pleinairists in Fontainebleau or in the open-air studios of various impressionists. The (French) academy, founded as a form of nationalization of the arts, had become obsolete at the latest when "artists were not really ready to serve again, and to serve not art but society."[30] This unwillingness to serve was characterized on the one hand by the Romantic idea, adapted from the *bohème,* of the role of the artist as savior, healer, or ruler of society and, on the other, by the struggle for the autonomy of all arts from the demands of both politics and the market.

True, the art academies survived all secessions in both the nineteenth and the twentieth century. They adapted, albeit hesitantly, to new forms of art and new perceptions of art. However, their role as opinion leaders in discourse on the arts dwindled, not least as a result of the separation between the discourse-oriented academy of peers and the edu-

14 b Jean Henri Uess, *The Studio of Jacques-Louis David*

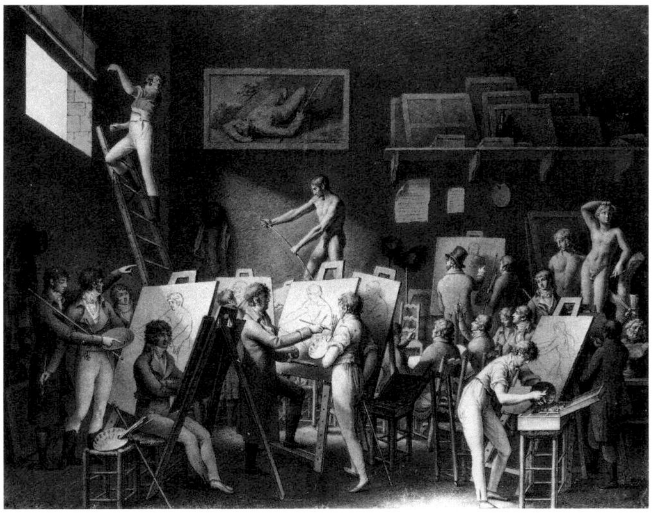

30 Ibid., p. 225.

14 c Gustave Courbet, *The Painter's Studio*, 1855
14 d Sculpture classes at the Académie Matisse at the Hotel Biron, 1909

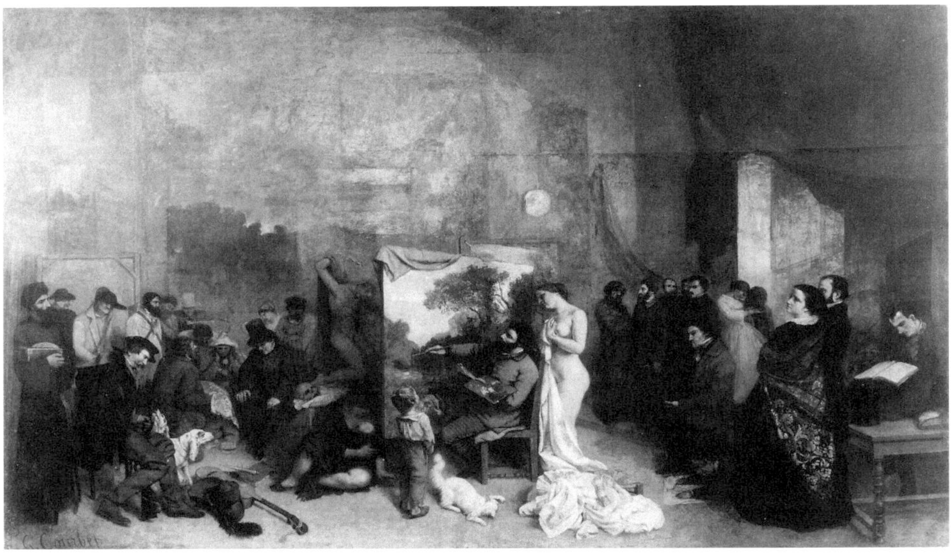

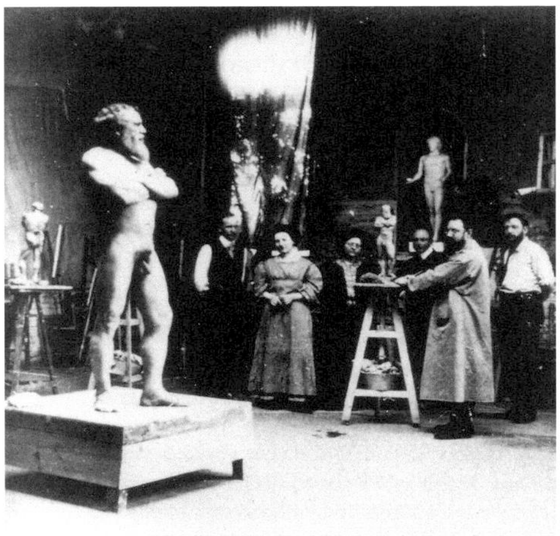

cation-oriented art school. This role passed to the secessionist avant-gardes who, as Bohemians, had formed a counterpole, albeit an indistinct one, to the established academicians in the mid-nineteenth century, and in the early twentieth century became the actual platform of artistic innovation. Not by accident did the word "academic" become synonymous with a dry, anemic, outdated concept of art that had coagulated into the classical. Innovative art had long been produced not inside, but outside the institutions. This applies even though Carl Goldstein, criticizing Pevsner, asserts in his book *Teaching Art* that the nineteenth-century academies contributed more toward the development of new artistic concepts than their secessionist or avant-garde critics would have us believe.

The thrust for a fundamental reform of art education came from a quarter that, as we have seen, had acted as a motivator once before, in the heyday of mercantilism and the founding era of modern academies: the economy. The industrial revolution in the nineteenth century had led to the extinction of craft skills that were still vitally important to product quality at a time when competition between up-and-coming industrial nations was increasingly fierce, and even in the epoch of mass production. The World Expositions staged at regular intervals from the mid-nineteenth century onward had demonstrated this to the world.

Yet the ubiquitous schools of applied arts that were established after the middle of the century were to be of no great significance to the reforming schools of the early twentieth century. Since most just aimed to train craftspersons, they were hardly closer to industrial production than the academies. Their curricula were usually geared to the three academic steps of drawing copies of originals, copying objects from antiquity, and study of nature. In the new schools founded in Central Europe, especially, workshops were frowned upon. So one can imagine how revolutionary Hermann Obrist must have sounded when he proclaimed, in 1901, "The only essentially right method of teaching Kunstgewerbe [applied arts] is by means of workshops."[31]

That same year, Peter Behrens established workshops in Nuremberg for a few makeshift master classes. Henry van de Velde, who was summoned to Weimar in 1902, built up an institute for applied arts there, with ceramics and weaving workshops. This later became the School of Applied Arts.

However, quite a lot was to happen before these reforms of the schools of applied arts and art academies, which were largely undertaken under the stylistic banner of Jugendstil, could take place. In England, William Morris founded the Arts and Crafts movement. While not actually focusing on industrial production, he elaborated the significance of production processes in arts-and-crafts training. Other pioneers of modernity, such as Gottfried Semper, were prominent in demanding a radical reform of art education, based on their experience with the new technologies of the day. These efforts at reform were not only, nor even primarily, aimed at improving the education of an artistic elite, but at the aesthetic education of the masses. In the mid-nineteenth century, the founding of the Kensington Museum in London as a consequence of the first World Exposition (the Great Exhibition of 1851) at Crystal Palace elevated industrial products to the ranks of culturally significant objects. Numerous similar museums were founded throughout Europe in its wake. Not long afterwards, some were transformed into training centers as schools of applied arts. fig. 15

True, the presentation of everyday objects as what H. U. Reck dubbed "functions of mass culture" was still somewhat reminiscent of the cabinets of arts and curiosities of the *ancien régime.* However, it had an immensely stimulating effect, if only as an opposing model, on those reform movements that aimed to bring the arts back together in

15 Charles Robert Ashbee, *Workshop of the Guild of Handicraft*, 1890

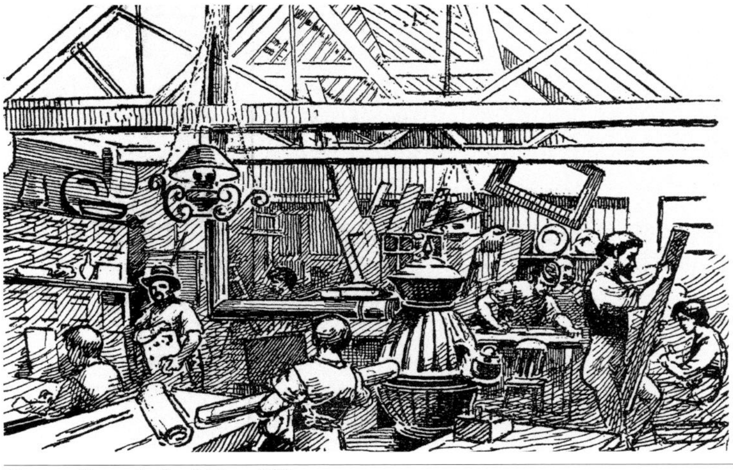

31 Quoted after ibid., p. 270.

Jugendstil, art nouveau, and in the symbolism of *La Revue Blanche.* Institutionally, this happened only very belatedly on the platform of joint, or at least interrelated, workshop teaching. Most notably, workshop teaching formed the basis of curricula at the few, generally very short-lived, reforming schools with an explicit social mission that were established in the first third of the twentieth century.

The Institutionalized Avant-Garde

The Higher Art and Technical Workshops (VKhUTEMAS) established in 1920 in Moscow aimed to bundle all artistic forces, as did, to an even greater degree, the UNOVIS (Champions of the New Art) group initiated by Kazimir Malevich at the Vitebsk Art Academy with the support of El Lissitzky, and the "creative group" around Vladimir Tatlin at the Academy in St. Petersburg. Moreover, they had more than the terrestrial sphere in their sights. A colleague recalled: "They always divided the world up between them—Earth, the sky, and interplanetary space. They established their sphere of influence everywhere. Usually, Tatlin took possession of Earth and tried to banish Malevich into space on account of his non-objectivity. Malevich did not reject the planets but did not want to relinquish Earth either, because he rightly thought that it, too, was a planet and thus perhaps nonobjective."[32]

Given the exorbitant nature of this *paragone,* it is no wonder that it gave rise to such exorbitant, utopian designs as Tatlin's monument to the Third International, a reconstruction of which reveals that it would have occupied an entire urban district, and Malevich's *Black Square.* In a way, the exorbitance of this painting led in the opposite direction, for it was to be the first of countless "last pictures" in which the early-twentieth-century avant-gardes repeatedly evoked the end of art. fig. 16/17

Despite significant excursions into theater and architecture, VKhUTEMAS and UNOVIS largely confined themselves to the visual arts, though they made use of the new media of the day. In the context with which we are dealing, however, a somewhat later creation, the Folkwang Schools, are significant. Naturally, they do not exude the same international charisma as the Bauhaus, which we will turn to shortly. Nonetheless, they played an important role in Germany in the decades after World War II, due to their distinctly interdisciplinary approach.

"Folkwang" was the name Karl-Ernst Osthaus gave the museum he founded soon after 1900 in Hagen, Westphalia, naming it after the hall of the goddess Freya in the Edda. Based on Osthaus's reforming ideas, in 1927 a school of music, dance, and elocution was established in the city of Essen in the Ruhr. In 1928, it was affiliated to the existing school of applied arts. From that time on, the name Folkwang in different disciplines was synonymous with a program unifying the arts. Rudolf von Laban in the late 1920s and Pina Bausch in the 1960s made dance the most prominent of the Folkwang arts, but an array of influential Folkwang graduates have graced the (West) German theater and music scene, while photographers such as Otto Steiner gave inspiration to visual design.

32 Nikolay Punin, quoted after http://demo.sfg_b.ch/TG03/suprematismus/4_nav_kuenstler/tatlin.htm (accessed June 12, 2007).

16 Kazimir Malevich, *Black Square*, ca. 1929

17 Tatlin's monument to the Third International, 1920, computer simulation, 1998

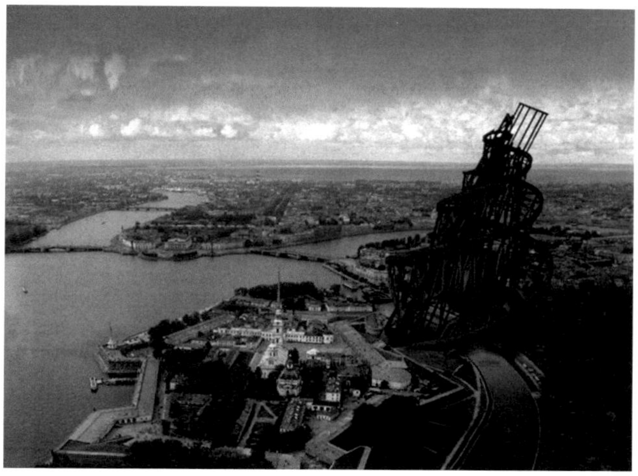

There was thus a host of concepts for reforming the institutional training of artists (by now including women artists).[33] However, no reforming school was as successful, or rather had such momentous consequences, as the Bauhaus.

The Bauhaus as a Cathedral

"Let us desire, conceive, and create the new building of the future together. It will combine architecture, sculpture, and painting in a single form, and will one day rise toward the heavens from the hands of a million workers as the crystalline symbol of a new and coming faith." This fragment from the Bauhaus manifesto is a great piece of expressive mythology for an institution that was preparing to learn how to solve

33 Cf. Hans M. Wingler, *Kunstschulreform 1900–1933* (Berlin, 1977).

the crises and problems of the modernization process by creative means. Despite its expressionistic wording it is reminiscent of aesthetic concepts in a comparable crisis that had hit industrial society a good century earlier. They, too, had preached the salvation of society through art.
To trace the tradition of the Bauhaus manifesto's second central motif, we need only recall Schiller's *Letters on the Aesthetic Education of Man,* or re-read No. 116 of the "Athenaeum Fragments" by Friedrich Schlegel, the chief ideologist of German Romanticism, which was written not long after, or Philipp Otto Runge's ideas on the unification of the arts through music. Whereas the Romantics thought that music would act as a catalyst in unifying all the arts, the Bauhaus saw architecture as fulfilling this role, followed later by theater and dance. It was probably due to this system of coordinates, consisting of demiurgic access to society on the part of the artist or designer (soon to include women artists) and curricula that treated the arts as a unified whole, that the Bauhaus, despite its relatively short lifespan, had such a tremendous impact on the entire field of design for living and the designed environment far beyond the borders of Germany. The Bauhaus ideology, which was never as one-dimensional as both its critics and its proponents would have us believe, was sustained from the outset by a prodigious concentration of prominent artists. These proponents of the latest artistic concepts acted as "Bauhaus masters" and argued among themselves over their often profound differences. fig. 18

The architect Walter Gropius in 1919 merged the Grand Ducal Saxon Art School with the Grand Ducal Saxon School of Applied Art (of which Henry van der Velde was director until 1914) to form the Bauhaus, whose first director he was. In the first two years of the school's existence he appointed distinguished, but highly antithetic, artists such as Lyonel Feininger, Gerhard Marcks, Johannes Itten, Georg Mucha, Oskar Schlemmer, and Paul Klee. After the last (conservative) professors, who had always been hostile to the merger, had left the Bauhaus, ironically in order to establish their own conservative school in the same complex of buildings, the first group of eminent appointees was followed by others. They included Wassily Kandinsky, László Moholy-Nagy, Ludwig Mies van der Rohe, Marcel Breuer, Herbert Bayer, Mart Stam, Ludwig Hilberseimer, the Swiss national Hannes Meyer, who succeeded Gropius as director in 1928, and Josef Albers, a former student who in

18 Lyonel Feininger, cover of the Bauhaus manifesto, 1919

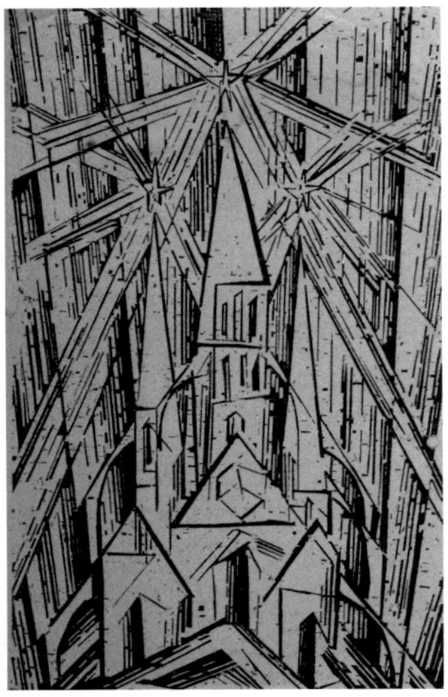

1923 was chosen to be the first “young master” at the Bauhaus. This —incomplete—list of illustrious names suggests another reason for the enduring impact of the Bauhaus, which in fact lasted throughout the twentieth century. It was that the National Socialist regime, more explicitly in some cases than others, forced all of these artists to emigrate. In exile, they shaped or headed diverse Bauhaus successor institutions in the United States—Ludwig Mies van der Rohe the Illinois Institute of Technology, Gropius the architectural department at Harvard, and Moholy-Nagy (as founder) the New Bauhaus, later the Institute of Design, in Chicago. Beyond the Bauhaus, they influenced pathbreaking institutes such as Black Mountain College, where Albers taught, and the Center of Advanced Visual Studies at the Massachusetts Institute of Technology, which was founded by Gyorgy Kepes, a student of László Moholy-Nagy’s.

The Bauhaus was persecuted from the beginning by nationalist forces, and later by the National Socialists. First, it was forced to relocate from Weimar to Dessau, where it staged a radiant resurrection in the form of the first modern college building in history. Subsequently, it was driven into private obscurity in Berlin, and finally into exile. Yet one of the most fortunate ironies of history is that after World War II, Bauhaus ideas returned to Europe in a variety of ways, on the side of the victors.

In our short history of higher education in the arts (which since the Bauhaus, if not before, have clearly included design), the Bauhaus plays an important role as a reforming school for another reason, too—the importance attached there to workshops and to production in general. As we said, one of the reasons why the academy concept was ailing was that, except in master classes, actual art production was sourced out, taking place only in academicians’ private studios. As a result, new, avant-garde concepts and methods were included in academic curricula only belatedly, if at all. Indeed, it became the rule (and some say still is) for art education institutions to be incapable of producing avant-garde or generally innovative concepts. Yet that had been the intention when academies were first developed, in an age when innovation no longer came from production workshops governed by guilds, but from the academic design laboratory. fig. 19–22

When stripped of some of its mystifying linguistic acrobatics, the Bauhaus manifesto makes it clear that its glorification of the workshop master should be judged in the light of this conflict. In “The Theory

19 Paul Klee, *Idea & Structure of the Bauhaus*, 1922
20 Walter Gropius, schematic representation of Bauhaus teaching, 1922

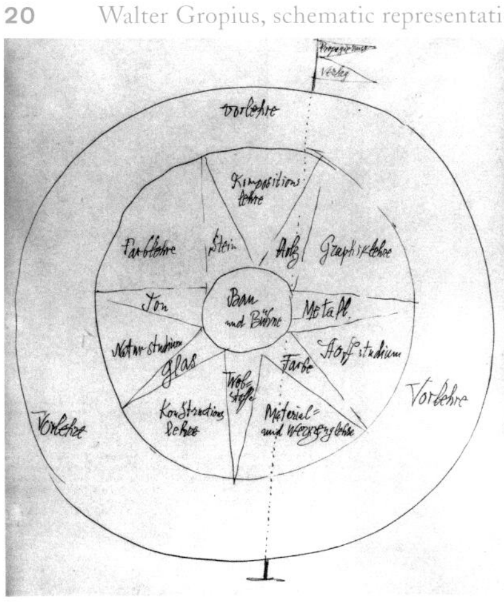

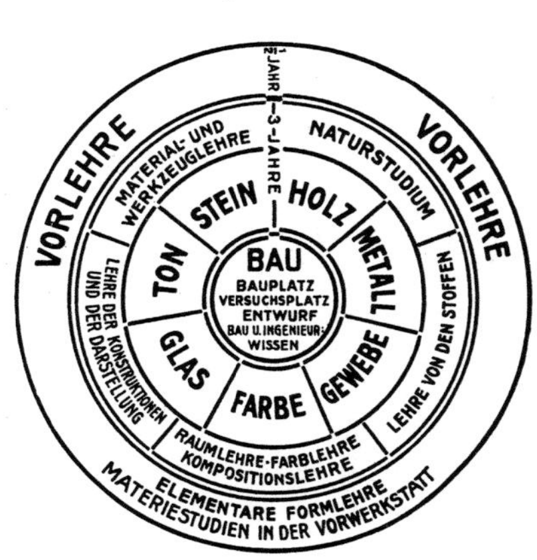

21 Oskar Schlemmer, *Man in the Circle of Ideas*, 1928

22 Johannes Itten, *Mazdaznan Principle*, 1921

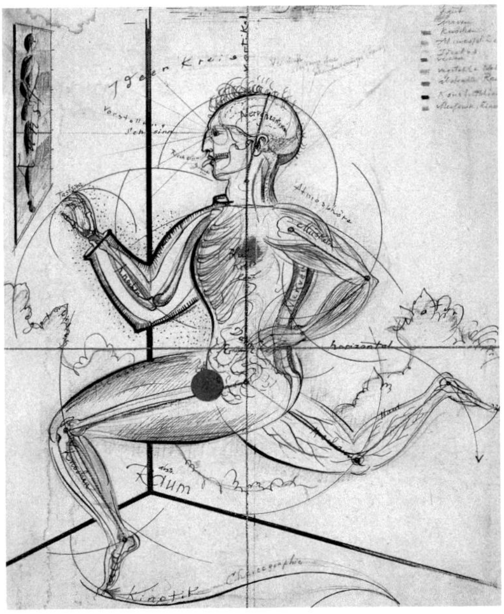

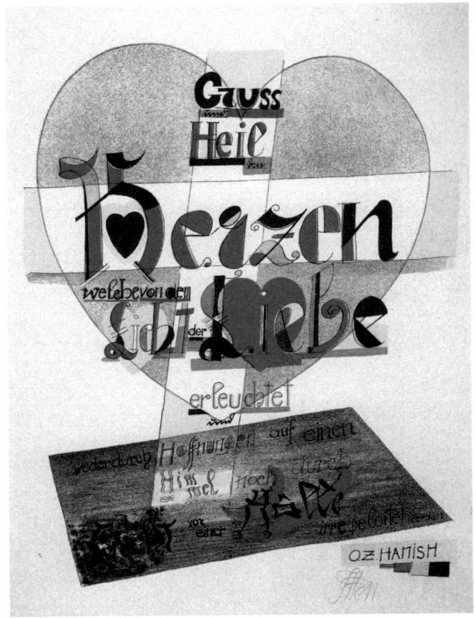

and Organization of the Bauhaus," published in 1923, Gropius explains the turnaround in curricular principles in plain language: "With the development of the academies genuine folk art died away. What remained was a drawing-room art detached from life. In the nineteenth century this dwindled to the production of individual paintings totally divorced from any relation to an architectural entity. The second half of the nineteenth century saw the beginning of a protest against the devitalizing influence of the academies. Ruskin and Morris in England, van de Velde in Belgium, Olbricht, Behrens (of the Darmstadt Artists' Colony) and others in Germany, and, finally, the Deutscher Werkbund all sought, and ultimately discovered, the basis of a reunion between creative artists and the industrial world. In Germany, applied arts schools were set up in order to develop a new generation of talented individuals trained in industry and craft. However, the academy was too firmly established. Practical training never advanced beyond dilettantism, and drafted and rendered 'design' remained in the foreground. The foundations of this attempt were neither wide enough nor deep enough to avail much against the old *l'art pour l'art* attitude, so alien to, and so far removed from life."[34]

Gropius's recipe for avoiding this (in his view) erroneous idea of art for art's sake was "thorough, practical manual work in productive workshops, closely linked to an exact teaching of the elements of design and the laws for assembling them."[35]

Most Bauhaus members were not craftsmen, but visionaries, and the instrumentalization of their visions for purely economic motives played a considerable part in the destruction of our environment by satellite towns worldwide with their building-industry functionalism, and in the totalitarian adaptation of their idea of the "unified work of art." But that is another story.

"The guiding principle of the Bauhaus was therefore the idea of creating a new unity through the welding together of many 'arts' and

34 Quoted after www.mariabuszek.com/kcai/Design%20History/Design_readings/GropiusBau.pdf.

35 Translated after www.kunstzitate.de/bildendekunst/manifeste/bauhaus_1923.htm.

movements: a unity having its basis in Man himself and significant only as a living organism."[36] This maxim, with which Gropius concluded his preface to the 1923 program, was actually impossible to realize in his day. Indeed, it would have been dangerous to realize it. Its affinity with political ideas of the gesamtkunstwerk in twentieth-century totalitarian systems has been discussed often enough. Nonetheless, this maxim was a starting point for the further development of public education in the arts, which we will outline using the examples of four institutes, the Ulm School of Design, Black Mountain College in North Carolina, the Center of Advanced Visual Studies in Boston, and the Center for Art and Media (ZKM) in Karlsruhe, which when founded was nicknamed the "electronic Bauhaus."

Max Bill versus Tomás Maldonado: The Ulm School of Design

The Ulm School of Design seems to have seen itself originally as the successor to the Bauhaus, perhaps even as compensation for the Bauhaus. Thus the school prospectus published in 1932 states in its characteristic lower case: "the school is the continuation of the bauhaus." This idea was put into practice through the principle of workshop classes in the context of which students and teachers were supposed to meet in "free association," and by building a campus on which teachers and students were to live. The link with core Bauhaus motifs was accomplished in 1955 when a new building designed by Max Bill was erected on Oberer Kuhberg overlooking the small town of Ulm in southern Germany.

However, it was not workshop classes alone that linked the concept of the Ulm school to Bauhaus ideas. Inge Aicher Scholl, who initiated the school, was the sister of Hans and Sophie Scholl, two shining lights of the German resistance who had been executed by the Nazis. Her intention from the outset was to make the reconciliation of art and life, which had led the Bauhaus (like other early-twentieth-century institutions) to the said demiurgic sense of entitlement, the program of the foundation she was planning to establish in memory of her brother and sister. "The school of design endeavors to channel the entrepreneurial spirit that surges to effect in youth, and to educate young people to cooperate in and share responsibility for life in society, to realize socially significant design tasks, and to cultivate the way of life of our technical age."[37]

However, Ulm was also linked to the Bauhaus by a fate that casts a significant light on the difficult situation faced by reformers in the 1950s, a period dominated by conservative restoration. The National Socialists had fought, and finally liquidated, the Bauhaus under the slogan of "cultural Bolshevism." Now, in the age of McCarthyism and the conservatism of the Adenauer era in West Germany, a charge of communism relayed to the U. S. High Commissioner by a former Gestapo agent almost brought about the downfall of the Scholl sister's enterprise. fig. 23

The U. S. occupation authority and conservative businessmen such as the Frankfurt banker Herrmann Josef Abs, who had had close

36 Quoted after www.mariabuszek.com/kcai/Design%20History/Design_readings/GropiusBau.pdf.

37 Bernhard Rübenach, *Der rechte Winkel von Ulm: Ein Bericht über die Hochschule für Gestaltung 1958/59*, ed. Bernd Meurer (Darmstadt: Verlag der Georg-Büchner-Buchhandlung, 1987), p. 11.

23 Magazine cover with Lufthansa corporate design, 1964, by Otl Aicher, Tomás Gonda, Fritz Querengässer, and Nick Roericht

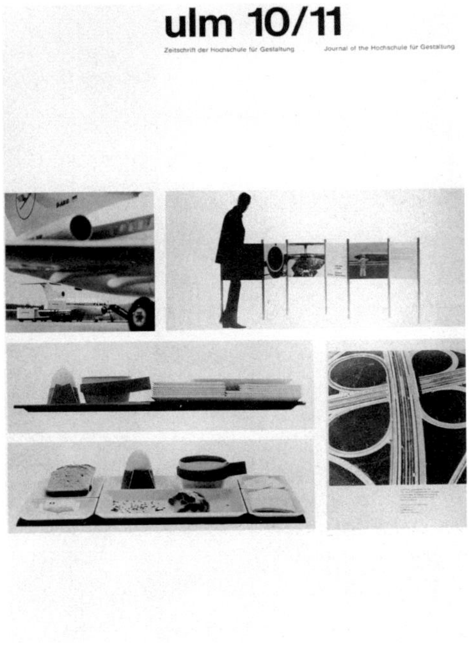

ties with the National Socialist regime, withdrew their support. Consequently, the Swiss national Max Bill, who was "unburdened by the fascist past and internationally presentable,"[38] took the lead in driving forward and specifying ideas for Ulm. Max Bill it was who, at the end of 1950, secured agreement that the school would be called Hochschule für Gestaltung (the subtitle of the Bauhaus) rather than Geschwister-Scholl-Schule, and who focused, but ultimately also constricted, the universalist education program of the Ulm group on "good form."

Whether this was an attempt to revive the academies' old claim to be the highest authority in matters of taste need not concern us here. Still, the principles of "good form" were an ambitious mission statement for Ulm to adopt in order to assert its status, catering for both exclusivity and popularity.

On the one hand, the claim to the Bauhaus legacy that Max Bill went to such extreme lengths to assert, including demanding that the majority of teaching staff should be recruited from among former Bauhaus members, contributed not a little to the young college's international reputation. On the other, it ignited the fierce disputes between the supporters of Max Bill and the Bauhaus tradition and the innovators headed by Tomás Maldonado. Fought out under the fascinated eye of the public, they entered the annals of Ulm and the discourse on design in the early days of the Federal Republic of Germany as the "querelles of Billists and Tomists."

Students even grumbled at the programmatic address delivered by Bauhaus founder Walter Gropius, who was invited to open the new college building designed by Max Bill in the capacity of "moral guarantor."[39] They sniggered at the "limbering-up exercises" that Johannes Itten, the legendary founder of the preparatory course at the Bauhaus and subsequently director of the Zurich School of Applied Arts, introduced at the start of his classes as visiting lecturer. By September, the Ulm director

38 Quoted after Eva von Seckendorff, *Die Hochschule für Gestaltung in Ulm: Gründung (1949–1953) und Ära Max Bill (1953–1957)* (Marburg, 1989), p. 56.

39 Ibid.

Max Bill had been forced to introduce a rectorate council to take over operative management of the school, despite his view that "a school of this kind, like all cultural things, can only be run with authorities."[40] The intellectual head of this management board, which was dominated by younger faculty, was the Argentine Tomás Maldonado, whom Max Bill himself had appointed several years previously and placed in charge of preparatory courses. One should see the real reason for Max Bill's exit from the Ulm stage on March 13, 1957, as lying in the divergent aesthetic concepts of these two key protagonists, aside from all subjective factors, personal sensitivities, and psychological subtleties that naturally made the conflict especially attractive to the news media of the day.

Max Bill argued as an artist when, in keeping with the Bauhaus tradition, he said that despite all rationality and affinity with business, "the creators of new forms are consciously or unconsciously under the influence of modern art."[41]

Tomás Maldonado, in contrast, opposed the concept of design as weltanschauung. "From coffee spoon to city: agreed, but without lapsing into the prejudice of a uniformly carpentered general image of reality. The designer should not be a grand inquisitor dispensing mercy and justice in the world."[42] From this he concludes: "The education of designers must place more emphasis on scientific disciplines that control operative processes in industrial production now and will do so in future, and that have an ever-greater impact on the end product."[43]

With Max Bill's departure, Maldonado's concept of techno-scientifically oriented education in design prevailed over artistically inspired design. This concept had a major influence on design education in general, an influence that endured well beyond the relatively early demise of the Ulm school (which the conservative government of the federal state of Baden-Württemberg closed down in 1969), even though its rigorous subjection of design to the industrial production process was not universally accepted. fig. 24

We see that the design schools we have looked at so far have one thing in common—they were relatively short-lived. The same applies to some extent to Black Mountain College in North Carolina.

24 Demonstration against the closure of the Ulm School of Design, 1968

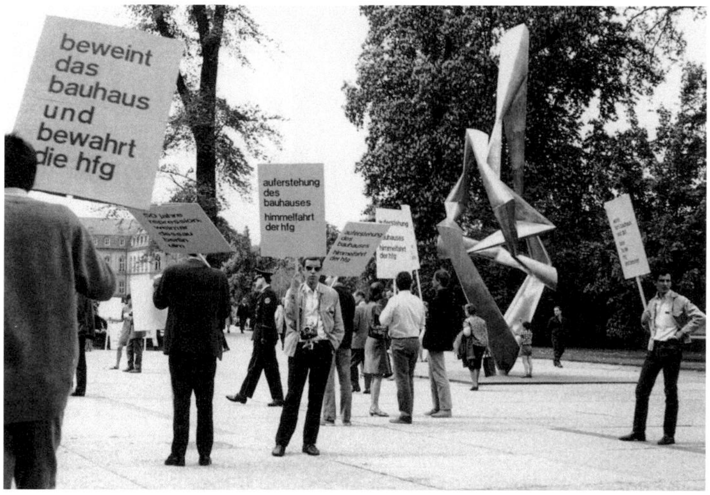

40 Ibid., p. 162.

41 Max Bill, "Bericht an den Schulvorstand der Stadt Zürich über das Projekt 'Institut für Gestaltung'," unpublished manuscript (Zurich, 1961), p. 10.

42 Quoted after Seckendorff, *Die Hochschule für Gestaltung in Ulm* (see note 38), p. 172.

43 Ibid.

Group Portrait with Ladies: Black Mountain College in North Carolina

Black Mountain College, founded by John Andreas Rice in 1933, continued its teaching activities until 1956. However, the period from 1940 until the mid-1950s is chiefly of relevance for our description of art education history. That was when it came closest to the ideal of a productive, innovative school, an ideal that is fundamental to the Zurich University of the Arts. In 1948, Buckminster Fuller produced the first geodesic dome there. John Cage and Robert Rauschenberg staged the first multimedia happening in 1952, and Allen Ginsberg's poems were first published in *Black Mountain Review*, the college newspaper, during that period.

These milestones alone illustrate how highly Black Mountain College ranks among the great twentieth-century art schools. The Bauhaus's late-Romantic idea of unity was realized there in the form of an interdisciplinary curriculum. The association between science and art was put to the test by experiment and not taken for granted in a doctrinaire manner as in Ulm, and space was given to the totality of the arts. Literature, theater, music, dance, visual arts, architecture, and design had their exponents at the college, in the persons of Buckminster Fuller, Walter Gropius (as a visitor), Alfred Einstein, Allan Greenberg, John Cage, and Merce Cunningham, Willem de Kooning, Robert Rauschenberg, Fritz Kline, Cy Twombly, and Josef Albers. Nor is this array of illustrious names mere name-dropping. Those artists are synonymous with a major part of the development that led in the 1960s to a great renunciation of the separatist purism of classical modernity in favor of crossover, to the contradictory cooperation between diverse arts, and later to intermedia concepts. fig. 25

Not by accident did this new beginning take place in what, to put it mildly, was a somewhat remote spot on the cultural world map. Black Mountain College's founder John Andreas Rice, after some very unpleasant experiences of the formalized college culture on the east coast of the United States, established in North Carolina an institutional set-up characterized by supremely democratic structures and highly informal curricula.

As Karl H. Füssl has elaborated in his article on creative educators at Black Mountain College, this led to the development of a host of

25 Lecturers of the summer academy at Black Mountain College, 1946, with Walter Gropius and Josef Albers

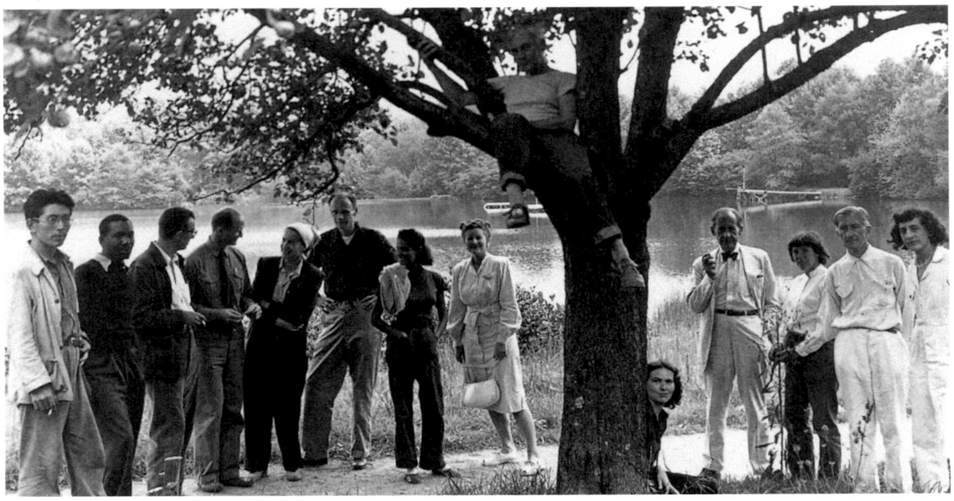

innovative education and training concepts that, after World War II, influenced, if they did not change, a number of traditional colleges, too.[44]

First, supervision arrangements were positively luxurious. The college had no governing body authorized to issue directives and to keep a check on it. Instead, it was headed by a board of fellows and an advisory board. The post of director was held by rotation. Curricula were so open that students had almost unlimited options. Life on campus, developed jointly by faculty and students, led to a situation where architecture was no longer executed in accordance with the classical modern design of Marcel Breuer and Walter Gropius, but built by the students themselves under the guidance of teaching staff. Naturally, a college that was constituted so informally had no state license to hold examinations. "But that was a deliberate part of the system, so as not to put an unnecessary strain on the relationship between faculty and students."[45]

This triad of democratic and egalitarian self-government, consistent interdisciplinarity, and artistic focus produced the climate in which it was possible for border-crossing as an artistic method to have such momentous consequences.

In League with Technology: The Center of Advanced Visual Studies

Border-crossing of a completely different kind was the leitmotif of the Center of Advanced Visual Studies (CAVS) established in 1967 by Gyorgy Kepes, a close associate of László Moholy-Nagy. Kepes had previously been head of Light and Color at the New Bauhaus in Chicago. To begin with, the CAVS was not a teaching institution but a fellowship program for artists at the renowned Massachusetts Institute of Technology (MIT). Its aim was to promote civic and spatial development projects in collaboration with the MIT School of Architecture and Planning. Gradually, however, more and more fellows brought their students to the center as members of project groups, so we can certainly regard the CAVS as a postgraduate studio, albeit one that was strongly research-driven. fig. 26

As early as the 1940s Kepes had worked on his "language of vision," geared to perception, or rather to Gestalt psychology. In his 1944 book

26 Gyorgi Kepes, *China*, 1942

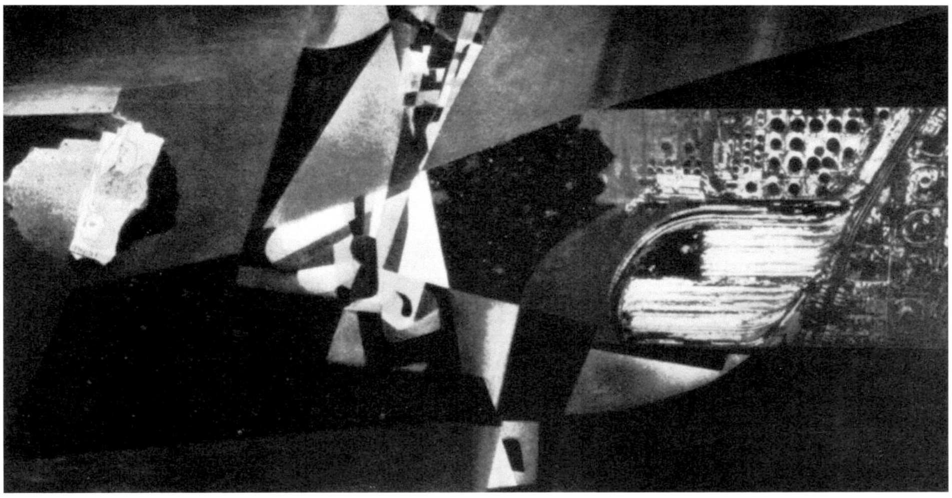

44 Karl H. Füssl, "Kreative Pädagogen am Black Mountain College College (1933–1949): Bauhausmeister Josef Albers—Ein Pestalozzianer im amerikanischen Exil," *Bildung und Erziehung* 56 (2003), pp. 3–22, at p. 6.

45 Ibid.

The Language of Vision he develops his theories of a new "dynamic iconography" that would arise from the transdisciplinary interaction of art and science: "The task of the contemporary artist is to release and bring into social action the dynamic forces of visual imagery. As contemporary scientists are struggling to liberate the arrested energy of the atom, painters of our day must liberate the inexhaustible energy reservoir of the visual associations. To accomplish this, they need a clear grasp of the social field, intellectual honesty, and creative power capable of integrating experiences into a plastic form. The goal will be reached only when art once more lives in inseparable unity with human life."[46]

Disregarding the fact that these lines were written before 1944, when only an initiate, if anyone at all, could foresee the devastating consequences that "liberating" atomic energy would have for the history of mankind, the link between technoscience, social ethics, and professional containment of creative ability that this suggests seems not only to take the ideas of the Bauhaus further, and to anticipate the Ulm curricula, but in some way to anticipate the actual dominance of technology in the revolution even in cultural aims in Western postindustrial societies. It comes as no surprise that no less a personage than Sigfried Giedion, who at the time was trying to come by further inspiration for *Mechanization Takes Command* by gaining experience in the United States, wrote the preface to Kepes's book. Kepes had already translated his pronounced interest in visual research into practice in classes and research projects at the New Bauhaus. Now he incorporated it into the structure and name of the Center of Advanced Visual Studies, thereby preparing the ground for a partnership that was to bring artists into extremely close touch with revolutions in media technology. Those revolutions at the MIT MediaLab and the Architecture Machine Group, including Ivan Sutherland's Sketchpad, the desktop-type monitor screen, and finally the interactive videodisk in the late 1980s, made the computer the most important challenge to the development of all arts since the invention of the art of printing.

By then, however, the German Zero artist Otto Piene was head of the CAVS. Piene propagated his Sky Art through truly monumental performances at Sky Art conferences, multimedia symposia combining discourse, performance, and large installations. Less spectacularly, but especially significant in our context, he collaborated with the architecture department, the Media Lab, and the MIT Film Section to establish the Interdisciplinary Master of Science in Visual Studies. Numerous artists who influenced the emerging media art were CAVS fellows. To name but a few, there are Peter Campus (interactive video), Douglas Davis (sound installation and computer music), Antonio Muntadas (media installation), and Charlotte Moormann, who became world-famous as a partner in the video performances of the Korean artist Nam June Paik.

With its emphatically interdisciplinary curricula, its foundations in advanced, socially relevant technoscience, and its role as a pioneer in the field of interactive media art, the CAVS represents the link between

46 On p. 201 in the 1995 reprint by Dover Publications, New York.

the 1920s Bauhaus and the Center for Art and Media (ZKM) in Karlsruhe, established toward the end of the twentieth century, which as mentioned earlier the media often call the "electronic Bauhaus."

Titanic of Media Art or Electronic Bauhaus: The Center for Art and Media in Karlsruhe

The Center for Art and Media (ZKM) in Karlsruhe, opened in 1997, had set itself the task of sounding out the creative possibilities of a connection between the traditional arts, design, and media technology.

The aim was to enrich the arts and not, as technophobic critics feared, to bring about their technological amputation. That is why an organism was set up that unites under one roof, as it were, the four major areas of the "operating system" of art—production, reception, research, and teaching. The abbreviation ZKM was soon to stand for research and production sites for music and the visual arts, for museums, media archives, and for a design school.

The ZKM's core area was the computer studios where artists back in the late 1990s were able to use what were still gigantically large and gigantically expensive machines to generate images, cultivate virtual worlds, produce interactive sound installations, and premiere multimedia operas. Jointly with the artists in residence, the technicians and computer scientists who worked at the ZKM studios created media technology platforms and experimental areas on which many of the large installations were based that defined the international interactive media art scene in the 1990s. fig. 27

Well-known artists such as Lynn Hershman, who may have been the first artist to produce an interactive video disk, Luc Courchesne with his virtual stage performances, the Californian Michael Naimark, who contributed to the first movie map—a precursor of today's virtual tours—at the MIT Media Lab, or Ken Feingold were artists in residence, as were the computer musician Ludger Brümmer, the Australian interactive movie director Jill Scott, and Knowbotic Research, the network art group that now holds important research and teaching posts at the Zurich University of the Arts. At the end of the 1990s the outlook for work at the Institute for Visual Media was described by its founder,

27 Otto Piene, *Sky Kiss*, Second Sky-Art Conference, Linz 1982

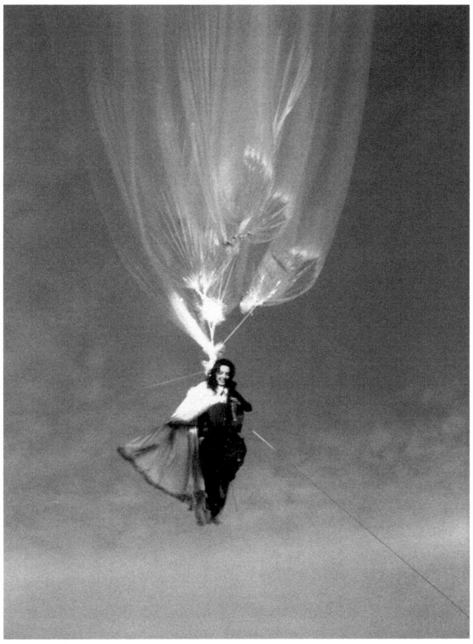

the Australian media artist Jeffrey Shaw, as follows: "If one considers the visions which have accompanied the development of contemporary art in the last thirty years—the kinetic art of the 1950s, the 'open art work' of the 1960s (happenings, environments, performances, land art, etc.), the conceptual and socially critical art forms of the 1970s—then one recognizes that these visions display interesting and astonishing parallels to the technological developments of the 1990s. Interactivity creates a close relationship between the work of art and the viewer, telecommunication makes far-reaching social interactions possible, simulation endows conceptual ideas with a material form. It appears to be only a short step from 'inter-media art' to multi-media technology. However, we cannot yet foresee whether technology will lead to fulfillment or to the final dissolution of these artistic Utopias. The Institute for Visual Media would like to be a place where artists can reflect on this question, and work on it."[47]

Similar in structure to the Institute for Visual Media is the Institute for Music and Acoustics at the ZKM, where a program of scholarships for composers and performers has taken shape that places at their disposal software and hardware that enables them to sound out problems of electronic music across their entire bandwidth.

The institute's greatest success has been the computer-aided composition environment that it developed jointly with the Center for Computer Research in Music and Acoustics at Stanford University. Johannes Goebel, founder of the Institute for Music and Acoustics, outlined his institute's research interests at the time as follows: "With the use of the computer in music we have reached the final stage of quantifiability for music. The purely physiological resolution capacity of the ear as a sense organ is confronted with an 'instrument' that is of equal quantitative value. That leads to a plethora of possibilities and questions, and all of them challenge us to express an opinion. For closer scrutiny the computer can be consulted with the techniques that it makes possible ... [That is why] we in our area no longer need just carpenters, iron founders, mechanical engineers, and master piano makers to make an instrument, but also electronics engineers, programmers, and experts in signal processing. At the Institute for Music and Acoustics they will jointly work on what 'holds the ear together in its essence' and on which artistic qualities can take shape from digital, quantifying technology."[48]

To realize laboratory findings up to their public performance and to test them under the sympathetic yet critical scrutiny of an audience, a media theater was set up with performance technology for interactive virtual space installations and a high-tech concert hall for musical performances that extend into virtual space. fig. 28/29

For sovereign rights reasons the State Academy for Design that was attached to the ZKM had to be built parallel to the Center, but was initially headed in personal union by the spiritus rector of the entire undertaking, the art and architecture historian Heinrich Klotz. Experiments by the media-art avant-garde were to be incorporated directly into its curricula. The design school's first professors were therefore recruited

47 Quoted from Schwarz, *Media, Art, History* (see note 17), p. 15.
48 Ibid.

from the media-art sector—from the Belgian media artist Marie Jo Lafontaine via the director and filmmaker Edgar Reitz to the media philosopher Peter Sloterdijk, the school's present president.

The museums were intended to function as shop windows for the entire ZKM, as it were. The Museum of Contemporary Art was to be a "museum of all genres" of the kind that Alfred Barr, the founding director of the MoMA in New York, had wanted his museum to be.

Along with the classical museum arts—painting and sculpture—the now classical media arts—video and sound installations—as well as architecture and design were included in the program of collections and exhibitions, which also includes a section housing works from southern German private collections of contemporary art.

The ZKM's central concern, however, was showcased at the Media Museum, which to this day can call the world's largest collection of interactive media art its own. And as the present writer was the museum's founding director, he may for once be allowed to quote himself: "While

28 Marie Jo Lafontaine, *Les Larmes d'Acier* (Tears of Steel), 1987
29 Fabrizio Plessi, *Tempo liquido* (Liquid Time), 1993

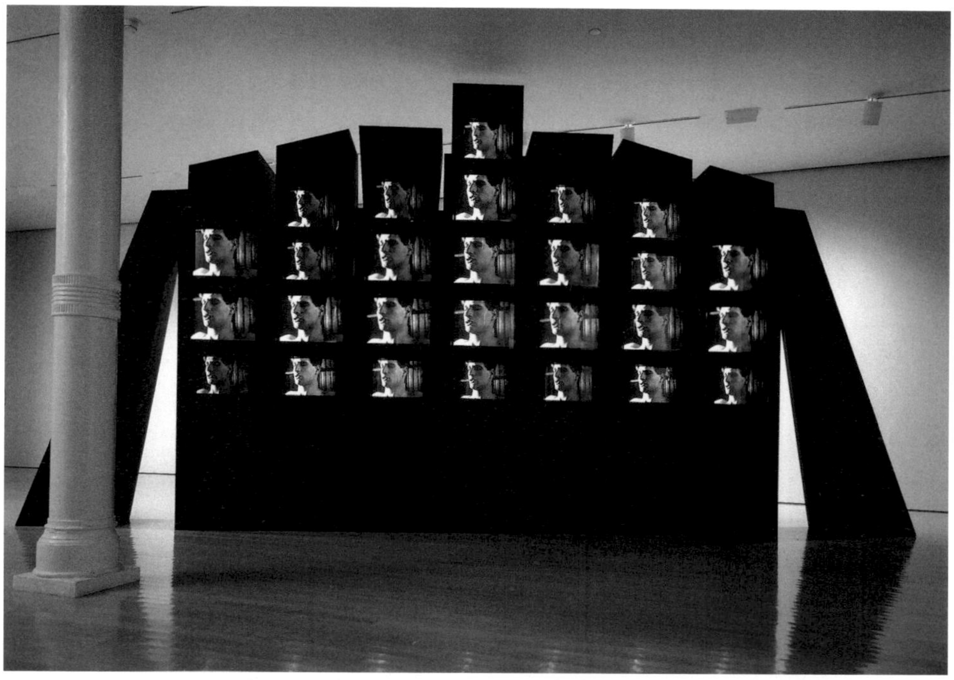

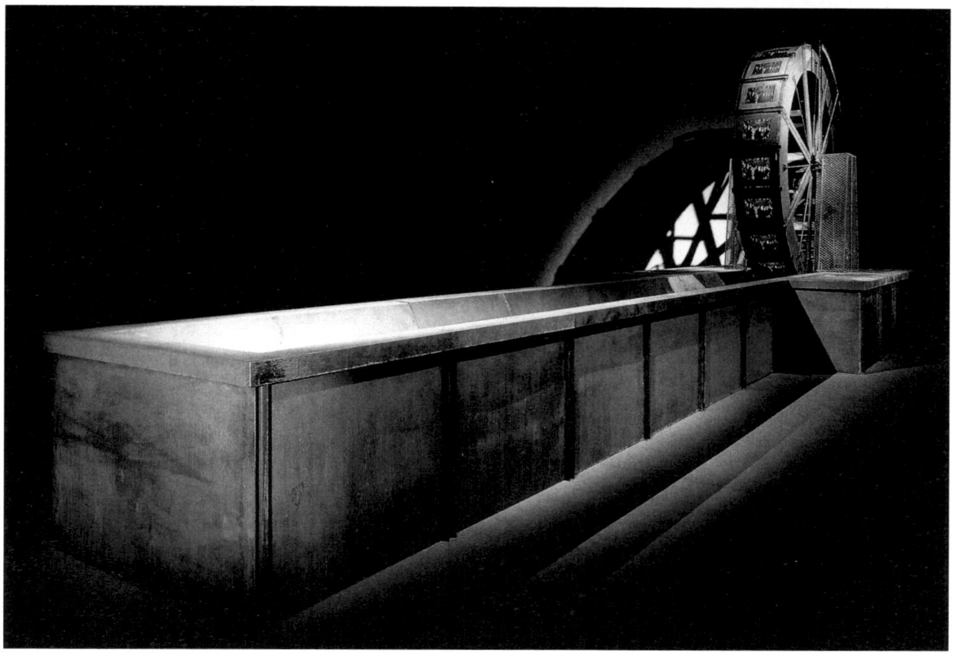

in other departments interest may focus on the artistic experiment in its often autopoetic self-awareness, analytical and therefore necessarily critical argument will prevail at the Media Museum. In spite of all the differences between current individual media technology concepts, their structure can be traced back to three basic functions: simulation, telepresence and, arguably most import of all for a museum, interactivity. The focus of interest at individual museum departments derives from these basic functions. Installations are currently being devised by international groups of artists and designers to take up these focal points with the aid of interactive media art and to present them to a wider public for the first time."

The Karlsruhe Media Museum was an innovation in several respects. It presented works of art not in gallery fashion as objects coagulated into artifacts, but as an interactive process of reception in accordance with Umberto Eco's "work in motion" model as defined in his poetics of the open work.[49] Works of art were specially produced, and the debate on media art was thereby influenced overall—a consequence of the coincidence of art theory and art practice that is not without its risks. The preconditions for media art relating to media aesthetics were made immediately available to visitors by means of action-oriented installations and not concealed in the work of art by way of the aesthetics of reception. That was an act of sacrilege in the history of the operating system of art, which still relies on the allegedly neutral and commentary-free white cube—but a successful act of sacrilege.

For someone so intensively involved in founding what went on to become an historic institution, it is difficult to classify it with the necessary detachment in a context such as ours and determine its place in the evolution of professional training in the arts. The Karlsruhe Center for Art and Media naturally does not represent the terminal point in a development in which the Bauhaus and Black Mountain College were also only some of the highlights. The Cologne Academy of Media Arts, which in my opinion focuses too one-sidedly on digitization, must also be mentioned, as must the fact that the ZKM's cofounders, Jeffrey Shaw and Johannes Goebel, have taken their ideas further forward in Sydney and Stanford in much the same way as I have sought to do in Zurich. But the ZKM definitely represented a milestone in the history of the production-oriented art schools of its day, which were geared to social communication structures. In its organic, albeit never friction-free combination of production, presentation, and education, it was arguably a little on the monumental side. Today, when the days of the "big machine" are long past in media art and elsewhere and the ZKM is being, as it were, re-museumized by its present director, Peter Weibel, there is something obsolete about it. fig. 30–32

From *Paragone* to Gesamtkunstwerk

The discourse in which the commonalities and differences between the arts find expression most clearly and, in media terms, most distinctively, is the so-called *paragone.* Starting with the medieval disputes between the *artes liberales* and the *artes mechanicae,* it was first formulated

49 See Umberto Eco, *The Open Work,* trans. Anna Cancogni (Cambridge MA: Harvard Univ. Press, 1989).

explicitly by Leonardo da Vinci. In his *Trattato della pittura* (*A Treatise on Painting*) Leonardo compares painting with sculpture and explicitly includes music and literature in his deliberations, given that they, as had often been emphasized, were especially ennobled as *artes liberales.* In a comparison of the individual arts in which he polemicizes against the competition, i.e. literature (he calls writers *bestiae*), he develops ideas of which the ramifications with regard to the aesthetics of reception and even media theory are often overlooked but of which the lines of argument went on to become paradigmatic. In this comparison he comes to the conclusion that painting is superior to the other arts because it is able to unite science and imagination in a unique manner. The *paragone* went on to become popular in the famous opinion poll in which Benedetto Varchi questioned the most highly regarded artists of his day on the subject and added the replies of Pontormo, Bronzino, Vasari, and

30 Jill Scott, *Frontiers of Utopia*, interactive cinema, Karlsruhe 1997
31 Jeffrey Shaw, *legible city*, 1989
32 Luc Courchesne, *Portrait No. 1*, 1990

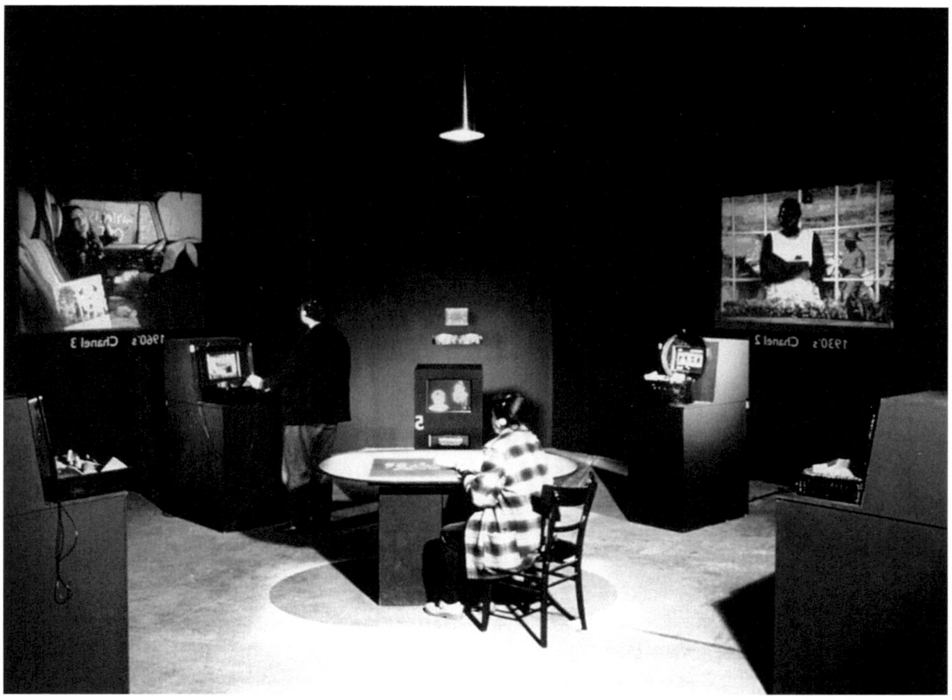

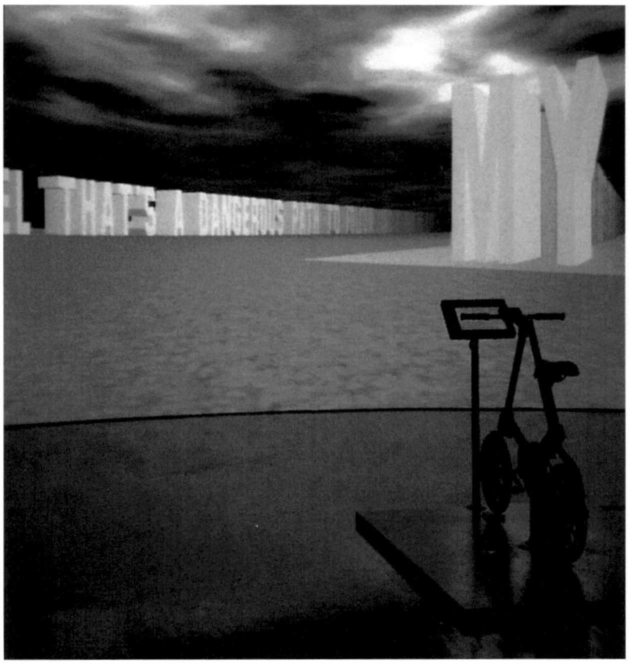

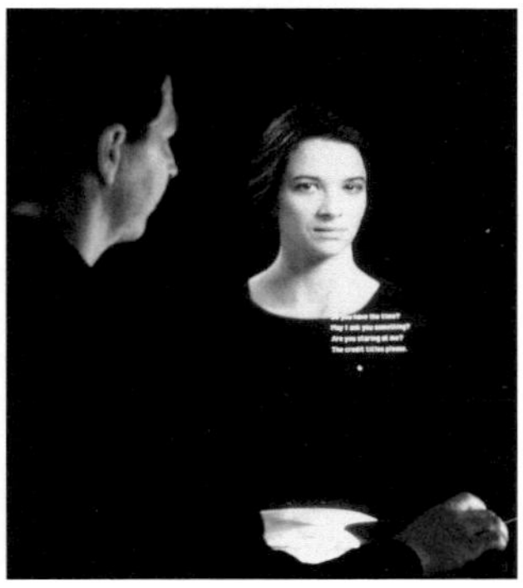

Cellini as an annex to the printed version of his academy lectures. All of these writers—whether they gave preference to sculpture, painting, or architecture—aimed first and foremost to enhance the social status of the visual arts, and succeeded in doing so. Literature and music, the methodology of which the (par)agonal champions of the visual arts sought to exploit in their pretensions to status, did indeed forfeit their status as the leading media until one of the best-known *paragoni,* Lessing's Laocoön, saved literature from being taken over by painting, and music was eventually declared to be the paramount art form.

What matters in our context, however, is that the *paragone* did not limit itself to verbal discourse; it also combined the genuinely artistic media into a kind of overall strategy. A whole range of sculptural and painterly works of visual art took shape as well as a special form of operatic prelude in which the arts, personified, competed against each other. Courtly society's large-scale events celebrated the *paragone* in the form of *trionfi, pompae,* and courtly festivities. Irony, too, became part of the paragonal argumentation strategy. The tale is told of an alleged experiment by Leonardo, who gave a blind man and a lunatic each a painting and a sculpture to judge. The painting was described to the blind man. It was a landscape with animals, woods, and mountains that so appealed to his imagination that he put to one side as uninteresting the sculpture, which he had identified by means of his sense of touch as a male nude. The lunatic, in contrast, who had been given the utensils of both artistic professions because he was incapable of an intellectual statement, was unable to make use of brushes and paint, whereas he had no difficulty in shaping human limbs out of a lump of clay.

Another likely instance of ekphrasis, or literary fiction, albeit in the context of a serious, unironic, and unsatirical line of argument, is Paolo Pini's 1548 example of a *paragone* that was aimed against sculpture and in favor of painting. It was an alleged virtuoso work by the hero of Venetian painting, Giorgione. His *St. George* is a knight in shining armor reflected by water in a spring, in two artificial mirrors, and in fragments of a suit of armor, thereby demonstrating the superiority of painting over sculpture.[50]

A genre which had a strong impact on artistic practice in connection with the *paragone* is the *trompe l'œil,* which was supposed to demonstrate painting's ability to achieve a supra-naturalistic, three-dimensional materiality. Sculpture's answer was to develop the *figura serpentinata,* a type of sculpture that was intended to emphasize the multifacetedness of an image that was not simulated by painterly means but actual and three-dimensional. Virtuoso works of art of this kind had a heyday in the late Renaissance in a phase we generally refer to as mannerism. We also find examples in the arts of the Baroque and neoclassicism of later centuries, which underscores the media-specific alignment of the *paragone* even before Lessing. fig. 33/34

In the course of our deliberations on what the arts have in common and what separates or distinguishes them we have repeatedly come across Lessing's Laocoön, so the title of Thomas Koebner's book *Laokoon*

50 See Christiane J. Hessler, "Maler und Bildhauer im sophistischen Tauziehen: Der Paragone in der italienischen Kunstliteratur des 16. Jahrhunderts," in *Wettstreit der Künste: Malerei und Skulptur von Dürer bis Daumier,* ed. Ekkehard Mai and Kurt Wettengl (Cologne, 2002), pp. 82–97, at pp. 83ff.

und kein Ende (Laocoön: A Never-ending Story), cited earlier, is borne out yet again. The figure of Laocoön made clear a trend in the *paragone* discussion that had always been there but now came to the fore—the analysis of the arts as media. Defining their specific mediality always formed a part of the argumentation on systematizing, hierarchizing, and reciprocally delimiting the arts, though it was instrumentalized to substantiate a claim to social standing. In the second half of the eighteenth century, mediality took center stage, and that is precisely what makes (art) theoreticians such as Lessing so topical today. Georg Frank was surely right in describing public attention as the key currency of the communication society, and current competition between the media as they seek jointly or antagonistically to catch that volatile beast, our attention, has placed categories other than those that are intrinsic to art in the center of paragonal evaluation concepts. However, that may be precisely why the *paragone* subdivided into countless individual media theories that are able—or seek—only to demonstrate their irreconcilability. Today we are engaged in a quest for means of creating a little more order in the confusion that postmodern media theories left behind. It is rather telling that large-scale art research projects are explicitly or implicitly dealing with the *paragone* once more.

From Lessing's Laocoön to the Death of the Author

But let us briefly go back to the time before Lessing's Laocoön and take a deliberate look at the cross-disciplinary collaboration inspired by the *paragone* that goes by the name of a phrase from Horace's *Ars poetica,* namely, "ut pictura poesis." The connection between painting and poetry may have been the most successful; it was certainly the most longstanding collaboration between two of the arts, each of which was understood in both the narrowest and the widest sense as visual arts or literature and may be taken to mean everything between poetry and textuality that is put down in writing. Lessing's Laocoön did not destroy this collaboration, either, but dissolved its simplifying equation of the two, which the young Goethe had still felt to be a mimetic straitjacket for the art of poetry. Since the early 1970s the quest for the language of images or the imagery of language has been back in favor, however. They were

33 After Giambologna, *Rape of a Sabine Woman, figura serpentinata*
34 Cornelis Gijsbrechts, *Quodlibet,* 1675

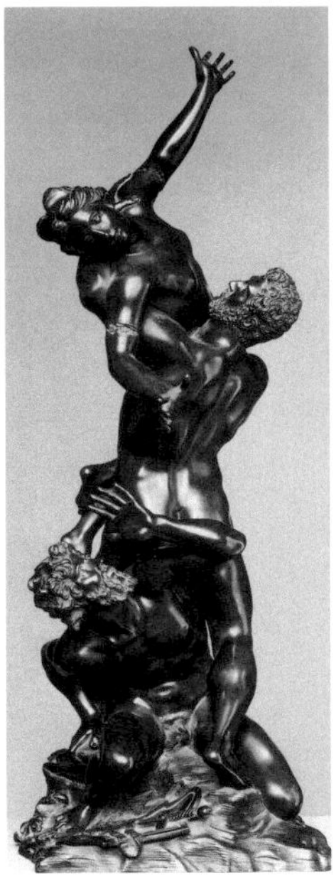

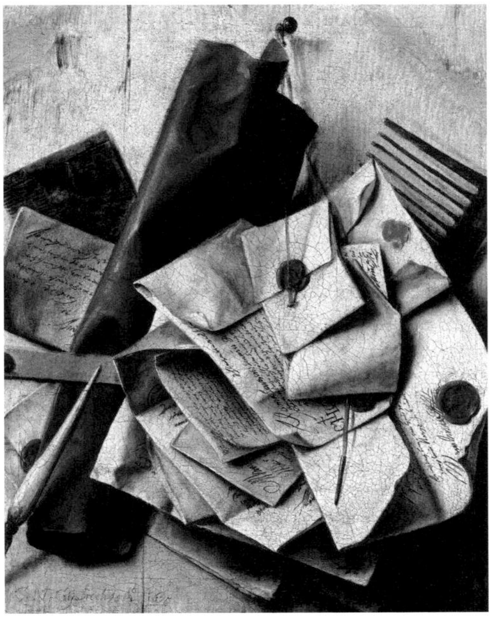

no doubt spread by the writings of Roland Barthes, which gained such a ready reception in the late 1960s, especially in the visual arts. In his essay "Rhetoric of the Image" Barthes rejects a "grammar of painting," but, in keeping with his concept of the birth of the reader brought about by the death of the author, he discovers the "grammatograph who writes the writing of the image."[51]

In our day the link between literature and art, or rather world and image, is closer than ever, as propagandists of hypertext literature never tire of stressing. "The next generation of digital literature [will] depend in equal measure on the design of image, sound, animation, and text," Jürgen Daiber writes in his hyperfictional *ars poetica*.[52]

Corina Caduff puts it more precisely, with reference to Sarah Kofman and Michel Foucault: "Ambiguous, metaphorical speech, according to the current imagery discussion, constitutes a linguistic representation of the gap between painterly syntax and semantics."[53] This relationship between the two art genres, which the semiologists mentioned above still based on difference, on the "leeway" between the "figurative order of the image and the discursive order of language,"[54] is then singled out by postmodern poststructuralists as the claim to general validity of the texualization of all art forms and genres. Everything becomes text. Architecture above all, the main field of action of the (con)textualization debates in the 1980s, is blamed for its alleged speechlessness, and regaining the legibility of architecture is hypostasized as the basic requirement for its renewal. In painting a similar development had taken place twenty years earlier with the triumphal procession of pop art—the antagonists and identification patterns were also similar, if one bears in mind that the gurus of classical modernity, such as Clement Greenberg or Ad Reinhardt, were only able to establish their purity requirements of art *ex negativo*. Revealingly, Ad Reinhardt's "Twelve Rules for a New Academy" all begin with the word "no"—from "no texture" in Rule 1 to "no object" in Rule 12.

Painted Poetry and Poetic Painting

For humanist art theoreticians like Petrarch and Policianus, the rediscoverers, as it were, of the *ut pictura poesis* postulate in the humanist Renaissance, to describe not Apelles, Zeuxis or, say, Protogenes, painters of the ancient world who are historically proven to have existed, but Homer as the first painter of the memorabilities of antiquity is in itself an indication of the paragonal alignment of the debate since the Renaissance, when poetry first held pride of place.

From Leonardo this state of affairs was reversed and painting, not to say the entire phalanx of visual art forms, took the lead in the sixteenth and seventeenth centuries until, as noted above, the elaboration of the medial characteristics of the arts by Winckelmann, Lessing, and others once more freed literature from the mimetic claim of painting. Subsequently the arts were approached via their individual medial character. Because it was seen as part of aesthetics and hence of philosophical

51 On this and the following see Corina Caduff, *Die Literarisierung von Mensch und bildender Kunst um 1800* (Munich, 2003), pp. 28ff.

52 Quoted after Jürgen Daiber, "Ut pictura poesis—oder: Ars poetica für Hyperfiction," www.dichtung-digital.de/Forum-Kassel-Okt-00/Daiber.

53 Caduff, *Die Literarisierung* (see note 51), p. 28.

54 Sarah Kofman, quoted after ibid.

systems, literature took the lead and retained it until the visual regained strength and no longer appeared solely as art, but in the mass-media flood of images.

For the while during which painting was displaced by literature, an art form came to the fore that since the early modern era had been only a third force. Music took center stage in the art systems of the Romantic movement: "At one pole of descriptive possibilities lay the natural sign as used by the representational fine arts (as a sensual sign of the tangible external), while at the other lay the immaterial and abstract musical sign (as a sign of internalization and of the absolute). Language moved between these two forms of artistic expression. It was able to imitate the painterly or musical sign by means of ekphrasis and musical description without actually becoming identical with them."[55]

In contrast to the relationship between painting and literature, which always has something usurpatory about it because it was used by painting and the other visual arts, as we have seen, to boost their social standing, the relationship between music and literature was sanctioned from ancient times, as it were, because both were part of the system of *artes liberales.* That is why in the history of ideas it has hardly ever been problematic to refer to a grammar of music. Harmony, prosody, canons, semiology—all of the terms borrowed from rhetoric were, from the sixteenth century onward at the latest, a fixed part of composition and have to some extent remained so to this day.

Even the e-learning programs of today's colleges of music still have very similar structures in their interactive courses.

This "abstract" vocabulary of form may be the reason why the finest examples in works of the music, literature, and art triad are to be found in so-called abstract art, from *Victory over the Sun,* by Malevich to *Yellow Sound*, by Kandinsky. But these projects already impinge upon the complex of synaesthesias discussed below. Let us first take a look at attempts to portray music directly by means of painting or painting directly by means of music. We can here only give marginal consideration to the role of language as a mediator in this connection, such as in art or music criticism, as ekphrasis or musical poetry.[56]

Ut pictura musica—A Romantic Idea

A key role in the first major attempt to unite the arts by means of music in the early Romantic period is played by the work of Philipp Otto Runge, and especially the *Tageszeiten* (Times of Day) cycle on which he worked between 1803 and 1807. "Music is always what we call harmony and peace in all three arts. Music must, for instance, be in a beautiful work of poetry, just as there must be music in a beautiful painting and in a handsome building or in ideas that are expressed in lines."[57] These are the words on which Runge based his endeavors to bring about an aesthetic reunification—words that are quite clearly written in opposition to Goethe, who in 1798 in the introduction to his *Propyläen* defined just the opposite as the core of his classicist manifesto: "One of the prime characteristics of the decline of the arts is the

55 Ibid., p. 31.

56 Cf. ibid.

57 Quoted from Michael Lingner, "Die Musikalisierung und die allgemeine Kunstwissenschaft," *Zeitschrift für Ästhetik und allgemeine Kunstwissenschaft*, vol. XXIV1 (1979), pp. 75–94, at p. 76.

mixture of the different kinds of them. Art itself and its varieties are interrelated. They have a certain inclination to unite and, indeed, to lose themselves in each other. But the obligation, the merit, the dignity of the true artist lies in the fact that he is able to detach from others the realm of art in which he works, to stand them on their own depending on their type and kind, and to isolate them as far as possible."[58]

Whether Runge with his tendency toward non-material work paved the way for absolute painting in the twentieth century, as Michael Lingner argues in his work on the musicalization of painting in the work of Runge,[59] must remain open. He certainly marks the beginning of a development that led more or less directly to Kandinsky, via symbolists like Odilon Redon, Jugendstil artists like Klimt, and fauvists like Matisse. Kandinsky saw himself as a synaesthetician and identified the color yellow, for example, with the sound of trumpets or a fanfare, orange with the viola and blue with the cello, double bass, or organ. One reason why he is of importance here is that in his pictorial compositions he referred not to Bach, Mozart, or other consonant musical concepts, but at a very early stage found Arnold Schönberg's emancipation of dissonance to be significant for himself and his painterly resolutions. fig. 35a–d

So it was that a unique situation came about at the beginning of the twentieth century when, more or less simultaneously in both genres, "musicians freed themselves from the system of tempered tonality ... and painters [broke] with the system of perspective in spatial unity and reproducibility."[60]

Kandinsky in his influential work *Concerning the Spiritual in Art* sang the praises of music as the leader of the arts and impressed the avant-garde artists of his circle with his synaesthetic admiration for Schönberg. So it comes as no surprise that in the *Blauer Reiter,* the almanac that Kandinsky edited jointly with Franz Marc and that gave the Munich group of artists its name, six essays about "primitive" art (Marc) were accompanied by four about music, and scores of music by Schönberg, Anton Webern, and Alban Berg were also included.[61]

The *Blauer Reiter* was intended as a synthetic manifesto to bridge the rifts between the arts (literature, music, and visual arts) that the "analytic" method had opened up, as Kandinsky put it in a 1936 essay in the *Cahiers d'art* on the work of his coeditor Franz Marc.[62] The line-up of composers who wrote for the almanac was particularly revealing. They included Nikolay Kulbin, who wrote about free music; Thomas von Hartmann, who was soon to be Kandinsky's closest associate in a "synthetic" work for the stage; and Arnold Schönberg, who contributed an essay on "The Relationship with the Text." Schönberg in particular here postulates—and his artist colleagues will have agreed—that a merely external, superficial equation of the arts could not be the aim of their

58 Johann Wolfgang Goethe, "Einleitung Propyläen (1798)," in *Werke,* 14 vols. (Hamburg: Wegner, 1953), vol. 12.

59 Lingner, "Die Musikalisierung" (see note 57).

60 Quoted after Karin von Maur, "Musikalische Strukturen in der Kunst des 20. Jahrhunderts," in *Vom Klang der Bilder: Die Musik in der Kunst des 20. Jahrhunderts,* exh. cat. Staatsgalerie Stuttgart (Munich: Prestel, 1985), p. 10.

61 See Jelena Hahl-Koch, "Kandisky und der 'Blaue Reiter'," in von Maur, *Vom Klang der Bilder* (see note 60), pp. 354–59, at p. 355.

62 Quoted after ibid., p. 357.

avant-garde reunification, but that “apparent superficial divergences can be necessary because of parallelism on a higher level.”[63]

The Blauer Reiter artists were not alone in giving ideas about the synthesis of art and (new) music an enthusiastic reception and in making them a main concern of their work. A veritable wave of audiovisual works surged through the avant-garde internationale of the early decades of the twentieth century, involving all of the “isms” and photography and cinema, too, which had only just been included in the canon of visual arts media. fig. 36/37

Old dreams of synthetic instruments and a common syntax of colors and sounds gained a fresh lease of life. Louis Bertrand Castel’s famous *clavecin oculaire,* which in the mid-eighteenth century was rarely given a real hearing but met with all the more of a response in literary criticism from Diderot to Goethe, experienced a widely regarded revival in the color organ of Hungarian composer Alexander László and the

35a–d Philipp Otto Runge, *Tageszeiten* (Times of Day), 1803

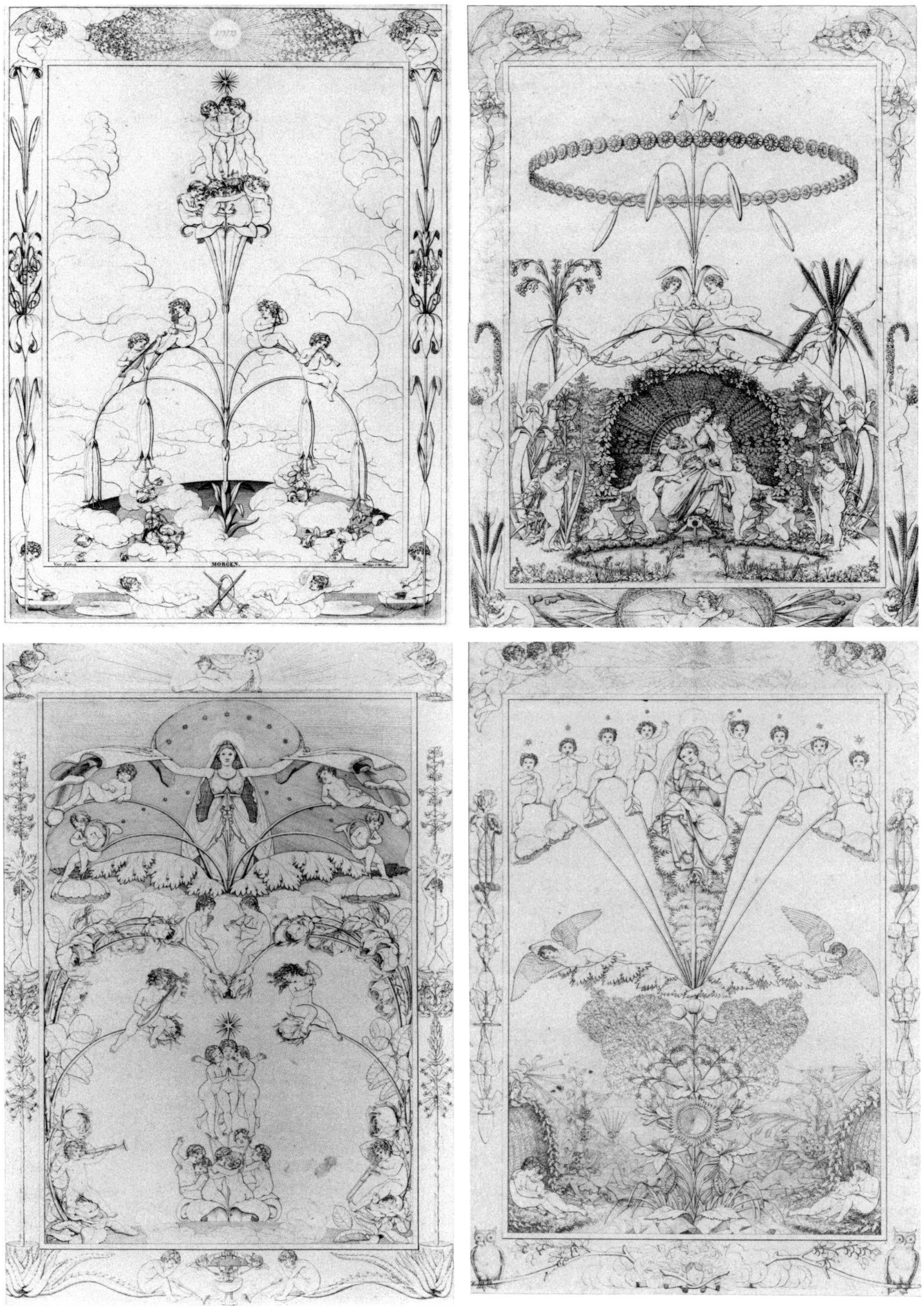

63 Arnold Schönberg, “The Relationship with the Text,” in *Style and Idea: Selected Writings of Arnold Schönberg,* ed. Leonard Stein, trans. Leo Black (Berkeley: Univ. of California Press, 1984), pp. 142–45, at p. 145.

34a/b Hans Richter, for *Film Sequences*, 1923

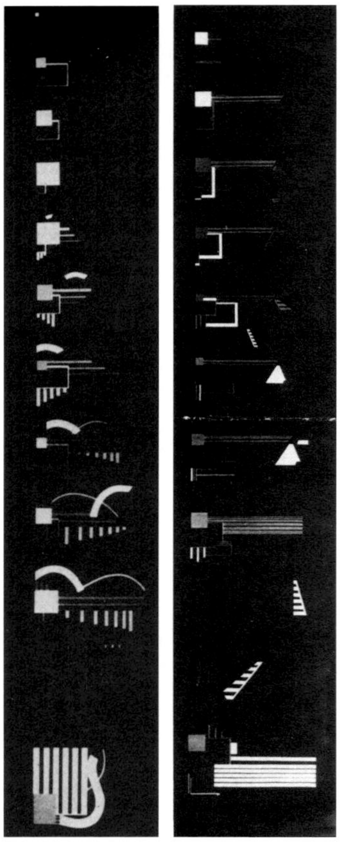

visual music experiments by the abstract filmmakers Viking Eggeling, Hans Richter, and Oskar Fischinger.

It is unnecessary to go into whether any, and if so which, of these synaesthetic experiments, which were crowned by Alexander Scriabin's formidable poem *Prometheus,* were truly based on psychologically and physiologically identifiable hearing of color or vision of sound. The pianist and Zurich University of the Arts teacher Natalia Sidler, who has taken László's color organ as the occasion for a further development and new interpretation of these concepts and in a large-scale research project at the ZHdK is engaged in academic and artistic research into the relationship between color, light, and music, is somewhat skeptical, as is her colleague Jörg Jewanski. They see visual works of music as tending more toward the Romantic trail that we laid initially.[64]

As for the question of what holds the arts together, the synaesthetic relationship between music and images that was not only given an enthusiastic reception by artists, sculptors, and architects, but was also taken up by what were then the new media, marked an intermediate stage. From this starting point two perspectives are possible for the further pursuit of artistic collaborations that I would first like to deal with separately. One illuminates modernity's "penchant for the gesamtkunstwerk" and consists of the provocative art concepts that we know as intermedia or multimedia. The other spotlights a collaboration that crosses the borders of the arts, that brings back into Western civilization the origin of the concept of art, as it were, and may be of even greater significance for our present and future than all other attempts at reuniting the arts: It is the relationship of the arts with technology, indus-

64 Cf. Natalia Sidler and Jörg Jewanski, *Farb-Licht-Musik: Synästhesie und Farblichtmusik*, Zürcher Musikstudien, vol. 5. (Bern, 2006), pp. 190ff.

37 Walter Ruttmann, photo sequences for *Opus III + IV*, 1923

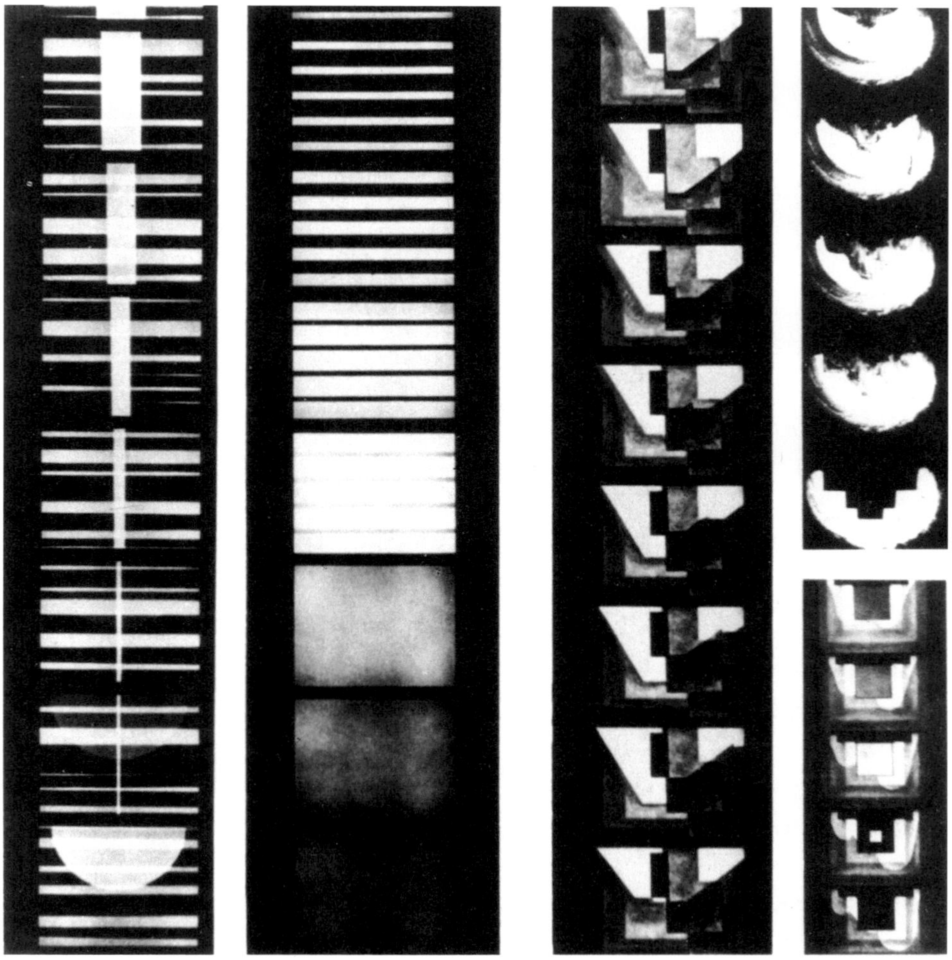

trial technology in any case, but even more so postindustrial media technology with its enormous effect on the entire social communication of our recent past, our present, and our future. fig. 38

Technological Localizations of the Arts

Friedrich Kittler, one of the best connoisseurs of media technology, expressed it wonderfully: "Like all the other words that make us think, art and technology are Greek gifts." Even so, in the context of this essay I do not propose to go into the history of the concept of *techné* at a time when art and artistry still coincided or into the theatrical machinery of Hero of Alexandria. I am also ignoring the wonderful world of courtly festivities for which Leonardo implemented several of his finest inventions, E. T. A. Hoffmann's ekphrastic machine men, the early automata of Swiss watchmaker Pierre Jaquet-Droz and Jacques de Vaucanson's mechanical duck, whose digestive processes so impressed Goethe.

For our deliberations on the interplay and possible inner connection between the arts, another of Kittler's observations is more important. There were many indications, he noted, "that the early modern era was epoch-making in transferring musical or mathematical knowledge to other arts."

Filippo Brunelleschi's dome for the cathedral in Florence, one of the greatest engineering achievements ever, was based on the mathematical studies of an architect who had trained as a goldsmith and

38 Matthias Holl, *Performance with Alexander László's Color Organ*, 1925

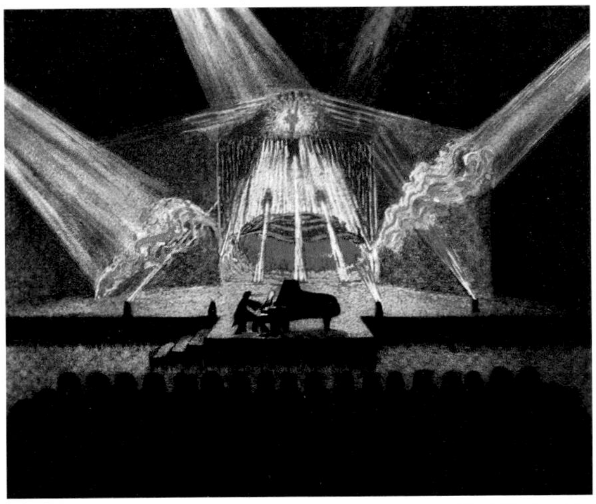

sculptor. Leon Battista Alberti in his *De pictura* (*On Painting*) united the liberal arts, mathematics and music, and parts of Euclidian optics to develop linear perspective. Simon Severin invented musical temperament. "Finally, in Euler's work optics and acoustics, the scientific technological bases of Romantic enjoyment of the arts, are merged into a single partial differential calculus..."[65]

Once again it is the Romantic era as the earliest age of modernity from which we plan to start out in our deliberations on the relationship between the arts and technology. We imagine the arts of that time as having been somewhat reserved about technology, and if we equate technology with industrialization, that was true. The invective against the "phantom color organ"[66] prove that the rationalistic component in technology was seen as either hostile toward the arts or at least irrelevant for them.

Yet Romanticism did call the aesthetic immediacy of the work of art into question by drawing a distinction between the work and the reception level that had not existed in the classical concept. Put simply, in the classical concept of art it was the artist who decided what the beholder saw.

Since the Romantic era, at least in central parts of the concepts developed at the time, the artist has done no more than produce the "instrument" with the aid of which the recipient can realize his visual hearing experience or his musical daydream. The work thereby becomes a joint enterprise by the artist and the beholder, the audience, the connoisseur.[67]

The disintegration of the unity of artist, work, and recipient—if it ever existed—led to a paradoxical situation. On the one hand, as autonomization with the tendency toward internalization that had its roots in and just before the Romantic era progressed, the arts increasingly moved away from socially agreed and sanctioned communication standards. Among the avant-gardes of the nineteenth and twentieth centuries especially, this led to a speechlessness that was felt to be traumatic and that drove them into isolation—a reciprocal isolation. On the other hand, both the modulation of emotion by the artist and the aesthetic experience of the recipient were subjected to a far-reaching process of

65 Quoted after Friedrich Kittler, *Optische Medien* (Berlin, 2002), p. 107.
66 Caduff, *Die Literarisierung* (see note 51), pp. 83ff.
67 Cf. Lingner, "Die Musikalisierung" (see note 57).

mechanization or even industrialization in which, with disruptions of course, the arts were reunited. Here, too, as in the avant-garde combination of music and image, the stage was the common ground, even if it appeared changed beyond recognition. Here, too, the aesthetic, artistic concept was theatricality. And theatrical it certainly was, the first mass-media and, in a sense, large-scale industrialized concept that was aimed explicitly at synaesthetic experience, namely, the panorama.

From Panorama to Cyberspace

Cult and ritual had also, of course, to a limited extent been immersive mass media, but a Roman Catholic mass, a courtly festival, or a dynamic ritual, even though they were regimented and thereby basically repeatable, were bound to a here and now. They were not media-driven to the extent of the panorama, which, significantly, was invented at the beginning of the industrial age. In his brief definition of the concept in the catalogue of the comprehensive panorama exhibition entitled *Sehsucht* (Addicted to Seeing) that was held at the Bonn Kunsthalle in 1993, Ulrich Giersch outlines this nineteenth-century "mass entertainment" as follows: "In the panorama, the beholder is shown the illusion of a certain real space, the borders of which are defined by the surrounding line of the horizon. To cover up breaks and interruptions, transitions from three to two dimensions are created by means of perspective techniques and light management. In an attempt to break the bounds of the whole picture as a window on the world and to make the orientation coordinates of real space work in an artificial space, all of the means of representational painting along with those of the stage and showmanship are put to use. The panorama's simultaneous show assembles what in principle are the techniques and elementary laws of optics in a single exhibition room."[68]

The panorama is therefore in our context—crossing borders between the arts—extremely significant with its mass-media orientation, its multimedia arrangement and its transmedial combination of advanced basic principles and methods of science and the arts.

That is why it is of some importance that the panorama can be regarded as the precursor of the synaesthetic mass medium par excellence of the early twentieth century—the motion picture. More important, however, is the fact that different pictorial, scenographic, and auditory media technologies were combined into a total work created with the aid of scientific inventions. New forms of perception were integrated, especially the type evoked by woodcuts and lithographs in illustrated newspapers, which strikingly conveyed information to the masses, whose ways of seeing changed accordingly. The latest physical medium of transport, the railroad, also changed perceptions, as Dolf Sternberger noted in his observations on the nineteenth century. "The railroad transformed the newly accessible world of lands and seas itself into a panorama."[69]

At the same time, new public spaces and concerns emerged that gave shape to new structures of perception: "Pleasure in the alternation of pictorial worlds, 'optical jugglery,' was satisfied with the panorama

68 Ulrich Giersch, "El Lissitzky: Prounen-Raum," in *Sehsucht: Das Panorama als Massenunterhaltung des 19. Jahrhunderts*, ed. Marie-Louise von Plessen and Ulrich Giersch (Bonn: Stroemfeld, 1993), p. 292.

69 Dolf Sternberger, *Panorama oder Ansichten vom 19. Jahrhundert* (1946; repr. Frankfurt a. M., 2001), p. 48.

as an art form of the revolution. Urbanization promoted public curiosity about the discovery of big cities, continents, and forms of life. These were the changing pictorial programs of a mobile profession that plied its trade wherever it wanted. The fascination of this new form of existence generated gigantic paintings in the round as a 'visual journey' to unknown locations beyond one's personal day-to-day experience. Historical events, mainly military to promote patriotic sentiment, were brought to the viewer, who by the panorama's deceptively faithful depictions on the circular screen was given the feeling of actually witnessing the event shown and experiencing for himself the validity and grandeur of patriotic events."[70]

Creating panoramas as the first mass media led not only to their production and distribution by stock corporations with enormous amounts of capital, but also to their continuous further development in terms of media technology. fig. 39

Depending on the different reception and distribution conditions in different parts of the world, the results included nausoramas and dioramas, double-sided moving panoramas known as pleoramas, cosmoramas and finally, at the 1900 World Exposition, the balloon cinerama as both climax and conclusion—the first cinematographic panorama in the round. The panorama was a hot tip on the stock market. Stock corporations founded specifically to produce panoramas financed lavish theaters and an advanced technological infrastructure. Miniature panoramas, construction manuals for young people and similar forms of merchandising were used, and the photographic devices became increasingly adventurous. In World War I carrier pigeons were equipped with panoramic cameras and sent on reconnaissance flights. But the invention that was most momentous for the history of audiovisual perception was and continued to be the panoramic viewpoint and the increasingly sophisticated media technology strategies aimed at involving the beholder more and more immediately in the pictorial action and making the events that were seen appear to be tangible.

39 Robert Mitchell, *Robert Baker's Panorama, London* 1801

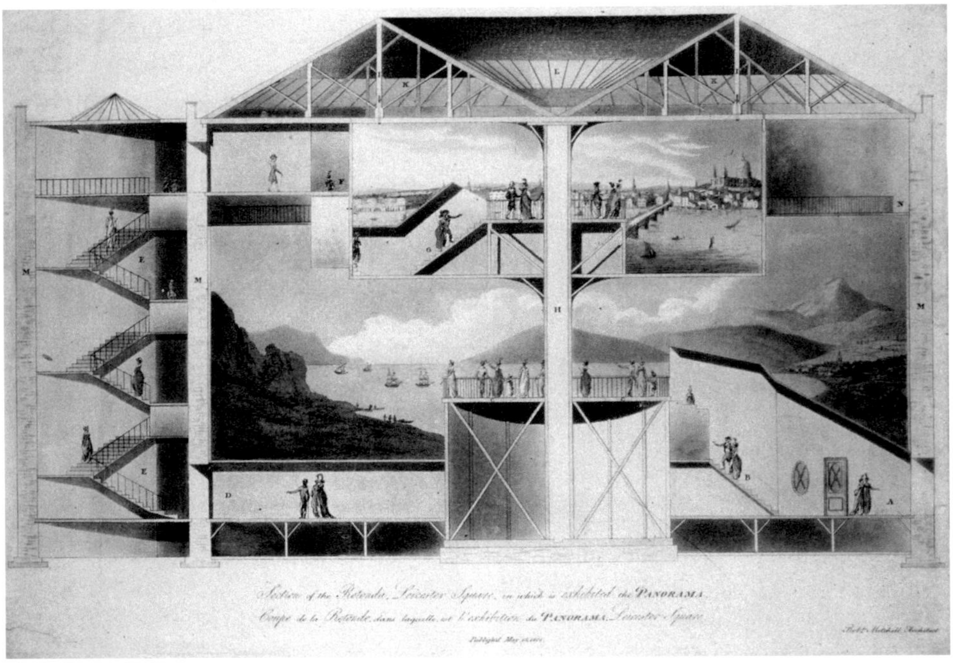

70 Marie-Louise von Plessen, "Der gebannte Augenblick: Die Abbildung von Realität im Panorama des 19. Jahrhunderts," in *Sehsucht*, ed. Plessen and Giersch (see note 68), pp. 12–19, at p. 13.

At the beginning of the twentieth century, collage and film montage literally dissolved the uniform concept of space that had prevailed undisputed in the fine arts since the Renaissance, and that had culminated in the panorama. Time-based strategies took the lead in the arts of audiovisual illusion. Gilles Deleuze deals with this process in detail.[71] Then, at the beginning of the second half of the twentieth century, groups such as the Expanded Cinema Movement countered by developing and experimenting with artistic strategies that sought to make the media concept of the cinema, developed paradigmatically in Hollywood for passive reception in a linear narrative time structure, more dynamic and bring it back into real space. It is plausible to assume that they resorted to the idea of the panorama in its various forms. The work of Australian media artist Jeffrey Shaw provides particularly good examples of this productive reversion to the prehistory of film, because the panoramic view became for him a central area of artistic experimentation—from his early Expanded Cinema projects in the 1970s via real-time computer-generated interactive panoramas such as *legible city, Virtual Museum,* or *Place: A User's Manual* and the Expanded Virtual Environment (EVE) that he developed to his interactive installation in the immersive Computer Aided Virtual Environment (CAVE) that was devised as a media technology concept by the University of Illinois and represents the high-water mark of immersive panorama, as it were. fig. 40

To see the panorama, the first synaesthetic multimedia mass medium, only as a staging post on the way to the big synaesthetic mass-media industries of film and television is to take too narrow a view. Yet it was the film and television industries that ruled the roost of aesthetic experience in the twentieth century. That they were outflanked toward the end of the century by the games industry, which transports the (inter)active reception behavior that was once the starting point of the disunification of art and recipient is one of the by no means coincidental paradoxes of (media) art history. But before that could happen the technological preconditions had to be developed for a concept by means of which industrialized mass culture and avant-garde art would

40 Jeffrey Shaw, *Place: A User's Manual*

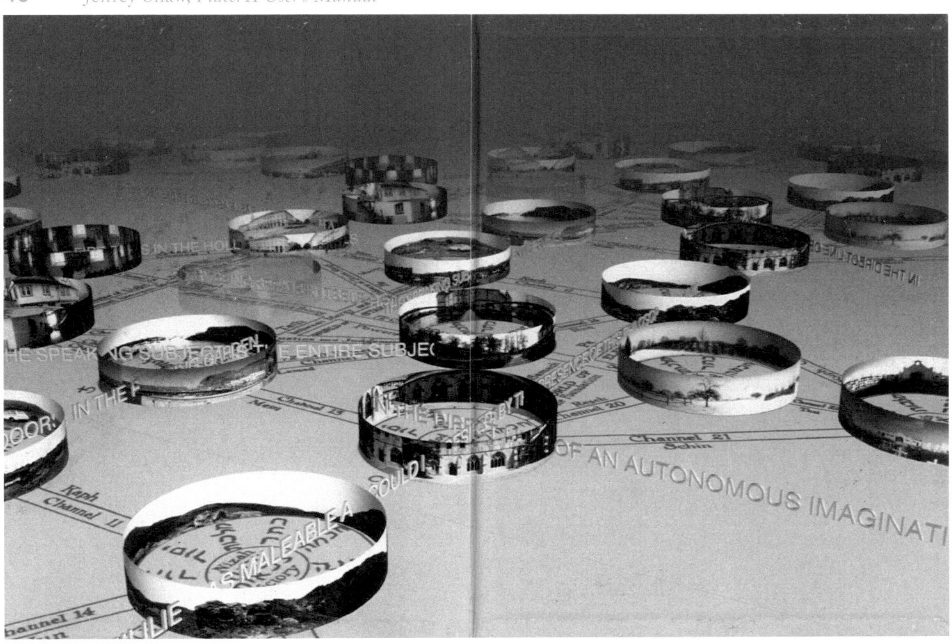

71 Cf. Gilles Deleuze, *Cinema 2: L'image-temps* (Paris, 1985).

influence each other and that as yet leaves the *paragone* between art and the (mass) media in utopia, or at least undecided for utopia. That concept is multimedia.

In Technology's Frenzy of Images—Multimedia as Avant-garde

Here, for once, developments began in the United States. Jointly with Robert Rauschenberg, the cofounder of the happening, the Swedish engineer Billy Klüver founded Experiments in Art and Technology (E. A. T.), a venture that in the early 1970s had six thousand members—artists and engineers in roughly equal numbers.

This venture institutionalized for the first time what had been in the making since the Bauhaus and comparable groupings such as the London-based Artists Placement Group. More and more artists were interested in learning about advanced technologies—not years or decades later when they had long become obsolete for industrial production, but as soon as they were invented. Douglas Davis in his book *Art and the Future* lists an entire phalanx of artists who were already making use of technological developments in their work before the general public was even aware of their main features, artists ranging from Bruce Nauman (hologram) to James Turell (laser).

The close connection between technology and art began to take shape, mainly in the United States, in the 1950s. There as elsewhere, the experiences of technology let loose that they had gained in World War II moved countless artists to withdraw to their studios and work with traditional materials in traditional formats. The members of the New York School were also among these artists. The counter-movement was due to a development that Davis describes as specifically American. He considers American artists not to be very receptive to aesthetic programs and ideologies. "The advent of Moholy and all he represented is only a part of the story that must be told about the growth of the fusion of art, technology, and science in the United States."[72]

The other part is based in the development of technology itself. This is where we finally come across the technological concept that took the place of the nineteenth-century "big machine" in the twentieth century—the computer or, to be more precise, the PC. We might not need to devote any thought to the relationship between art and technology today if it were merely a matter of the mainframe computer with its relevant computing capacities for large corporations, municipal administrations, or city telephone exchanges. But the PC's ability to control or even generate multimedia experiences and its resulting mass distribution are the real parameters of its revolutionary importance.

The legendary founding fathers in the evolution of the computer's multimedia capabilities, Vannevar Bush and Douglas Engelbart, still felt committed to the educational concept of expanding human understanding with the aid of technology. The one outlined the first multimedia desktop system, Memex, back in 1945, while the other invented or developed in the 1950s and 1960s everything that made the computer a mass-produced item, from the user interface via the mouse to the electronic mail system. "Augmenting the Human Intellect" was the title

72 Douglas Davis, *Art and the Future: A History/Prophecy of the Collaboration between Science, Technology and Art* (London: Thames and Hudson, 1973), p. 33.

of Engelbart's influential paper, and its author clearly belongs to a technophile wartime generation that had just experienced the triumph of diversified technologies over totalitarian ideologies. Both men had been employed in the American war industry, Bush as a science executive, Engelbart as a radar technician.

The next generation of multimedia strategists can be exemplified by Ted Nelson and his book *Dream Machines,* the manifesto of the multimedia movement and probably the original source of the term. Against ascetic intellectualism he sets the concept of a hedonistic "community of souls" between the hypermedia computer and the multimedia individual. This concept was to have an effect that went far beyond the bounds of science. In 1970 Gene Youngblood's *Expanded Cinema,* for which Buckminster Fuller, himself something of a multimedium, wrote the preface, compiled an abundance of events that had processed the model of a media concept that integrated graphics, film, video, theater, music, etc., into a comprehensive whole.

So we see that it was not, say, the computer's actual revolutionary but largely invisible computing power that was responsible for the widespread fascination with the so-called new media, but the opportunity to control a whole world of sounds and images that was now at the individual's disposal. Nelson cited its ostensible objective with his demand, "To see tomorrow's computer systems, go to the video game palace! Go to the military flight simulators! Look there to see true responsiveness, true interaction."

Interactivity had previously been merely an essential conceptual postulate, but it now seemed to have the potential to become a technological reality, and one that for the time being extended less to the contents than to the modes of reception of the multimedia ensemble. The reception devices, some of them a little strange, that have been developed for this purpose do seem to have a dangerous tendency. The interactive and simulational possibilities that are inherent in the multimedia concept have in general been reduced to a mere illusionism. That has made them a welcome treasure trove for the Hollywood entertainment industry or the Japanese games corporations that cream off the lion's share of their practical creativity and are largely to blame for extremely interesting image-generating programs leading to dubious results that have brought the computer's visual capabilities into overall disrepute, at least as far as art is concerned.

Admittedly, the aesthetics of reception based on technology concepts of this kind has since become global by virtue of the dominance of the Internet's communication structures and must at times be considered irreversible for the arts, too. To a certain extent, indeed, the precarious achievements of digital media technology only now seem to have delivered suitable hardware and the matching software to make the avant-garde dream of media or at least virtual reality come true, the dream that earlier on we left on the synaesthetic threshold of the "sound of images"—the penchant for the gesamtkunstwerk.

The Gesamtkunstwerk in the Modern Era

The concept of the gesamtkunstwerk or synthesis of the arts was introduced into the arts debate by Karl F. E. Trahndorff in the second volume of his *Ästhetik der Lehre von der Weltanschauung und Kunst* (Aesthetics of the Doctrine of Worldview and Art, 1827), popularized by Richard Wagner in his 1849 Zurich writings on *The Art Work of the Future,* and internationalized, as it were, by Charles Baudelaire. There have since been countless interventions on the subject of the gesamtkunstwerk in art theory and practice. Anke Finger, to whose recent work on the subject we owe the chapter heading, rightly says that "the over 150-year-old assimilation or, seen from outside, usurpation of the gesamtkunstwerk concept within individual disciplines [has] produced such a variety of forms that the number of interpretations of the concept that differ from the original reflects the aesthetic modern era in its polymorphy."[73]

Does that make the gesamtkunstwerk a mirror image of modernity overall? The gesamtkunstwerk is not an object, no matter how complex, but a highly complex process, depending on its degree of transdisciplinarity. It must be studied and portrayed less in its work aesthetics than in its production aesthetics and questioned in terms of reception aesthetics as to the degree of its effect on the players that take part in it. In the concept of modernity, the relationship of unity and fragment that is inherent in the gesamtkunstwerk is best described more as an oscillation than as a perfectly executed balancing act. Yet one must agree with Finger that it is "indeed the degree of cooperation and dedication to the work of art that is to be realized that fascinates and fires us on to this day. It is the quality and intensity in which the arts have merged and parted again over the centuries, parallel to the diversification and further development of disciplines and with or without borders being drawn."[74] At all events some of the most fascinating works of art of the modern era have taken shape as fragmentary units in this process of oscillation.

This is where two of the arts that in our previous investigations have put in only sporadic appearances—the performing arts of theater and dance—assume great importance. That is why we are returning to the threshold at which we left the collaboration of music and visual art, the avant-gardes of the early twentieth century and, more specifically, to Wassily Kandinsky. In the stage experiments that Kandinsky undertook with Thomas von Hartmann, his junior by twenty years, the combination of music and visual art was extended to the performing arts. fig. 41

As Jelena Hahl-Koch discovered, Hartmann and Kandinsky in their collaboration on the major stage compositions *The Yellow Sound* and *The Green Sound* struck such a balance between all of the elements that none dominated the other. Kandinsky had frequently criticized the dominance of music in Wagner's gesamtkunstwerk concept, although he otherwise admired Wagner and claimed to have had his first synaesthetic experience at a performance of *Parsifal.* Another interesting point in our context is Kandinsky's attempt, jointly with Hartmann and the

73 Anke Finger, *Das Gesamtkunstwerk der Moderne* (Göttingen, 2006), p. 12.

74 Ibid., p. 19.

41 Wassily Kandinsky, stage set for Mussorgsky's *Pictures at an Exhibition*, ca. 1930

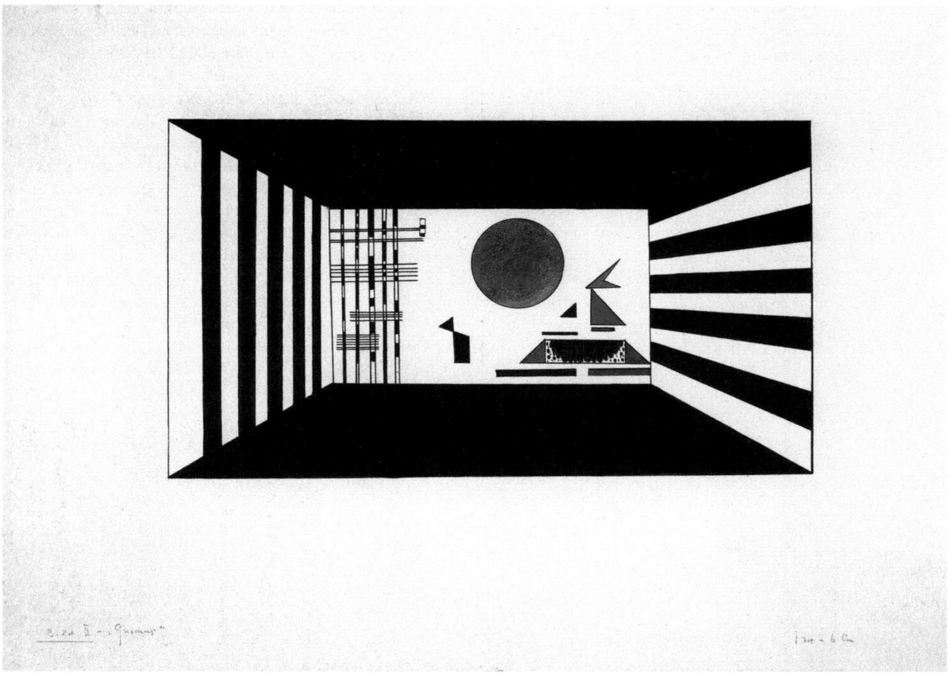

young dancer Alexander Sakharoff, to include dance in his experiments to sound out the interconnections between the arts.

In a lecture by Kandinsky that was published in 1921 in a Moscow journal, it all sounds like an amusing parlor game. "The musician selected from a number of my watercolors the one that seemed clearest to him from a musical viewpoint. In the dancer's absence he played this watercolor. Then the dancer arrived on the scene, the piece of music was played to him, he converted it into dance and then had to guess which watercolor he had danced."[75]

On the avant-garde stage the synaesthetic or synthetic twosomes expand into an ensemble. The Bauhaus, which itself intended to be a gesamtkunstwerk by the definition given above, brought together a whole number of celebrities who made the Bauhaus stage a brand name for synaesthetic experimentation. In addition to Kandinsky, they included Oskar Schlemmer, Moholy-Nagy, and Andreas Weininger, whose mechanical stage was reconstructed and presented for the collection of the Center for Art and Media in Karlsruhe.

Oskar Schlemmer's *Triadic Ballet* is surely the most spectacular solution produced for the synaesthetic Bauhaus stage, while his stage set for Hindemith's opera *Mörder, Hoffnung der Frauen* (Murderer, Hope of Women), composed after a one-act play by the painter Oskar Kokoschka, was probably the most popular. Moholy-Nagy's *Mechanical Eccentricity,* in contrast, refers to the technical aspect of the synaesthetic experiments, as does the total theater that Walter Gropius designed for Erwin Piscator. fig. 42–44

Not directly connected with the Bauhaus but with very similar intentions, Kazimir Malevich staged his suprematist visions in the play *Victory over the Sun.* Whether the theater really is the synthesizing model par excellence for an interplay of the arts, as Schelling noted in his 1802 *Philosophy of Art,* albeit with critical swipes at theatrical (opera)

75 Quoted from Hahl-Koch, "Kandisky und der 'Blaue Reiter'" (see note 61), p. 355.

42 Oskar Schlemmer, design for a stage set for the play Mörder, *Hoffnung der Frauen* (*Murderer, Hope of Women*), 1921
43 László Moholy-Nagy, score for *Mechanical Eccentricity*, 1924/25
44 Walter Gropius, plans for a total theater for Erwin Piscator

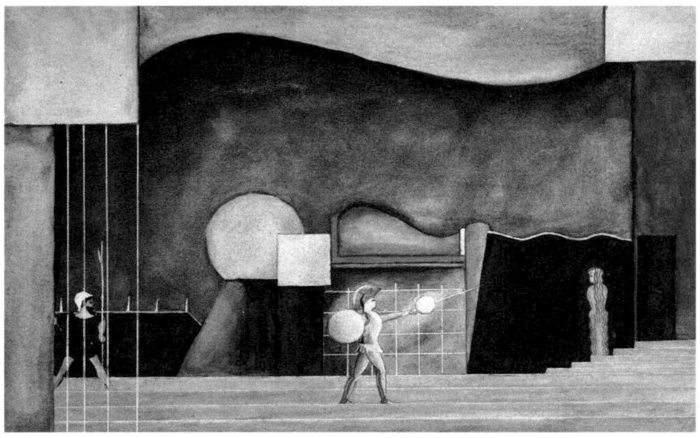

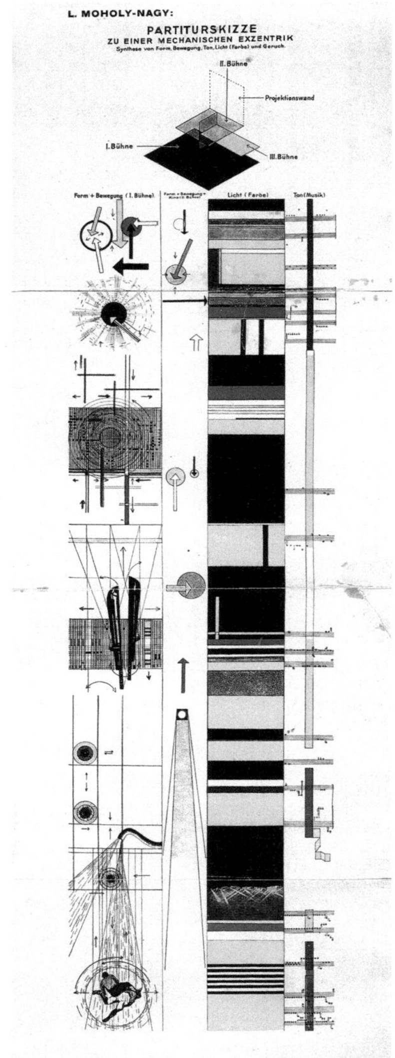

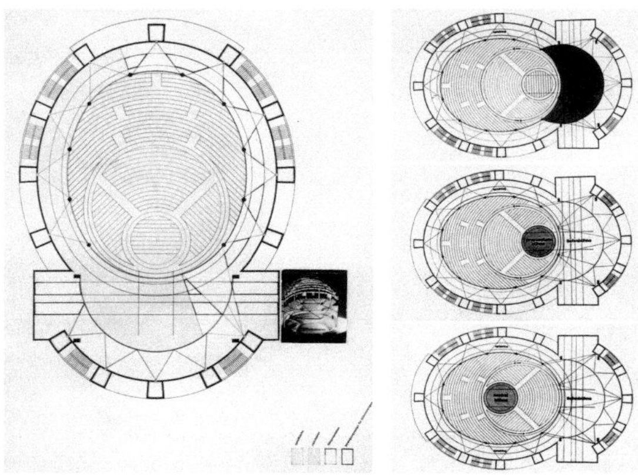

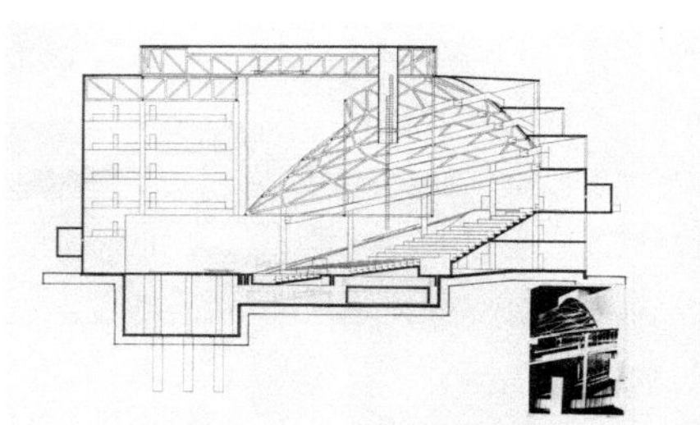

practice in his day, must remain a moot point. It could also be that the "performative turn" Erika Fischer-Lichte put forward with such verbal power over two hundred years later in her *Ästhetik des Performativen,* claiming the theater as the lead medium of the communication society, as it were, best describes the role assigned to the theatrical in our research into the lost interconnection between the arts. In her concept, immediate, sensual, physical experience plays the central role. Since the avant-garde reforms of the twentieth century have left the arts increasingly dominated by technological sound and image media, she writes, a new relationship between the (dead?) author and the recipient has emerged. The theatrical, performative interplay of the arts has brought about a form of aesthetic experience oscillating between unity and fragment and leading to the "productive uncertainty" (Hans Ulrich Gumbrecht) that removes not only the borders between the arts but also those between art and life.

This trend does not emanate solely from the stage, however. We may even be able to name a date and place where it began. In summer 1951, John Cage and Robert Rauschenberg staged, or rather brought into the world, at Black Mountain College, North Carolina, their *Theater Piece No. 1,* which was to go down in art history as the first happening. It is interesting to note that reports on what happened that summer evening in North Carolina differ widely, maybe because the audience or actors, seated in concentric circles, divided into four sections by Rauschenberg's white paintings and partly with their backs to the action, could only see different sections of the action that was taking place simultaneously in front of, alongside, or behind them. Mary Emma Harris gives a summary description in her work *The Arts at Black Mountain College,*[76] a summary description that I repeat no less summarily here. Cage, she says, sat high up on a ladder reading out sayings of Master Eckhardt, giving a lecture on Zen Buddhism and quoting from either the Bill of Rights or the U. S. Declaration of Independence; Merce Cunningham, accompanied by his dog, danced in a circle around the seats of the female members of the audience; and Robert Rauschenberg posed in front of his white paintings or played records of French chansons at the wrong speed. At the same time, films and slides were projected the wrong way around onto the walls of the college refectory where the event was held. Contemporaneously with Antonin Artaud's "theater of brutality," by which the writer sought to liberate the stage from the dictatorship of the written word and let "brute" life find its way into what was going on in art, Rauschenberg and Cage here advocated something that was to revolutionize all of the arts as pop culture and later to lead to a schism between art and event culture—the inclusion of reality in art. This was no longer undertaken, as the early twentieth-century avant-garde had postulated in the wake of their Romantic predecessors, to change reality as demiurgic gods of art, but to allow the gods of the arts to come into their own in the operating system of art, as it were. The multimedia ensemble of *Theater Piece No. 1* demonstrated this reality as a mediatized reality that could no longer be experienced directly by means of natural sense perception. The resulting inclusion of the quasi-actionistic surrounding communication structures in the work of art, which had previously been seen as an unacceptable disturbance of the "internal power lines" of the work, was later developed into a veritable movement by artists such as Allan Kaprow, who had gotten to know and embraced Cage's ideas at the New School for Social Research in New York. In an essay tellingly entitled "The Legacy of Jackson Pollock" Kaprow stated the new movement's intentions: "Pollock left us at the point where we must be preoccupied with and even dazzled by the space and objects of our daily life. Not satisfied with the *suggestion* through paint of our other senses, we shall utilize the specific substance of sight, sound, people, odors, touch."[77]

What Kaprow here calls for above all in relation to the happening was condensed into a movement for which the Fluxus artist Dick Higgins in 1966 coined the name "intermedia," by choreographers like New-York-based Alwin Nikolais; by filmmakers like Sven van der Bek, the advocate of Expanded Cinema; by painters like Milton Cohen, working on his Space Theater in Ann Arbor; by musicians like Nam June

76 Mary Emma Harris, *The Arts at Black Mountain College* (Cambridge MA: MIT Press, 1988), p. 228.

77 Allan Kaprow, "The Legacy of Jackson Pollock," *Art News,* vol. 57 (October 1958). Quoted after Davis, *Art and the Future* (see note 72), p. 38.

Paik, the founding father of media art; or dancers like Cage's confidant Merce Cunningham; and many others.

Higgins entitled his manifesto "Statement on Intermedia," which was uncommonly matter-of-fact for the Fluxus movement. In it, under the heading "Communication," he first called for the unity of all of the arts despite possibly widely diverging concepts, because "our real enemies are the ones who send us to die in pointless wars or to live lives which are reduced to drudgery."[78] That was surely a nod in the direction of the *zeitgeist.* Protest against the war in North Vietnam was at its height, as was the skeptical consideration whether psychedelic insights were important for the development of a new art that was to encompass all media. Higgins was, however, the first to postulate the importance of the mass media for the sensory experience of reality. Writing, the visual arts, and music—the triad of old—are here called upon by means of their contemporary media concepts. fig. 45/46

Tellingly, in view of the complexity of industrialized media complexes, Higgins called in this phase of intermedia art concepts for the new art to have a taste of simplicity. "As with the cubists," he wrote, "we are asking for a new way of looking at things, but more totally, since we are more impatient and more anxious to go to the basic images. This explains the impact of happenings, event pieces, mixed media films."[79]

Impatient they certainly were, the young media revolutionaries. In the intermedia 1960s and 1970s, a Bacchantic, Dionysian procession such as that which Richard Alewyn described so wonderfully for the Baroque era once more marched across Europe (and, a little, across North America, too). However, the waves of light that rose up into the sky and the fireworks shot into the night that made the stars pale were no longer the firework displays of courtly festivities, but the light-filled protest events against obsolete societal power structures performed as actions by, say, artists like Otto Piene. In music, too, the borders between high and popular culture fell, and the border-crossing was celebrated at ecstatic pop music film nights. The new locations where the arts celebrated at least for a while their new union with life were no longer museums but festivals, open-air concerts, and large-scale happenings. And these marriage ceremonies were in some cases gigantic. John Cage, who had made a somewhat minimalist start with his purist

45 Intermedia Heidelberg 1969, *America House Wrapped*
46 Intermedia Group at the Bielefeld University of Applied Sciences, 1969

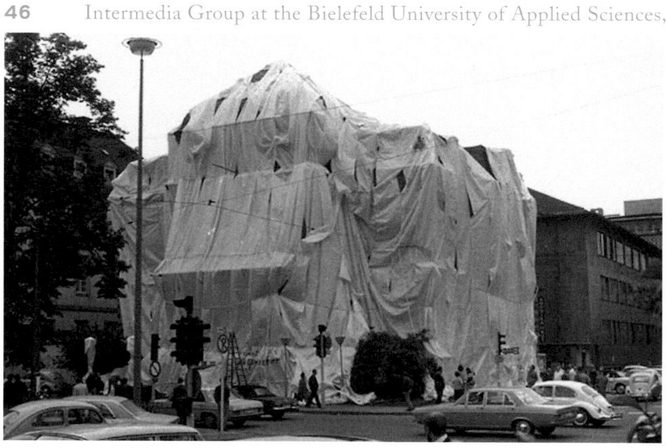

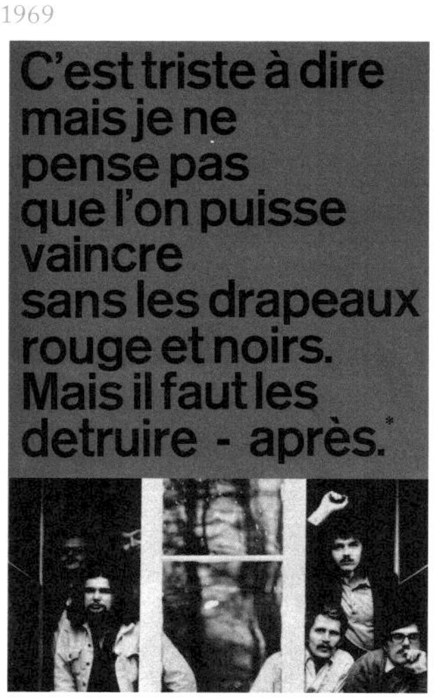

78 Dick Higgins, "Statement on Intermedia," *Something Else Newsletter* 1 (1966).
79 Ibid.

happenings *Theater Piece No 1* and *4'33"*, now staged a gigantic sound-space spectacle that he entitled *HPSCHD*, the computer abbreviation for harpsichord. Into one large-scale multimedia event he bundled five electronically amplified harpsichords, fifty-two loudspeakers, eight-thousand slides, and one hundred video projections

The high-water mark of this multimedia festival ecstasy, which lasted throughout the Roaring Sixties, was Expo 70 in Osaka, where the leading protagonists of intermedia and multimedia converged on the Pepsi-Cola Pavilion. Organized by the E. A. T. Group around Billy Klüver and Robert Rauschenberg, the first cybernetic intermedia total environment took place in the glare of international publicity and participation. fig. 47

In the decades that followed the *Intermedia* manifesto and intermedia manifestations, trailblazing new developments took shape off the beaten track of artistic institutions and with little contact with the art operating system that the critics of institutions had described as the ideal constitution and real location for the arts in the last third of the twentieth century. Media technology inventions, digital expansions of the production and combination of images and sounds, space, and texts were condensed into a global communications network into which not only the arts, but society in its entirety has been incorporated.

The Gesamtkunstwerk Revisited

That brings us back to the starting point of our portrayal of collaboration between the arts, the most comprehensive concept for interlinking them—the gesamtkunstwerk.

Today, despite Harald Szeemann's exciting 1983 exhibition *Der Hang zum Gesamtkunstwerk* (The Penchant for the Gesamtkunstwerk), discussion of the subject might still be limited to hermetic discussion groups with an interest in history, were it not that cyberspace and the World Wide Web, virtual realities and visionary total data compendiums, gigantic technosynaesthesia and immersive space operas had turned the visionary gesamtkunstwerk process into a techno-scientific overall plan, or even a media-technology feasibility study.

The gesamtkunstwerk in the modern era was, if not replaced, then at least overwhelmed by the total data compendium of the World Wide Web. The concept of digital convergence gave rise to the possi-

47 Billy Klüver and E. A. T., Pepsi-Cola Pavilion at the 1970 World Exposition in Osaka

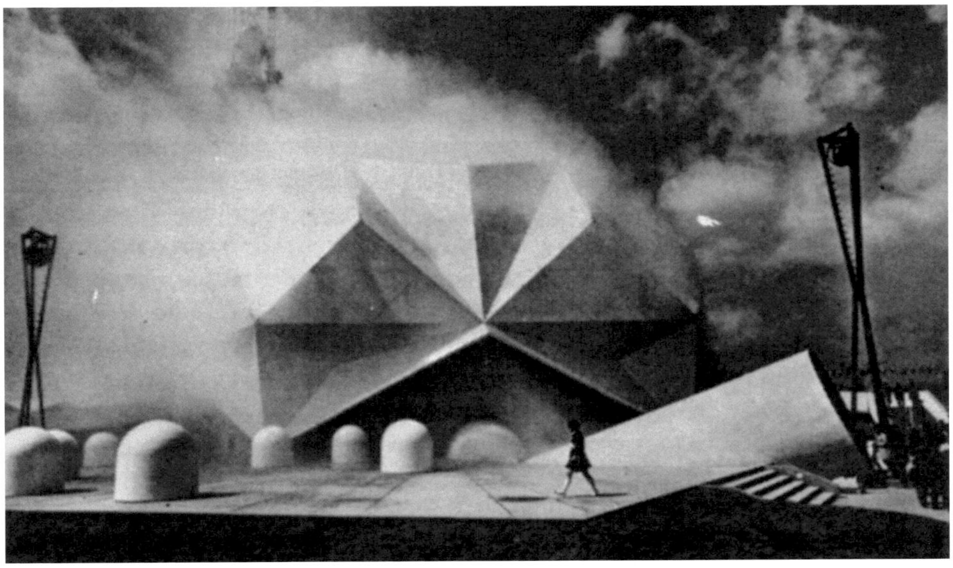

bility of networking the arts in a way that was not even remotely foreseeable at the time of the trailblazing *Der Hang zum Gesamtkunstwerk* exhibition. Hypertext seemed to put paid to the author much more finally than the academic literary debates fired by the forecasts of Roland Barthes or Michel Foucault could ever have imagined, and interactivity promised to make the utopias of reuniting the arts and their public in the "poetics of the open work of art" come true.

The 1990s experienced a technology euphoria especially in cultural areas such as had no longer been considered possible since the days of futurism and constructivism. Many interactive media art installations were proposed and a few were even realized. Like their 1960s intermedia precursors, they took shape beyond the bounds of the sanctioned art operating system. Cyberspace, named after the virtual wasteland in the novel *Neuromancer* and left by the technical concept of virtual reality for artists to cultivate, existed mainly at festivals, consumer electronics fairs, or congresses on media theory, and not in the exhibition programs of art institutions, let alone in the curricula of art, music, or drama academies. Yet some of the interactive media art installations of the time made important areas of experience available for an immersive art platform working on all of the senses in which music, film, theater, dance, painting, sculpture, architecture, and literature at least temporarily relinquished their respective specifics in digital convergence to unite all the more intensively the artistic vision and the dream of the beholder, who was now a user. In its innermost core the concept of interactive media art sought to penetrate the language barrier between it and the recipient. And it was prepared to resort to (almost) any means to do so.

Criticism of the ecstatic reconciliation of the arts in a multimedia spectacle was promptly voiced, however. How could it have been otherwise in the oscillating process of the gesamtkunstwerk in the modern era? Interestingly, one of these critical voices came from the center of the digital multimedia movement itself, Ars Electronica in Linz, Austria. Its director at the time, Peter Weibel, voiced the following warning: "An emphatically ecstatic fusion of the arts that drums on all of the sensory organs at the same time is … an illusory and false reconciliation … Art would be [more suited for] the task of developing subversive strategies of difference, absence, unlocking, and dissolution so as to recognize the social unconscious and to see through the masks of the social text and of media dramatization."[80]

Whether, for the oscillation between unity and fragment that we have chosen to describe the state of the gesamtkunstwerk process in the modern era, the communication society means the highest level of excitement or a standstill is a moot question. We are still in its early days. What can be said for sure, however, is that even after the waning of the maybe a little romantic, maybe a little avant-garde, maybe a little naive enthusiasm about the fascination of media technology that marked the last decade of the twentieth century, the arts are no longer what they once were. The borders between them have once more become permeable—the borders between disciplines in any case and

80 Quoted from Gottfried Hattinger, "Einleitung: Geschichtliche Extraktion zum Thema," in *Ars Electronica*, exh. cat. Ars Electronica (Linz, 1988), www.aec.at/de/archives.

now the intercultural borders, too. In this transparency lies the great opportunity to implement some of the unredeemed utopias of the modern era in overall artistic productivity, in part and especially within the framework of a university of the arts.

Admittedly, it is not the penchant for the gesamtkunstwerk as such, but the opportunities for transdisciplinarity that are implicit in it which now open up to us—now that we have made memory more precise, now that we have, at leaps and bounds, explored the historic meeting places of the arts.

It is indeed tempting to introduce the idea of the gesamtkunstwerk as a symbolic form of a university like the Zurich University of the Arts, at least in the university-specific debate, if not in its conceptual realization. If the quality of the gesamtkunstwerk in the modern era as an oscillating process between unity and fragment is correctly stated to be characteristic of the route that the arts have taken in the modern era, this model would appear to be an obvious choice for a place of comprehensive teaching and research. While disciplinary and adisciplinary theories, while aesthetics, art, music, and drama studies never tire of either calling into question or simply denying the applicability, the possibility, and certainly the feasibility of the gesamtkunstwerk, the practitioners and artists in all disciplines work no less tirelessly on its realization. And if they fail, it will be a grandiose failure that led at least in part to the most magnificent works of modern art and its postmodern siblings.

The Romantic beginnings of the gesamtkunstwerk concept were still relatively modest. Philipp Otto Runge's *Tageszeiten* cycle was mentioned earlier. What is less well-known is that he wanted to create an architecture of their own for the four large painted panels. Inspired by a visit to Meissen Cathedral, he discovered the identification-generating effect of the Gothic style for himself and planned "the unification of painting, music, poetry and architecture into a comprehensive, synaesthetic, plant-like body of art."[81]

Modern architecture, in keeping with a self-image characterized in equal measure by Romanticism and the avant-garde, comes up with more monumental gesamtkunstwerk concepts. They start with Karl Friedrich Schinkel's premodern plan for a Prussian Freedom Cathedral, a gesamtkunstwerk idea that was advocated after the Napoleonic Wars, and lead via the reform movement's Temple of the Earth, which was to have been built near Zurich shortly before 1900, and Rudolf Steiner's Goetheanum, which actually was built, to the Indian temple of which Scriabin dreamt for his mystery, the "universal liturgy of ecstatic world salvation" to which he gave first shape in his famous *Prometheus: Poem of Fire.*

Architectural gesamtkunstwerk projects include private ones, such as the Merzbau that Kurt Schwitters constructed in his Hannover apartment, and monumental ones, such as the city crowns and crystalline world city designs of Bruno Taut, Wenzel Hablik, and other members of the Gläserne Kette (Glass Chain) group.

81 Quoted from Roger Fornoff, *Die Sehnsucht nach dem Gesamtkunstwerk: Studien zu einer ästhetischen Konzeption der Moderne* (Hildesheim, 2004), p. 92.

48 Wilhelm Ahlbom (after Schinkel), *Gothic Cathedral on the Waterfront*, design for a Prussian Freedom Cathedral, 1914

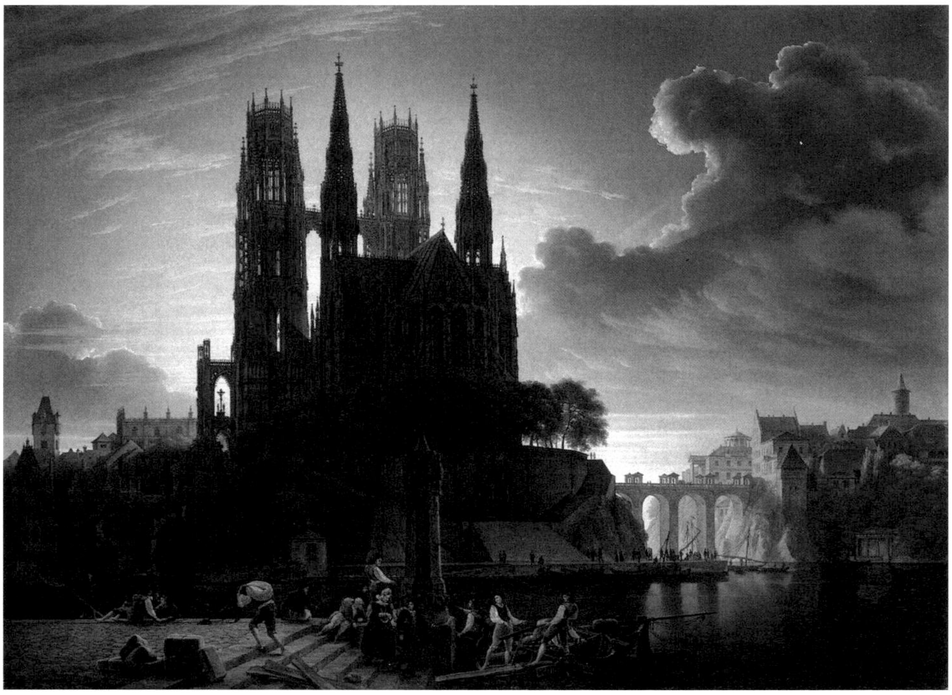

The seemingly so utopian designs of the Gläserne Kette, which was inspired by the science-fiction writer Paul Scheerbart, present the precarious sociopolitical objectives of what are often fairly esoteric gesamtkunstwerk projects of the avant-garde movements. fig. 48–50

The avant-garde movements that in Germany joined forces in the so-called Working Council of Art in the brief revolutionary period after World War I set the direction. "Art and people must form a unity. Art must no longer be the pleasure of a few but the happiness and life of the masses. A merger of the arts under the aegis of a grand architecture is the goal."[82]

And the Bauhaus manifesto proclaimed the Weimar School of Design itself to be a gesamtkunstwerk.

After the Pepsi-Cola Pavilion or Karl Heinz Stockhausen's geodetic Cathedral of Hymns, both built at Osaka in 1970, multimedia architecture such as was realized at world fairs in the 1970s and 1980s, though often only piecemeal, not only succeeded these gesamtkunstwerk concepts but sought to implement them, but this time in the virtual and not in the real world. They include the architectural designs for world cities in Cyberspace that have preoccupied the media-art avant-garde ever since William Gibson's 1984 science-fiction novel *Neuromancer.*

It was not just in architectural utopias that the avant-garde lived out to the full its penchant for the gesamtkunstwerk. Monte Verità near Ascona on Lago Maggiore was one of the liveliest artists' colonies at the turn of the twentieth century. It was where Rudolf von Laban staged dance dramas that he saw as building blocks for the "dreamed-of gesamtkunstwerk, the festival of dance."[83] The stage, as might seem obvious after Richard Wagner's festivals of consecration and Alfredo Appia's ingenious sets, played a major role in a concert of gesamtkunstwerk

82 Bruno Taut, "Ein Architekturprogramm," repr. in *Arbeitsrat für Kunst: Berlin 1918–1921*, ed. Eberhard Steneberg (Düsseldorf: Marzona, 1987), pp. 27–32.

83 Quoted from Harald Szeemann, *Der Hang zum Gesamtkunstwerk: Europäische Utopien seit 1800* (Frankfurt a. M., 1983), p. 153.

49 Otto Rietmann, the first Goetheanum, 1914

50 Wassily Luckhardt, *An die Freude* (To Joy), monument to work, 1919

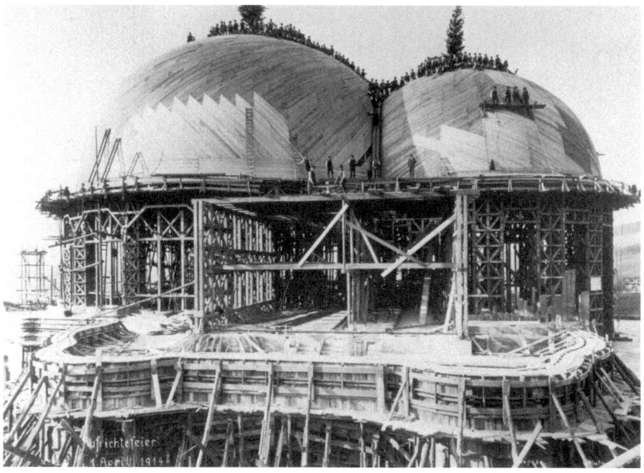

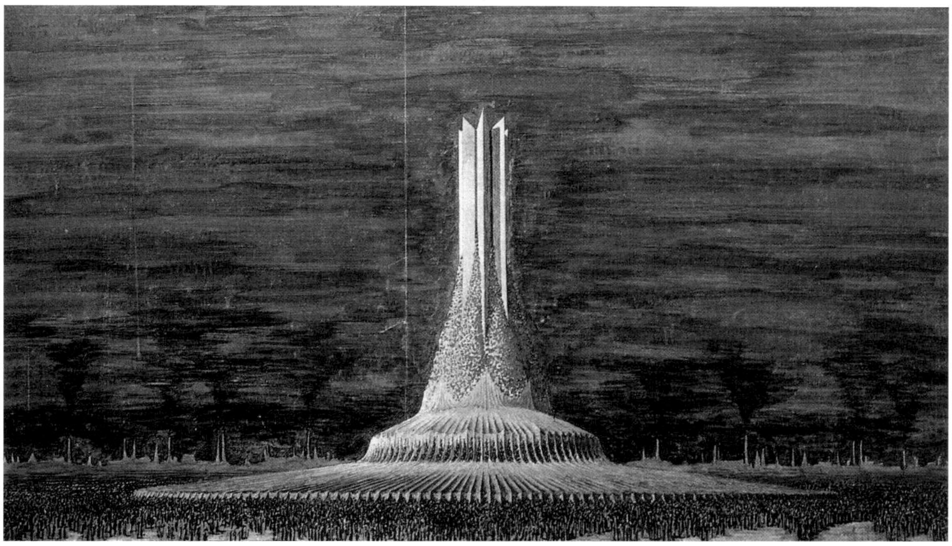

fragments that were a grandiose failure. It exerted an influence that was apparent even in media-art pioneer Roy Ascott's planetary fairy-tale *La plissure du texte,* written for the opening of the Centre Pompidou in Paris.

But I have let the dynamics of the fascinating concept of the gesamtkunstwerk carry me away from the admittedly somewhat more modest leitmotif for the construction of our house for the arts—transdisciplinarity.

Transdisciplinarity: Opportunity and Obligation

It has often been considered an imposition to have to leave the safe territory of one's own art or, conversely, to open up its borders to those of the other arts. That has not changed to this day. It has always been crises, within the arts or in society or both, that have made reciprocal border-crossing appear possible, desirable or, indeed, necessary. That has been the case for all of the bilateral and trilateral relationships among the arts. Crises motivated attempts to forge intermedia or interdisciplinary relationships, and crises justify the need to develop solution strategies in the artistic and cultural fields, as in others. For the acceptance of transdisciplinary strategies among artists it is not particularly helpful that they were originally devised at the academic level. The late 1960s and 1970s, a time when planners were optimistic and people were happy to participate, saw the first interdisciplinary attempt to correlate disciplinary areas more closely, especially in areas that were to form newly constitutive parts of public life, such as urban and regional planning, social policy and technological innovations, and—after the first oil crisis—resources planning. Later, as an outflow of the 1980s and 1990s risk society, ecology, technological impact assessment, and sustainability came to the fore. Today's issue is globalization. Research associations sound the alarm on major issues of the age—with varied success. The arts, with few intermedia exceptions, have remained strangely uninvolved, possibly in response to the naive overestimation of their own capabilities that characterized the historical avant-gardes. Either that or they have persisted in escapist, late-postmodern remoteness from society. Concepts of this kind, however, are no longer sustainable—for any of the arts. With the revolutionary communications technologies that since the end of the 1980s have made border-crossings a tangible phenomenon—as tourist travel flows and as flows of refugees, or virtual world travel—the quintessential sphere of action of the arts, the sensual ways of experiencing the world, are directly affected. Mediatization of all fields of perception has of course progressed steadily and been taken forward since the beginning of modernization. Here and there, however, a niche of direct experience seemed to have survived for the arts in particular. But not any more. Those days are over!

Music, design, performing arts (i.e. film, drama, and dance and, as a bridge, scenography), and the visual arts in their media specifics; art and cultural theory and art education for the various age groups; all in all more than thirty subjects, seven research institutes, and a museum, a theater, and a fully fledged concert organization make up the body of the new Zurich University of the Arts.

With the exception of architecture, the absence of which is painful and which ought soon to be returned to the panoply of the arts in Zurich, and of literature, which we offer in cooperation with the Institute of Creative Writing in Biel, the sum total of artistic professions that used to be known as the fine arts is now assembled, and assembled in all of its media variations, both traditional and state-of-the-art. This grandiose (re?)unification also spells out an obligation, however. The erstwhile fine arts have an enormous potential for contributing toward solutions to the highly complex challenges already posed by the globalized communication society that will determine our entire future.

The challenges of globalization affect aesthetic experience in its very core. They result from intercultural structures of perception, they reconstruct the problems of gender, and they aim at a sensory acquisition of the world with all of the senses, both negatively and positively. Inherent in global communication technologies are both the opportunity to enhance one's senses for communicative activity and the risk of reducing their faculties to that of passive consumption.

The many and varied cultures of visual, aural, and performative memory gain great significance. The risks of modernization, a term transferred from the cultural field to society as a whole, have if anything increased since Ulrich Beck in the 1980s condensed the reflexive modern era into the risk society. After all, the consequences of the various technological revolutions for both the human psyche and physical aspects of our planet are growing increasingly plain to see, and they are only some of the challenges that we face. For all of these problem areas solutions must be sought in transdisciplinary collaboration between the different professions, and for all of these problem areas artists, designers, cultural specialists, and media theorists are the experts per se.

Viewed in this light, higher education in the arts is not just of educational interest. The charisma of a university of the arts extends far beyond the educational sector to the entirety of culture and the central motivational forces of society. For that reason alone research plays an increasingly significant role alongside teaching, which has traditionally been the mainstay of work at art schools. In the past, innovations, including innovations in the arts themselves, were increasingly outsourced from the institutions to the avant-gardes of internationalized art. Today, the trend appears to be in the other direction. Outside of the universities, fewer and fewer resources—in other words, less and less money and less and less time—are available and infrastructures, if they exist at all, are subject to the rules of the culture industry and its mass-media demands. The role of research could be to offer innovations the institutional place that they deserve. That means providing excellent production facilities. A university of the arts is not just a place of teaching and research, of experiments and exercises. It does not just pass on tried experience and tested skills. It also composes and performs previously unheard works of music. New performative interpretations are researched on the dance floor and the rehearsal stage of the theater and at the Department of Cultural Analysis, and they are both published and performed. Screenplays are written, films are made, video games are designed, and they, too, are given public showings—in the movie theater in the best case and in any case at festivals or on the various platforms of mobile communications technologies. Pictures are still painted, posters are printed, installations are implemented, and they are shown both in the university's own museum and in galleries and at art associations.

A university of the arts is not just a teaching and research university. It is also, and above all, a producing university. It is not just a place of education, but also a place of culture. It takes the triad of teaching, research, and (cultural) production to make the university a sought-after partner in the network of transdisciplinary solution strategies, and transdisciplinary processes are the indispensable ferment of teaching, research, and production at a university of the arts.

The Motor of Innovation: The ZHdK's Transdisciplinary Studio

To test continuously a transdisciplinary transparency between the arts and between the arts, the sciences, technological systems, and the areas of society and the environment that are under special threat from the global risks of modernization, we have established the Transdisciplinary Studio at the Zurich University of the Arts (ZHdK). We did so very much in keeping with the transdisciplinary manifesto of Basarab Nicolescu, who is, as it were, the mouthpiece of the transdisciplinary internationale. "As the prefix 'trans' indicates, transdisciplinarity concerns that which is at once between the disciplines, across the different disciplines, and beyond all discipline," he wrote. "Its goal is the understanding of the present world, of which one of the imperatives is the unity of knowledge."[84]

Ever since the concept was launched into the academic theory and educational policy debate in the mid-1980s from the Bielefeld Center for Interdisciplinary Research, so much has been written and said about what distinguishes it from interdisciplinarity, multidisciplinarity, or even supradisciplinarity that the content for which it stood became vaguer and vaguer. Even so, transdisciplinarity is back on the agenda. The organizers of a conference on the subject held by one of the most influential German-language platforms for young academics, the Thesis Network, made the reasons clear. "If one were to exaggerate the point slightly, the generation of transdisciplinarity before us left with great hopes and ambitious drafts but, on the whole, with a rather frayed concept of transdisciplinarity and little that is tangible for implementing the grand ideas in academic practice. That, however, need not be to transdisciplinarity's disadvantage: we need it."[85]

For our purposes three basic requirements suffice to delimit our concept of transdisciplinarity. Transdisciplinarity relates mainly to specific projects that are passed on to the university from outside for research; in working on these problems it crosses borders between subjects and disciplines, and it changes the pattern of subjects and disciplines permanently.

These three foundations of the Transdisciplinary Studio indicate that teaching is not the first area to be affected by transdisciplinary changes that are imparted via transparencies in what have hitherto been subjects and disciplines delimited one from the other almost like nation-states. Research and production are affected first, and there we have good reason to expect exciting results. The curricula of the different disciplines must nonetheless be adapted to the societal conditions outlined above. The Bologna Process is sure to have made some headway here. It goes without saying that the necessary changes in curricular concepts must not liquidate the media specifics of the arts. Training for a concert pianist will always differ from training for a game designer, both structurally and in respect of methodical concepts.

Yet in one respect they are identical. They both pursue their profession in a society and must take part in its debates. Without this participation their art, their virtuosity, and their creativity would be ineffective. The autonomy to which the much-vaunted avant-gardes laid claim in such an exaggerated manner was more a defensive move against a reality that was felt to be hostile toward the arts than an attempt to regain a measure of opinion leadership in a societal process dominated more than ever by science and technology. Individual artistic disciplines can no longer achieve this on their own. Interdisciplinary collaboration

84 Quoted from Frank Brand, Franz Schaller, and Harald Völker, *Transdisziplinarität: Bestandsaufnahme und Perspektiven* (Göttingen: Göttingen Univ. Press, 2004).

85 Ibid.

is needed and has indeed existed for some time in artistic practice outside of the universities. A certain amount of movement has gotten under way in the practice of teaching and research at universities of the arts. The "grand coalitions" of individual arts described earlier exist on a small scale, too, and have been known to bear fruit where new subjects such as film music or scenography have taken shape. They are temporary joint ventures in which teachers in different subject areas have joined forces in projects, and they are always especially fertile where dialogue with the others suddenly brings home to someone the specific features of his own subject in an entirely new and fresh way.

Properly understood and in relation to the specifics of the arts, transdisciplinarity at the ZHdK does not, therefore, mean first and foremost that the contents of individual subjects are intermingled and that subjects fray at the edges, as Adorno feared in his early criticism of the gesamtkunstwerk.

The arts do, however, come closer together. Joint encounters with other professions, those of academics or other social groups, hone awareness of the specifics of one's own subjects. They can renew it and will certainly strengthen it. These encounters can lead to new subjects in their own right, just as visions always give rise to something new and usually better.

The House of the Arts

This essay is intended to contribute toward providing the Zurich University of the Arts with a sure theoretical foundation. Its title, "Making Memory More Precise," is intended to underscore the fact that historical experience is of special significance for an institution whose identity lies in conquering new horizons.

We have seen that there has never been a universally accepted order of the arts, but that repeated attempts have been made to (re)establish this order, and that these attempts at systematization have honed the self-awareness of the arts in question and encouraged their sense of specificity.

We have seen that teaching institutions in the arts have taken an active part in the process of change to which the practice of the arts was subjected, and that historical differences in the social status of the arts were mapped seismographically in their structures.

We have seen that the process of modernization in the arts can be described as an oscillation between unity and fragment. We have seen that the different attempts to restore the unity of the arts have failed. In the course of this grandiose failure some of the most impressive concepts in the history of art were imagined or even realized.

Finally, we have seen that the disciplinary borders drawn between the arts and between art and science and art and society must be disrupted especially at times of crisis in the arts and in the society that supports them (or, indeed, no longer does so), that a defensive, escapist view of autonomy does not lead to an improvement in the dynamics of the arts but to narrow-mindedness and standstill, and that art must in fact intervene in the societal debate, albeit as a partner and not as a demiurge.

All in all, history shows that the house of the arts we not only envision but intend to build will not be a palace such as the buildings to which the academies of the late eighteenth century laid claim. Nor will it be the cathedral by which the avant-garde reformers of the twentieth century sought to present their claims to absoluteness. It will have neither the flat roof of Ulm-style "good design" nor the engaging do-it-yourself appearance of Black Mountain College.

Our house of the arts is an open house. It has spacious rooms in which disciplinary specifics can take shape for virtuoso artists to mature. Above all, it has generously proportioned lines of communication and spacious meeting points where artists can meet each other as researchers, learners, and teachers, and where they can jointly contribute their respective competence, commitment, disciplinary dynamics, and transdisciplinary curiosity toward projects that can provide practicable visions of the future for a society that cannot even estimate the consequences of technology-driven globalization.

Viewed in this way, it has a certain similarity with the idea of Thomas Koebner, who sees the house of the arts as a "cavernous system of intricate pathways and surprising crossings," and especially because he concludes that "to get involved in this labyrinth seems to do more justice to the aesthetic and social practice of the arts than to play at being a border guard who wants to maintain rigid barriers."[86]

But as we, to use Koebner's metaphor, want to train neither anachoretic cave dwellers nor labyrinth explorers guided by Ariadne's normative clue of thread, we are taking on the unrestricted structure but placing our house of the arts in the light of the present day. Its roof rises high into the sky, offering protection from the icy winds of globalization, and it does so because its foundations are firmly rooted in the cultivated urbanity of a city such as Zurich.

86 Koebner, *Laokoon und kein Ende* (see note 4), p. 9.

Ackermann, J. S. "Ars sine scientia nihil est." *Art Bulletin* XXI (1949): 84–111.
Adorno, Theodor W. "Die Kunst und die Künste (1866)." Pp. 169–92 in *Parva Aesthetica.* Frankfurt a. M.: Suhrkamp, 1967.
Benthien, Julia. "Rezension von Corina Caduff, *Die Literarisierung von Musik und Bildender Kunst um 1800, München 2003.*" *Sehepunkte* 4, no. 2 (2004): www.sehepunkte.de/2004/02/3119.html.
Bill, Max. "Bericht an den Schulvorstand der Stadt Zürich über das Projekt 'Institut für Gestaltung'," unpublished manuscript. Zurich, 1961.
Caduff, Corina. *Die Literarisierung von Mensch und bildender Kunst um 1800.* Munich, 2003.
Conti, Alessandro. *Der Weg des Künstlers: Vom Handwerker zum Virtuosen.* Berlin, 1998.
Daiber, Jürgen. "Ut pictura poesis—oder: Ars poetica für Hyperfiction." www.dichtung-digital.de/Forum-Kassel-Okt-00/Daiber.
Davis, Douglas. *Art and the Future: A History/Prophecy of the Collaboration between Science, Technology and Art.* London: Thames and Hudson, 1973.
Deleuze, Gilles. *Cinema 2: L'image-temps.* Paris, 1985.
The Didascalicon *of Hugh of Saint Victor: A Medieval Guide to the Arts.* Translated by Jerome Taylor. New York: Columbia Univ. Press, 1961.
Eco, Umberto. *The Open Work.* Translated by Anna Cancogni. Cambridge MA: Harvard Univ. Press, 1989.
Finger, Anke. *Das Gesamtkunstwerk der Moderne.* Göttingen, 2006.
Fornoff, Roger. *Die Sehnsucht nach dem Gesamtkunstwerk: Studien zu einer ästhetischen Konzeption der Moderne.* Hildesheim, 2004.
Füssl, Karl H. "Kreative Pädagogen am Black Mountain College College (1933–1949): Bauhausmeister Josef Albers—Ein Pestalozzianer im amerikanischen Exil." *Bildung und Erziehung* 56 (2003): 3–22.
Giersch, Ulrich. "El Lissitzky: Prounen-Raum." In *Sehsucht: Das Panorama als Massenunterhaltung des 19. Jahrhunderts,* edited by Marie-Louise von Plessen and Ulrich Giersch. Bonn: Stroemfeld, 1993.
Goethe, Johann Wolfgang. "Einleitung Propyläen (1798)." In *Werke,* 14 vols., vol. 12 (Hamburg: Wegner, 1953).
Grasskamp, Walter. "Why Art Academies?" In *190 Years Academy of Fine Arts Munich.* Translated by Allison Plath-Moseley. Munich, 1999.
Groys, Boris. "Die dunkle Seite der Kunst; Rezension von Niklas Luhman: *Die Kunst der Gesellschaft.*" *Soziale Systeme* 2, no. 1 (1996): 172.
Hahl-Koch, Jelena. "Kandisky und der 'Blaue Reiter'." Pp. 354–59 in *Vom Klang der Bilder: Die Musik in der Kunst des 20. Jahrhunderts,* edited by Karin von Maur. Exh. cat. Staatsgalerie Stuttgart. Munich: Prestel, 1985.
Harris, Mary Emma. *The Arts at Black Mountain College.* Cambridge MA: MIT Press, 1988.
Hattinger, Gottfried. "Einleitung: Geschichtliche Extraktion zum Thema." In *Ars Electronica.* Exh. cat. Ars Electronica. Linz, 1988: www.aec.at/de/archives.
Hessler, Christiane J. "Maler und Bildhauer im sophistischen Tauziehen: Der Paragone in der italienischen Kunstliteratur des 16. Jahrhunderts." Pp. 82–97 in *Wettstreit der Künste: Malerei und Skulptur von Dürer bis Daumier,* edited by Ekkehard Mai and Kurt Wettengl. Cologne, 2002.
Higgins, Dick. "Statement on Intermedia." *Something Else Newsletter* 1 (1966).
Kemp, Wolfgang. "Disegno: Beiträge zur Geschichte des Begriffs zwischen 1547 und 1607." *Marburger Jahrbuch für Kunstwissenschaft* 19 (1974): 219–40.
Kepes, Gyorgy. *The Language of Vision.* 1944. Reprinted New York: Dover Publications, 1995.
Kittler, Friedrich. *Optische Medien.* Berlin, 2002.
Koebner, Thomas, ed. *Laokoon und kein Ende: Der Wettstreit der Künste.* Munich, 1989.
Kristeller, Paul Oskar. "The Modern System of the Arts: A Study in the History of Aesthetics." *Journal of the History of Ideas* 13, no. 1 (January 1952): 17–46.
Lingner, Michael. "Die Musikalisierung und die allgemeine Kunstwissenschaft." *Zeitschrift für Ästhetik und allgemeine Kunstwissenschaft*, vol. XXIV1 (1979): 75–94.
Maur, Karin von. "Musikalische Strukturen in der Kunst des 20. Jahrhunderts." In *Vom Klang der Bilder: Die Musik in der Kunst des 20. Jahrhunderts,* edited by Karin von Maur. Exh. cat. Staatsgalerie Stuttgart. Munich: Prestel, 1985.
Nelson, Ted. *Dream Machines.* San Francisco, 1974.
Nowotny, Helga, Peter Scott, and Michael Gibbons, eds. *Wissenschaft neu denken: Wissenschaft und Öffentlichkeit in einem Zeitalter der Ungewissheit.* Weilerswist, 2005.
Pevsner, Nikolaus. *Academies of Art, Past and Present.* Cambridge: Cambridge Univ. Press, 1940.
Plessen, Marie-Louise von. "Der gebannte Augenblick: Die Abbildung von Realität im Panorama des 19. Jahrhunderts." Pp. 12–19 in *Sehsucht: Das Panorama als Massenunterhaltung des 19. Jahrhunderts,* edited by Marie-Louise von Plessen and Ulrich Giersch. Bonn: Stroemfeld, 1993.
Rübenach, Bernhard. *Der rechte Winkel von Ulm: Ein Bericht über die Hochschule für Gestaltung 1958/59*, edited by Bernd Meurer. Darmstadt: Verlag der Georg-Büchner-Buchhandlung, 1987.
Schönberg, Arnold. "The Relationship with the Text." In *Style and Idea: Selected Writings of Arnold Schönberg,* edited by Leonard Stein. Translated by Leo Black. Berkeley: Univ. of California Press, 1984.
Schwarz, Hans-Peter. *Media, Art, History.* Translated by Freiherr Karl von Teuffenbach Translation Agency. Munich and New York: Prestel, 1997.
Seckendorff, Eva von. *Die Hochschule für Gestaltung in Ulm: Gründung (1949–1953) und Ära Max Bill (1953–1957).* Marburg, 1989.
Sidler, Natalia and Jörg Jewanski. *Farb-Licht-Musik: Synästhesie und Farblichtmusik.* Zürcher Musikstudien Vol. 5. Bern, 2006.
Sternberger, Dolf. *Panorama oder Ansichten vom 19. Jahrhundert.* 1946. Reprinted Frankfurt a. M., 2001.
Szeemann, Harald. *Der Hang zum Gesamtkunstwerk: Europäische Utopien seit 1800.* Frankfurt a. M., 1983.
Taut, Bruno. "Ein Architekturprogramm." Reprinted in *Arbeitsrat für Kunst: Berlin 1918–1921*, edited by Eberhard Steneberg. Düsseldorf: Marzona, 1987.
Ullrich, Wolfgang. "System der Künste." In *Ästhetische Grundbegriffe: Historisches Wörterbuch in sieben Bänden,* edited by Karlheinz Barck et al., 7 vols., vol. 3. Stuttgart: J. B. Metzler, 2001.
Vasari, Giorgio. *Lives of the Artists: A Selection.* Translated by George Bull. London: Folio Society, 1993.

Vorkoeper, Ute. *Hybride Dialoge: Kunstausbildung in der Medienkultur; Rückschau auf die Modellversuche zur künstlerischen Ausbildung an Hochschulen im BLK [= Bund-Länder-Kommission]-Programm Kulturelle Bildung im Medienzeitalter*. Hamburg, 2005. http://www.blk-info.de/fileadmin/BLK-Materialien/heft125.pdf.

Wingler, Hans M. *Kunstschulreform 1900–1933*. Berlin, 1977.

Zelger, Franz. "Revidiertes Bild der Académie Royale." *Neue Zürcher Zeitung*, no. 62, March 15, 2007, p. 62.

Credits

p. 11, fig. 1: Staatsgalerie Stuttgart; fig. 2: Staatliche Graphische Sammlung München, Inv.-No. 1991: 2D
p. 12, fig. 3: Photo: Heinrich Helfenstein, Zurich
p. 19, fig. 5: Deutsches Archäologisches Institut, Rome
p. 22, fig. 7: Staatliche Graphische Sammlung München, Inv.-No. 229582D
p. 23, fig. 8: from: Hans-Peter Schwarz, *Das Künstlerhaus* (Braunschweig, 1990), p. 140
p. 25, fig. 9/10: from: Hans-Peter Schwarz, *Das Künstlerhaus* (Braunschweig, 1990), p. 146 and p. 141
p. 27, fig. 11: Bibliothèque Nationale, Paris; fig. 12: Musée du Louvre, Cabinet de Dessins, Paris fig. 13: Walter Clinton Jackson Library, The University of North Carolina at Greensboro fig. 14a: École nationale supérieure des Beaux-Arts, Paris
p. 31, fig. 14b: Musée de la Ville de Paris, Musée Carnavalet, Paris
p. 32, fig. 14c: Musée d'Orsay, Paris; fig. 14d: The Museum of Modern Art, New York
p. 33, fig. 15: Musée d'Orsay, Paris
p. 35, fig. 17: Department of Architecture, Massachusetts Institute of Technology, Project UNBUILT
p. 36, fig. 18: © 2007, ProLitteris, Zurich
p. 37, fig. 20: from: *Bauhaus*, eds. Jeannine Fiedler, Peter Feierabend (Cologne, 1999), p. 183. © 2007, ProLitteris, Zurich
p. 38, fig. 21: © 2007, Nachlass Oskar Schlemmer, Munich; fig. 22: © 2007, ProLitteris, Zurich
p. 40, fig. 23: BHA
p. 41, fig. 24: Photo: Hans Kinkel
p. 42, fig. 25: Photo: North Carolina State Archives (Black Mountain College)
p. 43, fig. 26: Gyorgy Kepes, *Sprache des Sehens* (Mainz, 1944), p. 179
p. 45, fig. 27: Otto Piene
p. 47, fig. 28: Marie Jo Lafontaine, Brussels, ZKM; fig. 29: Photo: Helge Mundt, Hamburg, ZKM
p. 49, fig. 30: Photo: Jill Scott; fig. 31: Photo: David Allison, ZKM; fig. 32: Photo: Jason Levy, ZKM
p. 51, fig. 33: Staatliche Kunstsammlungen Dresden, Sculpture Collection, H4 154/27; fig. 34: Cologne, Wallraf-Richartz Museum, Fondation Carboud, WRM 2828
p. 55, fig. 35 a–d: Hamburger Kunsthalle
p. 56, fig. 36a/b: Marion von Hofacker Collection, Irschenhausen
p. 57, fig. 37: from: *Vom Klang der Bilder*, ed. Karin von Maur, exh. cat. (Munich, 1985), pp. 224–25
p. 58, fig. 38: from: *Vom Klang der Bilder*, ed. Karin von Maur, exh. cat. (Munich, 1985), p. 211
p. 60, fig. 39: The British Museum, London, Department of Prints & Drawings
p. 61, fig. 40: Jeffrey Shaw, ZKM
p. 65, fig. 41: Theatermuseum der Universität zu Köln, © 2007, ProLitteris, Zurich
p. 66, fig. 42: Theatermuseum der Universität zu Köln; fig. 43: © 2007, ProLitteris, Zurich; fig. 44: Theatermuseum der Universität zu Köln, © 2007, ProLitteris, Zurich
p. 68, fig. 45: Photo: Jochen Goetze; fig. 46: Private collection Hans-Peter Schwarz
p. 69, fig. 47: Private collection Hans-Peter Schwarz
p. 72, fig. 48: Staatliche Museen Preussischer Kulturbesitz, Nationalgalerie Berlin
p. 73, fig. 50: Akademie der Künste, Sammlung Baukunst Berlin

The Future of the Arts. Pers vision and technological innovat disciplinarity and transdisciplina to explore the transformations i and economic significance of art

ctives and scenarios of artistic
n, at the fault-lines of mono-
y in teaching and research, serve
he social, cultural, aesthetic,

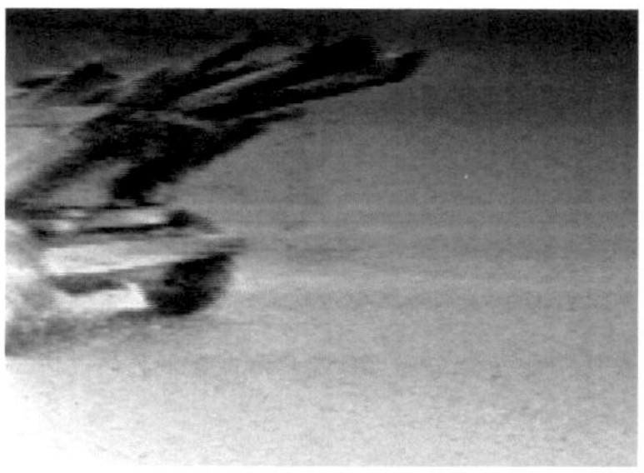

The Zurich University of the Arts 2022: A Vision Rooted in Reality

Hans-Peter Schwarz

Imagine a Tuesday morning in spring 2022. Flight EX480 has just landed at Kloten, one of the stellar hubs of the EuroStar Alliance. Ignoring the request to remain seated (nothing has changed there in fifteen years), Boris Medwed and Julian Blair, two choreographers from London's Goldsmith College, get up from seats 5F and 5E with the graceful movements of their profession, to fetch their hand luggage and its precious contents. But they respectfully make room for a graying German painter who was a major exponent of the famous New Leipzig School at the beginning of the century. Further back is the pianist Julia Barton, a young thing still, but already internationally famous. Klaus and Beatrix den Oudsten from Amsterdam, avowed fans of the still young genre of multimedia opera, have splashed out on a first class ticket and are already on the gangway, while a class of school-leavers from Mumbai, Zurich's biggest twin town, fidgets in seats 20F to 29D, itching to stretch their legs after the long flight.

Some things are still the same in the twenties of the twenty-first century. You wait for your luggage and set off into the city, by taxi-minibus or bus, depending on your means. Private cars are banned on Tuesdays because of the pollution. The passengers disperse to the city's renowned luxury hotels; the students from India stay at the International Student Residence of the Zurich Universities. Our protagonists go their separate ways. But—as allowed in visionary tales—the visitors we encountered at the airport meet again about two hours later, not by arrangement but not quite by coincidence either, at one of the Zurich culture scene's most attractive meeting points, the big foyer of the Zurich University of the Arts at the Züri-West Culture Campus. This light-flooded hall serves as a vestibule both to the opera studio where the multimedia opera *Caravaggio* has its world premiere today, and to the dance studios of the Department of Performing Arts and Film, the destination of the two choreographers from London. They have a very special reason for their visit. In the luggage they were watching so carefully at the beginning they have something very special—a gold medal from the European Ballet Association, which has been awarded to the Zurich Academy of Dance for its excellent work with young dancers. And the dance section at the Zurich University of the Arts can really be proud of its achievements. Since this residential dance school was set up fifteen years ago, more and more young Swiss dance enthusiasts have completed the grueling training program. The previous year a Swiss graduate of the Zurich Academy of Dance won a gold medal at the renowned Prix de Lausanne for the first time.

But let us return to the foyer of the Culture Campus. Here there are also signs pointing the way to the piano masterclass, a stony path that Julia Barton has bravely trodden, knowing as she does that she is unlikely to find such competent teachers for her discipline anywhere else in Europe, while at the same time enjoying the opportunity to attend such an excellent range of cultural studies lectures. For as she knows from her own family, you can become an outstanding virtuoso through talent and perseverance, but you will only become a great artist if you are open to the world outside your own specialty.

So we leave Julia Barton to her strict examiners and turn to our German painter. He is not normally a great traveler, but has come gladly to Zurich from his Amsterdam studio to attend an international conference at the invitation of the Institute of Art and Media Theory. The subject: Does painting still have a future in the third millennium? The Zurich University of the Arts is, after all, famous for its theory discussions, which began in the last century with the now legendary interventions that still continue to attract great public interest to the

Züri-West Culture Campus. Together with the Zurich University of the Arts' other research institutes (Design2context, Institute of Cultural Studies and Art Education, Institute of Computer Music and Sound Technology, Institute of Drama and Film, Institute of Design Technology), the Institute of Art and Media Theory has ensured that the Zurich University of the Arts has become a mecca of transdisciplinary research in the arts.

Just by the by, the Institute of Design Technology is celebrating a splendid anniversary. Exactly fifteen years ago it took over the Design Department of the Korean-German Institute of Art and Technology in Seoul, which has since become one of the most sought-after addresses for design training in the whole of Southeast Asia.

But theory discussions are by no means the only reason aficionados of avant-garde art forms like coming to Zurich. The Department of Art & Media has made a name for itself by taking the media arts that developed at the end of the last century and those visual arts that make use of traditional media and integrating them fully in a shared three-stage course of studies (Bachelor, Master, doctor of art) in such a way that each was able to retain its respective media edge. The grand old man of German painting is not alone in finding that unique.

Now the students from Mumbai arrive in the big foyer. Their destination is the exhibition hall on the Culture Campus, where today an exhibition of degree projects from the Design Department's Master's programs is taking place. Design was always a domain of Zurich's. Here Swiss design was able to hone its typical qualities to perfection. And the reforms of recent years that have focused design training at the Zurich University of the Arts on mobile communications and caused a furor worldwide have now borne tangible fruits. The program's reputation has reached far-off Mumbai, which long ago replaced California's Silicon Valley as the center of digital revolutions.

But the exhibition opening is not for another hour, so the class joins a charming hostess for a guided tour of the gigantic university building. With its cascades of rooms and its wide stairways and atria exhibiting prize-winning works by students, the building offers visitors a veritable treasure-trove. Wandering past, you gain fascinating insights into the design studios, dance studios, sculpture studios, sound-recording studios, and not least into the studio theater, where they are rehearsing the latest work by the young Swiss playwright Hansueli Marthaler. This way you get a grand impression of what the Zurich University of the Arts has been since its founding: a highly productive place. That applies above all to theater, for the performative aesthetic demands a very special relationship to viewer and audience. Not here the separation of bright activity on stage from a darkened passive audience. New communicative instruments have to be developed. And in this connection the drama program produces not only new actors, but a new audience, too.

This new audience is also found in the crowd standing in line at the Culture Campus's Experimental Cinema. Here, as part of the European Film Academies Festival, they are showing a retrospective of prizewinning films created in recent years by students or graduates of the Swiss Master's program in film, which the Film Department of the Zurich University of the Arts teaches as a leading member of the network. There are several Golden Leopards and Golden Tigers among the prizes. Public access to the cinema, incidentally, is via the building's impressive access ramp, where in the last century road tankers brought the milk of whole generations of cows to be turned into yogurt and other Swiss specialties. Now, with the aforementioned public cinema, the equally public theater, and the concert halls, the place has become a popular cultural venue in what is still Zurich's most dynamic neighborhood.

Now we have arrived at the end of our little trip into the future. As you can see, much of what was said fifteen years ago at the opening ceremony of the Zurich University of the Arts has indeed become reality.

It is the work of the imagination—to make the (hitherto) hidden visible, to make the previously unheard-of heard—that is at the heart of a school of the arts. When the as yet invisible is revealed, the inaudible made audible, this changes reality in a human, person-centered sense. Designers shaping the interaction of man and machine create new interfaces for new forms of communication, composers invent new tonal structures, filmmakers develop new time structures, theater directors present new communication structures; all of them alter the possibilities of perception. In an age where realities are mostly dominated by technologies, it is this potential—to contribute toward a future with human dimensions—that gives the Zurich University of the Arts its lasting significance and relevance.

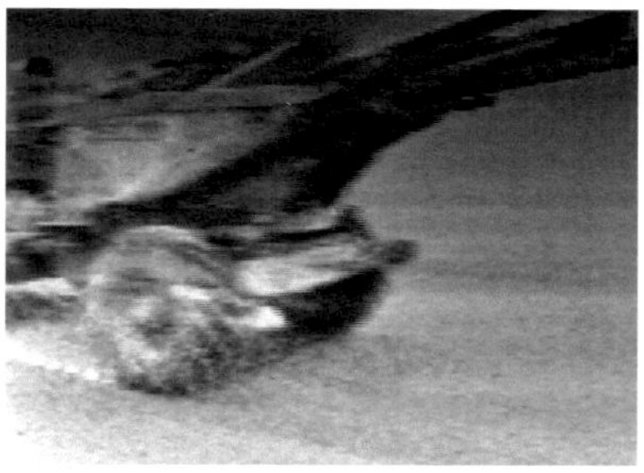

The Department of Music, 2007–2015

Daniel Fueter

Say goodbye to linear thinking! The future will not hinge on the simple discussion of whether technology is the end of the world or heaven on earth. It isn't about choosing between silver, pink, and black. It's about variety! The most important innovations are social ones. The most important changes are changes in attitude. Matthias Horx, Zukunftsinstitut, in an interview with the Gottlieb Duttweiler Institute, spring 2007

Fantasies which give rise to forecasts often have the sad tendency to project current developments onto the future without taking into account the possibility that unexpected forces may influence and deflect the predicted course of events. The following remarks, therefore, should be treated with appropriate caution.

Interrelationships

As complexity increases, so predictability declines. The Department of Music will be part of a complex network of forces, influences, and expectations of adaptability. Structural consolidation in the different sections of the Zurich University of the Arts will also generate a broad spectrum of possibilities and options for cross-sectional activities for students and staff alike.

International visibility will compel the universities of Switzerland to reexamine the courses they offer. This means that the Department of Music will confer with the other members of the Conference of Music Schools in Switzerland to continue developing its competence profile in a direction that is beneficial within the overall context of Swiss music schools.

Additionally, we will have to step up our cooperation with music schools abroad. Such joint international efforts will become increasingly indispensable, particularly in those areas of our educational programs which are centered in research.

In terms of challenges for the future, this means fostering joint efforts within the Zurich University of the Arts, finding cooperative concepts on the national level, and developing exchange programs with our peers worldwide.

The increases in complexity which we witness today are not limited to relations between different educational institutions. They also result from the growing importance of forming practical partnerships, not only during one's time as a student, but also in the working life of a musician. A program of study which incorporates production as a fundamental element gains added authenticity and credibility by focusing on practical work. Even more importantly, this focus increases the probability that graduates will be able to embark on a successful career.

In the working lives of music school graduates, the pace of change can be expected to accelerate in all areas. Varied professional biographies will become the rule. In general, we can expect to see growing polarization, increasing conflicts at all levels, and a continuous process of dissolution which will "medievalize" our educational structures. In the three core areas of music education, namely music pedagogy, performance, and composition, this could have the following consequences:

Pedagogy: In the increasingly colorful and conflict-ridden world of school and everyday life, music education in the widest sense will encounter new and challenging opportunities for action. Multilingualism in the figurative sense will be a prerequisite for making a living. At the same time, personal experience and personal attitude will increasingly become the only valid standards for self-assessment.

Performance: The divide between a musical culture based on commerce and aiming for increasingly spectacular events on various levels (including that of genre) on the one hand and a freely fluctuating everyday world of music on the other will grow wider, while the discrepancy between high and low is more likely to decrease.

Composition: Neither innovation nor adherence to tradition are sufficient to justify or explain one's compositional choices today. Musicians involved in the creation of new music must hold their own in a debate which centers around the issue of dissemination as an integral part of the work of art and its presentation.

Thus one of our tasks for the future will be to design our music education programs to help our students develop into competent professionals as well as to acquire flexibility, self-assurance, and openness to unfamiliar ideas.

Developments

Developments in the Department of Music during the coming decade will be dominated by trends which affect art schools in general:

1. The surge in development triggered by the technological revolution—the dawn of the digital age opened up vast new dimensions in the field of audio technology in particular—will continue and gain even more significance as an innovative force driving further changes.
2. The globalization of human resources, information, and problems will continue and will keep opening up new perspectives. In one of its oddest consequences, Asia will emerge as the primary force preserving Europe's cultural heritage, while in Europe itself there will be an increasing focus on issues of ethnomusicology and technology—along with a predictable trivialization of the music available on the market.
3. The line between high culture and popular culture will become increasingly indistinct. In the new dichotomy between a globalized market and regional manifestations, "elite" and "popular" phenomena will coexist on both sides of the divide.
4. The increasing complexity of issues will foster the development of cross-disciplinary trends. The work of the artist will increasingly call not only for networked thinking, but also for the ability to view issues from more than one perspective.
5. Music education and university administration will increasingly find that studying these issues and teaching students to cope with them will occupy a central role in their work. Anchoring creative artistic processes in a new social environment (multicultural surroundings, politically polarized structures, segmented audience) will require special effort and attention.

Specifics

It is easy to foresee the consequences which these five general considerations and the points considered in the "Interrelationships" section above will have for the specific training offered by the Department of Music:

1. The department must teach the use of new technologies and must provide the relevant infrastructure—from sound technology to e-learning, from film music composition to the development of new methods of dissemination.
2. All levels of training and organization must be compatible with international standards.
3. Our training must increasingly take the study of popular art forms into account.
4. Finally, the department must become more permeable and open within the Zurich University of the Arts and the educational and cultural infrastructure in the region.
5. At the same time, the task of disseminating art must be studied as an element of the artistic process.

Specialties

Aside from these five general topics which will dominate educational issues in the field of music and elsewhere—and the list, inevitably, is a fragmentary one—five very specifically musical issues must be mentioned here:

1. The Bologna Process calls for a stronger focus on individual profiles in student biographies, and this focus is mirrored in what could be called an increasing deregulation of the market, with nonlinear biographies, niche careers, and multiple professional profiles. These phenomena will remain the major challenge for the school, its teachers, and its students. All the members of the future Department of Music will be working within a highly charged environment between the poles of uniformity and individuality and will constantly need to reassess their positions.
2. The framework surrounding the Bachelor's and Master's degrees—pre-university music education at one end and post-graduate studies at the other—will have special significance for the Department of Music. For music to hold its own, the early phases of music training will have to be given more attention and greater efforts will have to be made to foster musical talent at the pre-university level. Additionally, the postgraduate phase must be given top priority as the guarantor of the highest level of musical training. The PhD program provides training for university teachers, especially in the fields of music theory and composition. The possibility of obtaining a PhD is indispensable, too, for the formation of individual professional profiles in the fields of performance

(specific repertoire, director of music) and pedagogy (general music pedagogy, methodology).

3. The issue of improvisation will become more important both from the perspective of repertoire—in Early Music and New Music alike—and as a prerequisite for all crossover projects and cross-disciplinary projects. The increased flexibility which professional musicians are being asked to develop is reflected on the level of musicianship by a natural competence in improvisation.

4. The focus on source research, which helped performing musicians bid farewell to traditional interpretations dictated largely by the force of habit, has already spread from the repertoire of Early Music to the early Romantic era. Source research will continue to gain ground and bolster the historical and analytical study of the canon of masterpieces, which will remain definitive for at least the next few decades. A spirit of research and enquiry on the part of performing musicians will find its counterpart in the support they receive from science and education.

5. In recent years, the didactic elements of music education have experienced a quantum developmental leap which has had immediate effects on the working lives of musicians and on music education in general. At the same time, we can now observe an increased sensitivity to and a growing awareness of the physiological aspects of musical training. Analogous to developments in sports, developments in instrumental technique will draw more heavily on movement science and techniques of mental practice. The standards of technical and mental requirements will continue to rise for at least the next several years.

Measures

In the prognoses we have made so far, we have described the future journey of the Department of Music mostly in terms of responses to wider trends. In so doing, we have followed a trend ourselves, namely, the trend by which processes in all aspects of life are becoming increasingly difficult to steer and control and are following laws which refuse to admit of analysis and change.

However, the dynamism of the Department of Music and the Zurich University of the Arts as a whole will certainly allow individual measures to be taken in order to ensure the specific quality of the work we do. We will mention five such measures affecting the field of music, without attempting to draw up a comprehensive list. In ten years, the following principles will still apply:

1. The working environment must be an exemplary one. The teaching activities of the Department of Music must reflect the increased social competence which music education is believed to help develop in young children.

2. Making and listening to music are physical activities. It is impossible to talk about music without taking physical experiences into account. Training body memory is one of the central goals of music education. The infrastructure and equipment of the Department of Music as well as training and preventive measures must be designed to foster careful body management.

3. Dogged persistence no longer has a place in the age of efficiency even though, on closer examination, it might prove to be a first-rate tool for increasing efficiency. Despite the duty and responsibility of a music school to select its students, it must be possible to permit developments which manifest themselves in blocks or quests or errors. Students must be given the opportunity to dismantle resistance rather than merely avoid it.

4. A music curriculum must have room for the new. Its focus on practical work and demanding peak performance must not undermine the courage to engage in experiments. Vigilance must be exercised to ensure that the curriculum always reflects current developments in every aspect of musical life.

5. The links between us and our history must not be allowed to break. Studying music involves an exploration of our own identity. We assume responsibility for a cultural heritage which represents the foundation of our training, and for the varied nature of that heritage both on a larger scale and, specifically, within the context of Zurich. For the expressiveness which enables us to tell stories through the medium of music, we are indebted not least to our opportunities to engage with the great narratives of music history.

These are also the prerequisites which enable the department to organize public concerts. Ideally, performances by our students and teachers should have a groundbreaking influence on the region's cultural scene through innovative, relevant programming, high artistic standards, and independent forms of presentation. This specific dialogue with the public will become increasingly important not only for society and educational policies, but also for re-evaluating the department's own positions.

One Detail

For some years, the Department of Music has become increasingly aware of the importance of the different sections, such as Brass, Voice, Theory, etc. The Zurich University of the Arts is the great hope for the future of the Department of Music. And the networking of the Department of Music within the Zurich University of the Arts is one of our most important objectives. In my experience, the crucial, long-term impulses will not come from the negotiating table, but from the sections themselves. I hope that the Zurich University of the Arts will examine the sections with great care and foster their future development. General potential will find its realization in specific activities. And it is precisely those forces which support the logic of the sections which will be able to overcome their restrictions and one-sidedness.

The most important "field of change" is related to people, who are becoming steadily more independent, more informed, more networked, and more decisive. We think we know all about them. In reality, though, how people will react to the current developments in the world is very much an unknown quantity. Friederike Müller-Friemauth, Sinus Sociovision, in an interview with the Gottlieb Duttweiler Institute, spring 2007

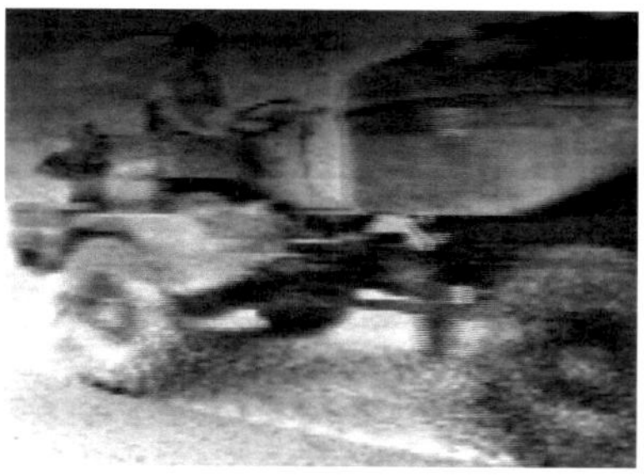

In the Year 2017: Reflections on Design in a University of the Arts

Jacqueline Otten

The task was monumental—to dismantle an old academy without losing anything. Far from being allowed to dissolve, existing disciplines were called upon to redefine themselves within a new context. Two hundred years after the publication of Hegel's *Phenomenology of Mind,* the recognition and application of dialectic—of reciprocal self-definition—had become the new institution's primary task.

The tenth anniversary of the Zurich University of the Arts this past year made it clear how much change had taken place, yet how little had been accomplished. The tremendous revolution occurring in the arts of the twenty-first century had begun to open the gates of design—but its doors were large and heavy. Let's take a look back to the future.

Intrinsic Design

The production of knowledge occurs in the mode of application. More than ever, designs are viewed within the context of their reception and users, with these relational networks serving as the point of departure for communication in society.

In this first decade, the mode of application acquired a distinct profile against the background of progressive technological developments. Correspondingly, the demands placed on design as an activity changed, which in turn affected educational concepts. For a mode of application is not a theory, but the experience of what happens: project work. With reference to the design process, one can no longer speak of a procedure that transposes knowledge and ability into commissioned work. Rather, design represents a kind of approach whose function it is to uncover differences, engage in communication, and provide material and non-material blueprints for the future. The status of media as tools has long been established; ever since, our interest has focused on design as a meaning-making process.

As Swiss sociologist and design theorist Lucius Burkhardt postulated in the 1980s, it is in a sense the invisible design that deserves our attention. A designed product possesses qualities that are not initially seen or noted; design and form-giving do not become visible until use. Although in 2007 the process was not yet complete, a paradigm shift did seem to be underway: solution-oriented design was giving way to scenarios, innovative application, and the integration of media strategies. These constitute what Burkhardt called the institutional-organizational component; good design takes account of the totality of the context. In some cases this can also mean ignoring problematics and parameters—and thus also limitations—and seeking to intervene in the underlying system.

At issue, therefore, is the intrinsic value of a design. Qualities emerging "from the inside out" belong to the object itself and make it what it is. Intrinsic actions are self-determined and require no external impetus. Nonetheless—and precisely for this reason—designers in the year 2017 had a job to do.

An old school bowed out while the new discovered itself

The Zurich University of the Arts did not emerge spontaneously or from the merger of two institutions and their capacities. While the fusion of capacities was indeed a first step in the direction of a university of the arts, its peculiar character, its uniqueness in the international educational landscape, was still largely undefined; those features that would one day be the distinctives of the new university were still in the formative stages. While such features did develop within the framework provided by the new institution—and the framework was a good one—the most significant impetus derived from the established sections facing the world of the future and its challenges.

It was in this context that the scenarios were played out which led to a positioning of design at the Zurich University of the Arts. Questions served as the basis for making decisions and forecasts for the future. Hegel had noted the end of the Romantic form of art, but what bonds were we dissolving? Does transdisciplinarity presuppose an altered concept of solidarity? And what is identity in transdisciplinarity? To consider the design of the future meant to establish the parameters of conceivable developments.

Not an easy task. Within the spectrum of potential developments for design at the beginning of the twenty-first century there were two strands that demanded closer consideration: technology and research.

"Applied Art"

Technological innovation has made it easy to separate the apparent from the existant. John Berger

Wasn't it Kant, too, who differentiated between the fine arts and the crafts? Design, however, participates equally in commerce and art. Accordingly, the crucial question is not whether aesthetic experience is a category reserved only for the arts, one that excludes design. In the past, the relationship between art and design has often been viewed as one of rivalry, but in the new millennium, a symbiotic relationship has developed under the influence of digitization. In the year 2017, what design and art share is the model of networking. Even at the beginning of the twentieth century, Paul Valéry foresaw immaterial, circulating works of art that could be downloaded anywhere: "They will not merely exist in themselves but will exist wherever someone with a certain apparatus happens to be ... so we shall be supplied with visual or auditory images."[1]

Technological development had generated a new class of demands on our attention. With the technological awakening of interactivity and, at that time, the zenith of user-generated content in Web 2.0, monocausalistic conceptions had become obsolete. While John Berger could still assert that it is a modern illusion to see the artist as a creator ("Rather he is a receiver. What seems like creation is the act of giving form to what he has received."),[2] the multifarious, reciprocal relationships between sender and receiver—to the point of continuous role reversal—required a completely new way of viewing modes of design and reception, and thus education as well, for these networks involve fundamental social changes. The clustering of transdisciplinary expertise lends a new and unique impetus to the drive for innovation.

A shift occurred from the creative individual to the anonymous collective.

For the crafts, this kind of creative work led to a performative, result-oriented, non-entrepreneurial culture. Jeremy Rifkin wrote in 2004: "Networks operate on an entirely different principle. Each party enters into the relationship based on the supposition that by optimizing the benefits of the other parties and the group as a whole, one's self-interest will be maximized in the process."[3]

Transdisciplinarity presupposes an altered understanding of solidarity; accordingly, in the course of collectivization, did everyone become a designer?

In the traditional view, designing meant the linking of intentions and considerations, but in a world seemingly generated more by digital systems than by designers, the function of design changed. At present, the discussion revolves around the question of how virtuality determines reality, but in 2007 we were talking about new roles for creators and actors: Myspace, YouTube, and SecondLife. While in the early days of design the boundaries were established by access to tools, today anyone can be a designer who has a computer at home. Thus the spectator has become a reporter, everyone is a web designer, and the children's bedroom has turned into a broadcasting station.

The year 2017 brought the all-clear signal. Evidently there does exist a culture of thought and action that originates in and corresponds to designing. In many areas, the application of design had become differentiated into a gestural vocabulary of play (and as so often in life, the object of the game is above all one thing: speed), but fortunately it has another characteristic as well: a tendency toward anarchy. Or, paraphrasing Baudrillard, one could say that design is in perpetual flight from technical structure toward its secondary meanings, from the technological system toward a cultural system.[4] Innovative design lies in properly connecting the technical-scientific with the cultural—an assignment for education. And to accompany it is the task of research.

1 Paul Valéry, "The Conquest of Ubiquity," in *Aesthetics,* trans. Ralph Manheim (1928; trans. London: Routledge and Kegan Paul, 1964), pp. 225–26.

2 John Berger, "Steps Towards a Small Theory of the Visible (for Yves)," in *The Shape of a Pocket* (New York: Vintage, 2003), pp. 9–24; repr. in *Left Curve,* no. 21, http://www.leftcurve.org/LC21WebPages/bergerelizam.html (accessed June 10, 2007). The epigraph to this subchapter is from the same source.

3 Jeremy Rifkin, *The European Dream: How Europe's Vision of the Future Is Quietly Eclipsing the American Dream* (Cambridge, UK: Polity Press, 2004), p. 186.

4 See Jean Baudrillard, *The System of Objects,* trans. James Benedict (London: Verso, 2005), p. 6.

All empirical explanations are only apparent ones and do not lead beyond the circle of lower, sense experience! Their will to know seeks to reduce the world to nothing more than the mechanical thumb-twiddling of so-called natural forces! Robert Musil[5]

The emphasis on industrial processes of production developed into an initial system design, and implicitly into a kind of science through methodology, the establishment of connections, and a process of systematization. The integration of technology, especially the digital media, into processes of design and products or services is also the expression of a cultural practice. The design development thus feeds off of technical conditions, among which the "connectionist model," interconnectedness in the broadest sense, is the most prominent. It has released a dynamism and a flexibility that has changed the concept of design and placed the focus on communication relationships.

The development of networked, transdisciplinary research in this area marked the founding of the Zurich University of the Arts.

From the perspective of design research, it was demonstrated that in the arts, identities that are bounded, stable, and unequivocal become fluid. In this open system, design becomes a continual process of redefinition and combination, essentially grounded in three areas of research:

– The field of materiality, or of sense perception, which concerns itself with the interrelationship of topics and with contextualization. It offers a way to focus on the exterior. What is meant are production processes, sequences, products, and presentations, in short: the constituting of the visible.

– Processuality, or more precisely: the observation of processes. This area of research opens up what can be perceived with the senses to expose shifts, openings, and technologies in the processes of design and transmission, as well as interactions in the broadest sense. It is, incidentally, an area that is carried primarily by multimedial connections.

– And, not least of all, identities—the "self" and the "other." Paradigms of generation, the ambiguity of things, cultural conditions such as intended audience and meta-representation, communication paradigms, and habits of use. Application (mentioned at the beginning of this essay) creates identity.

The explicit task of designers is to concern themselves with these areas. While research within the framework of the design process still involves given "sets of data," to "find" is to interpret, and that is a creative and exploratory act. This gives rise to demonstrative and cognitive concepts that perhaps in the first decade of the millennium are firmly rooted in the "performative turn"—it works when it works, and technology is the determining factor. To be sure, research focuses on knowledge "about" the design (asking how and why), but knowledge gained "through" the design likewise leads to new insights, new orientation, even a new order. For design in particular seems to assume a prominent role whenever a paradigm shift appears on the horizon …

…for example in the founding of a university of the arts.

Boris Groys postulated that innovation articulates itself less in physical products than in the making visible of the relationship between product and cultural activity.[6] Let us go a step further. In an academy that must concern itself in an extensive and prolonged fashion with the fate of its graduates after three (Bachelor's) or five (Master's) years, productivity in the area of design also implies economic productivity. Profession as social identity, rhythms of life, the value of work, belonging, loyalty: these values are changing. Creative behavior has become the model for the world of work; it is here that new determinants for economic growth and international viability are being developed. Of great significance in this regard is the conjunction of technologically innovative regions and creative people—a question of location.

Did the Zurich University of the Arts write the history of the future? Or in other words, did the year 2007 see the implementation of a utopia?

Two preconditions were crucial for the university's success:

1. The freedom, i.e. the possibility, to search for the new, unencumbered by ideological motives. This freedom determines the degree of innovation, and it includes the opportunity to take detours, to reject, to leave alone, or to anticipate. It is a long path, but that is a good thing. For when the future arrives, it ceases to exist, or, to quote Hegel: "The spirit only occupies itself with objects so long as there is something secret, not revealed, in them."[7]

2. Exchange and interconnection across disciplinary boundaries presupposed an altered conception of the arts. This relationship has freed itself from the former limitations of spe-

5 *Der Mann ohne Eigenschaften* (1930), vol. 1, chpt. 113.
6 Boris Groys, *Über das Neue: Versuch einer Kulturökonomie* (Munich: Hanser, 1992).
7 Georg Friedrich Wilhelm Hegel, *Aesthetics: Lectures on Fine Art,* trans. T. M. Knox, (Oxford: Univ. Press, 1998), vol. 1, p. 604.

cific disciplines and forms of expression. The transdisciplinarity made possible in this way is the compelling answer to the challenges of the new century.

If we in 2018 can now observe that after ten years of the Zurich University of the Arts, we have succeeded in conjoining a wide variety of disciplines—descriptive, guiding, designing, and performative—then we have succeeded in shaping the future of the arts. That is the spectrum of aspects implicit in the fusion of two educational institutions.

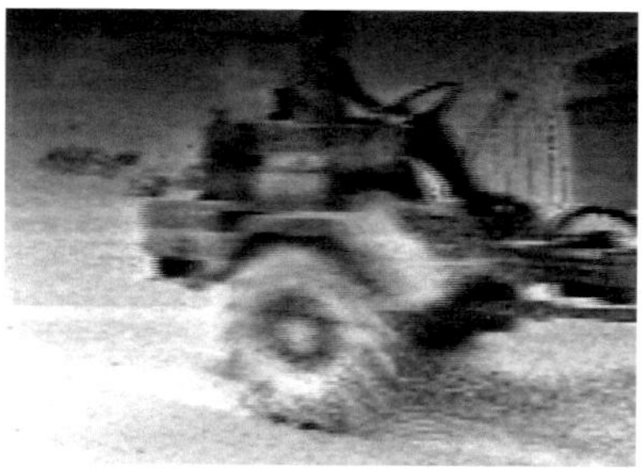

The Department of Cultural Analysis

Christoph Weckerle

The focus here is on a new department that is being established simultaneously with the Zurich University of the Arts (ZHdK). Anything we might say about this department, still in formation, must necessarily be couched in the future tense. But the sense of uncertainty arising from this situation should be taken in stride. Under the circumstances, it seems more useful to think in variable constellations than in fixed structures.

This unusual situation might even have its advantages—it could compel us to delineate the department's contours in a way that ensures its future viability.

Thinking Outside of the Box

From the perspective of the Department of Cultural Analysis, the Zurich University of the Arts corresponds to the equation 4+1=5. The School of Art and Design Zurich and the Zurich School of Music, Drama and Dance together comprise four departments, while one new department is born with the establishment of the Zurich University of the Arts.

The new department is intended to introduce dimensions that gain significance only with the merging of the two schools. Interfaces will be generated, transdisciplinary locations where competition between departments is emphasized less than the potential of their synergies. Hopefully, forward-looking strategies and approaches to problem-solving will emerge from the combination of opportunities now offered by the Zurich University of the Arts.

The Department of Cultural Analysis, however, is not constituting itself *ex nihilo.* It is being constructed from a series of renowned institutions. Among these is the Museum of Design Zurich, the largest Swiss design museum and one of the key European institutions devoted to the applied arts, design, and architecture. Its four collections—dedicated to design, poster art, graphic design, and applied arts—are world class. There is also the Institute of Cultural Studies in Art, Media and Design, a renowned and internationally networked transdisciplinary center for cultural history, cultural theory, and cultural analysis in the arts. And finally, there are the study programs in design and art education, which for almost a century have pursued an educational model that successfully integrates artistic and design-oriented with pedagogical and educational approaches.

The potential harbored by the structural amalgamation of these facilities is considerable. Equipped with a museum of design and degree programs in art and design education, the department is predestined to play a role in qualifying experts specializing in the broad domain of exhibition-related disciplines. Traditional university courses frequently fail to meet the demands in these rapidly evolving fields. The Department of Cultural Analysis, by contrast, will be capable of responding in a unique way to the emergence of new dimensions in the presentation and communication of objects and products. Classical roles will begin to blur as design and artistic knowledge are integrated with expertise in handling media, images, and texts. While such skills are traditionally assigned to various individual professional and disciplinary profiles, the Department of Cultural Analysis will open up the field of the public communication of art and design at the Zurich University of the Arts in a convincing way.

The long-term task of the researchers at the Institute of Cultural Studies and Art Education will be to attend to such profile development, to deepen knowledge through research, and to convey the results effectively. This will ensure the high quality and flexibility of studies while opening up exciting new possibilities of knowledge transfer.

To sum up the enviable set of tasks we face: A new department has been inaugurated together with the Zurich University of the Arts in response to a fundamental strategic need. This development coincides with the introduction of the Master's programs. For this reason, studies are to be fundamentally reconceived, given specific conceptualizations, and planned with an eye toward the future—at the level of content in teaching and research, as well as with respect to structure.

It would go beyond the scope of this essay to delineate the possibilities for exchange between the offerings within the new department. In the following, however, I should like to mention several key aspects of its future orientation. Besides profiling itself in the individual fields, the Department of Cultural Analysis must place itself in the service of the Zurich University of the Arts of which it is a part.

It is precisely this profile, with its deliberate shifts of perspective, its dedication to collaborative, future-oriented thinking, which assigns the Department of Cultural Analysis a crucial role within the Zurich University of the Arts.

Teaching Transdisciplinarity

Transdisciplinarity is a guiding idea for the Department of Cultural Analysis as a whole. The challenge lies in developing approaches which cannot be implemented within the individual departments of the Zurich University of the Arts. For it would be erroneous to imply that transdisciplinary aspects have hitherto played no role at the School of Art and Design Zurich or the Zurich School of Music, Drama and Dance.

The progressive disintegration of standard job descriptions encompasses nearly all of the fields represented at the Zurich University of the Arts. Transdisciplinary artistic and design practices are already in full swing: multimedia, crossover projects, intermediality in event culture—for instance video displays in concert halls, interactive electronic interfaces in performative formats, etc.

These transdisciplinary practices will only be accelerated by rapid technological developments, which often overtake capacities for reflection. We are confronted by a virtually omnipresent multimediality in artistic and design practices. But there exists a severe shortage of purposeful instruction that deals with the ways in which these various disciplines (theater–new media; music–art; design–music, etc.) interact to create meaning.

This discrepancy—the strong presence of transdisciplinary activities on the one hand, a virtual absence of reflection on them on the other—will no doubt be one of the department's main focuses. For the necessity of an institutional response to this phenomenon in the sphere of education is beyond dispute. What the department needs, therefore, are individuals who have profoundly grasped and mastered such transdisciplinary practices, who are themselves engaged in creative activity, and who are moreover capable of communicating and conveying these artistic or theoretical projects.

The challenges are considerable. Required skills include an analytical competence in the context of transdisciplinary fields of activity, practical competencies vis-à-vis individual transdisciplinary artistic projects, and the capacity to negotiate between the diverse discourses of the various disciplines—and in particular the capacity for bringing these disciplines into productive dialogue. For what musician is familiar with the production conditions of a photographer? Who knows how design processes function in the context of theater production, where to locate similarities, overlaps, and differences, and how to collaborate productively on the basis of such knowledge?

Such a conception of transdisciplinarity emerges now in a location where individuals from various disciplines collaborate as equals, and where, through transdisciplinary or interdisciplinary perspectives, other departments define problem-solving strategies as a new third term, thereby creating novel artistic formats.

This approach must do without any disciplinary center of gravity. No one discipline can provide its central point of departure or reference point. At the center stands the development and application of independent methodologies which—in contrast to existing interdisciplinary practices—do not simply transfer existing approaches to other disciplines, but which, instead, recognize the necessity for jointly developing newly-emerging hybrid art projects and new methods.

Given this model of equality, the Department of Cultural Analysis will probably be the first to define an innovative theoretical and practical approach to transdisciplinarity, one that will incorporate the disciplines of the performing arts, film, design, art, media, and music, as well as their respective socio-political and economic contexts.

The course offerings of the Department of Cultural Analysis will be all the more concretely useful because we will be drawing on instructors from other departments who have transdisciplinary experience in teaching and research; moreover, it will be possible to link teaching with practical and productive activities, including museum, theater, and concert work.

As the setting for a specific discourse of transdisciplinarity, one coordinated with the other departments, the Department of Cultural Analysis can be expected to expand the available instruction at the Zurich University of the Arts in a concretely useful and forward-looking manner.

Researching the Creative Scene

Research in the Department of Cultural Analysis will be characterized by its broad thematic diversity and its links to other departments in the Zurich University of the Arts. An example of this is the creative scene: current trends in public spending indicate that fewer and fewer graduates of the Zurich University of the Arts can expect to receive support from state cultural sponsorship programs. Discussions of the so-called creative industries with all its implications are having a growing impact on debates about education and cultural policy.

This production complex—one barely grasped in its real dimensions, and one that extends from the music industry to publishing, art, film, design, architecture, and all the way to private performing arts ensembles—is establishing itself at academies and universities both in Switzerland and abroad as an attractive research field. Still, only an art academy as large as the Zurich University of the Arts can claim that its preoccupation with creative industries also constitutes labor market research on behalf of its own graduates. The proximity to students, instructors, and graduates experienced here daily makes it possible to pursue highly promising approaches.

In fact, the "small" creative industries making up the creative scene where the overwhelming majority of ZHdK graduates will be active is an intensely multifaceted and interesting research subject. The fact that the creative scene is treated by most programs as a negligible quantity, at most a supplier for established enterprises, opens up an as yet unoccupied field of research.

The ramified trajectories of their specific professional and cultural competencies tie the protagonists of the creative scene together in a dense social network. They often anticipate social transformations toward hybridization; models of living and working developed by the creative scene thereby become exemplary in other areas.

Permanent reinterpretation, the opening up of fields of activity characterized by mutating and to an extent project-dependent definitions of the requisite qualifications and division of labor—this is how the creative scene appears today. Economic, cultural, and social dimensions are interconnected on an equal basis; approaches are motivated in a thoroughly pragmatic way, allowing flexible orientations. Because these three types of capital—economic, social, and cultural—constitute a unity and serve as joint capital, they can be set off one against the other in order to counterbalance deficits.

The creative scene, then, is more than a precarious, digitized bohemia. In particular, research should investigate whether and how the constellations and dynamics of the creative scene are of significance for other fields and branches, both in terms of direct impact and as a stimulus.

The flexible project context and carefully tended entrepreneurial freedoms of the creative scene give rise to attitudes, procedures, and products capable of reacting in positive and manifold ways on established enterprises. Creativity and innovation are closely associated, and working methods are oriented to the principles of experimental research, or else redefined. Because this market is one that need not always be taken into account in its full depth, approaches can be implemented that would never make it beyond the drafting table elsewhere. The outcomes are often astonishing.

But what does this have to do with an art school? The answer is as obvious as it is promising: given the special configuration of the Zurich University of the Arts and the pivotal function of the new department in terms of cultural analysis and art education, such reversals of perspective (from driver of culture to driver of innovation, and vice-versa) can be discussed pragmatically and innovatively in ways that makes them directly relevant to the curricula of all departments. For the interface between education and professional life is necessarily central for many Master's programs at the Zurich University of the Arts.

If we succeed in transferring such knowledge from the research context into cultural, educational, or even economic and political contexts, this will open up a multiplicity of new fields of argumentation and action at the Zurich University of the Arts which can be tested out with various discussion partners, thereby setting established argumentative structures on their heads.

This function of the Department of Cultural Analysis within the Zurich University of the Arts may also involve the provision of counseling services in a facility specially set up for that purpose. The department could thereby function as an additional and central interface between the Zurich University of the Arts and the professional lives of its graduates.

Exactly which forms this might take, and how such a Career Center might actually function, are questions for which concepts would have to be developed jointly. In any event, the Department of Cultural Analysis is an ideal setting for discussing these matters and establishing appropriate responses.

The objectives of this young department are ambitious, but nonetheless realistic in the framework of the Zurich University of the Arts. The criteria for evaluating the phases of its development must be defined in detail. In general, it will be regarded as a success if, three years after the publication of this text, students and instructors at the Zurich University of the Arts no longer perceive the Department of Cultural Analysis as an "add on," but instead as fulfilling an indispensable and pivotal function, as joining research, teaching, and communication. The equation $4+1=5$, then, would become the equation $4+1=5^{+}$.

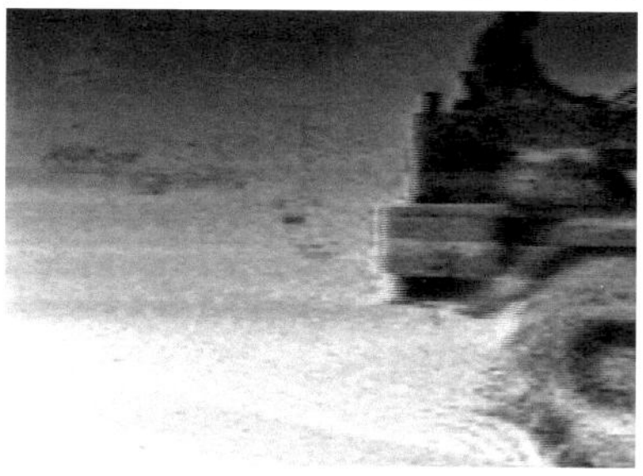

The Department of Performing Arts and Film: Drama

Hartmut Wickert

1.

The highest conjoint work of art is the drama ... The true drama is only conceivable as proceeding from a common urgence of every art toward the most direct appeal to a common public. In this drama, each separate art can only bare its utmost secret to their common public through a mutual parleying with the other arts; for the purpose of each branch of art can only be fully attained by the reciprocal agreement and cooperation of all the branches in their common message. Richard Wagner[1]

Just as the Zurich University of the Arts' film, dance, and scenography programs will profit from their physical proximity to the acting and directing programs, so the curriculum of its drama studies program will receive a crucial corrective from this same proximity. There will scarcely be any talk of traditional drama studies in future years. This much is evident from what has happened in Germany—at the Konrad Wolf School of Film and Television in Potsdam/ Babelsberg, at the Film Academy Baden-Württemberg in Ludwigsburg, and at the Institute of Applied Theater Studies at the University of Giessen, for example. fig. 1a/b

The education provided at the Zurich University of the Arts will be passionately committed to those areas in which the various departments overlap: We want dancers who can act and apply their verbalization and representational skills in modern dance theater, no matter what form it takes; we want actors who are skilled in music and movement and use this body-language proficiency to inject new ideas into the more physical and action-based forms of modern spoken theater. Our performers will have a keen interest in academic research as well as extensive experience of acting in front of the camera. Our future directors, meanwhile, will apprehend and use film as an integral aspect of modern theater and will learn not only to direct actors, but to confront the idiom of film with the demands of stagecraft.

Extending the students' repertoire of skills also means promoting the capacity for reflection, which on the terrain of the performing arts means learning to grapple with the protean processes of perception. What today's media society requires of the performing arts is not just a competitive awareness of the status of "old" in relation to "new" media, but rather the mediatization of traditional space. fig. 2

The inclusion of the scenography program in the same department will provide something akin to a system of coordinates for the performing arts, while acoustic and virtual space will provide new environments and terra incognita for performers to explore. Choreography, with its abstract systems of notation, will give film and theater directors a deeper insight into the relationship between space and time, while the work of the film studio will facilitate an

1a/b Adolphe Appia, *Rhythmic Space* (1909), "The Waterfall" and "Quay"

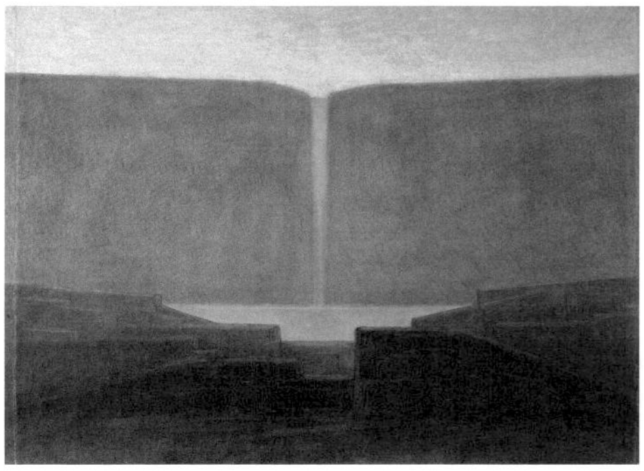

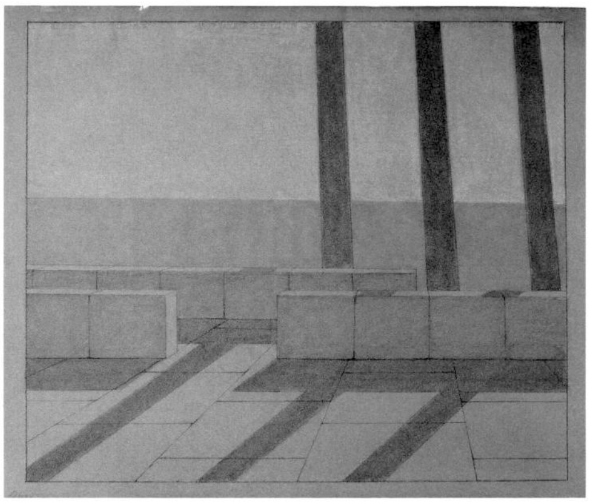

1 Richard Wagner, *The Art Work of the Future,* trans. William Ashton Ellis (1849; trans. 1895; repr. Kessinger Publishing, 2004), p. 85.

artistic approach to reality by creating—and demanding—opportunities for transformation and simulation of a very different nature indeed. fig. 3

Theater will be able to become film, film theater, scenography dance and dance scenography.

The performing arts will become performative in the sense that they will become self-referential and constitutive of their own reality. Artistic performance will no longer mean the representation of a different world, but rather the creation of a special, if possible unique, relationship between actor(s) and audience. The fact that something happens between the two groups will ultimately carry more weight than what happens. The players' and spectators' actions will have no meaning but what they mean in themselves.

Performative art, in other words, predicates the existence of an audience. Everything which takes place in progressive productions by performing artists has to do with the creation of a specific relationship with the audience. That this audience has long since moved beyond the confines of an auditorium neatly fenced off from what is happening on stage is of course common knowledge. What this actually means for new forms of performative artistic practice, however, has been neither exhaustively explored nor even tested. Where else, if not at a school of the arts, could we find the scope needed for the experimental, curiosity-driven development of the communicative skills required to this end? Where else could it be possible—for students and faculty alike—to constantly redefine and reassess this scope in relation to the discoveries that professional practice still has in store for us? fig. 4

For this, too, we need spectators—an audience that is both interested and alert. The department's own performance opportunities will become an indispensable vehicle of instruc-

2 Big Art Group, Ned Stresen-Reuter and Heather Litteer, *House of No More*, 2004

3 Station House Opera, *The Other Is You*, 2007

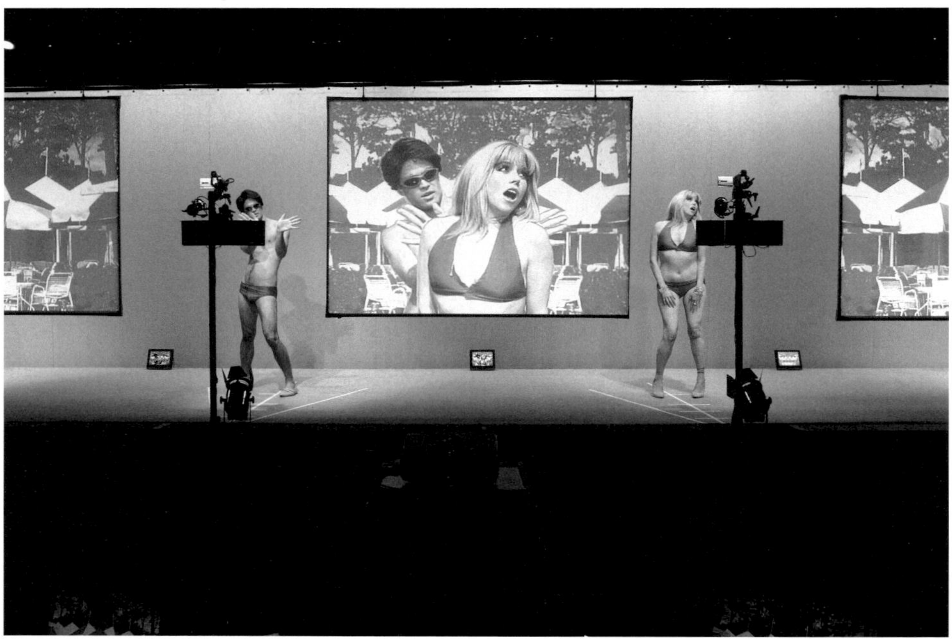

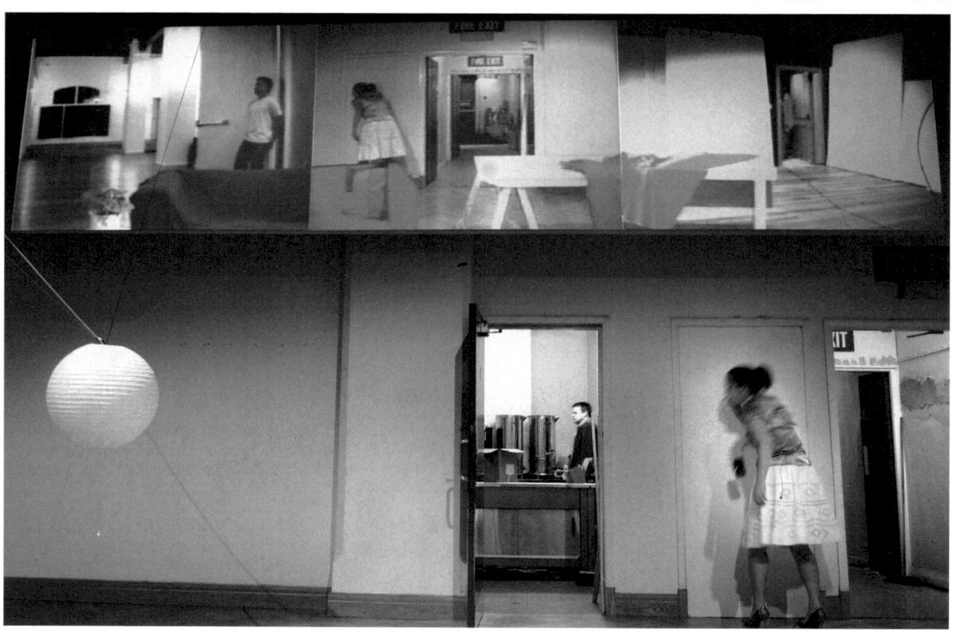

tion. Its professional-standard theaters, studios, and other premises will provide ideal conditions for these productions to generate practical overlaps between the various performative disciplines. Large-scale projects directed by artists of international renown will become a central part of the Department of Performing Arts' Master's program. The crossover concept and exploration of interreferentiality will both be enshrined in the hands-on curriculum, giving the department a unique status on both the national and international higher education scene.

2.

But to force his own specific nature to the highest blossoming of its contents in this one and highest art-work, the separate artist, like each several art, must quell each selfish, arbitrary bent toward untimely bushing into outgrowths unfurthersome to the whole; the better then to put forth all his strength for reaching of the highest common purpose, which cannot indeed be realized without the unit, nor on the other hand, without the unit's recurrent limitation ... This purpose, however, the separate art-branch will never reach alone, but only all together; and therefore the most universal is at like time the only real, free, the only universally intelligible art-work. Richard Wagner[2]

Teaching methods will inch ever closer to learning methods. Collective learning, such as any team of productive performers is likely both to facilitate and to necessitate, will further enhance the ability to communicate—with each other, with faculty, with the audience.

Teaching, in turn, fosters the ability to establish links between the practical aspects, the sheer craftsmanship that is the basis of proficiency, and production theory.

Students must also learn to direct a team; after all, the performing arts bring together artists from a variety of backgrounds and a wide range of artistic practices, so coordination and leadership skills are indispensable.

The tension generated as a result of the promotion of, and demand for, individual proficiency on the part of the performers themselves —a proficiency which will have the effect of minimizing their dependence on classical ensemble work—and their need to rely on their fellow performers is very great indeed.

As has already been noted, artistic practice in the years to come is likely to be shaped largely by the appropriation, application, and incorporation of new media techniques. This makes it all the more vital that the function and relevance of these same media to aesthetic practice become a core component in the curricula of the Zurich University of the Arts' various departments, just as it will be the job of its researchers to anticipate, stimulate, and indicate developments in this direction. If it is to extend beyond what few rudimentary and research-based attempts have been made to define performative space, any further research in this field will have to focus on those projects which seek to break new ground, to achieve what was previously deemed impossible, to transcend borders, and to broaden existing horizons. The art forms and media used to accomplish this will have to be constantly refined and scrutinized and their application in each particular instance questioned and analyzed. By seeking to reconstruct the theoretical underpinning of the media-driven changes which the performing arts are currently undergoing, researchers will engage in

4 White Trash, *Wir waren schon als Kinder Scheisse* (We Were Shit Even as Kids), 2005, degree theater project at the Hamburg School of Music and Drama

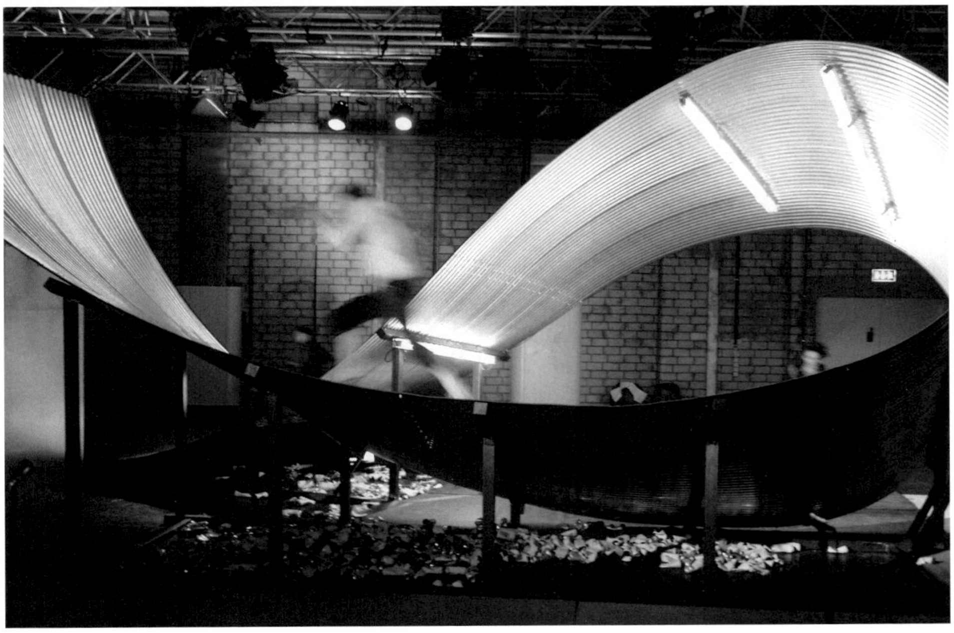

2 Ibid., p. 91.

reception research, too, pursuing a line of inquiry concerned with the place the performing arts occupy, or will yet occupy, in that mediatized space in which they are perceived and received. fig. 5

5 Het Zuidelijk Toneel, *Caligula*, 1996

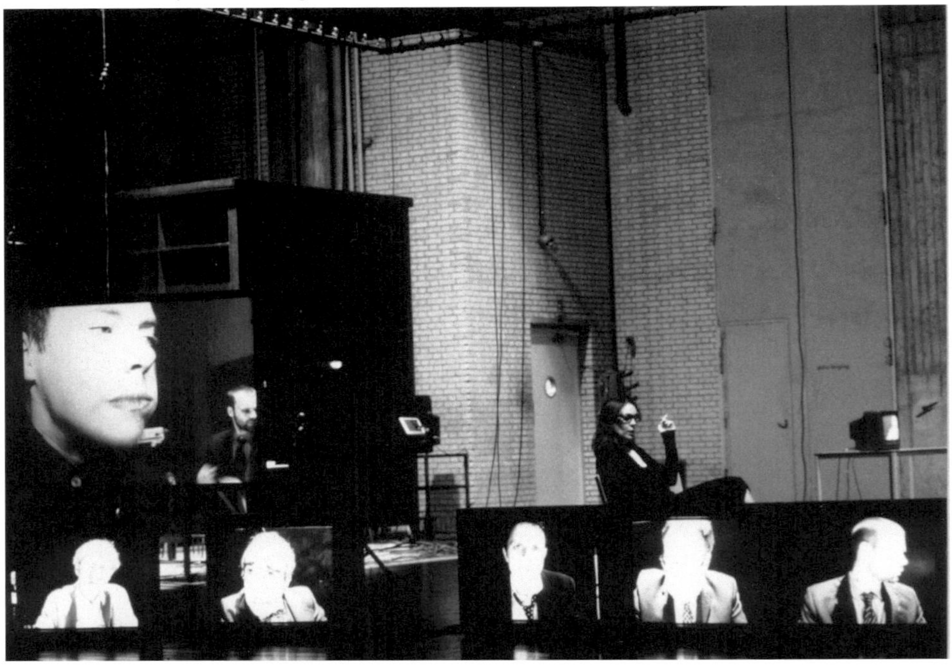

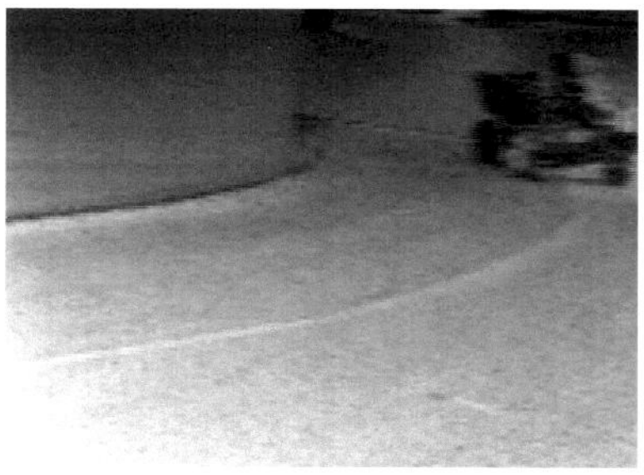

The Department of Dance: A Look at the Future

Oliver Matz

If you compare the training of dancers in Switzerland with that in other European countries it becomes clear that Swiss dance training is still in its infancy. Nevertheless, in recent decades Swiss dance has received a tremendous impetus. A highly creative dance movement, ranging from renowned ballet and dance companies to a whole host of independent contemporary dance companies, has begun increasingly to promote its own interests.

One of the most outstanding initiatives of this kind to be taken in recent years was the "Projekt Tanz." Seeing an urgent need to counteract existing trends, Pro Helvetia and the Federal Office of Culture together with cities, cantons, associations, and members of the dance profession launched a project designed to meet the needs of the future. The aim of the project was to improve conditions for members of the dance profession and thus preserve and enhance the quality of dance in Switzerland in a lasting way.

The first step toward realizing these goals is to make dance training more professional at all levels. The Department of Dance at the Zurich University of the Arts is eager to meet this challenge, which is of such primary importance for the future of dance in Switzerland. There is real pioneering work to be done here.

We are currently experiencing an era of extreme social contrasts, which also find expression in new trends in dance. The coexistence of a large variety of artistic forms testifies to these contrasts on both the national and the international dance scenes. With a spectrum ranging from advanced dance techniques to the non-dance movement, dance is becoming both more standardized and more individual and embraces mixed forms as well drawing clear distinctions. The use of media has served to negate the individual, turning the dancer into a technical being. A tendency to reemphasize the narrative aspect of dance may be observed alongside an interest in more abstract forms of movement and a striving for greater expressiveness. Choreographers from all the different styles of dance are reconsidering their approach to and treatment of traditional works and trying out new interpretations.

There are a variety of options for designing a training program that takes account of all these different currents, tendencies, and fashions in dance to prepare students for their future profession. Yet is it really possible to conceive a training program that will do justice to a dance scene continually in flux, or is this tantamount to trying to square the circle?

The only way to respond to the multiple challenges of the future is to teach to a standard of quality that will allow dancers to respond adequately to the highest demands. A dancer's training should emphasize individuality, learning the skills of the trade, and an artistic creativity that is not arbitrary. Whether the student is training as a performer or doing a Bachelor's or Master's degree in dance, these are the attributes that determine his or her real chances as a dance professional. Here instructors must pay close attention to both methodology and didactics, repeatedly questioning and updating them.

These tasks present a great challenge to both dance teachers and lecturers in dance, which in my opinion can only be met by working closely together in a team.

Transdisciplinary and interdisciplinary programs should be offered where they are sensible and where they help develop the profile of the individual student. In view of differences in training concepts it is important for the various programs to maintain their independence. While bearing in mind the need to be competitive internationally, it should at last be possible to offer Swiss dance students all kinds of training programs that have been running in Europe for decades.

Both the national and international debates about dance training are characterized by controversy. Hence there are a number of conceptual questions that may be answered differently depending on one's artistic or individual standpoint. I would therefore like to ask the directors of the three different study programs in the field of dance to speak for themselves.

The Zurich Academy of Dance taZ
Steffi Scherzer
Ideas for an Internationally Competitive Swiss Center for Ballet and Dance

Today, as the countries of Europe grow ever closer together, education and training have become one of the most important issues, for these are connected with bringing together widely differing cultures. A major challenge and responsibility for the directors, teaching staff, and other employees of the taZ is to give children and young people a sense of orientation and focus, to help them realize their dreams and ultimately to give their lives meaning.

In training dancers to become stage performers, the taZ aims to meet international standards in every respect. The training will take place in a building on the planned Toni campus, allowing us, at last, to offer excellent conditions for a training program that is important for the whole of Switzerland. The youngest dance students will enter the dance academy between the ages of ten and twelve and will train as dancers while pursuing their normal school education and residing in a boarding school. The integrated structure, which will enable students within the space of a single school day to move freely from general school education to training in dance as a practical and artistic discipline, is designed to compensate to some extent for the inevitable heavy demands made on students starting a professional training at such a young age. This kind of early training, however, is essential for furthering intellectual and physical development in parallel.

The dance curriculum is a broad one. Starting with basic training in all aspects of classical academic dance, it builds methodically to include the various styles of modern and contemporary dance. The final year of the course offers students the opportunity to work with international choreographers in order to prepare them as well as possible to work in both the Swiss and the international ballet and dance scenes.

A central feature of our school's profile is a team of professional teaching staff who are aware of their great responsibility and who aim to further the special talents of young dancers, recognizing and developing their individual qualities. The goal is to train students to become open-minded artistic personalities, free of dogma, and capable of making optimal use of their ability and creativity.

What makes the profession of a dancer attractive is not only the famous qualities of discipline, determination, and hard work, but also the fact that dance transgresses international boundaries and knows no language or cultural barriers. It is a fascinating profession, which draws young people, teaching them to take charge of their lives and to perfect their skills in order, ultimately, to prove themselves on the stage.

The Zurich Bachelor's Degree in Dance
Tina Mantel
Switzerland's First Degree Program in Dance: Visions of a Radical Normality

"I'm studying dance at the University of the Arts."

If in a few years a young person gives this answer when asked what he or she is doing, then the dance studies course at the University of the Arts will have become radical normality. It will be normal for people to nod their heads in recognition, knowing what dance as an art form means.

And it will be normal for students who are mad about dance to spend the whole day in the studio, absorbing what their teachers tell them with every fiber of their bodies and every cell of their brains, then going on to experiment with it themselves. In their free time they will satisfy their curiosity about dance in the library, in the media center, and in theaters in and around Zurich. Open to all directions in dance as an art form, they will actively explore the traditions of modern dance, the spectrum of contemporary dance, and the innovations of choreographers. These students will be equipped to analyze any form of dance in a discerning manner, to consider their own preferences, and to evaluate their own abilities in a realistic fashion.

"I'm studying dance at the University of the Arts."

In other words, in a place where students are invited to share their visions and are given the space to try them out and put them into practice. A place where performances combine contemporary trends with the repertoire of modern dance presented in an innovative fashion to win the enthusiasm of new audiences. A place where working with other art forms and artists is a normal and institutionalized process.

"I have a Bachelor's degree in dance from the University of the Arts."

An increasing number of motivated, professionally trained dance artists will be able to utilize this recognized qualification when looking for a job. They will know how to use the funding structures available all over Europe and be able to find performance venues suitable for their projects. They will vitalize and enrich the dance profession in Switzerland and take a passionate interest in shaping the future of dance. Absolutely normal. And absolutely radical.

The Zurich Bachelor's Degree in Dance

Philipp Egli

With Vision and Prudence

The Bachelor's course in dance trains dancers not only in a technical sense but also encourages their personal potential as performing artists and helps them integrate their work with that of choreographers.

The Supporting Leg

Instruction in a structured mixture of traditional and modern dance techniques provides dancers with a sound physical basis, while linear and non-linear impulses, a confrontation with traditional forms, *zeitgeist,* and current tendencies helps dancers to develop an open and flexible approach to their art—what in the context of dance might be called the supporting leg.

The Free Leg

This basis is then used to broaden a dancer's perception—his or her perception of outside and inside, of other and self, of being part of a whole and being a whole in this part. An awareness of the wherewithal, of the "how" of dance helps the dancer become a choreographic artist, an artist of movement—though not, or not only in an acrobatic sense:

What happens to me, what happens to the audience while I am dancing ? What am I projecting outside myself ?

Master of Advanced Studies in Dance Education, Zurich University of Applied Sciences

Sandra Nussberger

As part of its further education program in dance, the Zurich University of the Arts offers a Master of Advanced Studies in Dance Education at the Zurich University of Applied Sciences.

The Master of Advanced Studies in Dance Education offers dancers an important opportunity to obtain a further professional qualification or to start a second career. The course takes the form of an additional teaching qualification in dance. Students enrolling for this course will be expected to have completed a performance training in dance.

In 2004 the Zurich School of Music, Drama and Dance became the first institution to launch a postgraduate course in dance education. In introducing its Master of Advanced Studies, the Zurich University of the Arts is the only further education institution in Switzerland to offer a study program culminating in a qualification equivalent to a degree from a university of applied sciences. It has thus made an important contribution to giving dance teachers professional status.

There is a great need in Switzerland for highly-trained dance teachers with both professional and teaching skills. It is therefore essential to achieve a unified, high standard for professional dance teachers.

The aim is to enable above all children and young people, but also adults, to enjoy a professional level of instruction in dance and thus to further their enjoyment of physical movement, their creativity, and their technical ability. Dance education projects must be introduced in schools, which, like their counterparts in drama and music, will teach children to be creative and further their cognitive skills. The aim of professional instruction in dance is to sensitize students to dance.

Conclusion

The opportunity to work on a large campus, the Toni Areal, under the auspices of the Zurich University of the Arts together with teachers and students from other disciplines and study programs opens up new perspectives, which should be pursued consistently. It is a pleasure and a privilege to hold this responsibility, if it entails preparing the way for future generations of dancers of all styles of dance.

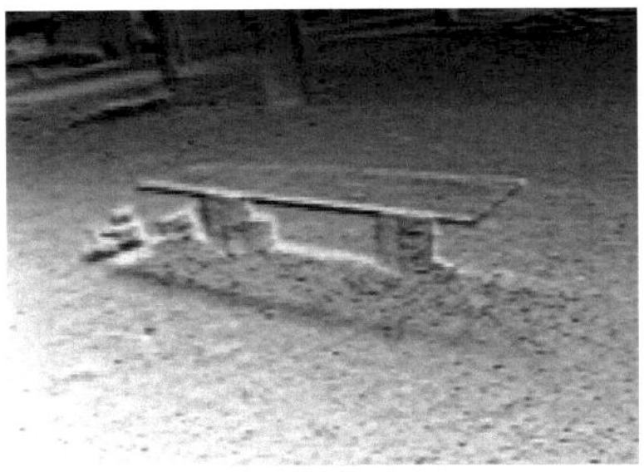

Film Training: Playground, Laboratory, and the Route to the Professional Job Market

Bernhard Lehner

The School of Art and Design Zurich—formerly the School of Applied Arts and now soon to be absorbed into the Zurich University of the Arts—has always been an important place for exploring the medium of film.[1] From as early as 1929, the Museum of Applied Arts adopted an innovative approach by showing the Deutsche Werkbund exhibition *Film and Photo*,[2] which examined film and photography within the context of modernism. In particular, however, let us not forget the seminal exhibition on film which in 1960 uniquely reappraised film history and film aesthetics—taking into account the way the artistic movements of European auteur cinema had changed the parameters.[3] Students from the photography class of the School of Applied Arts were involved in working on this exhibition. Shortly afterwards, they switched to film, developing even in their early works a personal conception of the medium that was more committed to artistic experiment than oriented on the standards of traditional cinema, which they rejected. Instead, they adopted positions that ran counter to the customary practices and aesthetics of Swiss film up to that point, which had been shaped by the moral and political values of the war and postwar years.

The legendary film classes that were conducted at the School of Applied Arts from 1967 to 1969 paradoxically number among the few points of contact between the Old and the New Swiss Cinema. This is where Kurt Früh and Hans Heinrich Egger, two outstanding figures in the "classic" 1940s to 1950s period of Swiss filmmaking, worked with a generation of young filmmakers who went on to decisively influence the New Swiss Cinema.[4] Equally memorable were the events staged in the lecture theater of the School of Applied Arts by the City of Zurich's Film Podium in the early 1970s—prior to the age of video recorders and DVD players—which significantly shaped the way a culturally aware audience perceived film history. Although these efforts to get film seen as a relevant artistic medium received widespread acclaim, they all came into being thanks to the initiative of individuals and were relatively short-lived. It took several attempts and decades of patient waiting before it was possible to permanently establish a comprehensive filmmaking program.

In the 1980s Urs Fanger, then head of the Department of Visual Communication, launched and headed another attempt to create a film training program. The project, which ultimately led to the current degree program in film, found support among renowned representatives of the Swiss film scene such as Georg Janett, Fredi M. Murer, Georg Radanowicz, and Hans-Ulrich Schlumpf. The first course plan—which Lucie Bader, then a junior lecturer and now one of the heads of the degree program, was also involved in developing—adhered to the image of the filmmaker as an all-rounder, an image that was also being propagated by Swiss auteur cinema.[5]
In 1991, after a number of political setbacks and nail-biting moments, Margit Eschenbach was elected to oversee the program. Extremely well-qualified in the field of filmmaking and art education, she immediately began planning the course and building up a team that had to fulfill both the requirements of an educational establishment and a production firm. The first entrance examination was held in the spring of the following year. Sixteen students were accepted;

1 The essay printed here is based on an article about the state of film training in Switzerland that was written for the annual periodical *Cinema*. See Jean-François Blanc, Fosco Dubini, Bernhard Lehner, "Filmschulen in Lausanne, Genf und Zürich," *Cinema*, no. 45 (Basel, 1999), pp. 136ff.

2 Deutscher Werkbund (ed.), *Film und Foto*, exh. cat. (Stuttgart, 1929).

3 Kunstgewerbemuseum Zürich (ed.), *Der Film*, exh. cat. (Zurich, 1960).

4 The film courses of 1967–69 are extensively documented in: Thomas Schärer, *Wir wollten den Film neu erfinden* (Zurich, 2005).

5 For example in an internal document from 1990 concerning the advanced film/video studies program at the School of Art and Design Zurich.

far more than one hundred had applied. Teaching began in fall 1992 in two separate classes.

The majority of people in the film world regarded the entry of film training into the groves of academe with benevolent interest, but there was also a degree of skepticism and ignorance. A good number clung to the naive idea that it is not possible to teach the essential part of an artistic pursuit, and that the teaching of acquirable skills would lead, at best, to off-the-peg film creations of no consequence. Now fifteen years have passed since the film program was set up at the School of Art and Design Zurich, and some one hundred students have graduated over that time. Most are now working in the field of film and audiovisuals. Female graduates from the School of Art and Design Zurich account to a large extent for the *Fräuleinwunder* phenomenon in contemporary Swiss cinema, which has been much propagated in the media in recent months. In passing, however, I would like to note that male graduates have also been successful as directors, screenplay writers, and cameramen, as well as in other filmmaking capacities.

The diploma program, which was initially a five-year course and was shortened to a four-year course in 1998, will cease at the end of the academic year 2007–2008. It is currently being phased out in favor of a program of study that is based on the Bachelor's and Master's degree system. The film training program is undergoing far-reaching structural change, as are the other study programs in the nascent Zurich University of Arts. Students were first accepted for the new Bachelor's course in 2005. A year later, the School of Art and Design Zurich set up a Master's program in filmmaking together with a number of other colleges and universities under the rubric of "CH Cinema Network." The founding of the University of the Arts in 2007 will bring a change of departmental structure, too, in that the Bachelor's and Master's programs in film will work together closely with the drama and dance programs which are currently departments in the Zurich School of Music, Drama and Dance. Another partner will be the new degree program in scenography.

The Bachelor's and Master's programs are being structured and redesigned in accordance with the current European requirements.[6]
The objective of the Bachelor's course is to teach students the basic principles of filmmaking and film theory, to enable them via project work to acquire personal experience of the medium of film, and to help them achieve the professional standard equivalent to a an entry-level assistant in a practical filmmaking field of their choice. The Master's program, in turn, aims to give a more thorough grounding in the areas of narrative (screenwriting, directing, editing), cinematography (camera), and production ("creative producing"). This new tiered course structure enables Master's projects to be more ambitious in production terms than the previous degree project films and to measure up to the productions made at important European and international film schools.

People such as my colleagues and myself, who have to deal on an almost daily basis with the vocabulary of an (art) school curriculum and issues of educational reform, may find these remarks about structure, qualifications, and aims to be fundamentally convincing, necessary, and important. However, they are probably only of secondary importance to young people who are interested in a career in film. Terms such as Bologna Model, ECTS points, and modules, or the distinction between seminar, workshop, and project teaching are for them, at best, troublesome side issues. They are interested in film, in developing and realizing their own ideas, rather than in course structures.

But what can one learn at an institute of higher education? What can a young person who wants a career in the field of film expect from a degree in film? How can the film training program prepare him or her for a career in film? What sets the institutional, academic approach apart from going straight into the profession and learning on the job? I often hear from students that they expect sound practical training first and foremost. This is something they could also learn on the job. The humility of this demand amazes me, and I cannot shake off the feeling that this is just the standard reply given to a lecturer because they do not want to demand the impossible. But really they do want more. They want to learn how good films are made, and because they are exacting and ambitious, they want to learn how to make good films themselves. They experience how difficult that is on a daily basis, and the lecturers know it only too well from their own experience.

The students' need—to make a film themselves and to do it well—should be taken seriously. Technical know-how, the correct handling of the equipment, the knowledge of work flows and work methods are an important part of filmmaking and are generally easy to teach.

6 As is documented in the internal documents of the years 2005–2007 concerning the Bachelor's and Master's study programs at the School of Art and Design Zurich.

At the heart of a creative program of study, however, must be the students' acquisition of a personal feeling for and understanding of the medium and film apparatus. It is of crucial importance that the students reach a point where film turns into their own means of reflection and expression. Two characteristics are particularly important in that respect: The ability to embrace utopian thinking and an enjoyment of play. Both have ideal and pragmatic consequences. Utopian thinking is about possibilities, the ability to see wishes, desires, and dreams as being on an equal footing with so-called reality. Play is about pure enjoyment, pleasure, and fun.

A utopia, if it is not to remain an idea only, requires language and images to be articulated and a medium in which to endure. Having plenty of ideas and a lively imagination is not enough. What is required is interaction with different kinds of media and forms, the will to make it happen, and the belief that it is possible to move mountains.

Adopting a playful approach is not always easy for students who want to achieve something and often want to achieve it quickly. It needs dedication and endurance. Special skills and promising strategies need to be developed and refined to maintain the enthusiasm. A clever and creative interpretation of the rules of the game is also required. To be able to recognize rules and their significance requires critical examination, a methodical, analytical approach, and reflection of the conditions and possibilities of one's own actions. But if you play a game, you are always confronted with the possibility of losing. Sometimes this can lead to the invention of a new game.

The transition from playground to laboratory is a fluid one. An essential feature of a program in filmmaking must be the opportunity to experiment. The most difficult thing about a professional filmmaker's day-to-day life is that often there is little room for experimenting or trying things out because solutions are expected to work at first go. The pressure of having to succeed quickly causes people to play it safe, to fall back on stereotypes and conventions that smother creativity. Training must be free of this kind of pressure which, however, must be addressed as a reality of future professional life. Students and lecturers are thereby confronted with the contradictions of the film world, in which uniqueness and universality are equally required.[7] The educational institution must prepare students for the demands and exigencies of professional life, but it must also call them into question. Students have to strive for a maximum degree of originality and quality in every single film project without neglecting production realities.

The lecturers cannot resolve these paradoxes for their students.[8] However, they should present strategies for dealing with them. They should also, by sharing their professional experience and conveying their own standpoint and perspective on these issues, create a climate of debate in which different and contradictory ideas about filmic qualities can be developed. It is the students' task to discover and develop from among the various choices and attitudes presented to them what concerns them and what encapsulates their strength and uniqueness. They themselves have to recognize and formulate the issues and connections that are important for their film work. Of course, this often involves going down difficult and labyrinthine paths where the criteria appear to blur and sometimes failure is inevitable. That makes it all the more important to keep mustering the energy to pull oneself together and carry on. It is the lecturers' task to use their expertise to accompany the students on the paths that they have taken, to highlight various possible directions to go in, and to provide encouragement. Sometimes they will also intervene, if someone has gone astray completely. Now and again, it is possible to indicate ways out of the problem. What the lecturers cannot afford to do is to present panaceas, or a career launching pad that is broad and obstacle-free.

7 There are hardly any introductory texts or textbooks about film production that do not make the contradictory claims on a film that it should be both "unique" and "universal."

8 Thomas Schadt, director of the Film Academy Baden-Württemberg, refers to paradoxes on a number of occasions in his observations about film training. He describes some fundamental demands made of students and film training as being contradictory: "We encourage egomania, a certain individual egocentricity, which is indispensable for the genesis of a film. However, at the same time we tell them films can only come about if they are able to work in teams. Or we announce, for example, a set of dramaturgical rules and in the same breath say that interesting, surprising films can come into being where these so-called rules are broken, where something explained as being right the day before is consistently done 'wrong'." Thomas Schadt, "Herzschlag oder zwischen Utopie und Realität", inaugural speech as director of the Film Academy Baden-Württemberg, Ludwigsburg 2005. Published in German at www.filmakademie.de.

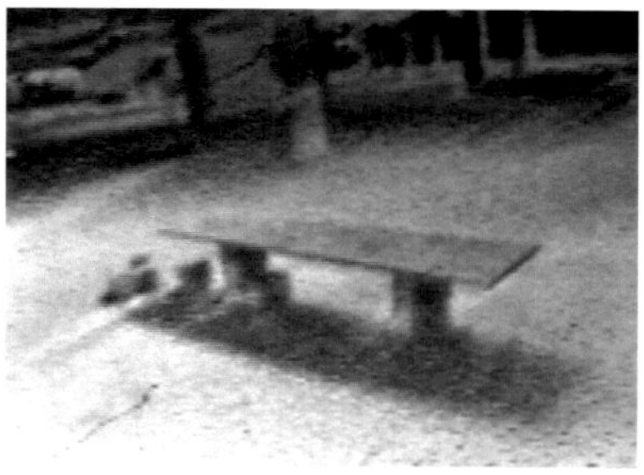

Art School Without Condition: Art Education in Postindustrial Society

Notes on a Neglected Discussion

Giaco Schiesser

We cannot foresee the future, but we can lay the foundations for future growth—because the future can be enabled. Antoine de Saint-Exupéry, French aviator and writer

As Though Our Work Were Done

I

Searching the Internet for literature on the future of art education yields an astonishing result: There is very little material to be found. One might think that most of our art education programs are hoping to survive the major social changes and reorganizations—on the economic, educational, and cultural levels alike—without making any major changes. Almost all of the various training programs at European art schools list the same mission statement on their Web sites today as they did in the past: To focus their training on the original and unique artistic individuality of their students and to teach critical and reflective thinking. What none of the mission statements questions is the function that artists and art must fulfill within society and the function that society ascribes to art and artists. The hermeneutic of continuity reigns supreme, while the hermeneutic of change is acknowledged by a minority only.

II

A symptomatic reading of the publications and Web sites which address the future of art education shows that only a very few exceptional cases fail to ignore the following gaps and problems:[1]

1. The immanence of art education

– Remarks about the way the arts have been taught to date tend to be based in a monadic way on the writers' own experiences with their

1 On the concept of "symptomatic reading," which treats the omissions within a text as indications of absence—as "absent presences"—with reference to the text's defining structure, see Louis Althusser, *Das Kapital lesen,* 2 vols. (Reinbek, 1972), pp. 31ff. and 112ff.—Important books which address the gaps mentioned here include the following: Ute Meta Bauer, Institut für Gegenwartskunst, Akademie der Künste Wien (eds.), *Education, Information, Entertainment: Aktuelle Ansätze künstlerischer Hochschulbildung* (Vienna, 2001); Beatrice von Bismarck and Alexander Koch (eds.), *Beyond Education: Kunst, Ausbildung, Arbeit und Ökonomie* (Frankfurt am Main, 2005); Ute Vorkoeper, *Hybride Dialoge: Kunstausbildung in der Medienkultur; Rückschau auf die Modellversuche zur künstlerischen Ausbildung an Hochschulen im BLK [= Bund-Länder-Kommission]-Programm Kulturelle Bildung im Medienzeitalter* (Hamburg, 2005), available online at http://www.blk-info.de/fileadmin/BLK-Materialien/heft125.pdf; Stefan Römer, "Kunst, Informatik, Theorie (KIT): Texte, Dossiers und Modellbausteine," commissioned by the Cologne Academy of Media Arts and KUBIM on behalf of the Bund-Länder-Kommission, unpublished manuscript (Cologne, 2002); Elke Bippus and Andrea Sick (eds.), *Industrialisierung <> Technologisierung von Kunst und Wissenschaft* (Bielefeld, 2005); Gerfried Stocker and Christine Schöpf (eds.), *Takeover: Who's Doing the Art of Tomorrow?* Trans. Mel Greenwald (Vienna and New York, 2001); Olaf Zimmermann and Gabriele Schulz (eds.), *Kulturelle Bildung in der Wissensgesellschaft: Zukunft der Kulturberufe* (Regensburg, 2005).—Important individual essays include the following: Giaco Schiesser, "Medien | Kunst | Ausbildung: Über den Eigensinn als künstlerische Produktivkraft," in *SchnittStellen,* ed. Sigrid Schade, Thomas Sieber, and Georg Christian Tholen, Basler Beiträge zur Medienwissenschaft BBM, vol. 1 (Basel, 2005), pp. 257–74; Beatrice von Bismarck, "Die Kunsthochschule als Spiel im Spiel," in *Bekanntmachungen: 10 Jahre Studiengang Bildende Kunst der Hochschule für Gestaltung und Kunst Zürich,* ed. Studienbereich Bildende Kunst / Departement Medien & Kunst and Kunsthalle Zürich, Jahrbuch 1 des DMK (Zurich, 2006), pp. 87–90; Ute Meta Bauer, "Was ist 'Knowledgeproduction'? Aktuelle Ansätze künstlerischer Hochschulbildung," in *Bekanntmachungen: 10 Jahre Studiengang Bildende Kunst der Hochschule für Gestaltung und Kunst Zürich,* ed. Studienbereich Bildende Kunst / Departement Medien & Kunst and Kunsthalle Zürich, Jahrbuch 1 des DMK (Zurich, 2006), pp. 105–109; survey "No guru no method no master: Zur Methode und Zukunft der Lehre," http://www.textezurkunst.de/NR53/tzk53_Umfrage2.htm; Simon Sheikh, "Räume für das Denken: Perspektiven zur Kunstakademie," http://textezurkunst.de/NR62/SIMON-SHEIKH_dt_2.html; Hans Dieter Huber, "Ästhetische Bildung in Europa," http://www.hgb-leipzig.de/ARTNINE/huber/aufsaetze/weiden.html; Wolfgang Coy, "Zukunft des Wissens—Zukunft des Lernens," http://waste.informatik.hu-berlin.de/coy/Zukunft_des_Wissens_12_97.html; "Pedablogy: Musings on the Art & Craft of Teaching," http://jerryslezak.net/pedablogy/?p=284 / http://jerryslezak.net/pedablogy/?cat=26/; Elke Bippus, "Aktuelle Debatten und künstlerische Ausbildung," in Elke Bippus, "Kurzer Abriss einer Geschichte der Akademien," in *Künstler in der Lehre,* ed. Elke Bippus and Michael Glasmeier (Hamburg, 2007), pp. 315–19.

own training concepts. No attention is paid to the experiences of other schools, historical experiences in art education,[2] or important findings from the humanities (for example, about technology and the media). Any remarks about the prospects for future educational reforms, too, tend to confine themselves to the subject of art education.

2. Changes in the function of schools of the arts

– None of these remarks address either the functions and changes in functions of art schools as educational institutions or the significance of art schools in today's postindustrial society.

3. Social changes

– Those publications that do address the wider economic, political, and cultural context—the transition from the industrial society to the information society[3]—within which art education takes place discuss it only in very general and overly simplified terms.

– These omissions have two grave consequences. For one thing, the concepts still fail to take into account the significance, ramifications, and functions of technology and the media in art and art education, even though these have become abundantly clear over the last thirty years. For another, any references to intermedial or transmedial art, interculturalism, globalization, etc., are limited to abstract considerations, even though the issues are crucial ones. The current discussions do address the significance of these epoch-making cultural changes and their consequences for education, but do not engage them to any productive purpose.

III

This is the background against which I will attempt to develop a theory, though I am fully aware that any such theory can represent only an approximate and simplified picture. My theory is not so much a thesis or an hypothesis as an attempt to discuss the issue in a public context, and it will raise more questions than it answers. Some readers may find this insufficient, but I hope a discussion which addresses past experiences in art education, the function of art schools as institutions, the significance of technology and the media for art education, and the present condition of postindustrial economies and post-medium cultural relationships will allow us to analyze our present situation and open up appropriate perspectives for the future.[4]

Past Experiences: The Black Mountain College (USA), the Academy of Media Arts (Cologne), and the Department of Media & Art at the School of Art and Design (Zurich)

IV

Located near Asheville in North Carolina, Black Mountain College (1933–57) only existed for twenty-four years, but brought forth an astonishing number of American artists who left an indelible stamp on the culture and arts of the United States, especially during the 1960s. These artists included John Cage, Merce Cunningham, and Buckminster Fuller.[5]

This chronically underfunded college owed its success to the fact that it offered vast scope for creative thinking, discussion, and experimentation, and that its faculty members represented a range of very different worldviews and ideas about art. There was no compulsory curriculum. The founders and their successors trusted that the combination of place and time and innovative teachers and students, who lived on campus during term, was enough to constitute a firm foundation for the training of its students. Teaching responded to conditions and situations. This is a model which is well worth reexamining in the face of the tendencies toward over-regulation that as a result of the Bologna Process are making themselves felt even in art education.

V

Art as experience, *art as experiment*, and *art as enactment* with the aim of fostering the "edu-

2 This is also related to the absence of an "archaeology of aesthetic concepts of education," the need for which is urgently stressed by Hans-Dieter Huber. See Hans-Dieter Huber, "Ästhetische Bildung in Europa," in *Die Neue Welt liegt mitten in Europa,* exh. cat. Kunstverein Weiden (Weiden, 2004). Quoted here from http://www.hgb-leipzig.de/ARTNINE/huber/aufsaetze/weiden.html.

3 "Information society," along with "postindustrial society," "Postfordism," "information age," "knowledge society," "postmodernism" (François Lyotard), "high-tech capitalism" (Wolfgang Fritz Haug), "cybersociety" (Achim Bühl), "network society" (Manuel Castells), "post-postmodernism," and "post-information age" (Nicholas Negroponte), is one of the most frequently-used terms of the present time. All these terms are problematic. As exploratory, audaciously certain, or normatively prescriptive as these terms may seem and as diverse as their theoretical and political implications are, they are all attempts to coin a definition for the far-reaching, epochal change which we are witnessing today.

4 The most differentiated attempt to analyze the complexity of art education today was made by Beatrice von Bismarck (see note 1). Attempts to include the complexity described below are also made in Römer, *Kunst,* Bauer, *Education,* and Schiesser, *Medien* (see note 1 for all three). A concise summary of the most important omissions in art education today, especially with reference to Germany, can be found in Bauer, *Education* (see note 1).

5 The history and development of Black Mountain College are detailed in Mary Emma Harris, *The Arts at the Black Mountain College,* 3rd ed. (Cambridge MA and London, 2002) and in Vincent Katz (ed.), *Black Mountain College: Experiment in Art* (Cambridge MA and London, 2003).

cation of head, heart, and hand" were the main elements that set the tone of the training at Black Mountain College.[6] We would do well to study these elements anew as a starting-point for rethinking today's art education.

VI

Founded in 1990, the Academy of Media Arts in Cologne played a pioneering role in the German-speaking world.[7] Its distinguishing mark was its focus on the significance of the media and the relationships between art, media, and technology as a special cultural skill and its adoption of these aspects as core elements of its curriculum.[8] A broad field of engagement, "the entire spectrum of interests [in] art in the age of its technological (re)production" was mapped out in the academy's foundation charter.[9] From the beginning, therefore, the Academy of Media Arts saw itself as a place which offers a home for experimentation, even wasteful experimentation, and which represents a contemporary alchemical laboratory whose graduates would subsequently be working in many different areas within society.[10] Assimilating and transforming the experiences gained in Cologne is another urgent task in the search for models of art education in the postindustrial society.

VII

At the School of Art and Design Zurich, the independent subjects of fine arts, photography, new media, and theory were amalgamated in the new Art & Media degree program.[11] The aim of this program, which seeks to train students to be authors, to work with the idiosyncrasies of different media, and to treat art as a process, is to offer scope and perspectives for a variety of different artistic practices, which are still being taught in separate departments or even separate schools elsewhere, to influence each other and interact with one another on an equal footing.

Technology, Mondialization, and the Postindustrial Society

VIII

Contrary to appearances, the significance and the effects on art education of the technology that developed at such breakneck speed in terms of both quantity and quality during the twentieth century have not yet been sufficiently examined.[12] To the extent that they have been addressed at all, the analysis has been explicitly or implicitly based on the points of reference and mental horizons set down some seventy years ago by Walter Benjamin in his essay *The Work of Art in the Age of Mechanical Reproduction.*[13] One does not need to share Peter Weibel's essentialist conviction that the secret code of all these art forms (video, cinema, literature, sculpture, GS) is the binary code of the computer and the secret aesthetics consists of algorithmic rules and programs[14] to acknowledge that all art forms have been dramatically changed by the digital age and that, like any other newly invented technology, these algorithms and programs may —or must —redefine themselves from scratch.[15] For example, how many art schools today would take it for granted that a fine arts student should study binary code in order to open up new perspectives for his paintings? The interrelationships between art, technology, and science have become a prerequisite for tomorrow's art and media work, and thus arts education cannot afford to disregard them.

IX

Today's arts curricula exhibit another blind spot in the matter of current social upheavals as society shifts from the industrial to the postindustrial phase. The changes in production

6 Harris in her table of contents uses these three concepts to characterize the various developmental phases of the college. See Harris, *The Arts* (see note 5). The quotation is from the same source, p. 246.

7 In her encompassing study on art education in Germany, Ute Vorkoeper writes, at so late a date as 2005: "Over and over again ... art schools thought themselves obliged to jettison the latest technological media for the sake of artistic freedom. This measure aimed to prevent the contamination of art by non-artistic institutions, i.e. newly developing media institutions, which not only operated under different production and presentation conditions, but were also subject to different economic principles than the art market is. New universities and faculties were created for photography, cinema, and television, and these schools took the applied arts as their role models, not the free arts." See Vorkoeper, *Hybride Dialoge* (see note 1), pp. 16–17. In Switzerland, the study program in new media which was introduced at the School of Art and Design Zurich in 1999 was the first art education program in the country to address this deficit. A preliminary analysis of its development is in preparation and will be published in early 2008 as *Jahrbuch 3 des DMK.*

8 Notes on the history and development of the Academy of Media Arts can be found in its yearbooks, *LAB,* and its current publication, *MedienKunst,* both published by the Cologne Academy of Media Arts, the latter in 2006.

9 See http://www.khm.de/institution/main_e.htm.

10 See Siegfried Zielinski, "Vorwort," in *MedienKunst* (see note 8), p. 5.

11 See dmk.hgkz.ch or dkm.zhdk.ch.

12 Cmp. the statement by Ute Vorkoeper quoted in note 7.

13 Walter Benjamin wrote *Das Kunstwerk im Zeitalter seiner technischen Reproduzierbarkeit* in 1936. An English translation is available at http://www.marxists.org/reference/subject/philosophy/works/ge/benjamin.htm

14 See Peter Weibel, "Postmediale Kondition," in *Postmediale Kondition,* exh. cat., ed. Elisabeth Fiedler (Graz, 2005).

environments and production conditions which are usually discussed in the context of "immaterial work," the changing demands on workers, and the concomitant changes faced by art and artists—more complex demands for skills, the significance of art in and for the postindustrial society, the pluralization of professions and the places where art takes place, and collaborative forms of working, to name only a few—are often dutifully mentioned as general preconditions that impact art. However, they have rarely been taken into consideration when designing arts curricula,[16] despite the fact that the "information society" plays an instrumental role in widening —or creating from scratch—the public fields of activity of art and the fields in which art school graduates subsequently find work.

Mediality and the Post-Medium Condition

X

While the last twenty years have seen an emerging consensus in the humanities that the "mediality of the media" (Georg Christoph Tholen) and the "idiosyncrasy of the media" (Giaco Schiesser) play a fundamental role in perception, experience, knowledge acquisition, and knowledge dissemination, most art schools have yet to follow suit in reflecting on, transforming, and utilizing these findings.[17] To date, art education programs have largely failed to consider the radical changes and breaks in the media and their effects on the restructuring of the previously dominant media ensemble.

XI

When the artist Peter Weibel, for instance, cited a series of graphic examples in 2006 to document changes in the media over the past twenty years and concluded that all art today is created according to a script dictated by the media and its rules, and that there is no life after the media in today's art world,[18] he was stating an opinion that is held only by a minority of art schools. And only rarely have such conclusions been assimilated by art schools or incorporated into arts curricula.[19]

XII

Most recently—tacitly adopting a term first used by Rosalind Krauss in 1999—Peter Weibel has revived the issue of the "post-medium condition" with explicit reference to the arts.[20] In his eponymous manifesto, he states that the new post-medium situation is defined by two phases with respect to art, the first being the equality of the different media and the second, the mixing of media.[21] Today, we find ourselves in the second phase, in which the artistic and cognitive objective is to mix the specific individual worlds of the different media.[22] Both Krauss and Weibel stress that, far from decreasing in importance under the post-medium condition, the mediality of the media in the arts is actually gaining added significance.[23]

The "Art School Without Condition"

XIII

Pondering ways to provide arts training adequate to our age also challenges us to consider the role of art schools as social institutions. What sort of renewed self-image do art schools want to develop? What stance will they assume in the postindustrial age?

XIV

In 2001, Jacques Derrida gave a famous lecture in Frankfurt which was titled "Die unbedingte Universität" (Art School Without Condition).[24] The *Frankfurter Allgemeine Zeitung* ranked this lecture on a par with the famous speeches of Kant, Schelling, Nietzsche, and Heidegger.[25] Derrida's point of departure was a simultaneously concerned and trenchant diagnosis of the postindustrial present which cuts

15 On the historical development of the relationship between technologies and the arts, see the fundamental contribution by Hans-Peter Schwarz, "Medien—Kunst—Geschichte," in *Medien—Kunst—Geschichte,* ed. Hans-Peter Schwarz and ZKM / Zentrum für Kunst und Medientechnologie Karlsruhe (Munich and New York, 1997), pp. 11–88. This extensive collection of material by the former director of the Media Museum at the ZKM in Karlsruhe, who is now president of the Zurich University of the Arts, traces the checkered history of the different arts and of technology since the eighteenth century and documents the inescapable significance of technology for the (media) art of today and tomorrow. For the current status of the debate, see especially Römer, *Kunst* (see note 1).

16 See Bauer, *Education* (see note 1), pp. 106–107; for further discussion, see von Bismarck / Koch, *Beyond Education,* and Schiesser, "Medien" (see note 1).

17 We have already mentioned the exceptions, namely the Cologne Academy of Media Arts and the New Media study program at the School of Art and Design Zurich. For this diagnosis, also see note 7.

18 See Weibel, "Postmediale Kondition" (see note 14).

19 The Art & Media degree program and the projected Master's program in fine arts at the Zurich University of the Arts both reflect these conclusions in their curricula.

20 See Rosalind Krauss, *"A Voyage on the North Sea": Art in the Age of the Post-Medium Condition* (London, 2000).

21 See Weibel, "Postmediale Kondition" (see note 14).

22 See ibid.

23 Rosalind Krauss developed the concept of the "post-medium condition" from the works of the Belgian artist Marcel Broodthaer. In her preface, she explains why she considers the concept of the medium to be indispensable for postmodern art and cultural studies—even though she really wanted to abolish the term because it is freighted with the unsolvable problems of the modern age. See Krauss, *"A Voyage"* (see note 20), pp. 5–6.

to the heart of the condition in which universities—and, in my view, art schools—find themselves today. Given the "new ... quantitative extent of an ... eerie process of virtualization, its accelerated rhythm, its breadth, its capitalizing potential" which we see today, the current "new technical 'stage' of virtualization (data processing, digitization, worldwide virtual availability of texts, teleworking, etc.) will lead to the destabilization of the traditional sphere of the university." Derrida continues: "It will unsettle the topology and disarrange the entire layout of the university—namely, the division of its territory according to research fields and subjects—as well as the localities of academic discourse, the battlefield of theoretical debates, and the socially cohesive structure of its campus ... It is impossible to avoid the impression that, in more radical terms, it is the topology of the event, the experience of unique occurrences, that is being cast into disarray."[26]

XV

In this situation, Jacques Derrida challenges the university to rediscover "the truth" and radically reinstate it at the focus of its attention.[27] To do so, it is necessary first of all for "the modern university to be an unconditional one, free of preconditions, and exempt from any limiting factors."[28] He explains: "What this university demands, what it requires, and what it should be granted is an unconditional freedom of questioning and assertion which goes beyond what we term academic freedom, and in addition it should have the right to state in public anything that needs to be stated in the interests of the pursuit of truth in research, knowledge, and discussion."[29]

Secondly, he says that this requires that the university should, "in principle and in its acknowledged calling," see itself as "a place of ultimate critical—and more than critical—resistance against any dogmatic attempts to take control of it."[30]

XVI

Derrida's incisive diagnosis and his suggestion for the foundation of a new type of humanities[31] represent an opportunity and a challenge which offers a great deal of scope for art schools and for the redefinition of their status. His ideas, therefore, should be given the attention they deserve.[32]

XVII

Derrida's seven "programmatic articles of faith,"[33] which were intended as impulses rather than solutions, proceed from the "human figure and 'that which is germane to humans'" and, additionally, address the core problems of "sovereignty," "*professer,*" "literature," the "profession of the professor," the "as if," and the "university that happens."[34]

XVIII

At first glance, it might seem surprising that Derrida takes the human figure and "that which is germane to human beings" as his point of departure in the age of mondialization,[35] but this is hardly sufficient grounds for supposing that the founder of deconstructivism had a naive view of human beings. Furthermore, he notes that "the concept of the human being is as indispensable as it is inevitably problematic." [36] One of his central tenets is that this concept "can be discussed and redefined as such without provisos and reservations, without limitations and prerequisites, within the context of *new* humanities alone."[37] It should be noted that this discussion should spread to the art schools as well.

XIX

Pointing out the many meanings of the concepts of *professer* and *professor,* Derrida notes that the history of the concept can be made fruitful in three different ways: As a *profession* (a calling and a public statement), as a *profession*

24 Jacques Derrida, *Die unbedingte Universität* (Frankfurt am Main, 2001). A concise breakdown of the Derrida terminology used in this text along with its implications and the philosophical discourse and traditions to which *Die unbedingte Universität* refers can be found in Erik Ode, *Das Ereignis des Widerstands: Jacques Derrida und "Die unbedingte Universität"* (Würzburg, 2006).

25 See Ode, *Das Ereignis* (see note 24), p. 19.

26 Derrida, *Die unbedingte Universität* (see note 24), pp. 25–26.

27 Ibid, p. 10.

28 Ibid, p. 9.

29 Ibid, pp. 9–10.

30 Ibid, p. 12.

31 Ibid, p. 20.

32 The more so as Derrida himself refers to the arts in this context, even if only in summary form. In his preamble, he writes that the lecture was originally given English at Stanford in 1998, when he "was invited to speak primarily about the future of art and the humanities at universities" (ibid., p. 8). The text itself focuses primarily on the humanities and touches on only one of the arts, namely, literature (ibid., pp. 69–68).

33 Ibid, p. 66.

34 See ibid, pp. 66ff. for a summary of the seven suggestions and the work to be done.

35 Derrida rejects the term "globalization" and insists on the concept of "mondialization" as the latter focuses on the world as its frame of reference. Globalization, on the other hand, refers to the globe and thus implies the idea of uniformity rather than differentiation. See ibid., p. 11.

36 Ibid.

37 Ibid.

of faith, and as a *confession* (of sin or of belief in a concept). This tripartite profession "transcends the order of purely technological and scientific knowledge by assuming a binding responsibility. *Professer* means to enter into a responsibility by declaring oneself, by exerting oneself for something—and by making a commitment in promising to be this or that …, in vouching for something by giving one's word."[38] Derrida is concerned with a new kind of professor, who views himself as a responsible creator of works rather than someone who merely applies and disseminates knowledge.

XX

Finally, Derrida makes the first six professions culminate in the seventh—"the university happens." The university is defined as a "place of happening"[39] in which activity centers around the occurrence and the study *in actu* of truth as declarative and performative knowledge.
The crucial thing is to allow things to happen. This simultaneously points toward the limits of performative acts of speech;[40] toward the dimension of not-knowing, and the dimension beyond linguistic knowledge, and thus toward the unavailability of such knowledge; toward the "second event," "the impossible" that manifests itself in the events of giving, confession, invention, or hospitality[41]—or, although Derrida himself does not directly refer to this, the event of the arts.

The Work That Has Yet to Be Done

XXI

In the light of past experiences in art education, the evaluation of the status of universities and art schools, and the necessary reevaluation of their status against the background of the epochal changes and breaks which are occurring in today's economy, culture, and politics, a promising perspective would be to develop approaches for designing art education systems against the background, and with the purpose, of the creation of a space.

Such approaches are rooted in the performative occurrence and development of events within this space—whether as a "space for action" (Beatrice von Bismarck),[42] new kinds of "spaces for knowledge production" (Simon Sheik),[43] a dense "enabling space" (Giaco Schiesser),[44] or a "place of occurrence" (Jacques Derrida). One might continue Derrida's train of thought by noting that, today, the main priority of art education and the new humanities is no longer the declarative dissemination of knowledge, but the creative and performative actions which bring forth their "truth" in the process of enactment. The function of art schools would be to enable the spaces which make this possible.

XXII

It is the theory of dense spaces and of the event, of allowing events to occur, that offers the opportunity of developing the questions addressed here along with other questions, experiences, goals, and our knowledge of art education—independently and confidently vis-à-vis the humanities and the sciences and with responsibility toward society. It would be a fruitful exercise to anchor these issues in this theory.

XXIII

An endeavor such as this has far-reaching consequences. The "art school without condition" affects the self-image of students, teachers, and the institution in general alike. The stakes are high. If art schools and arts training programs want to stay alive, they will have to rise to the challenge. The work has only just begun.

38 Ibid., p. 35.
39 Ibid., p. 23.
40 See ibid., pp. 72–73.
41 Ibid., pp. 73–74.
42 See von Bismarck ,"Die Kunsthochschule" (see note 1). It is characteristic of the relationally conceived "space for action" that "within it, the rules of the game themselves are brought into play" (p. 12).
43 Simon Sheikh, "Räume für das Denken: Perspektiven zur Kunstakademie," http://textezurkunst.de/NR62/SIMON-SHEIKH_dt_2.html
44 See *Master of Fine Arts: Eingabe zuhanden des Bundesamtes für Berufsbildung und Technologie (BBT) der Schweizerischen Eidgenossenschaft zur Einrichtung eines Studiengang Master of Fine Arts an der Zürcher Hochschule der Künste* (Zurich, 2007), p. 5.

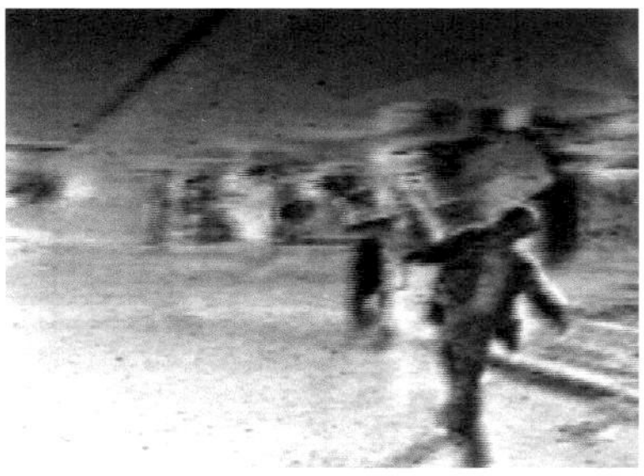

Art in the Here and Now of Higher Education: The Zurich University of the Arts' Centers of Production

Michael Eidenbenz

In the beginning was not the word, nor even the lesson; in the beginning was the deed. The oldest of all the many schools, institutes, and departments now being amalgamated under the one roof of the Zurich University of the Arts was originally a center of production—a museum. The precursor of today's Museum of Design was the Museum of Applied Arts and Design founded in 1875 on the Friedensgasse in Zurich-Selnau. Like all the other collections of applied arts and crafts springing up at that time—the Collection of Models and Patterns in Bern in 1871, the Winterthur Museum of Applied Arts and Design in 1874, the St. Gallen Museum of Applied Arts in 1878, the Basel Museum of Applied Arts in 1881, the Musée industriel Lausanne in 1884 and the Musée des arts décoratifs Genève in 1885—it served the purpose of providing models and samples for both handcrafted and industrially manufactured artifacts at a time when competition between the rapidly industrializing nations was becoming tougher all the time. Legend has it that the founding fathers got the idea for such an institution from the report of the Zurich delegation to the World Exposition in Vienna in 1873, whose exhibits had apparently drawn criticism for their remarkably poor design. That exhibiting exemplary objects alone would not suffice, but would have to be backed up by instruction, was clear right from the start. When Zurich's new school of applied arts opened in 1878, therefore, its founders ensured that it had its own department of design.

Certain aspects of today's University of the Arts—its globalization-inspired international thrust, focus on application and commitment to craftsmanship, for example—were present right from the start. What also happened right from the start was that the museum, by virtue of its very existence, set in motion that very same process of transformation which since then has repeated itself with remarkable regularity throughout the school's 132-year history. Removed from their original context and placed in an exhibitory framework subject to a very different perception of time and space, consumer goods and commodities tend to take on a life of their own; for not only do they invite inspection and analysis with a view to imitation, but they also acquire the perceptually enriching aura of a staged display. Objects of everyday use placed in an artistic context inevitably give rise to new questions.

The Zurich School of Music, founded in 1876 and renamed a conservatory in 1907, did not grow out of its own center of production. Yet in the person of Friedrich Hegar, the driving force behind the school's founding and its first principal for decades thereafter, it had at its helm a man who was both a composer in his own right and the principal conductor of the Tonhalle Orchestra, to say nothing of various choirs and vocal ensembles, and who therefore epitomized precisely that kind of involvement in the musical life of the city that was enshrined in number four of the school's statutes: "Support for Existing Musical Institutions." And that Winterthur founded its own conservatory even earlier, namely in 1873, is not so surprising when one remembers that the city had had an institutionalized concert culture sustained by its own *collegium musicum* since the seventeenth century. Underlying the founding of all these early schools and colleges was the realization that talent cannot be nurtured by imitation alone, but needs such reflection as institutionalized instruction promotes as well as the concurrence of society—best brought about by laying oneself open to criticism in public performances—that the results are artistically relevant.

The third center of production in the new Zurich University of the Arts combines both artistic and educational intentions, as is borne out in its own particular history. The Theater an der Sihl, which is to form part of the Department of Performing Arts and Film, started life as a children's theater. Founded in 1979 by Felix Rellstab, at that time the principal of what was then the Zurich Academy of Drama, the "Kitz, junges Theater Zurich" was at first obliged to lead a nomadic existence, moving from one temporary abode to another until in 1995 it at last became the "Junges Theater Zurich" with premises on the "Kulturinsel" on the river Sihl adapted to its needs. When, five years later, a new law providing for universities of applied sciences led to the theater's incorporation into the drama department of the Zurich School of Music, Drama and Dance, the name of the location became the name of an institution—the Theater an der Sihl—which will henceforth serve as the public portal to the new Zurich University of the Arts' interdisciplinary Department of Performing Arts.

This is not the place for a detailed history either of the many and various premises the school has occupied or of the uses to which they have been put; by the same token, it would be presumptuous of me even to attempt to do justice to the at times epoch-making significance of the Museum of Design in what little space is allowed here.

The current position of the Zurich University of the Arts in the cultural life of the city and region of Zurich is perhaps best conveyed by outlining the offering of its various departments, each of which has its own specific genealogy. The events alone make up an impressive list:

– Museum of Design: eight temporary exhibitions on design, visual communications, and architecture in the museum itself and in the gallery and vestibule, as well as three exhibitions from the poster and placard collection
– Museum Bellerive: three temporary exhibitions exploring the art/design, old/new dichotomies
– Theater an der Sihl: thirteen productions and coproductions, five guest performances plus the annual open-door drama festival, "Theater in allen Räumen"
– Biannual performances by the Dance Academy at the Schauspielhaus Pfauen (June) and Theater an der Sihl (November/December)
– Music: sixteen orchestral/choral/operatic productions (four by the school's own symphony orchestra, two by its Baroque orchestra plus four performances of contemporary music by the Arc-en-Ciel ensemble, three large choral concerts and one concert each by the vocal ensemble and the Kantorei, plus one opera); three concerts by the Studio for Ancient Music, eleven New Music projects, fourteen chamber music recitals, including a Zurich session of the ECMA (European Chamber Music Academy), seven master classes, four workshop performances of Music & Movement, four performances by the Zurich Jazz Orchestra, four projects by the electro-acoustic lab, weekly Multitrack Nights (live music/DJ acts), twelve Exchange Nights with other jazz academies plus the weekly JazzBaragge/Wednesday Jam

This list, of course, makes no mention of the countless panel discussions, lecture series, and forums to be held, nor of the several hundred instrumental and vocal master classes and public examination recitals to be held by the Music Department. Nor are the numerous publications in the Edition Museum für Gestaltung series and the Poster Collection as well as various collaborative projects with external publishing houses and a CD series with graphic, literary, and musical aspirations by HMT Records included.

The list, actually, does no more than outline the vehicles of production, while saying nothing at all about their content. Yet even this outer casing is enough to give one an idea of just how permeable the outer walls of the new Zurich University of the Arts will be. Indeed, the doors of its various departments will be literally open to the public several times a day. One indication of the extent to which this invitation is likely to be taken up is that provided by the annual visitor statistics: 60 000 for the Museum of Design, 16 000 for the Museum Bellerive, 17 000 for the Theater an der Sihl, and 70 000 for the concerts—all of which figures are cautious estimates, given that the exact numbers are not recorded.

Several times a day, in other words, an audience equivalent to the population of a medium-sized Swiss town will be able to observe that transformation which takes place when an artistic accomplishment leaves the context provided by practice, experimentation, or creative preparation and enters the context of strident interrogation, assertion, and publicly discursive exploration. Essentially, it is the same transformation as that which the founding fathers of the original Museum of Applied Arts witnessed when, 132 years ago, they transplanted craftsmanship and industrial design from the world of consumption into the world of contemplation.

This ongoing process of "claiming land" for art has of course experienced phases of heated debate; after all, any blurring of the hard-won distinction between art per se and objects of everyday use is bound to be controversial. The constancy underlying this process of transformation, however, is itself proof of how important it is to give artistic activity a firm footing in schools and colleges. For not only does it give the lie to the assumption that true creativity is possible only outside of an institutional framework—a platitude which is as old as the hills, but was recently trotted out yet again when the Music Department announced that it would be offering a course in pop music—but it also proves just how essential it is for teaching, research, and artistic production to interact.

One good example of this is the Museum of Design, which began exploring the interaction of all three levels at a very early stage in its history, both in pioneering exhibitions on art and design and by taking an interest in subjects such as the exhibition as medium and the communication of research findings. It is thanks to this work that it has acquired a status and relevance extending far beyond the Zurich region. Yet the museum can be viewed as exemplary in a much more general sense, too, if only on account of the collections it has held, or acquired, since its inception: the design collection, consisting of 10 000 products, the graphics collection set up in 1875, which now numbers some 100 000 objects from seven centuries, the poster collection, which also dates back to the museum's founding year and, having been systematically archived since 1955, now contains some 300 000 posters and placards, and finally, the Museum Bellerive, which houses a collection of applied arts consisting of some 15 000 artifacts. The history of the museum is borne out by its collections, which serve the present as a memory of the past. This also makes them a tangible manifestation of the principle underlying art history, a visual representation of those intellectual achievements that—with criteria depending on product and historical period—are deemed worth keeping. The concept of conservation is paradoxically premised on permanent renewal: Any artist who wants his or her works to be accorded widespread recognition is bound to offer something new. The inner logic of the collection can therefore be said to make it an engine of innovation.

In the performing arts, the dynamism generated by the collection as a vehicle of conservation and the exhibition as a vehicle of renewal finds its counterpart in the cultivation of an approach to the classical canon which encourages constant inquiry and creative reinterpretation. That the irretrievable reality of live performance is informed by both teaching and research was a known phenomenon long before the rehabilitation of "authentic" performance practices brought about the rediscovery of Baroque music—a development which in the cultural life of Zurich certainly did involve the early music experts at the School of Music, Drama and Dance. And if electronic music, for example, is perceived not just as a domain of autonomous creativity, but also as a subject of research and a means of acoustic environmental engineering, then the barrier between applied art and free art, the overcoming of which is one of the declared objectives of the Zurich University of the Arts, has already been breached, with the result that theoretical reflection and communication are already an integral part of the artistic vision. Always open, always receptive to the involvement of a potentially unlimited audience, as the Theater an der Sihl claims on its web site: "Which of us has not dreamed of playing the lead role (in life) for once? Theater is not just watching ... Theater is more than that! At the Theater an der Sihl you can yourself play a role."

A productive cultural institution, such as the Zurich University of the Arts will be, is bound to defy comparison in respect of both quantity and of the all-inclusive status it will claim within its own urban context. It will also become a trailblazer for the future development of those arts it teaches, nurtures, and promotes:

The collapse of the old high-low paradigm has left us with a vacuum which has to a large extent been filled by the cult of live experience and the instrumentalization of art for those decorative purposes to which our middle-class urban lifestyle has given rise. What yearning for the high-brow still exists—among traditional concertgoers, for example—tends to be satisfied, without dwelling any further on context, by attestations of the pianist's, director's, or installation artist's renown as a practitioner of "high art"—which in turn have the effect of absolving both audience and performers alike from the duty to engage in any more far-reaching discourse. Where deconstruction and the aesthetics of negation seek to provoke just such discourse—by continually ignoring taboos, for example—the reaction of an audience accustomed to the unlimited choice available from today's media will quite likely be a perfunctory "So what?" or at best a nod of approval. Yet art in all its many manifestations is dependent on audience involvement. If, therefore, a cultural institution such as the Zurich University of the Arts elevates the permeability between inside and out to the status of a principle on a par with the elementary incorporation of research and teaching discourse in the artistic production process, this could set in motion a process in the course of which art not only becomes a topic of conversation (again), but also one of the many interlocutors which actively shape the world we live in.

Even if we prefer to avoid such lofty postulates for "art's recovery," one immediate gain to be had from the amalgamation of the various centers of production henceforth to be known as the Zurich University of the Arts will be that experienced by the students themselves, who after all will always be the first "target audience" of any educational activity: Art production is not what comes later, is not something which has to be prepared for by the intensive, but largely imitative study of established artists. The consoling adage *non scholae sed vitae*—as if school were somehow not life at all!—has served its purpose and can now be laid to rest. In the beginning was the deed. Studying art means producing art. Here and now.

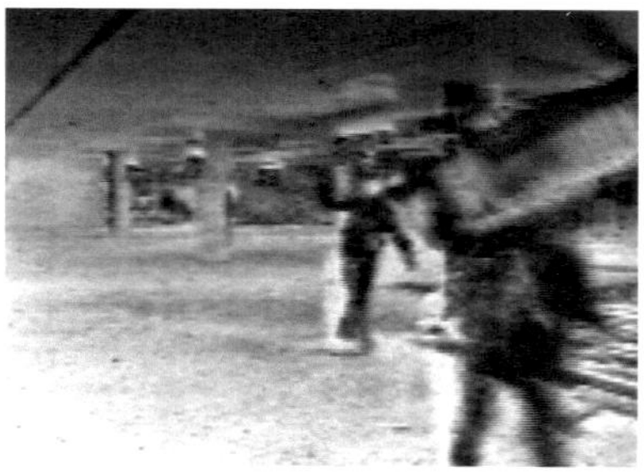

Research Between the Arts

Corina Caduff

Proximity Between Art and Research

Whenever I have an appointment in the Department of Music, I try to arrange things so that I arrive there a few minutes early. I then use that time to saunter along the corridors lined with practice rooms, from some of which I can be sure of hearing the muffled sound of music emanating. What I like most of all is to pause for a moment outside those rooms in which someone is playing the piano. Pacing up and down for a while, I sometimes listen hard in an attempt to identify the piece being played, while at other times I simply enjoy the somewhat muted fragments drifting through the door without asking myself anything at all. As short-lived as these moments may be, I always look forward to them; for me, they are a form of meditation, an experience which above all else gives me the feeling of being part of something real and substantial.

Naturally, I could just as well mention the drama students' workshops or the dancers' rehearsals, or the studios in which the design students, film and photography students are all busy at work. The sensuous proximity of the arts is a quality that all art schools share and one which the artists at the newly-founded Zurich University of the Arts (ZHdK)—whether they come and go as students, lecturers, guests, researchers, or friends—will soon be taking for granted. Their doing so will make the ZHdK an even more attractive research institution.

The merger of the Zurich School of Art and Design and the Zurich School of Music, Drama and Dance to form the Zurich University of the Arts will bring with it yet another attraction, which is a new proximity between the various artistic disciplines. For once photography, dance, theater, film, the fine arts, music, new media, and design are united under one roof; their new institutional proximity will inevitably have consequences for the transdisciplinary research that is done there. Another advantage will be the proximity of diverse research methods. The traditional distinction, of course, is that made between basic research and applied research—a barrier which today's universities of applied sciences are ideally placed to breach. That research by the arts in the arts can have an especially important role to play at a school of the arts is something we shall also see in due course.

The new Zurich University of the Arts, in other words, will combine three properties which not only are exceptionally conducive to research between the arts, but which, being simultaneously present in this one institution, promise to set it apart from those academies and schools of art which do not provide courses in several different artistic disciplines at once:

- Proximity between art and research
- Proximity between various artistic disciplines
- Proximity between various research methods and practices

But what does "research between the arts" really mean?

The Zurich University of the Arts houses various research institutes, each with various different lines of research, which in most cases are confined to one particular discipline. "Research between the arts," conducted in addition to the above, means transdisciplinary research which is at the same time, and to the same extent, relevant to the various different arts and to design. This kind of research knows no disciplinary center of gravity from which it operates and to which its conclusions pertain, nor does it have any specific disciplinary starting point or point of reference. To this extent, it could also be described as "adisciplinary research."

Such research between the arts presupposes an in-depth knowledge of several different disciplines at once, all of which must be accorded equal weight. It cannot possibly be the work of one individual alone, therefore, but instead calls for a transdisciplinary team made up of persons from different disciplines who come together to collaborate on specific transdisciplinary projects.

Although transdisciplinarity has been much talked of for more than two decades and doubtless is practiced in the most diverse places, the various disciplines involved in such projects can scarcely be said to carry the same weight. There is almost always one particular discipline which has to serve as the ultimate point of reference. In such instances, the prefix "trans-" means that one looks across at another discipline with the aim of eliciting from this process of exchange something of interest for one's own. Co-research, in contrast, in which researchers from various disciplines take part as equals and which therefore rests on absolute parity, aims at a third zone somewhere between the disciplines. This interdisciplinary zone can emerge only if the persons involved are curious, tolerant, and willing to relinquish whatever standard approach to a problem their own discipline has accustomed them to. This in turn gives rise to new, not yet established fields of work.

Proximity Between the Various Artistic Disciplines

So what might be the content of such research? Generally speaking, its thrust could be summed up as follows: transdisciplinary research addresses such social, political, aesthetic, technical, media-related, and economic issues as are relevant to all the arts. In our case, it will naturally focus on those disciplines that are represented at the Zurich University of the Arts. A multitude of topics and potential topics is just waiting to be explored. The first questions raised by any comparison of the arts are likely to be the fundamental ones: What are the conditions of production within the various arts and design? How can music, for example, criticize social realities, and how does a critical stance manifest itself in drama or in design? How is artistically produced knowledge communicated to society at large, and how do the various disciplines manage the knowledge they produce? Another interesting line of inquiry would be the numerous multimedia processes evident in the wide range of crossover projects we have witnessed in recent years, any detailed analysis of which tends all too frequently to be sidelined by other concerns.

In principle, therefore, research between the arts seeks to investigate how the various arts and design interact: What do they have in common and what not? This very basic question might be followed by an exploration of the potential and limits of each discipline in relation to certain transdisciplinary aspects—which in turn would raise the question of the extent to which any strengths and weaknesses are intrinsic to the medium or have to do with the technology used.

The really crucial question, however, seems to be this: what is it exactly that those who call for a transdisciplinary approach are trying to achieve? In principle, any comparison of the arts must pay equal attention to their similarities and differences, must take just as much interest in what they have in common as in what sets them apart. One important point that should be made, however, is that transdisciplinary research is certainly not about dispersing the various arts and design in a multidisciplinary emulsion. The point is not to combine or to homogenize and in doing so deprive the various disciplines of their salient and defining features. On the contrary, the advantage of the comparison is that it sets off the contours of each individual discipline and lends a distinct shape above all to *the differences between the arts.* The aim, in other words, is to expose these differences, including any historical manifestations of the same, and by comparing them render them clearly visible and distinct. Naturally, this focusing on the differences need not, and indeed should not, preclude a consideration of what the various arts and design have in common.

To show in rather more concrete terms how such research might proceed, I would like to present an example from my own work in basic research. An interdisciplinary team I worked with as part of a project sponsored by the Swiss National Science Foundation called "The Relationship between the Arts" was tasked with publishing a collection of essays.[1] The team was made up of a musicologist (Steffen Schmidt), an art historian (Sabine Gebhardt Fink), an expert in film studies (Florian Keller), and an expert in literature (Corina Caduff). Our first job was to formulate questions of transdisciplinary relevance, which for our purposes meant that they had to meet two criteria: To start with, each one of us had to be able to relate to the question from the point of view of our own particular discipline. In other words, we each had to be able to say: "Yes, this is an interesting question in music/art/film/literature." Secondly, we had to ensure that any similarities and differences which began to surface following our preliminary research and discussions were deemed worth pursuing by everyone involved.

1 Corina Caduff, Sabine Gebhardt Fink, Florian Keller, *Die Künste im Gespräch: Zum Verhältnis von Musik, Kunst, Literatur und Film* (Munich, 2007).

We agreed both on general themes ("sports in today's arts," "XTC"), as well as on specific motifs ("tears"), and specific products such as Stanley Kubrick's *Eyes Wide Shut,* a movie which relates to music, art, and literature in a very special way and hence offers plenty of scope for transdisciplinary reflection.

After defining our topics, we worked on the essays themselves by exchanging and discussing each draft and then realigning and rewriting them before once again submitting them for discussion and so on and so forth until we felt that each text was more or less finished. We frequently had difficulty mediating between two different definitions. This was particularly evident in the disputes over terminology; for what transdisciplinary discourse is very good at is enabling those on the inside to refute the superficial view of their discipline taken by those on the outside. By the same token, these same discussions from time to time had the effect of exposing our own blind spots in our perception of our own disciplines—as when a colleague from a completely different discipline asked a question which, owing to our own *déformation professionelle,* would probably never have occurred to us at all. Time and again we were shocked to discover the extent to which we each are encapsulated inside our own particular field. It transpired that Minimal Music theorists, for example, know almost nothing of the theory of Minimal Art and that the reverse is also true. One of the most intensive discussions we had was that about "tears" and the controversial question of which art form is most likely to move us to tears. As we were completely unable to reach a consensus on this point, it was decided not to raise this question at all in the written text.

The fact that only one person was assigned professional responsibility for each discipline and was therefore acknowledged as an authority in his or her own field turned out to be of tremendous benefit to the group dynamics.

The example cited here is just one possibility of how transdisciplinary research can be conducted. What seems important is that the experimental character of such projects be made explicit at all times and that they be properly evaluated—i.e. their strengths and weaknesses named by name so that any subsequent projects can build on the experience thus gained.

Proximity Between Various Research Practices

To the proximity between the various disciplines must be added the proximity between various research practices at the Zurich University of the Arts. According to the traditional understanding, basic research develops its lines of inquiry in the context and on the basis of existing research, and its results are not immediately applied. Applied research, on the other hand, derives its lines of inquiry from practice, and its results can be applied in practice or at least have the potential to be used commercially —i.e. they can be sold or at least offered for sale.

The demand that the barrier between basic research and applied research become more permeable is an old one and rests partly on the view that basic research has little hope of attaining universal validity in a world as complex and differentiated as ours. Basic research at universities of applied sciences is of course a relatively recent innovation, but precisely this could prove beneficial when it comes to redefining the balance between basic and applied research at the Zurich University of the Arts. This is where artists' own research comes into play, for research in the arts is research practiced by artists themselves using artistic media; its results for the most part are themselves works of art which in turn generate new and different forms of knowledge, reflection, and action. They point beyond purely scientific research in the narrower sense of the term.[2] If new paths are being sought among existing research practices, then research conducted by artists themselves could well have an important role to play, as this kind of research, by its very nature, oscillates between theory and practice. As research in the arts has so far been confined almost exclusively to the visual arts, a university of the arts could well provide an incentive to establish such research in the other artistic disciplines as well.

Musicians and photographers, for example, could team up to develop a project which explores the no-man's-land between music and image and culminates in a collective work of art. Similarly, researchers and artists could conduct joint research by focusing on those areas in which theater and design overlap and perhaps even consider the development of a joint product.

The convergence of arts and design in the new Zurich University of the Arts not only constitutes an exciting challenge for research between the arts, but is also an attractive experimental set-up, especially in view of the chance it offers of telescoping a whole range of research methods and practices. Despite, or perhaps because of this attractiveness, the Zurich University of the Arts would do well to exercise caution.

2 See Christoph Schenker, "Künstlerische Forschung," in *Zeichen nach vorn: 125 Jahre Hochschule für Gestaltung und Kunst Zürich,* ed. Hans-Peter Schwarz (Zurich, 2003), pp. 176–81.

After all, it is not just a playground for whacky ideas and mavericks, but a research center which demands both accuracy and constant checks on the work being done there.

What I have called "adisciplinary research" between the arts could have an institutionally integrative impact on the newly-founded Zurich University of the Arts. It could help bridge the gap between the new departments, arouse and enhance mutual interest among the various disciplines, and challenge the Zurich University of the Arts to nurture a new self-image as a research center. And because of its proximity to artistic practice, this type of research will most likely lend itself to communication to the public at large as well.

The simultaneity of all the proximities discussed here—that between art and research, that between artistic disciplines and that between research practices—is without a doubt a treasure of great value. Unearthing this treasure time and again, with both respect and relish, with both a cool head and a passionate heart —that is the art of research.

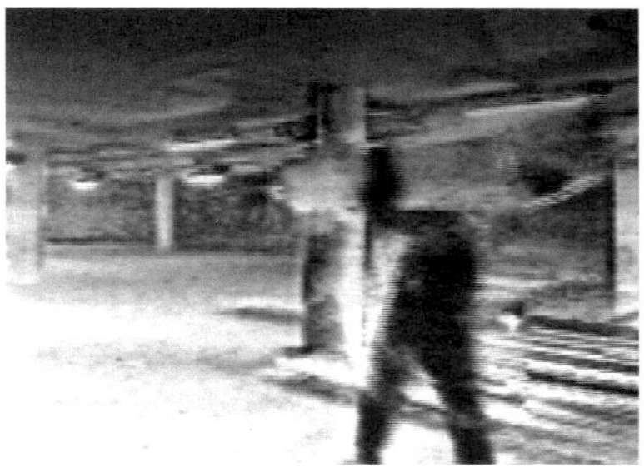

Under the Roof of Architecture: Building for Art Education in the Twentieth Century

Notes on a Piece of Unwritten Architectural History

Andrea Gleiniger

Painters and sculptors, break through the barriers to architecture and become fellow builders, fellow strugglers toward the ultimate goal of art: the creative conception of the cathedral of the future, which will once again be everything in one form.
Walter Gropius

In 1886, when Walter Gropius, the author of the epigraph,[1] was at the tender age of three, the Royal Academy of Fine Arts in Munich, whose origins, as we now know, extend far back into the eighteenth century,[2] moved into a formidable new building, after about ten years of planning and building. It was designed by Gottfried von Neureuther (1811–87). The imposing three-wing structure is located on Akademiestrasse, at the top of Amalienstrasse, which had been extended for that purpose and built out to form a kind of square, not far from the Victory Gate, which had been built in the 1840s (1843–50). It was a palace in the Italian Neo-Renaissance style.

A Palace for Art!

Until well into the nineteenth century, academies of art not infrequently had to make do with existing, often inadequate spaces. A shortage of space was the order of the day—a fate shared by applied arts schools institutionalized from the last third of the nineteenth century onward.

A new building like that of the Munich academy set new standards.[fig. 1] Considerable urban planning efforts had been undertaken to create an adequate (architectural) site for the academy. It seems that no effort was spared to stage it effectively: the aforementioned extension and expansion of Amalienstrasse to create a kind of square, or the raising of the terrain so that the façade facing the square would have two stories (three in the rear). Special planning regulations were established for new private buildings in the neighborhood of buildings that served the ends of science and the arts so as to ensure an imposing overall impression—and that was not all.[3]

1 Gottfried von Neureuther, Royal Academy of Fine Arts, Munich, 1886, view from the east, around 1900

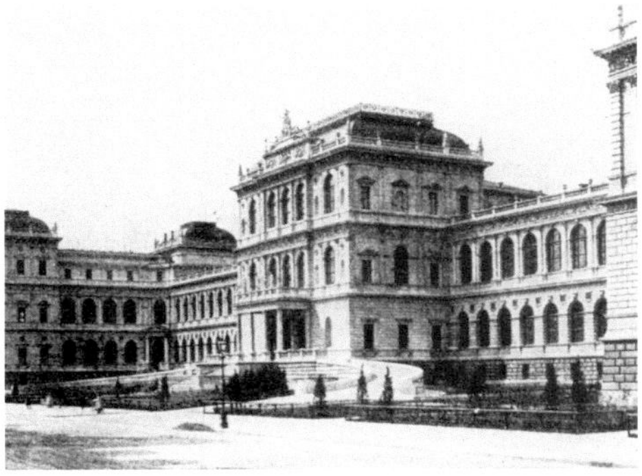

1 The epigraph is from a text Gropius wrote on the occasion of the *Exhibition of Unknown Architects*, “Ausstellung für unbekannte Architekten,” printed pamphlet (Berlin: J. B. Neumann, April 1919).

2 Monika Meine-Schawe, “‘…alles zu leisten, was man in Kunstsachen nur verlangen kann’: Die Münchner Akademie der bildenden Künste vor 1808,” http://www.goethezeitportal.de/fileadmin/PDF/db/wiss/bildende_kunst/meine-schawe_akademie.pdf, first published in Oberbayerisches Archiv 128 (2004), pp. 125–81.

3 Ibid., pp. 128–31.

4 http://de.wikipedia.org/wiki/Ferdinand_von_Miller: “Ferdinand Miller, from 1851 onward: von Miller (b. October 18, 1813, in Fürstenfeldbruck; d. February 11, 1887, in Munich) was a German metal caster and as inspector for the Royal Metal Foundry in Munich was responsible for the statue of Bavaria. He was a member of the Bavarian Applied Arts Association, from 1869 onward a member of the Bavarian Parliament and from 1874 onward a member of the German Parliament.”

When in 1873 Ferdinand von Miller, a cofounder of the Bavarian Applied Arts Association and future member of parliament,[4] launched his initiative to establish a new building for the art academy in Munich, he emphasized that "an academy building should not be constructed with the façade of a residential building, but even its exterior must express that its spaces serve the fine arts," adding that therefore "the creation of a more lavish, artistically designed façade cannot be avoided, and, even apart from that, it is required by the dignity of the state and of art."[5]

And now all of this was taken seriously: an elaborately conceived iconographic program with representations, allegories, and personifications of antique and modern art, of the three fine arts, of science and poetry, of art history, and so on, were of course absolute necessities.[6] The architect von Neureuther, however, wanted to do more than devise a program of paintings and statues to express an art academy's particular prestige. He was also concerned with formulating a functional and architectural character, with developing a meaningful architectural typology. All nineteenth-century architects, who were confronted with so many new architectural tasks, tried to do this in different ways. In the case of art academies, the architecture of museums suggested itself as an obvious reference. The museum had become one of the outstanding architectural briefs for a new bourgeois public. For example, the central room vaulted by a dome—the secularization of what had originally been a sacred motif—was repeatedly employed and varied as a way to ennoble the centerpoint of the building plan for art.[7] Another architectural motif of similar importance was the row of open arcades, which presumably evolved out of the context of the history of the development and significance of the loggia and gallery to become a beloved architectural element of buildings for museums and collections; von Neureuther made it the leitmotif of the main façade of the Munich academy.[8] In his study of the academy building Florian Hufnagl makes it clear "that von Neureuther not only designed a building for teaching and learning but also a building that went beyond the ephemeral ambition to create a monumental state building and signaled to the viewer the abstract concept 'art' by means of an overriding architectural motif."[9] That is also why it was above all the heyday of Italian Renaissance architecture and the associated high culture of art that provided the most convincing points of reference for architectural formulations of building for art.

As a contemporary of Gottfried Semper, whose new building for the Polytechnic in Zurich had earlier been a model for his plan for its pendant in Munich, what would later become the Technical University, von Neureuther with his Semperian programmatic reception of the Italian Renaissance triggered a turn in the architectural trends in Bavaria and Munich that had been influenced by Friedrich von Gärtner and Leo von Klenze, respectively.

The academy building has meanwhile begun to feel its age; after more than 125 years it has been refurbished and renovated. Most importantly, however, the old building, which remains intact and functional, has been supplemented by a new building by the Viennese architectural office Coop Himmelb(l)au, completed in 2005, which houses both the administration of the academy and new study workshops. The Austrian architects, who could scarcely be accused of having a conformist attitude toward architecture, juxtaposed an unconventional, almost unwieldy-looking new building to the existing bombastic three-wing structure. The awareness of context that the architects claim for this building is evident above all in an architectural stance that responds to the self-confident manner of the late nineteenth century with a no less self-confident declaration of post-postmodern contemporaneity. It is also and in no small measure an arrangement that reveals the principles of architectural formulation and urban planning positioning that guided architecture for art education for more than 120 years of architectural history.

Whereas the art academies, on the one hand, and the architectural academies, on the other—above all the new (poly)technical schools that were founded during the last third of the nineteenth century—established and institutionalized new public spaces for education in the

5 Winfried Nerdinger (ed.), *Gottfried von Neureuther: Architekt der Neorenaissance in Bayern, 1811–1887,* exh. cat. Architektursammlung Technische Universität München (Munich: Verlag Karl M. Lipp, 1978); on academy architecture, see Florian Hufnagl, ibid., pp. 119–44, esp. p. 120.

6 Ibid., pp. 128–131.

7 For example, one idea that von Neureuther wove through in one of his preliminary drawings for the academy—creating a central room vaulted by a dome as the focus of the grounds—goes back to a 1778–79 competition at the Académie de Rome for a museum project and was used repeatedly for museum buildings thereafter. Gottfried Semper was, however, the first to combine this motif with a longitudinally aligned building volume. See ibid., p. 132.

8 Ibid.

9 Ibid.

arts and architecture, for a time the applied arts rarely had their own site. Here, too, industrialization had, initially, left perplexity in its wake. The craftsmanship and practical approaches to design issues were taught in the educational contexts of existing workshops and were perpetuated in the training traditions of master workshops. There were, however, only hesitant responses to the improvement of industrially mass-produced commodities, and artistic instruction to enhance quality was for a long time limited to the teaching of draftsmanship. The pedagogical and artistic initiatives that sought to contribute to an aesthetic improvement of industrial products through concerted instruction and advice usually took the form of schools like the Normal School of Design, which opened in London in 1837 in the rooms at Somerset House that had formerly been the home of the Royal Academy.[10] They were often integrated into existing academies and museums, as was the case with the Zurich School of Applied Arts and its museum, which until they were moved to a new building by Karl Egender and Adolf Steger in the early 1930s were housed in the Swiss National Museum.

Torn between nostalgia for traditional craft methods, on the one hand, and the challenge presented by industrial mass production, on the other, the applied arts took nearly the entire nineteenth century to develop an autonomous status under the alternating hot and cold showers of the various reform movements.

Only against the backdrop of the reform movements in design—from the English arts and crafts movement to the Deutscher Werkbund—when the design of everyday objects became accepted as a serious task that could not be left either to crafts exclusively or to industrial mass production, did it become possible for this comprehensive approach to design to establish independent applied arts schools, which in turn created space for an autonomous evolution in their architecture. As we will see, however, this initially remained closely tied to the architecture of art schools, where impulses took hold and new energies were liberated that would begin to change the institutions.

Surely the most famous example of this was the transformation process that the Grand Ducal Saxon Art School in Weimar underwent in the early twentieth century. In 1902 the Belgian architect Henry van de Velde was appointed to the art school, which had been founded in 1860. In accordance with his contract he founded the Applied Arts Department, which in 1907—the same year the Deutscher Werkbund was founded—became the Applied Arts School.[11] As early as 1864 there had been a dialogue in Weimar between the art school and the applied arts association, but initiatives "to expand the profile of the art school in the direction of an applied arts school" remained unsuccessful.[12] That changed with Henry van de Velde.

Beginning in 1904, van de Velde was also involved in a series of new buildings. By 1911 the studio building for the Art School (after 1910, Art University), which is still the main building used by the Bauhaus University in Weimar, had been completed. fig. 2 In lieu of a new studio building for the sculpture department that had been planned across the street from the Art School, van de Velde produced a plan that would "unite the sculpture studio with the Applied Arts School designed by the architect in a single building."[13]

This resulted in one of the first—if not the first, though admittedly not formally unified—ensembles of buildings that related the two types of universities programmatically. Henry van de Velde's design for the Art School in Weimar became a milestone in the history of this evolution. Van de Velde's achievement has not been entirely forgotten in the shadow of the Bauhaus, with which Gropius succeeded him so brilliantly and momentously, but it deserves to receive greater attention again. It is not just that, at the institutional level, he managed to expand an (existing) art university by establishing a new applied arts department to create an applied arts school that was committed programmatically to collaborating with industry—a situation that would, after all, provide the essential prerequisite for its later conversion into the Bauhaus. Van de Velde also lent an inherently architec-

10 Nikolaus Pevsner, *Academies of Art, Past and Present* (Cambridge: Cambridge Univ. Press, 1940), pp. 247–48.

11 With van de Velde's appointment, Weimar established a connection to the reform movements in the arts that were coming from England. The Applied Arts Seminar, which opened on October 25, functioned as a central consulting office for small industry and craft workshops. It consisted of three sections: van de Velde's studio, a consulting office, and a kind of experimental and teaching workshop. The last of these became the nucleus of the new Applied Arts School. See Norbert Korrek, "Henry van de Velde und die Grossherzoglich-Sächsische Kunstgewerbeschule in Weimar," *Wissenschaftliche Zeitschrift Hochschule für Architektur und Bauwesen Weimar*, edition A, vol. 38, nos. 3–4 (1992), pp. 107–13.

12 Kerstin Vogel, "'Die Verbindung von Kunst und Industrie': Bemühungen um das Kunstgewerbe in Weimar im 19. Jahrhundert," *Wissenschaftliche Zeitschrift Hochschule für Architektur und Bauwesen Weimar*, edition A, vol. 38, nos. 3–4 (1992), pp. 149–54, esp. pp. 151–52.

13 Dieter Dolgner, *Weimar: Kunstschulbauten van de Veldes* (Leipzig: Seemann, 1981), p. 10.

tural expression to this cooperation between disciplines, this new constellation of schools.

At the time it was perhaps inevitably in the nature of things that the architecture of the Applied Arts School would be more modest than that of the Art School. The latter had caused a sensation at the time because of its subtly more objective Jugendstil forms and the large atelier windows with delicate muntins on the upper floor, which not only pass through the eaves and adapt to the form of the mansard roof, but are also an essential design element of the main façade. They have been the trademark of this unfussy studio building. Piercing the jamb wall of the strikingly-formed mansard roof, these windows effortlessly follow the transition from the vertical to the inclined plane while at the same time making a strong gesture in the direction of the overcoming of the window as "hole in the façade" in favor of dissolving the wall as a glass curtain, as was achieved so programmatically by Walter Gropius at the Bauhaus.[14] In general, the theme of lighting became an essential expressive motive, and the use of glass a central theme, and in some ways the point of intersection between service to art and utility for the crafts: for workshop-like industrial glazing was to the (art) trade school what the studio window was to the art academy.

Thus van de Velde had made a clear break from the art school buildings of the nineteenth century, which had essentially taken the lead for their main façades from historical architecture for palaces and thus banned to the rear of the building the rooms for studio activity and the associated large windows.[15]

We find no such breaks with convention in his building for the Applied Arts School, as, after all, its very construction amounted to a break with tradition, in that this architectural task had not even existed previously. In the way he articulated the pilasters and the visible steel forms of the lintels, van de Velde transferred essential design elements of the art school to the architecture of the applied arts school, making it seem like a kind of little sister. fig. 3

A two-wing figuration of buildings comprising a full story and a converted attic floor housed the sculpture studio on the ground floor of the east wing next to the rooms for the vocational school, which were accessed by central corridors. The largely unornamented building achieved its effect above all from the proportions and the makeup of the window, plaster, and stone surfaces and obtained its particular character not only from the angled layout (van de Velde had originally intended to extend the east wing, which would have produced a pendant to the Art School that was more effective architecturally and spatially), which provided space to design a square, but above all from the southern gable motif, succinctly framed by a horseshoe arch, which lent the otherwise single-story wing a "thoroughly unique, distinctive character."[16] Admittedly, even van de Velde could not get by without some kind of hierarchy, but his design of its relationships was subtle. The two-story building for the Art School, made even taller by the mansard roof, clearly towers above the single-story wing of the Applied Arts School. The arrangement of the buildings also recalls the relationship of a château or manor house to its coach house. fig. 4 But van de Velde had his own studio in the latter: on the upper story, where the gable façade was unusually emphasized by a horseshoe arch!

Artistic Program—Architectural Manifesto

Particularly in terms of this emphasized form of the studio windows, van de Velde went a step further than his Scottish colleague Charles Rennie Mackintosh had a few years earlier for the School of Arts,[17] previously known as the School of Design, in Glasgow, in which the art school building found a programmatically new architectural and design expression. It made it clear that the architectural decision was also a deliberate statement about the school's basic aesthetic and stylistic stance.

Mackintosh very pointedly worked out the contrast between, on the one hand, the studio wing and, on the other, the building volumes in which the museum spaces and above all the library were housed: whereas the studio wing facing north had wall surfaces with large openings that not only ensure the necessary light but also lend the northern façade, which is also the main façade, its unmistakable character, the library wing has a rather massive, almost medieval-looking unity that emphasizes verticals. Mackintosh did not go quite as far in breaking down his façades as van de Velde would later,

14 On the history and problems of restoration of the Art School windows, see H. Wirth, "Neue Atelierfenster im Hauptgebäude der Hochschule für Architektur und Bauwesen in Weimar," *Weimar Kultur Journal* 1 (1993), http://www.baufachinformation.de.

15 Dolgner, *Weimar* (see note 13), p. 14.

16 Ibid., p. 13.

17 Founded in 1845 as the Glasgow Government School of Design, it was one of the first schools of this sort to be founded by the state. It was renamed the Glasgow School of Art in 1853. From 1897 to 1899 a new building designed by Charles Rennie Mackintosh was constructed; it was expanded in a second construction phase in 1909. See http://de.wikipedia.org/wiki/Glasgow_School_of_Art.

presumably having been inspired by the Scottish architect.

"Under the Roof of Architecture": The Bauhaus Building and Its Consequences

The circumstances that led to van de Velde resigning his position were, as we know, more than simply unpleasant.[18] That he managed in the end to recommend (and push through) Walter Gropius, following their shared experiences with the Werkbund exhibition in Cologne in 1914, was a momentous achievement. Gropius's appointment represented the "de facto acknowledgment of a new kind of school, in which ... the educational institutions for fine arts and applied arts were merged,"[19] for which van de Velde had prepared the way.

After assuming office Gropius became involved in architectural activities in Weimar, and the university was soon renamed the Bauhaus. There was, however, no discussion of the possibility of a new building. That began in response to the threat of being driven from Weimar. After an initial period of openness toward the new institution, pettiness and narrow-mindedness prevailed in Weimar again. And after work at the Bauhaus was "gradually throttled by the Thuringian state government,"[20] the new beginning in Dessau offered a historic opportunity. Nowhere else did the emergent avant-garde movements obtain a real building site that enabled them to manifest their design ideas architecturally as well. The sites of the new movements mostly remained architecture on paper, settled into available buildings, and thus were at loggerheads with not only the rules but also the walls of existing institutions. The Bauhaus was built on the proverbial green meadow (of which no trace remains today); the new beginning of modern architecture thus had a real site but also a symbolic one. Under the banner of the new motto proclaimed in 1923, "Kunst und Technik: Eine neue Einheit" (Art and Technology: A New Unity), the ambition expressed there could reconstitute itself architecturally as well.

For Gropius, whose reputation at the time was built primarily on his buildings for the Fagus shoe-last factory in Alfeld an der Leine (1911–25) and the model factory at the Werkbund

2-4 Henry van de Velde, Art School and Applied Arts School in Weimar, 1904–11, view of the Art School, view from the east, and ground plan of the complex

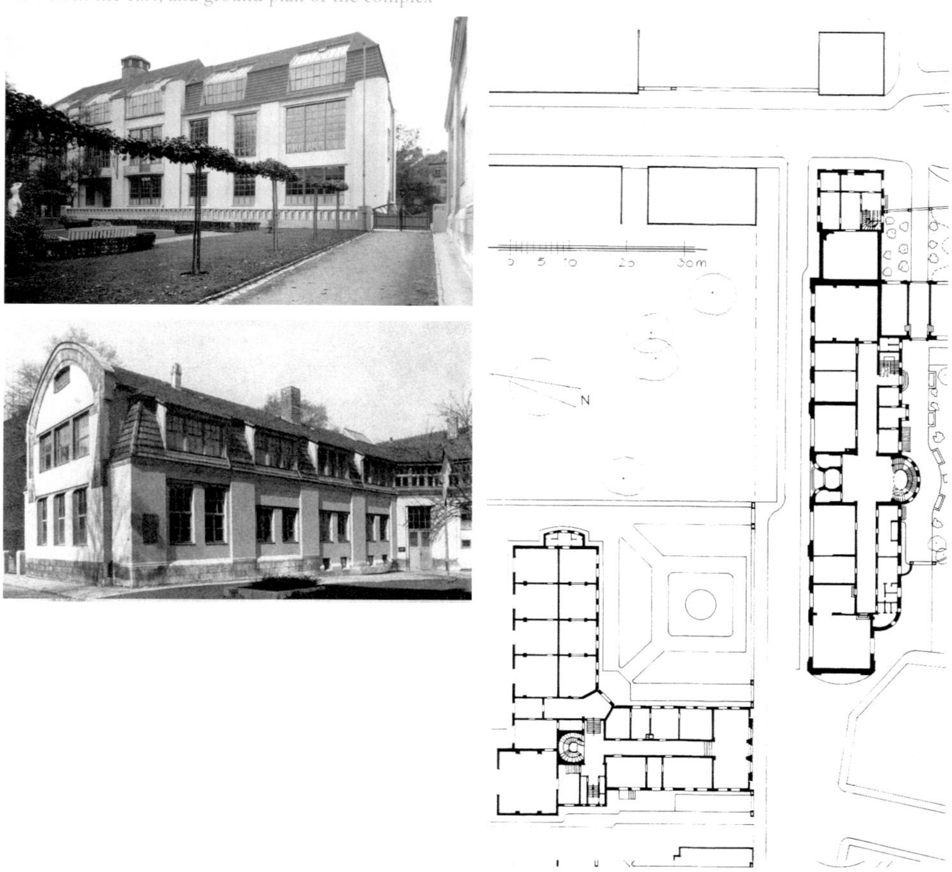

18 On this, see, among others, Korrek, "Henry van de Velde und die Grossherzoglich-Sächsische Kunstgewerbeschule in Weimar" (see note 11).

19 Andreas Haus, "Bauhaus: History," in *Bauhaus,* ed. Jeannine Fiedler and Peter Feierabend, trans. Translate-A-Book (Cologne: Könemann, 1999), p. 18.

20 Winfried Nerdinger, *The Architect Walter Gropius: Drawings, Prints, and Photographs from Busch-Reisinger Museum, Harvard University Art Museums, Cambridge, Mass., and from Bauhaus-Archiv, Berlin, with Complete Project Catalog,* trans. Andreas Solbach and Busch-Reisinger Museum, exh. cat. (Berlin: Mann, 1985), p. 70.

exhibition in Cologne (1914), the Bauhaus building was a unique opportunity to realize and showcase his design ideas.[21] The overall layout and formulation of van de Velde's new buildings for the Art School in Weimar had already demonstrated an effort to reduce the dramatization of an imposing façade in favor of the ensemble as a whole, which not only made it possible to identify the various uses and functions within an appropriately diverse spatial concept and appearance, but also related the parts to one another in a balanced whole. Gropius, however, gave this ambition a programmatic turn: "A building that is the result of the modern spirit departs from the representative appearance of symmetrical façades. Instead, one has to walk around this building in order to understand its corporeality and the function of its various parts."[22] fig. 5

But that is not all: the broadly spreading spatial form that is permeable on all sides also stands for an altered relationship of art and life. The claim to autonomy expressed in show and prestige that prevailed in the art school buildings in the style of the Munich academy, incrusted with programmatic visual slogans, was thus pointedly renounced. Instead, the new architecture called for art and life to permeate each other. In the Bauhaus building this claim is brought to a head in a kind of manifesto. At the same time, Gropius was moving on a tightrope, for the programmatically stated emancipation and redefinition of the disciplines within design was in turn also associated with a new claim to autonomy,[23] which left very clear traces in the shape of the floor plan of the Bauhaus, in the articulation of the individual building volumes, and above all in the design of the façade.

As we have seen, already in Weimar it was the large studio windows that gave the architecture its unmistakable imprint. Gropius went a crucial step further: by extending the glazing of the workshop wing to the entire surface, he produced a grand gesture that surrounded the entire wing. fig. 6 The point here, however, was not the workshop character as such, as would be the case, for example, a few years later with the Vocational School in Groningen, built in 1922 by Leendert Cornelis van der Vlugt and J. W. Wiebenga. Gropius was concerned with its aesthetic mise-en-scène. Although the Middelbare Technische School was not an applied arts school in the strict sense, and certainly not an art school, it seems to be an interesting example in our context. fig. 7

The architect, who five years later would build the Van Nelle factory in Rotterdam, one of the quintessential incunabula of modern industrial architecture, arranged the training rooms and workshops between two long, extended, terraced horizontal reinforced concrete bands, creating a glass layer dissolved between filigree steel profiles that transform the nature of a workshop glazing into a dynamic motif that grasps the entire building in its horizontal lines. The school becomes an arrangement of glass boxes on a kind of industrial shelf. It can be understood as the pointed formulation of what Sigfried Giedion would sum up a few years later under the keyword "industrial school" and advocate, to no avail, as the guideline for the new building for the Zurich School of Applied Arts.

Henry van de Velde had emancipated architecturally the concept of an applied arts school and elevated it in its juxtaposition with the Art School in Weimar. Walter Gropius had at the very least left a monumental mark with his glass façade of the workshop building, which operated somewhere between oversized studio windows and functional industrial glazing. Its pathos no doubt outstripped the rigorous and objective implementation of the industrial idea as practiced in Groningen in 1922, which nevertheless achieved an unusually memorable expression of the architectural brief for a vocational school.[24]

An "Industrial School"?!

When in Zurich the first competition for a new building to house the School of Applied Arts and the Museum of Design under a single roof was held in 1926, the Neues Bauen movement was just beginning its heyday, which would be as brief as it was intense. In early summer 1926, an impressive number of proposals were submitted for the new building.[25] The topping-out ceremony for the new Bauhaus building in Dessau, designed by Walter Gropius's

21 Ibid.

22 Walter Gropius, *Bauhausbauten Dessau,* ed. Hans M. Wingler, 2nd ed. (Berlin: Gebr. Mann, 1997; facsimile reprint of *Bauhausbücher,* vol. 12); quoted in Nerdinger, *The Architect Walter Gropius* (see note 20), p. 74. Sigfried Giedion took up and interpreted this description from Gropius when he wrote: "The eye cannot sum up this complex at one view; it is necessary to go around it on all sides … The ground plan lacks all tendency to contract inward upon itself; it expands, on the contrary, and reaches out over the ground. In outline it resembles one of those fireworks called 'pinwheels,' with three hooked arms extending from a center." See Sigfried Giedion, *Space, Time and Architecture: The Growth of a New Tradition* (Cambridge, MA: Harvard Univ. Press, 1941), p. 493.

23 The three-wing motif swinging wide out into space as a symbol of opening and a new ambition to penetrate space on all sides is still juxtaposed with the commitment to an overall form whose opening cannot yet go quite as far as the dynamic and open structures of Ulm or Nuremberg (or even the linear development of the original design for Black Mountain College in North Carolina).

architectural office, had been held three months earlier, and the first houses for the masters were occupied in June.

The Bauhaus building in Dessau was a spectacular architectural symbol of the profound change in arts and design education that had been proclaimed there. Given the sensation that the building caused at the time, it is difficult to imagine that the future architect of the new School of Applied Arts in Zurich, which would not call itself a university for some time yet, would not have been familiar with it. All the more so as Sigfried Giedion, one of the most committed propagandists for Neues Bauen, was living in Zurich; he not only maintained active contact with the protagonists of the movement but never missed an opportunity to report on the achievements and perspectives of Neues Bauen and to reflect critically on them. As early as 1923, in the Swiss architectural journal *Das Werk,* he reported on the activities and objectives of the Weimar Bauhaus on the occasion of the first large Bauhaus exhibition in late summer of that year.[26]

Yet not a trace of these new developments can be sensed in the designs for the first round of the competition. Seeing the conventional results, Giedion tried to get involved in the discussion of the new building, but with no great success. His committed postulate of an "industrial school" met with little or no response. More than that, as we now know, a text was rejected by the *Neue Zürcher Zeitung* in which he stated: "It [the school] has to be a testing ground

5/6 Walter Gropius, the Bauhaus in Dessau, 1925–26, ground plan of the winged complex and view of the building and workshop wing
7 Leendert Cornelis van der Vlugt and Jan Gerko Wiebenga, Groningen Vocational School, 1922

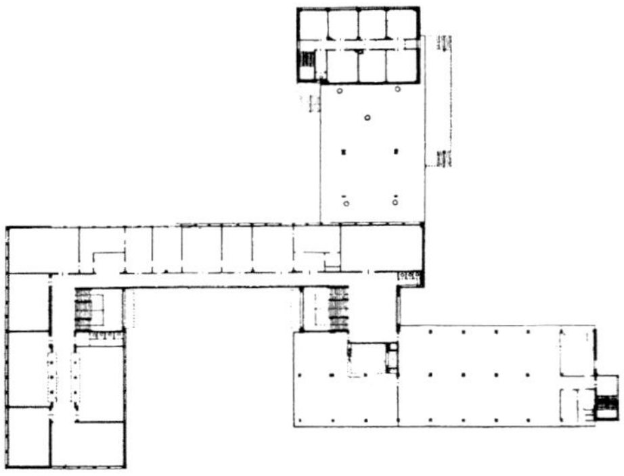

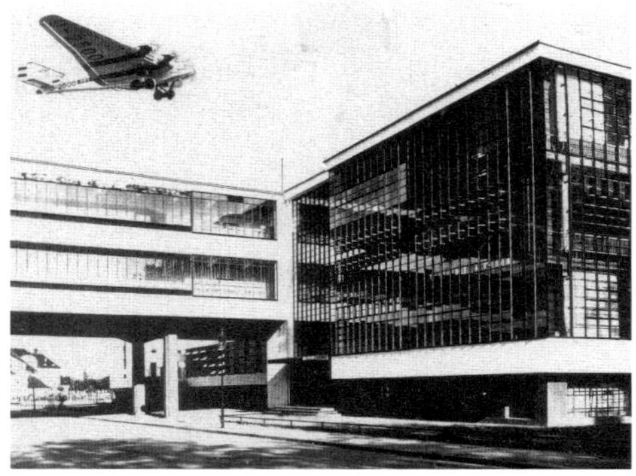

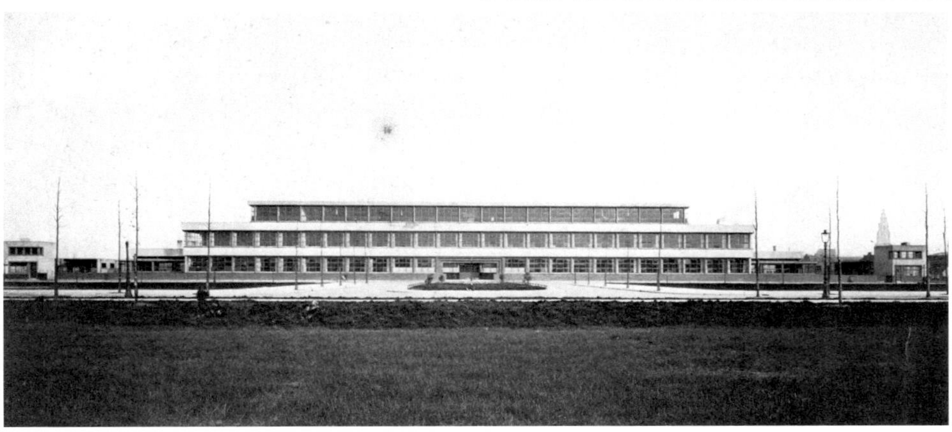

24 Surprisingly, it has been little discussed; on this, see Gustav Adolf Platz, *Die Baukunst der neuesten Zeit* (Berlin: Propyläen, 1927), p. 404; Julius Vischer, *Der neue Schulbau im In- und Ausland: Grundlagen, Technik, Gestaltung* (Stuttgart: Hoffmann, 1931), p. 96; Jeroen Geurst and Joris Molenaar, *Van der Vlugt, Architect, 1894–1936,* 2nd ed. (Delft: Delftse Univ. Pers, 1984), pp. 26–27. Using the example of the school in Groningen, Gustav Adolf Platz supported what he claimed in general for the essence of modern architecture and specifically for the genuine power of the modern school building: function as creative principle. "Seen in this way, modest work on the standard type becomes … a cultural achievement. The school with its components—classrooms, corridors, workrooms, and gymnasiums—articulates its various objectives. The characterization of the parts becomes an artistic impulse, providing an opportunity for effective contrasts." See Platz, *Die Baukunst der neuesten Zeit*, p. 112.

25 Claude Lichtenstein, "Werkstatt und Labor: Ein Bau der Architekten Egender & Steger, 1930–33," in *Zeichen nach vorn: Zum 125-jährigen Bestehen der Hochschule für Gestaltung und Kunst Zürich,* ed. Hans-Peter Schwarz (Zurich: Hochschule für Gestaltung und Kunst Zürich; Museum für Gestaltung, 2003), pp. 39–53. Luzi Dosch, "Neues Bauen in der Schweiz: Gewerbeschule und Kunstgewerbemuseum Zürich, 1930–33," thesis, University of Zurich, 1979–80.

26 In August and September the *Bauhausausstellung* (Bauhaus Exhibition) was held in Weimar as the "first extensive progress report" from the Bauhaus; see Bauhaus-Archiv, Museum für Gestaltung (ed.), *Experiment Bauhaus: Das Bauhaus-Archiv, Berlin (West) zu Gast im Bauhaus Dessau,* exh. cat. Berlin/Dessau (Berlin: Kupfergraben-Verlagsgesellschaft, 1988), p. 410. Giedion reported in *Das Werk* 10, no. 9 (1923), p. 232, under the title "Bauhaus und Bauhauswoche zu Weimar" (Bauhaus and the Bauhaus Week in Weimar).

for theater, film, and advertising. That is, a laboratory. For that it has to look like a factory, a laboratory, a school."[27] It is thus all the more striking that the design by Egender and Steger has so little to do architecturally with the Bauhaus building and so much more in common with the "normal" modern school building of the 1920s. Only in the second round of the competition did the designs take on more "modern" forms, and the decision in favor of the design by Karl Egender and Adolf Steger sent an even clearer signal. fig. 8 Still, the planned new building typified a textbook school building, and the architectural position taken by Egender and Steger seems to me to shed light on how the School of Applied Arts in Zurich saw itself.

Interestingly, there has never been a detailed comparison of the architecture of the school building in Zurich with that of the Bauhaus. That would not be possible within the framework of this text, however. The generally acknowledged relationships presumably refer above all to the circumstance that the model of the Bauhaus must naturally be mobilized when trying to establish the position of an educational facility built at almost exactly the same time and with a similar educational brief.[28]

The differences between the two buildings are at least as great as what they share. If we want to determine why that is, it is enlightening to allow one's gaze to roam once again across the sparse landscape of similar new buildings at that time in order to establish a position on the architecture of the applied arts school. In doing so I would like to direct attention once again to the motif that seems to provide information about the function and self-image of the new schools in a significant way: the window—or perhaps more accurately—the approach to glazing.

In the second volume of the architecture series *Die Bauaufgaben der Gegenwart* (Contemporary Architectural Briefs), published in 1931 and devoted wholly to new school buildings, the Zurich school is illustrated next to the Vocational School in Groningen, though not yet in photographs but in perspectives and plans.[29] This juxtaposition reveals a striking contrast. While the school building by van der Vlugt and Wiebenga defines itself almost pointedly as a workshop and laboratory building through the manner of glazing described above, the Zurich design positions itself firmly within the landscape of modern architecture for school buildings that was emerging at this time under the influence of the committed and comprehensive concepts of modern reform pedagogy. The regular, unbroken rows of windows suggest an equally regular arrangement of well-lit and ventilated classrooms and workshops. fig. 9

Comparing the Bauhaus, on the one hand, and the Vocational School in Groningen, on the other—which more than all the others seems to represent an example of the "industrial school" that Sigfried Giedion advocated in response to discussions of the new building for Zurich—makes the differences clear: the Zurich school was located above all in the spectrum of modern school building including, for example, the work of Martin Elsaesser, such as his school for the Römerstadt in Frankfurt (1928),[30] the design for the primary school in Eschweiler by Walter Schwagenscheidt (1927),[31] or the school

8 Karl Egender and Adolf Steger, Zurich School of Applied Arts, 1926–33, November 1929

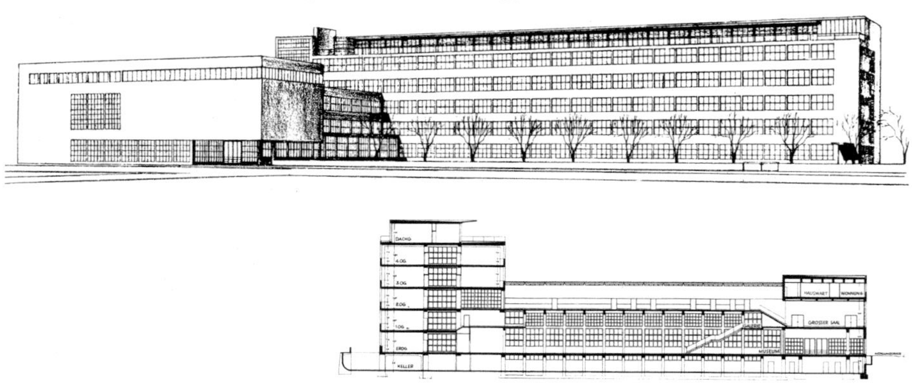

27 Quoted in *Sigfried Giedion, 1888–1968: Der Entwurf einer modernen Tradition,* exh. cat., Institut für Geschichte und Theorie der Architektur Zürich, with essays by Jos Bosman et al. (Zurich: Ammann, 1989), p. 155. Henry van de Velde had already spoken of a "laboratory" in the context of his school in Weimar; see Korrek, "Henry van de Velde und die Grossherzoglich-Sächsische Kunstgewerbeschule in Weimar" (see note 11), p. 108.

28 Thus Claude Lichtenstein remarks, somewhat tersely and without more detailed justification, that the building by Steger and Egender can be compared to and measured against the Bauhaus in its aesthetic and spatial effects, but "the Zurich building, despite being less radical, is superior to the Bauhaus building in terms of architectural substance." See Lichtenstein, "Werkstatt und Labor" (see note 25), p. 46.

29 Vischer, *Der neue Schulbau im In- und Ausland* (see note 24), pp. 96ff.

30 Now known as the Geschwister-Scholl-Schule. See Vischer, *Der neue Schulbau im In- und Ausland* (see note 24), p. 73, and, among others, Christoph Mohr and Michael Müller, *Funktionalität und Moderne* (Frankfurt am Main: Fricke, 1984), p. 299.

buildings by Otto Haesler. fig. 10 The stereometric articulation and interpenetration of building volumes marked by flat roofs of the sort that began to emerge in the second design for the competition; the horizontal dynamic of the rows of windows; and the planar relationships between the wall and window openings—all these things do not simply point to basic dispositions or a modernity articulated with modesty and presented with restraint. They have also become essential features of modern architecture for school buildings of this period—to say nothing of the large clock that accentuates the severe planes like a single abstract ornament.

The Studio Window; or, Art Opens Up to Life

With his spectacular curtain façade for the Bauhaus in Dessau, Gropius emphasized and staged the workshop and the studio character of this educational facility. The "industrial façade" thus meets with the oversized studio window that had, as a large opening in the wall, marked the appearance of art academies until the time, even if architects had not directed it outward as demonstratively as Henry van de Velde had done so ingeniously at the Art School in Weimar. For there van de Velde had not only broken down the true façade into a series of large window surfaces with delicate muntins that in a sense reduced the remaining sections of the walls and turned them into articulating elements that function like pilaster strips, vaguely reminiscent of Behrens's turbine hall for AEG. The way these window surfaces penetrate the jamb or mansard roof and the transition from the vertical to the inclined plane had, after all, even beyond any functional objective, suggested "an aesthetic intention" by which "the windows no longer manifested themselves as filled holes in the façade but as negations of the eaves or

9 Karl Egender und Adolf Steger, Zurich School of Applied Arts, 1926–33, view across the river Limmat

10 Martin Elsaesser, elementary school, Frankfurt-Römerstadt, 1926–28

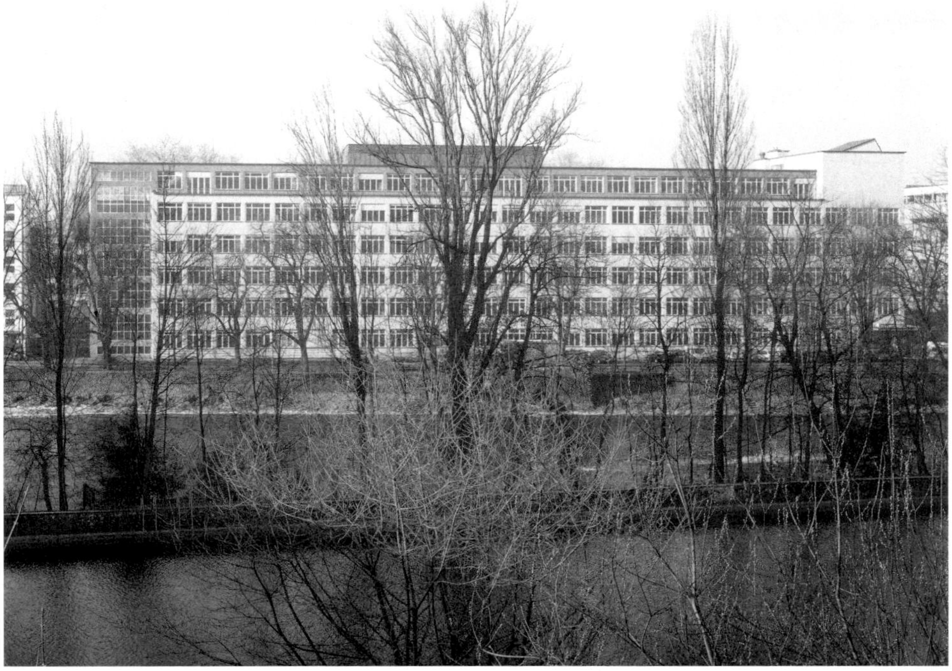

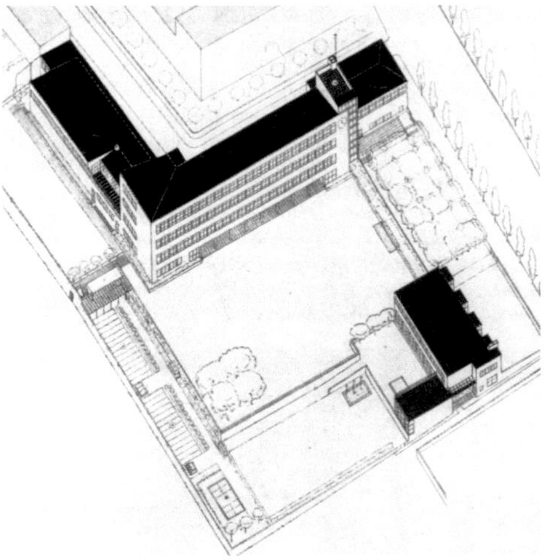

31 See Vischer, *Der neue Schulbau im In- und Ausland* (see note 24), p. 11, and Burghard Preusler, *Walter Schwagenscheidt, 1886–1968: Architektenideale im Wandel sozialer Figurationen* (Stuttgart: Deutsche Verlagsanstalt, 1985), p. 65.

32 See H. Wirth, "Neue Atelierfenster" (see note 14).

bend of the mansard roof, as a kind of autonomous element of a glass facade."[32]

This motif is all but nonexistent on the new building in Zurich, which is dominated by the regular rows of classrooms and workshops; only the large studio window of the room for life drawing underscores the tower-like effect of the building volume on its west flank. fig. 11 Interestingly, this view from the west nonetheless recalls a design that was never built but sets us off on another trail.

The "Frankfurt Bauhaus"; or, Modern Architecture as Educator[33]

"The Applied Arts School that is, on the one hand, a school of fine arts (painting, sculpture, architecture, and interior design) and, on the other, a trade school for all areas of the applied arts, is to be constructed on a site at the Wilhelm Bridge on the Main River. The layout of the rooms thus includes, in addition to rooms for the administration, large studios for teachers and students, on the one hand, and, on the other, workshops for carpentry, metalworking, bookbinding, book printing, weaving, textile work, fashion, ceramics, enamel work, scene painting, photography, and so on, as well as the necessary lecture halls, library, and refreshment rooms. The urban planning regulations for the site permit a high-rise-like tower in which the large studios were planned. In this way all of the studios can receive northern light. The workshops of the trade school are arranged around a courtyard."[34]

That is Martin Elsaesser's description of his project for a new building for the new Frankfurt Art and Applied Arts School of 1926–27, almost exactly contemporaneous with the first competition in Zurich.[35]

The building site for the school was a lot near today's Friedensbrücke, not far from the Städel-Museum. That is perhaps what makes it so astonishing from today's perspective, causing our gaze to turn from Zurich to Frankfurt and back again: the positioning of an art school on the bank of the river Main, which, much like the river Limmat, establishes the dynamic of movement in the building volumes and dramatizes the perspective of their arrangement. fig. 12 Nevertheless, the comparison of these two examples—keeping in mind that one project was realized and the other not—makes the difference clear: the elongated volume of the school building in Zurich facing the river is determined by a regular rhythm, the serial alignment of window formats that remain constant; the only formal counterweight are the large openings in the wall for the south/east stairwell. The staggering of the building volumes seems much less pointed than in Frankfurt; a tower motif is barely suggested and is more or less evident depending on one's perspective, perhaps most clearly from a perspective analogous to the one Elsaesser chose to present his Frankfurt design. With the glass volumes and planes that penetrate the building in the Frankfurt design, Elsaesser not only made a clear statement about the studio and workshop character of the new school, but also programmatically made reference to the Bauhaus building in Dessau and thus expressed the conceptual relationship between the two schools.

The "Morality of Architecture" and "Building for the Open Society"

The Bauhaus building in Dessau, built more or less on the proverbial green meadow, had signaled with is windmill-like wings extending out into the landscape that it was an "art

33 Fritz Wichert, director of the Frankfurt Art School in 1923, in the journal *Das Neue Frankfurt,* which he edited with Ernst May; see *Neues Bauen, neues Gestalten: Das neue Frankfurt, Die neue Stadt; DNF, dns; eine Zeitschrift zwischen 1926 und 1933,* ed. Amt für Industrielle Formgestaltung, intr. Heinz Hirdina (Berlin: Elefanten Presse, 1984); also see Mohr and Müller, *Funktionalität und Moderne* (see note 30), pp. 319ff.

34 Martin Elsaesser, *Bauten und Entwürfe aus den Jahren 1924–32,* pts. 1–3 (Berlin: Bauwelt-Verlag, 1933), n. p. Quoted in Mohr and Müller, *Funktionalität und Moderne* (see note 30), p. 284. From 1920 to 1925 the architect Martin Elsaesser (1884–1957) was director of the School of Applied Arts in Cologne (later known as the Cologne Work Schools), for which he designed an extension on the Hansaring in brick, his preferred building material, between 1922 and 1924. In 1925 the new director of Frankfurt's municipal planning and building inspection office, Ernst May, brought him to Frankfurt to head the structural engineering office (until 1932). See http://de.wikipedia.org/wiki/Martin_Elsaesser.

35 Hardly any other German city was as comprehensively planned during the Weimar Republic as Frankfurt, which as "the new Frankfurt" had become a kind of institution for architecture and social reform in the brief span between 1925 and 1930, under the leadership of Ernst May as director of Frankfurt's municipal planning and building inspection office.

In addition to the famous, exemplary housing developments created during this brief period, Neues Bauen in Frankfurt turned to schools and kindergartens, homes for the elderly and other care facilities, and "urban furnishings." In a bid to foster education May himself and above all Martin Elsaesser built a series of schools. But their interest was not limited to reform pedagogy in public education but also concerned creating places in Frankfurt where the newly acquired basics in artistic education could be brought in and brought to life. The City of Frankfurt had deliberately taken over facilities for education in the arts that had been established by private means or foundations in order to keep them from closing: that included the Städel School and the School of Applied Arts of the Polytechnic Society. For more detail on this, see Rosemarie Höpfner, "'das publikum wird gebeten, auf den stühlen platz zu nehmen': Frankfurter Kulturverflechtungen," in *Ernst May und das Neue Frankfurt,* ed. Heinrich Klotz, exh. cat. Deutsches Architekturmuseum Frankfurt (Berlin: Ernst, 1986), pp. 25–34; Mohr and Müller, *Funktionalität und Moderne* (see note 30), pp. 284–85.

space" open to its surroundings on all sides. And the interlocking, the (symbolic) intertwining of different spaces and spatial qualities became a paradigm of modernism. It signified the opposite of what had been embodied by the monolithic building volumes of the imposing academy buildings of the nineteenth century.

This kind of spatial thematizing of the interlocking of art in life found its true continuation in the university buildings of the 1950s, such as the new building by Sep Ruf for the Art Academy in Nuremberg or the Ulm School of Design by Max Bill, for whom the legacy of the Bauhaus had become a special obligation.

"There is no view like any other. Walking around the school means setting it in motion. There is no point toward which a central façade could have been built. From each point around the school the masses of the building appear to have been articulated differently, though they always offer a seemingly coherent, final image. There is no concentration of volumes anywhere, and nowhere is a center evident. Apart from the four-story residential tower, all of the buildings are two stories at most. Terrace-like, they ascend the slope. The dominant impression: gracefulness, movement, multiple meanings."[36] fig. 13

If we recall the descriptions of the Bauhaus building by Gropius and Giedion cited earlier, their relationship to this depiction by Bernhard Rübenach, from his legendary radio feature "Der rechte Winkel von Ulm" (The Right Angle of Ulm),[37] broadcast in summer 1959, is obvious. In it Rübenach not only described vividly the architectural effect and composition of the school, but also worked out the contradictory emotions and impressions it triggered; in doing so he offered an inimitable portrait of the school, its spirit, and its members.

In Max Bill, an architect was calling the shots in Ulm whose artistic versatility not only embodied modernism's ambition to design comprehensively, but who also continued the Bauhaus tradition at a crucial point and made it his concern to create dialogue with industry in every respect. In architecture, too—finally—the idea of industrialized building, which even in the 1950s, despite numerous experiments during World War II, had only been realized in rudimentary form, would finally be expressed in more than a symbolic way.[38] For the ensemble of buildings "armed in concrete"[39] on the first Danube terrace of the Kuhberg in Ulm, Bill developed his own systematic method based on a rigorously sustained reinforced-concrete construction. The austere aesthetic of exposed concrete was omnipresent and was forcibly brought out by the calculated geometries of the spatial relationships. That was an incomparably more rigid stance than that of the academy in Nuremberg,

11 Karl Egender and Adolf Steger, Zurich School of Applied Arts, 1926–33, view from the northwest
12 Martin Elsaesser, project for a Frankfurt Bauhaus, Frankfurt, 1926–27
13 Max Bill, Ulm School of Design, 1950–55, isometric projection

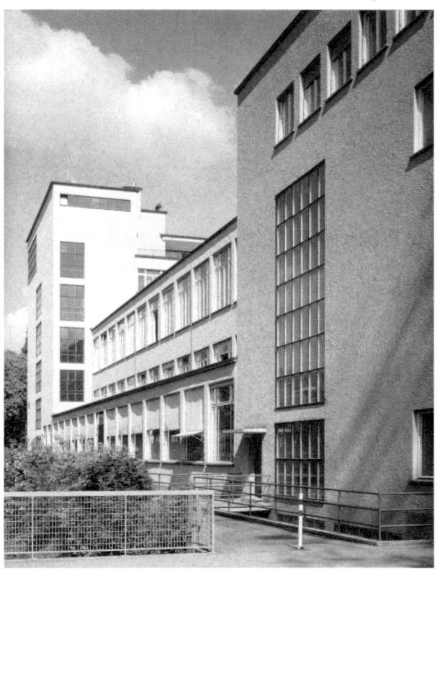

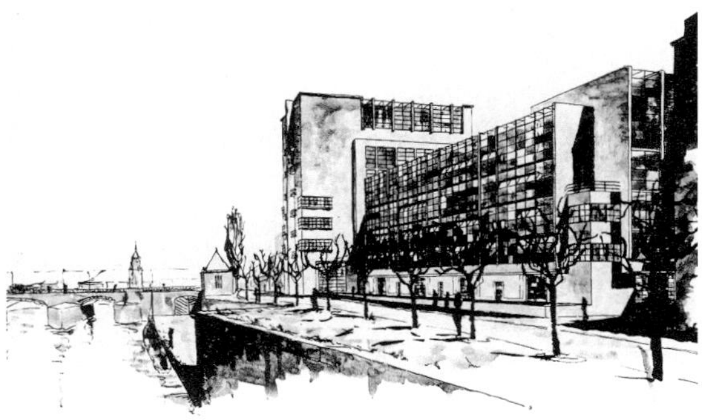

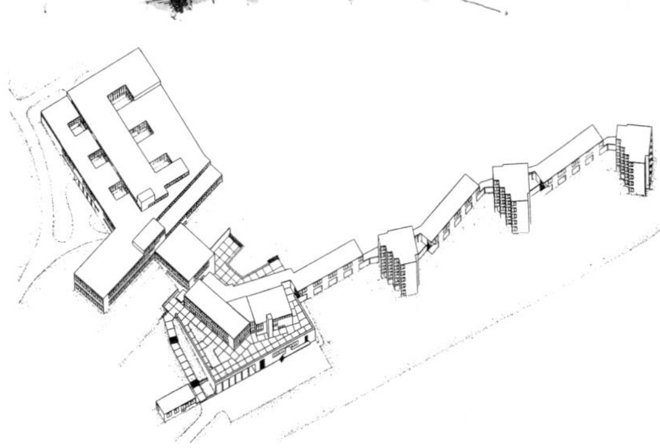

36 Bernhard Rübenach, *Der rechte Winkel von Ulm: Ein Bericht über die Hochschule für Gestaltung, 1958–59*, ed. Bernd Meurer (Darmstadt: Verlag der Georg-Büchner-Buchhandlung, 1987), p. 24.

37 From 1958 to 1962 Rübenach was guest lecturer on broadcasting at the Ulm School of Design and head of the culture and radio play section of the Südwestfunk (Southwest German broadcasting).

38 See, among others, Herbert Ohl, "Industrialized Building at Ulm," in *Ulm Design: The Morality of Objects*, ed. Herbert Lindinger, trans. David Britt (Cambridge, MA: MIT Press, 1991), pp. 197–213.

39 Rübenach, *Der rechte Winkel von Ulm* (see note 36), p. 17.

which we will address later, which not so much played with symbolic legerity as with a sparse presence, often described as "monastic," dominated by the sober workshop and laboratory character of the buildings. That is an "industrial school" in the truest sense of the phrase!

In Ulm the goal was to put a roof over the head of the exiled Bauhaus ideas yet again, to repatriate them in a sense, to continue to think about and develop the by no means completed project of modernism, and to do so in Germany. In exile in the United States, the former Bauhaus architects had created famous university buildings—one need only think of Mies van der Rohe's buildings for the IIT campus in Chicago—but none of them addressed a similar profile of artistic demands as the Bauhaus had earlier and the Ulm School of Design would later. There was one exception: Black Mountain College. The college had been founded in 1933 on an artificial lake in North Carolina, originally in sixteen individual buildings that had proven unable to withstand the rigors of winter, so a design was commissioned from the office of Walter Gropius and Marcel Breuer in 1938–39.

Thanks to his friendships with Josef Albers and Xanti Schawinsky, both of whom taught there, Gropius had excellent connections to Black Mountain College after his arrival in the United States in 1937, and he was familiar with its project for artistic education, which was also largely concerned with creating new forms of communal "training."

The design of the new campus, however, was essentially the responsibility of Marcel Breuer, who until 1939 continued to refine the project in collaboration with students and teachers.[40] The result was a four-part complex of buildings on one-story-tall pillars that followed, with several bends, the bank of Lake Eden. Its linear sequence embraced a complex program of spaces, but it also meant decidedly long paths. This kind of linear spatial articulation, which took advantage of an exposed topographical location to produce the gesture of an expansive prospect, seems to have found its echo a good decade later in the Ulm School of Design, though the building complex of the latter was on the whole articulated in smaller parts. Breuer's project was not realized. Although it was revised and simplified, in the end it was rejected, presumably for reasons of cost. fig. 14

A new, highly simplified design, developed by A. Lawrence Kocher, who would later join the faculty, ultimately became the point of departure for a kind of self-help and do-it-yourself project that the students realized themselves. But even of Kocher's plan only one wing—known as the Studies Building—could actually be built, in 1940–41.

In view of the explicit program for education based on community that Gropius and Breuer, by their own account, had wanted to make the basis of their design, under the motto "letting the life form the house,"[41] the students' concept gets more to the point. They viewed constructing it themselves as part of the training program and on that basis appealed to potential sponsors to support the building of their college on the basis of share certificates—a procedure that was extremely unusual at the time but anticipated later self-construction and participatory projects.[42]

Whereas the architecture of the school in Ulm programmatically worked with the "morality of architecture" and of "good form," Sep Ruf's new building for the Nuremberg Art Academy, which was also planned and realized in the early 1950s (1950–54), became a torch for "democratic" architecture, of architecture for the open society.

For Ruf, who had been appointed professor at the historical Academy of Fine Arts in Nuremberg in 1947, the goal was once again to set an example. The academy in Nuremberg, founded in 1662 by Joachim von Sandrat, was the oldest academy of the arts in a German-speaking country, but after the inglorious role the city had played under the Nazis, above all through Albert Speer's party conference grounds, the formulation of a new architecture for the art school held special significance.

Ruf was one of the most important architects of the period of rebuilding Germany after

14 Marcel Breuer and Walter Gropius, Black Mountain College, North Carolina, second project, 1938–39, photo collages

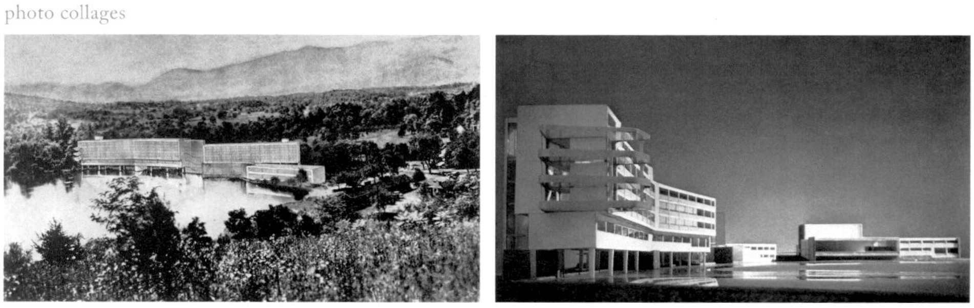

40 Nerdinger, *The Architect Walter Gropius* (see note 20), p. 198.
41 Ibid.

the war. In such significant buildings as the West German pavilion for the first World Exposition since the end of World War II, in Brussels in 1958, or later above all the chancellor's bungalow in Bonn of 1963–64, Ruf shaped and expressed architecturally the democratic self-image of the young republic: open arrangements of building volumes, flowing, transparent spatial figures, graceful steel-skeleton constructions—all in all a loosely articulated legerity of the new democratic essence for which his pavilion seemed to be the appropriate form of architectural expression, weightless and ephemeral, far from any claim to eternity. fig. 15 In comparison with the brutalist concrete aesthetic of the Ulm School of Design, his university grounds, in a place as highly contaminated politically as Nuremberg, confirmed exemplarily the new principle of architecture freed of the ballast of history. The figuration of glazed corridors and studio pavilions became the symbol of a transformed self-image: "In the addition, the result was a group of largely autonomous sections, a free association of individuals."[43] The legerity of the mise-en-scène in Nuremberg became a metaphor for the political self-image of the still young republic and pointed the way in the spirit of art.

With Max Bill and Sep Ruf (both born in 1908), a new generation of architects emerged from the shadows of the grand masters of modernism. The latter, however, continued to be active. Crown Hall, the architecture school in Chicago by Mies van der Rohe, was constructed at the same time as the buildings for Ulm. That is yet another, very different concept. With this enormous hall with glass on all sides, Mies produced the very thing he recommended to his colleague Hugo Häring, according to an anecdote, when Häring was grappling with his elaborate floor plans: "Make your spaces big enough, man ... that you can walk around in them freely, and not just in one predetermined direction! Or are you all that sure of how they will be used? We don't know at all whether people will do with them what we expect them to."[44] The "space" in Chicago had a floor area of about 120 by 220 feet, the largest interior that Mies ever built. A clear structure, a "splendid openness," whose obvious inconveniences did not interest Mies—this too was a confession, an idea of teaching and learning, for which the relationship of spatial freedom, openness on all sides, and intellectual dominance were crucial.[45]

Synthèse des Arts and *Promenade Architecturale*

The alternative program to Mies's conception for Crown Hall derives from another hero of modernism. At the instigation of Josep Lluis Sert, Walter Gropius's successor as dean of the architecture department at Harvard, Le Corbusier was commissioned in the late 1950s to design the new building for the Carpenter Center for the Visual Arts. Built between 1960 and 1964, it would be Le Corbusier's only building in North

15 Sep Ruf, new building for the Nuremberg Art Academy, 1950–54, view into the pavilion complex

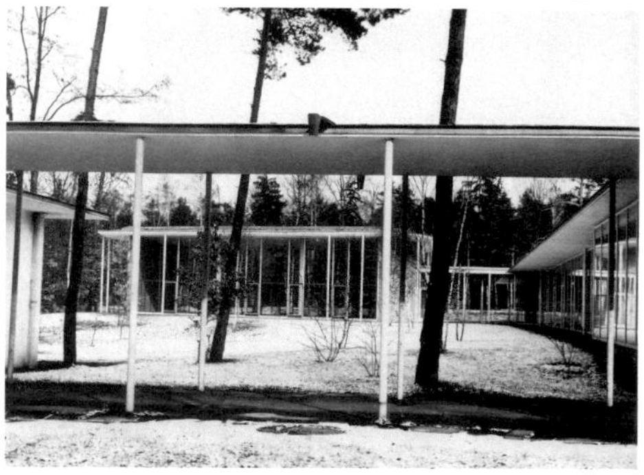

42 The text of one such share certificate read: "Unlike other colleges we derive no income either from taxes or endowment. The college has managed to exist and grow on fairly modest student fees and on gifts from its friends ... In order to meet our present problems—preparing a permanent location for the college—we have cleared land, diverted a stream, cut away half a hill-side, we have cut the timber for piles, blasted and hauled rocks for walls, mixed and poured concrete; we have learned to build stone walls and lay flooring. Yet the importance of actual building is but a part of our whole educational program. In order to continue that program, we need your help." The share certificates referred to units for walls or floors, to a door or two windows, to a stairway, and so on.
On another occasion, in 1946, a new approach was taken to another new building. At the invitation of Theodor Dreier, one of the founders of Black Mountain College, Norman Fletcher worked out a layout of spaces and later a plan for a dormitory to house 150 students. See Nerdinger, *The Architect Walter Gropius* (see note 20), p. 280.
On Black Mountain College, see, among others, Mary Emma Harris, *The Arts at Black Mountain College*, 3rd ed. (Cambridge, MA: MIT Press, 2002), and Vincent Katz (ed.), *Black Mountain College: Experiment in Art* (Cambridge, MA: MIT Press, 2002).

43 Wolfgang Pehnt, *Deutsche Architektur seit 1990* (Munich: Deutsche Verlagsanstalt, 2005), p. 303.

44 Franz Schulze, *Mies van der Rohe: A Critical Biography* (Chicago: Univ. of Chicago Press, 1985), p. 109.

45 Ibid., pp. 261–64.

America and one of his last—he was already over seventy at the time.

The Carpenter Center was created in the middle of a campus marked by a diversity that had grown together from more or less solitary buildings. Le Corbusier reacted to this context with a figuration of buildings that is as compact as it is communicative, in which he once again offered an exemplary presentation of the elementary convictions of his conception of architecture: the aesthetic effects of exposed concrete and its sculptural qualities, which determine both the overall contour of the building and the modulations and structures of the planes; the interpenetration of exterior and interior space that is thematized in the dramaturgy of the incidence of light and the spatial movement; and hence, all in all, yet another mise-en-scène of his *promenade architecturale* as an elaborate artistic dialogue between constructive elements, architectural forms, and different spatial characters. fig. 16

This building, this architectural brief, summarizes the themes that always occupied the great masters of modernism.[46] As a facility for studies in the visual arts it offered the genuine material for Le Corbusier's principle of a *synthèse des arts*,[47] formulated here not only in the architectural and sculptural adaptation of a motif that is painterly at its core: the "double guitar,"[48] which we believe we recognize in the traditions of cubist painting. Above all, however, it was the architectural brief itself that demanded that the various arts be brought together under one roof.[49]

In these contexts the ramp that Le Corbusier placed in the center of his design takes on tremendous significance: for in addition to the sculptural qualities of brutalist concrete architecture, which after all characterize all of the architect's later work, it is above all the motif of this ramp that thematizes the interrelationships of interior and exterior not only concretely but also symbolically. fig. 17

In its concrete function the ramp is a continuation of and response to the campus's pedestrian system and becomes the backbone of the interior circulation: it rises in a broad arc, penetrates the building volume on the level of the second story, and then continues out of the other side of the building again. Le Corbusier wanted this arrangement to be understood as an invitation to, on the one hand, cross the building, using it as a deliberately spatially staged connecting route for the various areas of the campus, and, on the other, as a kind of panoramic path through the various teaching areas for the artistic disciplines represented there.

It would turn out, however, that these theoretical expectations of the concept did not come across and were not accepted in reality as he had imagined: the ramp's invitation to take a *promenade architecturale,* and in this case presumably *artistique* as well, was only accepted by the public when a café and a gallery were added to supplement the functional and abstract-architectural qualities with social and cultural ones.[50] Since the Villa La Roche (Paris, 1923–25) and his contribution to the Weissenhof residential development in Stuttgart (1927), Le Corbusier had repeatedly extemporized anew on the theme of the *promenade architecturale.* The Carpenter Center represented not just an interpretation of it but also a new dimension, as the ramp became the architectural backbone of the

16 Le Corbusier, Carpenter Center, Harvard University, Cambridge MA, 1960–64, southeast side with ramp

17 Le Corbusier, Carpenter Center, Harvard University, Cambridge MA, 1960–64, isometric drawing

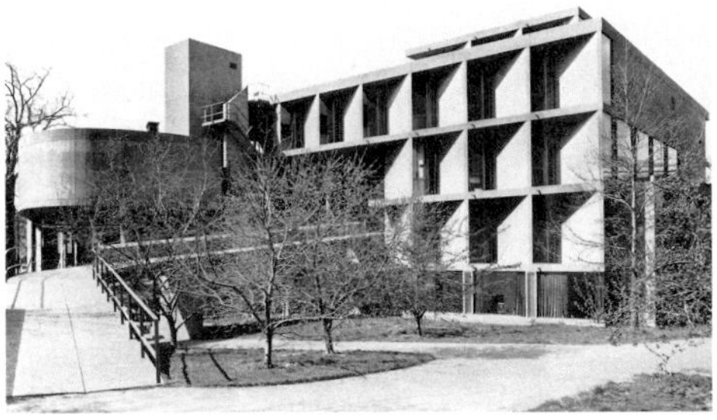

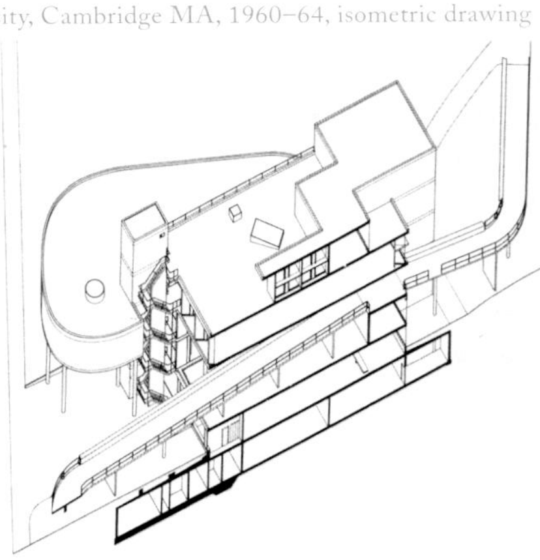

46 A comprehensive presentation of the Carpenter Center may be found in the study by Eduard Sekler and William Curtis, *Le Corbusier at Work: The Genesis of the Carpenter Center for the Visual Arts* (Cambridge, MA: Harvard University Press, 1978).

47 On this, see, among others, Badischer Kunstverein Karlsruhe, Andreas Vowinckel et al. (eds.), *Le Corbusier: Synthèse des arts; Aspekte des Spätwerks, 1945–1965,* exh. cat. (Berlin: Ernst, 1986).

48 Adolf Max Vogt et al., *Architektur, 1940–1980* (Berlin: Propyläen, 1980), p. 247.

49 The Carpenter Center housed the various genres of two- and three-dimensional art, from photography and video to sculpture.

synthèse des arts that Le Corbusier had favored and advocated since his early days. And what could be better suited for that than a building for education in the arts?

Contextualizing and Interpenetrating: New Architecture for Education in the Arts

In the forty-odd years that have passed since the Carpenter Center was completed, and especially since the late 1980s, a wealth of architecture has been built for a university landscape that repeatedly finds itself diversifying and becoming more highly differentiated. In addition to extensions or new buildings for the academies of art in Münster and Munich, there have been universities for film and media and buildings for education in design and dance. Whether in Berlin, London, Münster or Munich, Turku, Essen, or Cologne, the variety of architectural briefs has unfolded in a diversity of architectural concepts that express not only the variety of training in artistic and design disciplines but also—and perhaps above all—that of the architectural concepts. In the process, thanks to the paradigm shift in architecture and urban planning introduced by the discourse on postmodernism, an important new architectural brief involved grappling with, on the one hand, the existing building fabric of institutions and, on the other, the conversion of abandoned industrial areas. The architectural themes of spatial penetration and interlocking that had become so central to modernism and the twentieth century generally thus obtained a new facet: contextualization.

Particularly informative in our context, therefore, are two concepts developed at nearly the same time that thematize, each in its own way, the approach to existing architectural and urban planning structures and yet make reference in different ways to the Bauhaus: the new buildings for the Academy of Art and Architecture in Maastricht by Wiel Arets and the conversion of a former munitions factory, by the architectural office of Schweger und Partner, for the State Academy for Design established along with the Center for Art and Media (ZKM) in Karlsruhe.

"Virological Architecture" and "Alabaster Skin"

In the late 1980s and early 1990s Arets realized an expansion of the existing Rijkshogeschool in Maastricht which also served to bring the art and architecture departments together. The complex is in the middle of the city, a multipart ensemble of existing buildings and new ones that is shaped by the intricate, partly medieval layout of the city.

The urban planning situation of the academy in Maastricht was thus diametrically opposed to that of the Bauhaus. Nevertheless, Arets not only carried out his own architectural and urbanistic program, but also made explicit reference to the "historical" Bauhaus built almost seventy years earlier. fig. 18

The concept of contextualizing and interpenetrating the architectural volumes that is evident in the Maastricht project—which Arets himself characterized with the somewhat trendy

18 Wiel Arets, Academy of Art and Architecture Maastricht, 1989–93, view

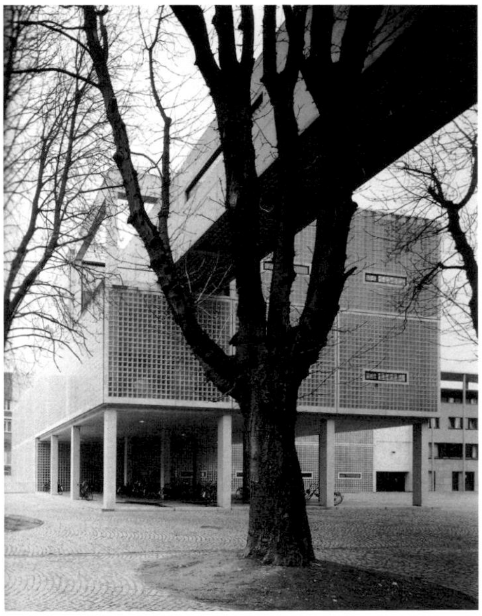

50 "The ramp was intended to be the centerpiece of the building, taking people directly to its center. Le Corbusier envisioned the ramp as becoming a major campus pathway, with students constantly flowing between Quincy and Prescott Streets. Unfortunately, Le Corbusier did not understand that few students have any need to travel this route (not to mention that they are lazy and would never walk up an inclined ramp just to walk down the other side). The University has done a commendable job in adding the Sert Café and revitalizing the Sert Gallery, giving people a reason to use the ramp more often." Zachary R. Heineman, "Understanding the Carpenter Center," *The Harvard Crimson Online,* Opinion, Monday, April 7, 2003, http://www.thecrimson.com/article.aspx?ref=347414

biological metaphor "virological architecture"[51] —is not that unique. We have already encountered the transformation process that reflects the idea of interpenetration as parallel to the postulate of the interlocking of art and life as an essential parameter of the architectural and artistic constitution of space in modernism in general. Arets supplements this somewhat sociopolitical demand with the aesthetic postulate of mutual interpenetration of urban planning and architectural energies. What is intended by that becomes clear above all in the way he cites the architecture of the Dessau Bauhaus in his concept for Maastricht.

It was perhaps necessary to have the earlier postmodern discourse—and above all the relaxed and confident approach to the legacy of High Modernism that has always characterized Dutch architecture—to react again in as contemporary a way to the architectural parameters of the Bauhaus building as Arets did in Maastricht, where he presented large-scale façades of square glass bricks as an homage to the curtain façade of the workshop wing of the Bauhaus building. fig. 19 At the same time, the architect superimposed it with new interpretations by adopting the square grid of the concrete skeleton for the formats of his glass bricks and by suggesting that the glass bricks were a transformation of the typical brick of Maastricht's architecture.[52] In doing so, Arets added another facet to the thematization of a material that—as we have seen—played a very special role in the formulation of the workshop and studio character of the art school.[53] By materializing and arranging glass in this way, many different layers of historical meaning and spatial interpretation overlap. The wall becomes a membrane of many layers and meanings that in the end is exemplary of a concept of architecture that the Dutch architect described as follows in his text *An Alabaster Skin*: "a between, a membrane, an alabaster skin, a thing, that is at once opaque and transparent, meaningful and meaningless, real and unreal."[54]

Industrial Architecture and Art: A New Unity

In Karlsruhe in the early 1990s, by contrast, the reference to the Bauhaus would be less architectural than institutional. When the long-cherished plans for the Center for Art and Media in Karlsruhe began to take shape in the late 1980s, Heinrich Klotz, the founding director of the ZKM, had the unique opportunity to give them a genuine perspective and a concrete site. After the original plan for a new building by Rem Koolhaas in the immediate vicinity of the main train station in Karlsruhe had been rejected for a variety of reasons, a new option came into focus: an industrial building of enormous dimensions, a former munitions factory in the southwest part of the city.[55]

This decision no doubt meant passing up for the moment the opportunity not only to create a striking architectural situation for those

19 Wiel Arets, Academy of Art and Architecture Maastricht, 1989–93, view

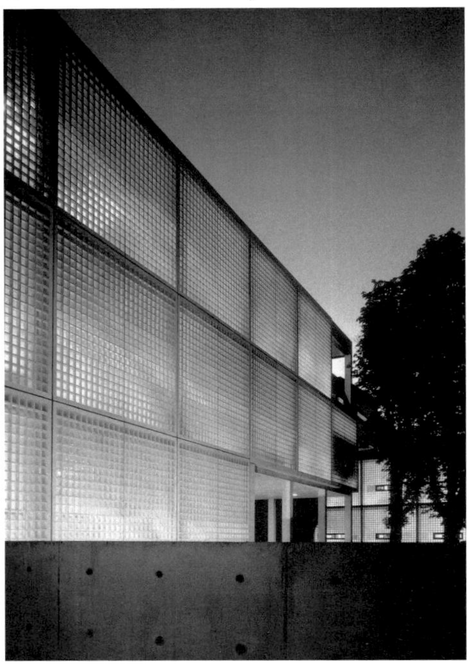

51 Wiel Arets, "Een virologische architectuur," *Architect thema* 57 (1994), pp. 42–48; on this, see also Greg Lynn, "Intensive Disappearance," in *Wiel Arets, Architect: Maastricht Academy of the Arts and Architecture* (Rotterdam: 010 Publishers, 1994), pp. 35ff.

52 Glass venting doors are built into the glass brick walls to provide ventilation. On Arets's new academy building, see Arets, "Een virologische architectuur" (see note 51), and "Wiel Arets 1993–1997," special issue of *El Croquis* 85 (1997), pp. 44–61.

53 In Maastricht, too, the workshops are behind glass brick façades.

54 Wiel Arets, *An Alabaster Skin* (Rotterdam: Uitgeverij 010 Publishers, 1991), p. 5.

entering the city but also, and above all, to formulate a first programmatic contribution to the theme of media architecture through an institution that was intended to focus on new approaches to digital media and information technologies in art.[56] At the same time, however, it also offered unanticipated potential space to develop the planned institutional diversity.

The decision in favor of the former factory building also meant that the State Academy of Design associated with the ZKM would be understood as a new, resurrected "electronic" Bauhaus under the sign of the digitalized information society. Moreover, it meant that an architectural monument was established to the old Bauhaus ambition of reconciling art and technology, design and industry.

The decision in Karlsruhe against a spectacular new building and in favor of an existing building with immense space potential is typical of a paradigm shift in urban planning and architecture that began over the course of the 1970s, in which new buildings were not necessarily the aim. Just as postmodernism shifted the focus to the historical city, above all of the nineteenth century, the many buildings of an industrial culture that had been orphaned and abandoned for various reasons but had since been declared historic landmarks were now being converted to new uses in various ways. The examples are legion. In Karlsruhe it was a former munitions factory, whose spatial features and enormous dimensions made it the object of a planning for diverse offerings including museums, research institutes, and a design school.

Converting historical industrial architecture only succeeds if the leitmotif of the architectural interpretation is not simply a filtering out and development of the potential space but also brings to bear a living relationship of mutual illumination on the future uses and content. Such a brief fires the imagination especially in the case of a design (and art) university.

In the case of the project in Karlsruhe, one thing was obvious: The gesture, as monumental as it was spacious and open, of a hall structure a thousand feet long incorporating ten atriums with glass shed roofs, was to be made the point of departure of all the architectural and functional decisions that affected the new uses. The architects, Schweger und Partner, staged the encounter between the spatial features of the historical building fabric and the innovative tasks and content of the ZKM and design school as a relationship of tensions. In the case of the hall structure, its existing spaces were explored in terms of their transitory, sequential character and related to the views into the spaces of imagination and creation of contemporary visual production and design. Within the framework of the spaces for the museums, the twentieth-century evolution of spatial perception was made evident. In the case of the university there was a dovetailing of various qualities of public, production, and representation spheres. fig. 20

Given the specific nature of the existing architecture, the main theme became movement as an aspect of the visual and physical penetration of a vast space with many perspectives and layers. The keyword here was accessibility as an urban principle for developing spatial connections and atmospheric obligations in dealing with the architectural and urban planning context.

20 Peter Schweger und Partner, Center for Art and Media (ZKM) and State Academy for Design, Karlsruhe, conversion of a former munitions factory, Karlsruhe, 1993–97, aerial view (detail)

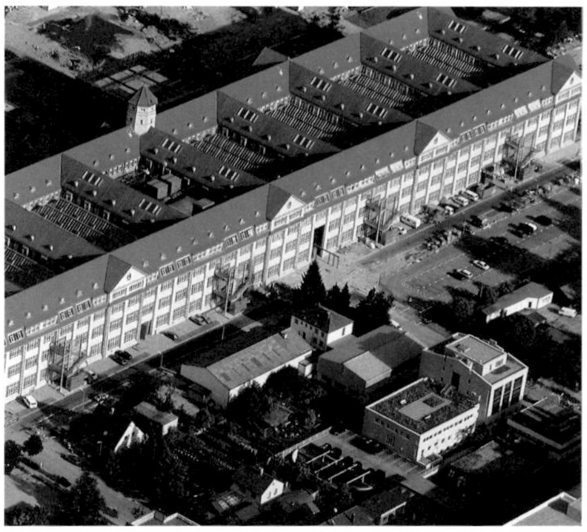

55 On the architecture and history of the origins of the ZKM, see, among others, Andrea Gleiniger, "From the Blue Flower to the Blue Limbo: The Zentrum für Kunst und Medientechnologie in Karlsruhe," in *Architekten Schweger + Partner: Zentrum für Kunst und Medientechnologie Karlsruhe,* trans. Michael Robinson (Stuttgart: Menges, 1999), pp. 6–19.

56 Perhaps it was better that way: the architects abandoned an early idea for a symbolic representation of a situation that was still completely open and under development, and the ZKM's significance as a place where projections, visions, and scenarios of a future still being determined are supposed to be drafted, explored, and discussed remained unimpaired by the proclamations of media architecture, however that be construed. See Gleiniger, "From the Blue Flower to the Blue Limbo" (see note 55), p. 10.

Promenade architecturale, interpenetration, and contextualizing—in their approach to the conversion of the Toni Dairy for the newly-founded Zurich University of the Arts, Daniel Niggli and Matthias Müller introduced the concept of perforation to this architectural, urban planning, and artistic principle. fig. 21 If the concept for the Toni Dairy that EM2N developed makes us think of the Carpenter Center,[57] that is probably due to the motif of the ramp and the way Daniel Niggli and Matthias Müller thematized its function as a backbone and extended and developed it into a boulevard of culture. fig. 22

From the perspective of the design, the way they brought this analogy to the surface under the circumstances and with the spatial potential which the Toni Dairy has to offer seems very convincing. In this case, however, it is not just the ramp in its real and symbolic qualities as the nucleus of a complex structure of relationships between inside and outside that was used to provide for access and internal circulation. fig. 23–25 Even if the givens of the Toni Dairy differ fundamentally in many respects from a spatial sculpture as deliberately calculated as Le Corbusier's, there are other points of connection, above all the material qualities of the architecture: the rough and raw makeup of the concrete —which in Le Corbusier's building is an artificial, artistically reshaped product—is in the case of the Toni Dairy the usual legacy of workaday industrial architecture. Yet this materiality is omnipresent, both in the surfaces and in the structure and construction; it characterizes the appearance and is also intended to be an essential element of the design. The calculated and artificially thought-out complexity of a figuration of buildings like that represented by the Carpenter Center is juxtaposed in the Toni Dairy complex by the inherent logic of a complexity

21/22 EM2N (Matthias Müller and Daniel Niggli), conversion of the Toni Dairy in Zurich for the Zurich University of the Arts, project beginning in 2006, urban planning model of the complex, and conception model

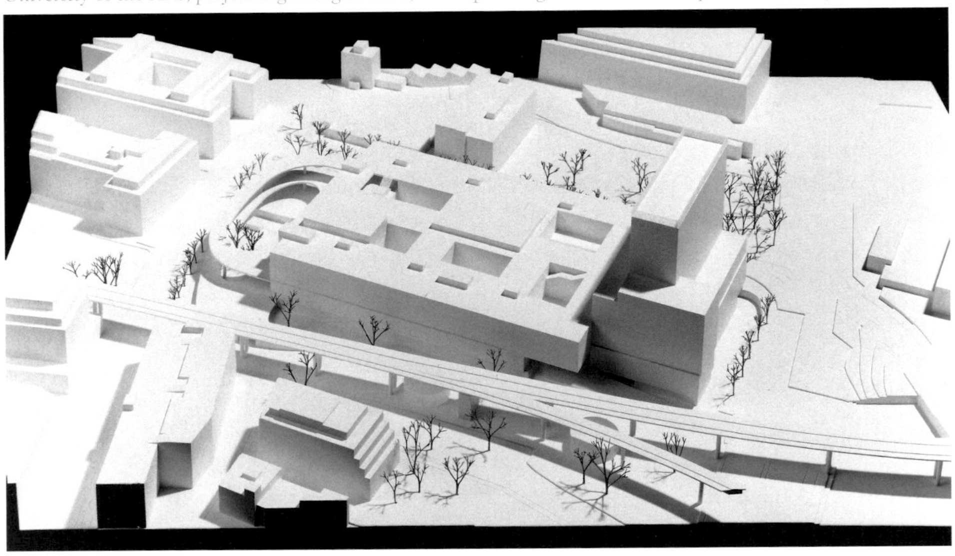

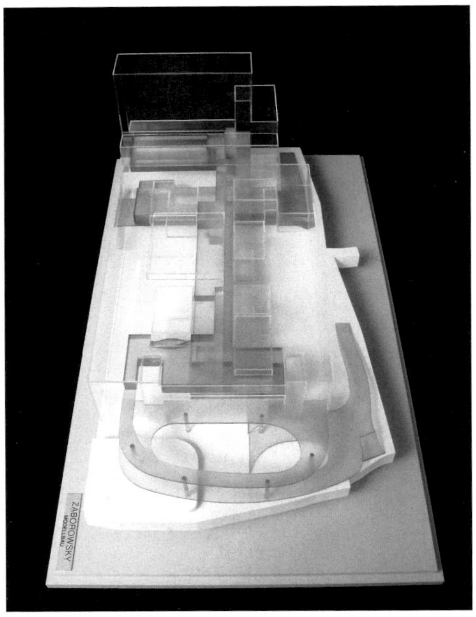

57 And the architects are well aware of this analogy, as was evident in a conversation with the present author.

that emerged from completely different functional contexts—a complexity that can be interpreted programmatically for the complexity of the functional and semantic contexts of this new university constellation and its urban, social, and cultural connections.

These new functions not only turn the building volumes into a highly complex cultural cosmos, they also penetrate it in many ways, "perforate" it, and thus thematize a tension between the opened and opening areas and the closed and sealed-off areas—both in terms of content and in a very concrete spatial sense. On the architectural plane the existing building fabric of the Toni Dairy offered a broad palette of glazing and window motifs ranging from banal industrial glazing to such characteristic window motifs as the vertical glass ribbons on the western flank.

Wiel Arets's elaborate homage to the façade of the Bauhaus can scarcely be improved upon, and a wall design as sculpturally conceived as that typical of the late Le Corbusier, which in the wall openings of the Carpenter Center thematized the modulation of interior and exterior relationships down to their details, could scarcely find a foothold or connecting point on the smooth and planar reinforced concrete volumes of the Toni Dairy. Against the backdrop of the inherent logic of a history of architecture that has repeatedly expressed the particular relationship between the artistic content, the disciplinary concepts, and the institutional constellations and made itself felt in so many ways in architectural and urban planning configurations, it may be possible to find an adequate expression today in a concept for a façade that takes into account the discourse on the

23–25 EM2N (Matthias Müller and Daniel Niggli), conversion of the Toni Dairy in Zurich for the Zurich University of the Arts, project beginning in 2006, view of the ramp from the southeast, view of the ramp from the northeast, and Culture Boulevard

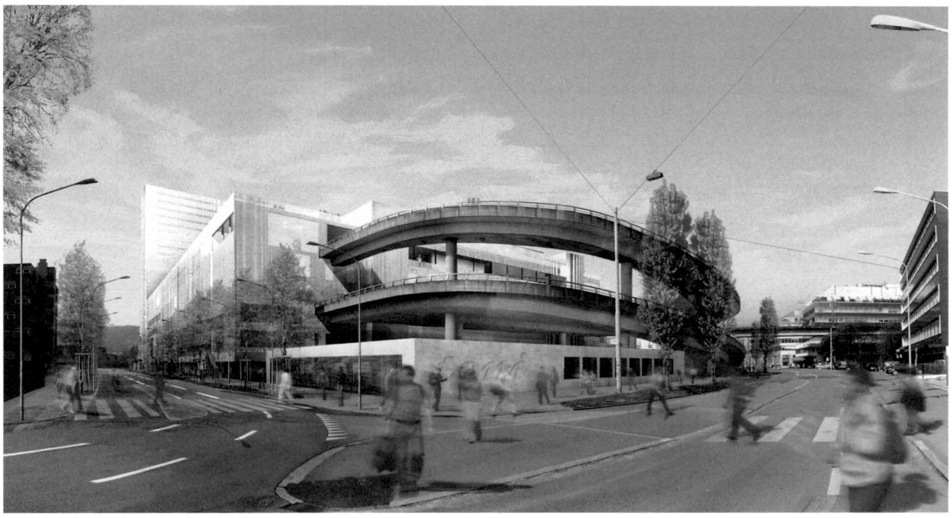

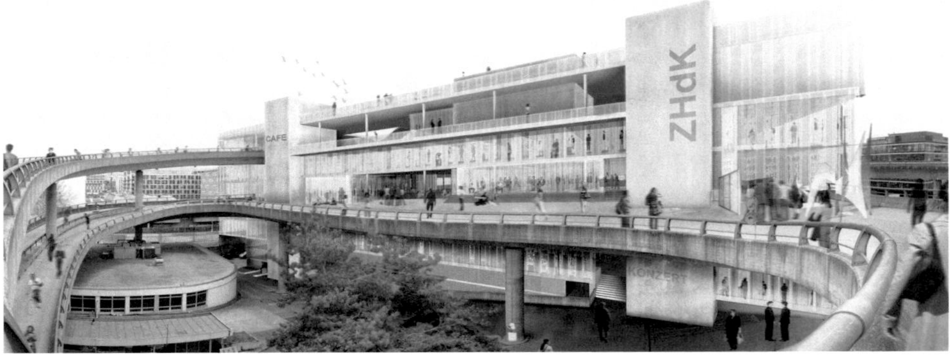

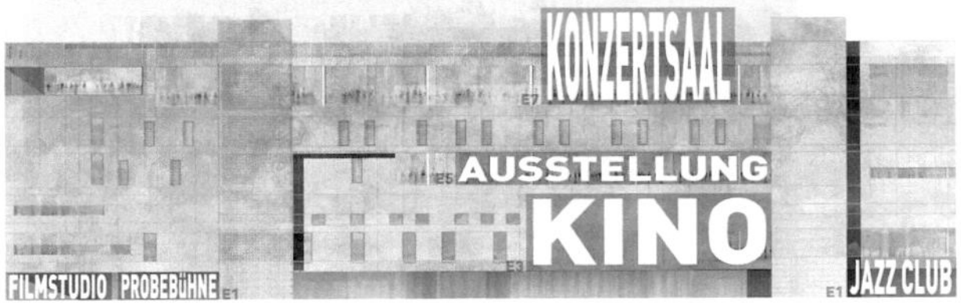

architectural visualization and spatial thematization of the experience and perception of space as transformed by media and information technologies—and to do so in a place that to a large extent adopts this discourse: "In the way that architecture at the time of the Modern Movement attempted to respond to produce techniques then in vogue, so architecture today should provide an answer to the simulation techniques now emerging."[58]

Synthèse des Arts Revisited

In the roughly eighty years between the new building for the School of Applied Arts in Zurich in the early 1930s and the architectural and urban planning redefinitions for the future Zurich University of the Arts at the beginning of the second decade of this century, an architectural transformation has taken place that does more than cast a spotlight on the specifics of the development of the former Zurich School of Applied Arts. It also represents exemplarily the change in principles that shaped education in the arts and crafts over this period and were expressed in the choice and shaping of the sites for that education.

The Toni Dairy is a monolith and a kind of architectural objet trouvé. In terms of its architectural and urban planning parameters and in the institutional and disciplinary constellations of the future Zurich University of the Arts, it offers an exemplary experiment. Its potential will permit a new interpretation of what has preoccupied the modern history of education in the arts from the outset: exploring and thematizing the connection between art and life in continually new ways—spatially, aesthetically, and institutionally: as *promenade architecturale* and *synthèse des arts.*

58 Arets, *An Alabaster Skin* (see note 54), p. 7.

Credits

p. 99, fig. 1a/b: Schweizerische Theatersammlung Bern

p. 100, fig. 2: Photo: Caden Manson, http://www.bigartgroup.com/honomo.htm;
fig. 3: Photo: Peter Atkinson, http://www.stationhouseopera.com/Current/theotherisyou.htm

p. 101, fig. 4: Photo: Thalia Theater Hamburg, http://www.thalia-theater.de/frame.php

p. 102, fig. 5: Photo: Het Zuidelijk Toneel

p. 123, fig. 1: Akademie der Bildenden Künste München

p. 127, fig. 2/3: Photos: Klaus G. Beyer, Weimar;
fig. 4. Site plan drawn by Lutz Waler, Weimar

p. 129, fig. 5: BHA, © 2007, ProLitteris, Zurich;
fig. 6: Postcard from a private collection, © 2007, ProLitteris, Zurich;
fig. 7: Archiv van den Broeken en Bakema, Rotterdam

p. 130, fig. 8: Archive of the Media and Information Center ZHdK

p. 131, fig. 9: Photo: Heinrich Helfenstein, Zurich;
fig. 10: from: Christoph Mohr, Michael Müller, *Funktionalität und Moderne* (Frankfurt, 1984), p. 284

p. 133, fig. 11: Photo: Heinrich Helfenstein, Zurich;
fig. 12: from: Christoph Mohr, Michael Müller, *Funktionalität und Moderne* (Frankfurt, 1984), p. 299

p. 134, fig. 14: from: Winfried Nerdinger, *Walter Gropius* (Berlin, 1985), p. 199 (BRM-GA, 87.4 Stoller, New York)

p. 135, fig. 15: from: Hans Wichmann, *Sep Ruf: Bauten und Projekte* (Stuttgart, 1986), p. 72

p. 136, fig. 16: Le Corbusier; photo: Robert Frisbee;
fig. 17: from: *Le Corbusier at Work: The Genesis of the Carpenter Center for the Visual Arts* (London, 1978), p. 16

p. 137, fig. 18: Photo: Hisao Suzuki, Kim Zwarts

p. 138, fig. 19: Photo: Hisao Suzuki, Kim Zwarts

p. 139, fig. 20: ZKM

p. 140, figs. 21/22: © EM2N

p. 141, fig. 23–25: © EM2N

Videograms: Hannes Rickli

The videograms *Retina* are part of the "Arena, Überschuss" Collection, an open-ended art project which since 1992 has been bringing together audio-visual material from scientific research laboratories. The video sequences are generated by measurement and steering media used in experiments. As technical things of the experimental system they have no further function in the research process. By transferring these media worlds into the context of art, a surplus of signs becomes visible that points beyond functional and instrumental use: scientific facts are produced in a permanent calibration between human and social, technical, medial, animal, and architectural actors.

The videograms are part of the research project "Scraps: Videograms of Experimentation" to be launched in fall 2007 at the Institute of Contemporary Arts/Zurich University of the Arts (SNF/DORE; partners: ZKM Karlsruhe, Max Planck Institute for the History of Science Berlin; project manager: Hannes Rickli).

Video Stills

Retina: In the eye, the retina processes visual stimuli and transmits selected data to the brain. Only moving objects are registered. This process is emulated in an analogous artificial retina with silicon receptor cells. The images resulted from a first test outside of the laboratory, in which the artificial retina was exposed to visual stimuli on the building site of a parking garage (images recorded by Jörg Kramer, Institute of Neuroinformatics at the University and ETH Zurich, 2002).
pp. 85–123

The Structure of the Zurich University of the Arts (ZHdK)

The President's Office and the Administration form the foundation of the Zurich University of the Arts. There are five largely independent departments, which are linked through various cross-sectional functions organized in the Dossiers. At the head of the Zurich University of the Arts is the University Board, consisting of the founding president, the head of administration, and the five heads of department.

Department of Performing Arts and Film

The Department of Performing Arts and Film encompasses the drama, dance, and film programs. It offers a Bachelor of Arts in Drama program with majors in acting, stage directing, dramaturgy, scenography, and drama education; a Bachelor of Arts in Film with majors in directing, cinematography, screenwriting, and editing; a Bachelor of Arts in Dance is at the planning stage. The Master of Arts in Film program has been running as a pilot project since fall 2006. A Master of Arts in Drama program is scheduled to start in fall 2008. The department also includes the Zurich Academy of Dance (taZ), the research-centered Institute of Performing Arts and Film, and the Theater der Künste, which offers a stage to students and serves as a place of public performance for the productions created in the study programs.

Department of Design

The Department of Design houses study programs in art and design for prospective designers. The Bachelor of Arts in Design program offers majors in casting, industrial design, interaction design and game design, scientific visualization, style and design, and visual communication. A Master of Arts in Design program is scheduled to start in fall 2008. Research on design is carried out at the Design2context Institute, while the Institute of Design and Technologies focuses on technological innovations at the interface of man, machine, technology, and design. The Design Department also hosts an annual Junior Design Department with courses for children and young people aged twelve to sixteen.

Department of Cultural Analysis

The Department of Cultural Analysis trains specialists for art and design education in its Bachelor's program. From fall 2008, it will also be possible to enroll for a Master of Arts in Art Education (with special focuses on education, exhibition, and publication). Moreover, from 2008 the transdisciplinary potential of the Zurich University of the Arts will be brought together in a new Master of Arts in Multimedia program. Research at the department takes place in the Institute of Cultural Studies and Art Education. The Museum of Design Zurich, the Museum Bellerive, and the four collections (Design Collection, Graphic Design Collection, Applied Art Collection, Poster Collection) provide a public platform for presentation and showcase the creativity of the department and the university as a whole. The department also accommodates outreach programs and continuing education programs.

Department of Art & Media

The study programs at the Department of Art & Media train future artists and media authors. The Bachelor's program offers majors in fine arts, photography, new media, and theory of media, art, and design. Graduates are awarded a Bachelor of Arts in Media & Art. In fall 2008 a Master of Arts in Fine Arts program is scheduled to start. Research at the department takes place in the Institute of Contemporary Arts and the Institute of Theory, which together form the Institute of Art and Media Theory. The activities of the two research institutes focus on aspects of research in and through the arts and on non-discourse-based forms of knowledge.

Department of Music

The Department of Music offers programs in the three basic fields of musical activity: creation, interpretation, and education. The more general Bachelor of Music program is designed primarily to prepare students for the Master's programs that follow, while the Bachelor of Arts in Music and Motion qualifies students to teach music and motion arts for children. Four Master's programs are scheduled to start in fall 2008. The Master of Arts in Music Performance will train students as instrumentalists in a concert or orchestra context, and as singers, conductors, and church musicians, while specialist soloists and opera singers will be trained in the Master of Arts in Specialized Music Performance. Courses for teachers of musical instruments and singing will be taught in the Master in Music Pedagogy, and composers and sound engineers will be trained in the Master in Composition/Theory program. The Institute of Computer Music and Sound Technology concentrates on applied and practical research in the context of music and media technologies.

President's Office

The President's Office supports the founding president in all his activities and projects. It includes a Legal Service, the President's Staff Office with the Communications Officer, the International Office, and the Equal Opportunities Officer.

Administration

The administration is responsible for all administrative and technical work that concerns the Zurich University of the Arts as a whole. This includes finance and human resources, university administration, logistics and university operations services including utilities, coordination, and maintenance, as well as university information systems (business applications).

Dossiers and Support Centers

In order to promote exchange between the departments and develop a shared understanding of the core concerns of the Zurich University of the Arts, each head of department has been allocated one particular Dossier. These Dossiers are Strategy, Teaching, Research (incl. Libraries, Databases, Archives), Outreach and Continuing Education Programs, Quality, and Production. Within some of these Dossiers, specific Support Centers (SUZ) have been defined, e.g. SUZ Information Technology, SUZ Media and Information Center (MIZ), SUZ Continuing Education, and SUZ Production. The latter combines the workshops of the theater and the museum, photographic studios, and other production sites.

Heike Pohl, Communications Officer

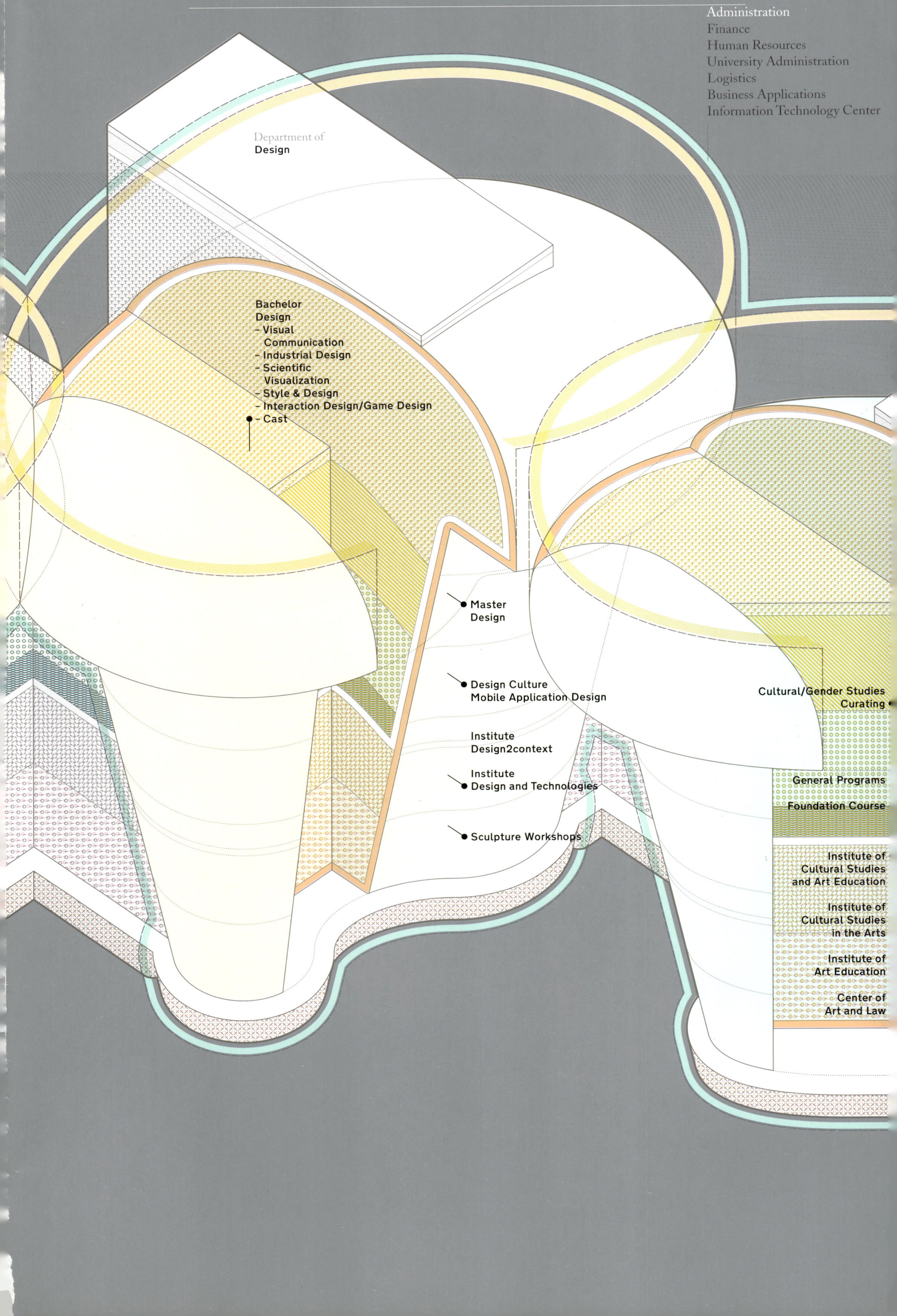
Administration
Finance
Human Resources
University Administration
Logistics
Business Applications
Information Technology Center
Department of
Design
Bachelor
Design
– Visual
Communication
– Industrial Design
– Scientific
Visualization
– Style & Design
– Interaction Design/Game Design
– Cast
Master
Design
Design Culture
Mobile Application Design
Institute
Design2context
Institute
Design and Technologies
Sculpture Workshops
Cultural/Gender Studies
Curating
General Programs
Foundation Course
Institute of
Cultural Studies
and Art Education
Institute of
Cultural Studies
in the Arts
Institute of
Art Education
Center of
Art and Law

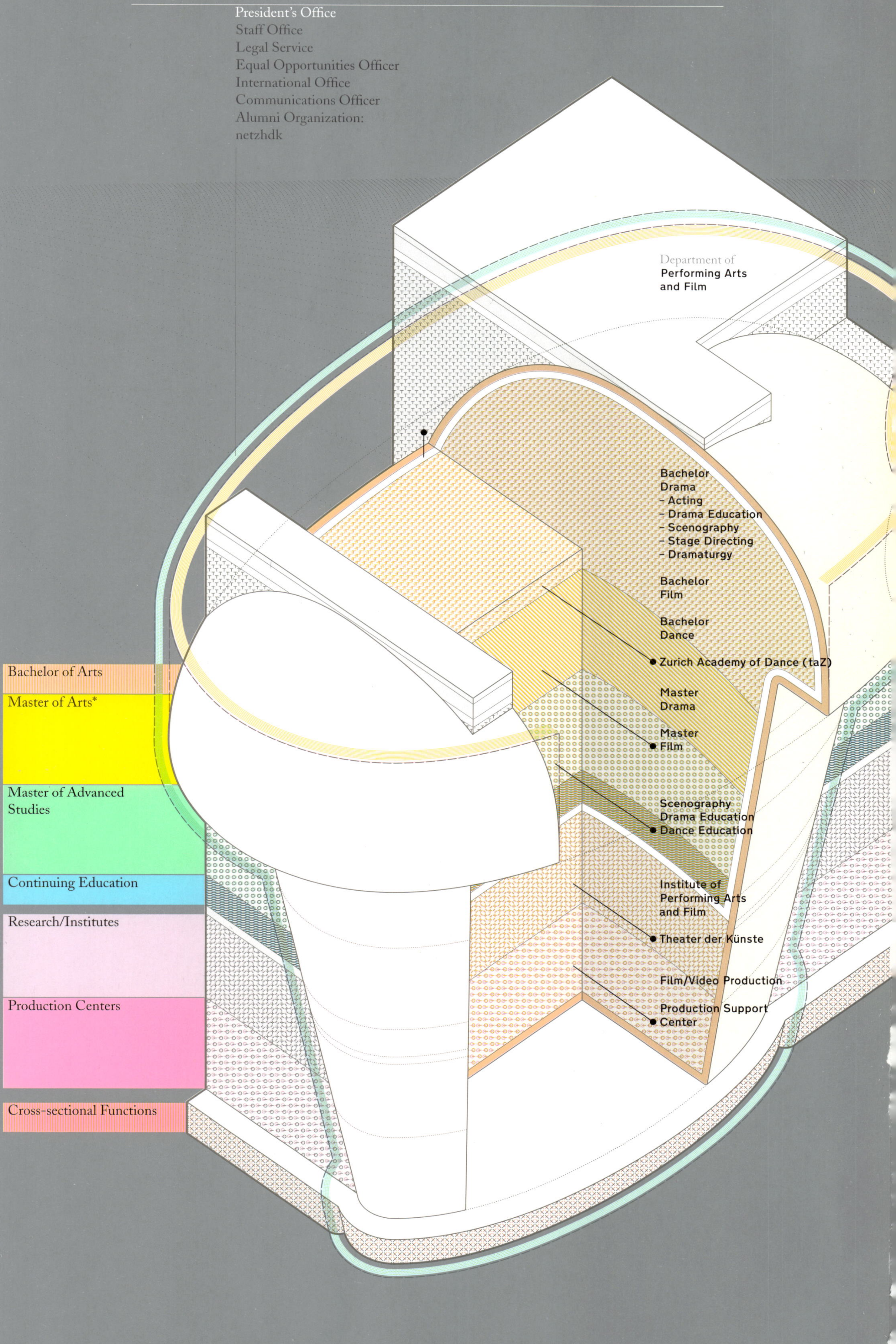

* Master programs will be offered from 2008, MA Film has been running as a pilot project since fall 2006

I

Regionality and internationality are complementary commitments that open up various perspectives of the same horizon.

The Zurich University of the Arts combines a regional base with an international outlook. We enliven and enrich, integrate and develop, consolidate and alter Zurich as a place of culture, enhancing its international profile and broadening its global horizon.

II

Art and design take shape where talent, knowledge, technical skill, and productive experience meet. Forward-looking curricula foster these competencies within an integrated educational concept that enables all actors to combine education and experience, expertise and experiment at all times.

The Zurich University of the Arts is a place of education, research, and creative production. The juxtaposition of these three objectives guarantees innovative, continuous, and sustainable performance throughout the university.

III

Impacting the cultural scene and the general public with results from teaching and research that are interlinked not only on the theoretical and thematic level but in concrete projects requires an excellent, publicly accessible infrastructure.

The Zurich University of the Arts stages productions in its own museums, dance and drama theaters, and concert halls, where students and lecturers, laypeople and experts, creative professionals and the general public in ever-changing roles and relationships meet and exchange ideas.

IV

Art and design generate explications and implications of human thought, emotion, and action. In a professional context this explicating and implicating calls for constant personal engagement in intellectual, aesthetic, and ethical discourses. This engagement is the basis for fruitful collaboration in private and public, economic and cultural partnerships.

The Zurich University of the Arts trains personalities whose creative and design activities are predicated on professional commitment to cogent interests, attitudes, and opinions which, for that very reason, may also change and adapt.

V

Work within disciplines generates competencies, work between disciplines generates dialogue about these competencies, work across disciplines lends them meaning.

At the Zurich University of the Arts these three forms of knowledge assimilation and production have equal status, with basic research and applied research depending on one another, exchanging and interlinking with regard to shared objectives.

VI

In a cultural climate marked by openness, curiosity, and thinking aimed at development, transdisciplinarity is far more than a conceptual desideratum. It is reality and everyday experience.

At the Zurich University of the Arts, the boundaries between the disciplines, between teaching and research, between discovering the world, passing on knowledge about the world, and shaping the world are wide open. Sense, meaning, and orientation take form at points where boundaries are crossed.

VII

The classic focus on the work of art has made way for a transmedial orientation on the event. Art and design manifest themselves in dynamic and interlinked processes extending from initial idea to draft to medial expression.

The Zurich University of the Arts is a multiplex event space whose overall dynamic is owed to a complexity of independent parts, their conflicts and collaborations, and to an organizational structure predicated on participation and equal opportunities.

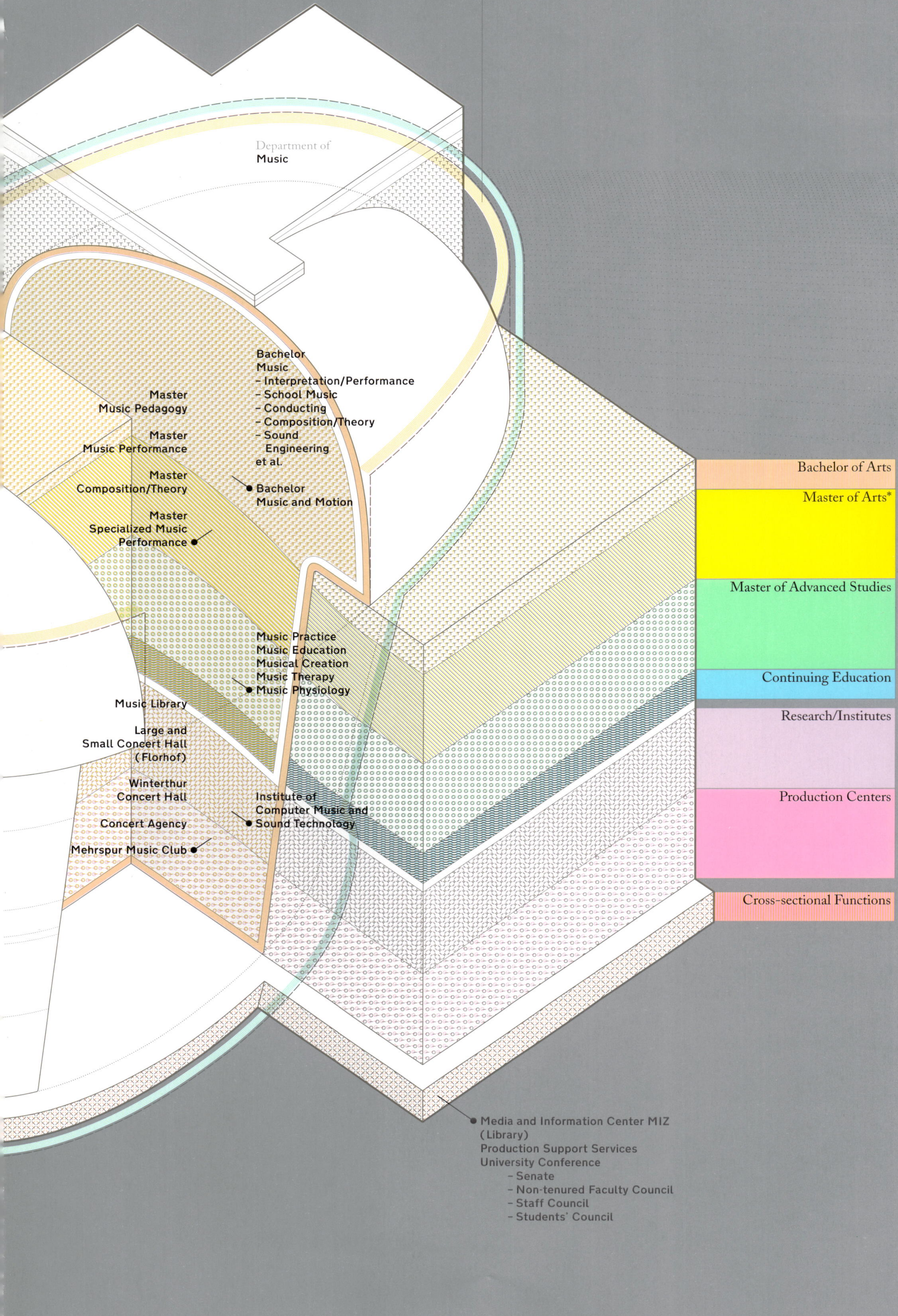
Department of
Music
Bachelor
Music
– Interpretation/Performance
– School Music
– Conducting
– Composition/Theory
– Sound
Engineering
et al.
Master
Music Pedagogy
Master
Music Performance
Master
Composition/Theory
Bachelor
Music and Motion
Master
Specialized Music
Performance
Music Practice
Music Education
Musical Creation
Music Therapy
Music Physiology
Music Library
Large and
Small Concert Hall
(Florhof)
Winterthur
Concert Hall
Institute of
Computer Music and
Sound Technology
Concert Agency
Mehrspur Music Club
Bachelor of Arts
Master of Arts*
Master of Advanced Studies
Continuing Education
Research/Institutes
Production Centers
Cross-sectional Functions
Media and Information Center MIZ
(Library)
Production Support Services
University Conference
– Senate
– Non-tenured Faculty Council
– Staff Council
– Students' Council

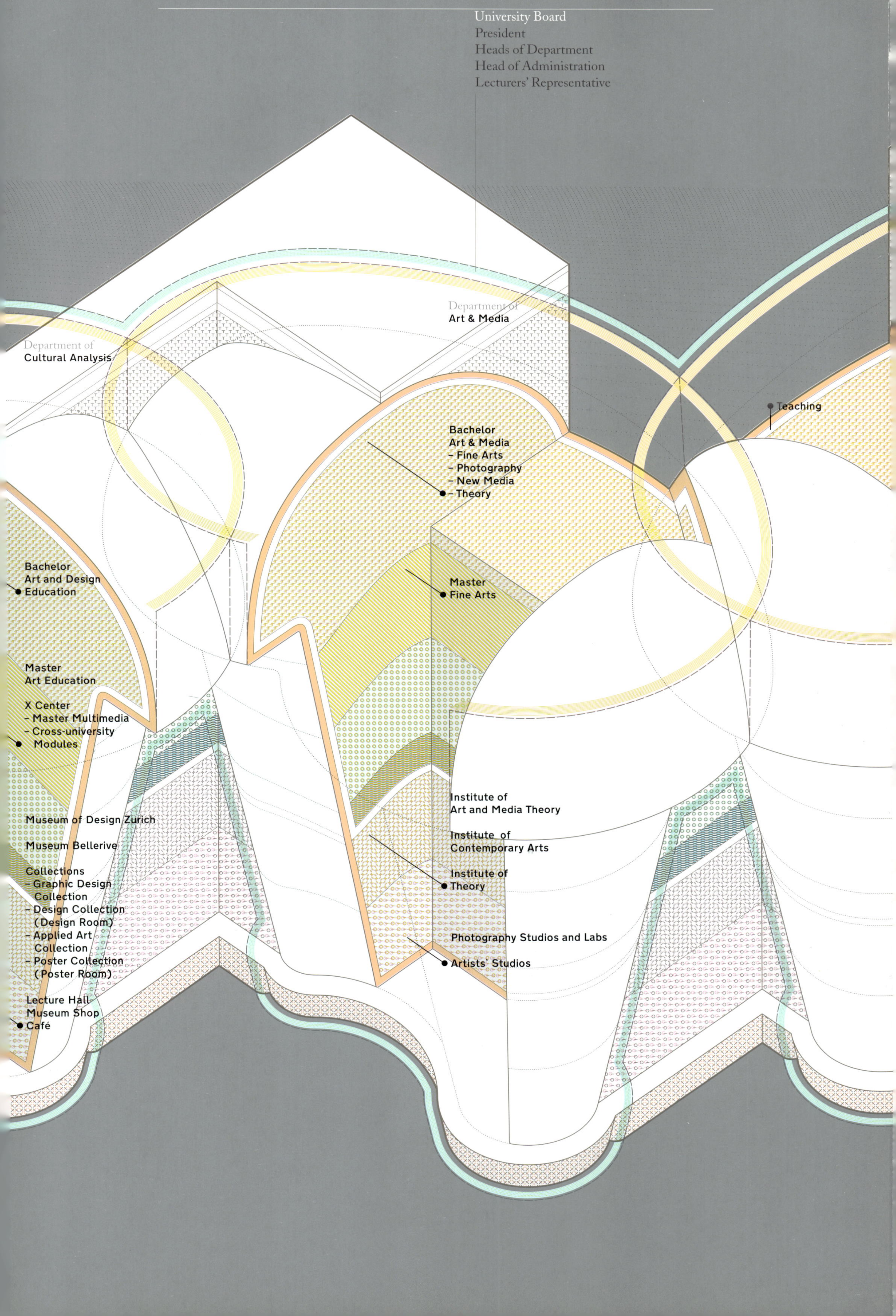
University Board
President
Heads of Department
Head of Administration
Lecturers' Representative
Department of
Art & Media
Department of
Cultural Analysis
Teaching
Bachelor
Art & Media
– Fine Arts
– Photography
– New Media
– Theory
Bachelor
Art and Design
Education
Master
Fine Arts
Master
Art Education
X Center
– Master Multimedia
– Cross-university
Modules
Institute of
Art and Media Theory
Institute of
Contemporary Arts
Institute of
Theory
Museum of Design Zurich
Museum Bellerive
Collections
– Graphic Design
Collection
– Design Collection
(Design Room)
– Applied Art
Collection
– Poster Collection
(Poster Room)
Photography Studios and Labs
Artists' Studios
Lecture Hall
Museum Shop
Café

The members of the board of the Zurich University of the Arts (ZHdK) in the staircase of the university's theater.

Standing on stairs, from top to bottom:
Giaco Schiesser, Vice President, Head of the Department of Art & Media
Hartmut Wickert, Vice President, Head of the Department of Performing Arts and Film
Martin Schlumpf, Lecturers Representative

Sitting on steps, from top to bottom:
Hans-Peter Schwarz, President ZHdK
Jacqueline Otten, Vice President, Head of the Department of Design
Christoph Weckerle, Vice President, Head of the Department of Cultural Analysis

Sitting next to the staircase on the left:
Michael Eidenbenz, Vice President, Head of the Department of Music

Standing next to the staircase on the right:
Daniel Waeber, Vice President, Head of Administration

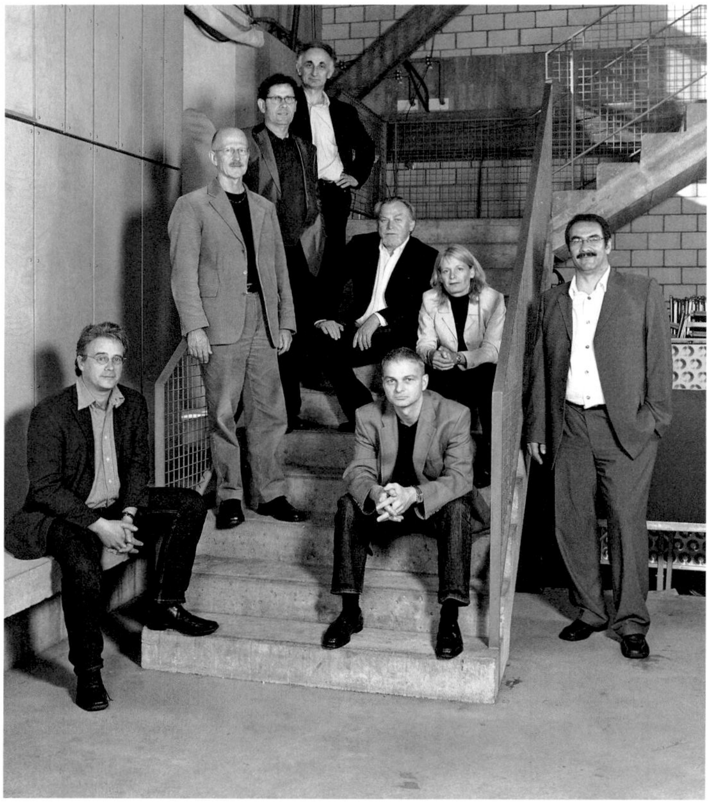

Visual Worlds. A colorful ka

year history of the institutions t
University of the Arts offers insi
the exponents. Not dry historica
aura of institutions and protago
phonous medley.

doscope from the five-hundred-
t now make up the Zurich
t into the lives and works of
acts but the atmosphere and
ts are reflected in this poly-

Introduction

This kaleidoscopic image-text collage is intended to offer a presentiment of what might ultimately emerge from this confluence of the diverse arts, and from this new academy of the arts, within whose magnetic field artistic profiles and cultures will be in a state of permanent evolution. This presentation chronicles the personalities who have emerged from and decisively shaped their respective former institutions, which now combine to form the Zurich University of the Arts. Their biographies and their works combine to produce larger constellations of potential and synergies, featuring the atmospheric, the ferment, the oscillations, the invisible: opalescent, oscillating, iridescent. Yet we always remain aware that heterodox cultural spaces such as the Zurich University of the Arts cannot be depicted as unities. The phenomenology of music, dance, the visual arts, theater, film, and design, of the most divergent modes of presentation and expression—pictorial, theatrical, tonal and atonal, factual, virtual, staged—highlights the sheer multiplicity and complexity of this enterprise.

This polychrome collage is capable of providing neither a representative nor a historically correct image of the over 500-year history of the respective institutions of the Zurich University of the Arts. That would be a very different—and doubtless also highly rewarding—project.

This selection, then, is aleatoric in nature. It features those elements that a necessarily selective memory has retained, minus the boundless abundance of names and images which had to be omitted for reasons of space and time—regretfully—and those that fell prey to the limited capacities of memory, or to the decision to forego the systematic historical approach.

Omitted almost entirely are those persons currently responsible for representing and shaping these institutions—and the few exceptions only confirm the rule.

The order of the entries is neither alphabetical nor chronological. Instead, free constellations—clusters—have been composed of the diverse contributions to art, music, dance, and theater, constellations designed to articulate and foster a vision of the Zurich University of the Arts as a transdisciplinary archipelago.

These constructed clusters are not airtight; they tend to leap between epochs, even fraying the edges or straining the limits of their affiliations. The pictorial arts are visually predominant, while for medial reasons, the acoustic and performance arts have been "relegated" to a DVD and a CD.

The overall arrangement resembles a carefree narrative that revels in fragmentary recollections.

This "symphony of shapes, images and sounds" is a display of pride and pleasure, and of gratitude for the passion with which the key people who have worked in and shaped these institutions—and in particular their students—have made their contributions to culture. Gratitude as well toward a society that has been willing to sustain such institutions, granting them support even when their critical impulses have occasionally brought them into disrepute.

Written by various authors, this portrait collection betrays a heterogeneous texture, while the supporting process of researching images has at times resembled an attempt to divine the presence of concealed—and in some cases long dried up—wellsprings.

"The mission of photography is to explain man to man and each man to himself." *The Family of Man* was a touring exhibition by Edward John Steichen. It offered a wide-ranging portrait of humanity, subdivided into thirty-seven themes, including love, faith, birth, work, family, war, and peace. It was seen all over the world, and enjoyed long-standing preeminence. The show was based on a vision of love and humanity overcoming hate, violence, and destruction.

An entire generation of photographers and their successors has pursued this "realistic" and humanist image of humankind, one that has also admittedly been deployed and diffused as a choreographed image in advertising.

He traveled to every conceivable scene of human misery, creating the definitive icons of the human condition in the twentieth century **1**; his images and portraits display a profound knowledge of humanity; he traveled half the world for Magnum, and his signature stamped the photographic universe of the *Neue Zürcher Zeitung* for decades **2**; his experiments in color photography won him the undisputed title of "master of color" **3**; his fashion photography manifests the highest excellence and stylish elegance **4**; his archive collections constitute a photographic memory bank of Swiss provenance **5**; he portrayed the world famous, and yet his lapidary trademark was "photographer of people" **6**; his images of humanity are provocative, even scandalous **7**; he travels the world, photographing and communicating elementary questions of human existence **8**.

1

Werner Bischof (1916–1954)

His photographs became iconic representations of the human condition in innumerable posters and publications. Turning his back on his teacher and erstwhile mentor Hans Finsler, who focused on new photography and its functionalism, Bischof turned to the "family of man" and to a style of photography that is centered on human beings—in short, to the art of photojournalism. He was a member of the world-famous Magnum photo agency.

It all began when he toured the ruins of Europe after the end of World War II. His pictures reveal the agony and destruction of the war with oppressive urgency: "The point is not to turn photography into an art form in the traditional sense. The important thing is the profound social responsibility of the photographer, who uses the elementary tools of photography to do a job that would be impossible by other means. The photographer's work must become an authentic document of temporal reality."

In Bischof's work, aesthetic differentiation, the elementary power of form, and human compassion came together to form an inner whole: "I was driven to go out and get to know the true face of the world. Our comfortable, satiated life blinded many people to the unbelievable deprivation beyond our borders."

From the early 1950s onwards, he traveled in the Middle and Far East (famine in Bihar). In 1953, he began what was intended to be a lengthy journey through the American subcontinent. He died near Trujillo when his off-road vehicle tumbled down an incline in the Peruvian Andes near Peña de Aguila.

2

Ernst Scheidegger (*1923)

Ernst Scheidegger is a photographer, painter, filmmaker, gallery owner, and publisher. Most importantly, he is the photographic face of the *Neue Zürcher Zeitung*, for which he worked as an influential and formative photo editor—or, more accurately, photographic impresario. He trained in Hans Finsler's photography class. He frequented the Paris studio of Alberto Giacometti not only as a photographer, but also as a friend. He created the best portraits of Giacometti, showing both the man and his work through the eyes of a friend, using barite paper and dispensing with the photographer's usual arsenal of flash, artificial lighting, and tripods: "pure reality" —animated photography born of a profound knowledge of human nature. As a photojournalist for the Magnum agency, he traveled throughout the Arab world as well as India and the Far East.

As an artist, his work brought him into contact with Fernand Léger, Cartier Bresson, Max Bill, Werner Bischof, Richard Paul Lohse, and Man Ray, compiling an impressive oeuvre. As the founder of Scheidegger & Spiess publishers, he is the "copublisher" of the present book.

3

René Groebli (*1927)

René Groebli has been dubbed the master of color. He caused a stir with his depictions of moods and movement, and especially with his experiments in color photography, where he explored and stretched the frontiers more colorfully than anyone before him. After a short period of training in the photography class of Hans Finsler, Groebli worked as a globetrotting photojournalist before directing a famous studio of advertising photography in Zurich.

In his exhibition *N.Y. Melancholia* at the Kunsthaus Zurich in 1999, he edited and concentrated early negatives from his New York years to create a coherent portfolio that was printed in a limited edition. Contrasted with symbolic photographs of burnt trees, this series becomes a ballad of life and death, a dirge for modern civilization. Other selected themes too document the photographer's dedicated quest for subjective expression and photo-

1

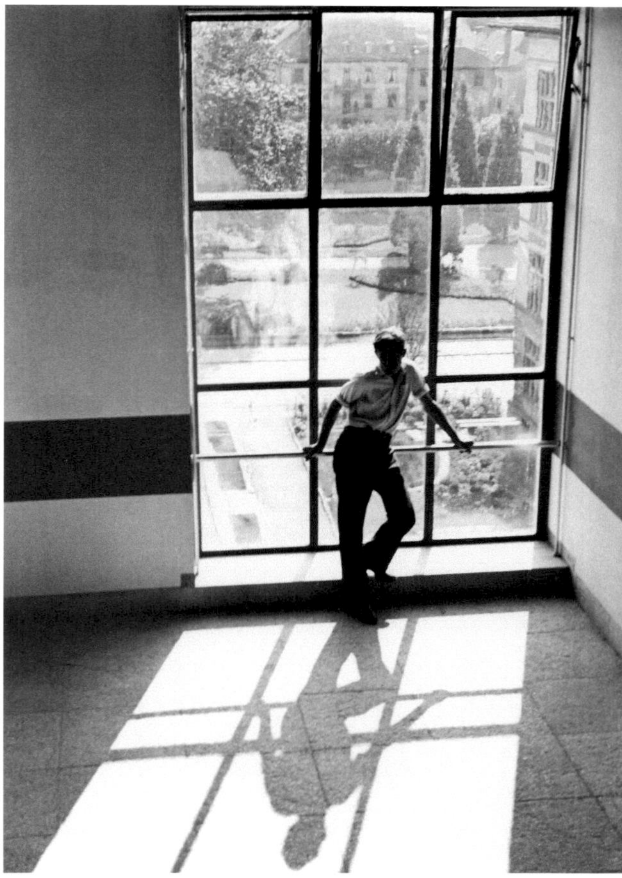

3

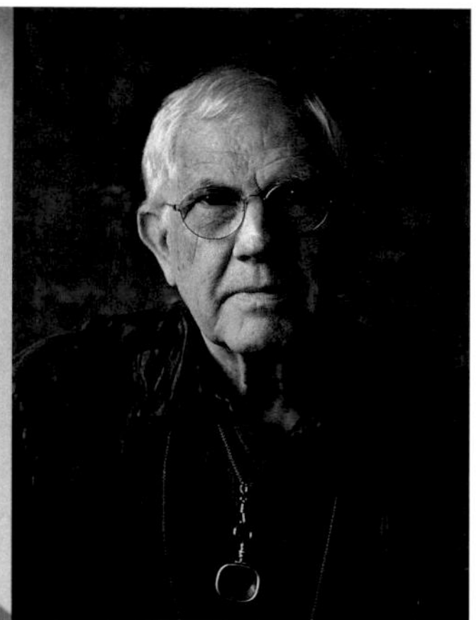

2

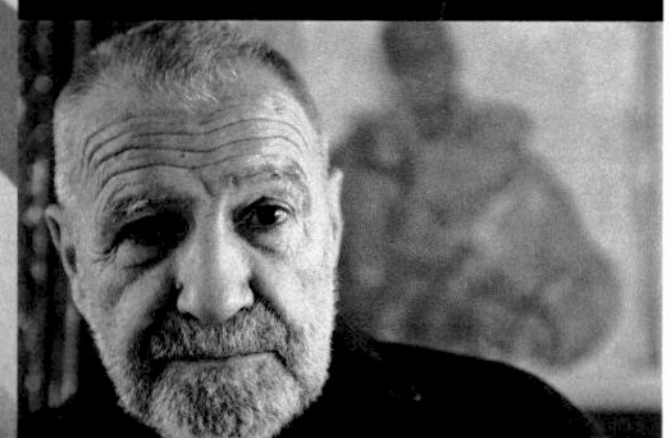

graphic poetry between monochrome and color, between movement and "still(nes)s," between reality and dreams, between magic and melancholy.

4

Peter Knapp (*1931)

His picture series entitled *Three Minutes of a Flag*, which was exhibited in 1964 at the regional Expo in Lausanne, has become an emblem of cosmopolitan Switzerland. The series celebrates the Swiss flag not out of chauvinism or patriotic motives, but out of a fascination with form and the changes of form exhibited by the white cross on its red background while the flag billows and creases Knapp's photography, however, cannot be reduced to this one masterpiece. Rather, his fashion photography has become the advanced gold standard of the genre for *tout le monde.*

Peter Knapp attended the graphic arts course from 1946–50 and later became art director of Galeries Lafayette. He has worked for all the most important fashion magazines, and especially for the fashion mogul Courrèges.

5

Walter Binder (*1931)

In 1948–1952, Binder studied with Hans Finsler in the legendary photo class. He first earned his spurs as the "court photographer" of the Museum of Applied Arts and Design, before succeeding Finsler in 1957. He directed the photography class, was a founding member and head of the Swiss Foundation of Photography. In this function, he organized important exhibitions, among them *Französische Fotografie 1840–1871* (French Photography 1840–71), and *Fotografie aus der Sowjetunion* (Photography from the Soviet Union). He also coedited the series *Schweizer Fotografie* (Swiss photography).

His real life's work is the Swiss Foundation of Photography in Winterthur. Emerging from a committed circle and beginning with the modest investment of 500 Swiss francs, Binder, collaborating with Roselina Burri-Bischof, among others, created a cultural institution without parallel. Through tireless work, this small, almost conspiratorial circle succeeded in creating a photographic "memory" which, together with the foundation's own exhibition galleries and the Winterthur Museum of Photography, has become a focus of national and international photography. The foundation is committed to the preservation, display, and broader presentation of photographic works. It maintains an archive and a collection which to date encompasses more than thirty artist's estates and around thirty thousand original prints by outstanding photographers, in particular those of Swiss provenance.

6

René Burri (*1933)

He is most frequently and laconically characterized as a "photographer of people." His portrait of Che Guevara smoking a cigar became the latter's trademark, and he shot his first celebrity portrait—of Winston Churchill—at the age of thirteen. What followed was a who's who of world celebrities: Eisenhower, Kennedy, Fidel Castro, Makarios, and Maria Callas. Photo series of Picasso, Le Corbusier, and the rest are indelibly imprinted in our minds as landmarks in the history of photography.

Burri, who trained in the legendary photography course of Hans Finsler and Alfred Willimann, soon created a pictorial cosmos of his own. He was more interested in people than in his teacher's eggs and coffee cups. There is barely any place in the world that he has not photographed. As a member of the world's most important agency, Magnum, he traveled tirelessly to the scenes of the events in the news, producing intense reports characterized by succinctness and excellence of photography. His Leica captured social upheavals and chronicles of everyday life alike.
A comprehensive retrospective was produced in 2005 in close cooper-

6

5
4
8

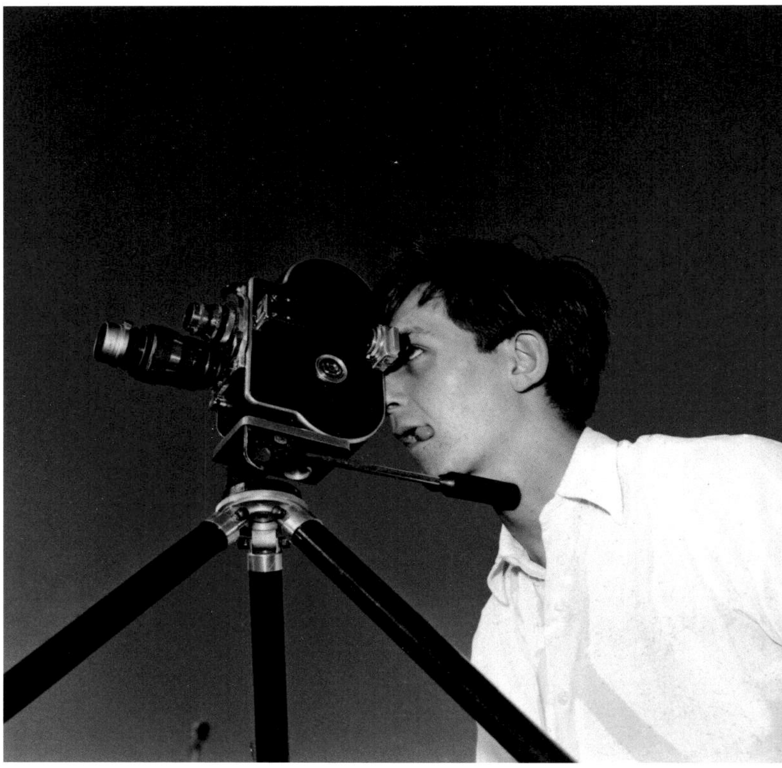
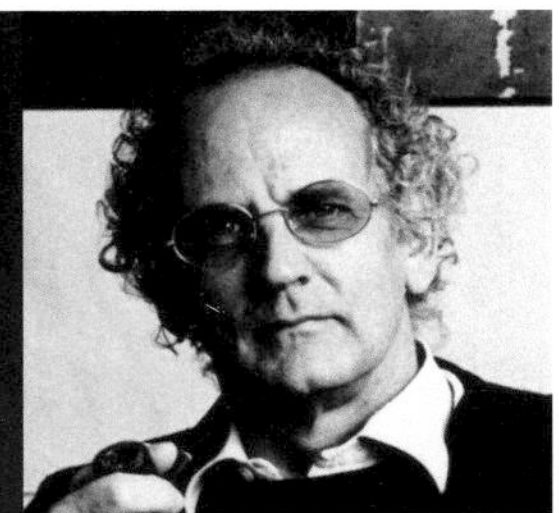
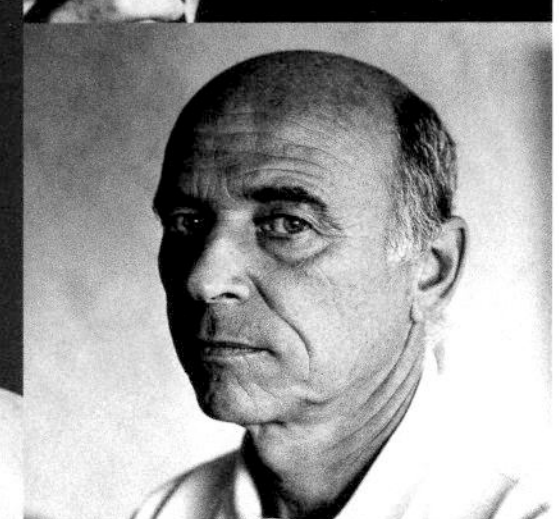
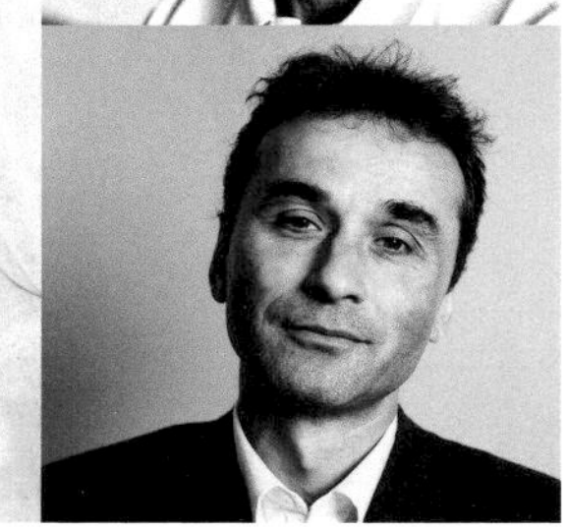

ation with René Burri at the Zurich Museum of Design.

Burri is one of the world's most important contemporary photographers.

7

Oliviero Toscani (*1942)

Oliviero Toscani is an *agent provocateur* who succeeded in moving from the street—with his Benetton posters—to the Haus der Kunst in Frankfurt. He studied photography and graphic arts at the School of Applied Arts from 1961–65 and then became one of the most sought-after commercial photographers of the present day. His portfolio includes photography for *Elle, Vogue, Uomo Vogue, Lei, Donne, Mademoiselle, Harper's*, and many more. His spectacular (and scandalous) advertising campaigns for Benetton caused great controversy all over the world.

While advertising in general aims to implant an awareness of its products by means of aesthetically pleasing images, Toscani the troublemaker prefers to use shock tactics, and sometimes shock therapy. He says that the purpose of these tactics is to make people think and to provoke discussions. And his portrayals of newborn babies covered in blood, dying Aids patients, war scenes with soldiers in tattered uniforms, and birds covered in tar certainly succeeded in doing just that. His declared philosophy is to use all the power of the advertising industry to make society aware of issues that are usually repressed. His strategy could be described as a paradoxical intervention in which advertising abandons beauty and the aesthetics of consumer products to instrumentalize the aesthetics of ugliness. Oliviero Toscani trained in the photography class of Walter Binder and Serge Stauffer. Stauffer's influence on Toscani appears to have been considerable.

8

Daniel Schwartz (*1955)

A graduate of the specialist photography course, Daniel Schwartz was a member of the Lookat photography agency (1996–2004) and is a regular contributor to the arts magazine *du*. In his work, Schwartz deals with "long durations." His art is informative, and his photojournalism does not simply respond to events, but rather identifies and pursues political developments and their social consequences over longer periods of time, in larger geographical areas, and in their historical contexts. His best-known works are *The Great Wall of China* (1991, revised edition 2001) and *The Perils, Profits, and Politics of Water in South and Southeast Asia* (1997). Two books on his work over the last ten years in Central Asia, Iran, Afghanistan, and Kashmir will be published in 2008. Schwarz has held many individual exhibitions (including in the Kunsthaus Zurich, 1986) and participated in numerous group exhibitions (including the Venice Biennale, 1993, and Encontros de Fotografia, Coimbra 2003). Schwartz lives in Zurich.

7

1a Werner Bischof, "St. Margrethen on the German/Swiss Border," 1945, shortly before the end of World War II

1b "St. Louis, Missouri, USA," 1953

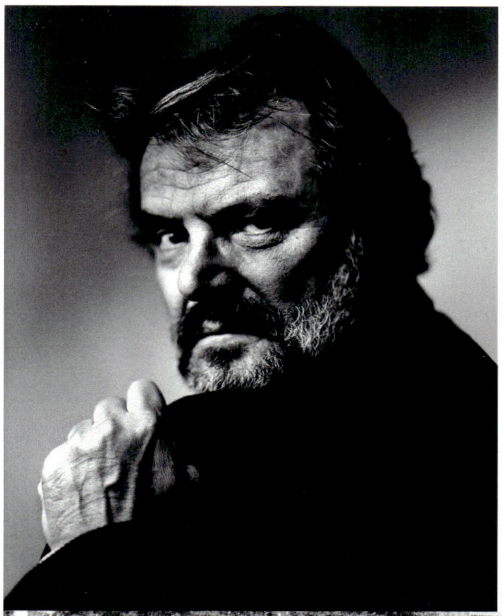

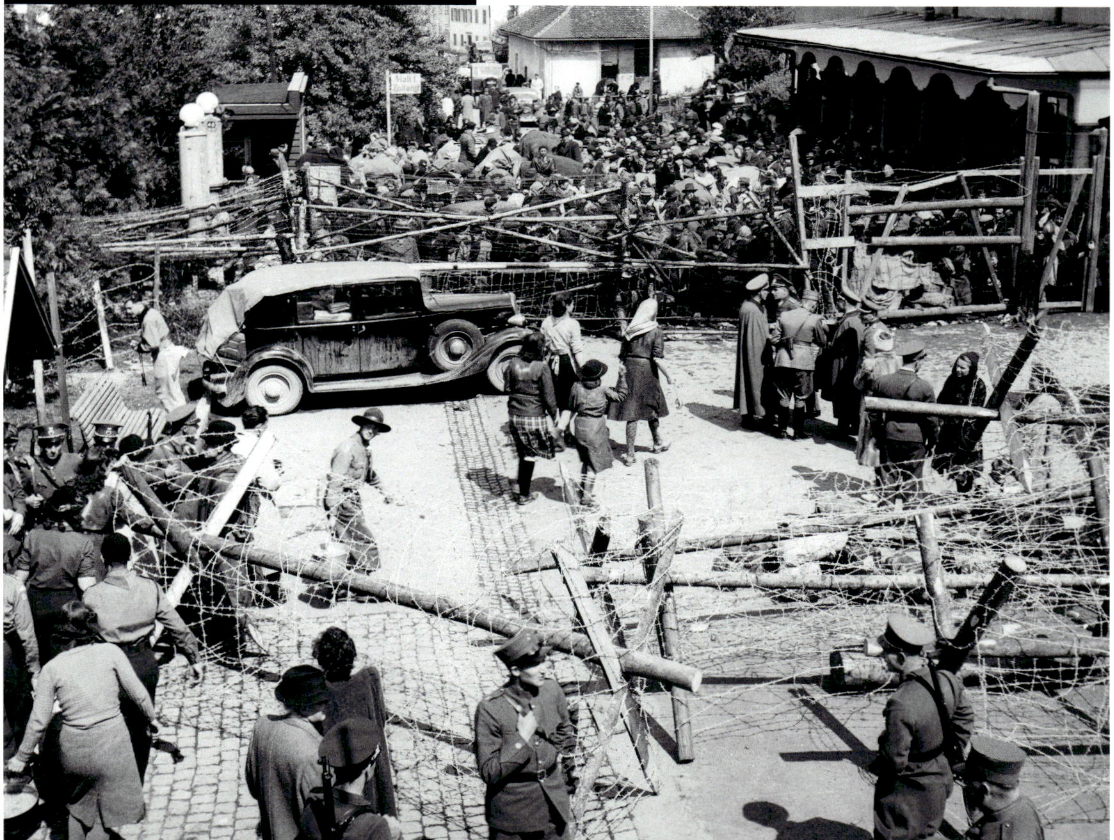

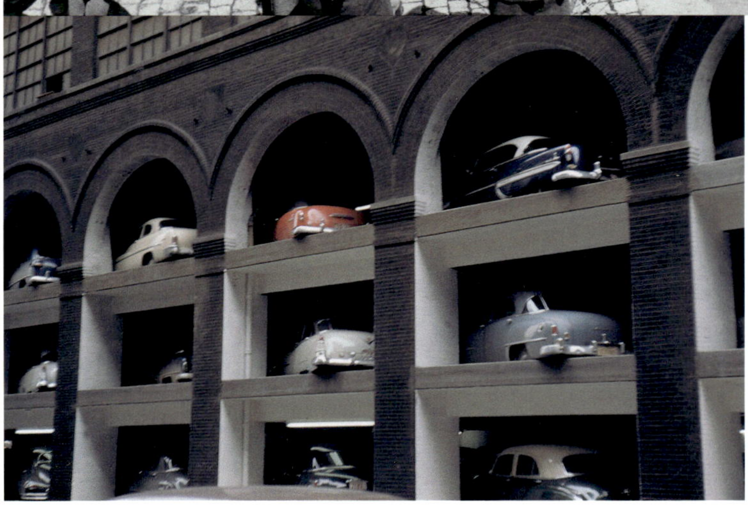

1c Werner Bischof, “Damodar Valley,” 1951/52 1d Cover of DU, no. 5, 1946
1e “Warsaw in Ruins,” 1948
1d “Mexico City,” 1954

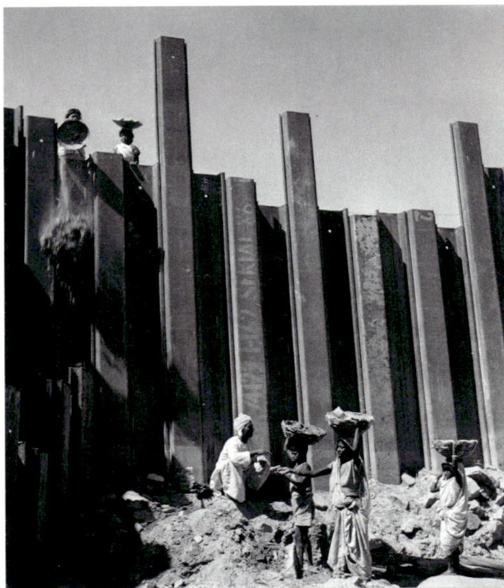

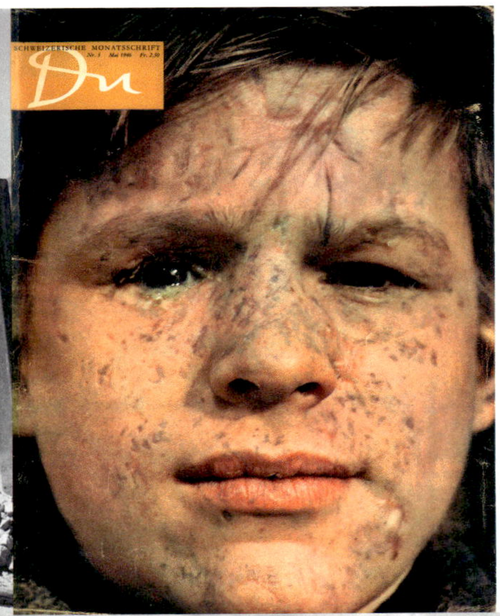

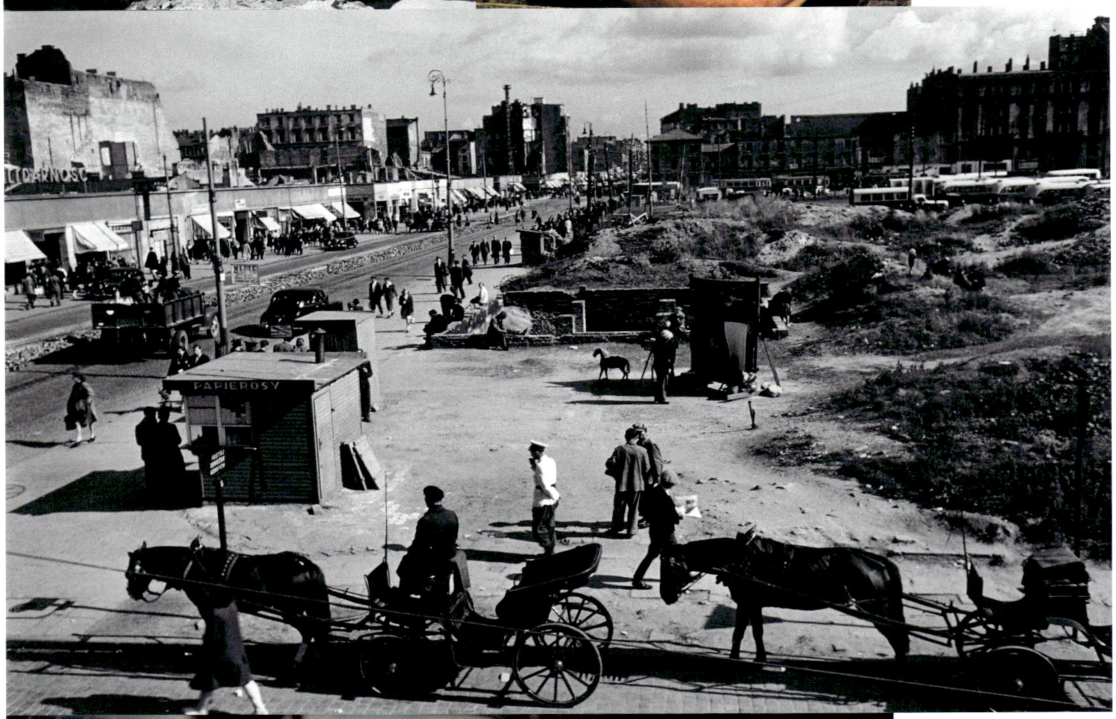

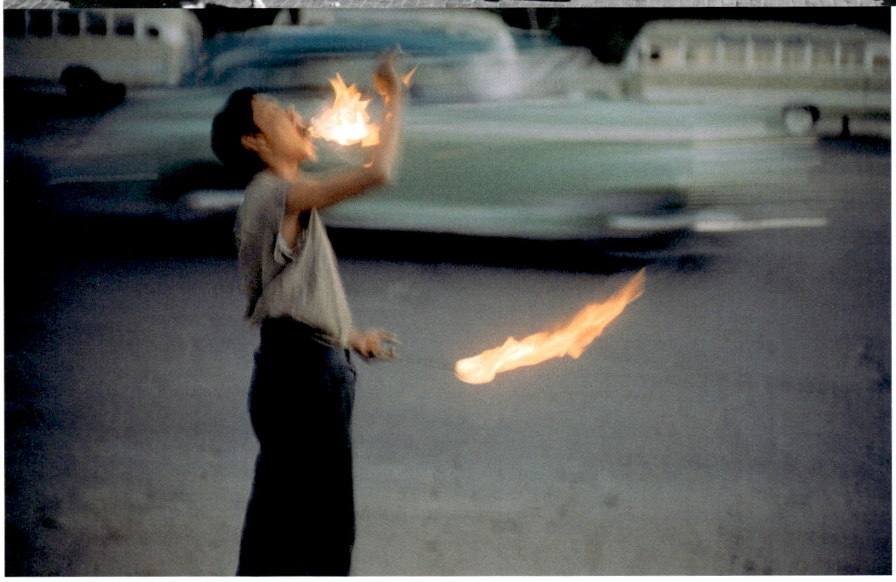

2a Ernst Scheidegger, “Alberto Giacometti in His Studio,” winter 1948/49

2b *Neue Zürcher Zeitung*, February 20, 1963 edition of the weekend supplement, of which Ernst Scheidegger was coeditor (1960–88)

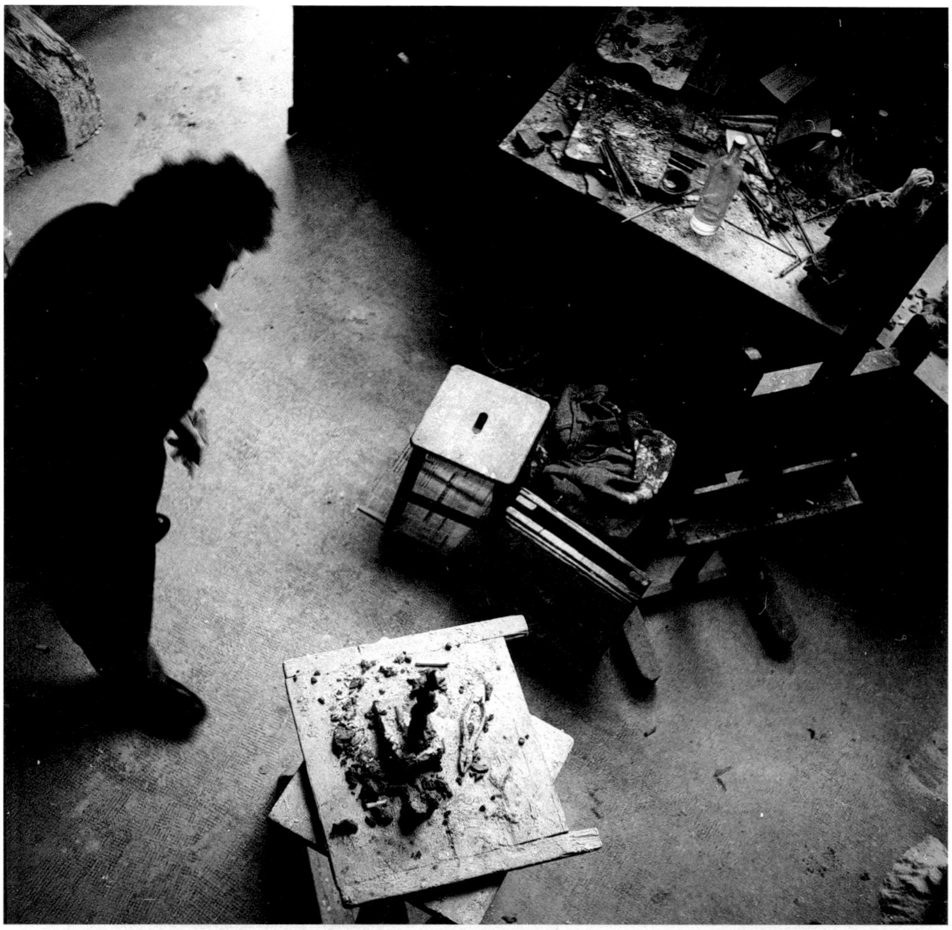

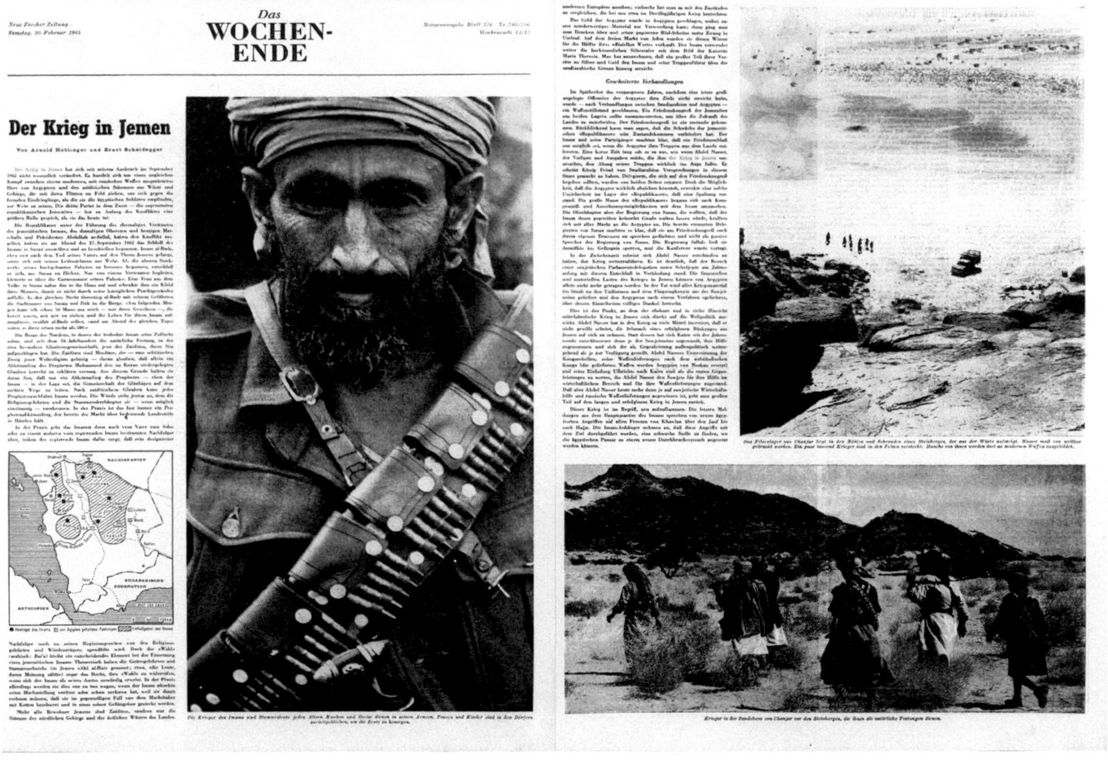

Neue Zürcher Zeitung
Samstag, 20. Februar 1963

Das
WOCHEN-
ENDE

Der Krieg in Jemen

Von Arnold Hottinger und Ernst Scheidegger

2c Ernst Scheidegger, “Aga Khan, Egypt,” ca. 1950
3a René Groebli, “Locusts in Eritrea,” 1952. Gelatin silver print
3b From *Magie der Schiene,* first edition, 1949. Gelatin silver print
3c/d In the 1950s René Groebli became famous as “master of color” for his experiments in color photography (1953–81).

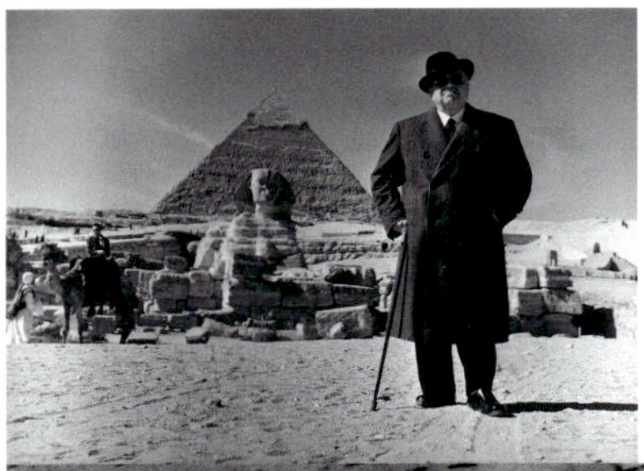

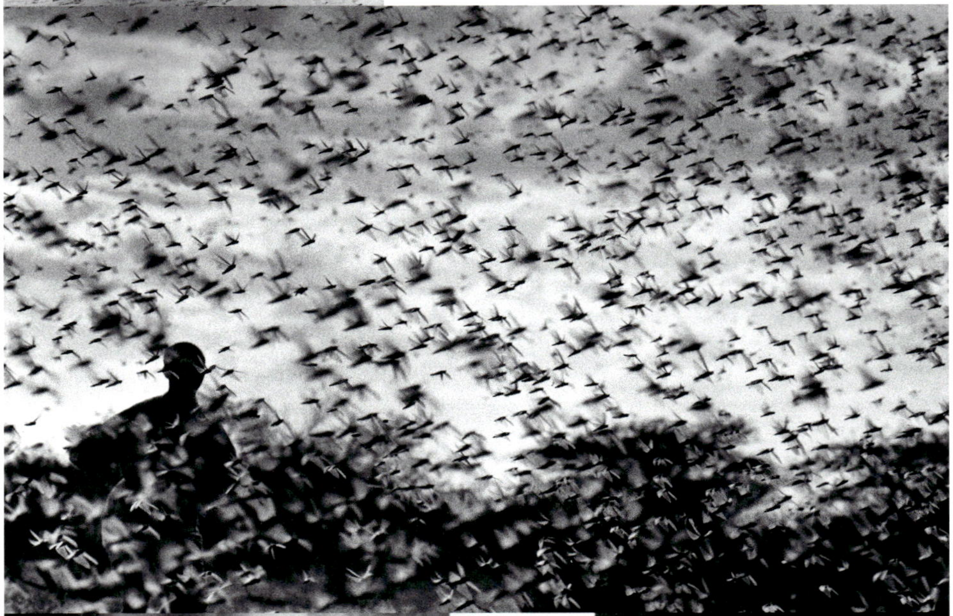

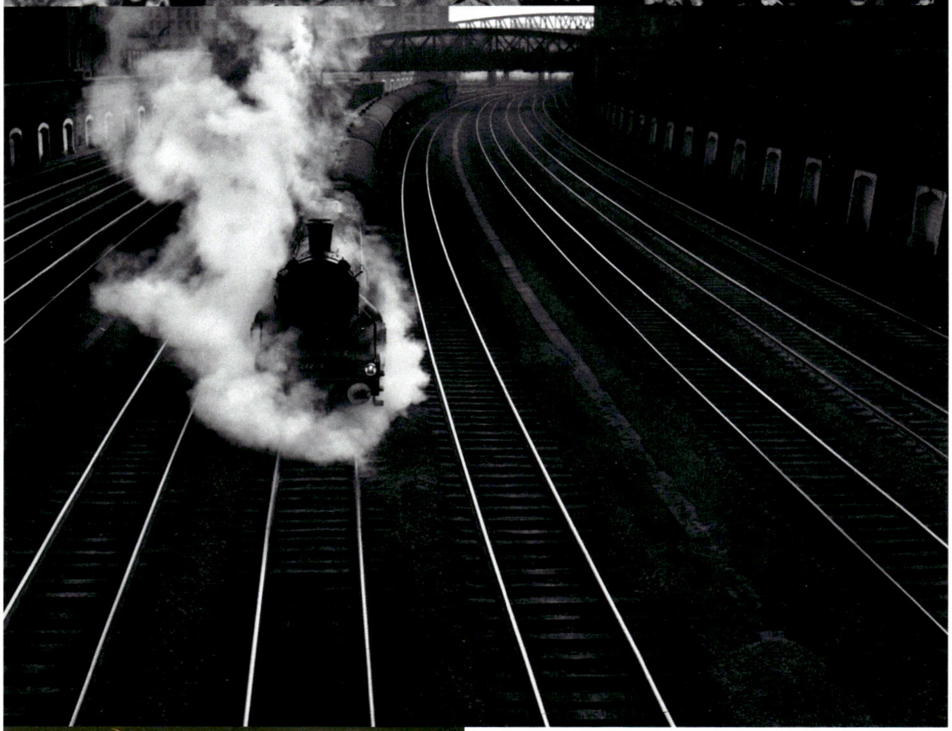

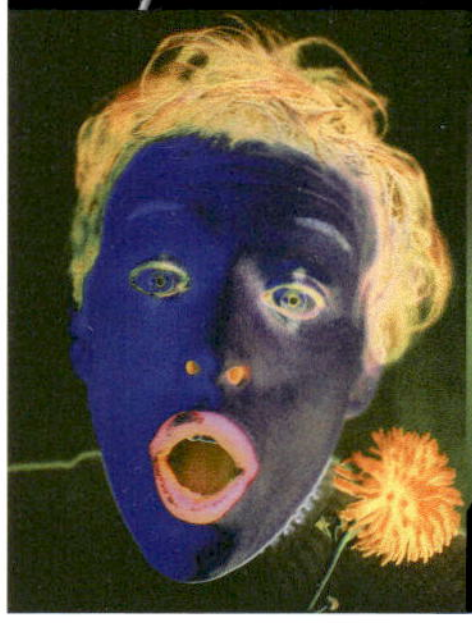

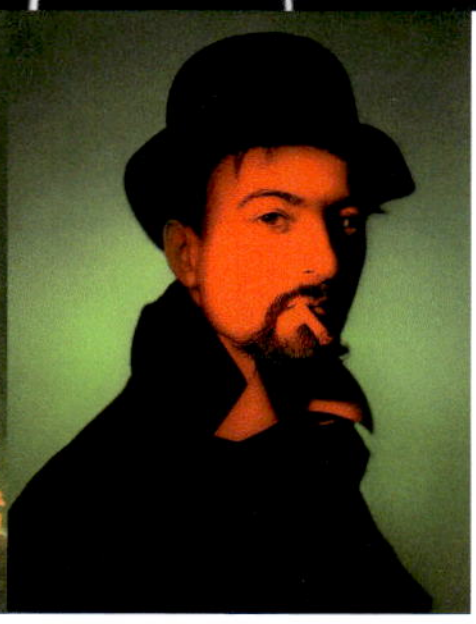

3e From René Groebli, *Das Auge der Liebe,* 1954, various editions. Gelatin silver print

3f From *Magie der Schiene,* 1949 edition

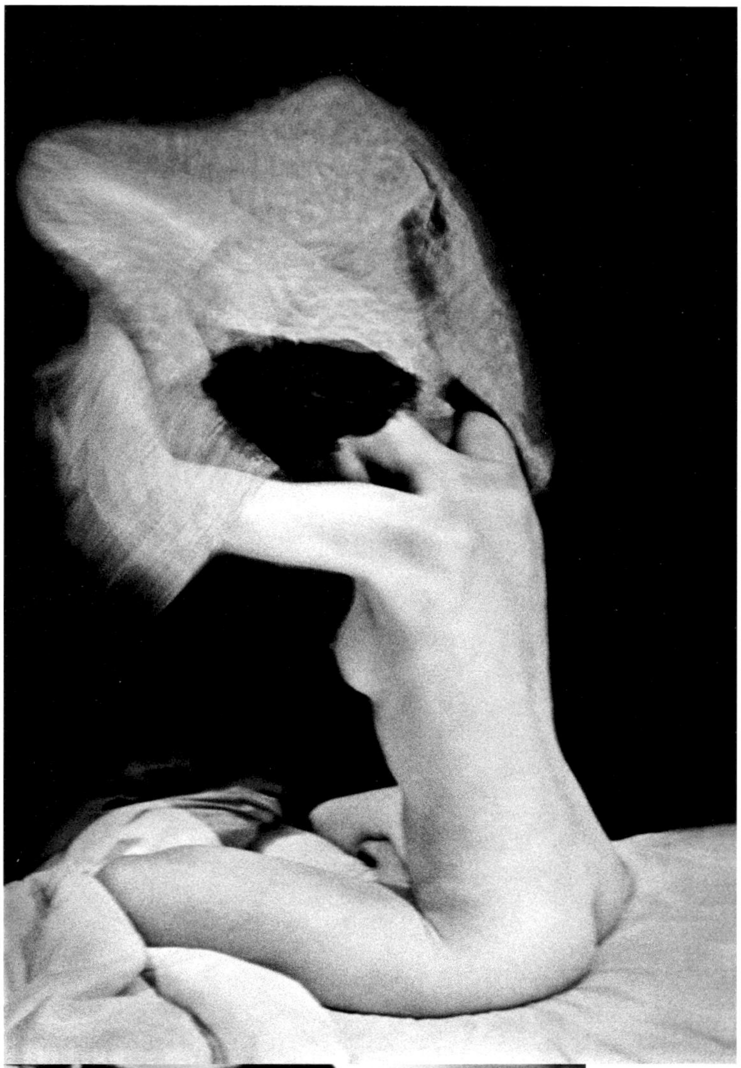

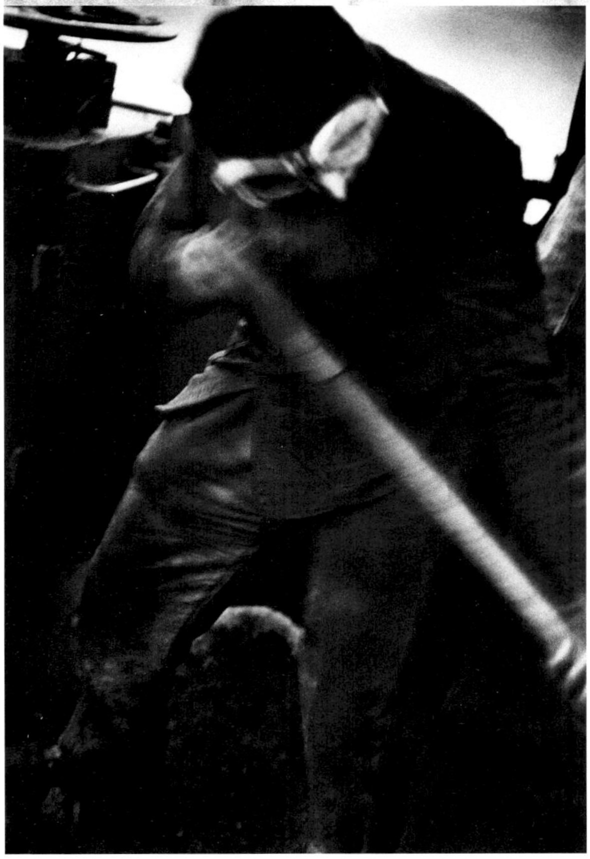

4a Peter Knapp, “Saki à Etretat,” 1980

4b Fashion photograph, 1978

4c “Rita.” Fashion by André Courrèges, Tokyo, 1967. Photographed for *Vogue*

5a “Der Höllensturz der Fotoklasse,” 1951. Collective work based on a concept by Serge Libiszewski/Alfred Willimann (hand resting on bust: Libiszewski [left] and Binder [right]; holding the camera: René Burri)

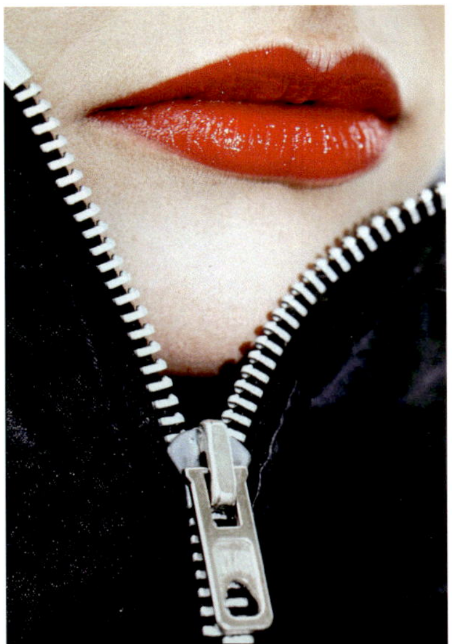

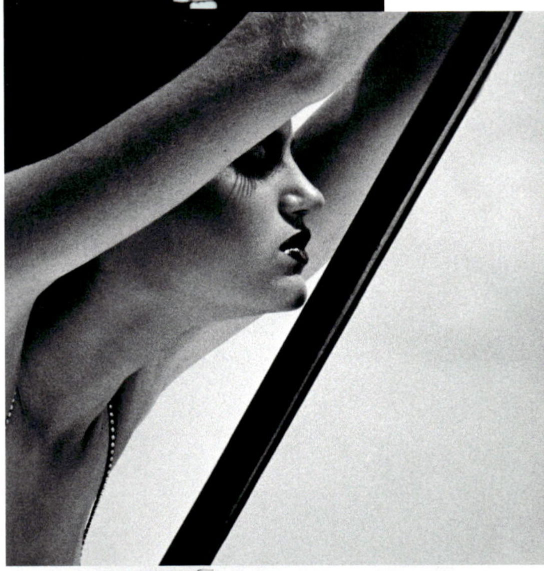

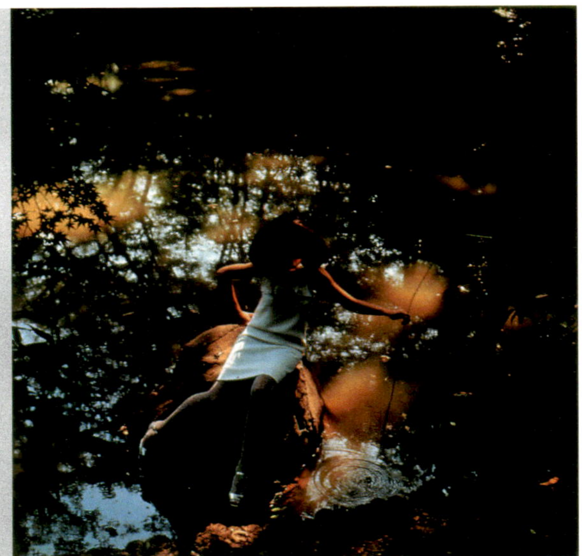

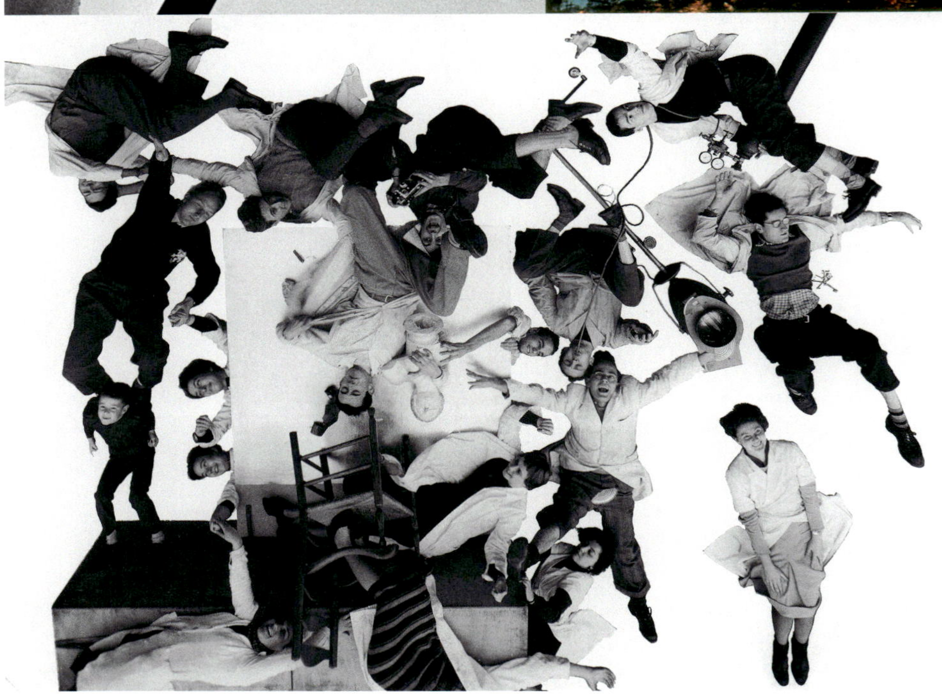

5b “Photography Class on the London Underground,” 1962. Wearing a necktie: Walter Binder; over his shoulder: Serge Stauffer; behind them: Hans Knuchel, Oliviero Toscani, and others. Photo Christian Gartmann (accidental developing error)

5c/d Zur Palme, commercial building. Architects HMS, Zurich, 1967. Photo Walter Binder

5e Hans Fischli, *Grosse Gruppe,* 1967. Sculpture at the entrance of Triemlispital. Photo Walter Binder

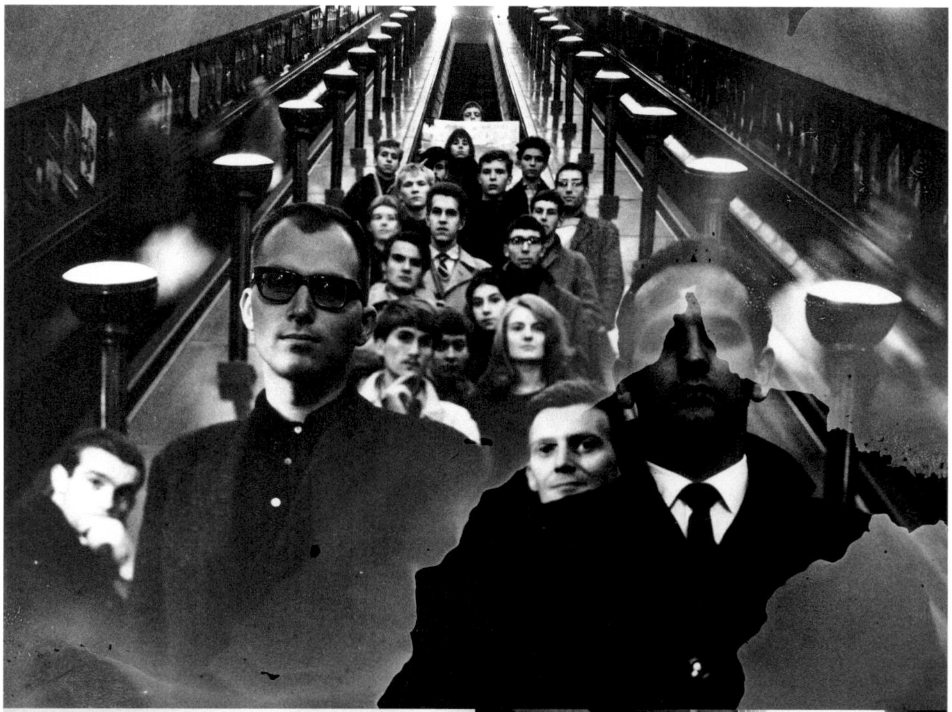

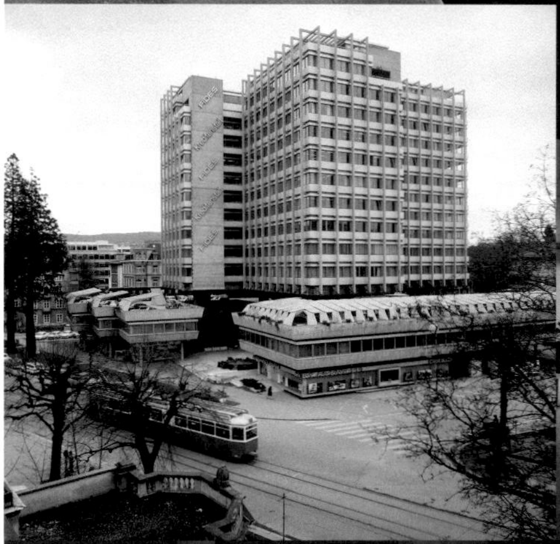

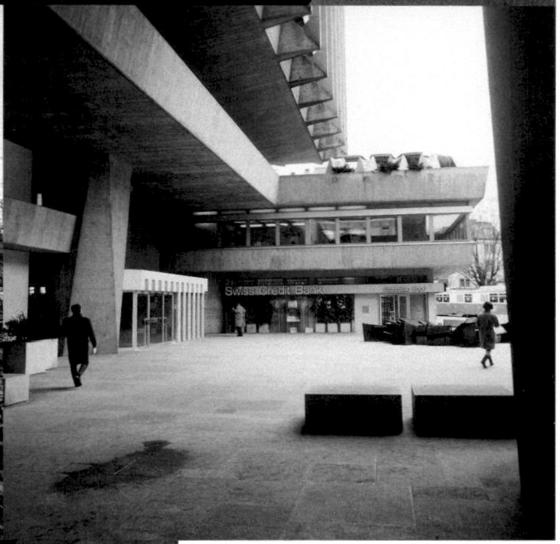

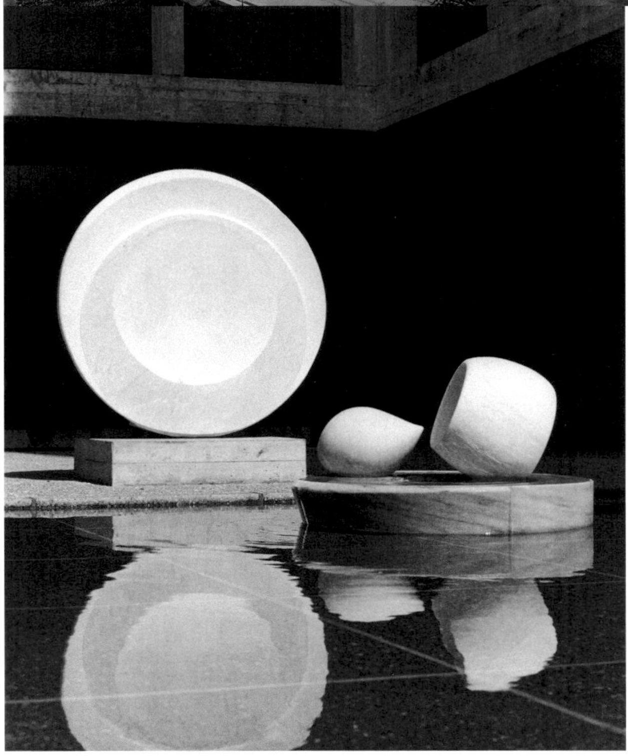

6a René Burri's first photo, taken when he was thirteen, showing British Prime Minister Winston Churchill when in Zurich during his *Europe Arise!* lecture series, 1946

6b "Ernesto 'Che' Guevara." From a series taken in his office in Havana, Cuba, 1963, when he was Minister of Industry (1961–65)

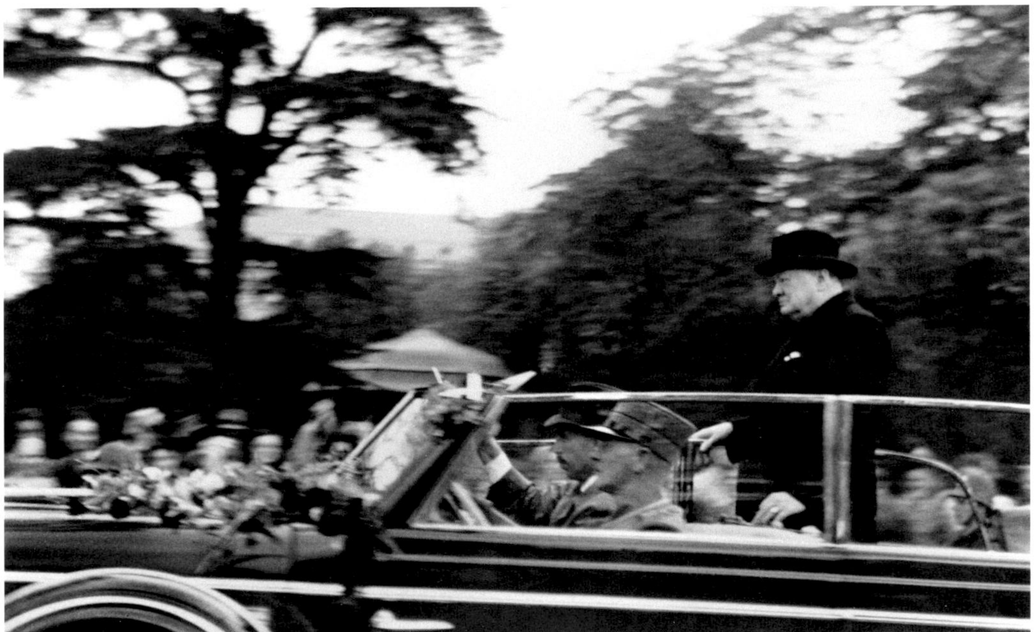

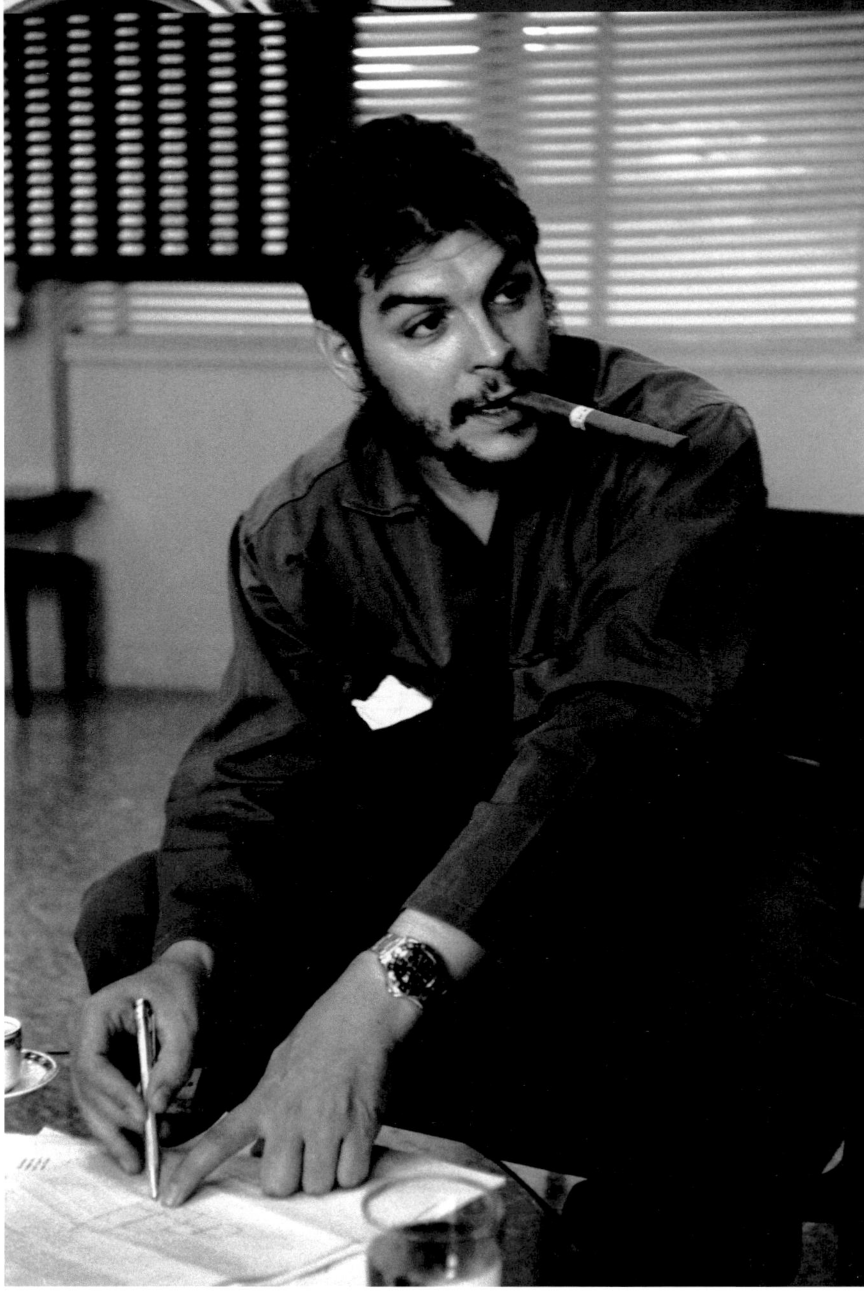

6c René Burri, "The Six-Day War." Taken after the destruction of all of Egypt's 536 tanks by Israeli Mirage fighter planes on Mitla Pass, Sinai, June 8, 1967

6d "Maria Callas," Pennsylvania, USA, 1959. On the right, conductor Eugene Ormandy; on the left, journalist Elsa Maxwell

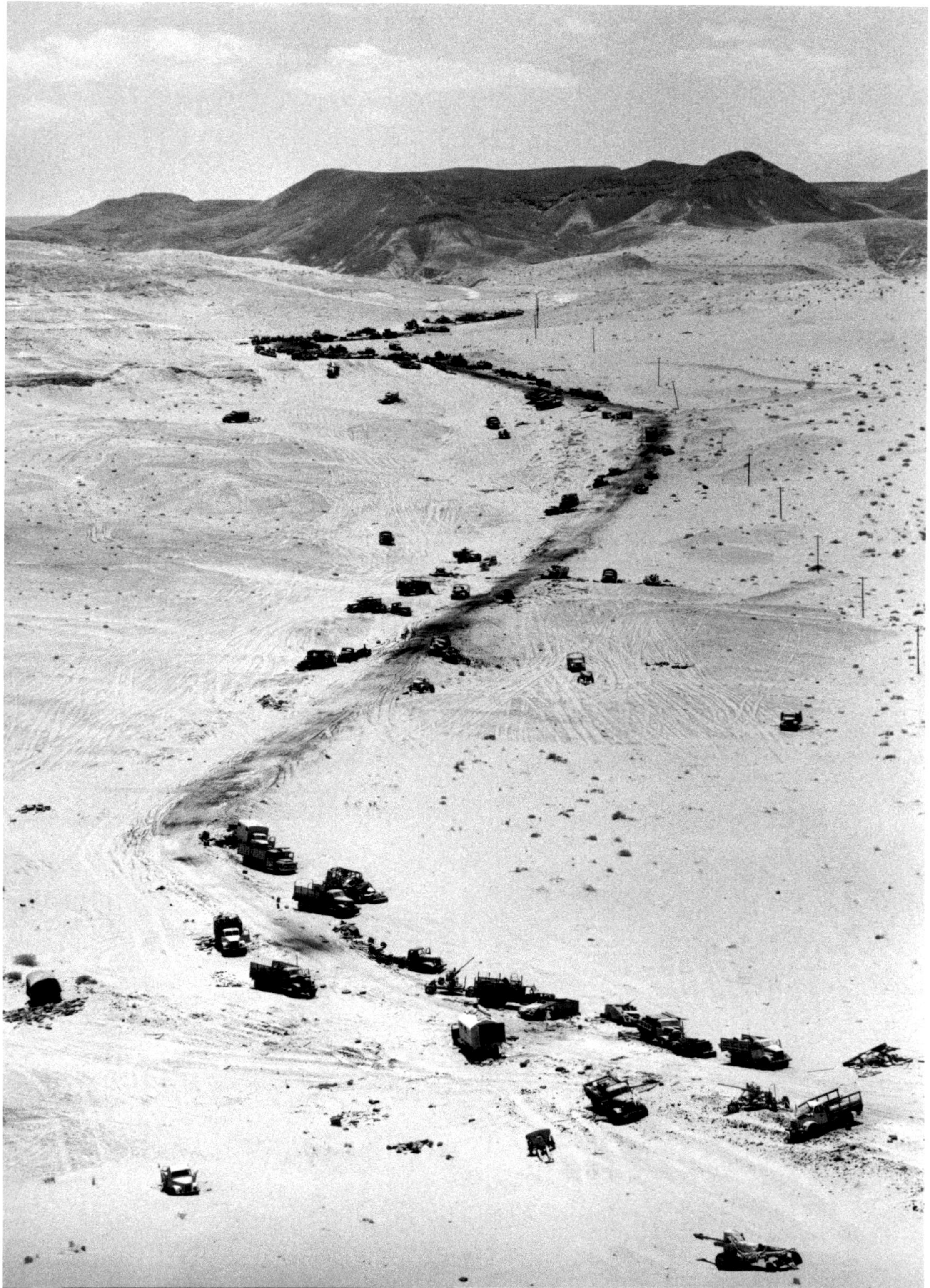

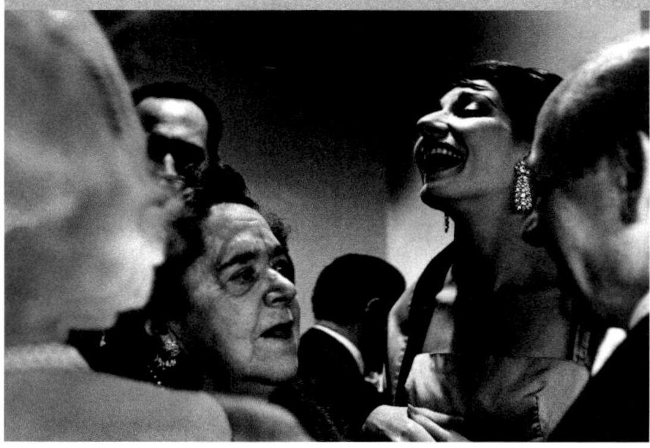

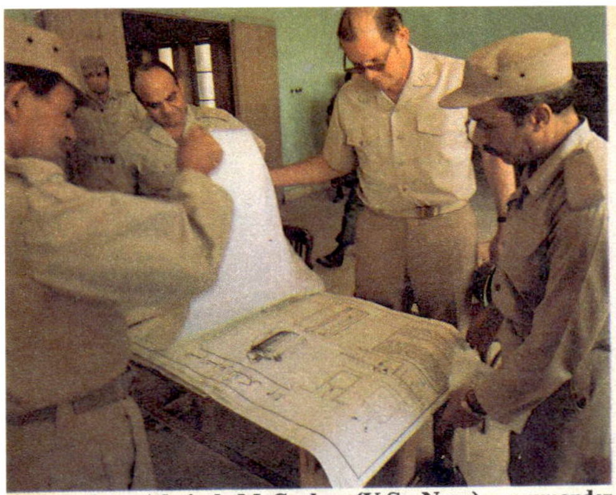

Rear-Admiral McCauley (U.S. Navy), commander of the Mine Warfare Force, looks at details of mines

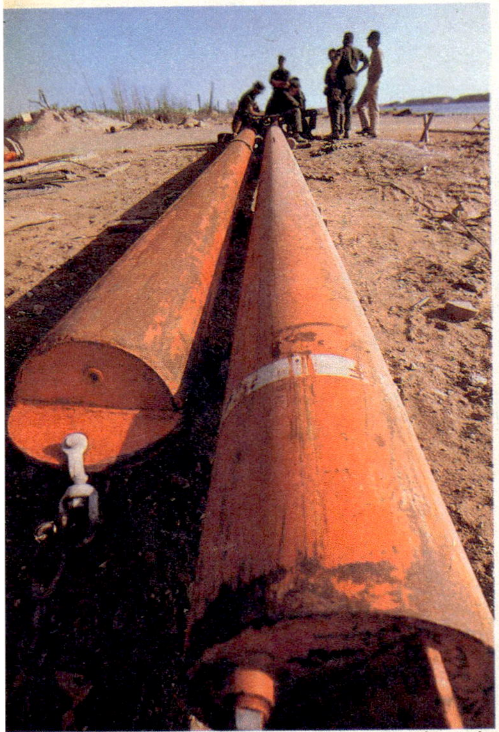

Above: mine-sweeping rods. Below: Egyptian units clear an Israeli-built causeway. Right: thousands of salvaged mines, piled up with 4000lb. of TNT, are detonated by McCauley (left) and Egyptian troops

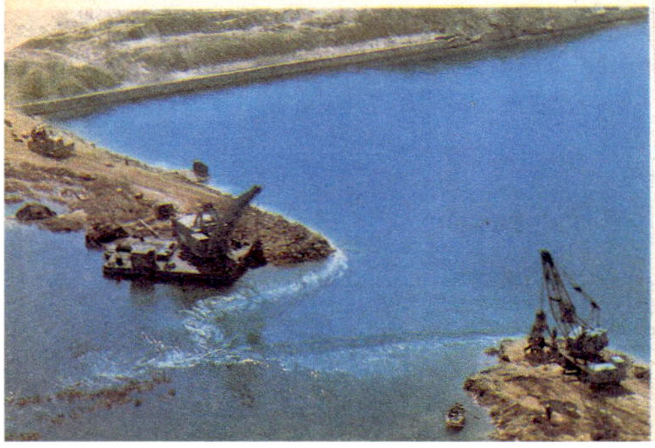

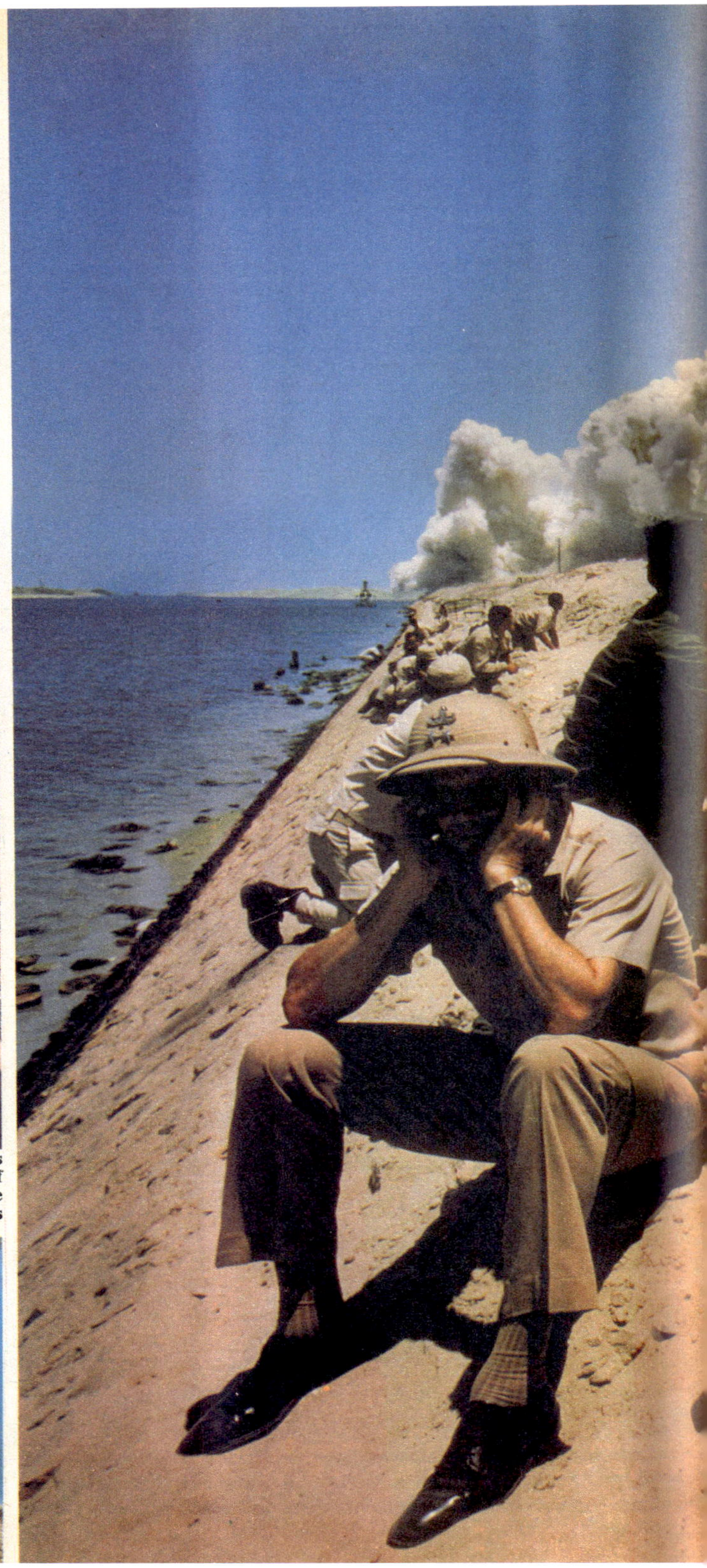

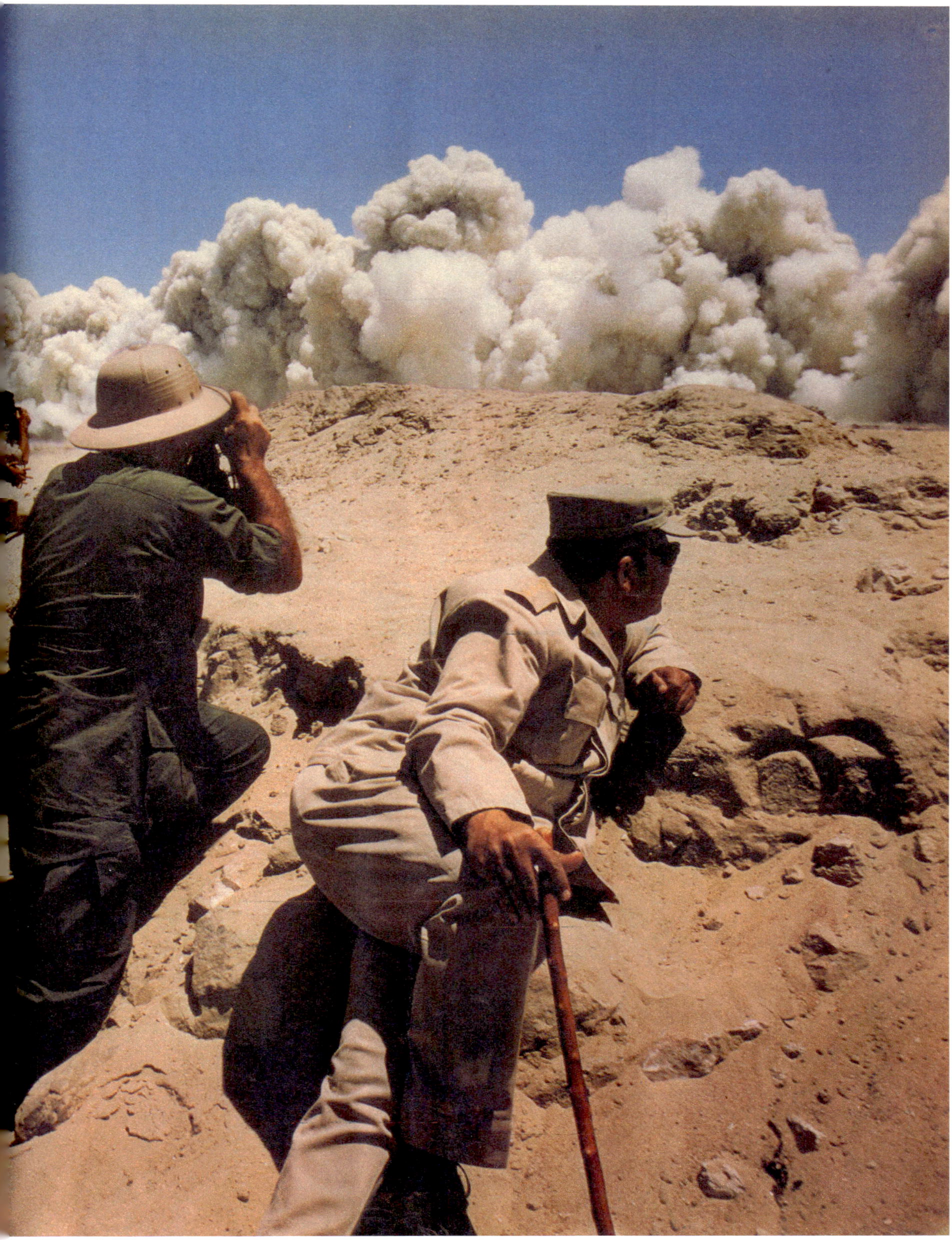

6f René Burri, “Space Museum,” Washington D. C., USA

7a Photo of dying AIDS activist David Kirby taken by Therese Frare for LIFE, 1990, and used by Oliviero Toscani for a 1992 fashion ad campaign

7b From the EPOCA Reportage on Somalia, 1993. Photo Oliviero Toscani

7c Fashion ad campaign, 1992

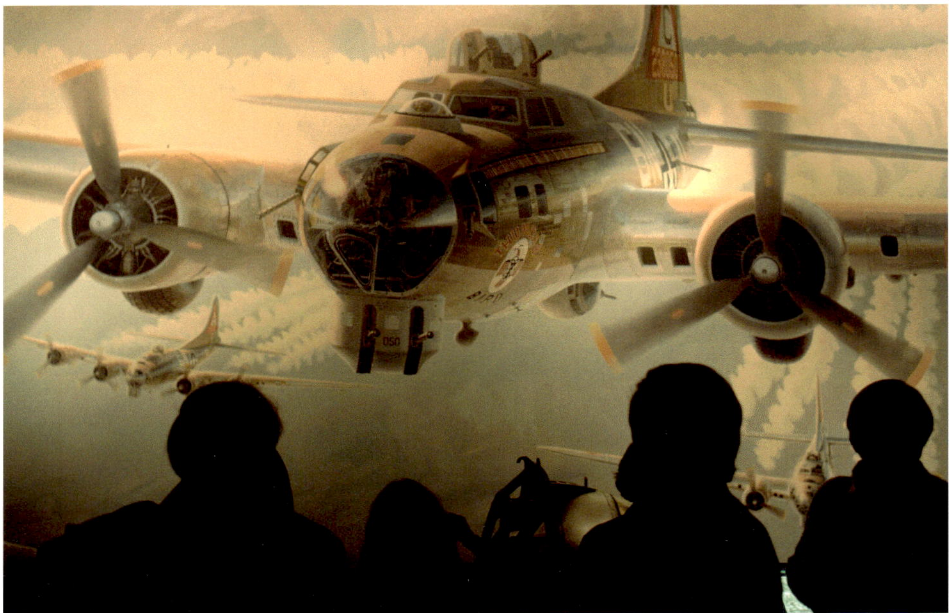

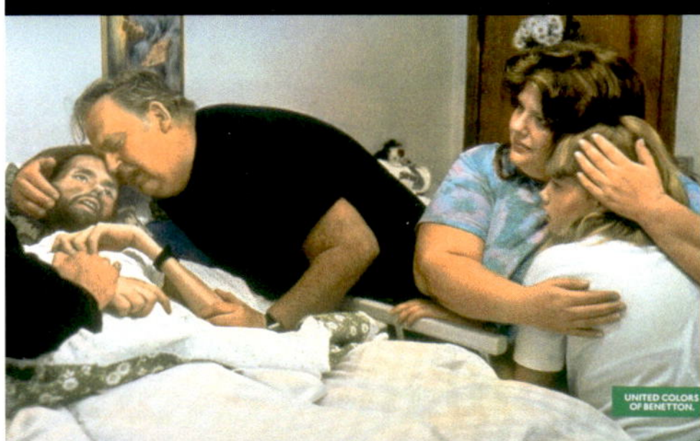

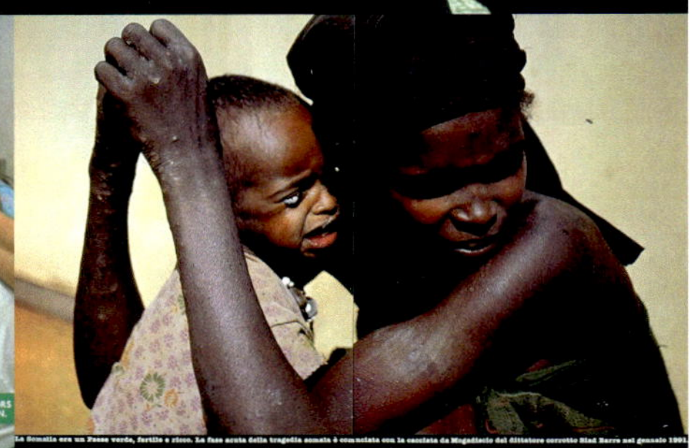

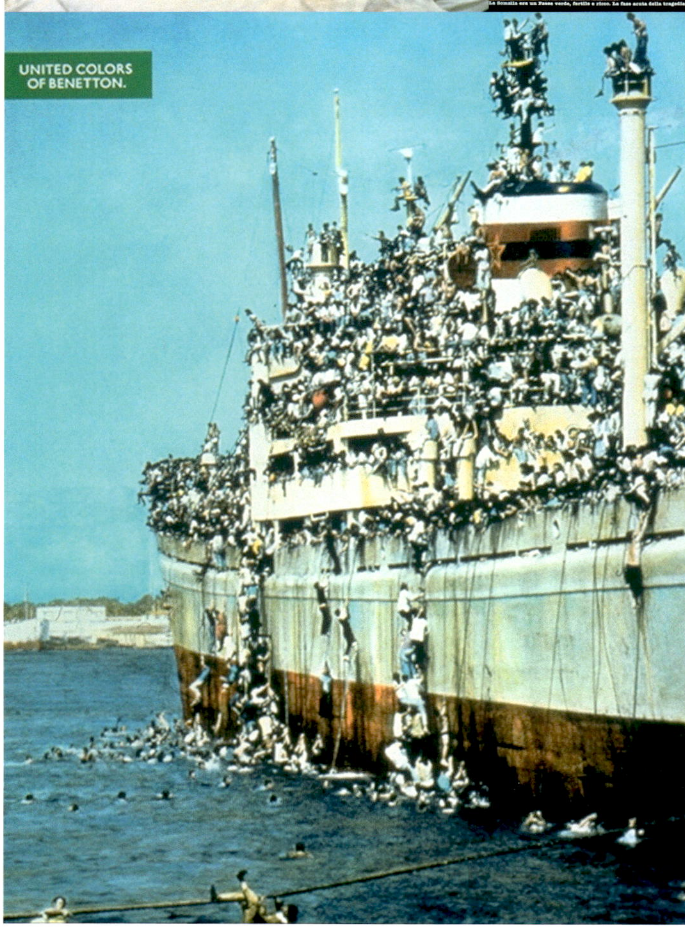

8a Daniel Schwartz, "Market in Osh," Kyrgyzstan, 2004
8b "Erection of a Billboard," Ho-Chi-Minh-City, Vietnam, 2001

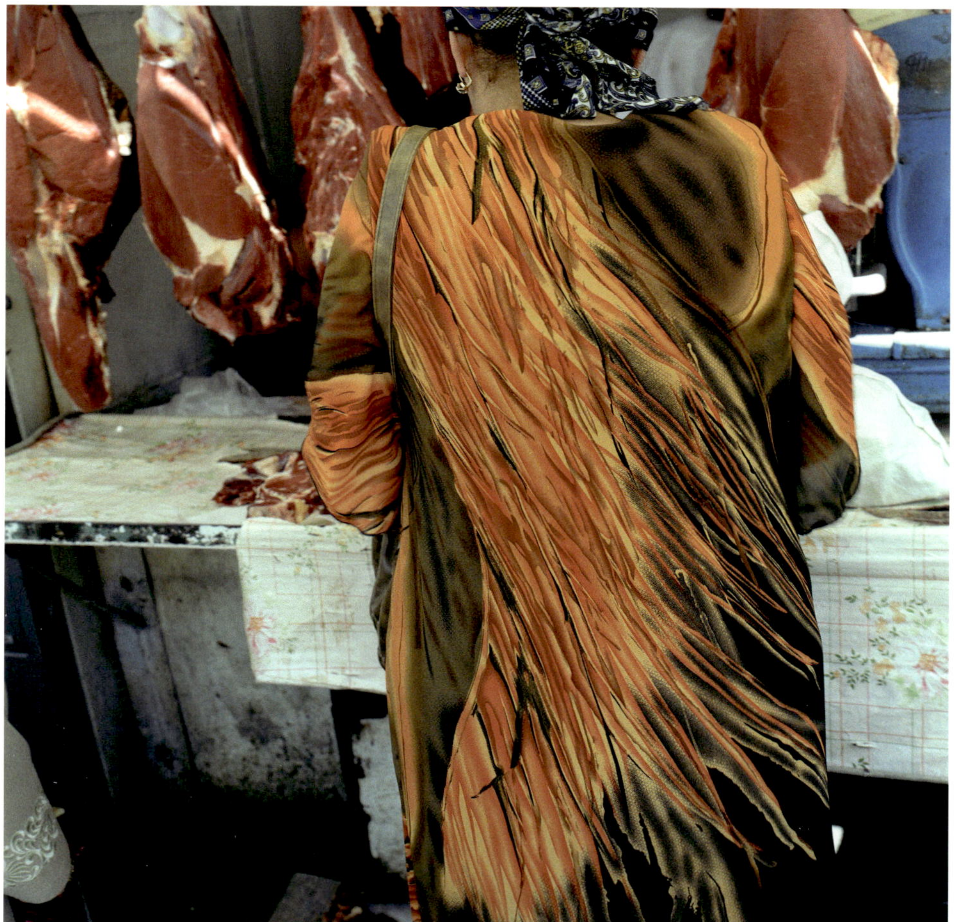

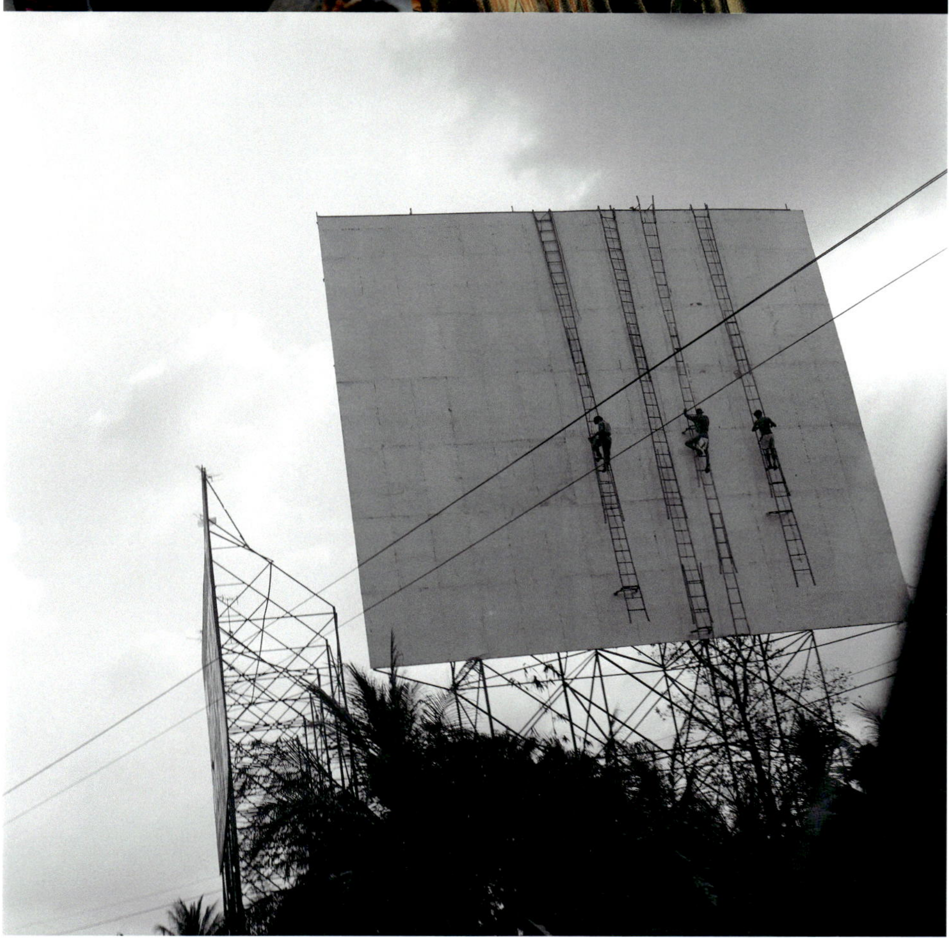

Their materials are wood, metal, plastic, porcelain, glass, fabric, which they translate into objects and products of everyday use. They are "materialists" in neither the philosophical nor the ethical senses of the term. They strive neither toward basic epistemological principles nor toward material possession. Instead, they design the "interspace" that resides between us and our environment, between us and the worlds of objects and symbols. They combat the dysfunctional, the insincere, and the obsolete traits of our artefactual world. They design the most immediate expressions of our culture: now aesthetic, now playful, but always inspired by the desire to explore, by powers of renewal: thinking and forming for the sake of accomplishing the idea, of necessity, constructive, technicist, innovative.

He developed, among other things, a "bachelor machine," a studio apartment of maximal functionality 1; his chairs are well-used and ubiquitous inventions 2; his objects are brilliant marriages of aesthetics and technology 3; her fabric creations interweave aesthetics with functionality, and her teaching activities generated a baroque multiplicity of textile expressions 4; his design creations are hip, oscillating between art and design 5.

1

Wilhelm Kienzle (1886–1958)

In 1916, Kienzle became head of the newly-established class in interior architecture in the Department of Applied Arts at the Zurich School of Applied Arts. He was one of Switzerland's first industrial designers, and was responsible, among others, for a model for a one-room bachelor's apartment; a legendary, easily disassembled bookcase (that has been re-released recently); and above all for his cactus watering can, whose striking, brightly colored form still graces many design-conscious residences. Today, Kienzle's motto might be revised as "reduce to the max," that is to say, the maximum reduction of materials combined with maximum functionality and variety = good form at its purest. The surface of the base of his watering can, for example, is oval = space saving; the handle is raised = perfect equilibrium when watering; the spout = precise guidance of the water stream; the can as a whole = charming object, a strange bird in the vicinity of the cactuses. Kienzle is the ultimate designer of classical modernism. Good form: made in Switzerland.

2

Willy Guhl (1915–2004)

Willy Guhl's medium was the chair. His Schleife (Loop) garden chair is now fifty years old. Quintessentially modernist, it was originally made of fiber cement. After being maligned for its asbestos content, it was redesigned in 1997, and today's asbestos-free version continues to adorn countless public facilities and private gardens. Willy Guhl was the doyen of Swiss design instruction, a man who achieved worldwide recognition, and whose works are exhibited in the Olympia of art and design, New York's Museum of Modern Art. He designed the first plastic bucket chair in Europe. Back then, he was in competition with one of the most renowned designers worldwide, the American Charles Eames (1907–78). Unlike Guhl, Eames had access to the relevant production conditions.

As a teacher of hundreds of interior architects and designers, he was the most influential designer of his generation. Willy Guhl's credo could hardly be illustrated better than through one of his own statements: "First, praise and take joy in the drawing (a chair design) you see before you. Then ask yourself: What is hidden behind it? What kind of a joint is that? What kind of a wooden segment? Investigate the construction point by point and examine its intended application. Who is going to sit there? And if it flops, there remains one advantage, namely that wood burns—especially birchwood, which doesn't give off sparks."

3

Franco Clivio (*1942)

His designer portfolio contains names such as Lamy, Gardena, ERCO, Rodenstock, Siemens, all firms whose corporate cultures prioritize superior design. He draws his design philosophy, his competence, and his creativity from his cabinet of curiosities, which, in its selectivity and excellence, is itself an expression of intelligent design. It is a museum of good form, of ingenious technique, handicraft skill, and adequate materiality, assembled globally at flea markets, junk shops, and warehouses—wherever everyday products and objects can be found. "Many people go to the market at seven o'clock in the morning, but I often go around three in the afternoon. The things I search for are always there." This different point of view constitutes the charm of his collection, an accumulation of curiosities, marvels, a cabinet of rarities composed of dead objects that come to life and become instructive design exemplars the moment Clivio takes them in his hands and holds forth—swept up in fascination and enthusiasm—on their forms, functions, constructions, materialization, haptic qualities, and ergonomics. His students profit im-

1
3
2
4
5

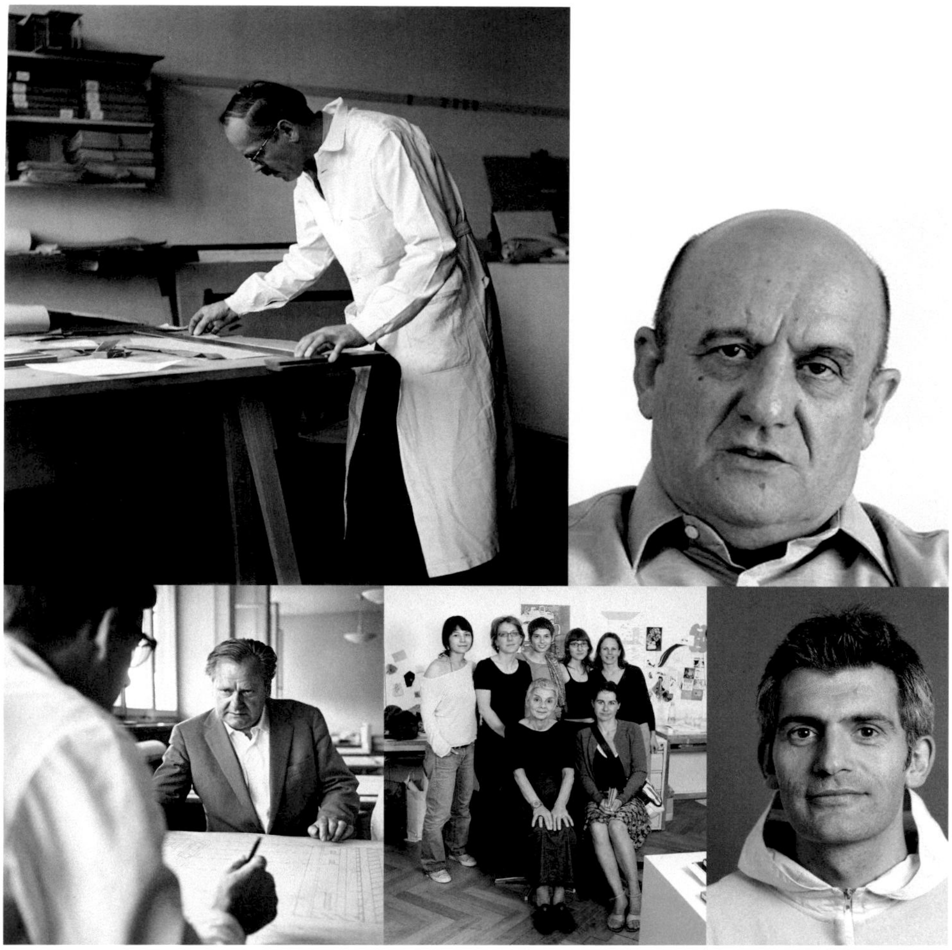

measurably from his collecting zeal and from the best possible illustrative material—always accompanied by his brilliant commentary.

Clivio was an instructor and head of the industrial design program at the School of Art and Design Zurich.

4

Bärbel Birkelbach (*1943)

With almost every fiber of her being she created a textiles culture that was not to be based on free-floating authorship, but was rather fully interwoven with progressive everyday culture. The catalogue to the *Tuchfühlung* exhibition in the Museum for Design in Zurich remains valid as her legacy—with its own vocabulary of textile design, and her uniquely "knitted" educational principles. She took a great interest in theory from an early stage, establishing important principles and transferring content into form. The result was cloth creations in velvet, silk, felt, metal: embroidered, crocheted, knitted, interwoven: flat, iridescent, shiny, glistening, abstract, figurative, tufted, plush, impudent, stolid, noble, or bold and cheeky, and over and again powerfully surprising.

In 1998 the threadbare and completely frustrating decision was made to close the Textiles Department in Zurich and substitute a link-up with Lucerne. Right to the end she brought her "weavers" to their explosive graduations. Piles of promotional prizes are the proof. She was the influential director of the Textiles Department at the School of Art and Design Zurich for many years. She freelanced for renowned companies, curated exhibitions such as *Tuchfühlung*, and *Verner Panton* and sat on national and international juries.

5

Alfredo Häberli (*1964)

He is sometimes labeled the "Swiss Philippe Starck," and it is not certain whether that suits him or bothers him. Häberli is a designer of objects that leave their mark on our world. They have style, a cultivated, precise, and functional formal language—as is appropriate for a Swiss designer. The Spanish element in his first name—the o in Alfredo—harkens, however, to his Argentinean origins and is possibly the key to the elegance and temperament of his designs. His trademark is stylistic certainty: the remarkable balance between redundancy and innovation, with a stronger pull toward the latter, and cultivated materialization, derived from innumerable experiments with materials, nuanced coloration, and a keen eye for detail.

In his book *Design Live*, published by Birkhäuser Verlag (2007), there is a perfect summary of his views on design: "The difference between right and really good is beautiful."

Alfredo Häberli graduated from the Department of Industrial and Product Design.

1a Wilhelm Kienzle's interior design class: model-building lesson using the example of Aalto's cantilever chair, ca. 1948

1b *Das Neue Heim,* 2nd exhibition, 1928, Museum of Applied Arts and Design Zurich. Exhibition design by Wilhelm Kienzle

1c/d Heating device, design 1934, Therma AG; shoe cabinet, design 1951, Blattmann Metallwarenfabrik AG, MEWA Wädenswil

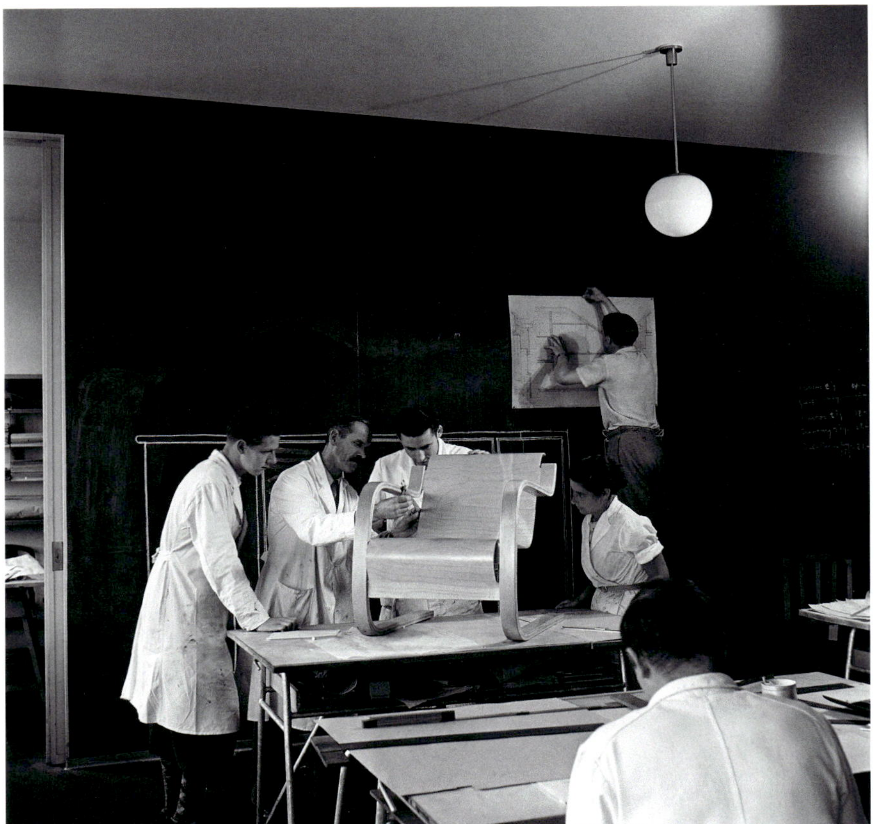

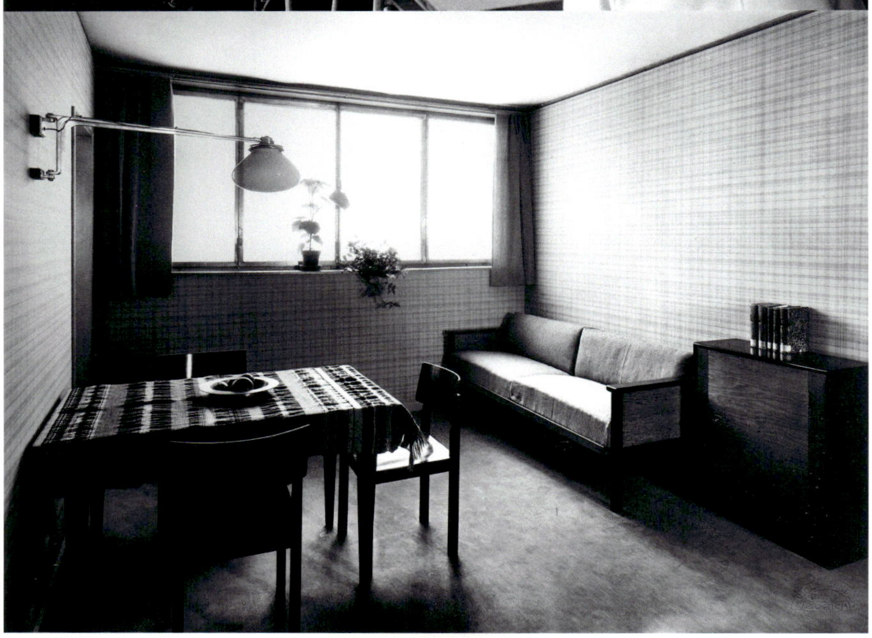

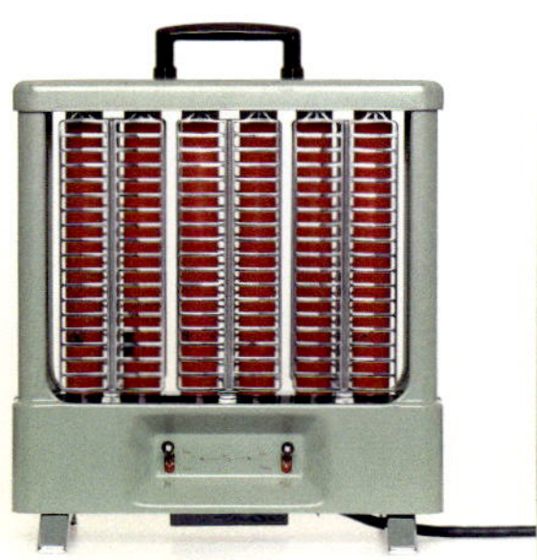

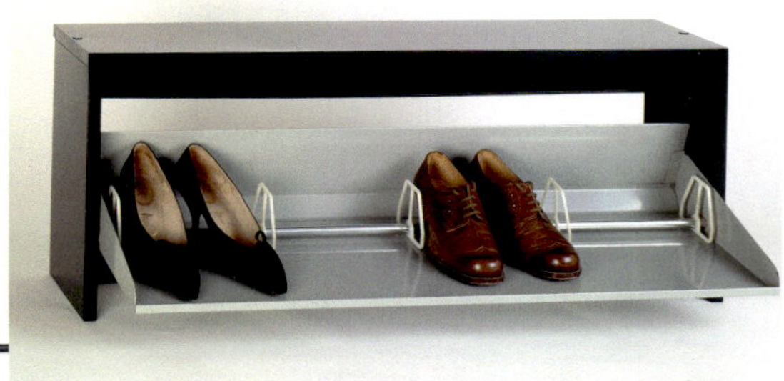

1e/f Cactus Watering Can, design 1935, MEWA Wädenswil; Kienzle Bookcase, design 1930, model 132, Embru-Werke Rüti **1g** Wilhelm Kienzle teaching interior design, ca. 1948
1h Poster for the sixth exhibition in a series on Swiss design pioneers at the Museum of Design Zurich, 1991. Design Jürg Brühlmann

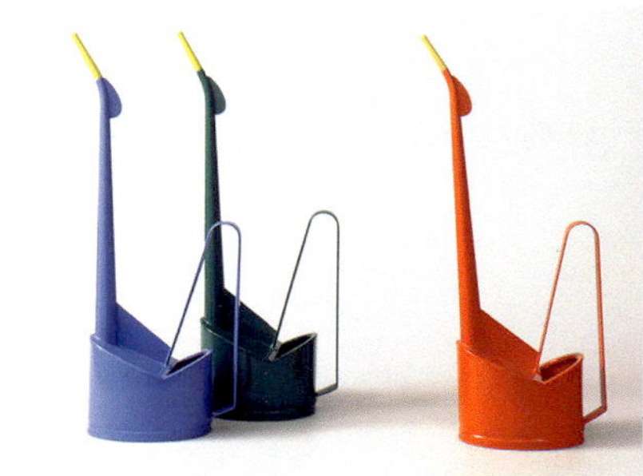

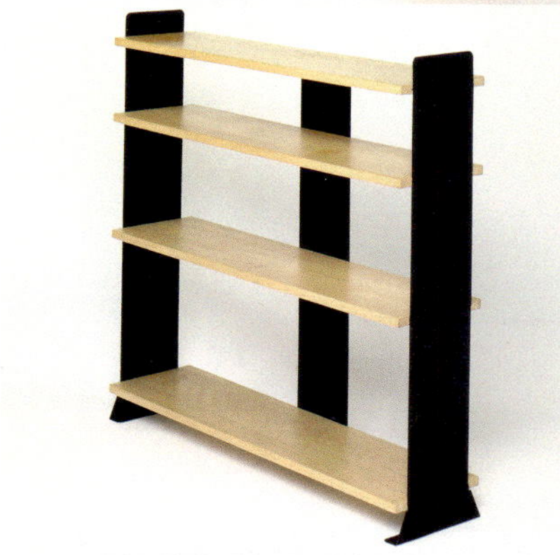

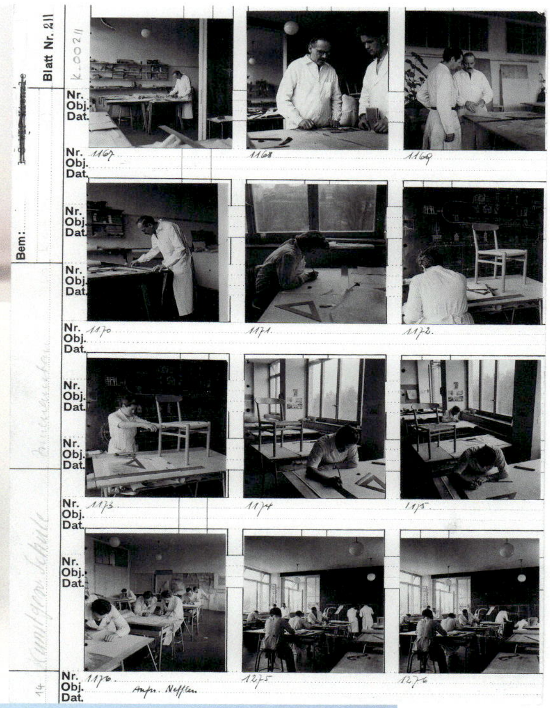

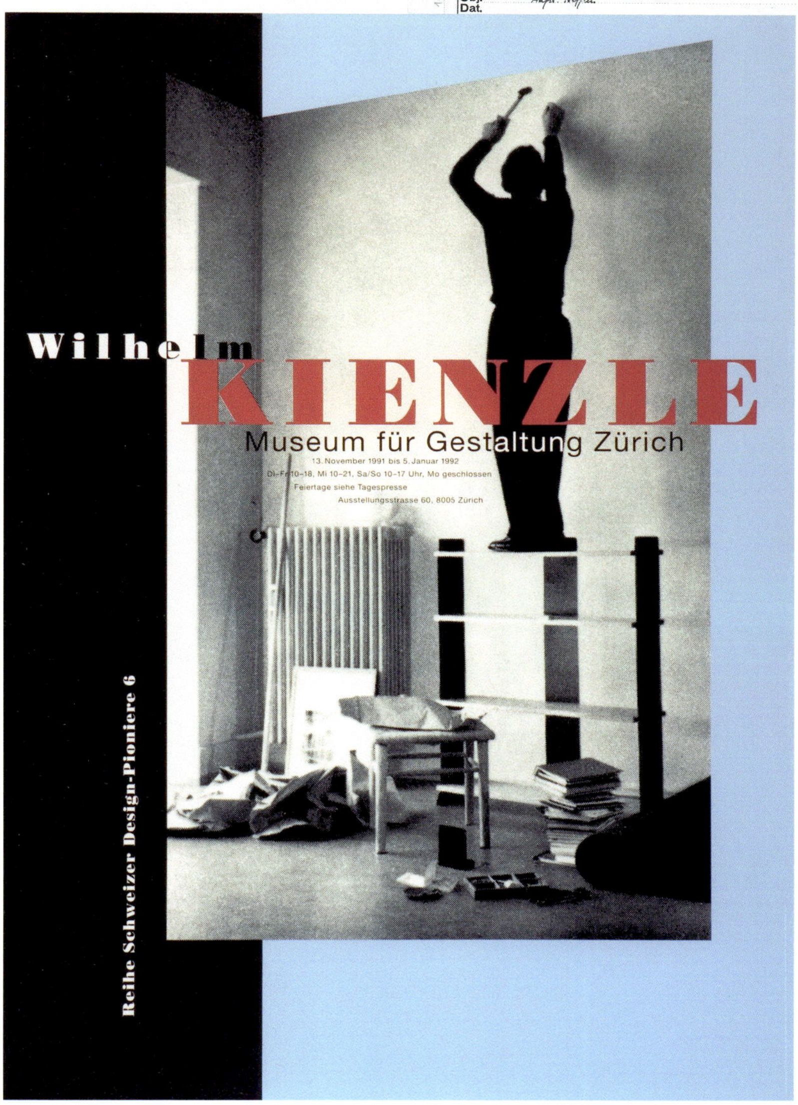

2a Willy Guhl's plastic bucket chairs, made of Scobalite and aluminum, were awarded the 1952 Die Gute Form Prize.

2b Tractor for steep slopes and challenging terrain: Aebi Terratrac TT77 implement carrier, 1976

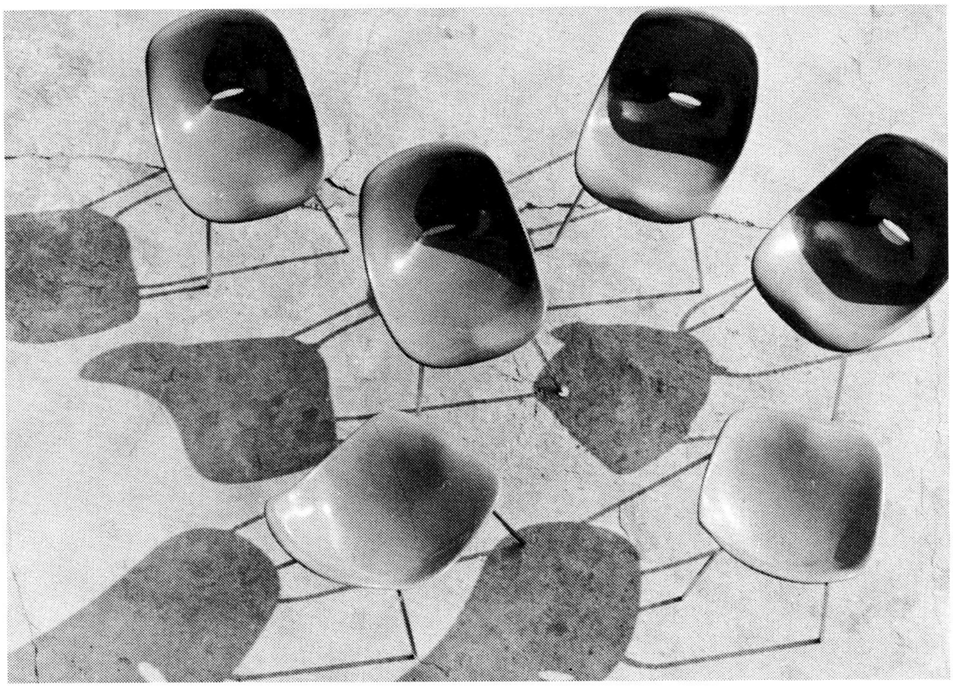

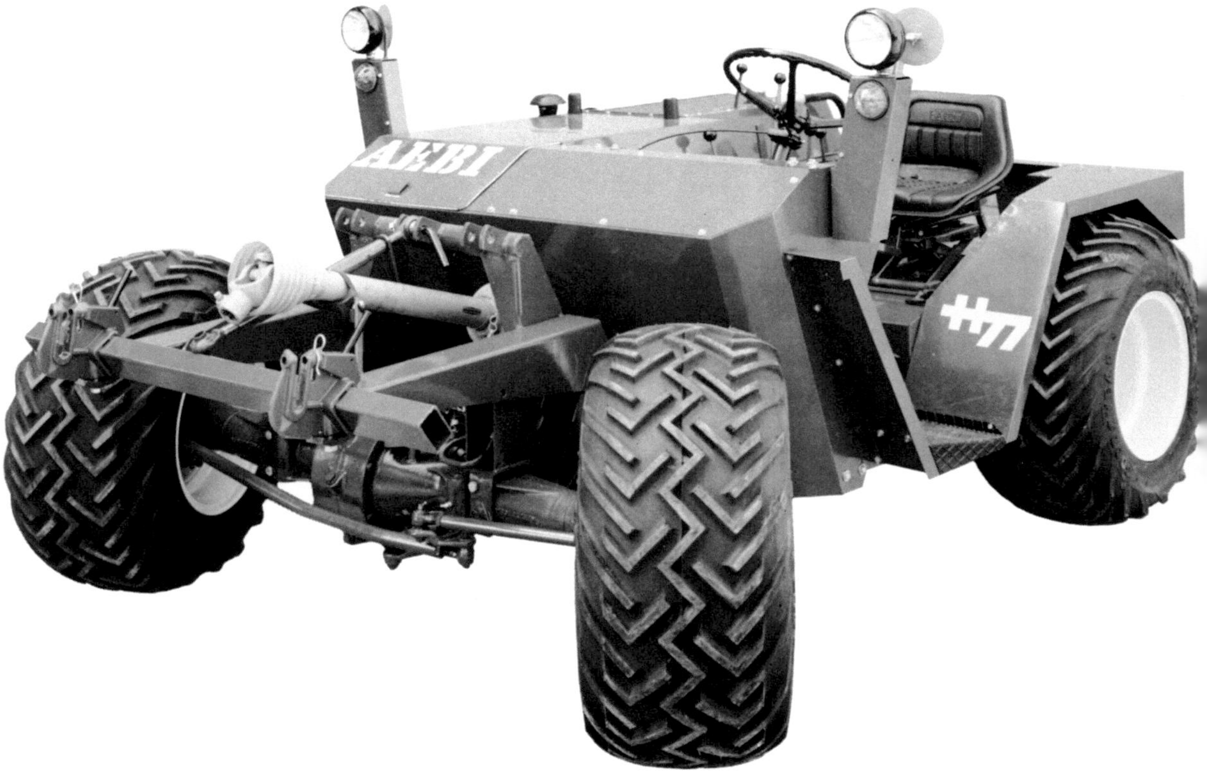

2c Willy Guhl was the first European designer to create a plastic bucket chair. Chairs 1947–69

2d Beach and garden chair shaped from a single fiber board. Eternit AG, 1954

2e–g Foundation studies: exploring different ways of sitting through clay models, 1947

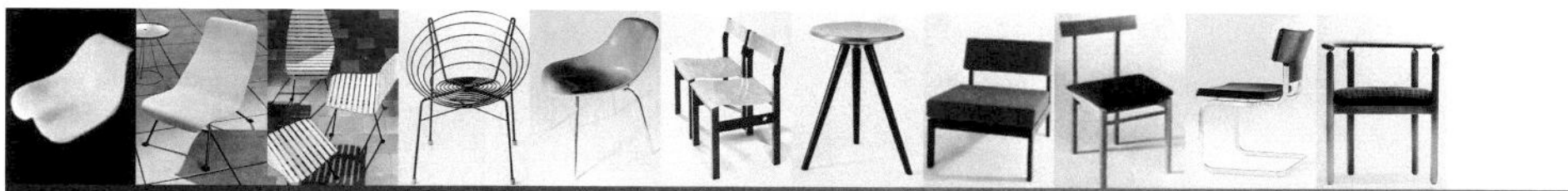

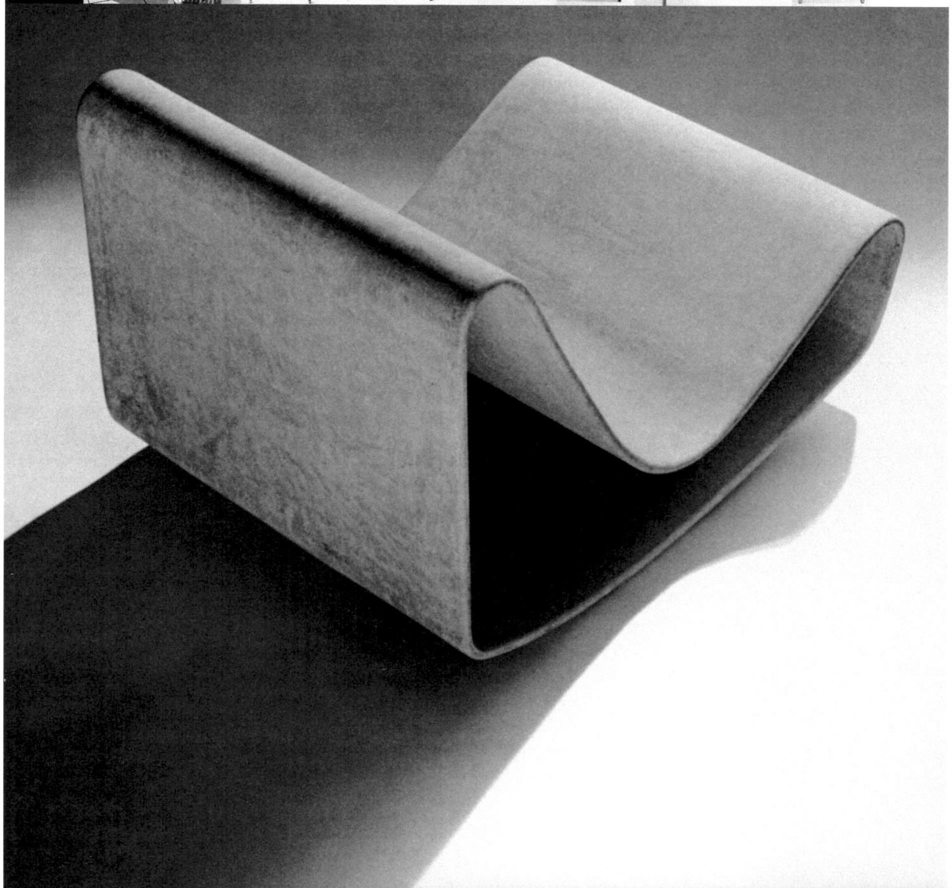

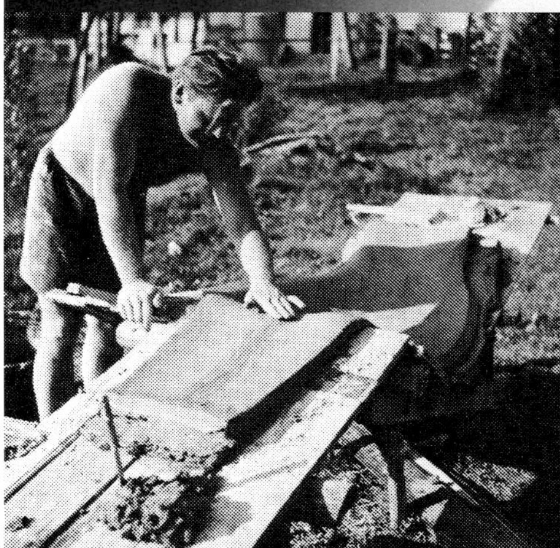

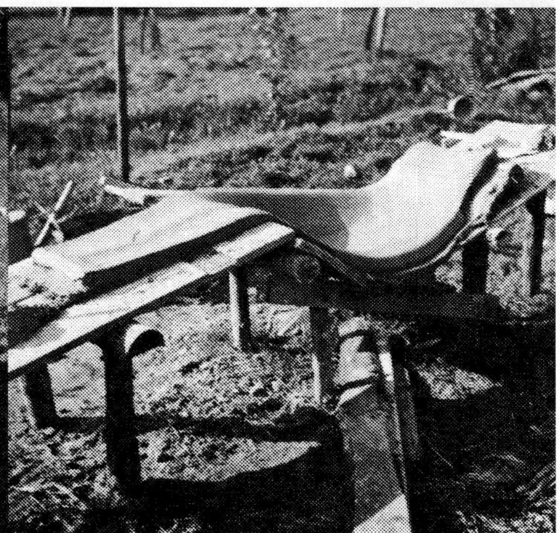

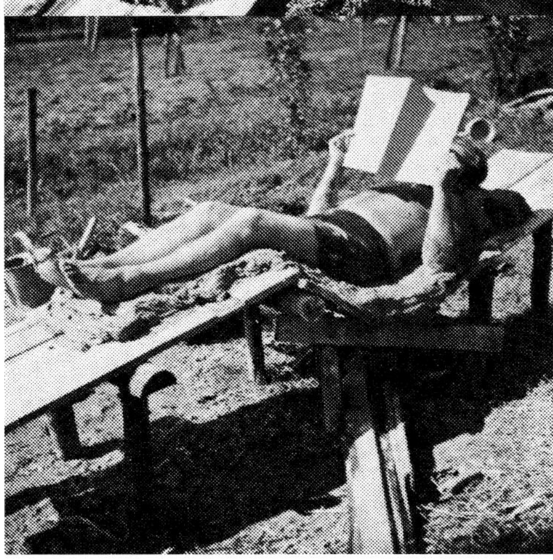

2h Exhibition poster, 1985. Design Jörg Hamburger and Georg Staehelin

3a Franco Clivio and his design collection

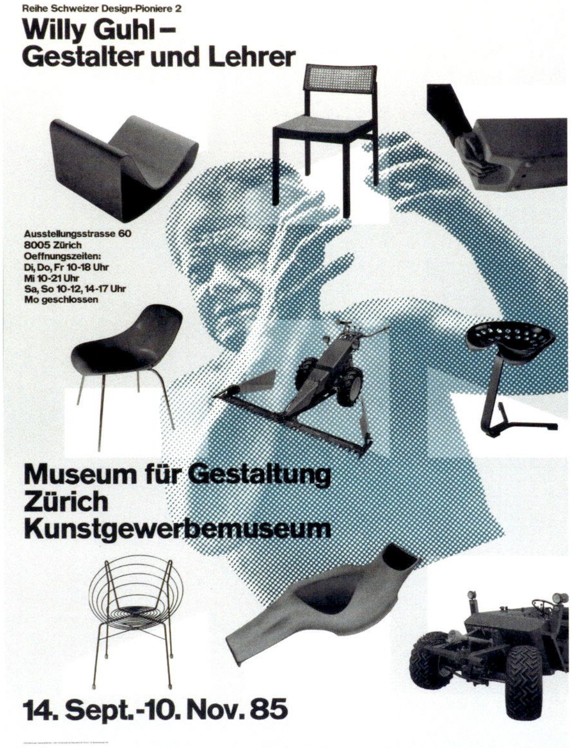

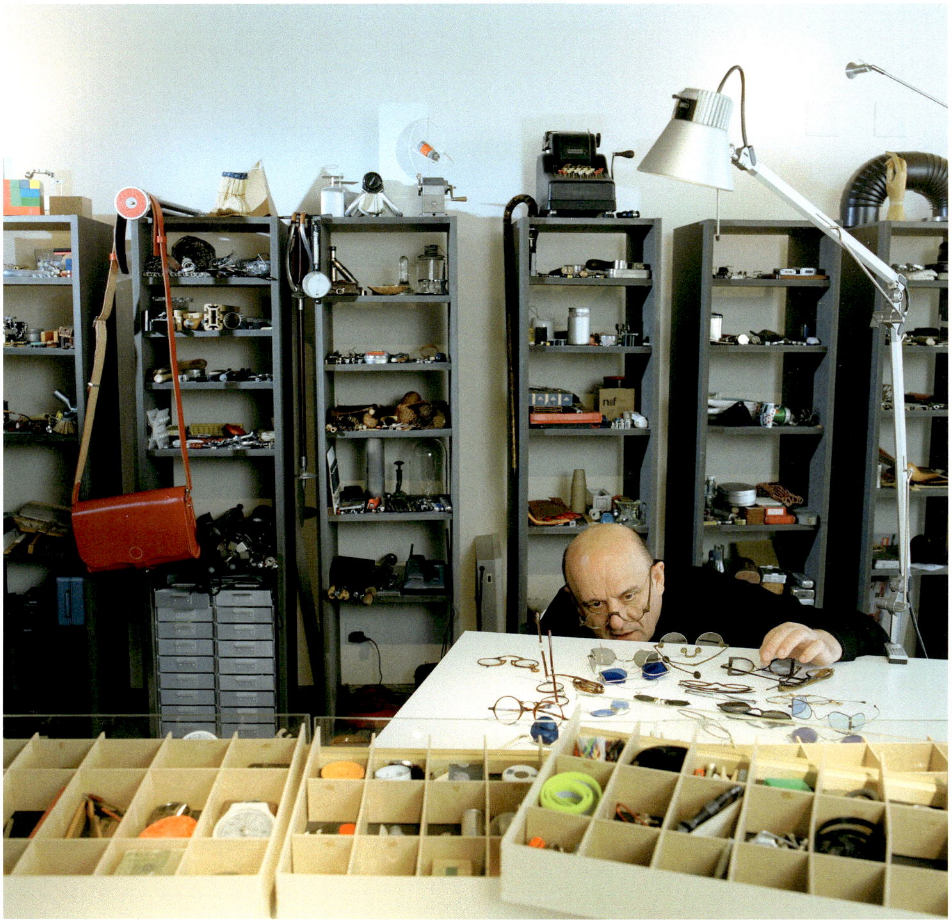

3b Franco Clivio, sprinkler designed for Gardena, 1977

3c The Stella spotlights designed for ERCO were developed in 1997 for the Bilbao Guggenheim Museum and the Reichstag building in Berlin.

3d The Lucy task lights designed for ERCO combine high-quality technology and high-quality design.

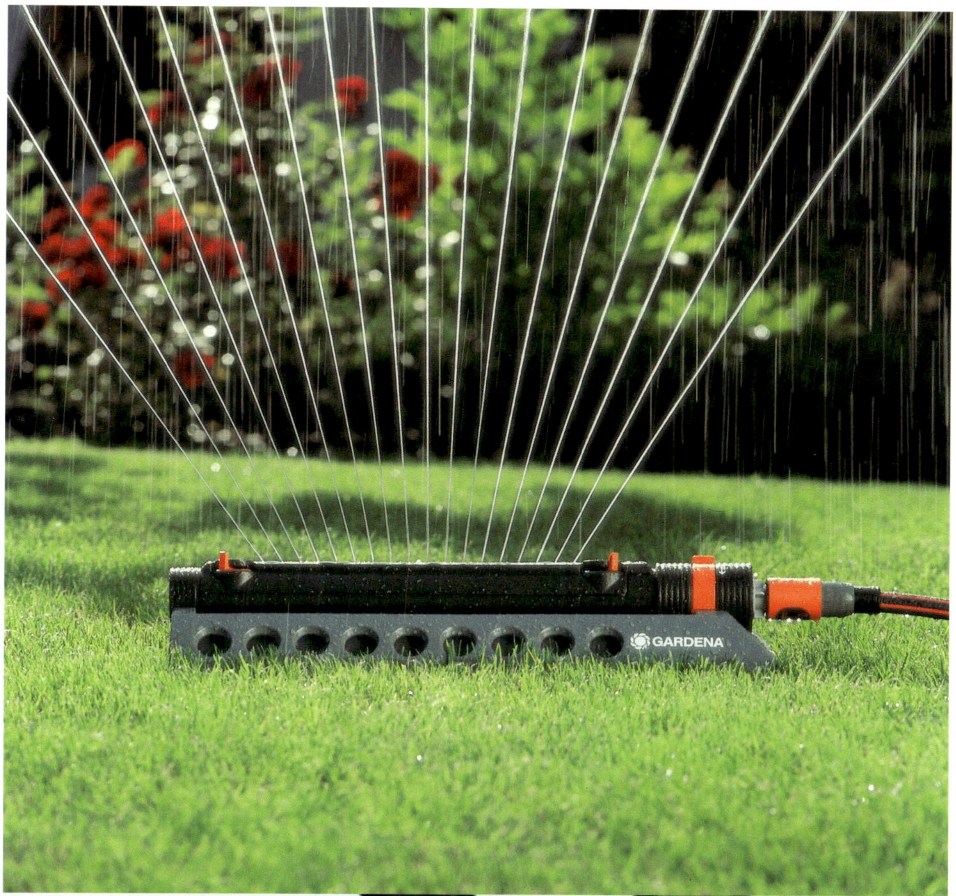

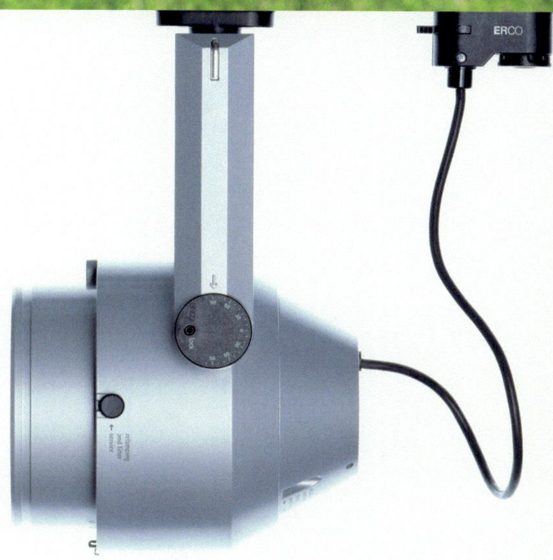

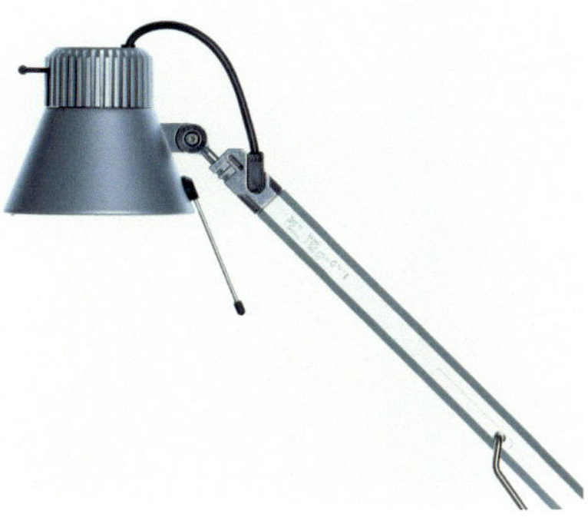

4a Scarf screenprinted by Sonnhild Kestler, former student at the Textile Design Department of the School of Art and Design Zurich, headed by Bärbel Birkelbach (1981–2004)

4b "Elephant," 2004. Foulard sample, screenprint by Sonnhild Kestler

5a Alfredo Häberli, various works shown in *Design Live*. Photo Walter Pfeiffer

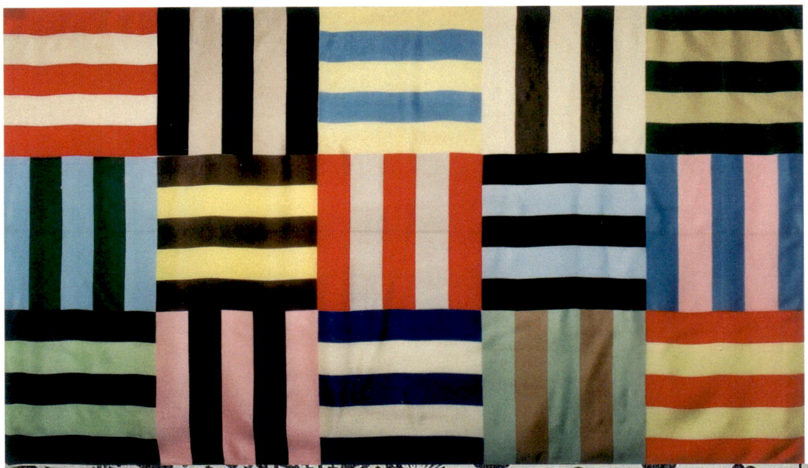

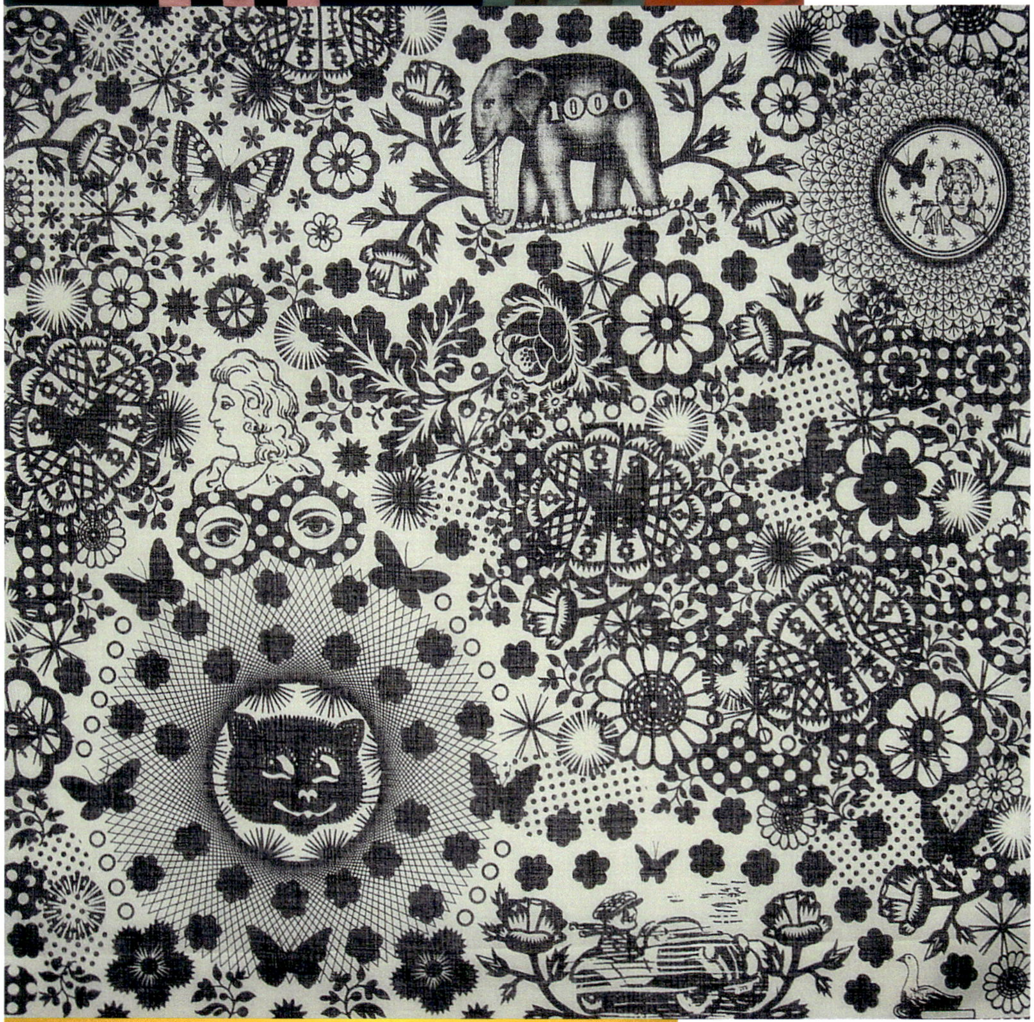

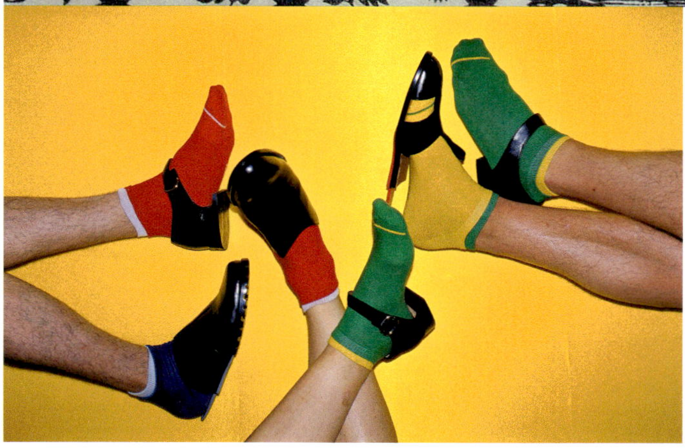

5b/d Alfredo Häberli, various works shown in *Design Live*. Photo Walter Pfeiffer

5c Alfredo Häberli with model of the multifunctional chair *Segesta*, developed 2002

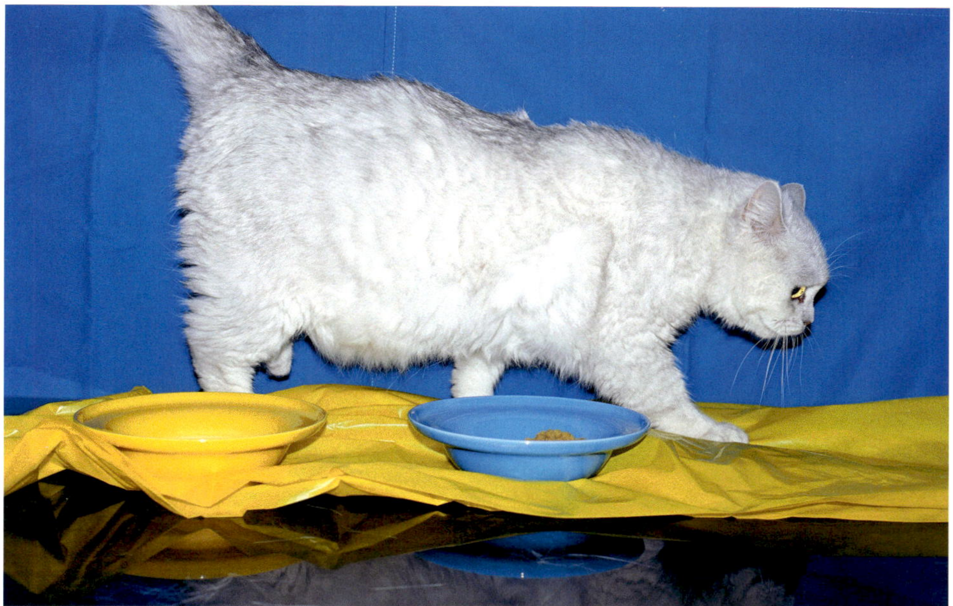

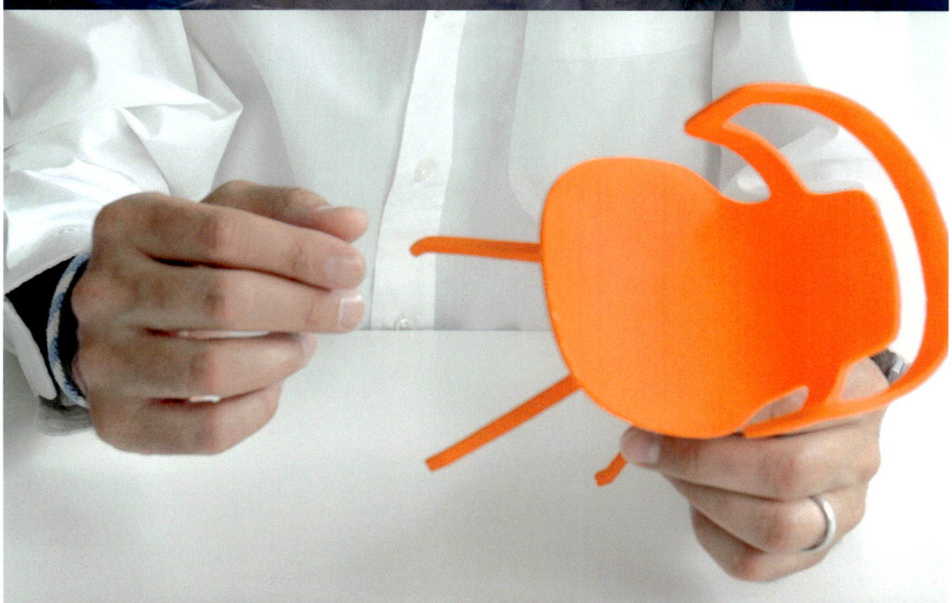

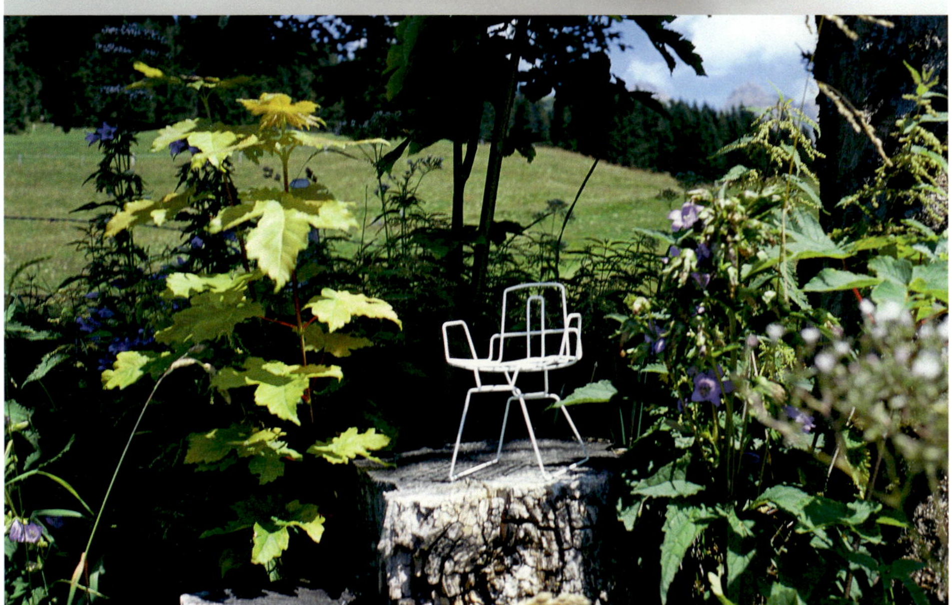

The time of utopian and totalitarian aesthetic doctrines, of *the grand récits*, is at an end—in any event, such discourses enjoy no resonance among these young stars. They pursue no universal aesthetic that might purport to possess general validity. Instead, their artistic programs oscillate between demystification and re-enchantment, although on occasion, aesthetic pleasure is permitted to betray ethical or political implications.

They are the future, they celebrate the new, the young. This is the fresh, eager generation that makes the preceding one suddenly seem like "yesterday." With them, musicality and noise are mutually accommodating, artistic beauty and ugliness make simultaneous claims, and that hypermedium, the computer, that black box, provides illumination.

He is the recipient of the Young Director's Award, along with international critical acclaim **1**; she is our best young actress, and now increasingly in demand for lead roles **2**; he is a ubiquitous presence in the reveries of teenage girls **3**; they interact virtually and capture the Goldener Hase prize **4**; she is a prize-winning star violinist who plays silken strings **5**; she yodels to the sound of her own echo **6**; he sings in the baritone's mid-range, and is met by a full chorus of praise **7**; he dances his way from Armenia to the world's most glamorous metropolises **8**; he has conducted important orchestras around the world from the tender age of twelve **9**; she is the incarnation of the sympathetic shooting star—albeit without star allure **10**.

1

David Bösch (*1978)

David Bösch was born in North Rhine-Westphalia. He opted for a civilian alternative to military service, and attempted unsuccessfully to do this in Israel. He did, however, spend six months in Israel looking after and observing a German-Jewish actor. He then spent a year at the free Theater Total and a further year studying theater and film at the Athanor Akademie Burghausen. From 2001 to 2004 he studied theater direction at the Zurich School of Music, Drama and Dance—submitting a production of *Spring Awakening* by Frank Wedekind for his final examination.

Early in his studies Bosch was already a source of some concern and also great hope and excitement for his teachers. One of his early sketches was an "eruptive" outburst using just a few disjointed words from Arthur Schnitzler's play *Reigen (La Ronde)*. In 2003 the directors of the school sent an adaptation of Georg Büchner's *Leonce and Lena* that Bösch had written outside the normal study program to a meeting of German-language drama schools in Graz. Its playful verve brought the young team the ensemble and the audience prize. This was followed the same year by three further productions in Zurich: *Fluchtpunkt* (Vanishing Point) by Jessica Goldberg, and two plays by Andri Beyeler, *Je ne m'en souviens plus (mais ce n'est pas vrai)* (I Don't Remember, but It Is Not True) and *Kick and rush*. *Fluchtpunkt* won the first prize in the Körber Studio Young Directors award; part of the prize was a chance to stage the play with the Hamburg Thalia Theater. Bösch realized this project together with Simon Stephen's *Port* as a co-production in the Young Directors Project at the Salzburg Festival. The production won the Montblanc Young Directors Award and finally succeeded in gaining Bösch the attention of the national theater critics.

There followed productions in Bern, Bochum, Hamburg, and Zurich. In 2005 David Bösch became house director at the Essen Theater, directing two plays a year. *His Leonce and Lena: A Better Day* was included in the theater's repertoire and in 2007–2008 will be in the program for the fifth season running.

2

Johanna Bantzer (*1978)

Johanna Bantzer was born in Zurich and grew up in Hamburg. After an internship with the costume department of the Thalia Theater in Hamburg, she worked as a costume assistant at the Zurich Schauspielhaus. Then came a detour to Berlin, and return to Zurich, this time to begin training at the Zurich Drama School. Late in her studies, she appeared in the Langstrasse project *Strähl* under the direction of Manuel Hendry. In 2004, she received the Max Ophüls Prize as best young actress for her role as Carol, a young female junkie, and in 2005, the Swiss Film Prize for best supporting role.

In 2003–2006, she was a regular ensemble member at the Theater Basel and appeared in the short film *Herr Goldstein* under the direction of Micha Lewinsky; the film received the Pardino d'oro for best Swiss short film at the International Film Festival at Locarno. Most recently, she played the female lead in a television movie *Havarie* (Loss at Sea) shown on Swiss television in spring of 2006. In early 2007, again under the direction of Micha Lewinsky, she took on the main role of Nora Mahler in the film *Mein Freund* (My Friend), which deals with the delicate topic of assisted suicide in Switzerland.

3

Mathis Künzler (*1978)

After studying metalworking, Künzler made a career of his hobby, studying at the Zurich School of Music, Drama and Dance. As formulaic as it sounds, he was indeed "discovered" during a director's audition and catapulted overnight from student to jetsetter, appearing in *Verliebt in Berlin* (In Love in Berlin) and becoming a teen idol in the German-speaking world. In this TV novella, he embodies to perfection a snobbish and slightly nasty young man, incisively portraying the requisite character traits.

4

Christian Iten (*1978)

Daniel Lüthi (*1968)

Although winning no prizes for their degrees, they did receive the Goldener Hase in 2007, one of the most important, and perhaps most prestigious, Swiss design prizes, which is awarded and publicized

1

3

2

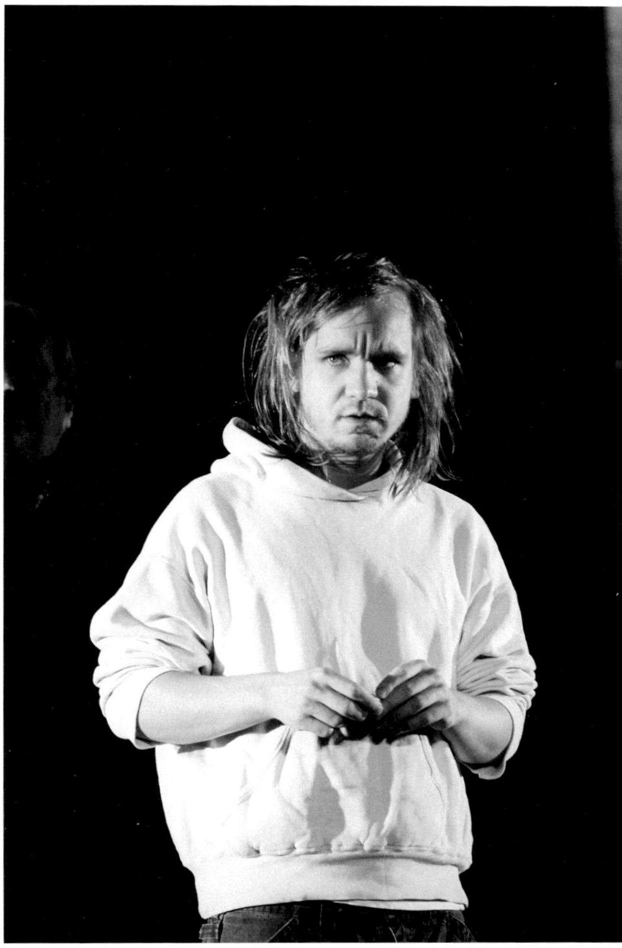

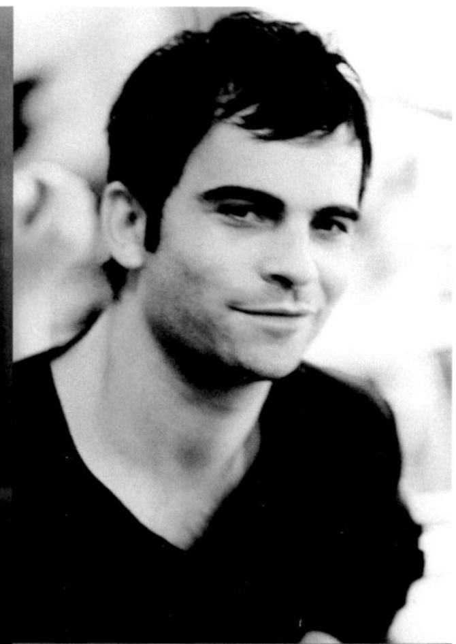

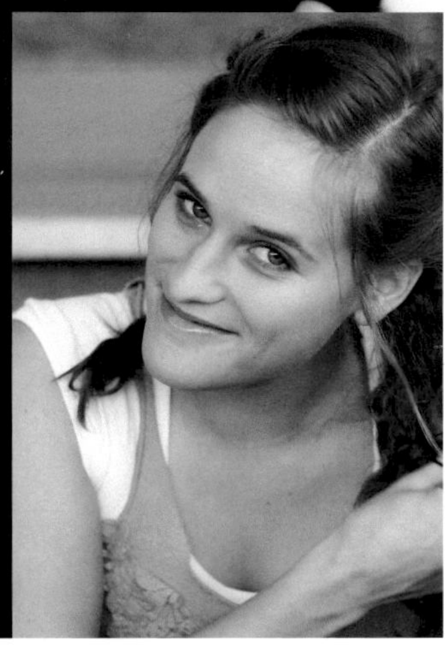

annually by Swiss Television and the architecture and design magazine *Hochparterre.* The award was for a virtual workbench with the ingenious name Tangent—a forward-looking invention promising much for future forms of work and interaction.

The jury commented: "Tangent is a virtual tool, a multi-touch research platform. It is operated by hand, without mouse, keyboard, or writing implements. Interactive techniques can be developed, tested, and intuitively used on the monitor, and can to an extent be operated by all fingers simultaneously. Conceivable are applications for design tasks, games, but also in medical and technical fields. Tangent was conceived as a design construction kit. As a research tool, on the one hand, Tangent evaluates new paths of interaction. In the jury's opinion, however, it also harbors the potential for wider dissemination, because Tangent is based on the standard interface of a jointly usable monitor."

Gerhard Buurman, the program director, commented: "To convey new potentials for interaction with the computer in such a playful manner, means becoming an ambassador on you own behalf: interactive design as an object of design. No more and no less!"

5

Yuka Tsuboi (*1979)

Yuka Tsuboi was born in Tokyo in 1979 and was admitted to England's Yehudi Menuhin School in 1994. She gave several concerts while still a student there, including some in the Royal Albert Hall and Wigmore Hall. In Zurich, she was the 2002 winner of the Schenk Foundation Prize and since then has performed as a soloist with the Aargau Symphony Orchestra, the Academic Orchestra of Zurich, the Orchestra of the Zurich School of Music, Swiss Television, and TV España. Tsuboi has won numerous competitions and is currently working as an assistant of Zakhar Bron in the Music Department of the Zurich University of the Arts.

6

Nadja Räss (*1979)

Nadja Räss is one of the best known personalities on Switzerland's yodeling scene. A highly versatile musician (who plays the *Schwyzerörgeli*, piano and double-bass), Räss is equally at home in the most diverse genres, in both folk music and classical, as a soloist, duettist, or as a member of various ensembles. Since 2004, she has been on the committee of the Swiss Folk Music Society (GVS), which endeavors to promote and preserve Swiss folk music in various different areas. Her own role in this organization is that of public relations officer with a focus on folk music education.

7

Ruben Drole (*1980)

There he was on stage—and there he was backstage as well! What Ruben Drole was doing was making Swiss media history—as Papageno in a production of Mozart's *Magic Flute* at Zurich Opera House broadcast on Swiss Television's DRS channel in 2007. And anyone who chose to flip channels half way through would have seen him on DRS 2 as well, this time in a "making-of" program that gave viewers a glimpse behind the scenes of the same production. Switzerland's TV viewers, in other words, had a unique opportunity to get to know a singer who not only has a remarkable stage presence and is an extraordinarily gifted singer, but who approaches the complex world of opera with a refreshingly heartwarming lightness of touch. The production in question, incidentally, which was directed by Martin Kusej and conducted by Nikolaus Harnoncourt, has since then come to be seen as Drole's breakthrough. Born in Winterthur to Slovenian and Spanish parents, his rise to fame has been almost meteoric. He had his first singing lesson in 1999 and now, just eight years later, after studying with Jane Thorner-Mengedoht at the School of Music, Drama and Dance, is considered one of the best baritones on the circuit.

8

Tigran Mikayelyan (*1980)

After completing his second season as a soloist with the Bavarian State Ballet in Munich, Tigran Mikayelyan can be considered to have made it. Outstanding performances include the Golden Idol in *La Bayadère*, Prince Siegfried in *Swan Lake*, Romeo and Mercutio in *Romeo and Juliet*, and Forsythe's *Limb's Theorem.* Following his triumphs as Ali and Konrad in *Le Corsaire* he was pro-

6 5
4

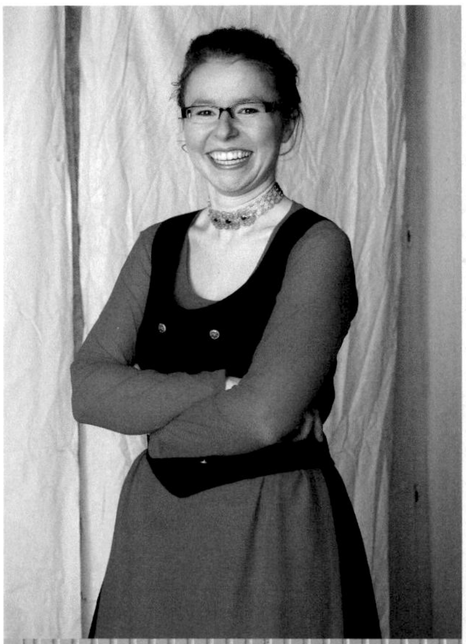

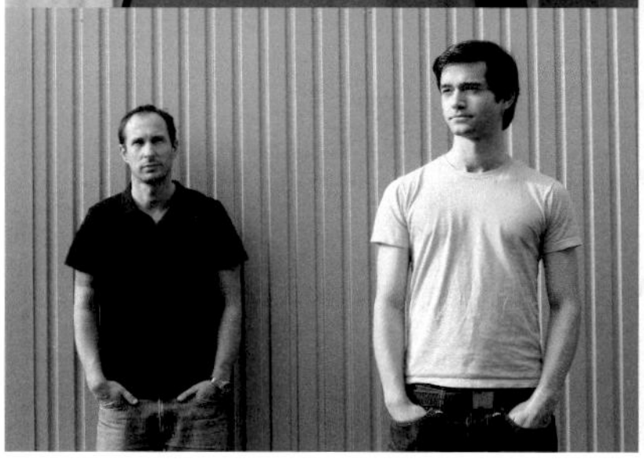

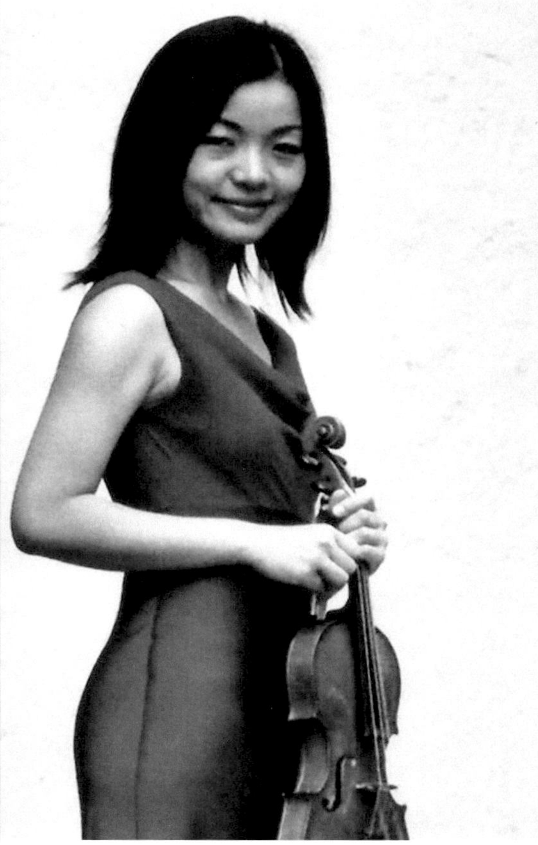

moted to principal soloist and has also been nominated for this year's Merkur theater prize. His strong and elegant stage presence enthralls the public. His road to the top began in his native Armenia in 1989 at the Armenian Ballet School in Erevan.

Mikayelyan began studying at the Swiss Professional Ballet School (SBBS) in 1997 on a Nureyev Foundation scholarship. A year later he won the Prix Niveau Professionnel of the Prix de Lausanne, and after completing his studies was engaged by the Zurich Ballet. He danced many solo roles in ballets by Heinz Spoerli and guest choreographers, rising to become second soloist and then soloist. His courageous decision to join a large company with an extensive repertoire came at just the right time.

9

Patrick Lange (*1981)

Patrick Lange was born in Germany and began his musical career as an eight-year-old chorister in the famous boys' choir, the Regensburger Domspatzen. He had his first conducting lesson at the age of twelve and conducted his first major production at the Stadttheater Regensburg at the age of sixteen. After leaving school, he studied at the Würzburg and Zurich Schools of Music and in the spring of 2005 was admitted to the Conductors' Forum of the German Music Council. That summer, Claudio Abbado appointed him assistant conductor of the Gustav Mahler Youth Orchestra, where Lange prepared the orchestra for forthcoming tours and collaborated closely with conductors such as Abbado, Ingo Metzmacher, Philippe Jordan, and Myung-Whun Chung.

Lange has conducted a number of European orchestras, including the Beethoven Orchestra Bonn, the MDR Symphony Orchestra, the Mahler Chamber Orchestra, the Janácek Philharmonie Ostrava, the orchestra of the Theater Vanemuine Tartu in Estonia, the Camerata Zurich, and on several occasions since 2004 the Simón Bolívar Youth Orchestra of Venezuela, with which he conducted the opening concert of the Beethoven Festival as well as opening the 2006/2007 season.

In addition to symphonic music, Lange has long concerned himself with the operatic repertoire as well, conducting Mozart's *Le nozze di Figaro* and Massenet's *Cenrillon* in Würzburg, and Ravel's *L'Enfant et les Sortilèges* at the Theater an der Sihl in Zurich. He was also in charge of rehearsals for Wagner's Rheingold at the Teatro dell'Opera in Rome.

10

Laura de Weck (*1981)

Laura de Weck is the quintessential and sympathetic shooting star of 2007. Born in Zurich, her path took her to Hamburg, Paris, and back to Zurich again, where she began her studies in acting at the Zurich School of Music, Drama and Dance in 2001. When she graduated in 2005, no one suspected that she would attract national attention as an author. At the Frankfurt Authors' Forum of 2005, she took part as an actor in a reading of her own piece *Lieblingsmenschen* (Favorite People), attracting the notice of the Autorenagentur publishing house. Interest was expressed in performances, and in spring 2007 her "firstborn" was realized as a joint premiere in Basel (director: Werner Düggelin) and Mannheim (director: Marcelo Diaz). "It is more a question here—I mean, you search for someone who loves you, or simply for something that gives you a hold in life, which is what everyone wants."

In spring 2008, the play returns to its place of origin, the Zurich Theater School, in a workshop production by directing student Daniel Kuschewski, played by current acting students. Hopefully, Laura de Weck can be present that evening instead of appearing on stage in her first regular acting engagement at Junges Schauspielhaus Hamburg. Alongside her writing, she would never want to give up acting. She belongs wholly to the theater.

10 9

7 8

1a David Bösch directed *Kabale und Liebe* at Schauspielhaus Zürich in 2007. The picture shows Catherine Seifert and Fabian Krüger.

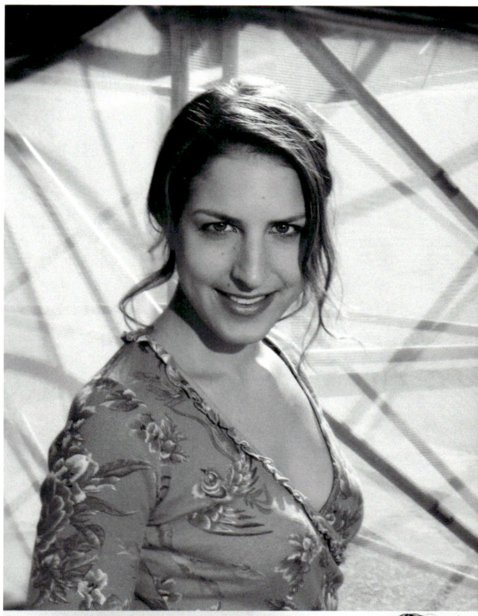

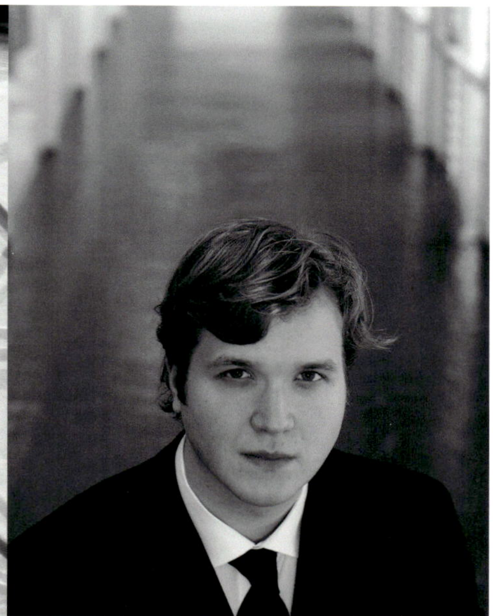

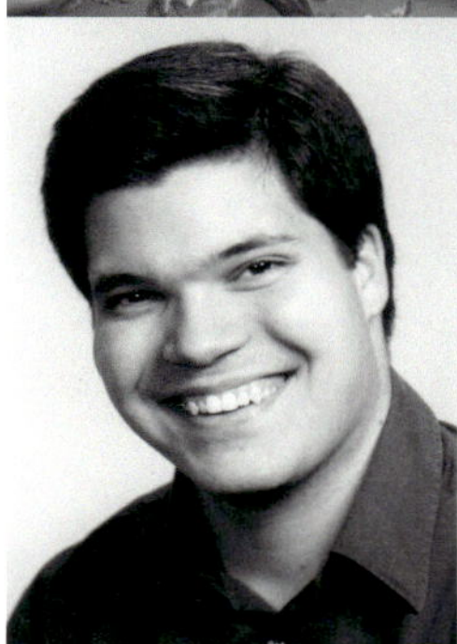

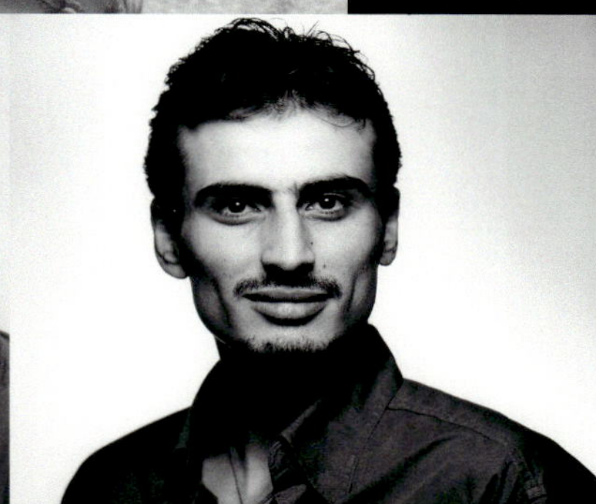

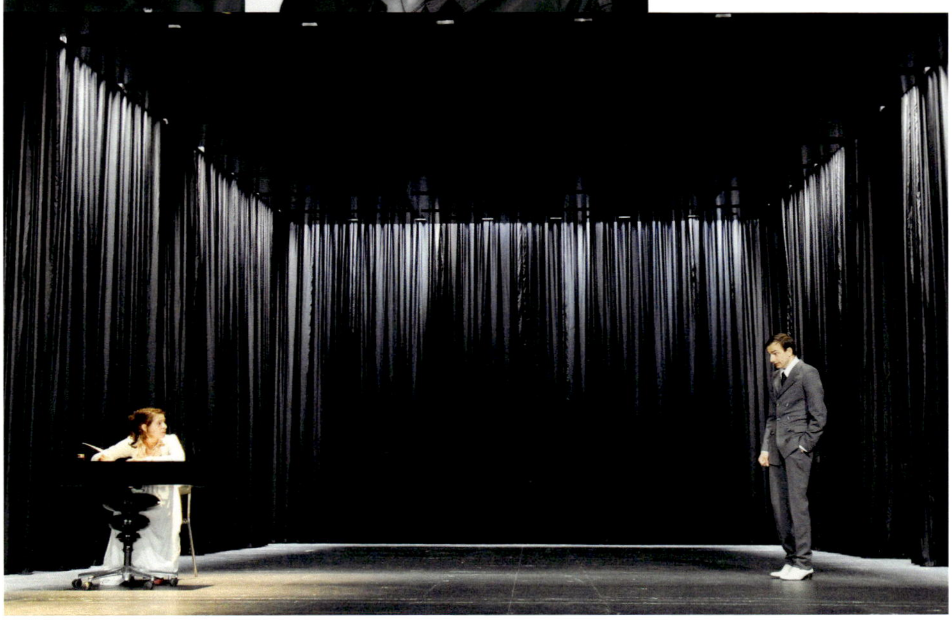

2a Johanna Bantzer as drug addict Carol in *Strähl* by Manuel Flurin Hendry, 2003

3a–c Mathias Künzler in the TV novella *Verliebt in Berlin*, 2007

4a Christian Iten/Daniel Lüthi, *Tangent: An Interactive Multitouch Surface*, degree project at the School of Art and Design Zurich, 2006

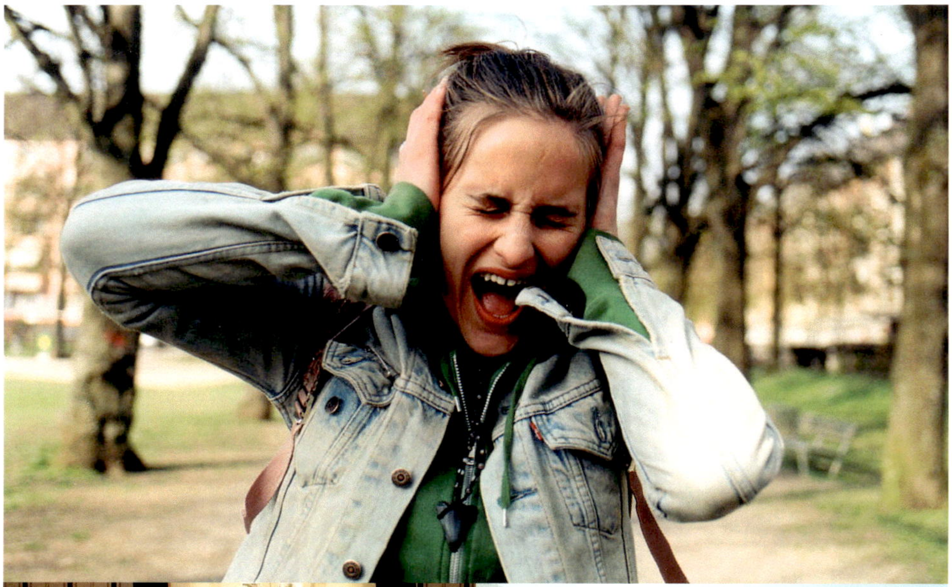

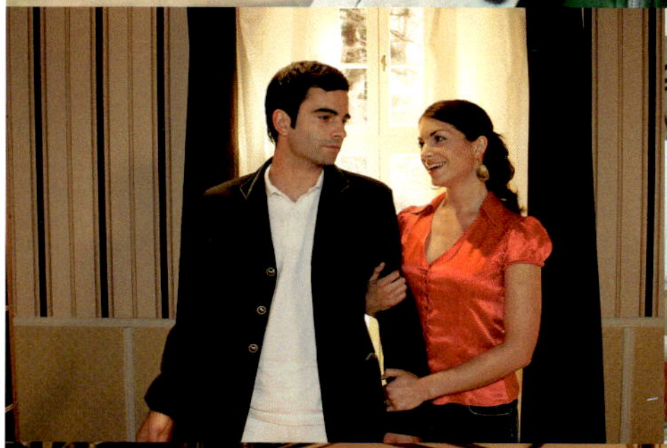

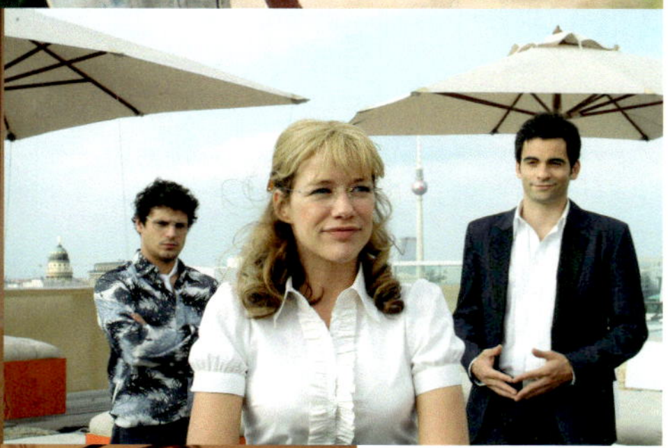

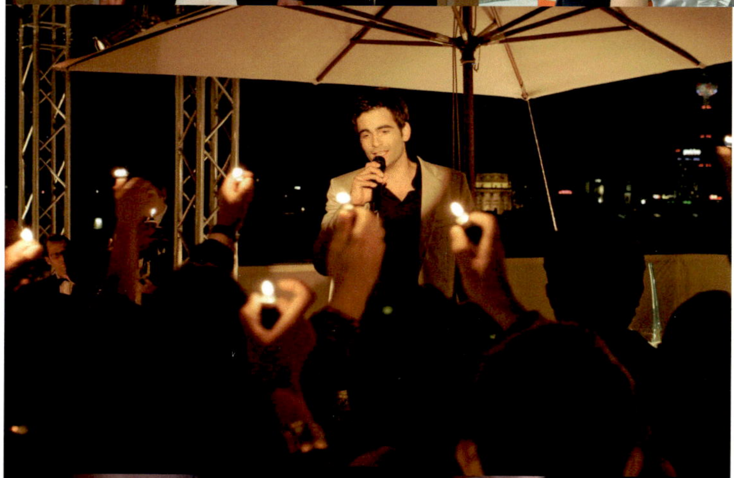

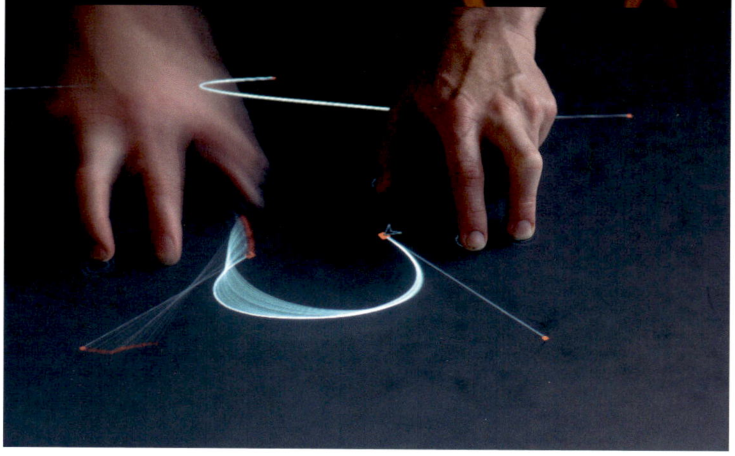

4b/c *Tangent: An Interactive Multitouch Surface,* degree project at the School of Art and Design Zurich, 2006
7a Ruben Drole plays Papageno in *The Magic Flute* at the Zurich Opera House, 2007

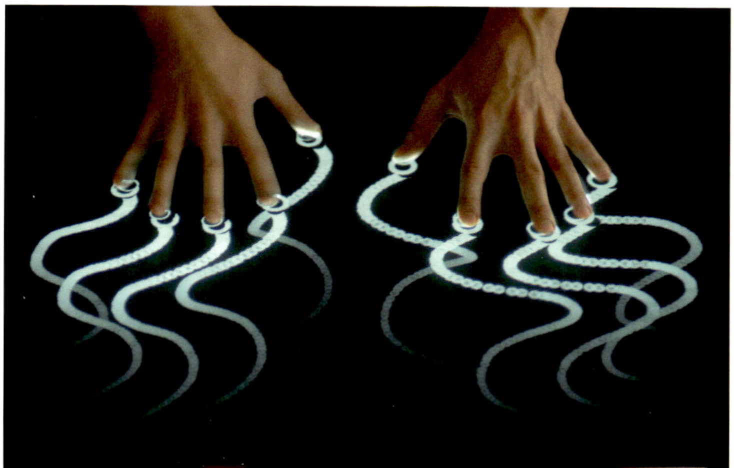

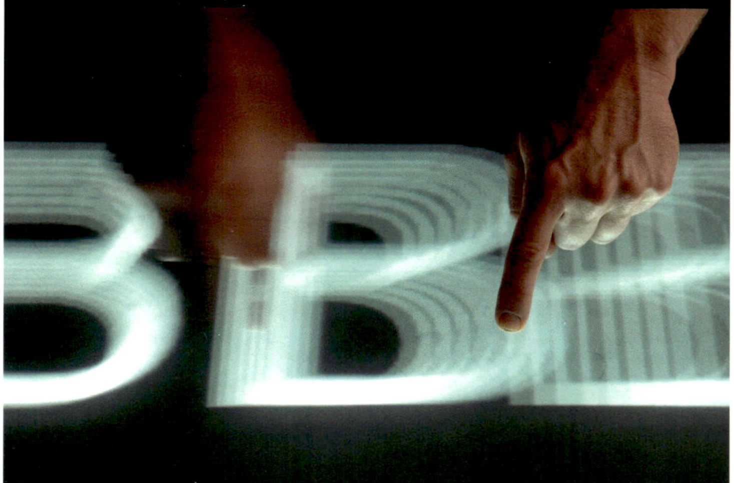

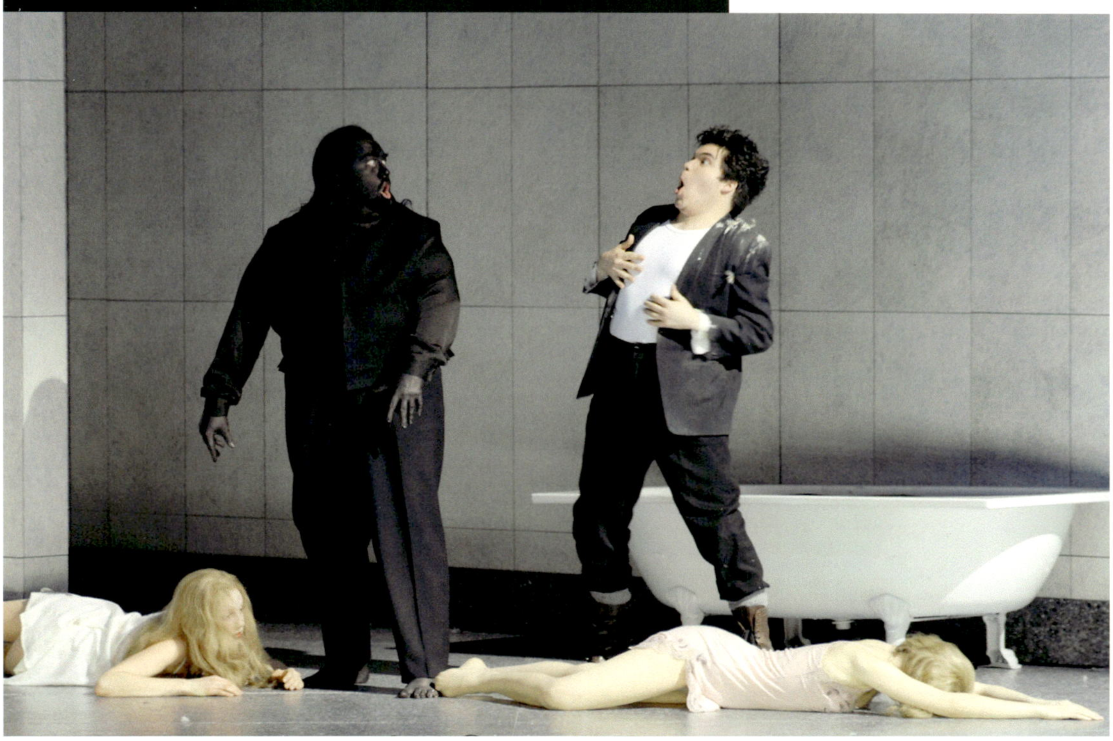

8a Tigran Mikayelyan in *Le Corsaire* at the Bavarian State Ballet, 2007
9a Patrick Lange conducting Ravel's *L'Enfant et les Sortilèges* at the Theater an der Sihl, Zurich, 2005

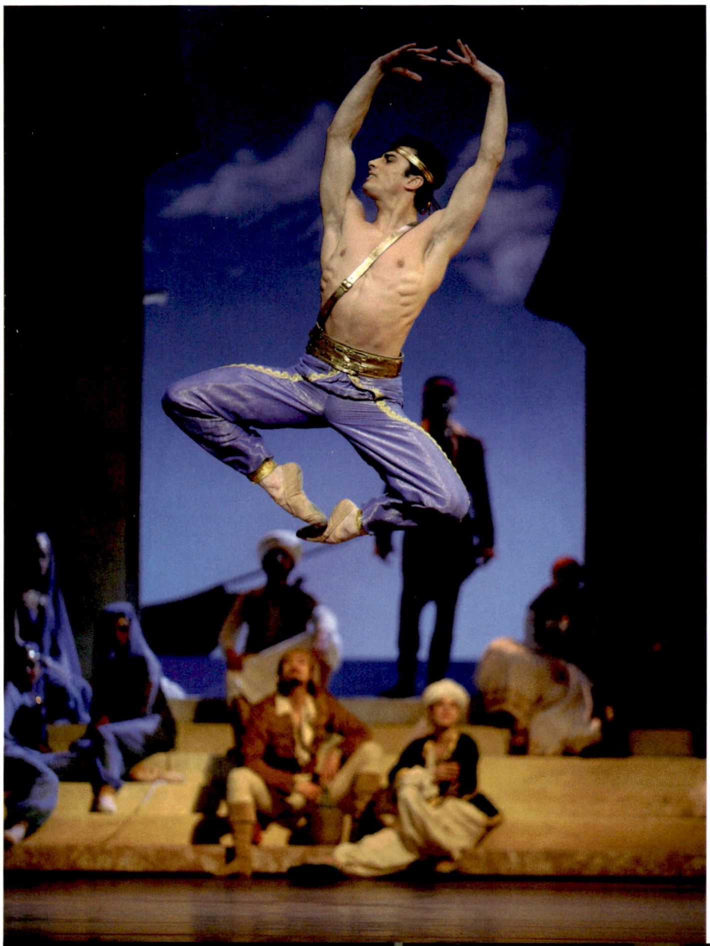

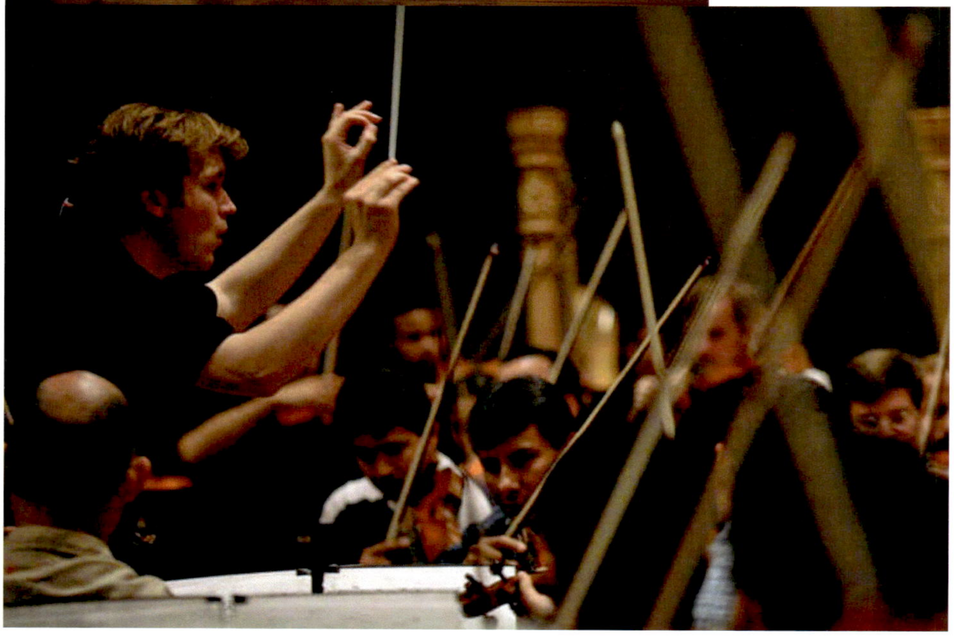

10a–c Premiere of Laura De Weck's debut play *Lieblingsmenschen* at Theater Basel and in Mannheim, 2007, with Jan Bluthardt as Sven. Directed by Werner Düggelin

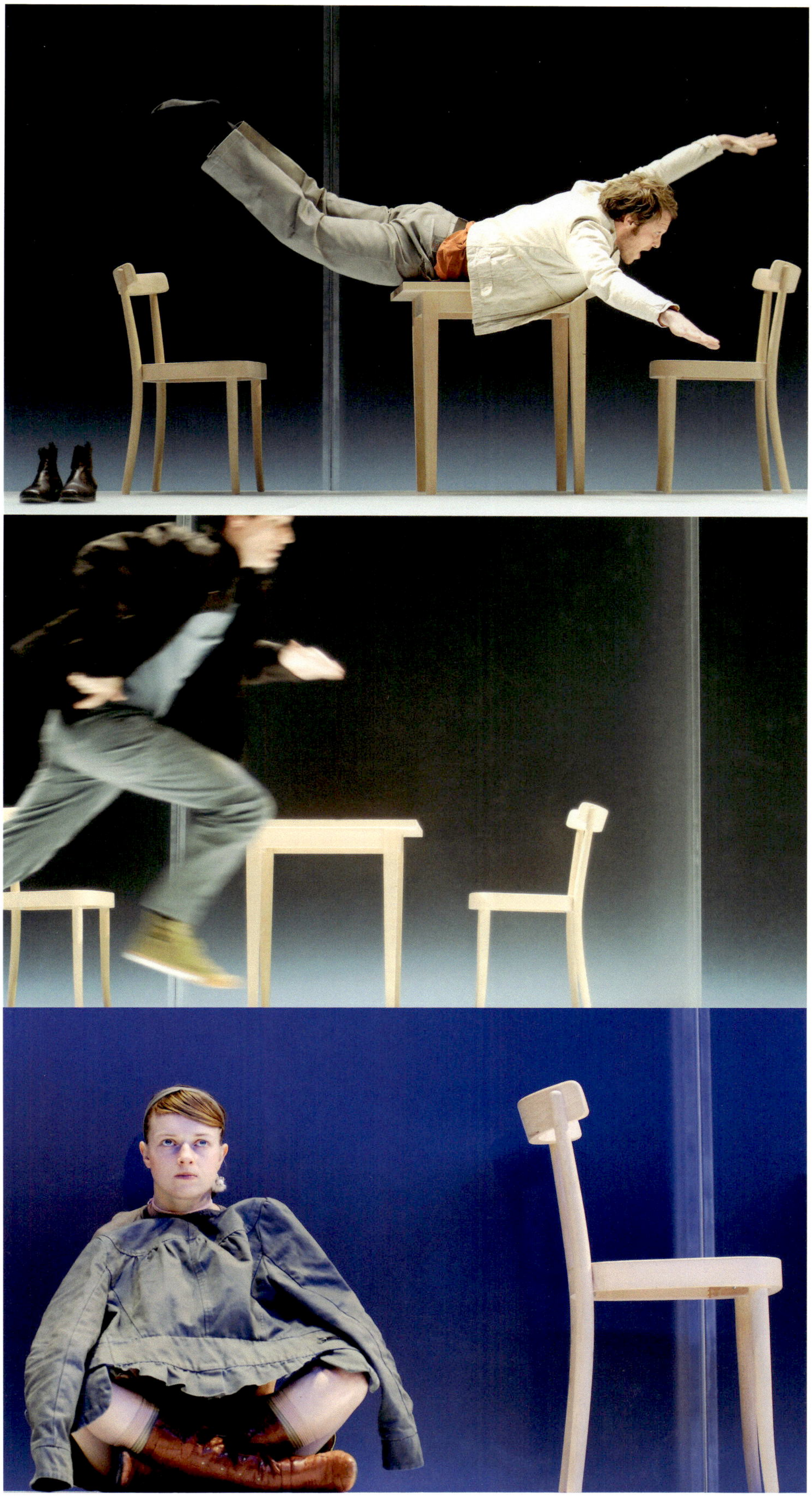

Shots, sequences, films, increasingly fugitive shadows. They create pictures, scrupulously framed, illuminating, inventing images that are coarse, filthy, accidental, placing their trust in the power of the moment, the acting, the screenplay. They fix time on the ephemeral eternity of celluloid, magnetic tape, and hard drives. They devour recipes in order to create their own. They master technique, entering the scene in order to revolutionize their predecessors. They take advantage of expectations, organize communities of belief, factions, networks. Bolex and Arriflex, Cinéma Copain and Leutschenbach, low tech and high definition, quality and popularity, or: what was that again? All of them have stories to tell, all are searching for financial sponsorship and an audience—and with increasing frequency, they are finding both. They are met with enthusiasm, scandal, success, indifference, censure, wonders, even girl wonders. With their creative independence, each of them enriches the local, inter-cantonal, and global cinematic landscape.

He composed his music of the spheres for global success in the movies, and created an enormous musical oeuvre **1**; they attended the legendary film courses at the School of Applied Arts **2**, **3**, **4**, **5**; he documents and transforms his prize-winning directorial competence, from theater to silver screen **6**; they attend the Higher—and highest—School of Design **7**, **8**, **9**, **10** and are now creating awe-inspiring cinema.

1

Robert Blum (1900–1994)

Marie-Louise won an Oscar in 1944; Leopold Lindtberg's *Letzte Chance* (The Last Chance) was a box-office success worldwide, including in the USA, and *Uli der Pächter* (Uli the Tenant), *Heidi* and *Wachtmeister Studer* have all gone down as milestones in the annals of Swiss cinema. One man who had a hand in all these cinematic success stories was Robert Blum, who composed the music not only for these movies, but for countless others made in the 1940s and 1950s by the legendary production company Praesens-Film. Blum, for whom composing for the silver screen was merely a sideline, was not spared the fate of so many other composers of film music, for while his compositions became famous, the man who wrote them did not and almost all the other works in his vast oeuvre have long since been forgotten. Blum was taught composition first by Volkmar Andreae and later, alongside Kurt Weill, by Ferruccio Busoni in Berlin. In Zurich, he worked as a conductor and began teaching composition at the Conservatory in 1943. It was in that capacity that he trained several generations of young Swiss composers.

2

Jacqueline Veuve (*1930)

Jacqueline Veuve is a careful chronicler of vanishing professions and ways of life. With her training in anthropology, she discovered cinema history in the film clubs of Geneva and Lausanne. In 1956–58, she was Jean Rouch's assistant at the Musée de l'homme in Paris. After marrying and having a family, she turned to film in 1966, realizing *Le panier à viande* (Schlachttag; Slaughter Day) jointly with Yves Yersin: a subtle non-acceptance of a village day of slaughter in the canton of Vaud. In 1967, she attended her first filmmaking course at the Zurich School of Applied Arts, where she filmed the short film *Dimanche de pinguins* (Sunday of the Penguins). After a directing course with documentarist Richard Leacock at MIT in 1973–74, she established herself solidly as a filmmaker. Since then, she has made more than fifty films. Among them are important films such as the 1997 *Journal de Rivesaltes 1941–1942* (The Diary of Rivesaltes 1941–1942) and the 1999 *Chronique Vigneronne* (Vineyard Chronicle). In her latest film *La nébuleuse du cœur* (The Heart's Nebula) of 2005, inspired by her own illness, she portrays the human heart in a sovereign and original way.

3

Fredi M. Murer (*1940)

Fredi M. Murer is one of the most individual and at the same time popular Swiss filmmakers. At seventeen, he moved to Zurich, befriending artists and free spirits in various group residences. In the photography class at the School of Applied Arts, he developed a distinctive experimental tendency that allowed him to disrupt the static quality of the freeze image. While on excursions, he filmed with a 16 mm Bolex and, after concluding his studies, realized numerous experimental portraits. Playful and anarchic, marked by the vitality of cultural upheaval, these short films remain accessible. Murer never shied away from accepting commissions and, in the 1970s, turned increasingly toward narrative and documentary cinema. His sympathetic portrait *Wir Bergler in den Bergen* (We Mountaineers in the Mountains) is by no means an isolated milestone in his production. It was his 1985 feature *Höhenfeuer* (Alpine Fire) that brought him his international breakthrough. *Vitus,* his most recent success, is an ode to dreams. *King Melchior* is an astonishing film, both witty and sincere, and satisfies without being ingratiating.

4

Markus Imhoof (*1941)

Markus Imhoof was born in Winterthur. His socially committed, documentary and feature films are simultaneously accessible and grounded. His second love is the stage: Imhoof directs throughout the German-speaking world. After his studies in German languages and literature and history, and a stint as Leopold Lindtberg's directorial assistant at the Schauspielhaus Zurich, he acquired his cinematic technique from Kurt Früh in the filmmaking courses 1 and 2. His portrait of a prisoner, produced during the second course and influenced by Brecht, was banned and acquired cult status: Jean-Paul Sartre himself was a supporter of the film

3 2
4 1

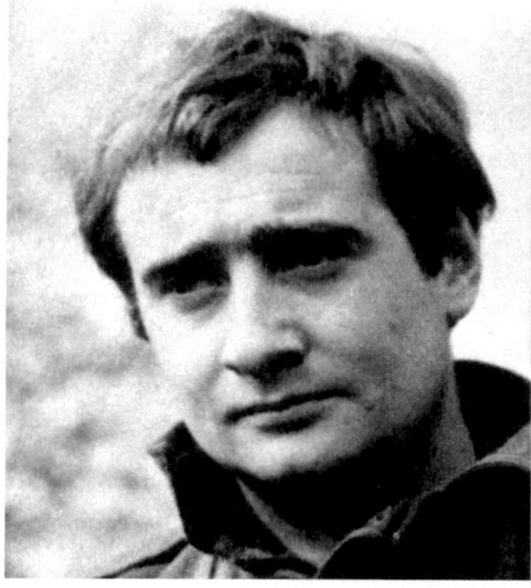
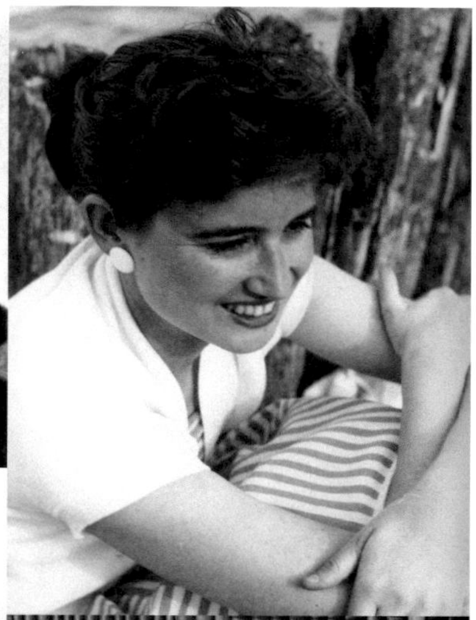
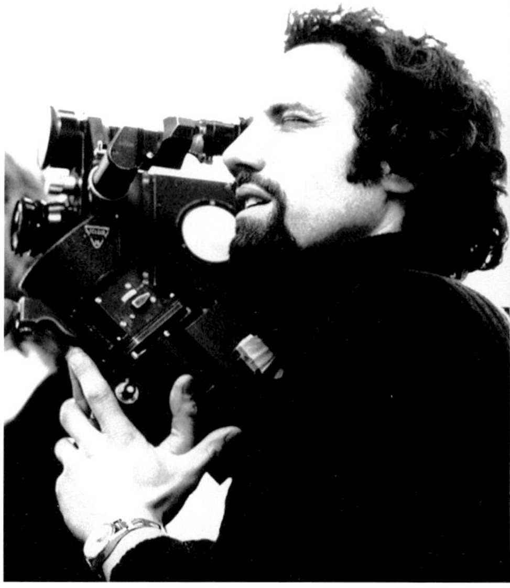
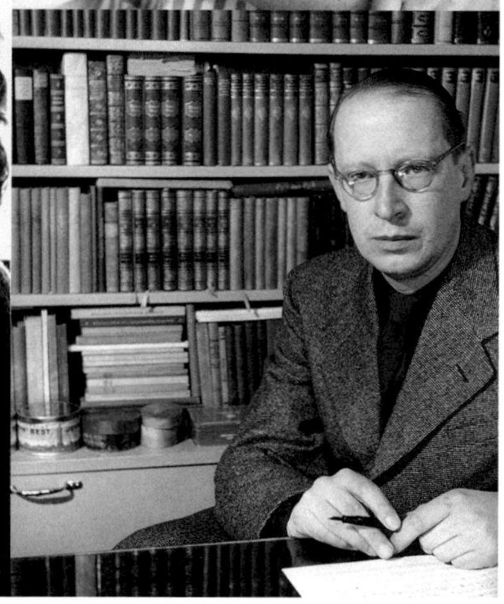

Rondo. Also sensational was *Ormenis 19 9+69*, his uncompromising documentary on the cavalry. In 1981, long before Swiss dealings with refugees during World War II were discussed more broadly, Imhoof produced *Das Boot ist voll* (The Boat is Full), a masterwork uniting historical and social sensibility, scrupulous analysis and broad appeal. His comparatively elaborate, classical narrative cinema allows him little respite, and occasionally elevates creative risks and the danger of blind alleys, such as *Flammen im Paradies* (Flames in Paradise).

5
Clemens Klopfenstein (*1944)

Clemens Klopfenstein was born in Täuffelen. The intrepid painter, author, cameraman and director works quickly and spontaneously. His "buddy films," most of them produced with minimal resources, focus on the Swiss condition. Beginning in 1962, he produced mainly cheeky, ironic short films as a member of the author's collective AKS. In 1967, after attending the Basel School of Applied Arts, he attended filmmaking courses 1 and 2 of the Zurich School of Applied Arts, and in 1974, with his *Fabrikanten* (Manufacturers), realized an ambitious finance world thriller. Its financial failure led Klopfenstein back to more artistically radical positions. In 1976, in *Geschichte der Nacht* (Story of the Night), he forced the sensitivity of the film material beyond its limits. Nighttime, streets, and later dialogue play important roles in his work, which in *Füürland* (Land of Fire) and others becomes an implicit chronicle of social utopias and a confrontation with their failure. At the same time, his work is full of vitality and wit. This is illustrated by his latest caper, *Die Vogelpredigt* (The Bird Sermon).

6
Stefan Haupt (*1961)

In 1985, Stefan Haupt began studies in theater education at the Zurich Academy of Drama. At first, he was an independent theater instructor and director, later achieving recognition as a filmmaker. In 2004, he founded his own production firm in Zurich, Fontana Film GmbH. In 1998, he made the documentary film *I'm just a simple person*, and in 2000 *Increschantüm* (Homesickness). Then came projects such as *Utopia Blues*, a feature film for which he won the Swiss Film Prize 2002 (best feature, best actor), the Zurich Film Prize, the EDI Study Prize (Swiss Federal Department of Home Affairs), the Max Ophüls Preis 2002 (best screenplay), and Grand Prize Molodist at the Kiev International Film Festival. In 2002 followed the demanding documentary film *Elisabeth Kübler-Ross: Dem Tod ins Gesicht sehen* (Elisabeth Kübler-Ross: Death Looked in the Face); here too, he was responsible for the screenplay, direction, and production. The film was nominated for best documentary film for the Swiss Film Prize of 2004, and shown widely in movie theaters in Switzerland, Germany, Austria, and Spain. In 2003 came *Moritz*, his first television feature film, for which he is coauthor, director, and coproducer, and in 2004 the documentary *Downtown Switzerland*, codirected with Christian Davi, Kaspar Kasics, and Fredi M. Murer. In 2006, he made the documentary *Ein Lied für Argyris* (A Song for Argyris); here too, he was responsible for screenplay, direction, and production.

7
Sabine Boss (*1966)

The synopsis of her diploma project, *Endspurt* (Final Sprint), runs as follows: "A couple have a fight that makes a few tentative attempts at getting off the ground, then quickly gathers impetus and reaches a conclusion that is a beginning." Stretching the point a little, one could interpret this synopsis autobiographically using a quotation from Sabine Boss: "It was the very first class, and I handed in a really bad film!" While her diploma film was still rather too tentative, she quickly gathered impetus as an assistant director at the Hamburg Schauspielhaus, where she began with her own, highly successful production of *Creeps*. Subsequently she worked in the theaters of Hanover and Lucerne and then came into top form with *Studers erster Fall* (Studer's First Case) and *Kein Zurück, Studers zweiter Fall* (No Going Back, Studer's Second Case), both of which feature a policewoman. These productions were followed by *Crisis in Havana* with Victor Giacobbo, with over 300,000 box office tickets sold, and *Undercover*. Today, Sabine Boss is one of Switzer-

5

7

6

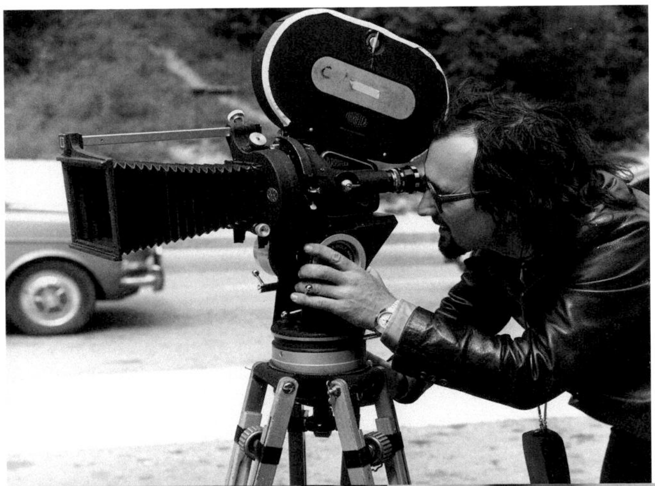

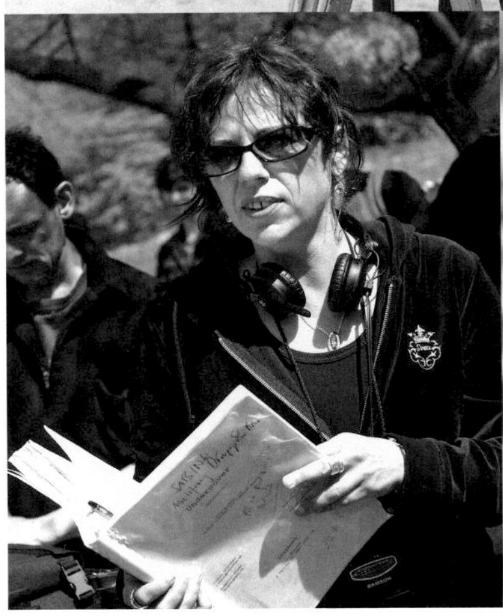

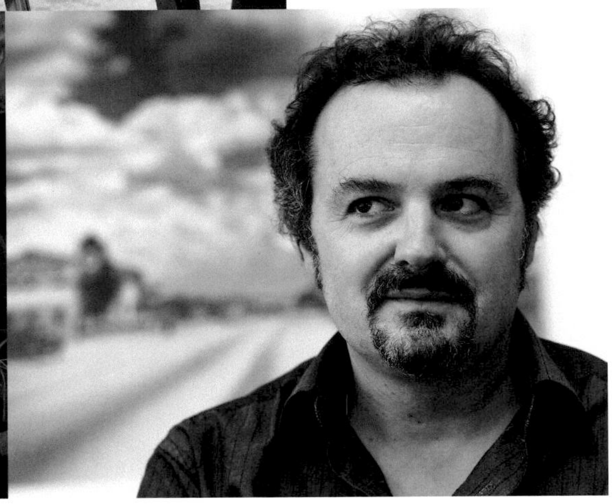

land's established filmmakers. Thus her final performance at the School of Art and Design Zurich, where her diploma project barely received a passing grade, marked the beginning of an impressive career as a director that can only be described as outstanding.

Sabine Boss studied in the Department of Film and Video between 1992 and 1995.

8

Bettina Oberli (*1972)

Das Fräuleinwunder (The Girl Wonder)—the title of which is a nod to the title of Andrea Staka's film—refers to the four women graduates of the film class, Sabine Boss, Anna Luif, Bettina Oberli, and Andrea Staka, the "wonder women" of the Swiss feature film scene in recent times.

One of the products of these "wonder women" is Bettina Oberli's second feature film, *Late Bloomers* (2006), which drew an audience of over half a million viewers. The film tells the story of four women who blossom late in life and cause a stir in their village by opening a lingerie boutique. Oberli meticulously describes the intoxicating effects which these ladies—with their white hair tinted to the pale purples and violets of meadow saffron, their fine wrinkles, and the hint of pink on their lips—unleash on their village, pitching the stolid Emmental valley into a frivolously cheerful chaos worthy of the works of Friedrich Dürrenmatt.

This movie, which is geared toward a broad viewer base, is a precise depiction of human longings, dreams, fears, and behavior patterns. It would be wrong, however, to say that Oberli courts the public. Rather, her first feature film, *Im Nordwind* (In the North Wind), is an extremely sensitive treatment of the theme of unemployment. And when asked about her future plans, she says that her next project could easily turn out to be a "depressing arthouse movie."

9

Anna Luif (*1972)

With her short film *Summertime*, Anna Luif earned over twenty prizes at film festivals in Switzerland and abroad and also won the Swiss Film Prize for best short film. This film already reveals her sensitive affinity for coming-of-age stories, her leisurely narrative style, and her intense focus on the ages of puberty and adolescence from the female perspective.

Blue Girl Blue was her rite of passage in feature film format and high-definition video—a level of image quality that can compete with classical film material. In a memorable visual language that is carefully balanced in form, Luif uses intensified, dramatically accentuated and garish color to describe the emotional tumults of a love story between two young people against the background of severe family problems in an atmosphere that is intense, emotional, and cheerful at the same time. As in *Summertime*, the protagonist is a pubescent girl, who is caught with her dreams and fears in a sterile atmosphere and the social dynamics of teenage girls.

Anna Luif is a director, screenplay writer, and graduate of the Film and Video Department.

10

Andrea Staka (*1973)

Andrea Staka studied in the Department of Film and Video between 1993 and 1998. Her diploma project, *Hotel Beograd*, became one of the most successful short films to emanate from Switzerland in recent years. In thirteen minutes she tells the story of a night of love: a brief encounter between two young people whose life stories are characterized by uprooting and longing. The film tells of migration, of the traces of a lost time in which memory always comes off worst in the face of alienation through war and displacement. The Yugoslavia of the past and its people's lives exile is the common theme that dominates all Staka's works to date, from *Hotel Beograd* through *Jugodivas* to her greatest success, *Fräulein*. However, her films represent more than mere descriptions of people's perceptions and memories of their former home countries; ultimately, they are universal messages. *Fräulein* won the Golden Leopard at the Locarno Film Festival in 2006, earning Staka the most important award to date in her already impressive list of prizes.

9

10 8

1a *Matto regiert*, 1947. Film music Robert Blum, screenplay Leopold Lindtberg

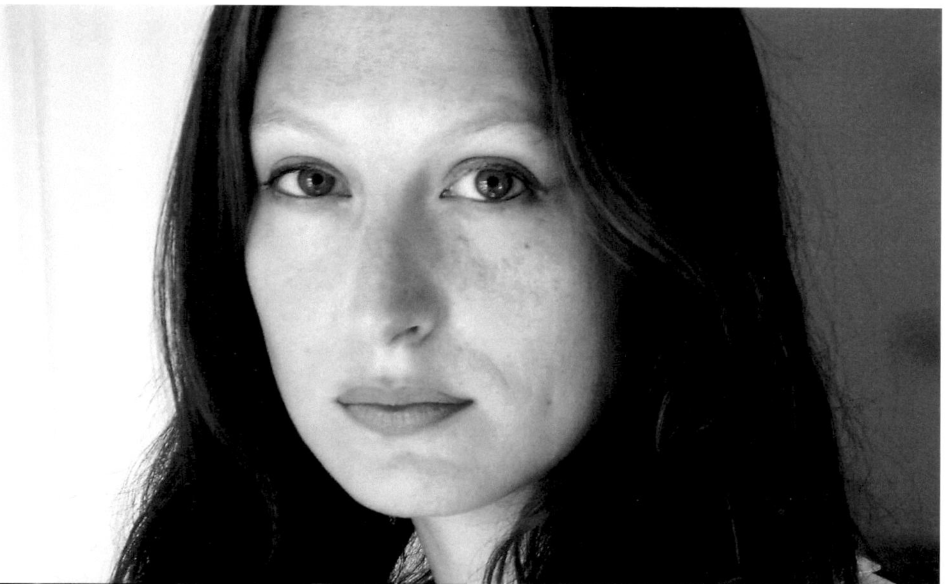

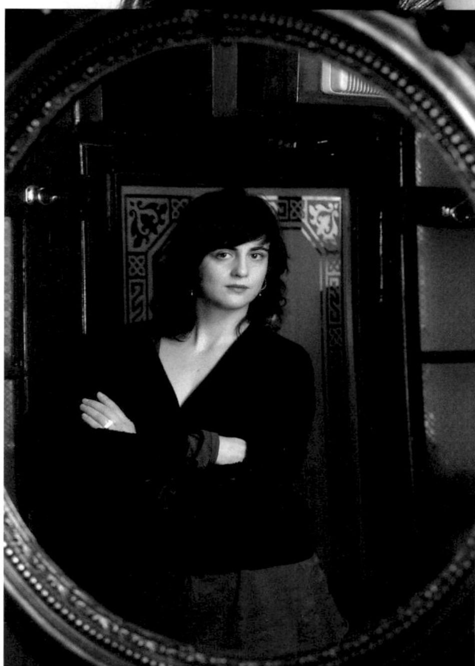

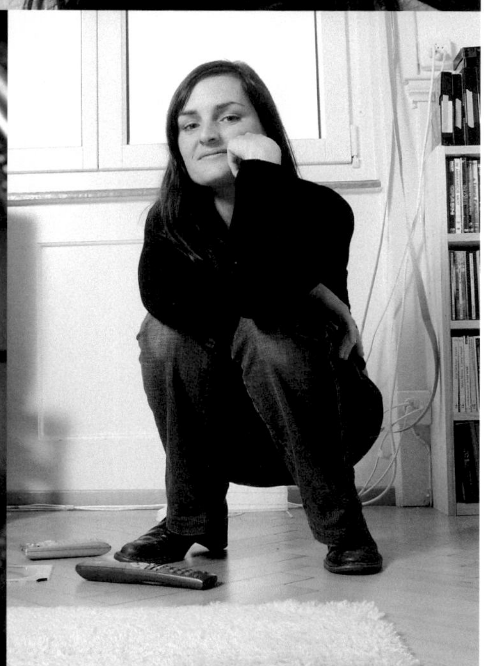

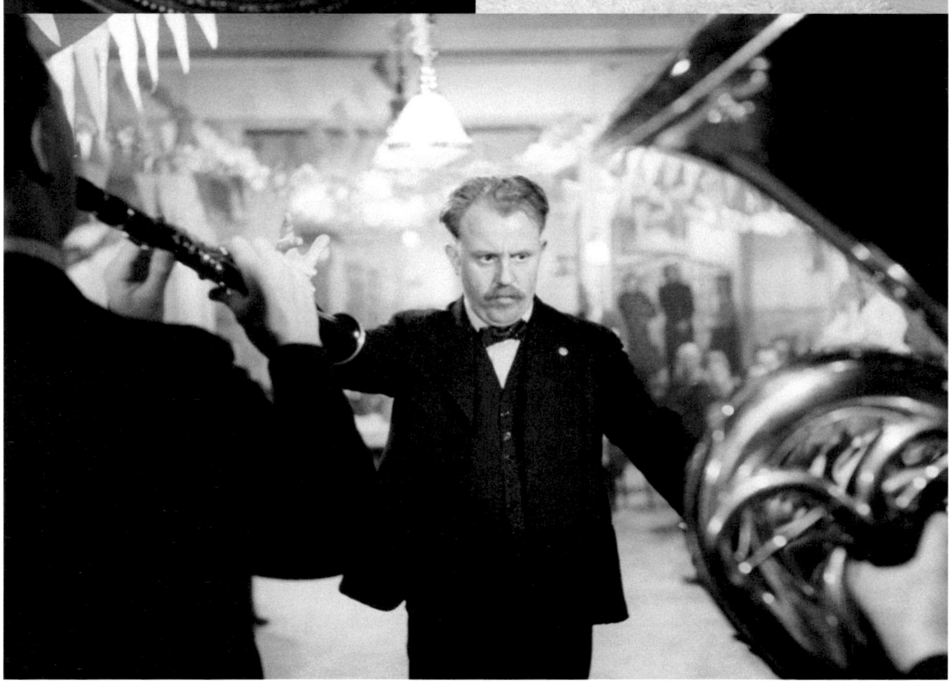

1b *Die missbrauchten Liebesbriefe*, 1940. Film music Robert Blum, director Leopold Lindtberg
2a/b Jacqueline Veuve, *La Nébuleuse du cœur*, 2005. Film still
2c Delphine Seyrig in *Porträt einer Kometin*, 2000

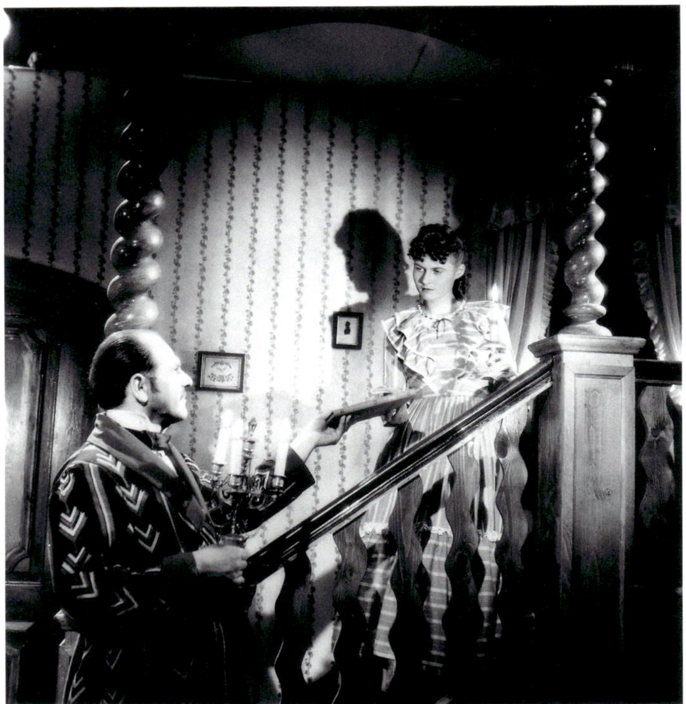

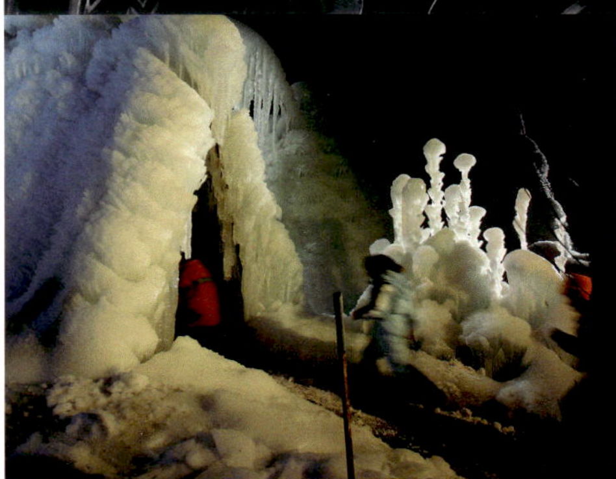

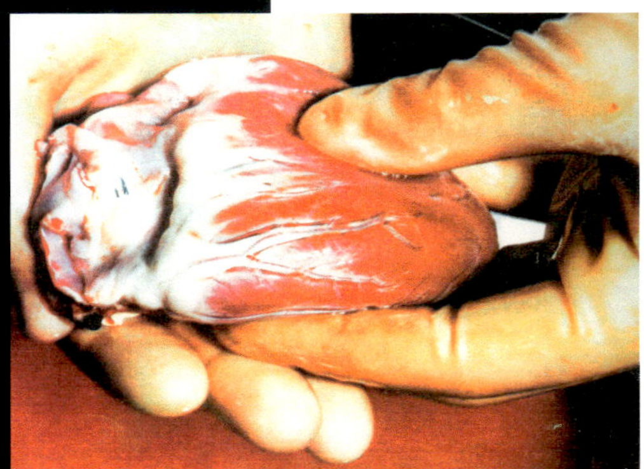

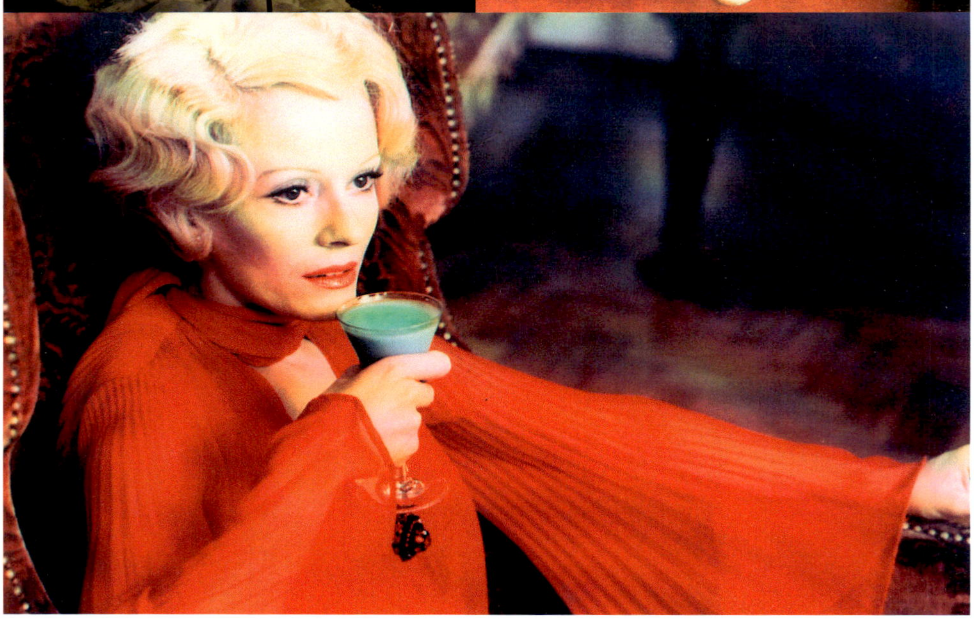

2d Jacqueline Veuve, *Parti sans adresse,* 1982

3a Fredi M. Murer, *Wir Bergler in den Bergen sind eigentlich nicht schuld, dass wir da sind,* 1974

3b *Höhenfeuer,* 1985

3c Poster for *Grauzone,* 1978

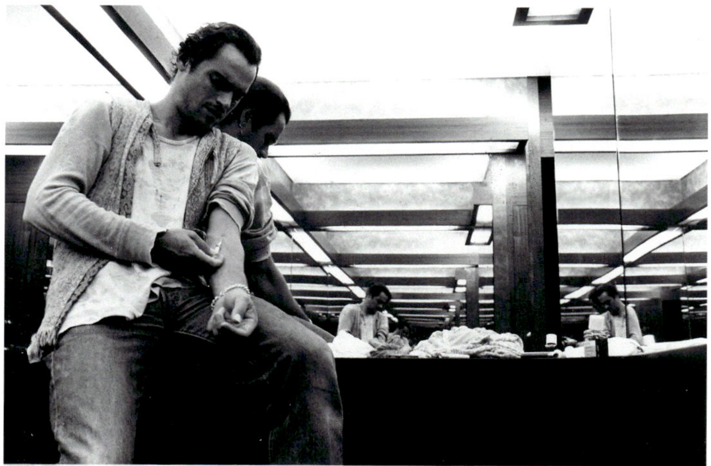

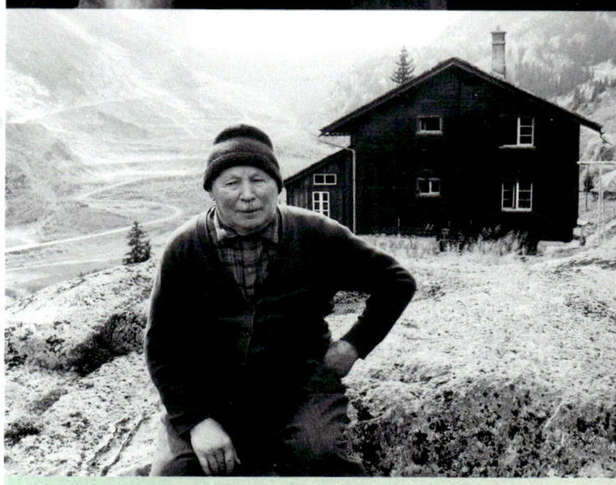

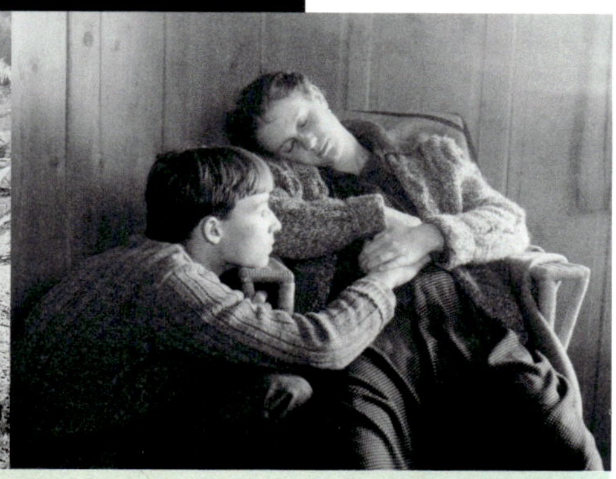

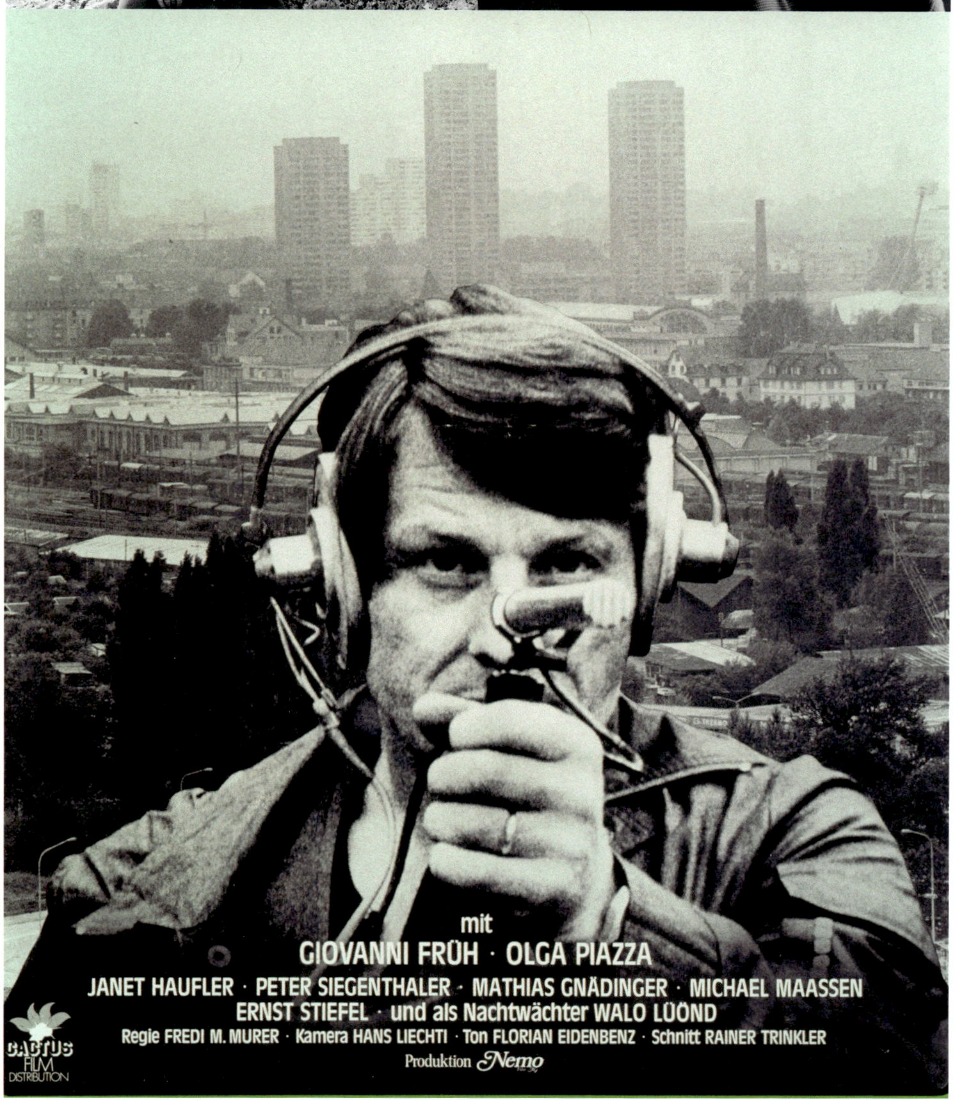

4a Shooting on location on Mount Pilatus for Markus Imhoof's *Der Berg*, 1990

4b *Das Boot ist voll*, 1981. Michael Gemphart, Mathias Gnädinger, and Tina Engel

4c Markus Imhoof in New York City

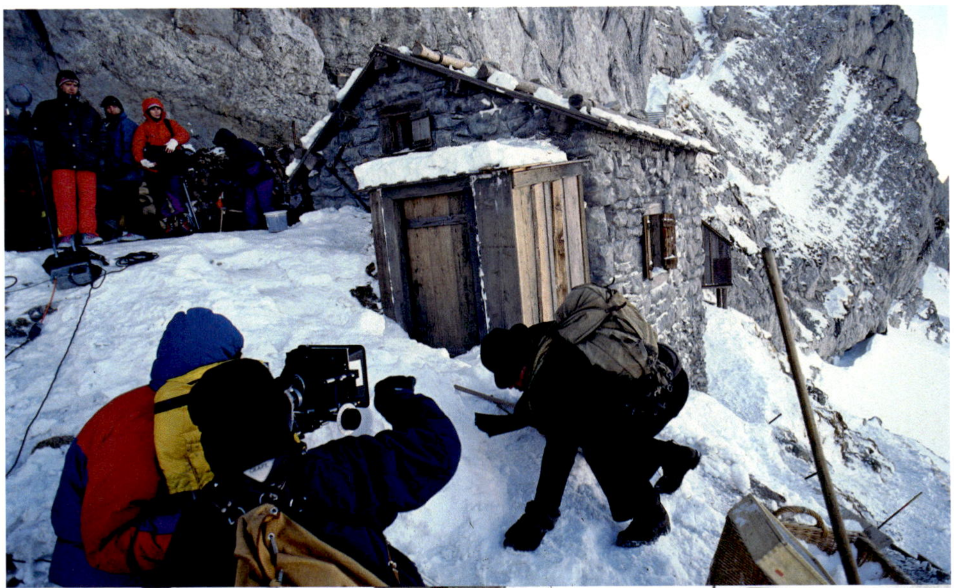

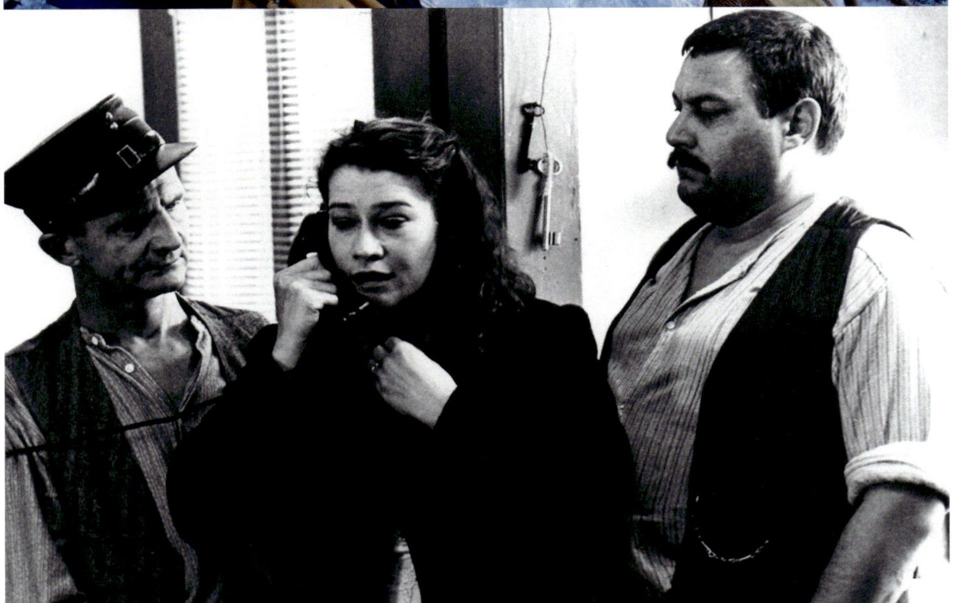

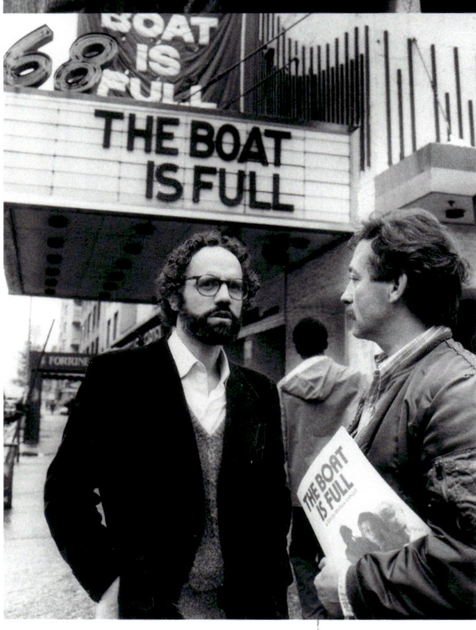

5a Clemens Klopfenstein, *Geschichte der Nacht*, 1979
5b *E Nachtlang Füürland*, 1981
5c *Das Schweigen der Männer*, 1996

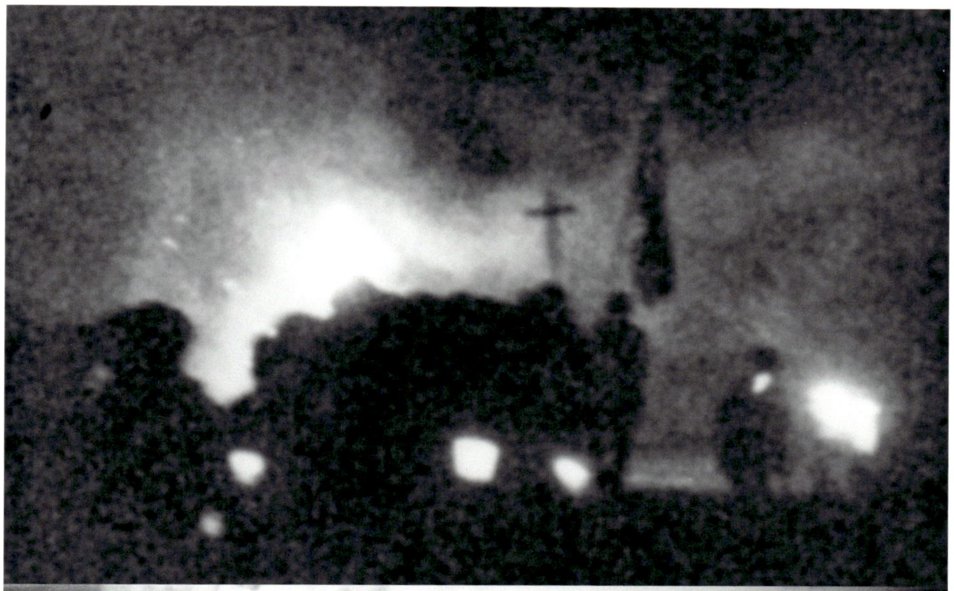

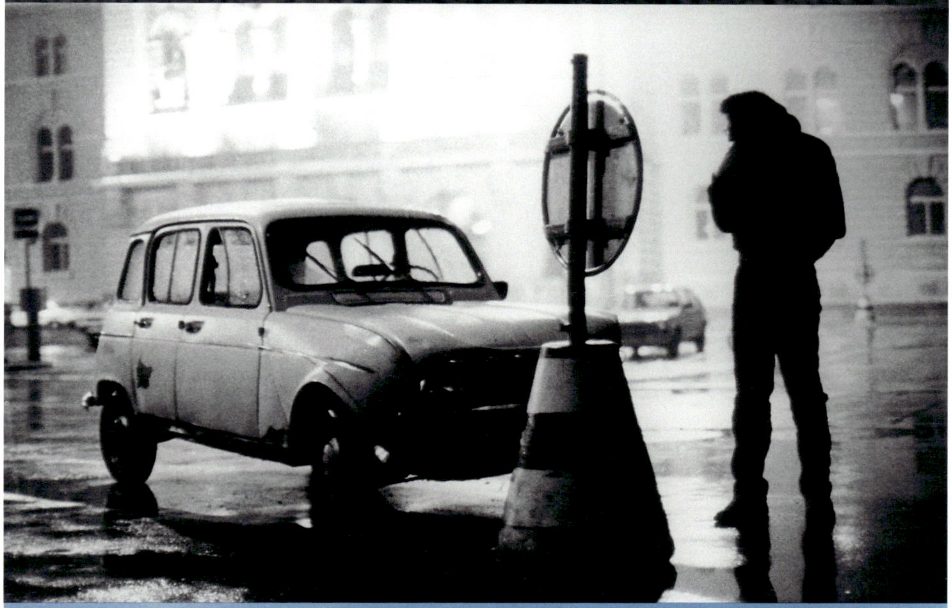

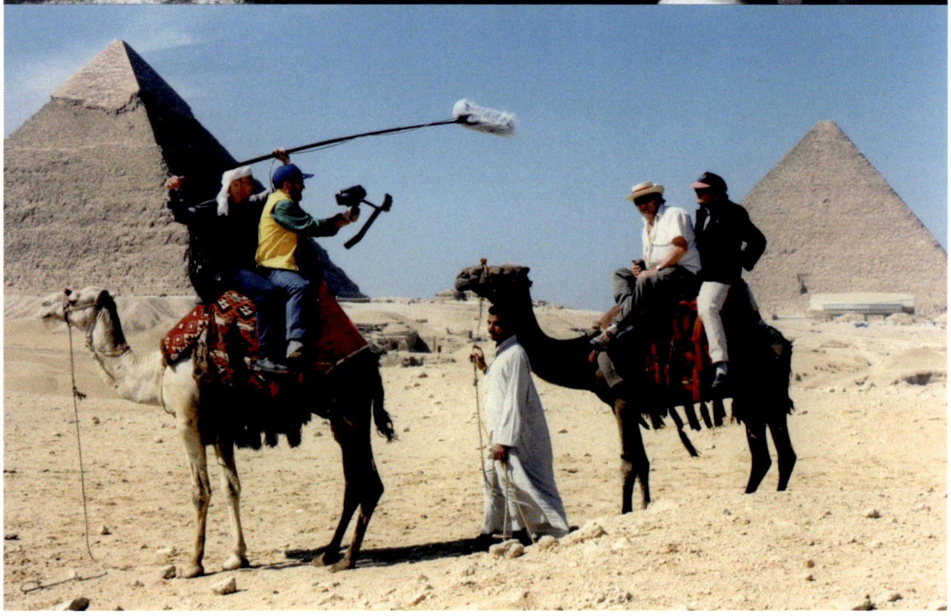

6a Stefan Haupt, *Ein Lied für Argyris*, 2006. Delphi

6b *Ein Lied für Argyris*, 2006. The Nazi massacre in Distomo on June 10, 1944

6c *Utopia Blues*, 2001. Babett Arens, Ettore Cella, Bruno Cathomas and others. Screenplay with Michael Finger

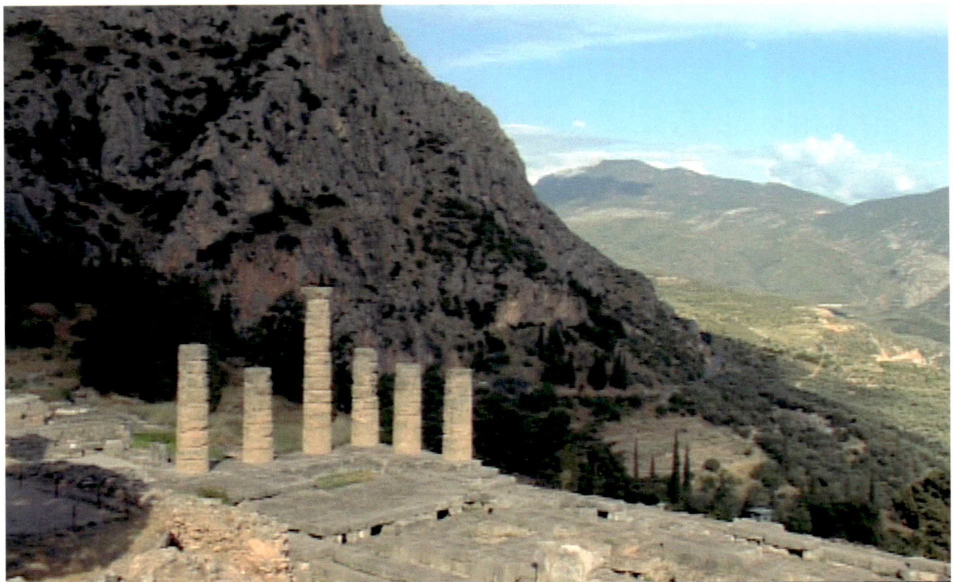

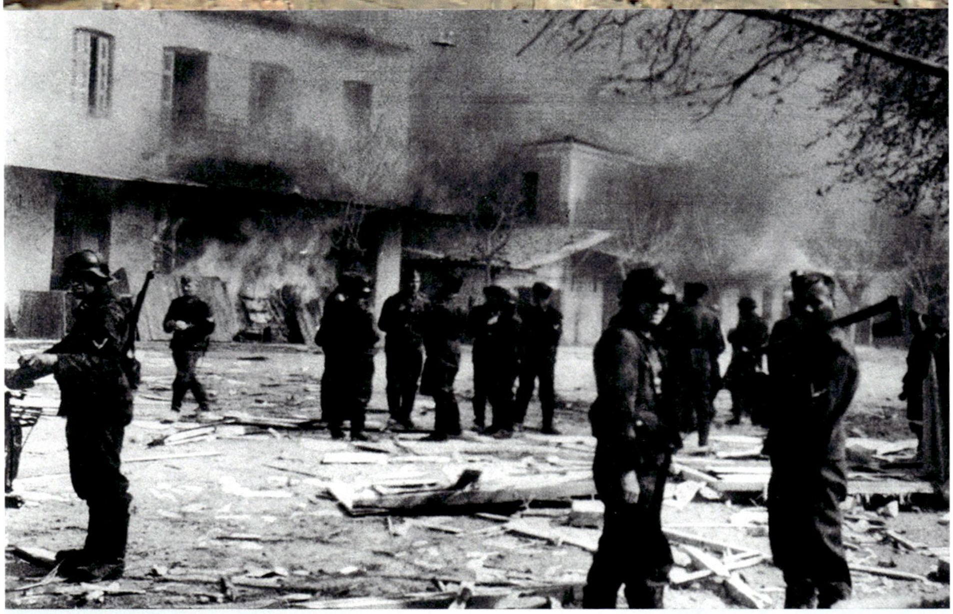

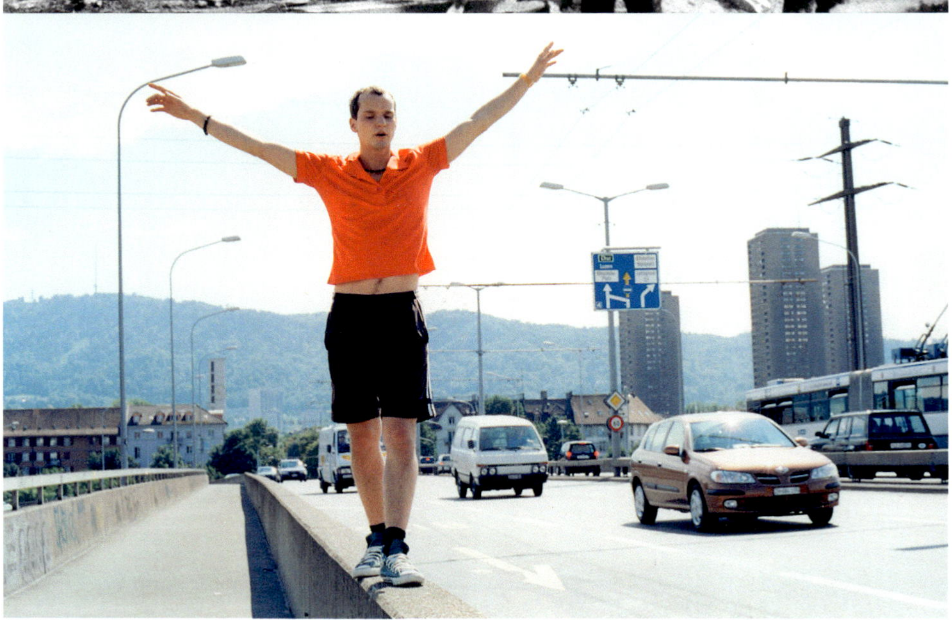

7a–d Sabine Boss, *Ernstfall in Havanna*, 2001. Victor Giacobbo with Carla Sanchez and Sabina Schneebeli

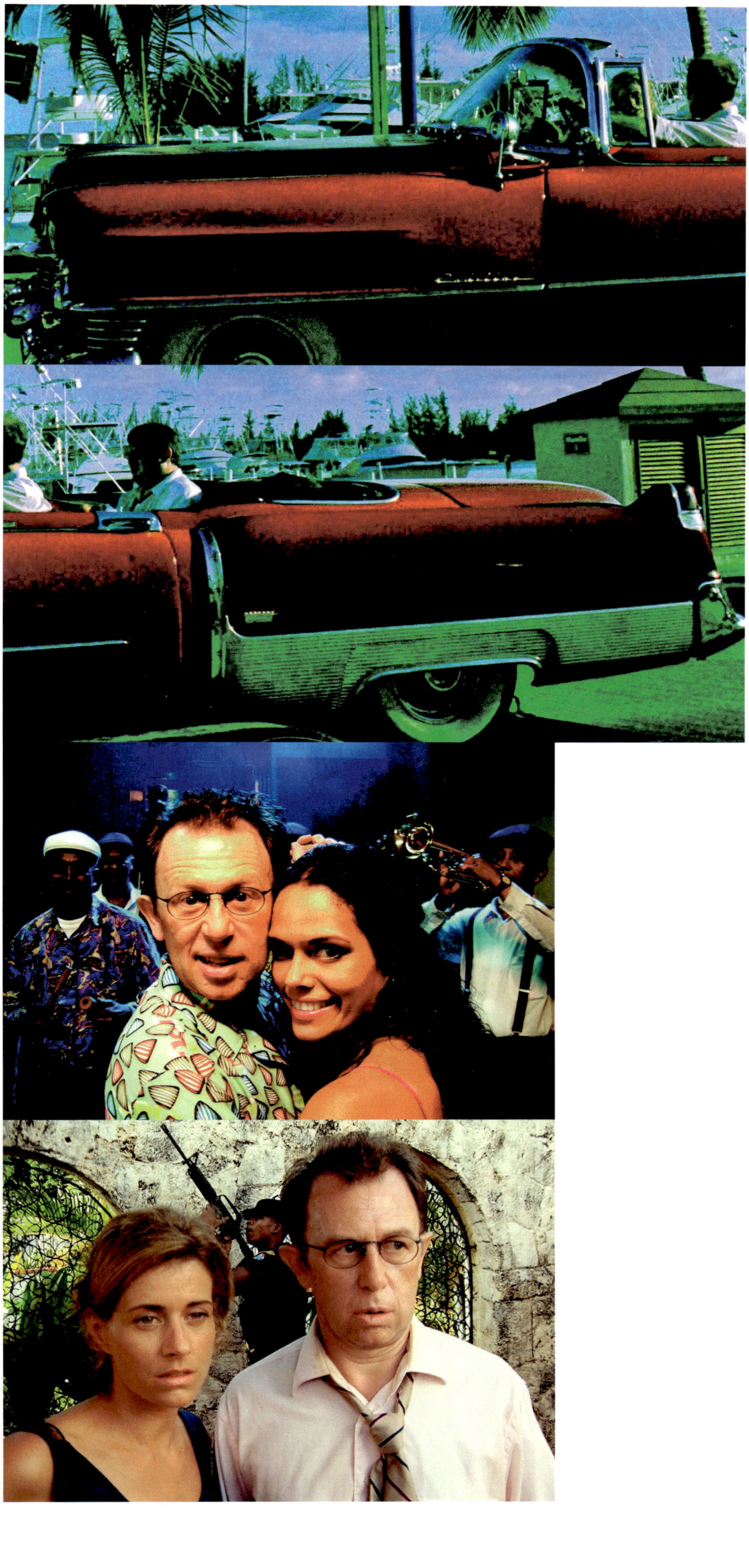

8a/b Bettina Oberli, *Herbstzeitlosen*, 2007

9a Anna Luif, *Summertime*, 2000

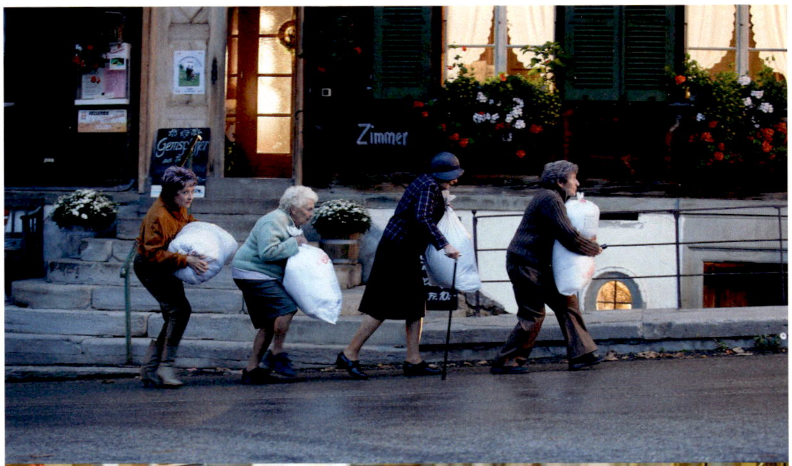

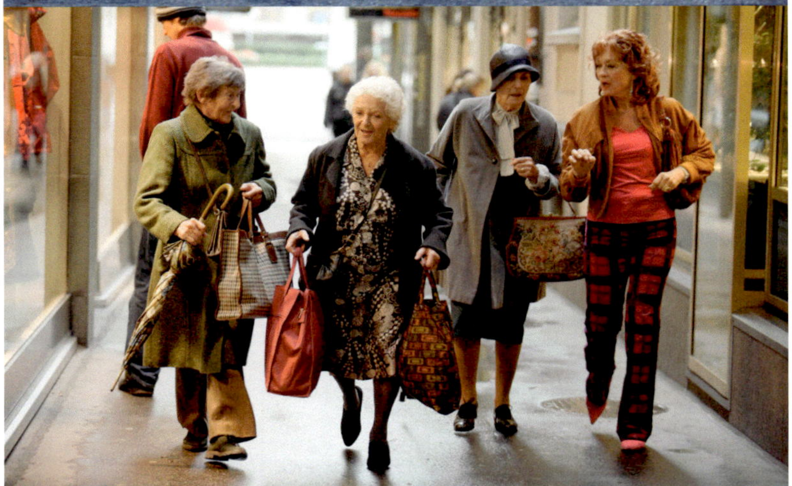

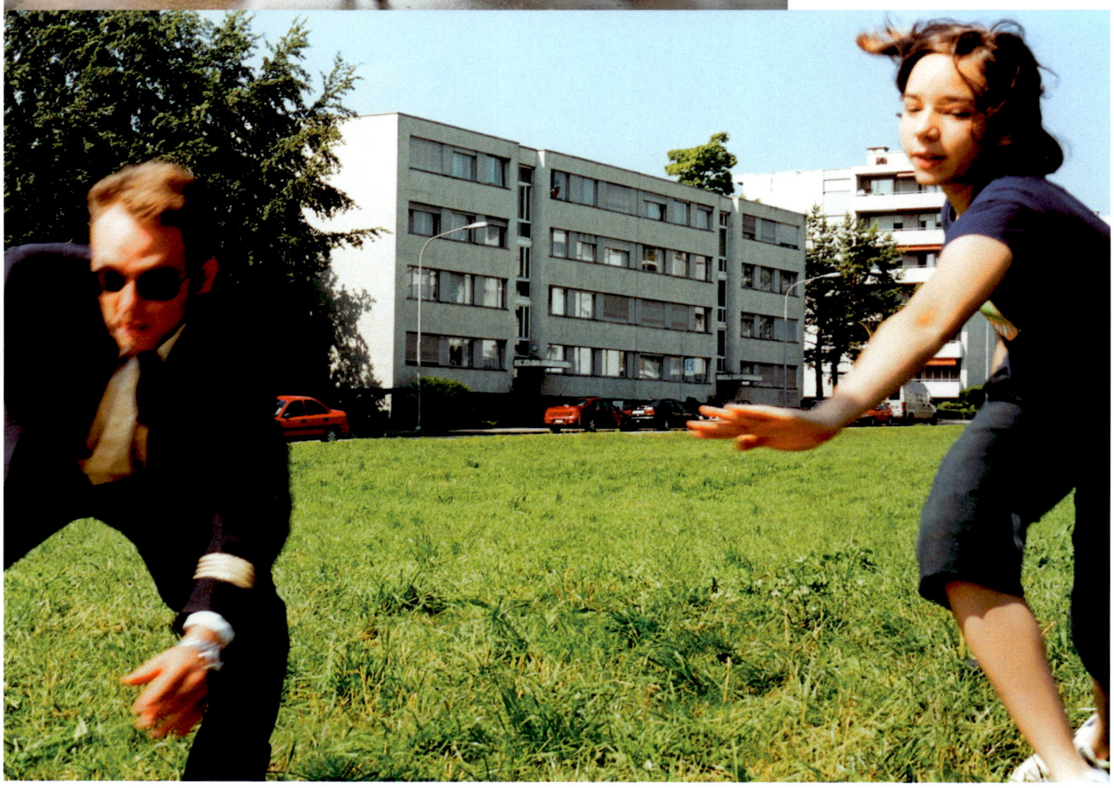

9b/c Anna Luif, *Little Girl Blue*, 2003. Screenplay with Micha Lewinsky
10a Andrea Staka, *Das Fräulein*, 2006

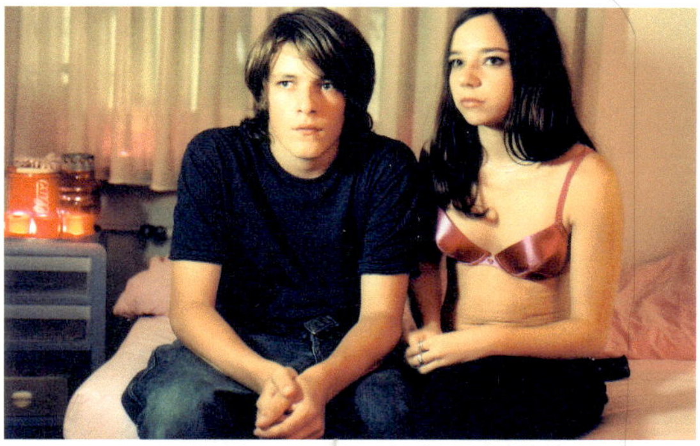

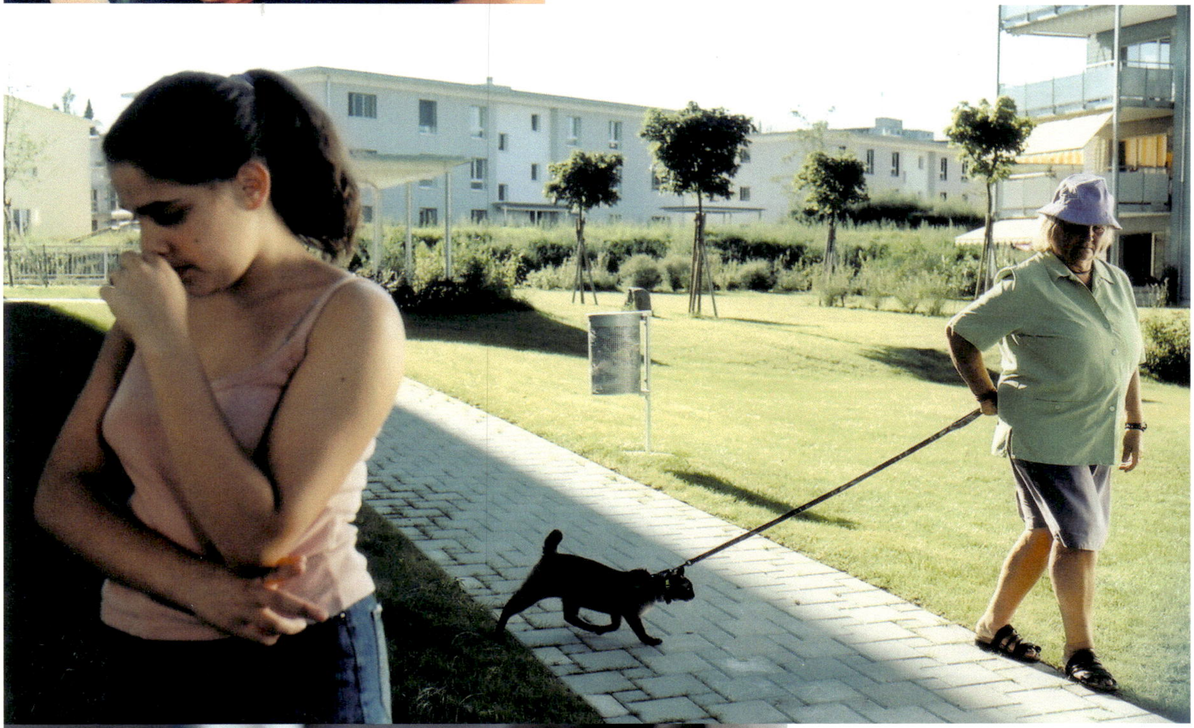

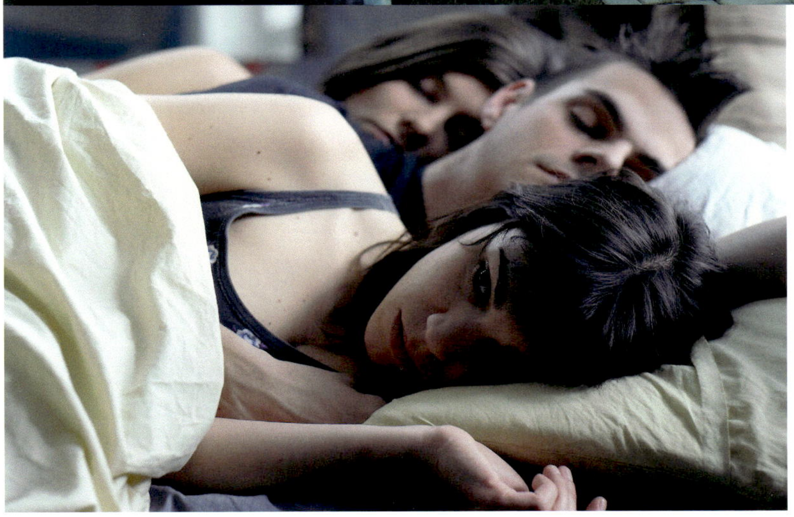

They are the yeast, the leaven, they embody the "activating energy" for the radical conversion of artistic material. They set the rules of grammar and syntax into a state of fermentation, allowing new scenic, visual, linguistic, and sound worlds to emerge. They rupture conven-

1

Serge Stauffer (1929–1989)

"An agitator's agenda, a trouble-maker, someone who deliberately provokes the other teachers and the students of the School of Applied Arts, was the official verdict leading to the closure of the Color and Form (Form und Farbe = F+F) class." Serge Stauffer was both the cofounder and, by his withdrawal, the coliquidator of the class. The vision of the F+F, which was inspired by the movement of 1968, had a markedly modern and avant-garde thrust. It demanded debates about social issues, group-dynamic learning processes, and the right of students to have a say in organizational matters. The class was a rock of offence, made still more offensive by Stauffer's Dadaist impetus. He is the translator and commentator of what is probably the largest edition of Duchamp in Geman (*Duchamp's Schriften,* 1981), a meticulous production which he created in cooperation with the publisher Theo Ruff. He is the doyen of Duchamp research and a passionate and determined art researcher.

He received his photography training in the school's photography class. He was an excellent ambassador for the French language and culture. He was the first to translate Ionesco into German. Calling himself a feminist, he examined social and artistic questions from the perspective of gender determination. He was one of the earliest gender researchers.

He taught the photography class from 1957–70 and subsequently taught in the F+F.

2

Aldo Walker (1938–2000)

His biography is unusual. He was trained as an electrician and managed his parents' electrical appliance shop. He was a cross-border commuter between art and philosophy. His influence developed not only as an important artist but also as the point of contact and mentor of colleagues and students at the school of art and design where he headed the Department of Visual Design and never shied away from a dispute. He was known for his one-man and group shows in Switzerland and abroad. He was the first Swiss artist to reside for one year at the studio maintained by the Swiss Federal government at the PS 1 art center in New York. There followed representation of Switzerland at the Venice Biennale and added fame with the award of the Art Prize of the City of Lucerne. Aldo Walker's works are not solitary works of art but rather more like vehicles and "explosive material" for a far-reaching emotional and intellectual investigation of the position of the people of the world.

3

Gerald Bennett (*1942)

Gerald Bennett has no difficulty dating his fascination with the tonal possibilities of music conceived and generated using electro-acoustic means. Apparently it began in 1972, when he heard a piece by the French composer Jean-Claude Risset—the experience was so direct and sensuous that he was instantly won over. A native of New Jersey, USA, Bennett the composer did not have to wait long to be discovered. No less a person than Pierre Boulez himself invited him to help set up the famous Ircam Institute in Paris, which Bennett joined in 1976 and where he was head of research until 1980—alongside such illustrious colleagues as Jean-Claude Risset, Vinko Globokar, and Luciano Berio. Bennett brought this experience with him on his return to Switzerland, where he not only worked as an exceptionally inspiring teacher, but also became one of the pioneers of Swiss computer music. His founding of the Institute for Computer Music and Sound Technology at the Zurich School of Music, Drama and Dance marked the culmination of his career and even today continues to make waves far beyond Switzerland itself.

4

Berndt Höppner (*1942)

Berndt Höppner is a continuing source of inspiration to his students, an agitator and instigator, radical in his judgments and in his demands for the development of a multiplicity of ideas and expressions.

As an artist, stupendous craft skills and overflowing inventive powers make him a highly gifted *bricoleur*, who creates his unwieldy and poetic installations from urban refuse. He is a collector and assembler of plywood, PVC panels, scrap wood, wrapping paper, plastic canisters, and other items. By means of wire, tape, and clamps, all of these discarded elements are submitted to an inspired and never-ending process-oriented transformation, often executed in situ in the exhibition gallery over a period of weeks, and even during the exhibition itself as a performative element.

In collaboration with Luigi Archetti und Peter Emch, Berndt Höppner founded the visual arts program, which he headed for many tions, calling into question and undermining the existing conditions and manifestations of art, searching for new expressive forms and a new aesthetic consensus. They discovered new languages. They were and are quintessentially contemporary, revising and developing new, different models and standards. Probing, inventive, and thorough, they dig deep in their search for the authentic. They embody that which is referred to as artistic willfulness. They live from the concordance of person and (life) work. They stir things up, challenge us with subversive strategies, their indeterminacy, rupture, fragmentation. Their greatest horror is compilation and copying. The ultimate challenge is the new.

He is the embodiment par excellence of the spirit of Dada and of French culture **1**; his philosophical treatises on art are themselves verbal artworks **2**; he toils over his electro-acoustic researches on a computer **3**; he both lives and communicates artistic willfulness **4**; he unites tactless music with tactless design **5**; his theater projects truly merit the term avant-garde **6**; his artworks oscillate between glamour and shock **7**; his oeuvre, acclaimed worldwide, cannot be reduced to some provincial Swiss scandal **8**; her ornaments constitute a "crime" **9**; his installations are sparkling bricolage, as intoxicating as a kir royal **14**; his bags are a match for any others **13**; his performance art flaunts normalcy **11**; he attains ecstasy via asceticism **12**; his stage productions are found throughout the German-speaking world **16**; he combines maximum complexity with the most innovative aesthetic expressions **10**; she has danced, exceptionally well, in the classic Swan Lake, as well with the limb-dislocating Forsythe Company **15**.

years, under the innocuous but meaningful title of Drawing and Painting. He took responsibility for discovering artistic individuality in students, and is himself an exceptionally gifted draftsman. His style came to be known as the "new sensibility." *Grüne Nächte* (Green Nights), his sensitive volume of illustrations of American poetry, was published in 1974 by DuMont Verlag.

5

Ruedi Wyss (*1949)

The tenor of Ruedi Wyss's posters is suggested by the name of an avant-garde music festival he cofounded: "taktlos" is a musical pun meaning both "tactless" and "unmeasured." His graphic works are both, for they experimentally and dissonantly rupture the canon of "moderate" design, incorporating the ephemeral, the marginal, the fugitive, avoiding any definite "key"—to invoke the second avant-garde music festival cofounded and codirected by Wyss ("tonart," or musical key).

Improvisational, process-oriented, in search of new visual stimuli, his posters exist outside of graphic conventions. They pose more questions than they answer, opening a space for interpretation, rejoicing in their distance from the familiar, brilliantly improvised or "incorrectly" assembled. They embody acts of stylistic liberation and ironization, and only the typefaces remain as recognizable constants—at least for the most part. The visual repertoire contains reinterpreted mass-media refuse, while both text and typography, and even more so grid structures, are attacked by "clumsy" paste-ons and shrill colors. Ruedi Wyss's posters anticipate the provocative interactions between contemporary music and design that are conceivable in the context of the Zurich University of the Arts.

Ruedi Wyss is head of preparatory studies at the School of Art and Design Zurich.

6

Stephan Müller (*1951)

Stephan Müller began as an extra, a directorial assistant, and then as dramaturg under Werner Düggelin in Basel, and from the mid-1970s he dedicated himself to theatrical and dance studies in the USA. In 1978, he was appointed head of the lab at the Zurich Schauspielhaus. In 1980–83, he worked as an independent director and received recognition as a specialist in avant-garde projects and experiments. In 1993–99, he was codirector with Volker Hesse of the Theater am Neumarkt in Zurich. The two complemented one another ideally, and the Theater am Neumarkt enjoyed an artistic and public heyday. Among Müller's directing achievements are *Phaidon* after Plato; Peter Weiss's *Marat/Sade; The Black Rider* by Waits/Wilson/Burroughs; and Goethe's *Faust II*. Müller currently works at the Vienna Burgtheater, the Maxim Gorki Theater Berlin, and the Theater Basel. He worked as an adviser for the Zurich Schauspielhaus during Marthaler's tenure, and for the Stadttheater Bern during Gramss's directorship. He has been active as an opera director since 1989, directing Walter Zimmermann's *Die Blinden* (The Blind) in Frankfurt at Gary Bertini's invitation, as well as Purcell's *Dido and Aeneas* in Lucerne in 2005–2006, and Jules Massenet's *Werther* in 2007. At the Zurich University of the Arts Stephan Müller teaches at the Department of Performing Arts and Film and heads the Directing study program.

7

Daniele Buetti (*1955)

Glamor and horror contrast in Daniele Buetti's art into a ghastly and beautiful synthesis on our consumer and lifestyle cult. One of his strategies is to injure the immaculate beauty and perfection of supermodels using fake scars that trigger confusion and permanently latent unease. With minimal means the portrayal of the most beautiful people of our time as we see them on the covers of fashion magazines is "disfigured" with terminology and text. These reproductions show deceptively real looking growths and scars. Where Buetti actionistically plastered these in city spaces as world-format posters without commentary or context, the worlds of make-believe and reality rose precariously into a cosmos of the ugly. Another project, *Lightboxes*, involves writing over the bodies of beautiful women using light-emitting diodes; these works recall the devotional candles at pilgrimage sites, the glitter worlds of Broadway and Ginza or the flickering neon of red-light districts like Patong Beach. They bewitch and enchant in their blinding glitter and simultaneously celebrate the negative beautiful—the abnormal and the suppressed.

Buetti attended the photography class at the School of Applied Arts, where he already initiated actionistic projects together with Thomas Hirschhorn. Today he is a professor at the Münster Academy of Art.

1 2
3 4

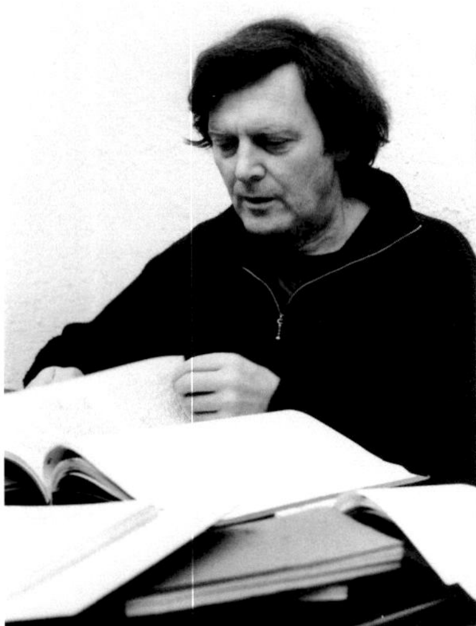
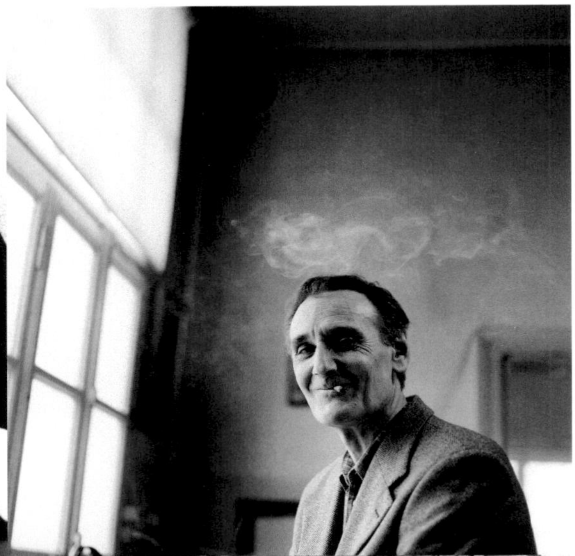
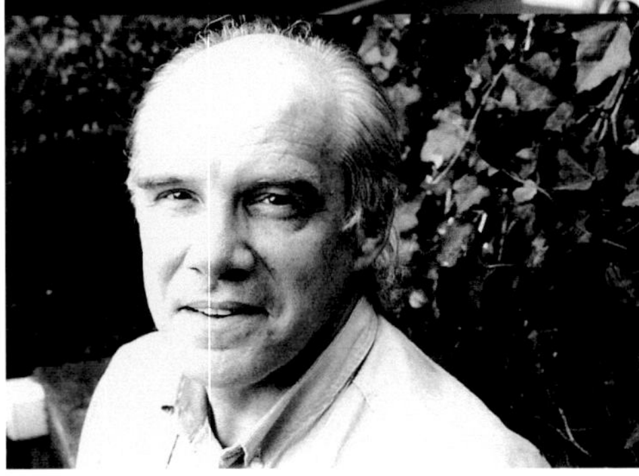
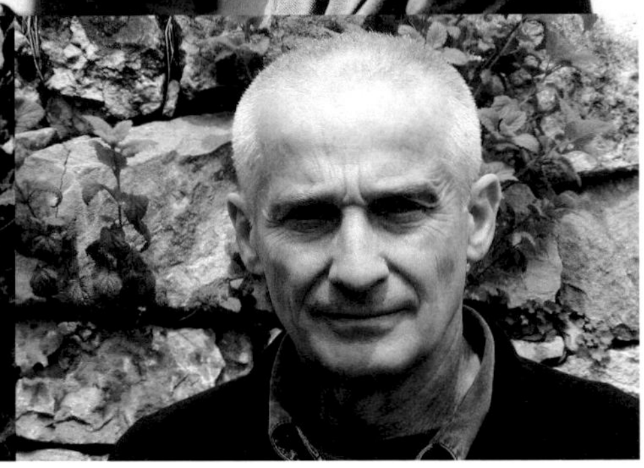

8

Thomas Hirschhorn (*1957)

On 12 June, 1980, visitors using the main entrance of the School of Applied Arts unexpectedly found themselves immersed in an extremely poetic, pink atmosphere. The floor was painted pink and, flooded with morning sunlight, reflected its color onto the white ceiling to bathe the entire lobby in a uniform pink glow. The School of Applied Arts building, which was rather old and in need of repairs at the time and had all the charm of a military barracks, acquired a more cheerful atmosphere through this surprise stratagem.

The person responsible for the frivolous prank was soon found. It was none other than Hirschhorn. This was probably the first controversial public gesture by the leading *agent provocateur* of the international art scene. As the perpetrator of this act of vandalism of public property, he was punished by having to remove the "mess" with his own hands. Since then, Hirschhorn has performed his provocative repertoire with cardboard and brown adhesive tape at the *Documenta*, the Biennale, and in the hotspots of social upheaval in the *banlieus* of Paris, "sticking" his art together with manic political dedication according to his personal creed: "In art the impossible triumphs over the possible. This is the triumph over narcissism, depression, resentment, and fear. I want to be uncompromising, because art does not come about through consensus. Art is not diplomatic; it is impossible to create art by lame compromises." Accordingly, ever since his controversial appearance at the Centre Culturel in Paris and its cultural and political aftermath, he has been uncompromising in his refusal to participate in exhibitions in Switzerland. However, his popularity on the world's leading art market portal "artnet" is steadily growing. He currently ranks in fifty-seventh place, ahead of Henry Moore, Keith Haring, Gustav Klimt, and John Cage.

9

Karin Wälchli (*1960)

By the criteria of Adolf Loos, Karin Wälchli would be considered a criminal. In the exacting prose of *Ornament and Crime*, his perhaps most celebrated essay, Loos excoriates the use of ornament as one of the greatest transgressions. According to Loos, the plague of ornamentation, one approved and even subsidized by the government, is responsible for unspeakable damage and desolation to the aesthetic development of humankind. Only under postmodernism did design succeed in ridding itself of the procrustean bed of such rigid, formalist reductionism.

Together with her partner Guido Reichlin, Karin Wälchli has used her label Chalet 5 to endow ornament with a new dignity. It is mainly the investments in terms of content, the patterns, so rich in images and associations, the links between abstract and concrete—through the introduction of photography, of the ordinary, of the everyday—that have provided ornament here with new spaces for projection and association. Karin Wälchli began as a pioneer, realizing her ornamental and textile concepts in foulards and materials according to the highest manufacturing standards. Today, she designs and produces wallpapers and even entire façades in the context of modern and contemporary architecture and interior architecture—the latest thing in unfettered art.

She attended the textile program of the School of Art and Design Zurich.

10

Martin Woodtli (*1971)

Martin Woodtli is one of the central figures in *Graphic Design Wonderland* and in the rhetorical inflammatory *Benzin* (Gasoline)—to cite two book titles used to characterize the young Swiss design scene. The motto here is pure joy in the design process in contrast to desires for monetary compensation. Woodtli regards visual design as a medium through which one can create friction within the world as it exists. To work in this world, to intervene in it, and to bring it slightly out of equilibrium, impels him to rejoice in the greatest affronts.

Woodtli is obsessed. He seems to have taken the lines from Brian Eno's diary to heart according to which a good way to create something original is to do something that is so painstaking and time-consuming that no one else would even bother. Woodtli's designs manifest themselves in complex typographic games and manically layered, dense patterns of everyday objects, which he produces in astonishingly precise silkscreen prints.

He studied first at the Bern School of Design, before continuing his studies at the School of Art and Design Zurich. He worked in the offices of David Carson and Stefan Sagmeister in New York before establishing his own studio in Zurich in 1999. His independent, experimental

6

7

5

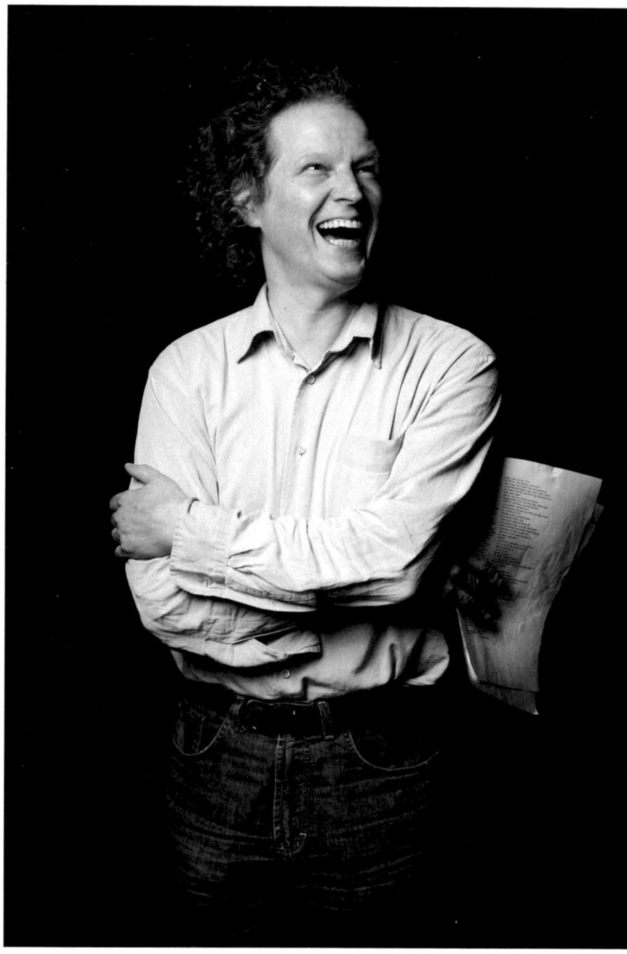

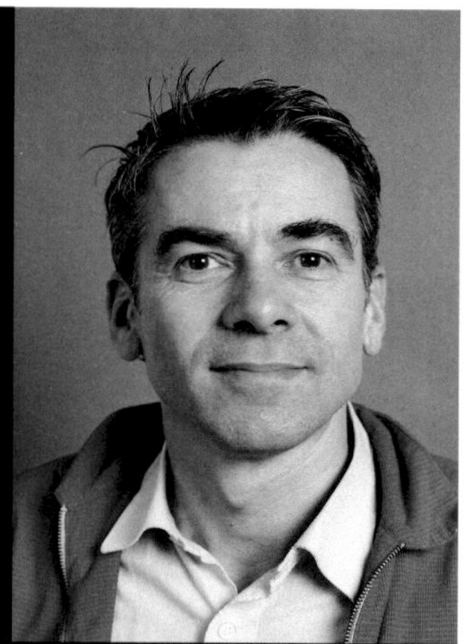

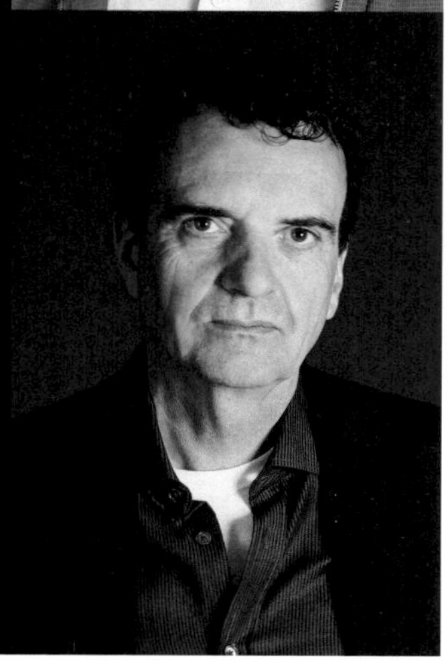

visual language has been awarded numerous design prizes. He is a member of the Alliance Graphique Internationale AGI.

11

San Keller (*1971)

His artistic projects, whether taking the form of objects or actions, operate in public spaces—usually intermingling art and the real (the everyday), private and public. He dances with great suppleness, and with great success, often reaching the heights: entertainer, provocateur, scholarship-holder, commissioned artist, moving between art as a calling and art as service provision. He is amused by his own failure, isolates himself, and occupies first place everywhere, makes himself ridiculous, successfully varies projects as far as he can take them, creating incessant talk about himself.

His trademark is art-as-event, all the way to the carnivalesque: "The carnivalesque is a way of turning the world upside down, breaking down the established order and doing away with all of the forms of fear, respect, piety and etiquette that have emerged from it" (Mikhail Bakhtin). San Keller thrives on it.

Keller is a graduate of the visual arts program.

12

Nik Bärtsch (*1971)

Nikolaus Bärtsch was born in Zurich and now lives in Zurich and Berlin. He began learning jazz piano and percussion at the age of seven and in 1997 completed his piano diploma at the Zurich School of Music. Having spent the years 1998 to 2001 studying philosophy, linguistics, and musicology at the University of Zurich, Bärtsch now works freelance as a pianist, composer, and scenographer of his RITUAL GROOVE MUSIC. He is leader of a group called MOBILE, which performs ritualized groove ceremonies lasting several hours combined with multi-media set-ups of the surrounding space. Bärtsch is also leader of the zen-funk quartet RONIN (with Kaspar Rast, Björn Meyer and Andi Pupato) and since 2001 has been working on a solo project called *Hishiryo* scored for prepared piano and percussion. Bärtsch's aesthetic aims to achieve maximum effect with minimal means and to use the ascetic as a gateway to the ecstatic.

13

Markus Freitag (*1970)

"The Freitag bag is an urban tool—the urban cowboy's saddlebag." The waterproof shoulder bags cobbled together from old truck tarpaulins, bicycle inner tubes, and car seatbelts are *the* brand, the hallmark of the urban lifestyle of the men and women who have been using them for some ten years now, and not only in Europe but also in the USA and Asia. Each is unique, made by hand, marketed in the Container Tower, an iconic building in Zurich West, and displayed in opulent picture catalogues published by Verlag Lars Müller. The Freitags celebrate their everyday culture—in-your-face, ecological, critical.

Markus Freitag was enrolled in the Visual Design course but when production of Freitag bags soared he hung up his studies and shouldered his Freitag bag to join his brother and devote himself exclusively to inventing and producing the Freitag label —with a degree of success that has made it an icon worthy of exhibition in the Museum of Modern Art in New York.

14

Urs Fischer (*1973)

Kir Royal—that mélange of sparkling wine and sugary creme de cassis—was the title of Fischer's bold premiere at the Kunsthaus Zurich, which in 2004 made the large Bührle Hall available to this shooting star for a monographic spectacle. He produces his sculptures, large-format pictures, and proliferating installations through acts of sheer will. His headstrong expressive forms appear improvisational and process-oriented, with their debt to the weighty gesture and the spectacular. Audacious constructions emerge from his battle with the material (often in situ), towering up like bricolage, jauntily painted, grotesque, abstruse, mystifying constellations.

He began his training in the folk photography class at the Higher School of Design Zurich, but broke off his studies early. Then he attended the sought-after de ateliers in Amsterdam and lived as an artist in residence at Delfina Studios in London. His works have been seen in numerous exhibitions, including the Venice Biennale.

15

Kusha Alexi (*1976)

Kusha Alexi is an exceptional phenomenon. Born in Switzerland, she danced her first Giselle in Munich at the age of nineteen, causing a sensation only two years later as Odile/Odette in *Swan Lake*. Such a precipitous career as a stylistically sound and technically skilled interpreter of the great roles of the ballet repertoire

10 9 12
8

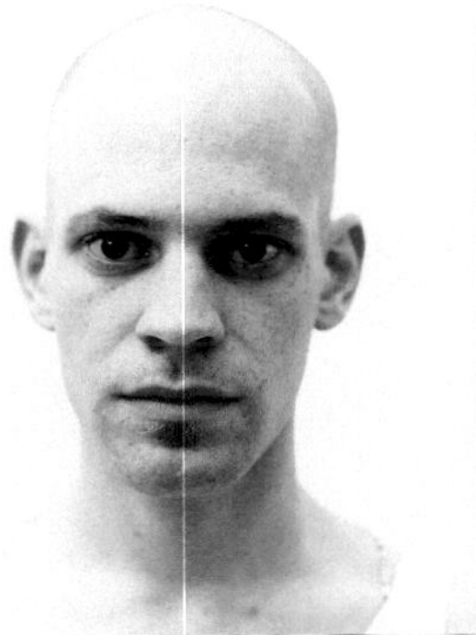
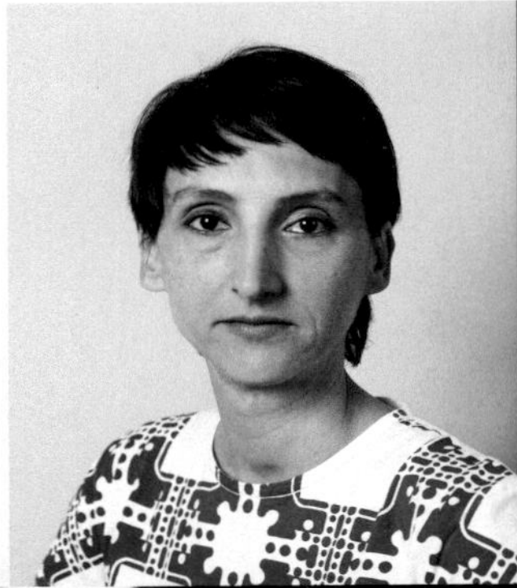
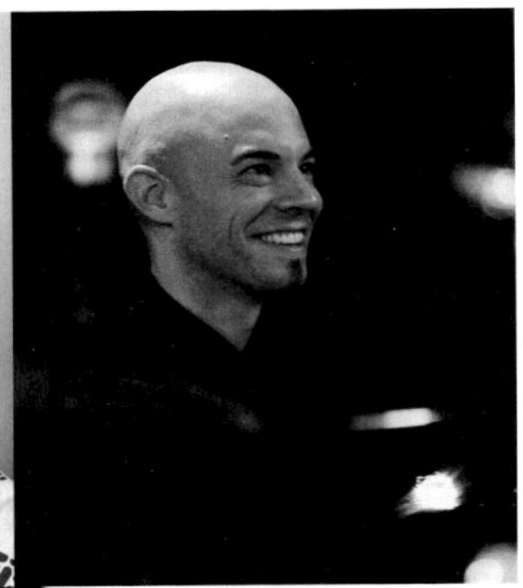
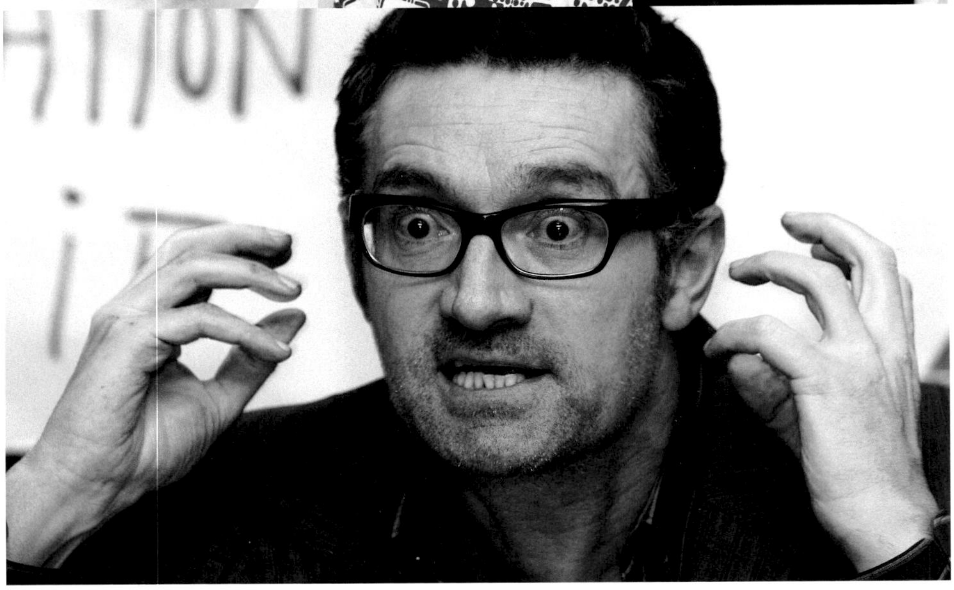

is by no means a foregone conclusion. Kusha Alexi began her professional training at the Swiss Professional Ballet School (SBBS) with Anne Woolliams, going on to study at the Heinz Bosl Foundation in Munich, where she was engaged by the Bavarian State Ballet in 1994. She won prizes at competitions in Aarau, Lausanne, Stockholm, and Jackson USA and went on to become a striking and versatile ballerina with a very modern stage presence. Apart from the classics she has also given highly successful performances in ballets by Balanchine, van Manen, Kylian, Forsythe, Lucinda Childs, Mats Ek, Saburo Teshigawara, and many others. After a short period at the Ballet de Monte Carlo she was a soloist at the Zurich Ballet under Heinz Spoerli from 2004 to 2006 and now dances at the Hamburg Ballet under John Neumeier.

16

Tomas Schweigen (*1977)

After studies in theater, philology, philosophy, and art history at Vienna University, Schweigen earned a degree in directing from the Zurich School of Drama in 2000–2004. He then founded the independent theater group FAR A DAY CAGE together with actress Vera von Gunten; participated in the director's platforms Freischwimmer and Gipfelstürmer, and has continued his work with the Theaterhaus Gessnerallee in Zurich.

FAR A DAY CAGE was seen at international festivals; the Schiller Project *Polizey* (Police) won the Premio 2005; and Schweigen's diploma production *Parzivality Show* won the Audience Prize and the Ensemble Prize at the SKS-Theatertreffen in Hanover. His productions have been seen in Zurich, Bern, Vienna, Berlin, Hamburg, Munich, Frankfurt, Düsseldorf, Stuttgart, Mannheim, Neuchâtel, Strasbourg, Lisbon, and Amsterdam.

Tomas Schweigen works independently and at municipal theaters, and most recently at Stadttheater Bern, Staatstheater Schwerin, and the Munich Kammerspiele. In the coming season, he will be working at Theaterhaus Jena, schauspielfrankfurt, and Vienna Schauspielhaus.

11
13 16 15
14

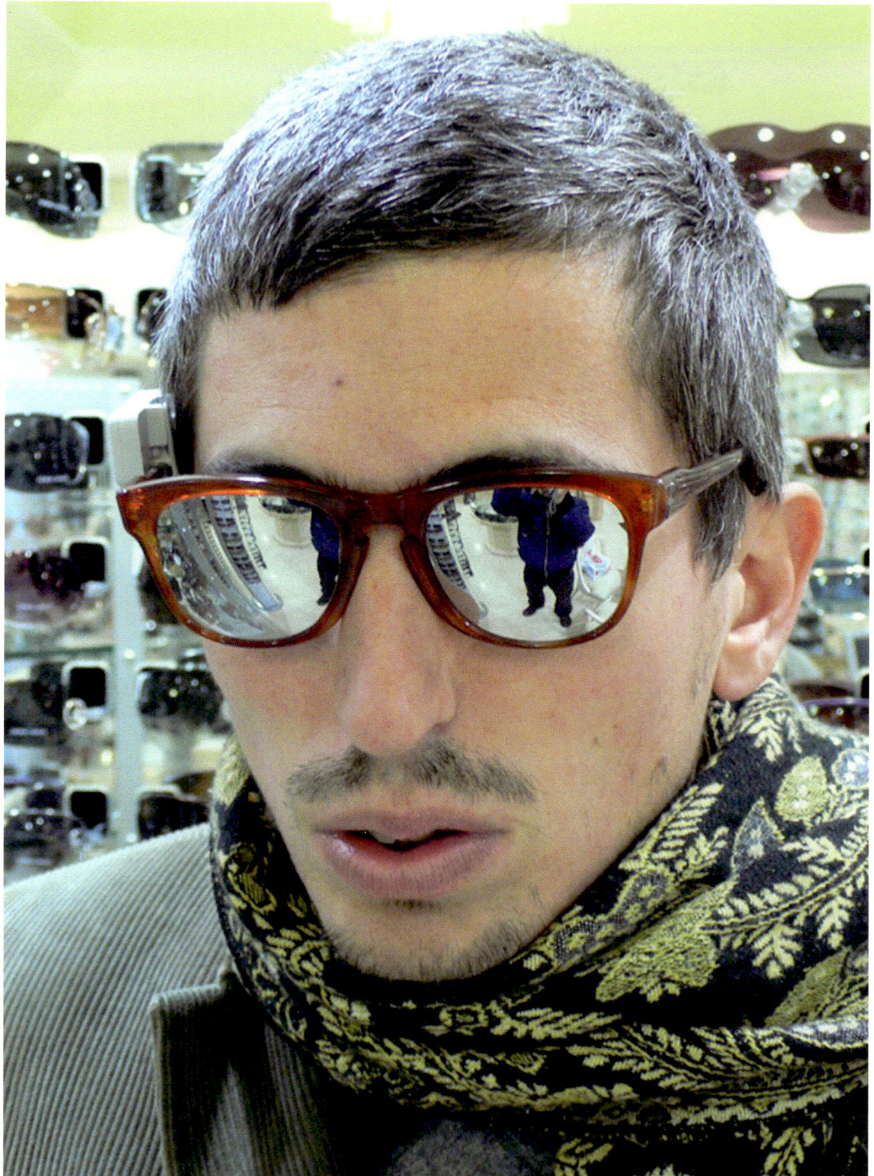

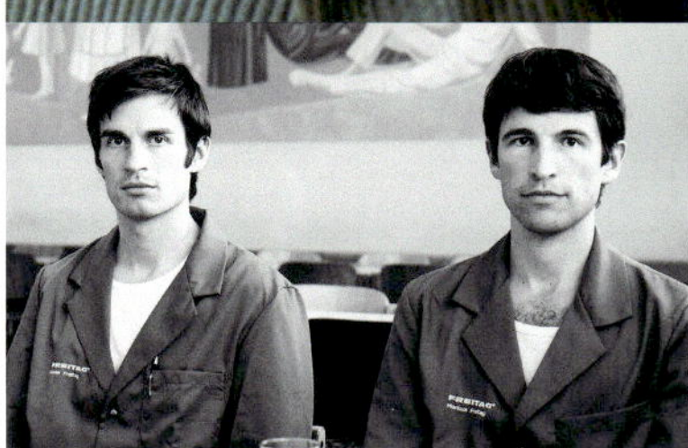

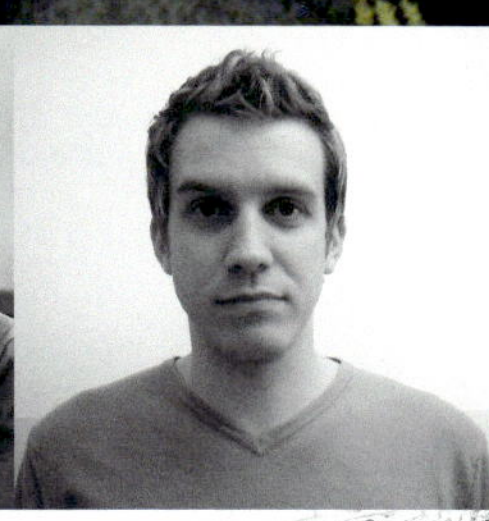

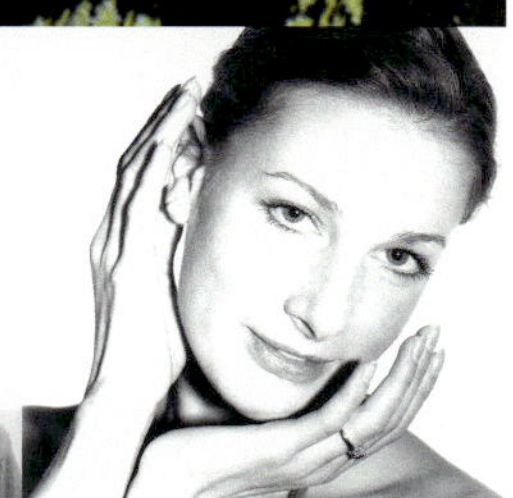

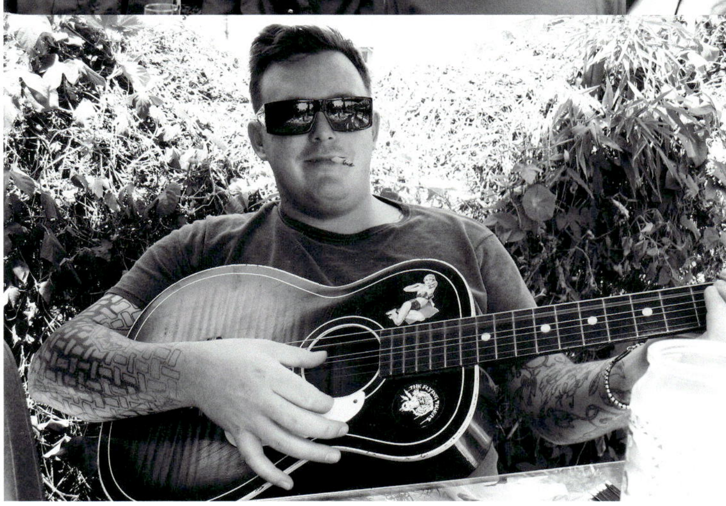

1a Serge Stauffer (bottom left) and the Color and Form class council, Zurich School of Applied Arts, 1968
1b Anagram by André Thomkins, 1985
1c Serge Stauffer's German edition of Marcel Duchamp's writings, vol. 1. Published by Regenbogen Verlag, Theo Ruff, Zurich/Cochabamba, 1981

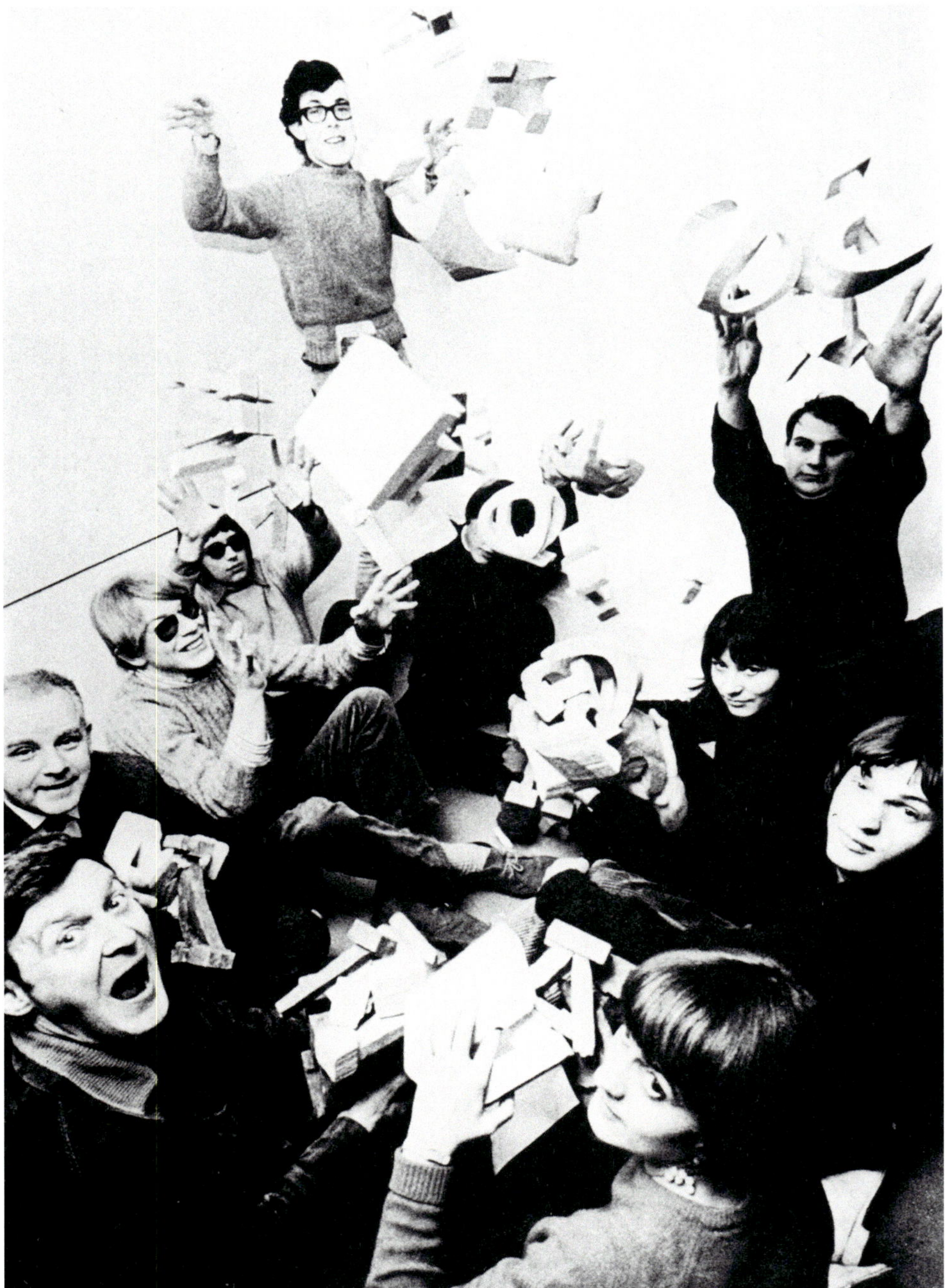

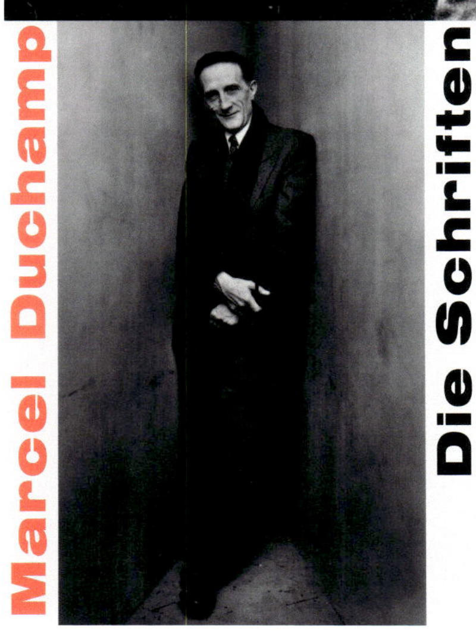

serge stauffer

frage es, es ruft
rufe es, es fragt.

gefasster rufe
ursage, es treff
argus, treffe es!

fueger erfasst
urfragefestes;
gefaess ruft er
erfasster fuge.

gestus erraffe
urraffgeste, es
gaffte uresser
saeugers treff,
affe gruesst er.

essfrage freut
esser, affe trug
urfaesser, fegt
gefraesse, ruft:
»fresstagfeuer
suffes ertrag'!«

festrufer sage
fegfeuers star:
»feuergraf esst!
faust reg ferse,
gret fass feuer,
regt feuerfass,
suff gaere erst!«

»arges uferfest!«
seegraf ruft es,
frag seefuerst:
»frustgefasere!«
ruegt fee, frass
uferstegfaser,
esser traf fuge,
frass teerfuge.

»ursee raff steg!«
seegraf freut's,
grasfee freut's:
»frag's reuefest,
fuerst seegraf!
sturseegaffer
gaff erst reuse,
gaff reuserest,
ufers festrage

2a Aldo Walker, *Die Greifbarkeit der weiblichen Masse (als magisches Quadrat)*, 1975/86
2b *Der Vater und sein Sohn*, 1981/82
2c *Untitled*, 1985. Latex on cotton
Exhibition catalogue, Helmhaus Zurich, 1989
2d *Lettre d'images par aldo walker.*

argus treff see-
gaffers treues
feuer; fragst es,
rufst seefrage:
»steuer reff?« sag
gast: »reff's eure
ufergastferse!«
fussreferat ge-
aeffter gruess.

ufergefasster
feuerfersgast
fege afterruss,
feefuss ertrag,
feeaftergruss.
see trug seraff,
fuesse fragt er,
fers' aeugt fers'.

fueg rares fest,
erst fuge fraes',
fraeser fuegt's,
faesser fugt er,
teerfassfuger
raffe teerguss,
fuge erfasst er.

straffer geuse
fasst gurrefee;
fee gurrt: »fass,
freugerte fass,
fass fegerrute,
rege fut erfass!«

»rassefutfeger
feg raserstufe,
surre fegesaft!«
fee traf erguss;
festfeger raus.

asseruf fegte
treue ss gaffer:
»rassegut reffe!«
gruefte erfass.

frass gefeuert,
es aergert suff«
grasfee ruft es,

fresst gar efeu!«
gret frass efeu:

streue es gar f+f.«

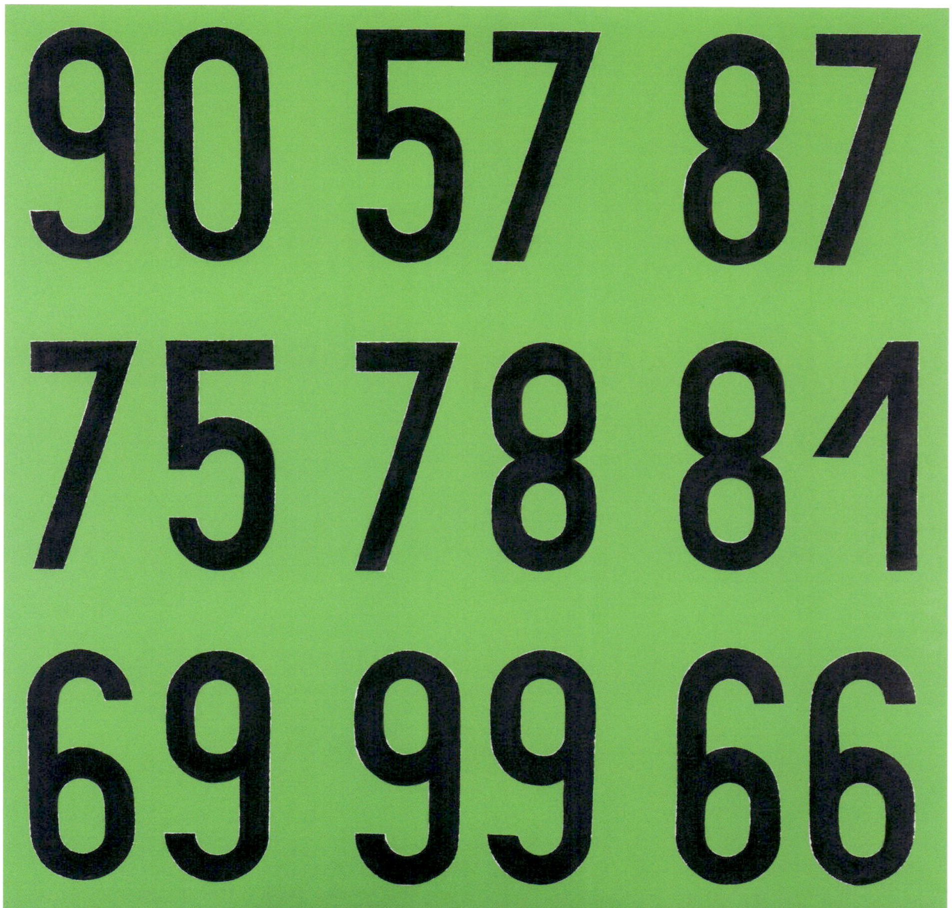

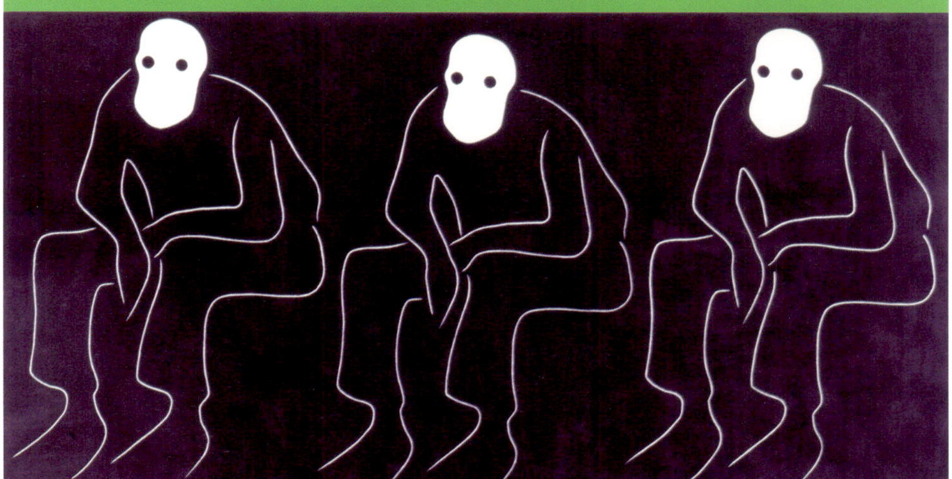

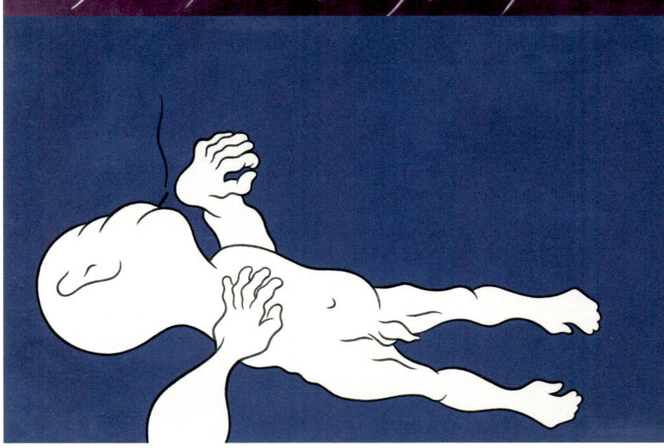

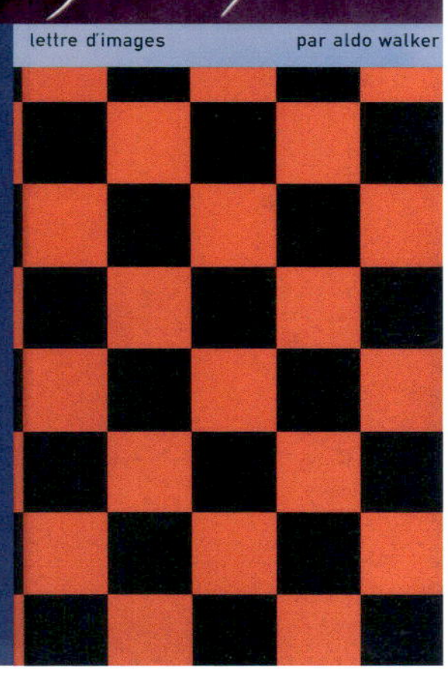

4a Berndt Höppner, *Posteggio.* Genoa
4b Installation. Exhibited at Karin Schiesser's, 2003
4c Rug. Acrylic

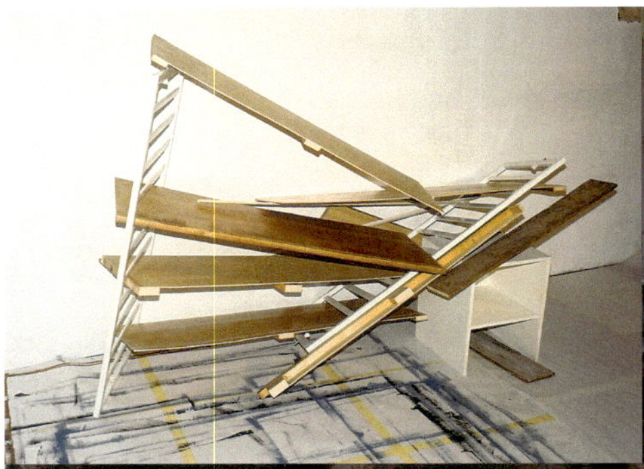

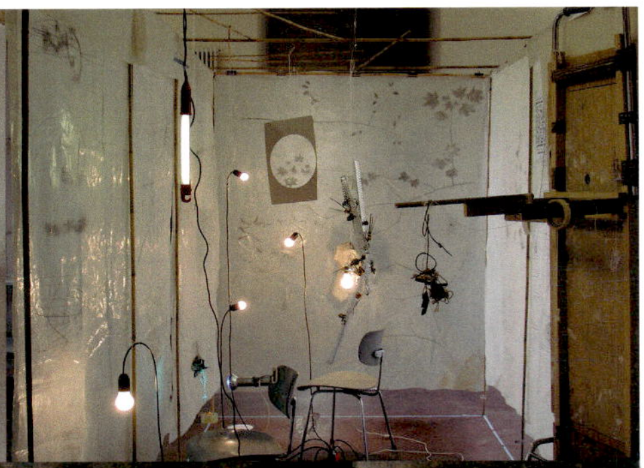

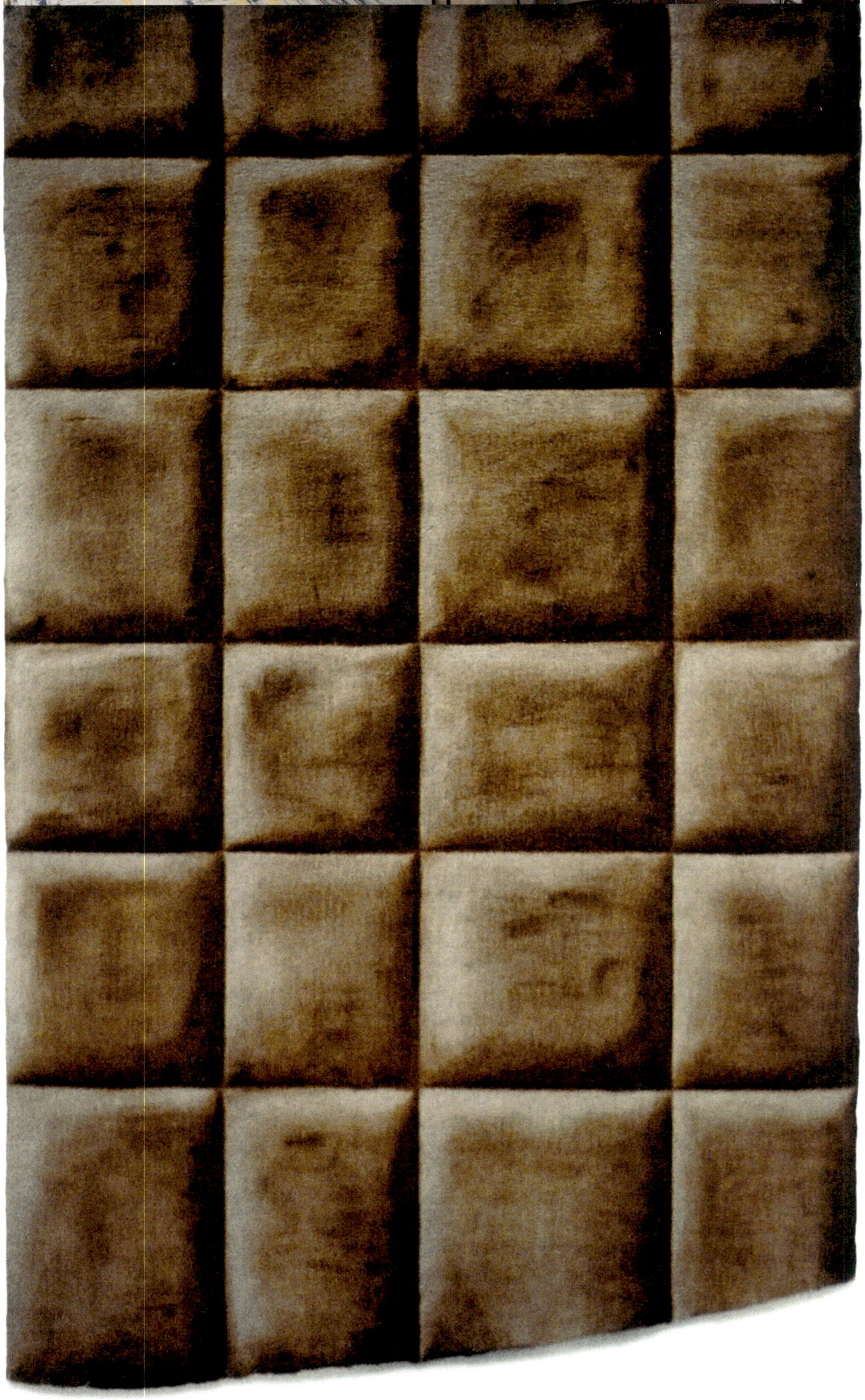

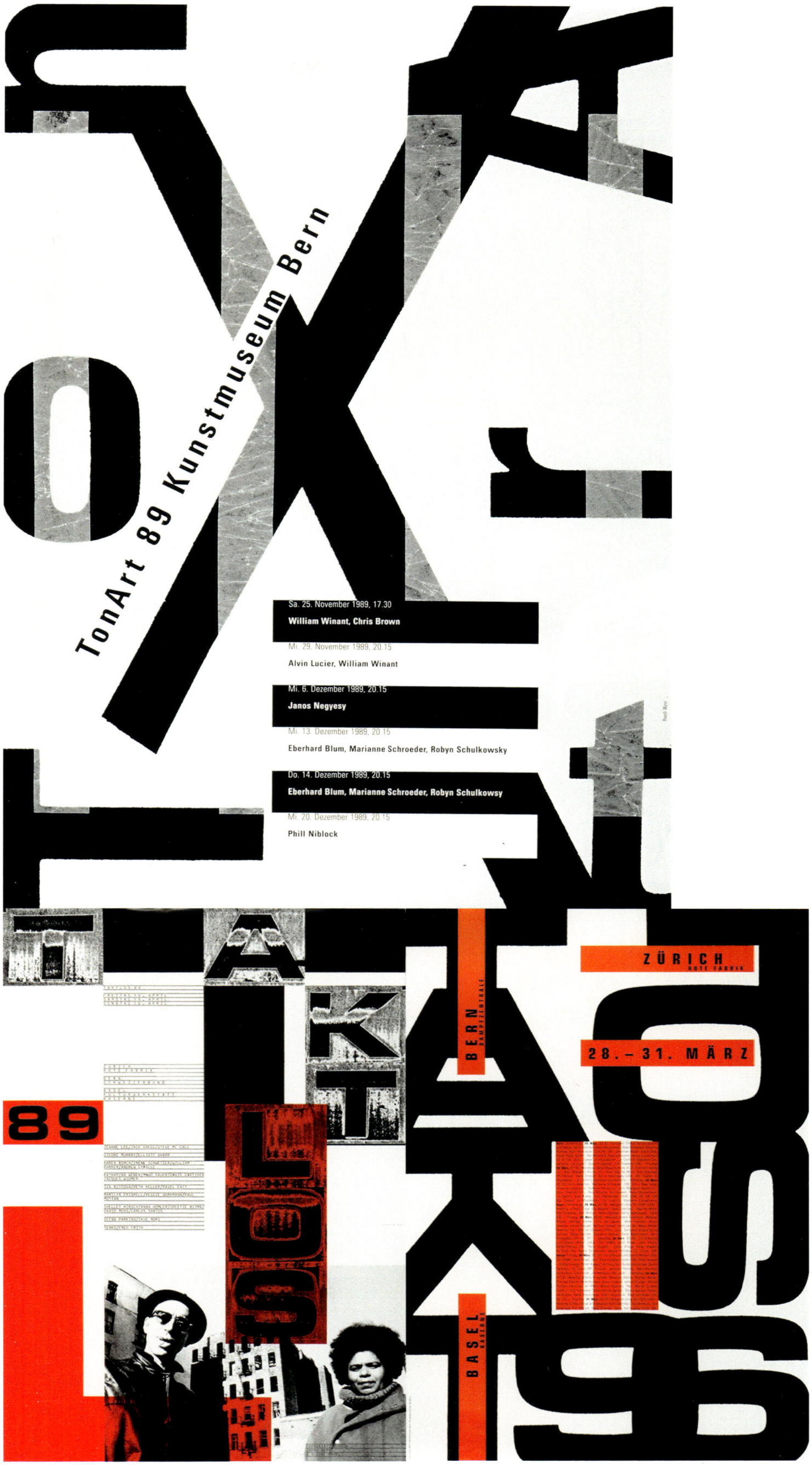

5a–c Ruedi Wyss, concert posters for TonArt 1989, Taktlos Festival 1989 and 1996

7a Daniele Buetti, *Looking for Love.* Pinwall, 2004

8a/b Thomas Hirschhorn, *Stand-alone.* Exhibition at Arndt & Partner Berlin, 2007

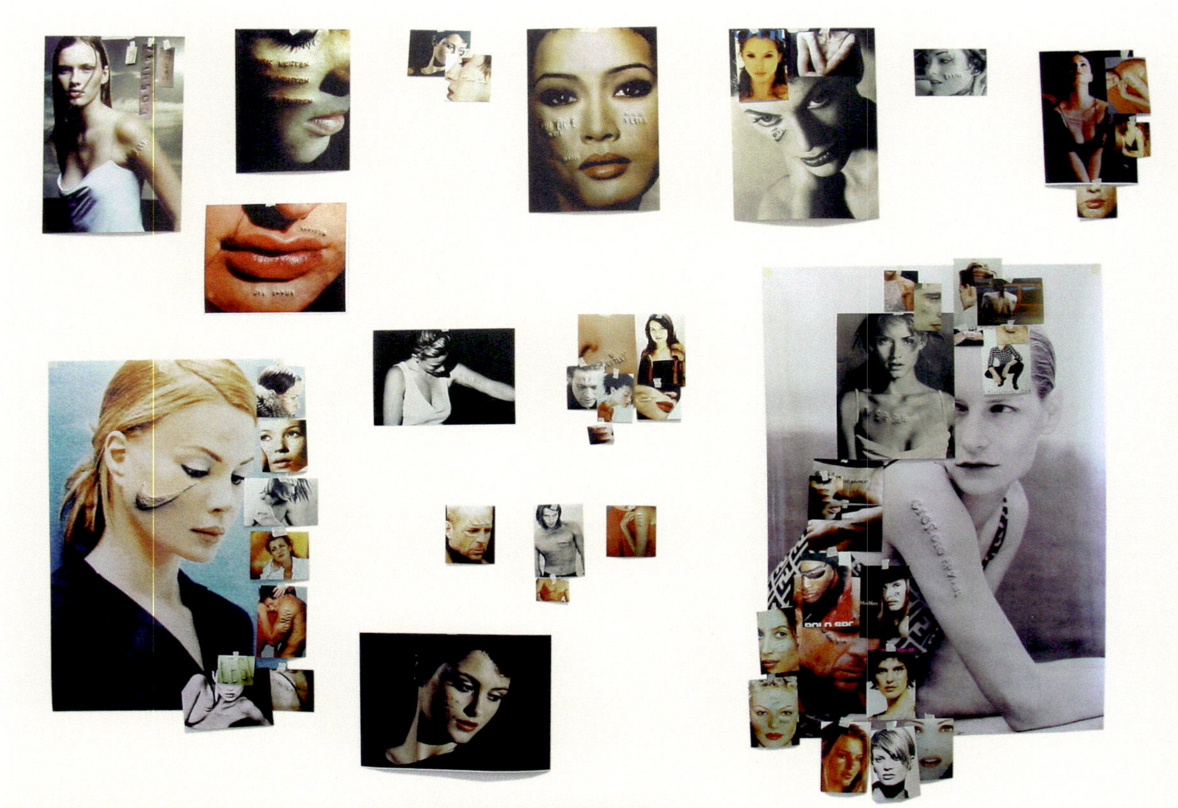

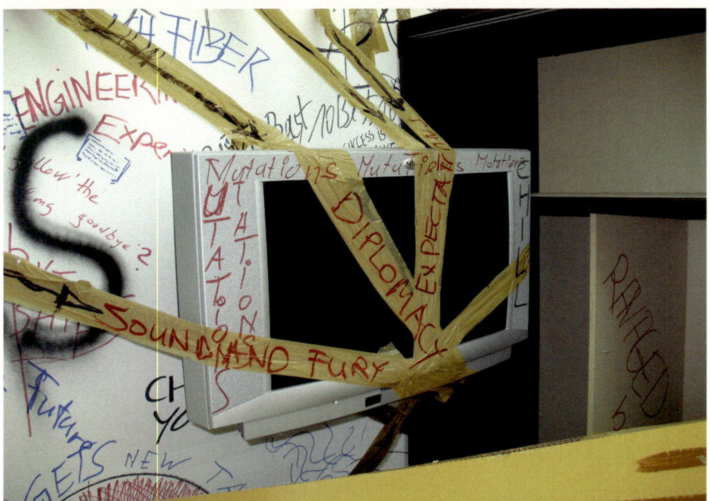

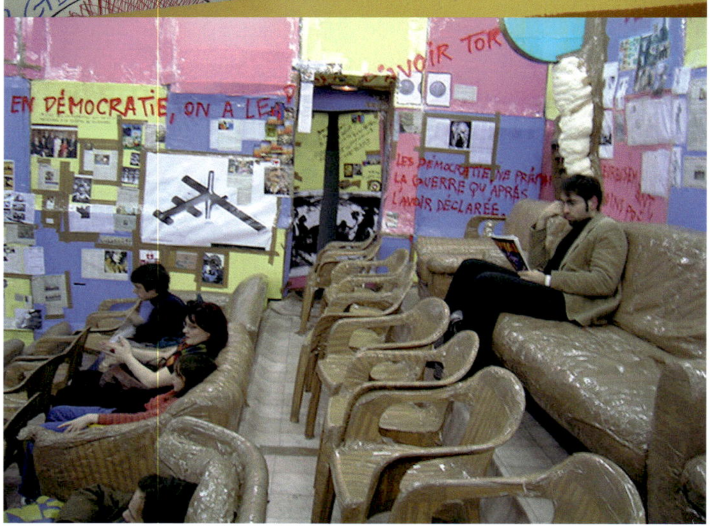

8c *Swiss-Swiss Democracy.* Controversial installation at the Centre culturel Suisse. Paris, 2004
9a Karin Wälchli, Guido Reichlin, *Cairo,* 2006. MPEG video still
9b *sPaGaT 20050801_12:43,* 2005. Photo collage

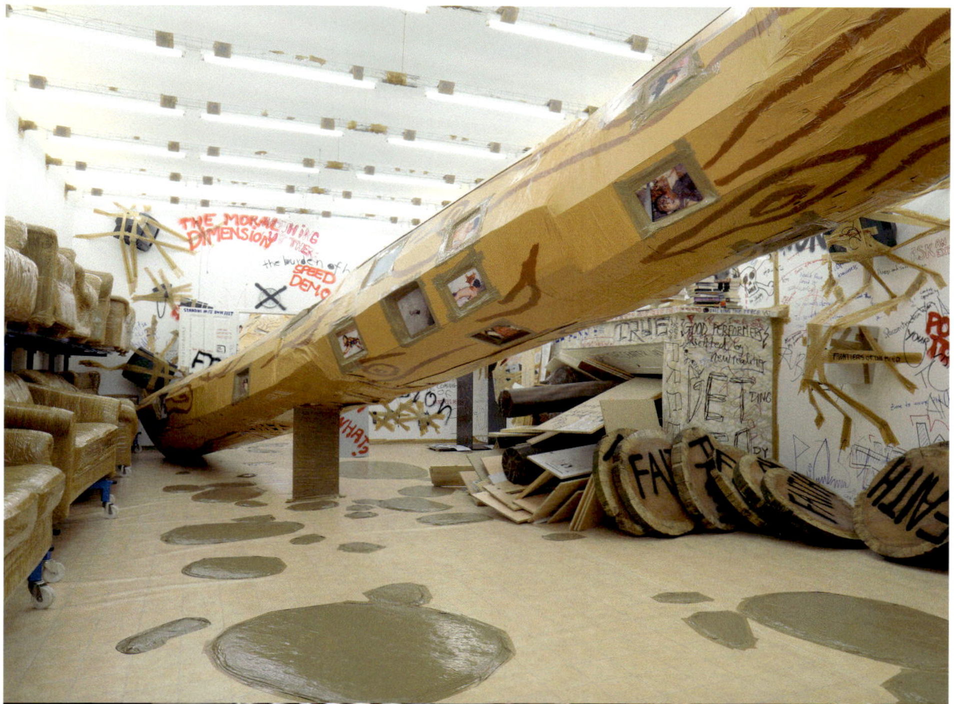

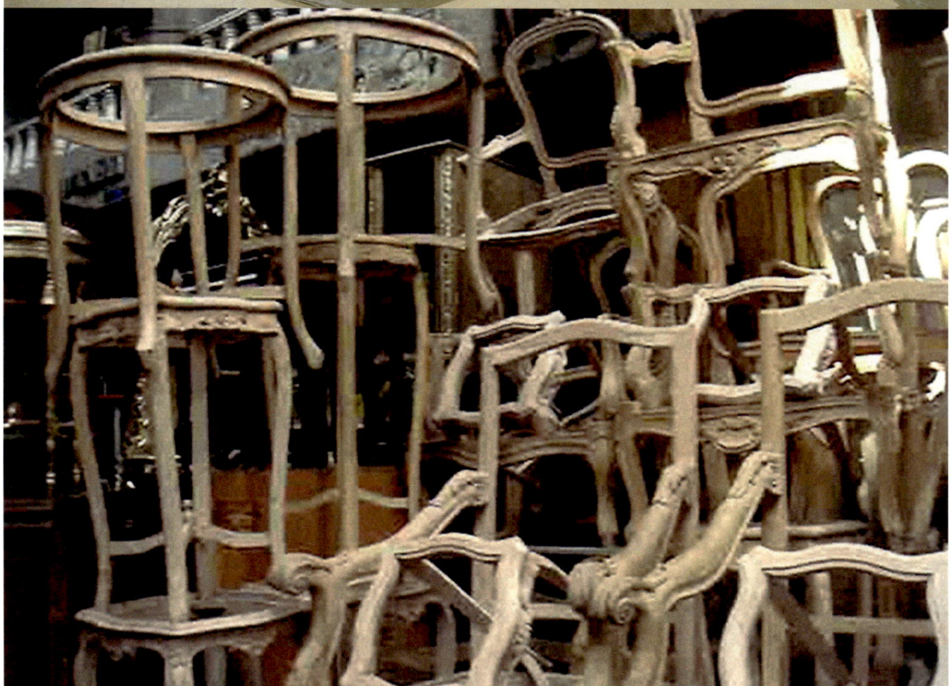

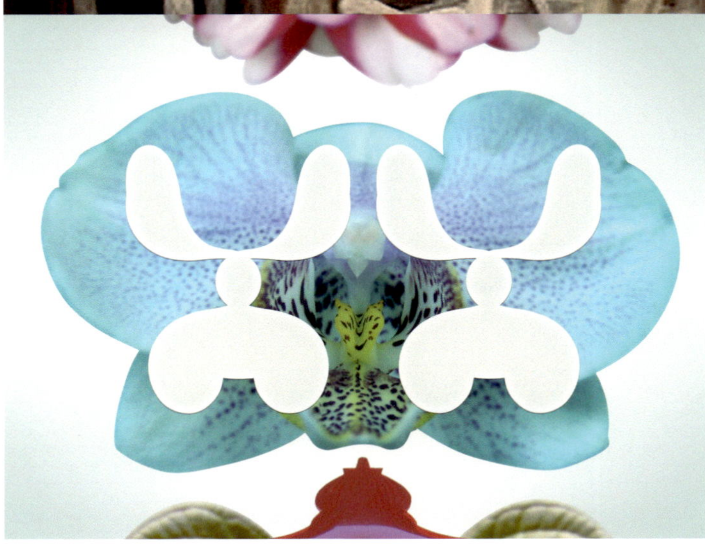

9c Karin Wälchli, *Cairo, happy new year 2007*, 2006. Mixed media

10a Martin Woodtli, *WoodtliUnivers*, 2000. Detail

9d *Cabina 2005*. Lambda print

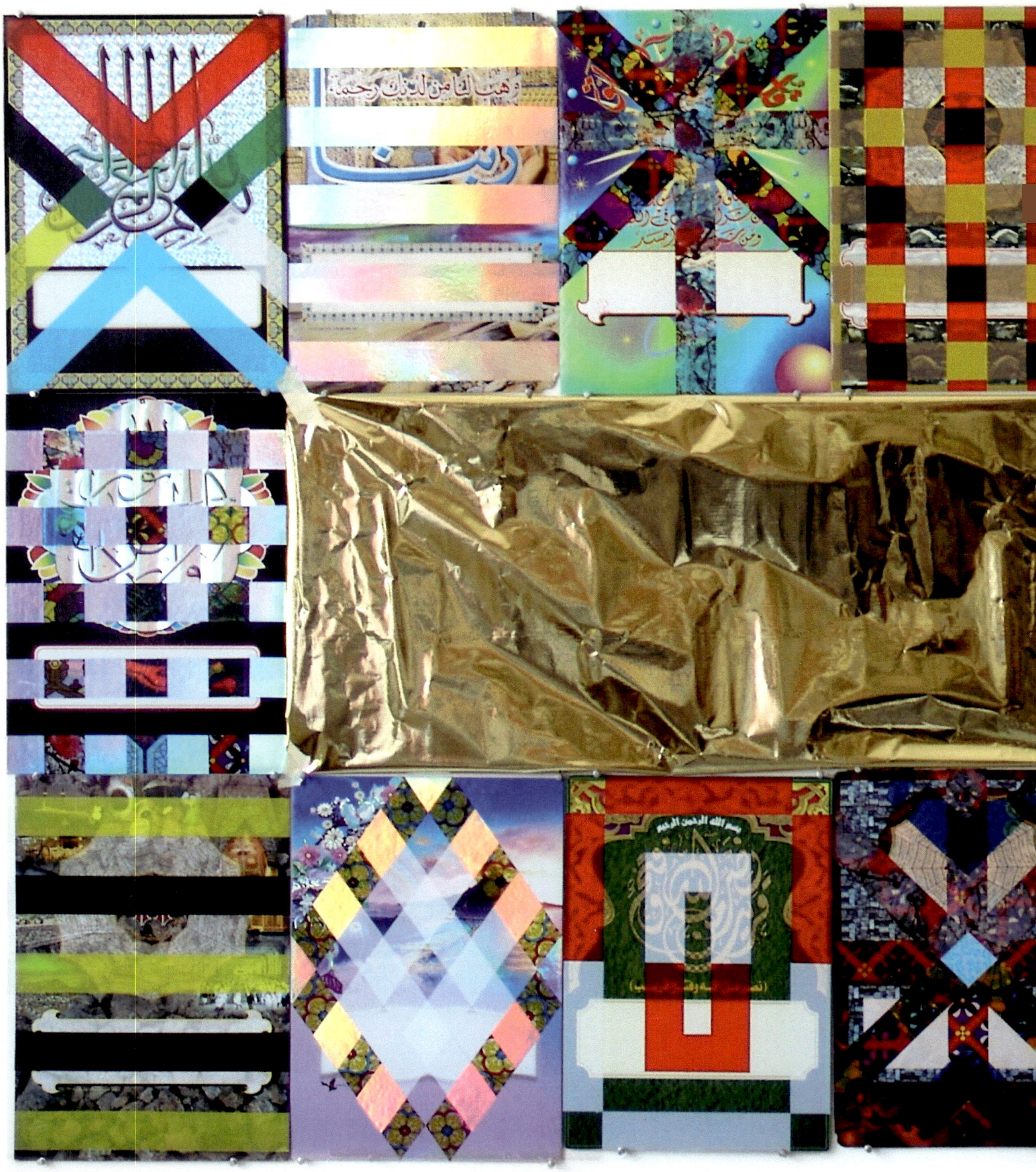

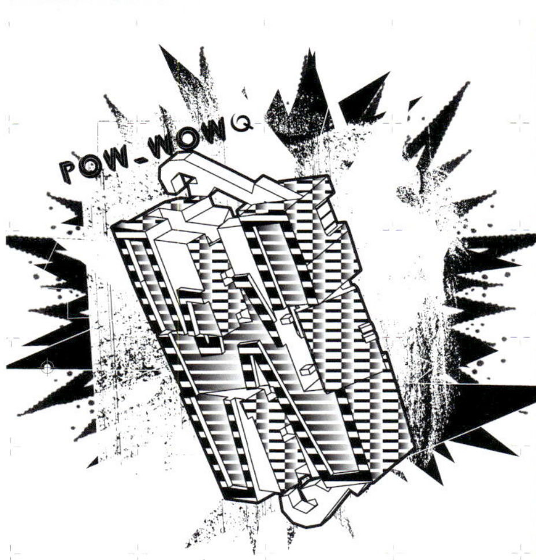

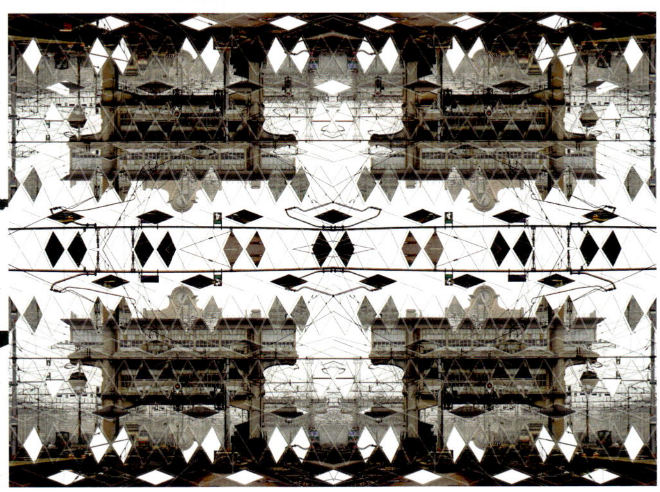

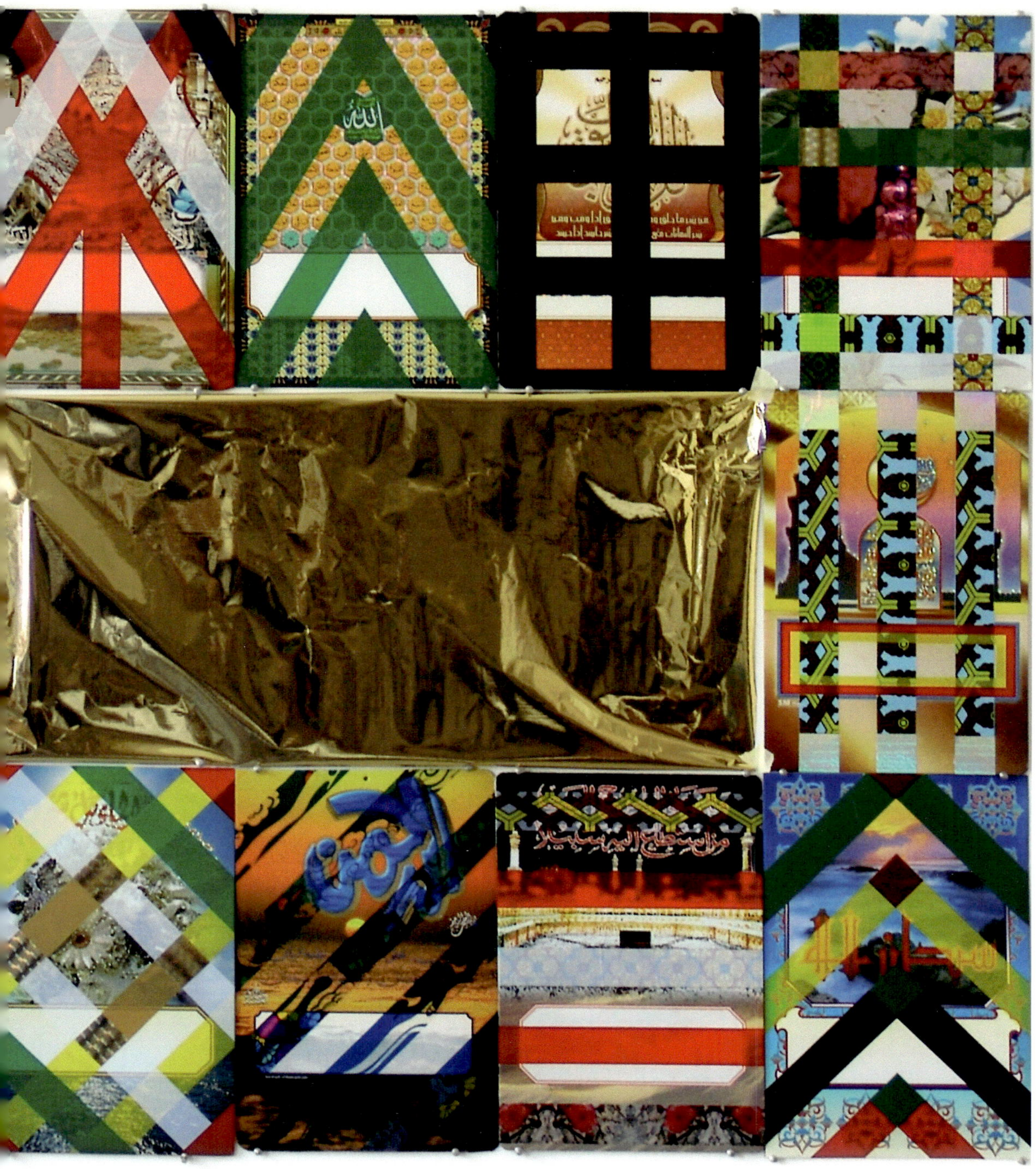

10b Martin Woodtli, *WoodtliUnivers*, 2000

10c Poster for Schaffhausen Jazz Festival, 2003

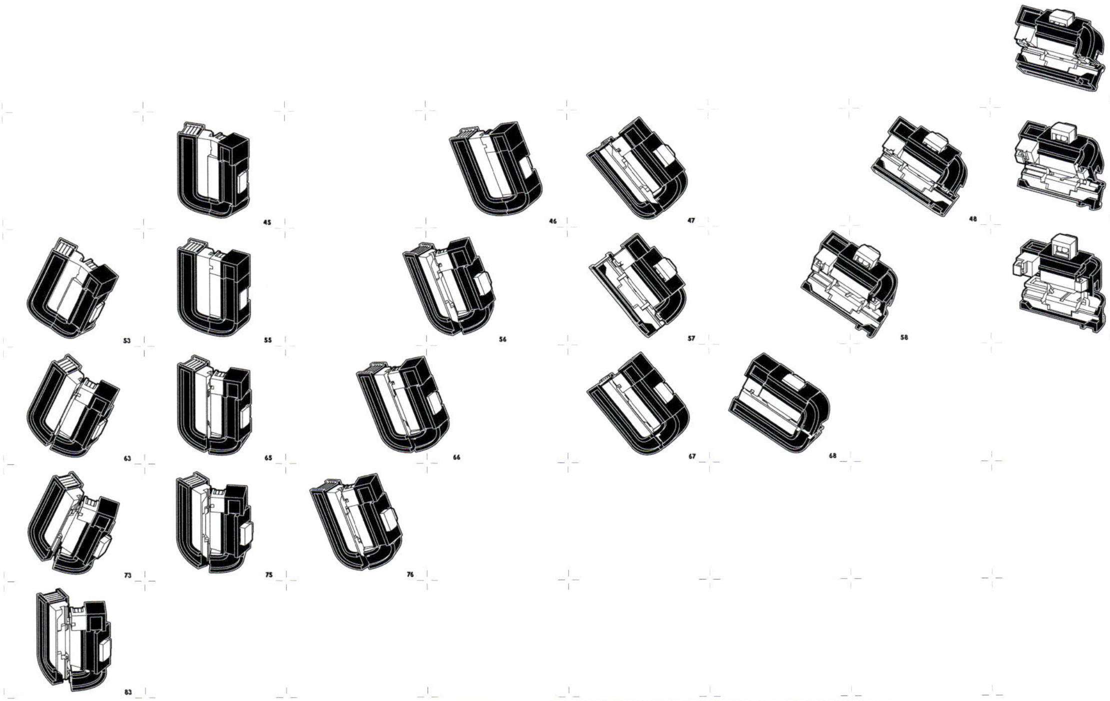

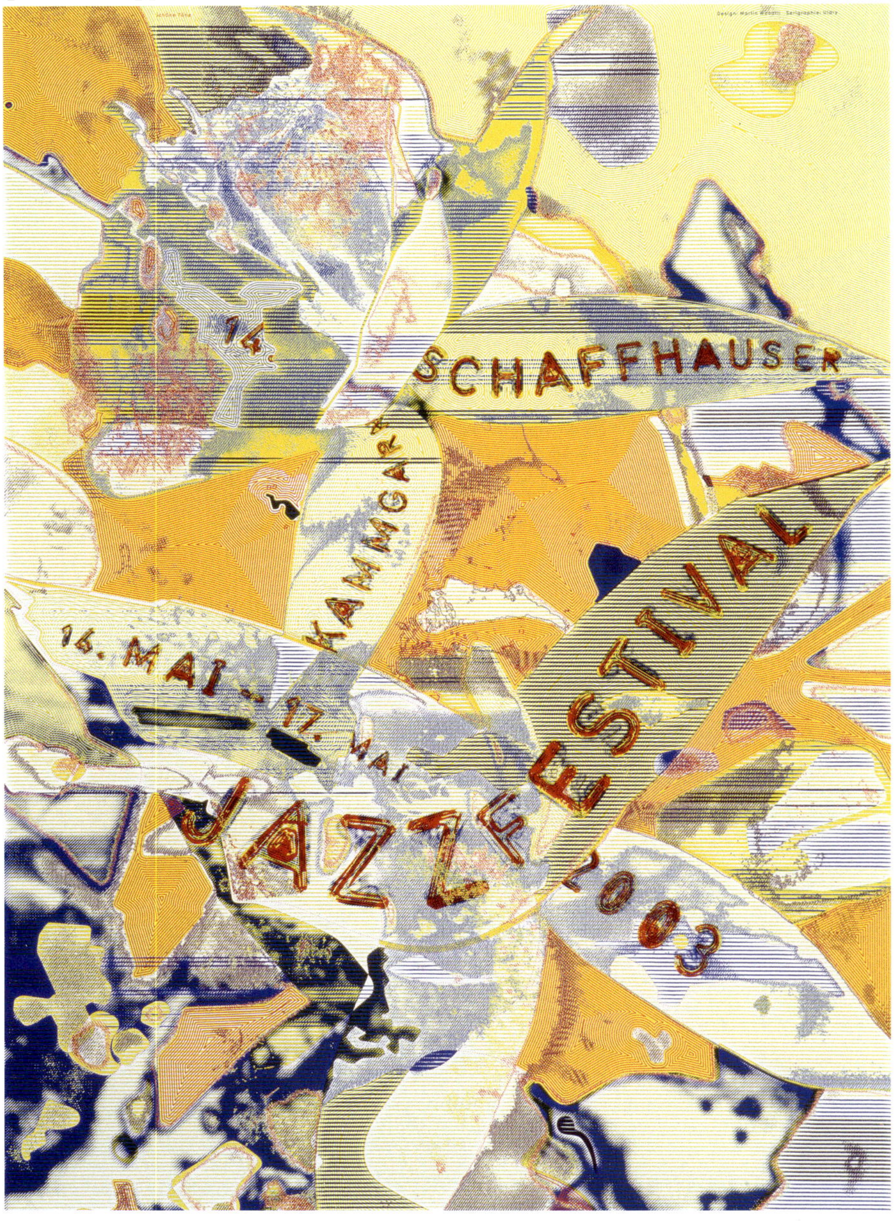

10d/e *Play.* Poster for an exhibition at the Museum of Design Zurich, 2005.—*Video-Ex.* Poster for the International Experimental Film & Video Festival, 2003

11a San Keller, *Wer schläft zuerst.* Video installation at Galerie Brigitte Weiss, Zurich, 2005

11b/c *Clever and smart,* 2007. Screenprinted poster board (Challenge: Find 47 English adjectives from critiques on the work of San Keller)

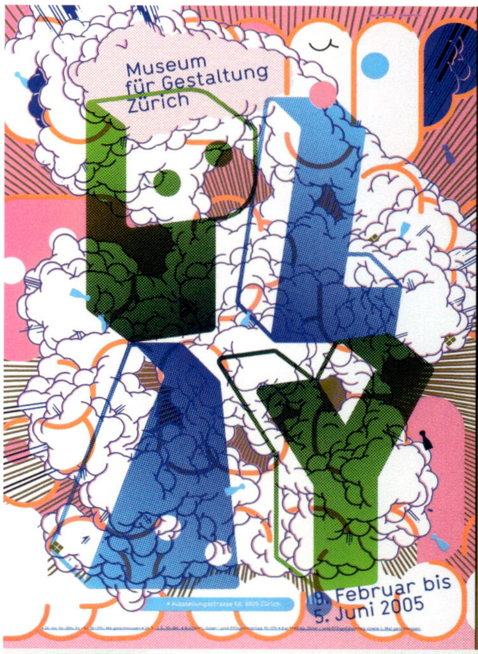

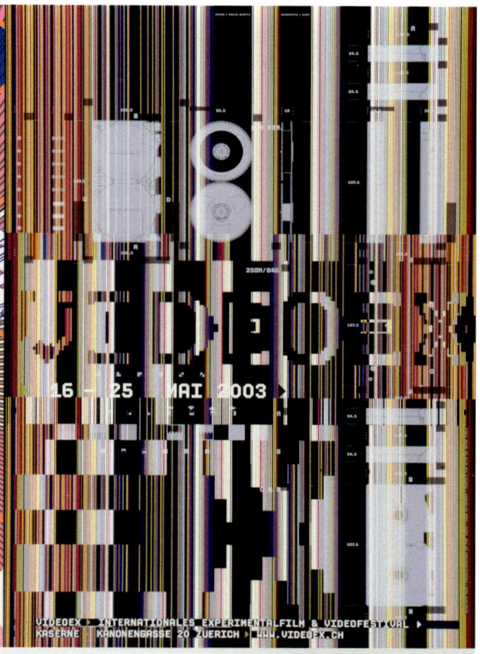

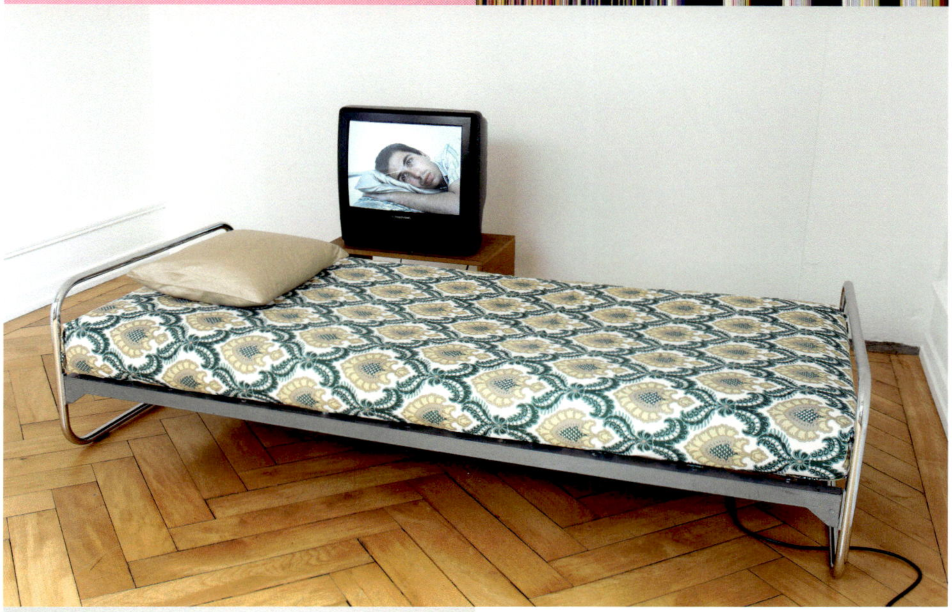

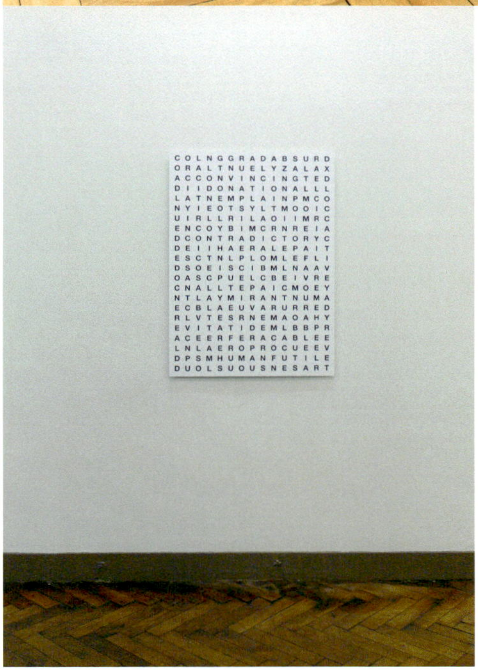

C	O	L	N	G	G	R	A	D	A	B	S	U	R	D
O	R	A	L	T	N	U	E	L	Y	Z	A	L	A	X
A	C	C	O	N	V	I	N	C	I	N	G	T	E	D
D	I	I	D	O	N	A	T	I	O	N	A	L	L	L
L	A	T	N	E	M	P	L	A	I	N	P	M	C	O
N	Y	I	E	O	T	S	Y	L	T	M	O	O	I	C
U	I	R	L	L	R	I	L	A	O	I	I	M	R	C
E	N	C	O	Y	B	I	M	C	R	N	R	E	I	A
D	C	O	N	T	R	A	D	I	C	T	O	R	Y	C
D	E	I	I	H	A	E	R	A	L	E	P	A	I	T
E	S	C	T	N	L	P	L	O	M	L	E	F	L	I
D	S	O	E	I	S	C	I	B	M	L	N	A	A	V
O	A	S	C	P	U	E	L	C	B	E	I	V	R	E
C	N	A	L	L	T	E	P	A	I	C	M	O	E	Y
N	T	L	A	Y	M	I	R	A	N	T	N	U	M	A
E	C	B	L	A	E	U	V	A	R	U	R	R	E	D
R	L	V	T	E	S	R	N	E	M	A	O	A	H	Y
E	V	I	T	A	T	I	D	E	M	L	B	B	P	R
A	C	E	E	R	F	E	R	A	C	A	B	L	E	E
L	N	L	A	E	R	O	P	R	O	C	U	E	E	V
D	P	S	M	H	U	M	A	N	F	U	T	I	L	E
D	U	O	L	S	U	O	U	S	N	E	S	A	R	T

11d San Keller, *Baden in der Menge.* Action object at the highLOW symposium on the relationship of high and popular culture, organized by ICS, School of Art and Design Zurich, 2006

12a *SEE.* Live music spatial image composed by Nik Bärtsch for MOBILE. Architecture by oos. Theaterspektakel Zurich, 2005

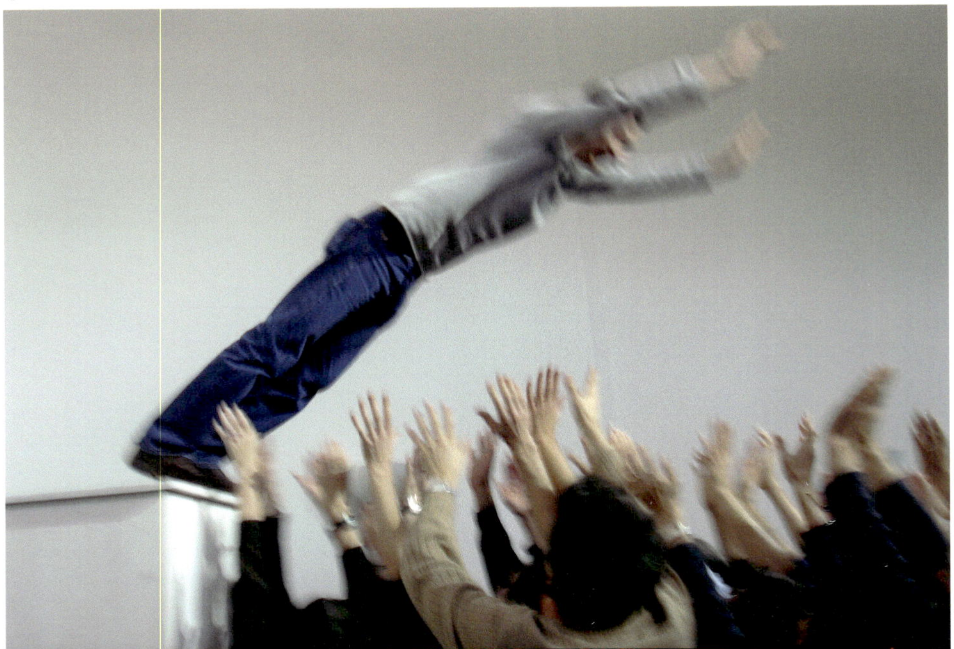

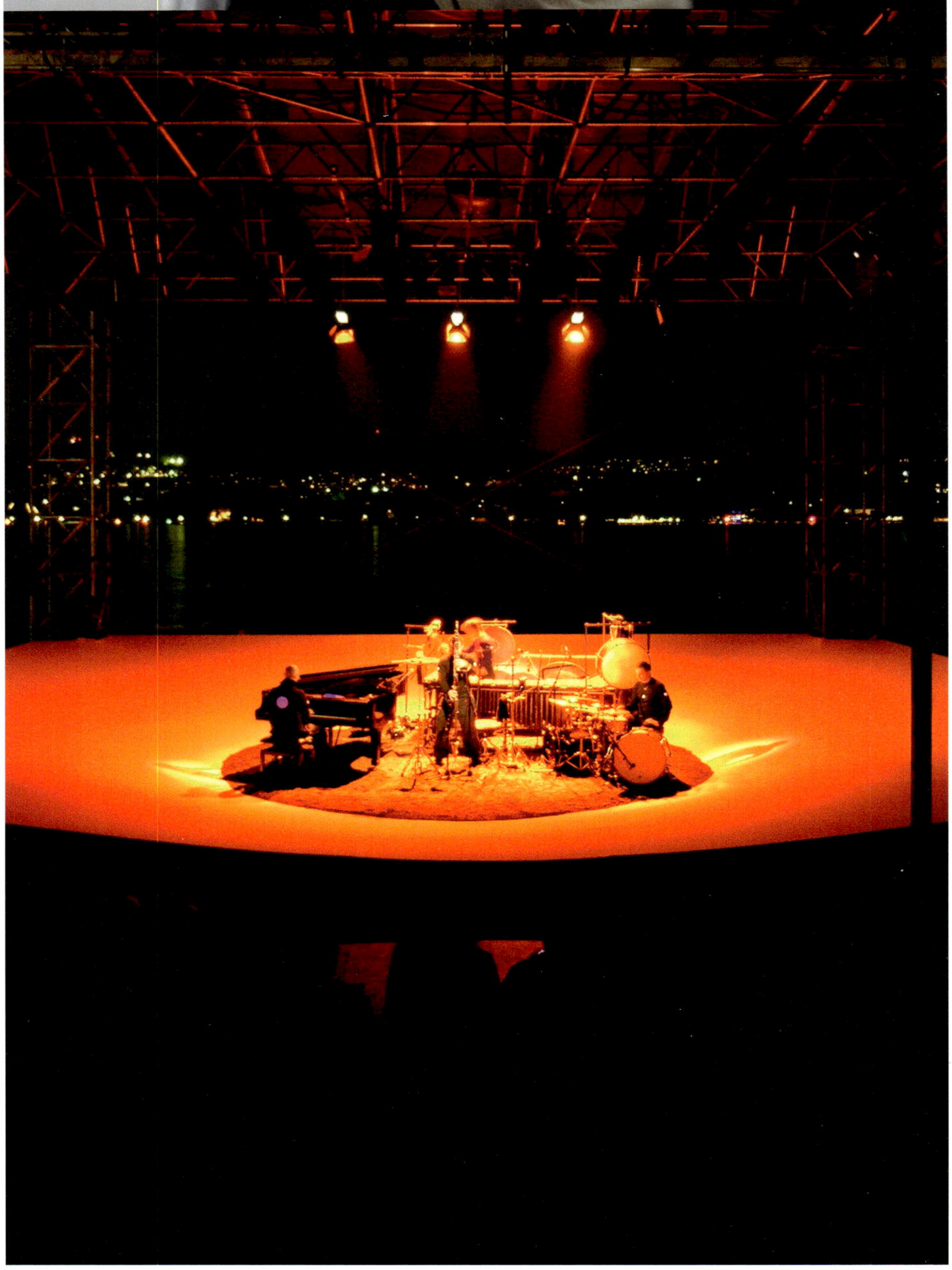

13a Freitag®, *Iconic Building*. Construction of the Freitag Container Store, Zurich, 2006
13b/c *On the road, travel solution group*. Set of bags
13d Freitag bags

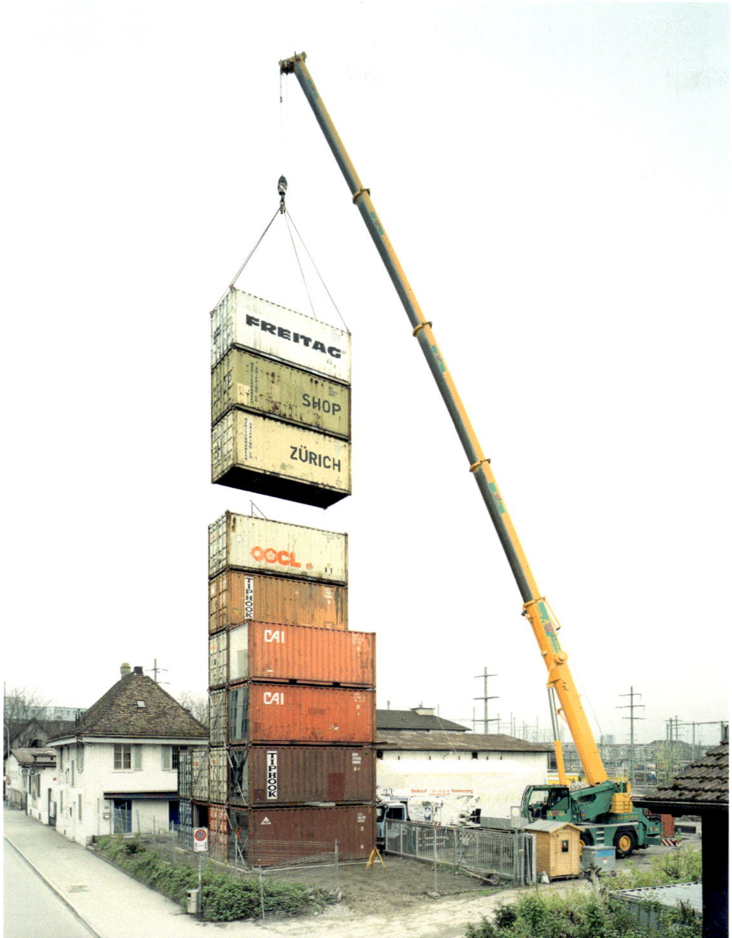

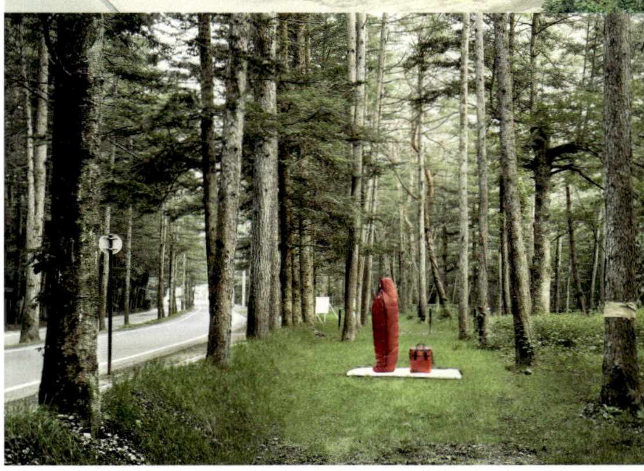

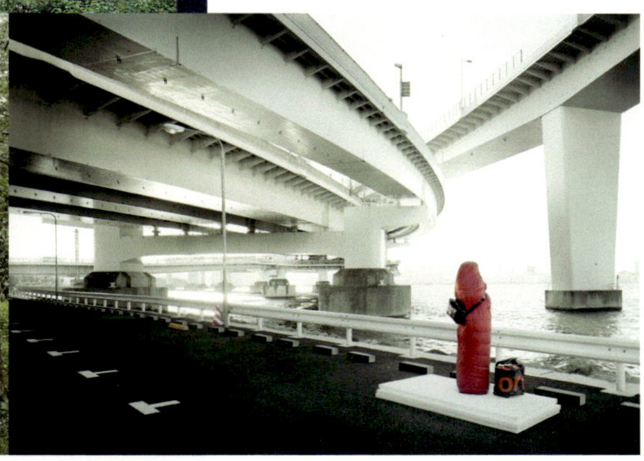

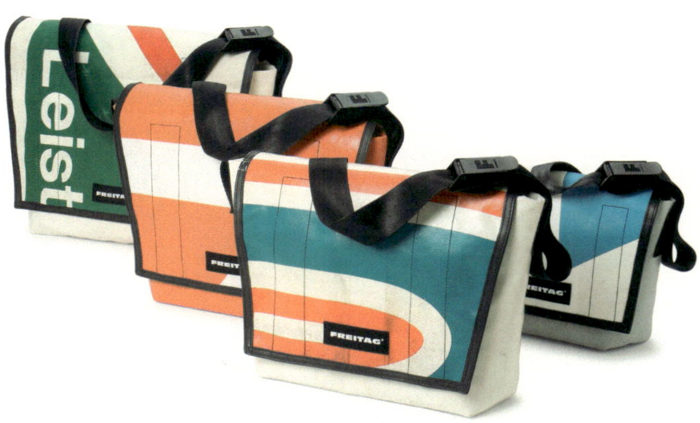

14a Urs Fischer, exhibition architecture for *Kir Royal*. Kunsthaus Zurich, 2004

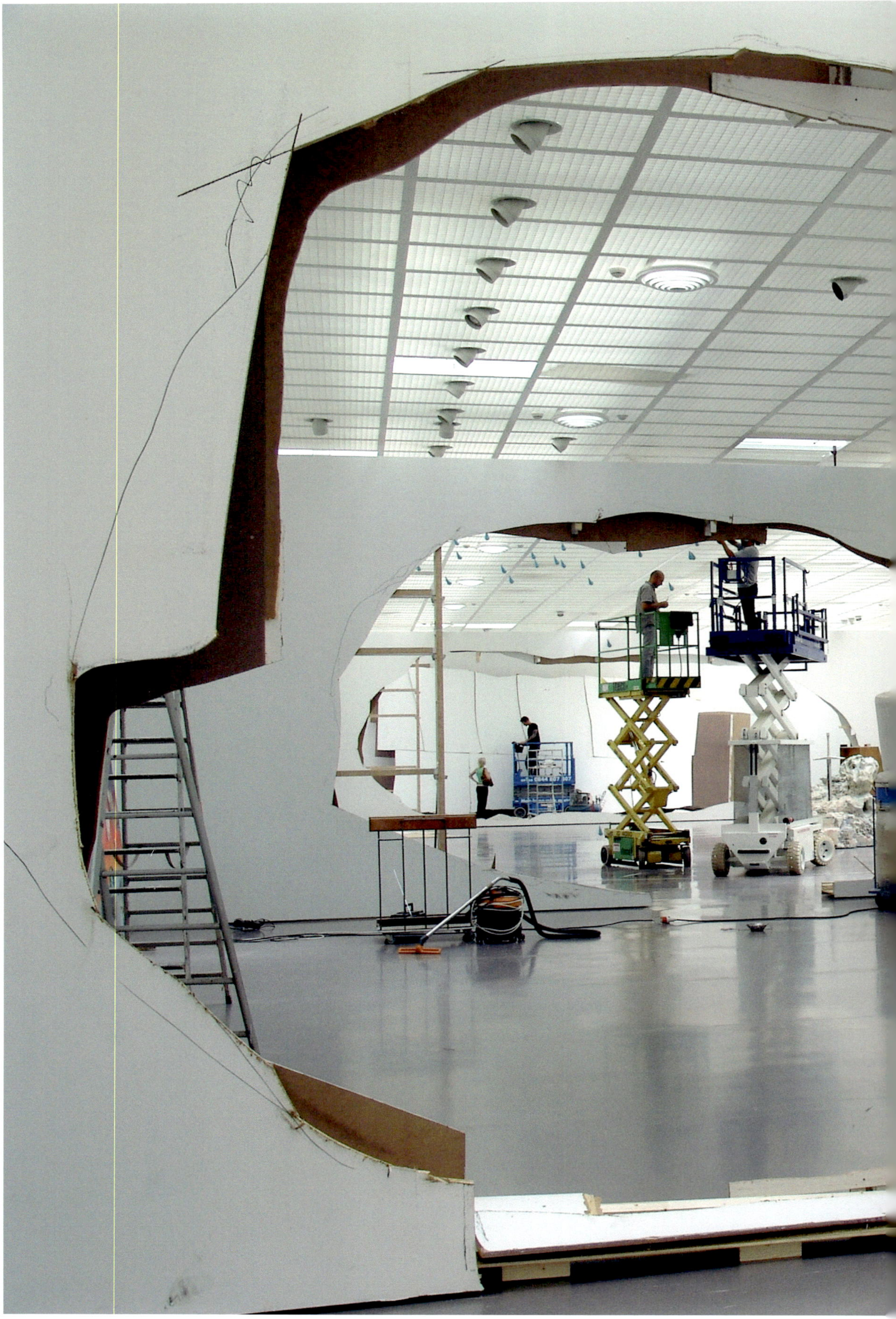

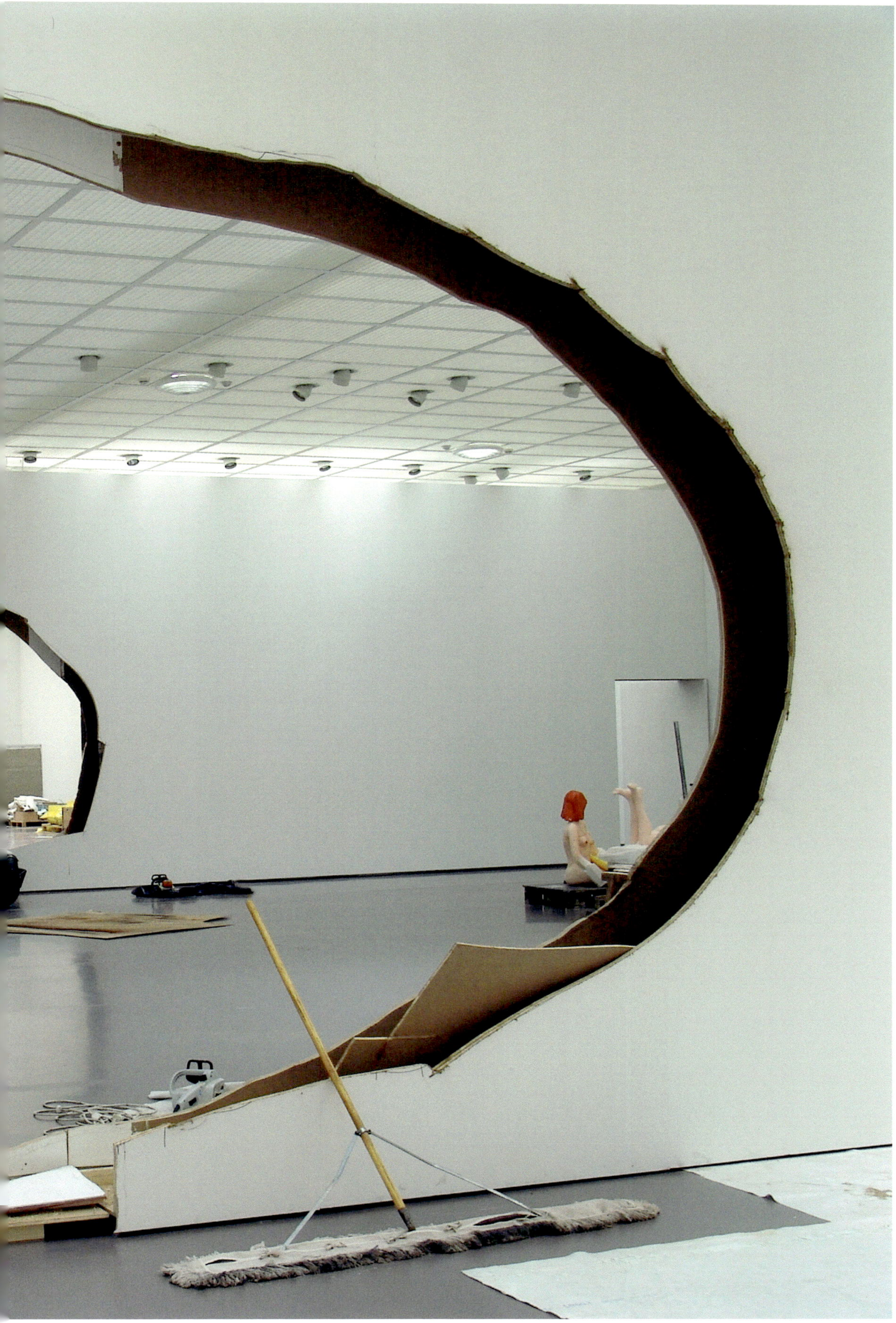

14b Urs Fischer, *September Song,* 2002

15a Kusha Alexi (left) with Sherelle Charge, Caroline Geiger, Beate Vollack, *Grosse Fuge.* Bavarian State Ballet, choreography by Hans van Manen

14c Urs Fischer, *What if the Phone Rings,* 2003. Three-part sculpture. Wax, wick, pigment

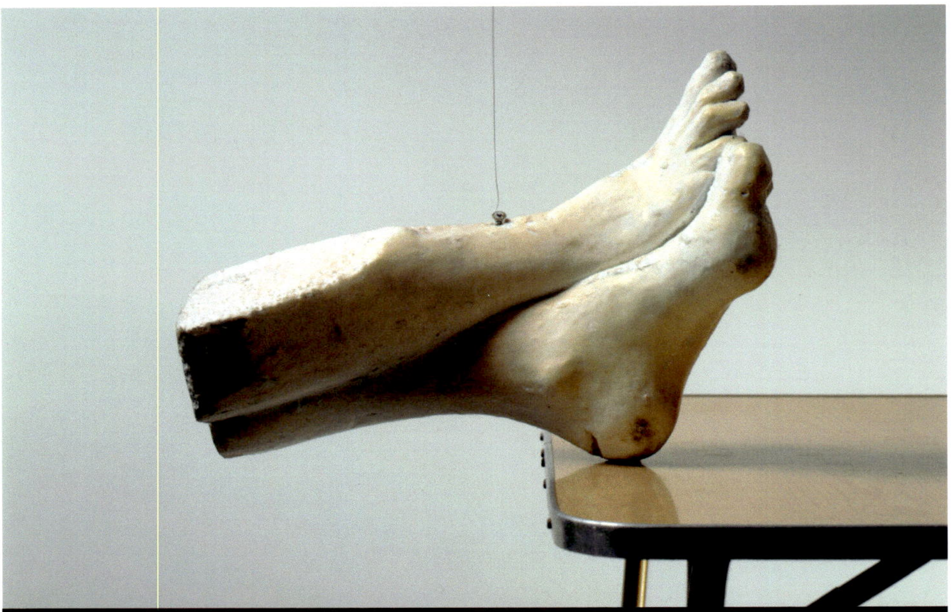

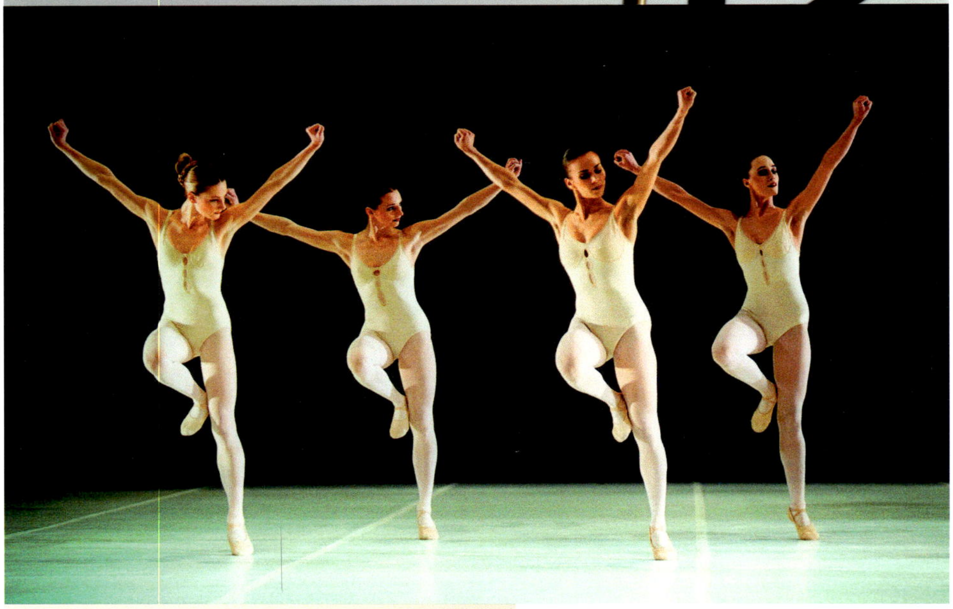

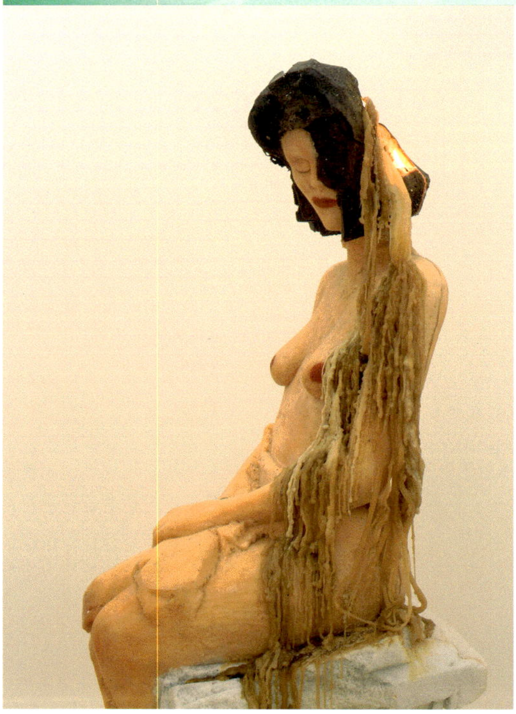

14d Urs Fischer, *Stuhl für einen Geist: Urs,* 2003. Sand cast, aluminum, paint, enamel paint, string

15b Kusha Alexi with Oliver Wehe, *La Dame aux Camélias,* Bavarian State Ballet, 2001

14e *You Can Only Lose,* 2003. Styrofoam, acrylic paint, resin, screws, fiberglass

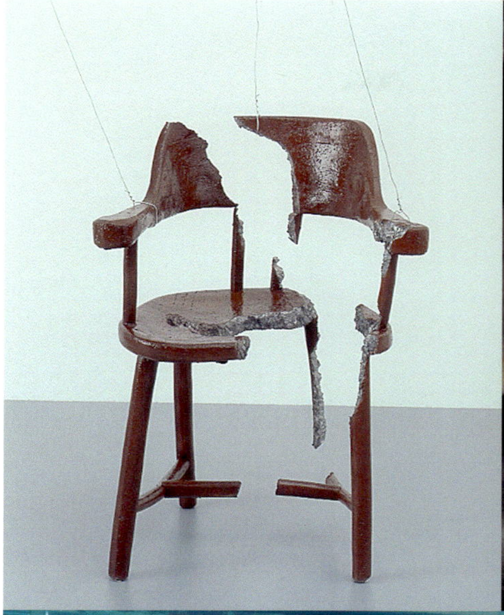

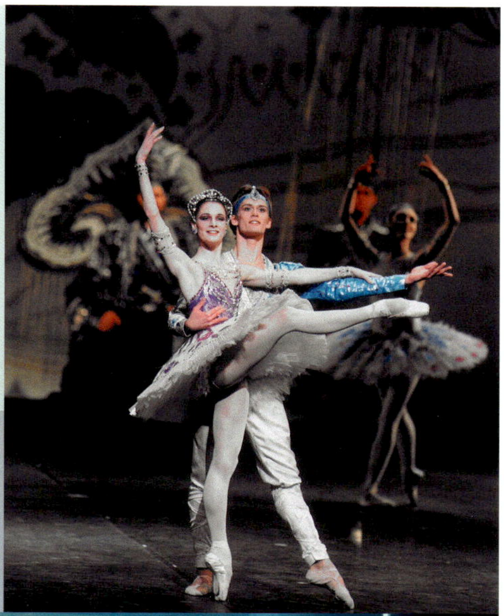

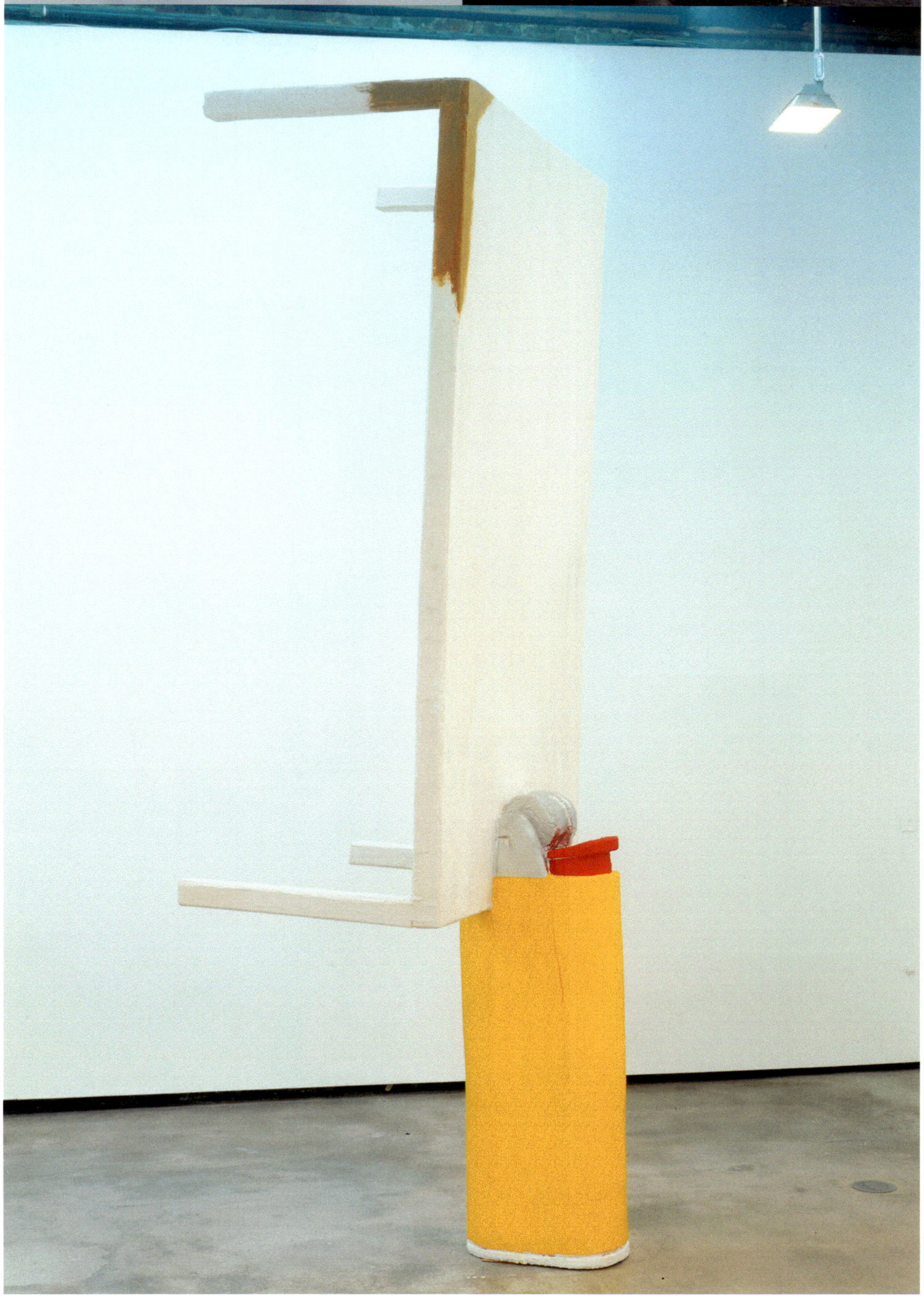

They are in control of their art down to the smallest nuance and detail, striving toward and celebrating consummate mastery. They are distinguished by inventive gifts, skill, passion, and conspicuous talent. They seduce us on their enchanting adventures with sharp narratives and allegories of love and death, with playful *guilloches* 1; with illustrative waywardness and a joy in visual storytelling 2; with a virtuoso signature in perpetually new variations of lapidary and powerfully expressive forms 3, 5; with gender-oriented literary impetus and the interlacing of language and image 4; no battle was too much for him, he challenged everything 6; he lent his musical support to the word, accompanying great singers at the piano 7; she thrills us in the oratorios and lieder that have survived their own times, and teaches voice 8; she captivates with her scientific scrupulousness and graphic skill 9; he bewitches his audiences with improvised and transposed organ music, evoking all of life's spheres 10; he provokes with phenomenal perceptual sensations 11; as the "man with stupendous qualities," he astonishes with multifaceted textual interpretations 12; as clown-like globetrotter, she tours in tents and cultural centers 13; he astonishes via chameleonic self-staging 14; she lends Switzerland her voice 15; he stands for the perfected mastery of the body, for dreamlike expressive dance 16.

1
Pierre Gauchat (1902–1956)

Together with Willy Eidenbenz, Ernst Hiestand, and Jörg Zintzmeyer, Pierre Gauchat is one of the four Swiss "money makers" of the School of Applied Arts in Zurich. To complement the 10 and 20 Frank bills by Willy Eidenbenz, Gauchat designed the 50, 100, 500, and 1000 Frank bills using allegories for universal values like fertility, motherhood, brotherly love, and—to the consternation of many people at the time—death. One of the peculiarities of the high-quality banknotes was their large "sheet-like" dimensions.

Like Eidenbenz, Gauchat attended the graphic arts class of Ernst Keller and Otto Baumberger. His graphic art work was characterized by his liking of balance and appropriateness, which followed the example of the New Functionalist artists who were his models.

2
Warja Honegger-Lavater (1913–2007)

This painter, draftswoman, and graphic artist attended the graphic art course at the School of Applied Arts from 1931–35. Her graphic artwork included the seal of the Swiss State Exhibition of 1939. In 1962 the Museum of Modern Art published *Wilhelm Tell*, her first children's book. In her fold-out books ("imageries") she illustrated her own fairy tales and those of the brothers Grimm. She received the Hans Christian Andersen Prize for children's literature. As a self-described "image maker," she operates at the intersection of literature and the visual arts. With her experimental treatment of printing processes and paper (papier modulé) Lavater created picture books and artistic works in the shape of *Leporello* folders that can be stood up and folded out. Her stories, above all *Tur di di* (1971) and *Sketchbook: Der Ungehorsame* (Sketchbook: The Disobedient; 1968) are not only entertaining and decorative but are also laced with commentary on politics, cultural criticism, and the philosophy of history.

3
Celestino Piatti (*1922)

His cover design for the dtv (Deutscher Taschenbuch Verlag) paperback book series is inscribed into the visual memory of all German-speaking readers. The white covers, with Piatti's simple, slightly abstract, drawn and colored illustrations set standards for presence and identity that were hitherto unknown in the publishing world—which had used mostly text-based logos. Up to then there was no real aesthetic identity or brand awareness for whole series of paperbacks. His designs were a milestone of elegant and high-value book art in paperback.

A motif that runs throughout his entire work is the owl, which in all its manifold associations remains a symbol for reading and wisdom. Piatti's take on it: "You can draw the owl a thousand times and you will not learn its secret."

4
Erica Pedretti (*1930)

The author and painter arrived at her grandmother's home in Switzerland on a Red Cross transport from Czechoslovakia in 1945. She attended the School of Applied Arts from 1946–50. Since 1970 Erica Pedretti has been among the most multifaceted personalities of contemporary Swiss literature, in particular women's literature. She has been awarded many important literary prizes including the Ingeborg Bachman Prize in 1984 and the Marie Luise Kashnitz Prize in 1996.

Erica Pedretti is also a successful artist. Superscripts, a combination of literature, art, and sculpture, represent just one of her original forms of artistic expression. Her public installations include the 7.5-meter-tall wing at Zurich's Kloten airport.

5
K. Domenic Geissbühler (*1932)

The precursors of the theater poster were the posters of traveling entertainers in the sixteenth and seventeenth centuries. Later, eye-catching theater posters became widely used in the larger cities. The large-format, colored lithographs of the *belle époque* mainly served to announce theater performances, variety shows, and circuses; in other words, they were used chiefly as advertisements for independent, frivolous entertainments. The posters of Toulouse-Lautrec bear witness to this genre.

Geissbühler made his mark on the urban landscape of Zurich over several decades with his prize-winning posters for the Opera House. His work is in the tradition of Burkhard Mangold, Otto Baumberger, and Emil Cardinaux, whose theater posters caused a stir throughout Europe in the early twentieth century. Geissbühler's posters, however, do not use straightforward images to

1 2
3 4

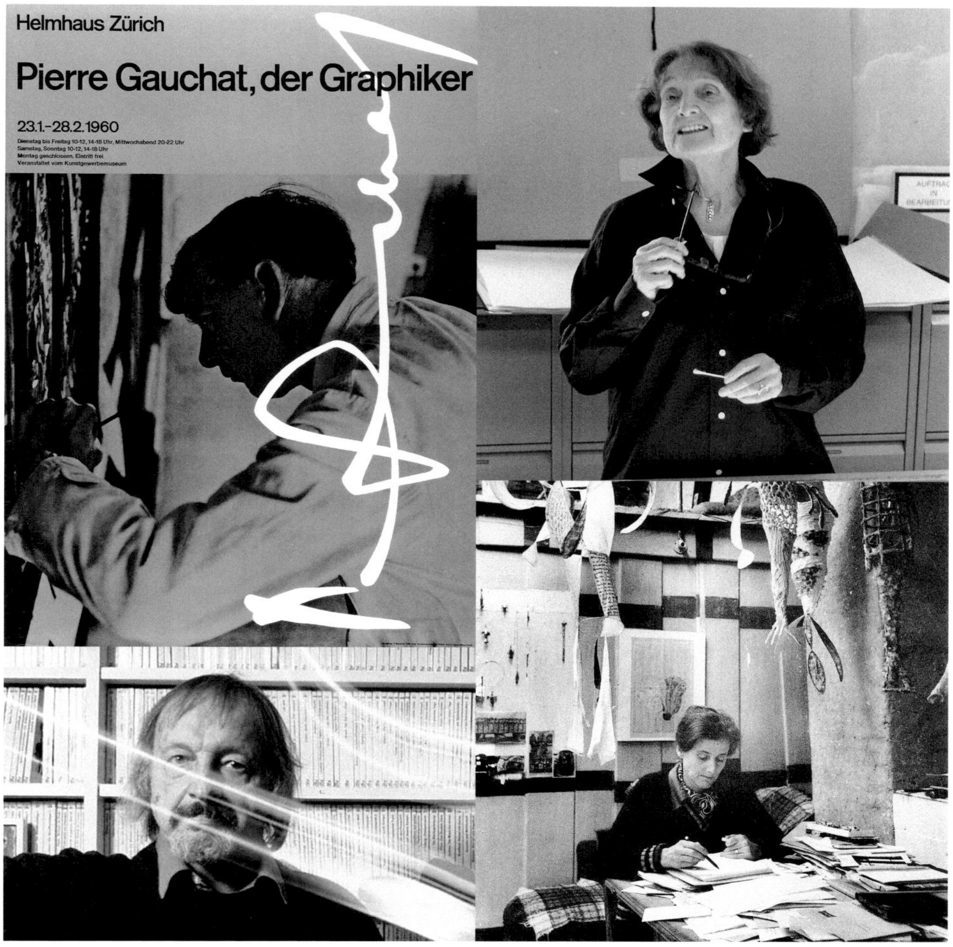

convey their message. Rather, he uses the tools of irritation and defamiliarization to illustrate the true nature of theater and opera, which should aim to unsettle, irritate, and seduce by illusionist means—holistically and plurimedially. The posters arouse interest and serve as announcements for both spectacular performances and elite cultural events. Geissbühler created hundreds of posters which express the symbiosis between art and music, between opera and its representation in graphic art.

He was a student of Ernst Keller at the School of Applied Arts and also studied art in Berlin. His posters were shown in solo exhibitions in New York, Mexico, Sydney, Warsaw, Tokyo, Berlin, and elsewhere; the prizes he received include the Toulouse-Lautrec Medal and awards from the Triennial of Posters in Tokyo and the Centre Pompidou in Paris.

6

Charly Lang (*1939)

In 1963, Charly Lang received a degree in acting from the Hamburg School of Music and Performing Arts. From 1963 to 1972, he was engaged at the Freies Schauspielhaus der Hansestadt Hamburg. He began there as an actor and directorial assistant before rising to the position of artistic director. In 1973–74, he was director at the Freie Volksbühne Berlin. Beginning in 1977, Charly Lang specialized in fight choreography. He became a director of movement in the true sense. In this capacity, he worked together with directors such as Peter Stein, Peter Zadek, and Luc Bondy. From 1981–2003, he was assistant professor of stage combat at the Berlin University of the Arts, but at the same time choreographed movement for a wide range of theaters. He worked in Zurich as an instructor in stick fighting and stage combat from 1989 onward. In 2003, Charly Lang retired, and now lives in Ticino.

7

Irwin Gage (*1939)

Sometimes he gave lieder recitals without the accompaniment of the sung melody. "Songs without singers" was also the name the pianist Irwin Gage gave to a series of recordings of lieder by Schubert and Brahms in the 1980s. Accompaniment, for Gage, is an art in its own right. "I play words," he says—an assertion that is borne out by his sensitive and impulsive style of playing. Meanwhile, the list of singers he has accompanied reads rather like a "who's who" of recent vocal history and includes both veterans such as Cheryl Studer, Brigitte Fassbaender, Dietrich Fischer-Dieskau, and Peter Schreier, and also much younger singers, such as Christoph Prégardien, Juliane Banse, and Christine Schäfer. Between 1979 and 2005, Gage was able to pass on his vast knowledge of playing with words and of the connection between words and music to countless students at the Zurich School of Music, Drama and Dance, where his lieder class attracted international interest.

8

Kathrin Graf (*1942)

Originally a student of Lorand Fenyves in Geneva, Kathrin Graf began her career as a violinist in the Tonhalle Orchestra in the late 1960s. She then decided to do something completely different, however, and enrolled to study singing in Frankfurt am Main and later in Berlin. It was not long before she had acquired a vast repertoire of works, ranging from Baroque to avant-garde pieces and including such diverse genres as oratorio, chamber music, orchestral works, and lieder. Graf's numerous concert tours have taken her all over Europe and as far away as Canada and Japan. She has been teaching singing at the Music Department at the Zurich University of the Arts since 1977.

9

Cornelia Hesse-Honegger (*1944)

Heteroptera: Das Schöne und das Andere (Heteroptera: The Beautiful and the Other) is the title of one of her publications. "Heteroptera" means nothing more than "bug," and it is bugs in particular whose mutations, severe mutilations, grotesque deformities, and overgrowths Hesse-Honegger draws with great care and meticulous precision, using the "harmless" aesthetic of scientific illustrations to create a veritable chamber of horror. She seeks her "protagonists" in the areas around nuclear power plants or the scenes of nuclear catastrophes like Chernobyl (1986) and Sellafield (1992). She is combative in her commitment to the environment. She picks fights with "science," which reacts defensively and slanderously, and also with the art world, which treats her work skeptically.

She attended the preliminary course in the early 1960s and taught herself to be a natural science draftswoman at the Zoological Institute

5 9
6 7

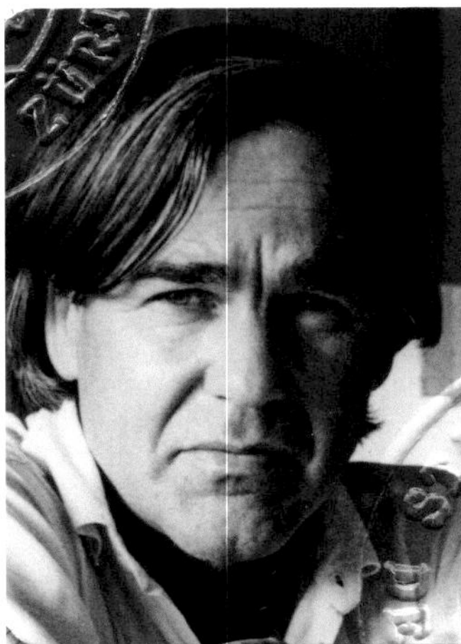
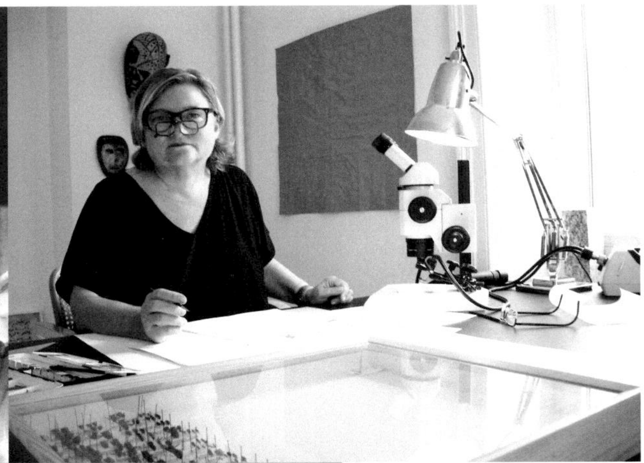
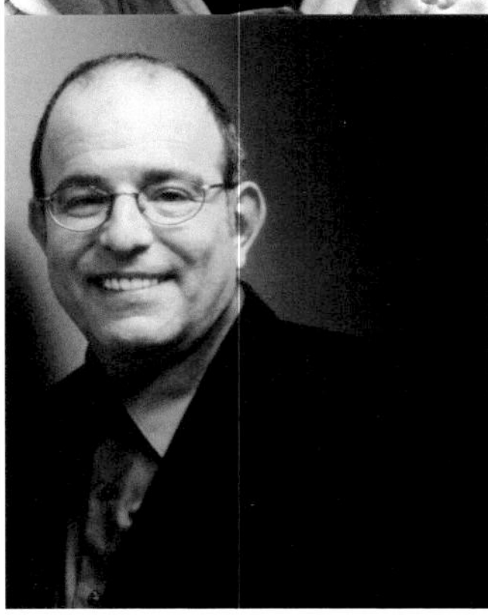
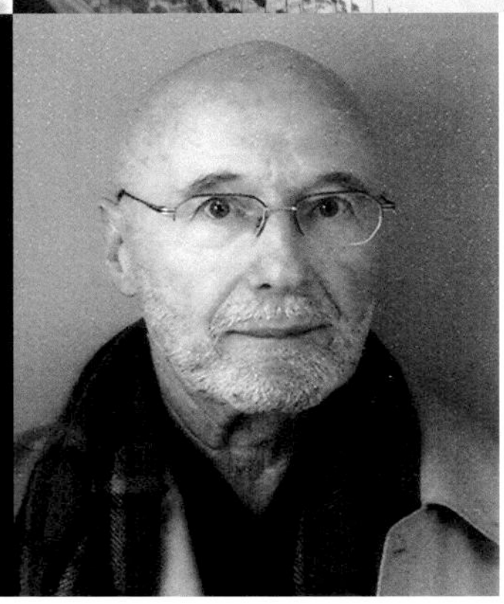

of the University of Zurich. In 1992 she represented Switzerland at the 18th Triennale in Milan. Her pictures have been included in standard works of natural science as well as in the *History of Modern Science* (2003).

10

Rudolf Meyer (*1943)

Born in Küsnacht on Lake Zurich, Rudolf Meyer trained as an organist at the Zurich Music Academy and Conservatory and from 1976 to 2001 was both first organist of the City Church and a lecturer in organ playing, improvisation, and chamber music at what was then the Winterthur-Zurich School of Music. In an age in which the music business is just as globalized as any other, Meyer's career seems remarkable above all for his topographical constancy. Yet he is certainly not as sedentary as might at first appear. He has been a guest lecturer in Sydney, at the Schola Cantorum Basiliensis, and at the Cologne University of Music. He also organizes international organ conferences in Winterthur and has been working as a freelance composer since 2001, composing both sacred and secular music for various ensembles.

11

Hans Knuchel (*1945)

It is truly remarkable how black paper cuttings, fragments of photographs, abstract patterns, or mirrors can lead to technical designs for previously unknown optical spaces, and how new ways of looking and forms of perception miraculously transform our image of the world into the fantastic. Hans Knuchel expands, elevates, and defamiliarizes our ways of seeing in his fictitious, abstract, and three-dimensional spaces. He breaks through our everyday, stereotypical perception with stereoscopic pictures, unfamiliar color schemes, seeing machines, and sight installations. This is the field in which he researches, experiments, and publishes. The result includes pictorial events that bring our visual confidence to the verge of collapse: perceptual sensations, optical wonder worlds, dizzying spaces that trigger both astonishment and disorientation in the viewer.

Knuchel was a graduate of the photography program and the Visual Designer pilot course at the School of Applied Arts and the Higher School of Design.

12

Wolfram Berger (*1945)

Born in Graz, Wolfram Berger is a man of multiple talents and a jack of all trades who seems to be successful at whatever he turns his hand to. After a dream career as an actor at mainstream theaters in the 1970s, Berger decided in 1980 to give up permanent engagements and to travel, alone or with friends, performing a large variety of programs, singing and playing musical instruments as well as acting. His repertoire stretches from literary cabaret inspired by Karl Valentin to radio readings ranging from short poems to Robert Musil's novel *The Man without Qualities*.
As a speaker, actor, and director he has devoted himself to the work of a large number of distinguished authors.
His talent for playing with language, for black humor, and for both charming levity and deep melancholy make him an outstanding interpreter of sensitive literary texts. Since 1973 Wolfram Berger has acted in many films. Since the early 1980s Berger has worked as a teacher at the Academy of Drama for many years.

13

Gardi Hutter (*1953)

Beginning in 1981, Gardi Hutter has toured half the world with her clown theater. To date, she has given 2,700 shows in twenty-two countries, created six evening-length theater pieces and a circus program, and won nine art prizes. She received her training at the Zurich Academy of Drama, and spent her apprentice years in Milan at the CRT (Centro di ricerca di teatro). In her virtually wordless solos and duos, performed in clown costumes in front of oddball stage sets and accumulations of common objects, she invents miniature, absurd universes whose characters struggle boldly if futilely for happiness.
The tragicomic aspect is exaggerated mercilessly, to the amusement of the public. She performs in theaters and barns, concert halls and cultural centers, at festivals and in favelas, and is received everywhere with enthusiasm by public and press alike.

14

Andreas Schertenleib (*1960)

After his school-leaving examination, this native of Kandertal attended the Zurich Academy of Drama. Beginning in 1986, he has been an independent author and actor,

8 10
11

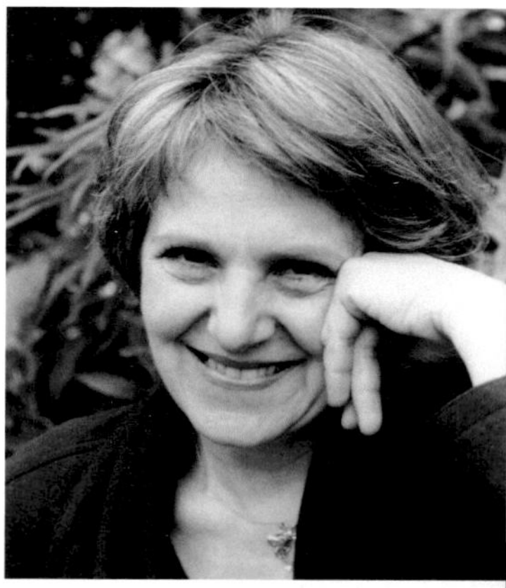

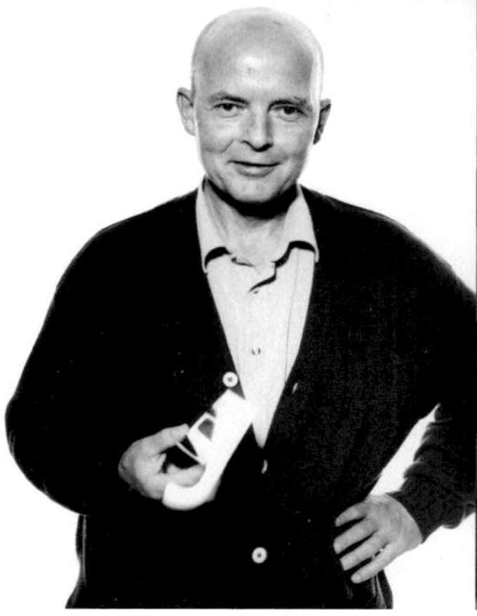

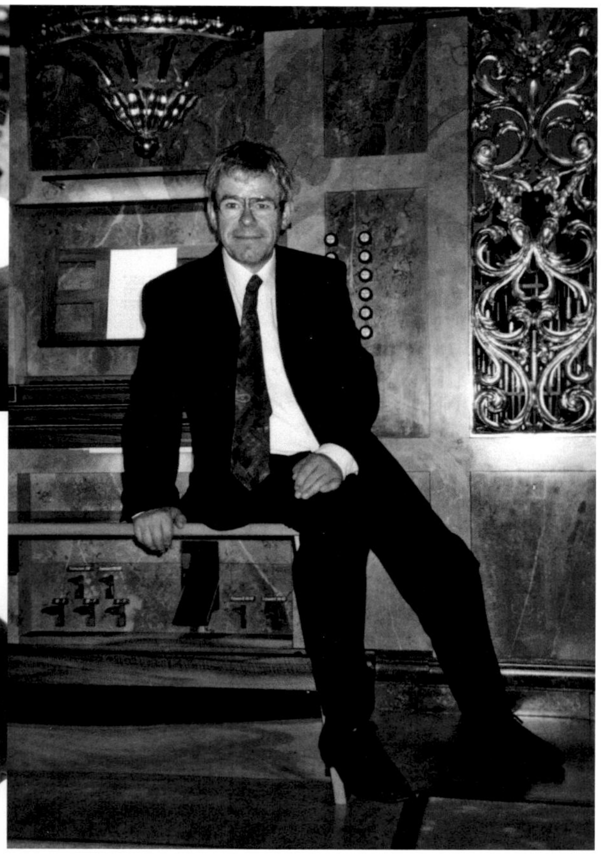

writing new pieces for his own use and appearing for years in various small theaters in German-speaking Switzerland. His witty and evocative label is Schertenleib&Seele, a play on his own name involving the German words for body and soul. Schertenleib certainly makes plentiful use of both body and soul in his performances, and adds his own whimsical humor when relating the states of being of his "self-referential" protagonists. These figures are inscribed on Schertenleib's own body, and pose questions relating to their/his spiritual condition(s) and needs in touchingly funny ways. In the process, he switches identities and roles like costumes, constantly appearing as new characters. Schertenleib's performances include music and his own songs, which effectively add to the dramatic atmosphere. As an actor, he has worked for the momoll theater, the Theater Zamt & Zunder, and the Nina Theater. As a musical actor, he has participated in musical theater productions of *Der Rock'n'Roll-König* (The King of Rock'n'Roll) and *Pepper*, and is a member of the trio Männertreu, which toured in the early 1990s with his staged concert *Kei Esel u keis Ross* (No Ass and No Horse). In 2004, Andreas Schertenleib received the canton of Solothurn Theater Prize.

15

Irina Schönen (*1960)

Irina Schönen is the anonymous yet omnipresent voice of Switzerland. Her incisive and cultivated voice can be heard in announcements on the SBB, in regular television announcements on programs such as *Quer, Rundschau, DOK, 3Sat Kulturzeit*, and *Kino aktuell*, in radio plays, and other announcements and readings.

Still, it would be wrong to assume that she hides permanently behind a studio microphone. Alongside film roles and work for the stage, she contributes her vocal talent to Trio Single Belles—a group whose brilliant shows for voice and theater stand for "serious" entertainment. They sing everything imaginable, from somewhat ill-reputed songs about *Heimat* to pop classics and hit parade numbers. Their voices are unique and omnipresent, and whether singing classical or jazz, their range and skills are remarkable. The program is reminiscent of a Saturday evening spent in front of the TV channel hopping, as the Single Belles will use any format from live talk shows and weather reports all the way to catastrophe alerts. *Wir leiden mit Spendenkonto 85-338880-1* (We Suffer with Donations Account 85-338880-1) is the name of their latest program. The Single Belles have existed as a regular group since 1995—they are Brigitte Frey (Petty), Marie Louise Grunder (Lilly), and Irina Schönen (Fabienne), and director Caroline Schenk. Irina Schönen studied at the Zurich Academy of Drama.

16

Félix Duméril (*1971)

Félix Duméril is a dancer and choreographer who has made his own way between institutionalized companies and the free dance scene. He did his initial professional training at the Swiss Professional Ballet School (SBBS) in Zurich from 1988 to 1990, where he learned from Anne Woolliams how to make his body speak and how to use his perfect control as a medium of expression. After completing his training in Stuttgart and The Hague, Duméril began his career with contemporary dance companies under Daniela Kurz, Amanda Miller, and Ivan Wolfe. He then joined the ballet of the Bern Municipal Theater under Martin Schläpfer, where he made a name for himself as a powerful dancer equally at home in classical and modern dance. Following his first choreography in 1997, Duméril was ballet director and in-house choreographer in Bern from 1999 to 2004, subsequently returning to freelance work. He is never one to do things quickly, doggedly pursuing his own productions and exchange projects. As a dancer he works painstakingly to achieve a precise and intense mode of expression.

12 13
14
15
16

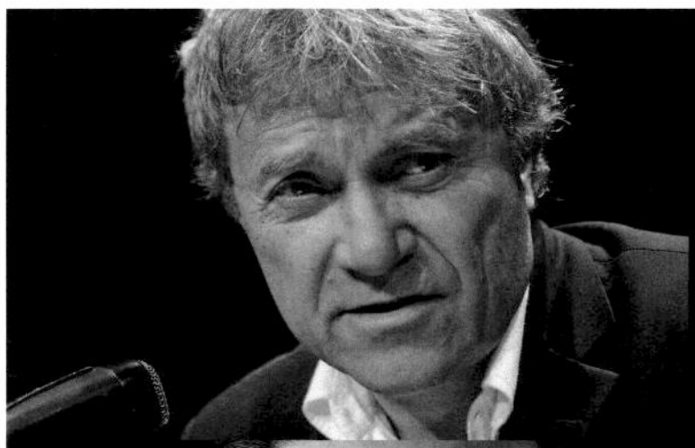

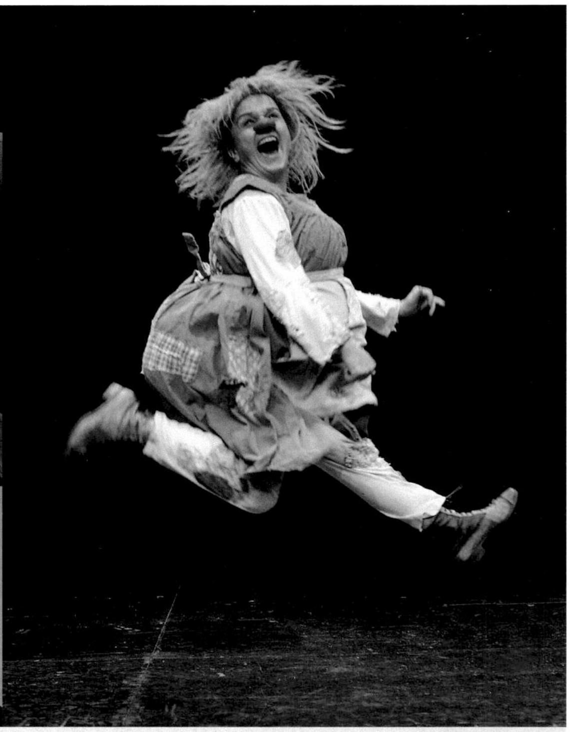

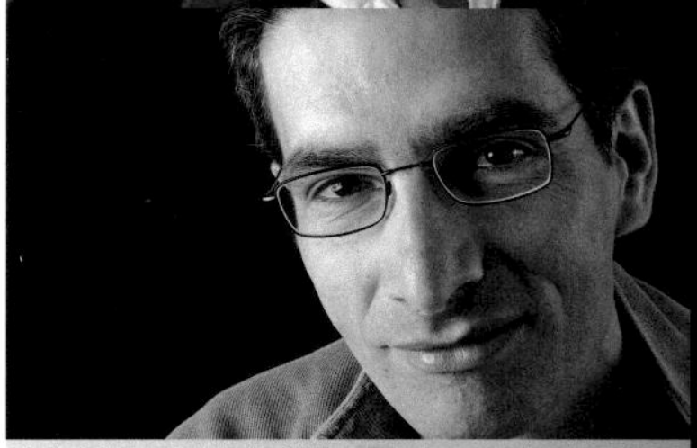

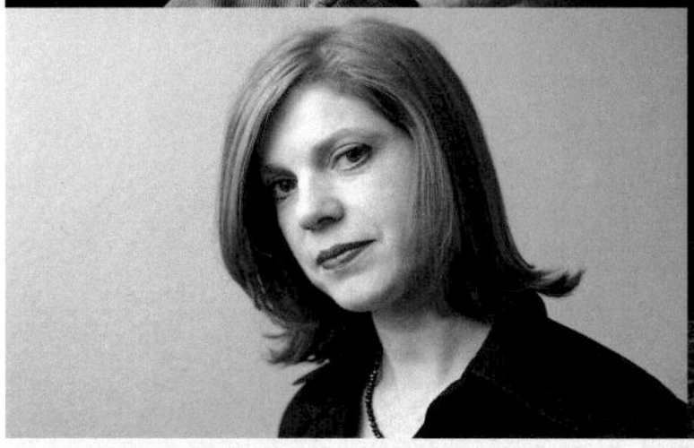

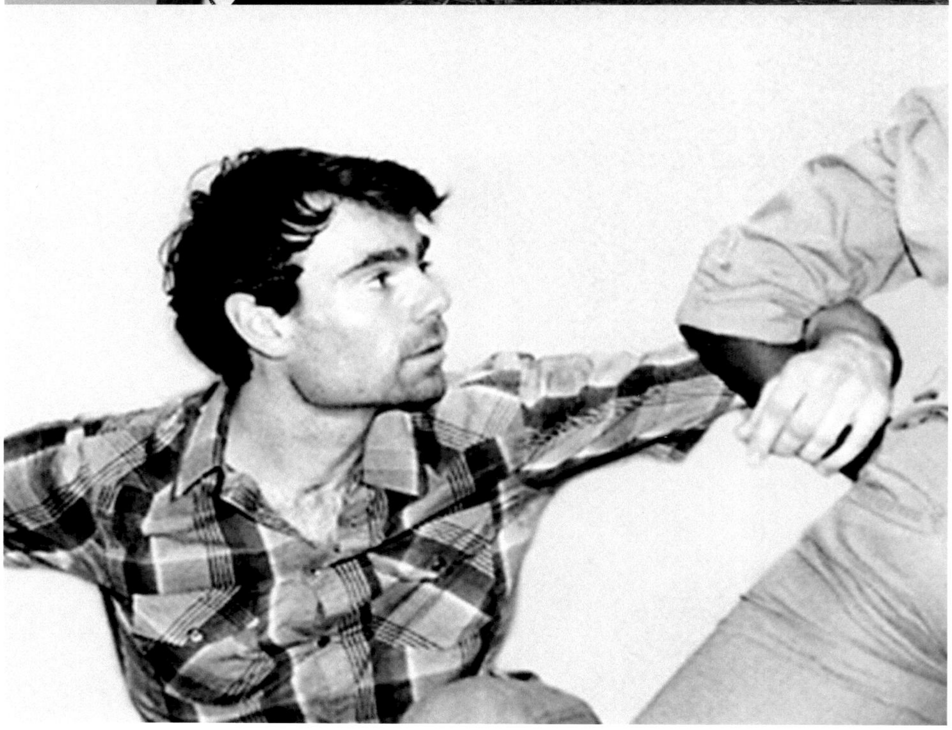

1a–e Swiss banknotes, fifth emission (1956–76). Design Pierre Gauchat and Hermann Eidenbenz. Detail showing St. Martin

1f Design (jacket cover) of the photo book *Fabrik*. Zurich, 1943

1g Poster design for Bally International AG. Caslano, 1935

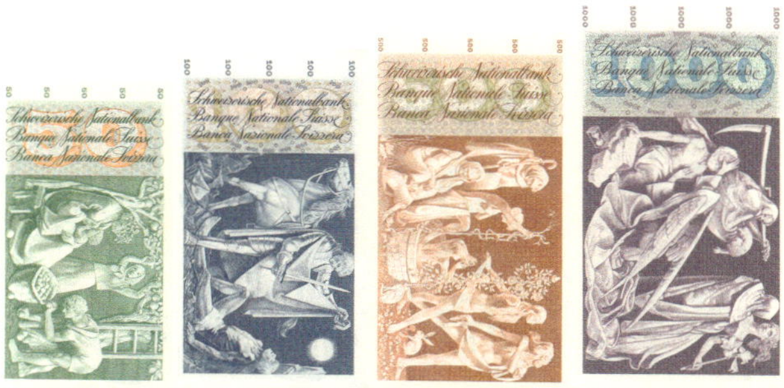

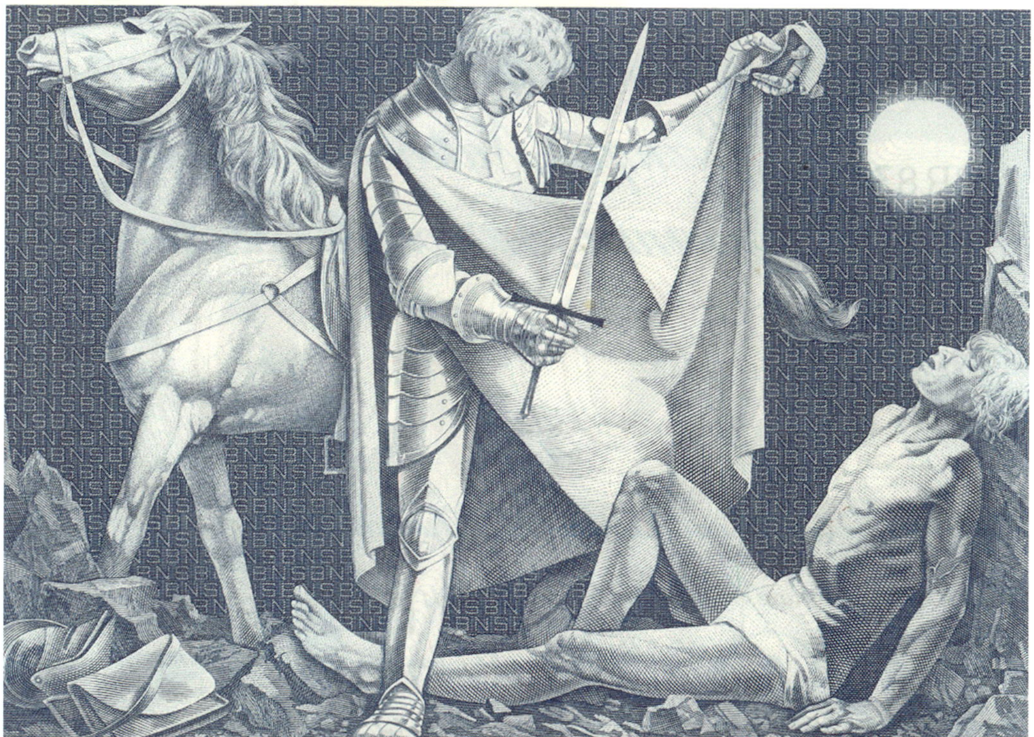

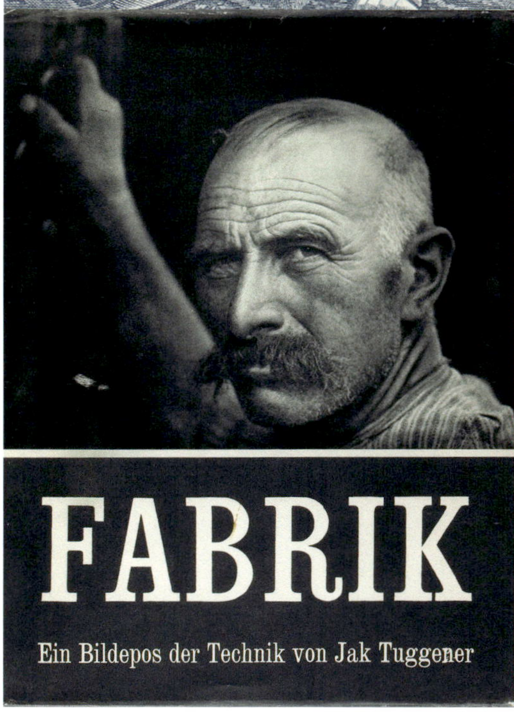

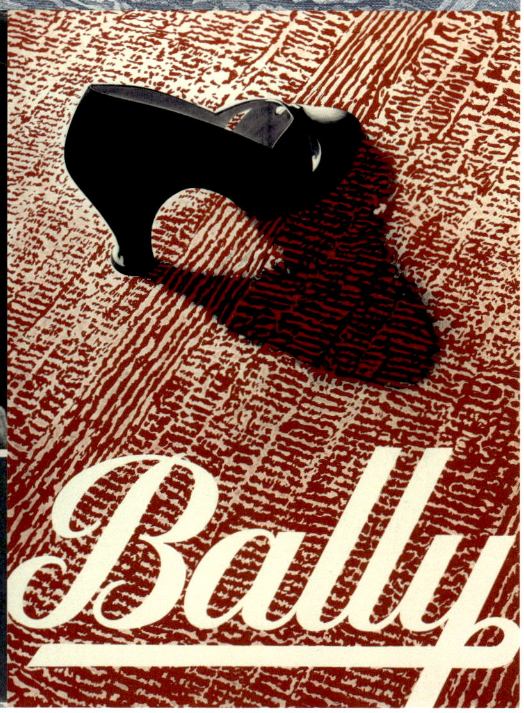

2a/b Warja Lavater, *Le Petit Poucet: Une imagerie d'après le conte de Charles Perrault.* Leporello with lithographs, detail and full view. Adrien Maeght Editeur, Paris, 1979

3a Celestino Piatti, poster

3b–e Selection of cover designs. Piatti designed all of Deutscher Taschenbuch Verlag's covers from its founding in 1960/61 to 1990.

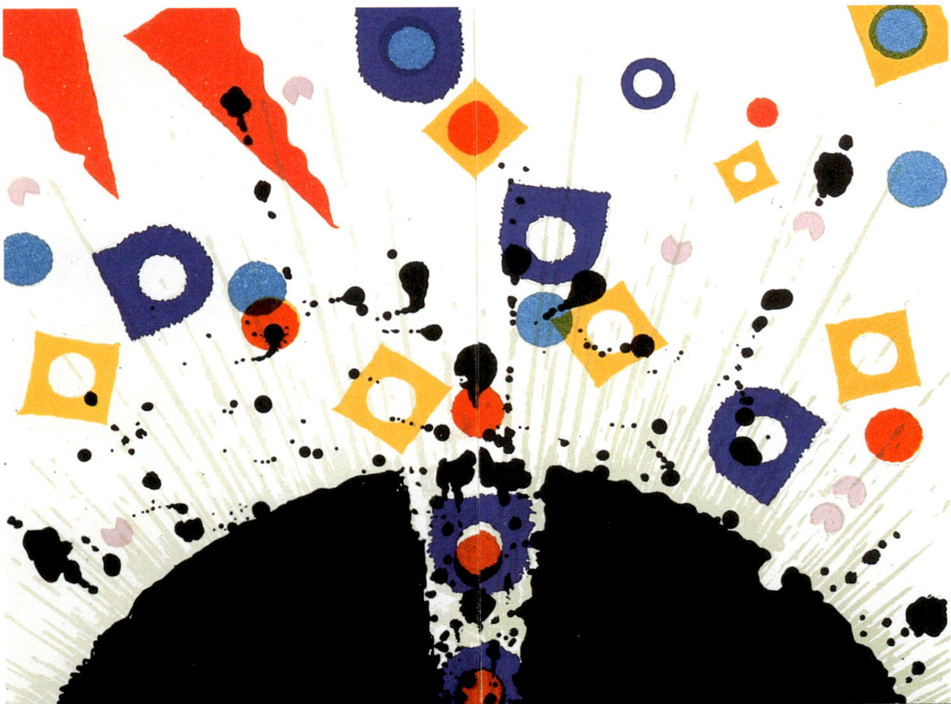

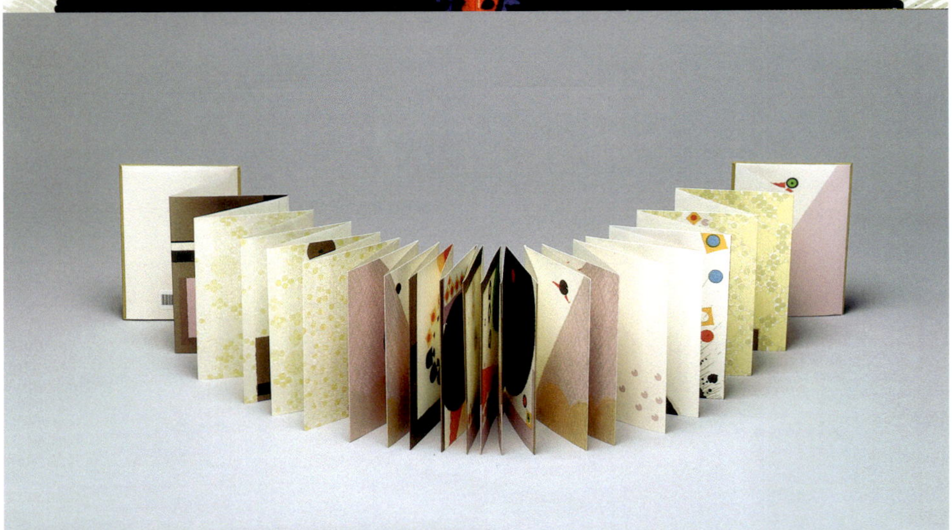

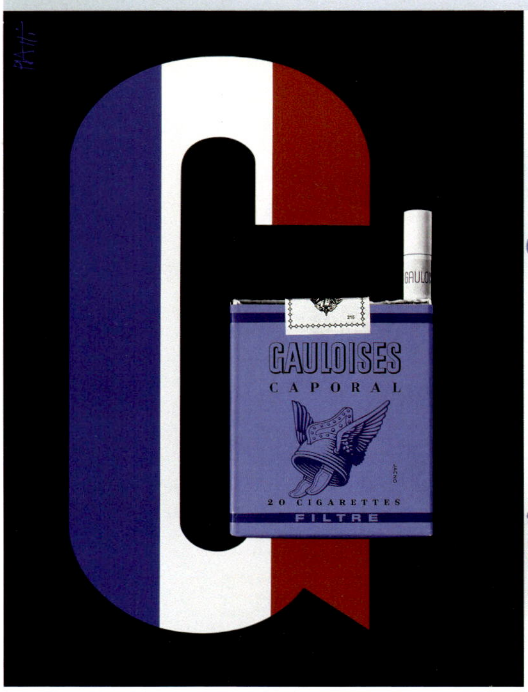

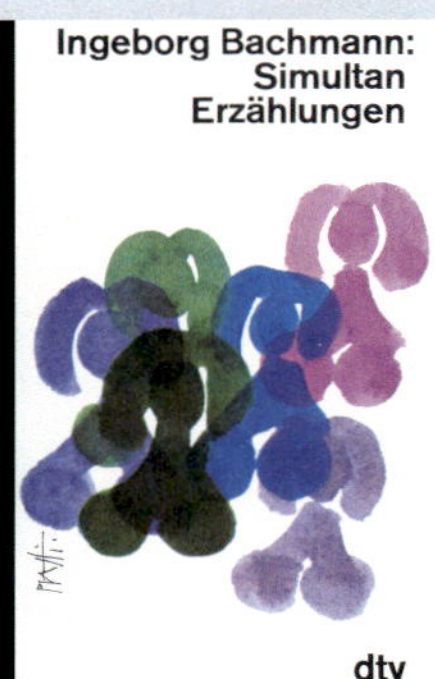

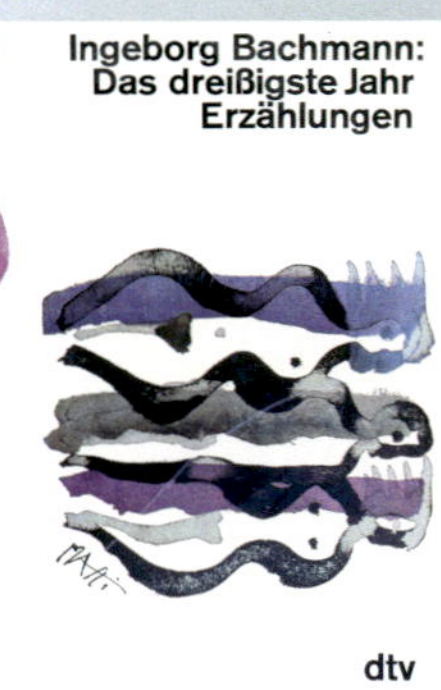

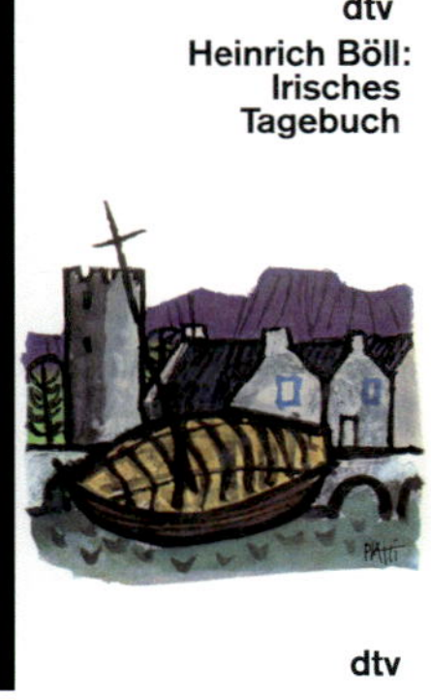

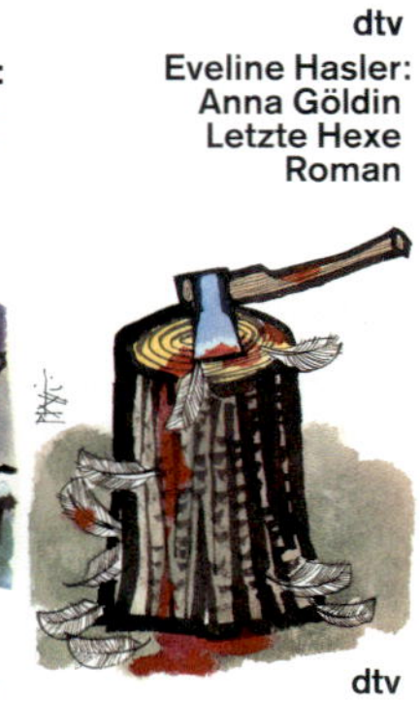

5a–m Since 1976 K. Domenic Geissbühler has designed more than 150 posters for the Zurich Opera House. *Oper im Bild*, exhibition at the School of Music, Drama and Dance, 2005

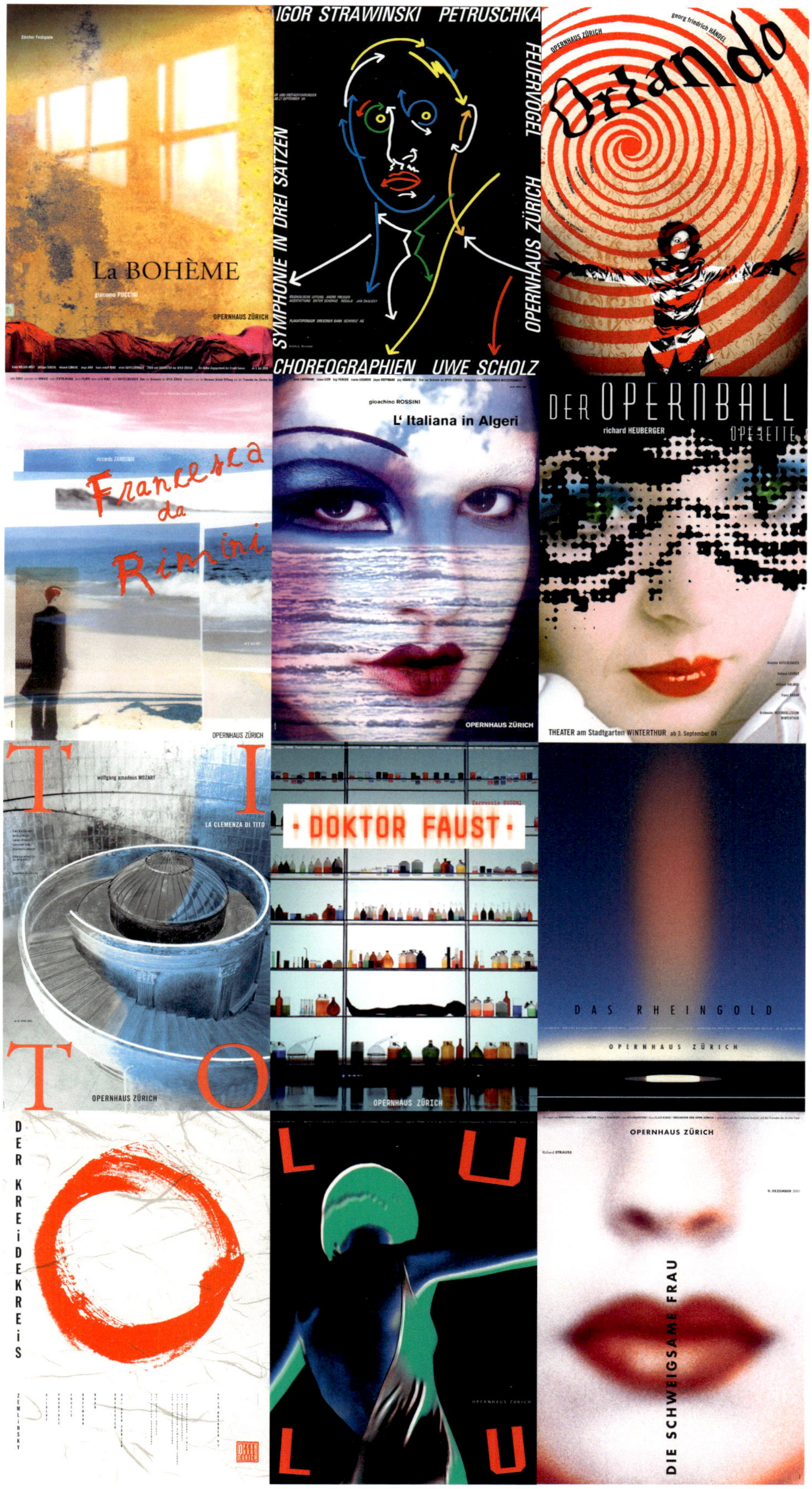

8a Soprano Kathrin Graf with the Greenwood Harmony Choir and conductor Kunio Imai. Performance of Fauré's *Requiem*, Japan, 1994

9a–e Cornelia Hesse-Honegger, scientific illustrations of morphological deviance in insects exposed to radiation in the vicinity of nuclear power stations: Stink bug, Slavutych, Ukraine, 1991.—Assassin bug, Othello, Washington State, USA,1998.—Stink bug, Parvin Road, Washington State, USA, 1998.—Bug of the *Miridae* family, Prypiat, Ukraine, 1990.—Wings of a stink bug, La Hague, France, 1999

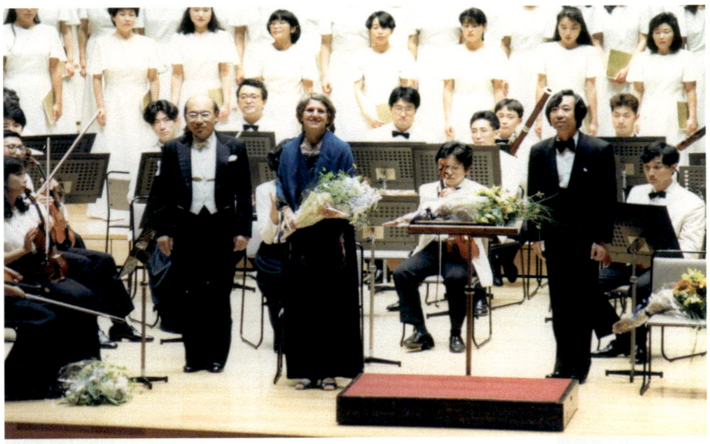

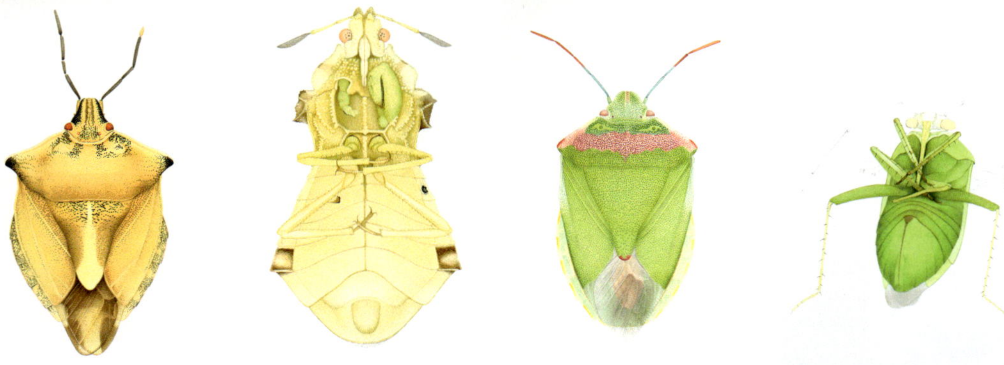

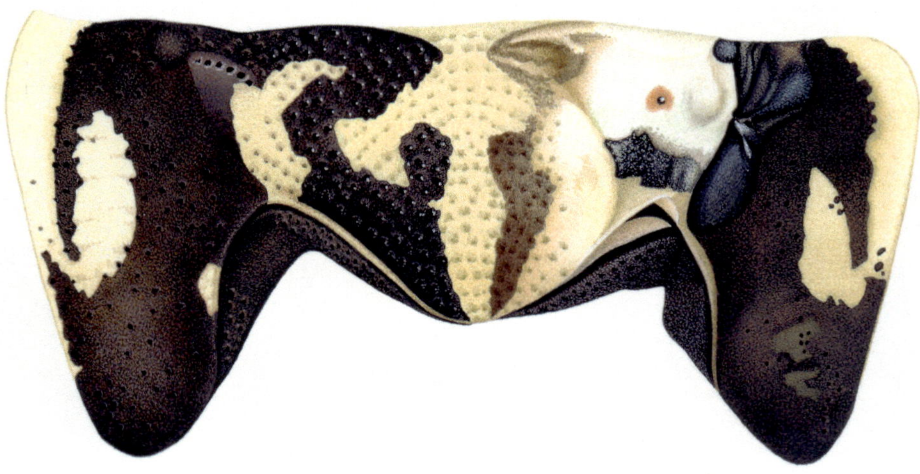

11a Hans Knuchel, “Experiments with a Pinhole Camera”

11b–e 3D motion figures in the staircase of the School of Applied Arts and Design. Hans Knuchel and Peter Bosshard, Visual Designer pilot course, 1985

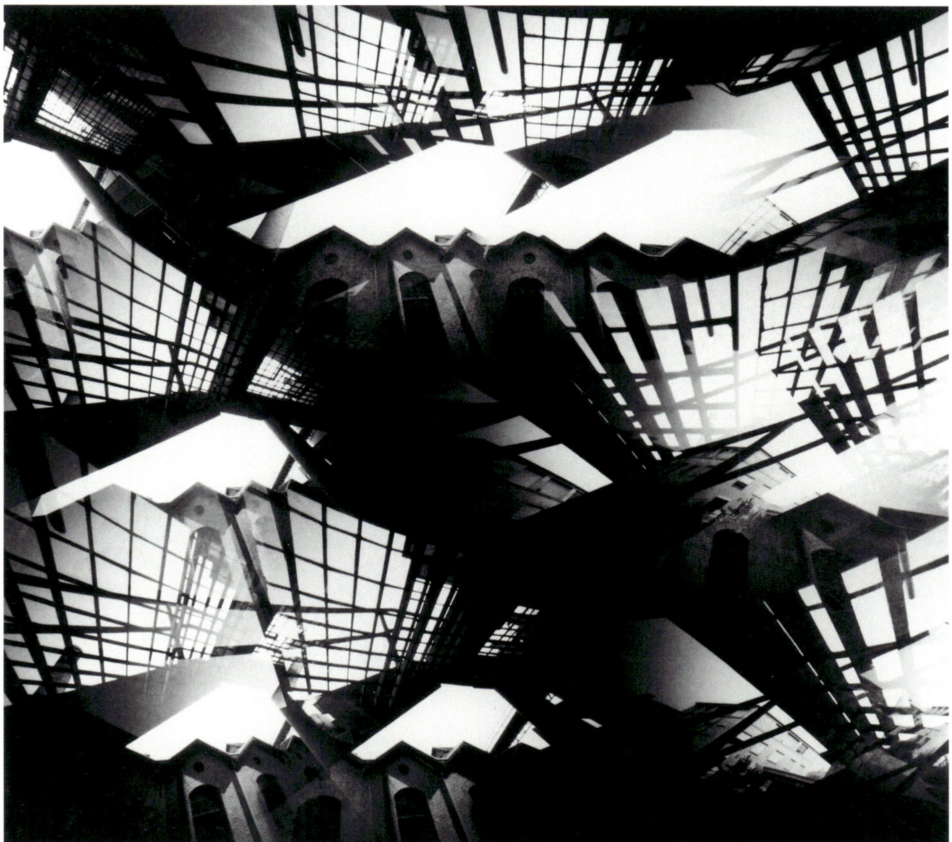

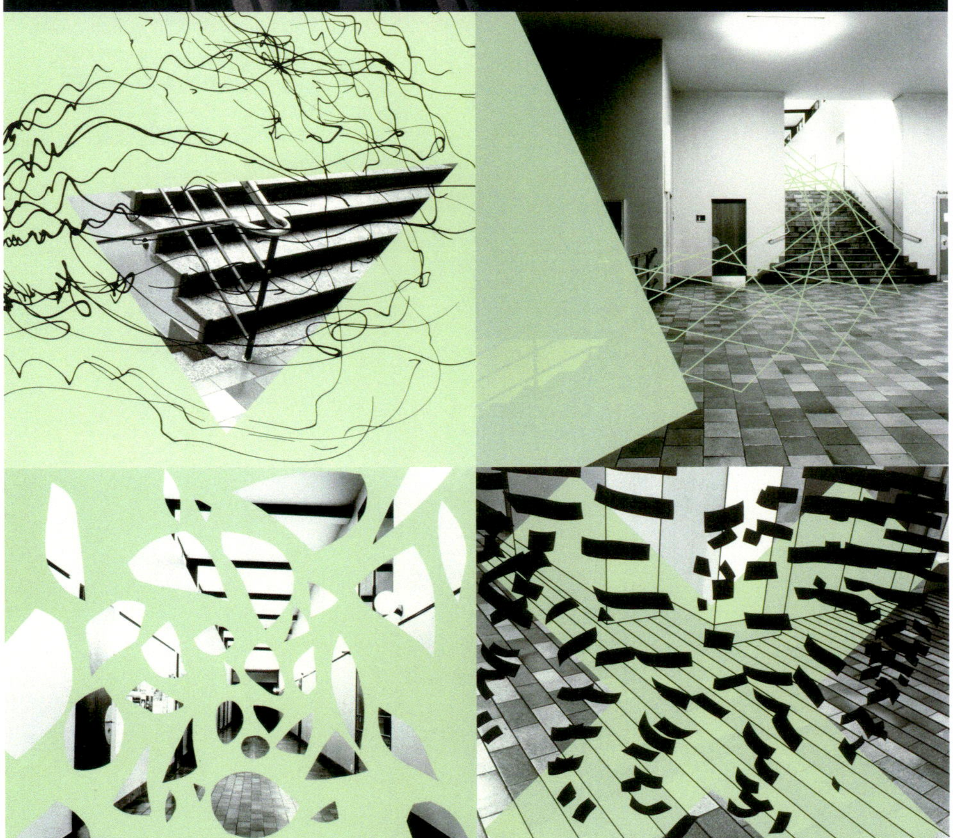

11f Hans Knuchel on a field trip in Brittany, with the Photography Class 1963. Photo Andrée Binder

11g "Frauendoppel," Berlin Central Station, 2007

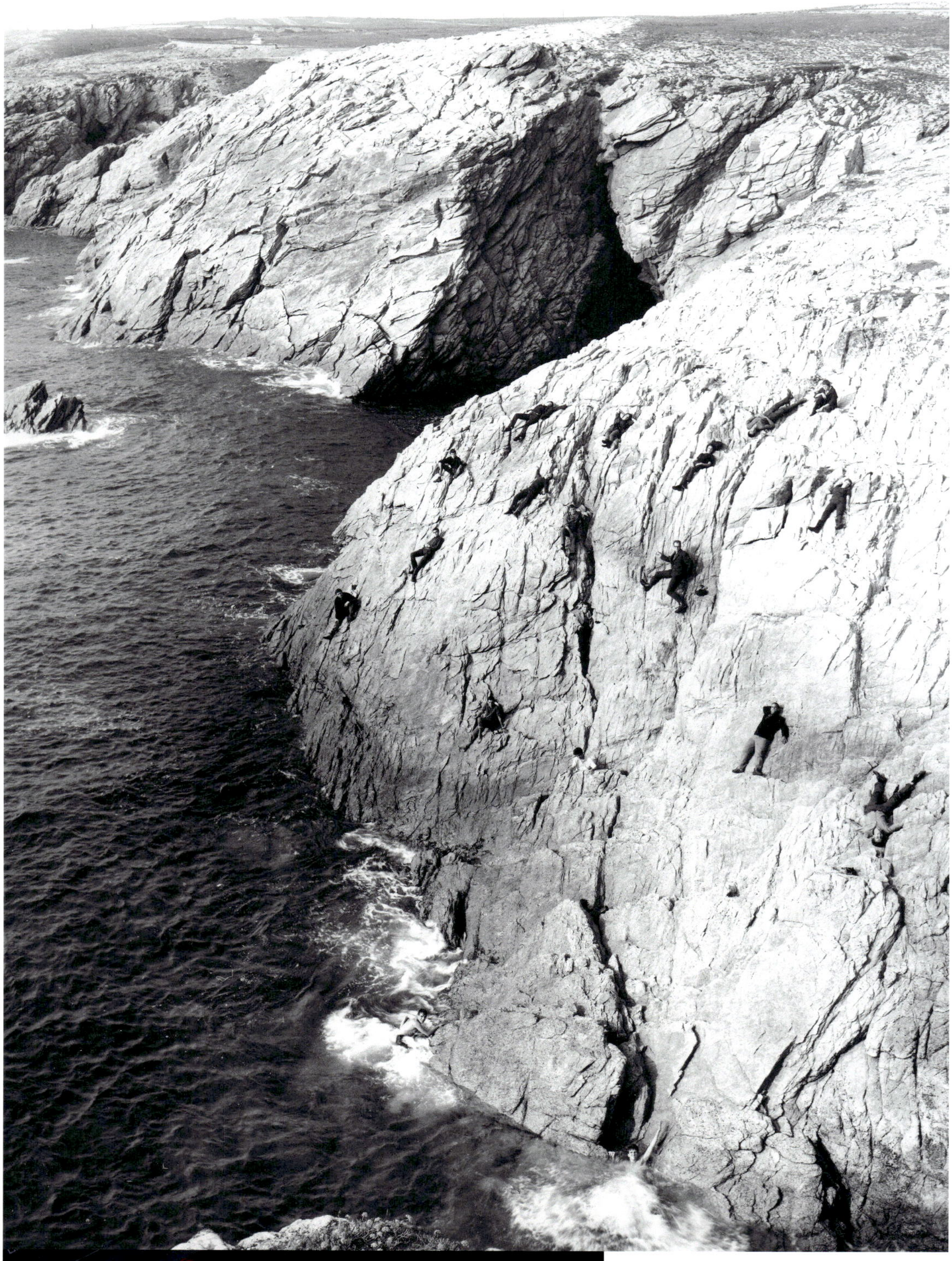

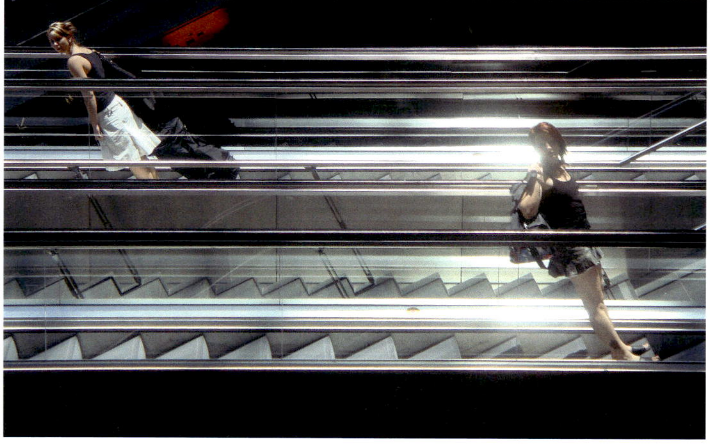

11h Hans Knuchel, neon color spreading effect from *blelb*, Interactive Visual Perception Lab

12a Wolfram Berger, *Come Back Liza*, 2005. Voice Wolfram Berger, harmonica Ruedi Burkhardt, Theater Ticino Wädenswil

12b *Acropolis Now*, 1984. Wolfram Berger, Dominique Laffin, and Max Rüdlinger. Director Hans Liechti

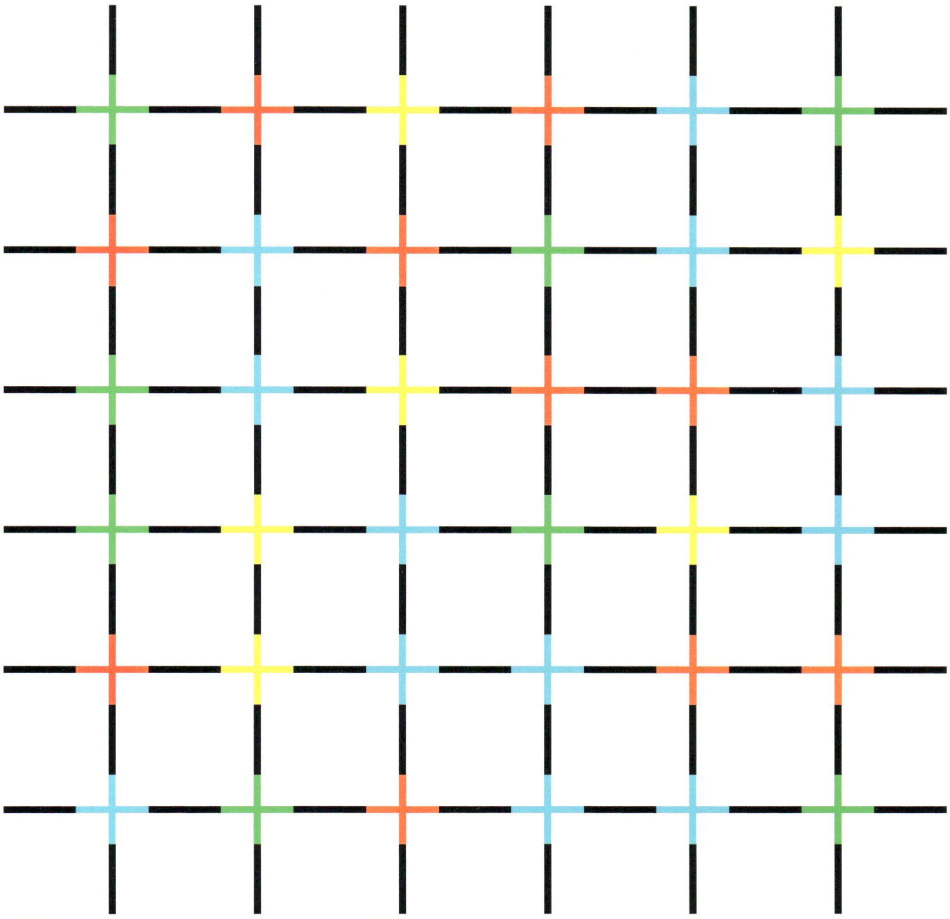

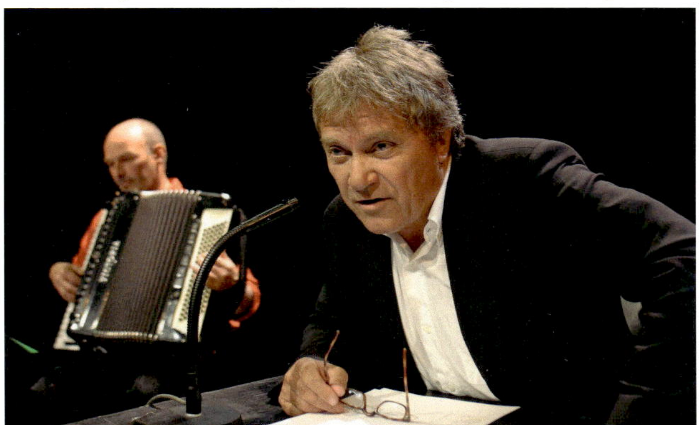

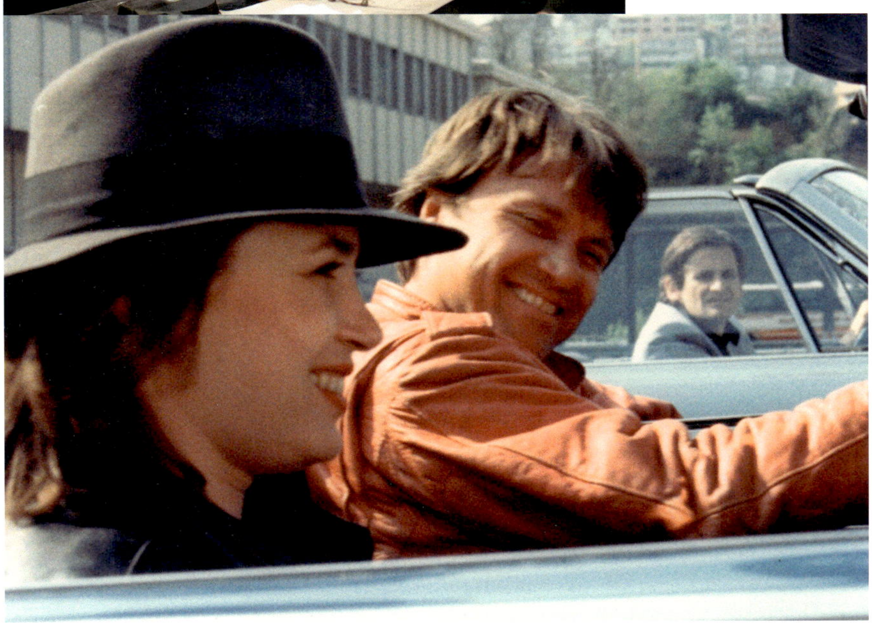

13a Gardi Hutter as Hanna the Washerwoman in *Jeanne d'Arppo—die tapfere Hanna.* Lucerne, 2001

14a/b Andreas Schertenleib, *Onkel Ernst.* Theater event with music, 2003

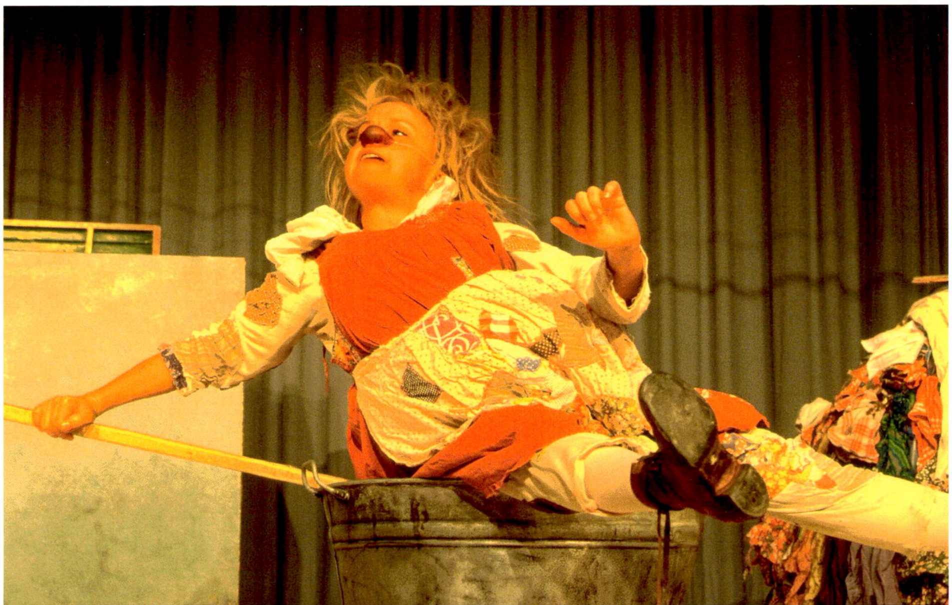

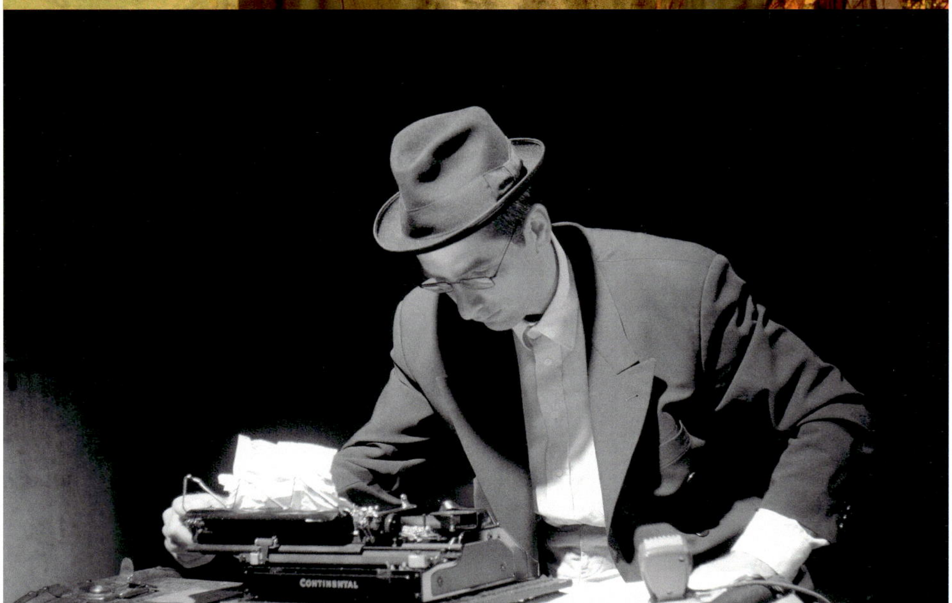

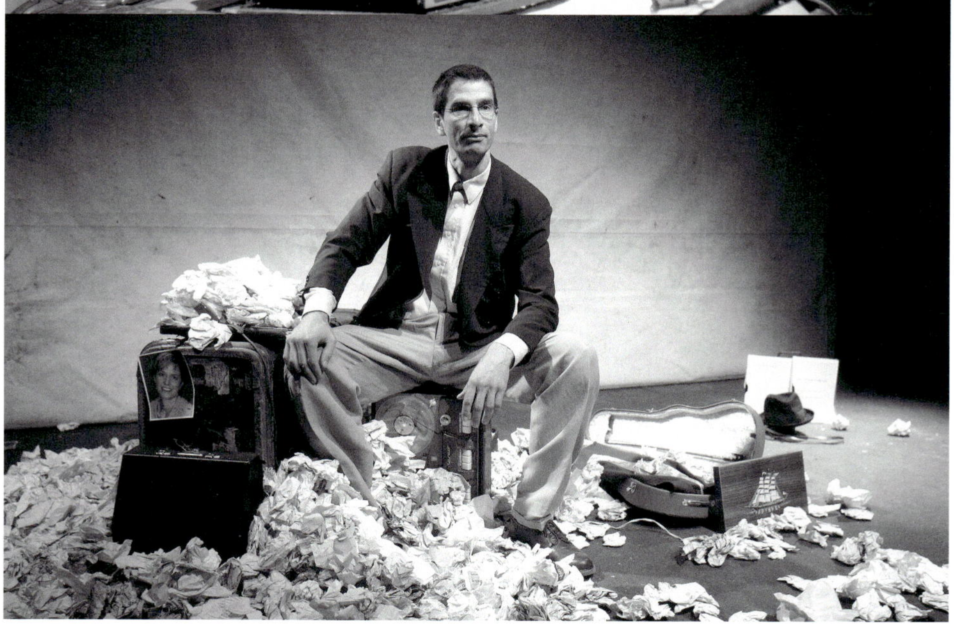

15a Irina Schönen (right) with the Single Belles. Tenth anniversary event, 2007

16a/b Félix Duméril, *Soliloquy*. Rehearsal with Sipho Manashe. Choreography Lucia Baumgartner. InFlux Dance Company, Durban, Maputo, 2006; Bern, 2007

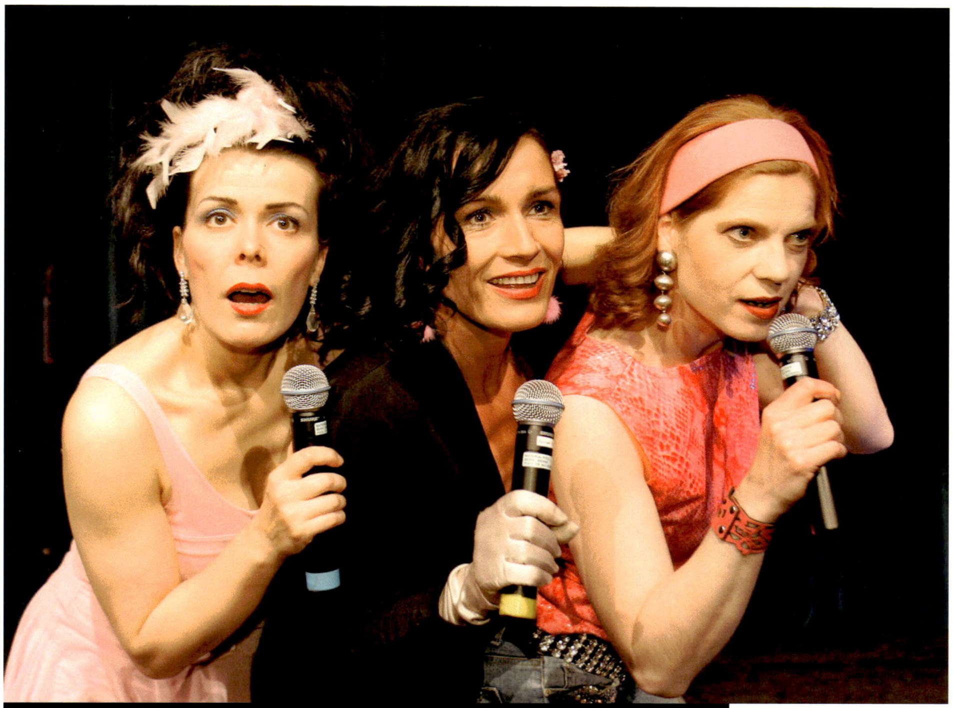

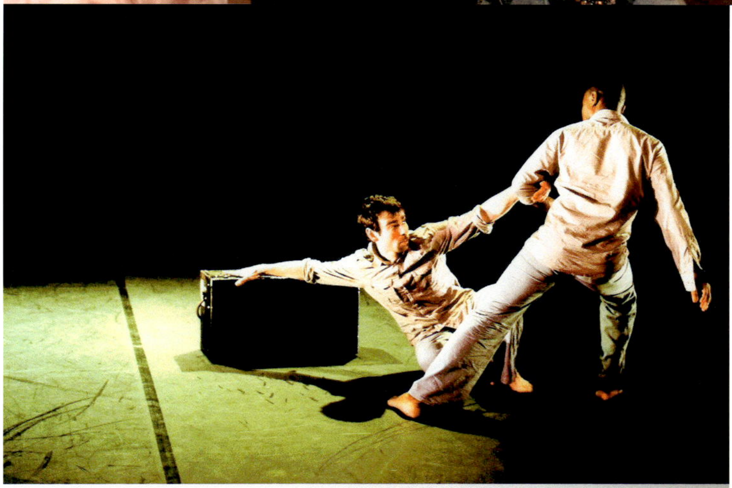

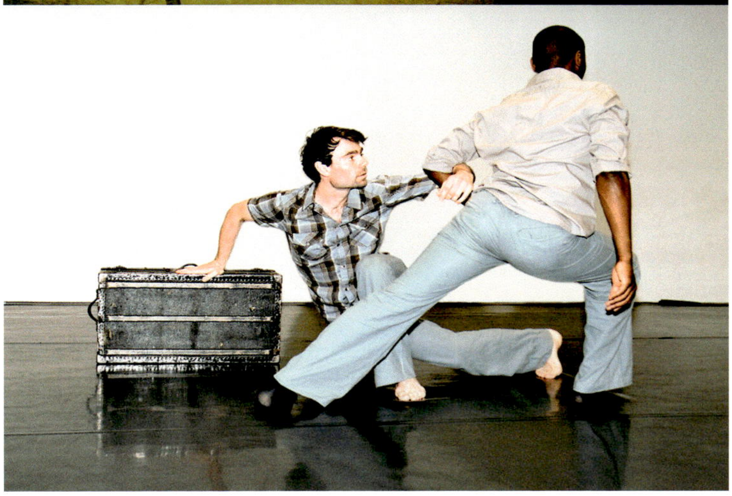

Primeval rocks appear in grandiose or elemental formations, are unwieldy, dark apparitions that convey some notion of the temporal immensity of the earth's history. These are the actors and actresses who can be referred to without irony as "primeval rocks," the "character actors" who depicted complex and contradictory individuals in grotesque and abysmal depths or comical highs and lows. They constitute petrified stage and film pathos.

She appeared in oppressive films about delusional child murderers, and taught rhythmic speech to apprentice actors and actresses **1**; with his massive size, he was an unforgettable and roguish public favorite on stage and cinema alike **2**; he achieved international celebrity as a director of classic Swiss film, and was simultaneously ostracized as a "nest fouler" *(The Last Chance)* **3**; he embodied *The Sudden Loneliness of Konrad Steiner* so convincingly that it became impossible to decide where Sigfrit Steiner stopped and Konrad Steiner began **4**; he played all characters and roles with sovereign skill and elemental force **5**; the hero, and simply indescribably good **6**.

1
Ellen Widmann (1894–1985)

Swiss actress Ellen Widmann appeared on various Berlin stages, as well as in movies, among others Fritz Lang's celebrated *M—eine Stadt sucht einen Mörder.* She was also famous for founding the Zurich Kammersprechchor (Chamber Speaking Choir) in 1951, a unique institution in the German-speaking world. After World War II, Ellen Widmann began practicing choral, rhythmic speech with acting students, and in the Chamber Speaking Choir she developed these techniques into a powerful expressive instrument. Her work was widely esteemed—graduates of her course were encountered wherever good public speakers were found. The chorus was used in various ways by directors, among others by Leopold Lindtberg in his staging of *Faust I und II* at the Zurich Schauspielhaus. As time passed, the Chamber Speaking Choir was heard increasingly on concert stages—composers such as Vladimir Vogel wrote works for them.

2
Gustav Knuth (1901–1987)

Gustav Knuth was the ideal embodiment of a popular actor. With his stocky build, sharp little eyes, and earthy, warm, and humorous approach to his roles, he quickly won people over and became a favorite with the audience. At the same time he would rise to any challenge, playing the major villains of the theater repertoire or unwieldy modern roles. Born in Braunschweig, he left home at the age of seventeen and began acting in provincial theaters and with travelling troupes of actors. During World War II he played under Gustav Gründgens in Berlin and from 1949 until well into the 1980s he was a member of the various ensembles of the Zurich Schauspielhaus. He gave brilliant performances in productions of Hauptmann, Shakespeare, and Brecht, and helped to make the premieres of plays by Max Frisch and Friedrich Dürrenmatt major successes. Knuth appeared in more than fifty films, including character studies and *Heimatfilme* (often sentimental regional films), and also shallow farces. He became even better known after he began appearing in popular television series in the 1960s. During the 1940s he taught for a modest salary at the Zurich Stage Studio. Gustav Knuth died in Zurich in 1987.

3
Leopold Lindtberg (1902–1984)

Leopold Lindtberg, an actor, theater and film director, and a theater manager, was born in Vienna. He took acting lessons while studying German language and literature and the history of art, and from 1924 onward pursued a stage career as an actor and director at German theaters. In 1933 he fled from the Nazis, first going to Paris and then to Zurich, and during and after the war he was a member of the legendary Zurich Schauspielhaus company as both an actor and director. He also made a name for himself as a film director. His films included highlights of Swiss film of that era, such as *Wachtmeister Studer or Die letzte Chance* (The Last Chance). After the war Lindtberg began a precipitous international theater career, which took him as director to Vienna, Salzburg, Berlin, Hamburg, and Munich and on tour to Tel Aviv and Tokyo. From 1965 to 1968 he was manager of the Zurich Schauspielhaus, but was rather unsuccessful in this role. For some time he was in-house director of the Stage Studio, where he directed plays for schools. He is buried in Sils Maria.

4
Sigfrit Steiner (1906–1988)

Sigfrit Steiner was among the great actors and directors of Swiss film and theater. He studied at the studio of the Théâtre de l'Atelier in Paris, and later at the acting school of the Deutsches Theâter in Berlin. He supported himself by working as an extra at Ufa: "Thanks to a relative, I was able to get work with the high-class extras crowd, where I earned 200 German marks per day. That was a lot in those days, I was able to live on it for an entire month. But I was drummed out before long, since the other extras had a tight organization and really stuck together. I was able to work in four or five films, then it was over." With Hitler's seizure of power, Steiner returned to Switzerland, where he at first headed an embroidery works. Then came his first appearances in Swiss theaters, after which he became a regular member of the Zurich Schauspielhaus.

His first film appearance was *Füsilier Wipf* (Fusilier Wipf) in 1938. In 1941, he directed a movie for the first time: *Der doppelte Matthias und seine Töchter* (The Doubled Matthias and his Daughter), which made a loss. *Steibruch* (The Quarry), for which he was both director and

4 2

1 3

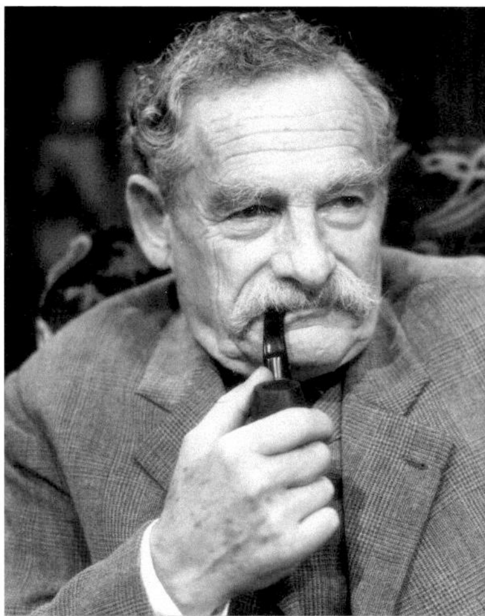

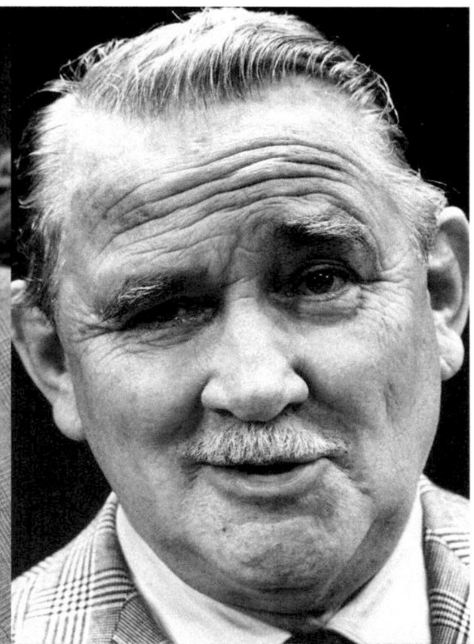

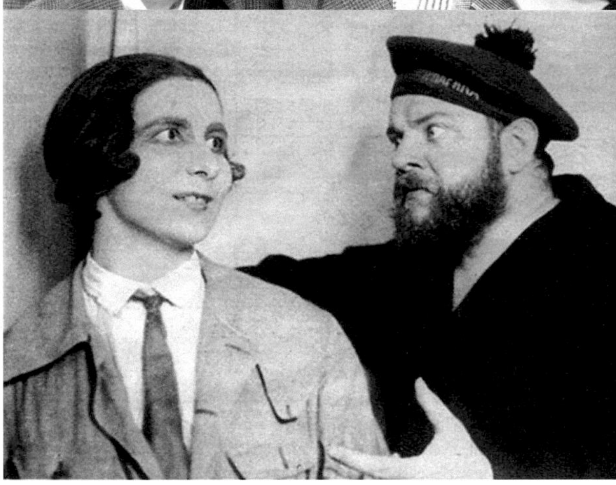

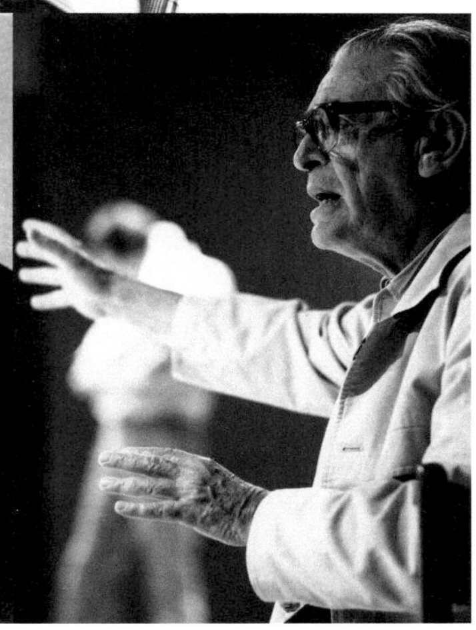

screenwriter, was then a success, but Steiner really only achieved great popularity as an actor. At the end of his career came his first great if belated success. In *Die plötzliche Einsamkeit des Konrad Steiner* (The Sudden Loneliness of Konrad Steiner), the directorial debut of Kurt Gloor (a graduate of the arts and crafts school), he played an old man who stubbornly refuses to enter an old folks home—virtually playing himself. In 1988, this appealing actor died in his Munich apartment. Sigrit Steiner taught at the Zurich Stage Studio.

5

Matthias Gnädinger (*1941)

Matthias Gnädinger, born in Ramsen, in Schaffhausen Canton, today lives in Stein am Rhein, just seven kilometers away from his birthplace. But this does not mean he is a provincial man. To Gnädinger acting comes naturally, and he can be considered a born popular actor. After abandoning his profession as a typesetter, Gnädinger trained at the Zurich Stage Studio and in his subsequent career became a seasoned theater and film actor, showing the same dedication to his art whether he was playing weighty or comic roles, farce or drama, television soaps or character studies in serious feature films. His career began at the Theater am Neumarkt in Zurich, later taking him to Peter Stein's Schaubühne in Berlin. Michael Grüber and Luc Bondy are among the many directors he has worked with. Bubbling with energy, almost to the point of exploding on the stage, Gnädinger has been seen in many different roles. Swiss film directors, in particular, often cast him in their productions. He has played the police commissioner in the TV detective series *Tatort* as well as Jörg Schneider's Commissar Hunkeler. But for the majority of the Swiss-German population he is best known as farmer Ruedi in the endless soap series *Lüthi und Blanc.*

6

Bruno Ganz (*1941)

Bruno Ganz is one of the German-speaking world's top theater and film actors. Born in Zurich, he trained at the Zurich Stage Studio. A formative influence and key figure in his career was the German director Peter Stein, with whom he acted in Bremen in the mid-1960s. In 1969–70 Ganz was part of the team at the Zurich Schauspielhaus that caused major political controversy in the city and was given its marching orders after only one season. For Ganz there followed glorious years at the Schaubühne in Berlin under Stein's direction, including tours all over Europe. From the mid-1970s onward Ganz alternated between the stage—playing at all Germany's major theaters—and film. Among his most recent achievements was his performance as Faust in Stein's thirteen-hour production of Goethe's play in 2000. One of his most difficult and controversial film roles was his performance as Hitler in the film *Downfall.* In 1996 Ganz received the Iffland-Ring, which is considered the highest German acting award.

6

5

2a Gustav Knuth, *Die Nylonschlinge,* 1963. Crime film

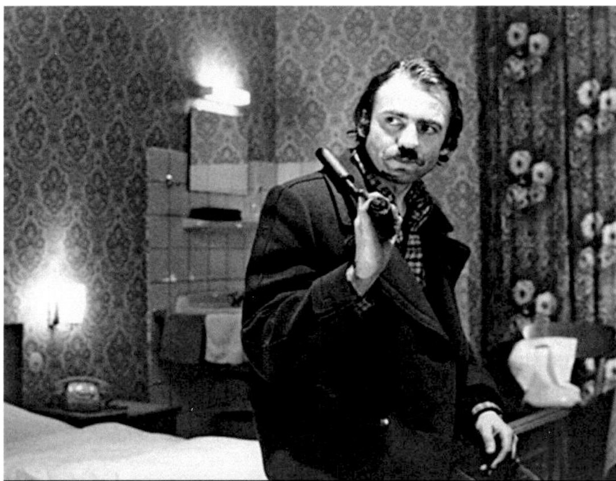

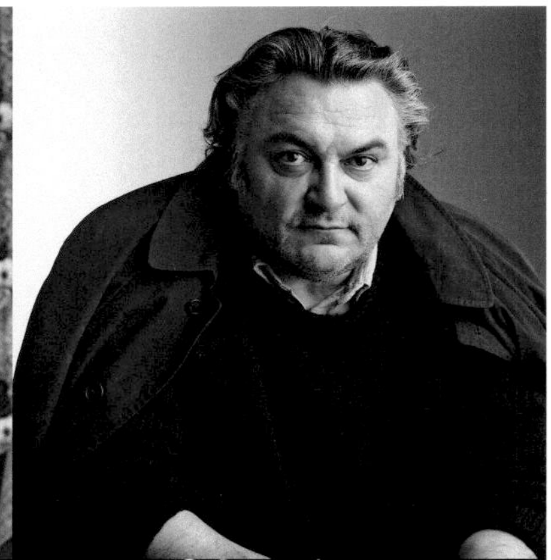

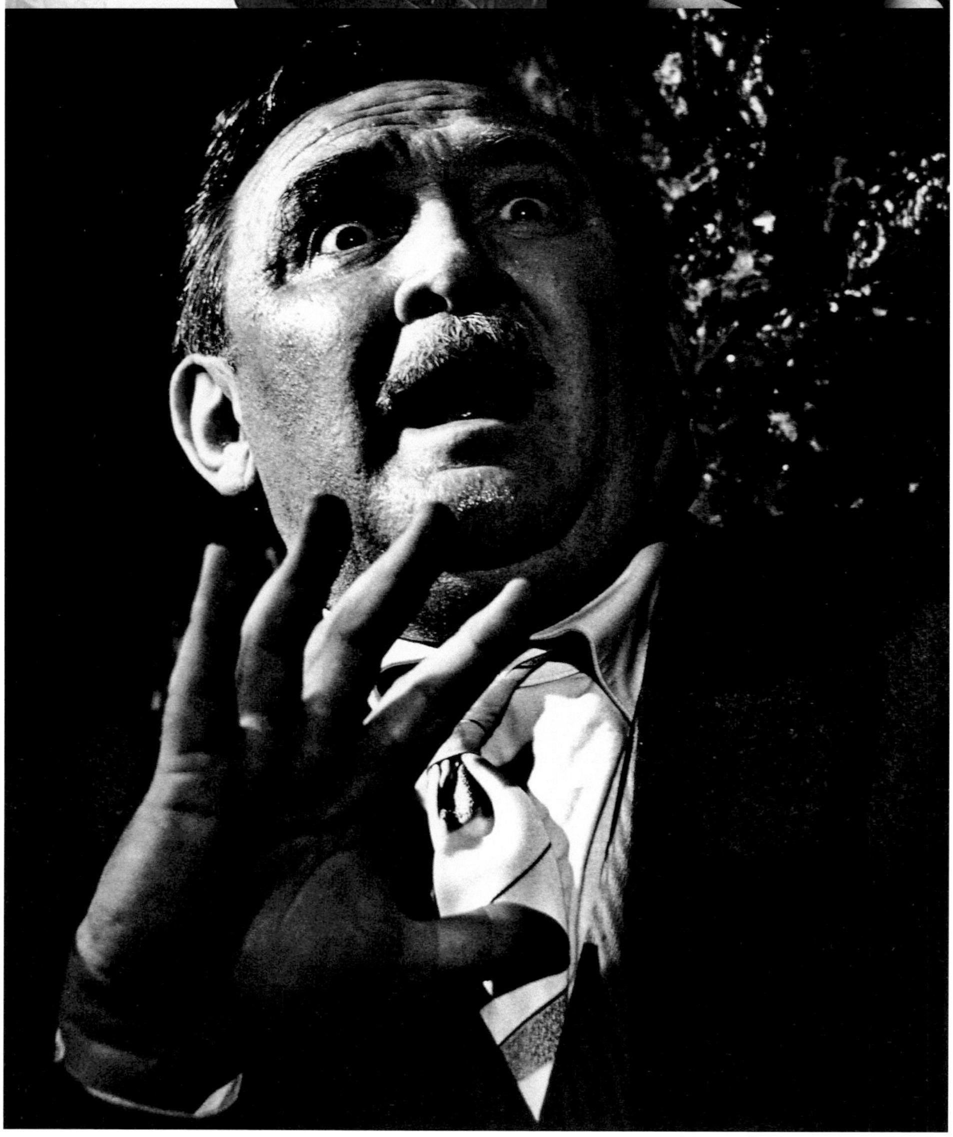

3a Leopold Lindtberg (top right) with the cast of *Sacco und Vanzetti*, which he directed in 1927.

3b–d *Derrick*, 1974. TV series

4a Sigfrit Steiner, *Krock und Co.*, 1976. Crime film with Hans Moser

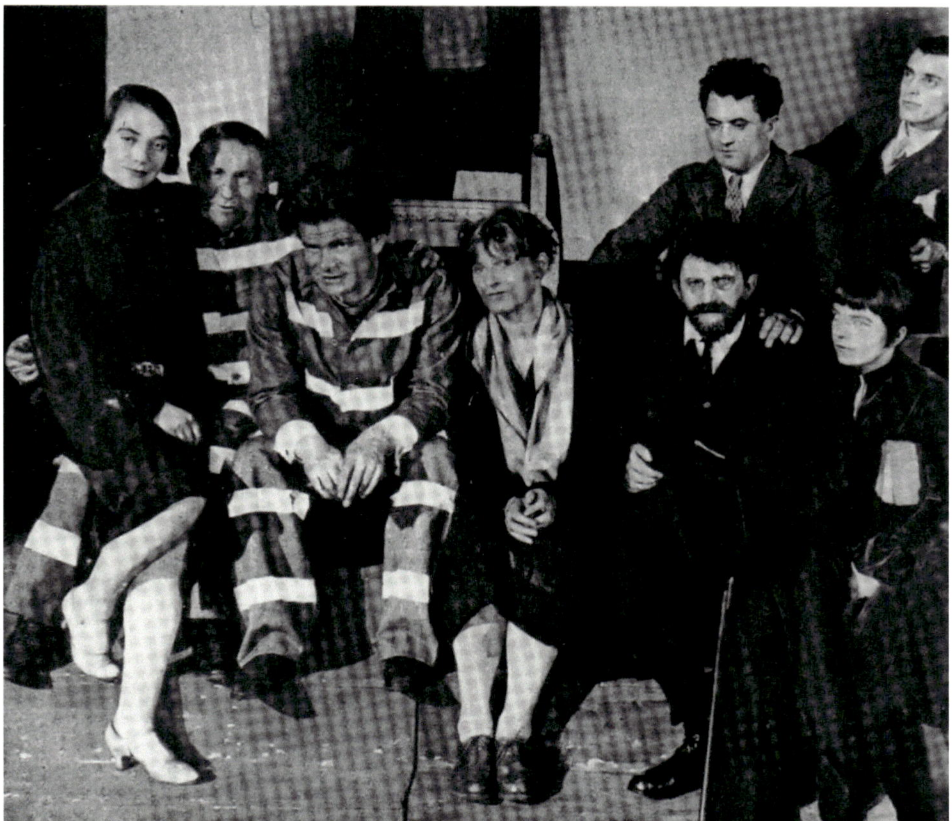

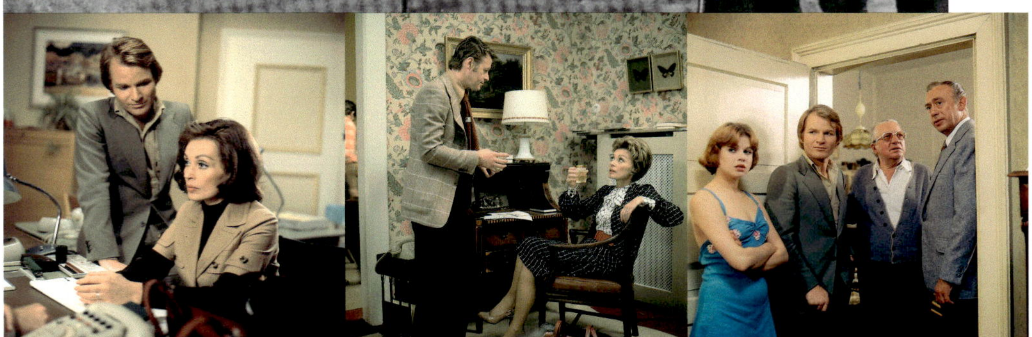

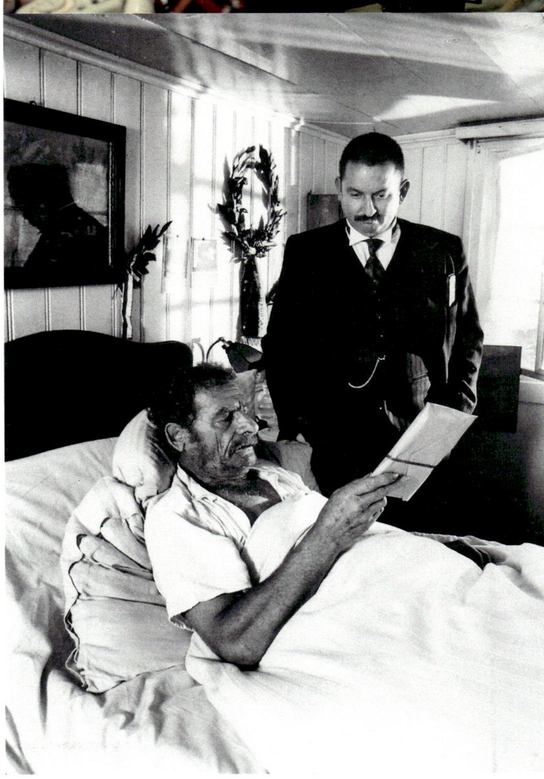

4b Sigfrit Steiner in *Es geschah am helllichten Tag*, 1958, with Michel Simon, Heinz Rühmann, and Siegfried Lowitz

5a Mathias Gnädinger at Schauspielhaus Zürich, 1995/96

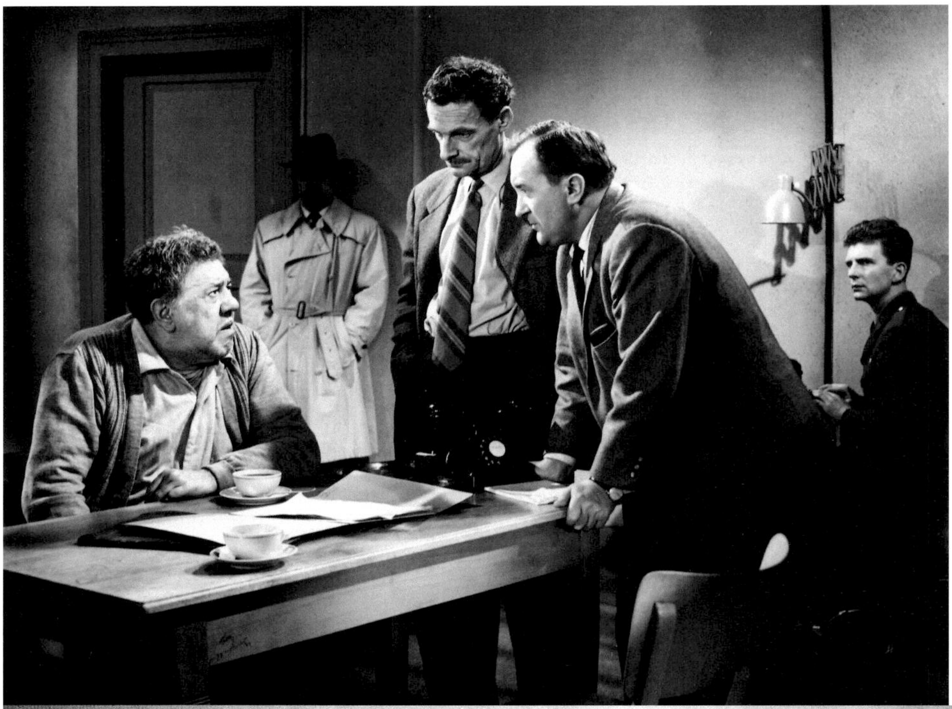

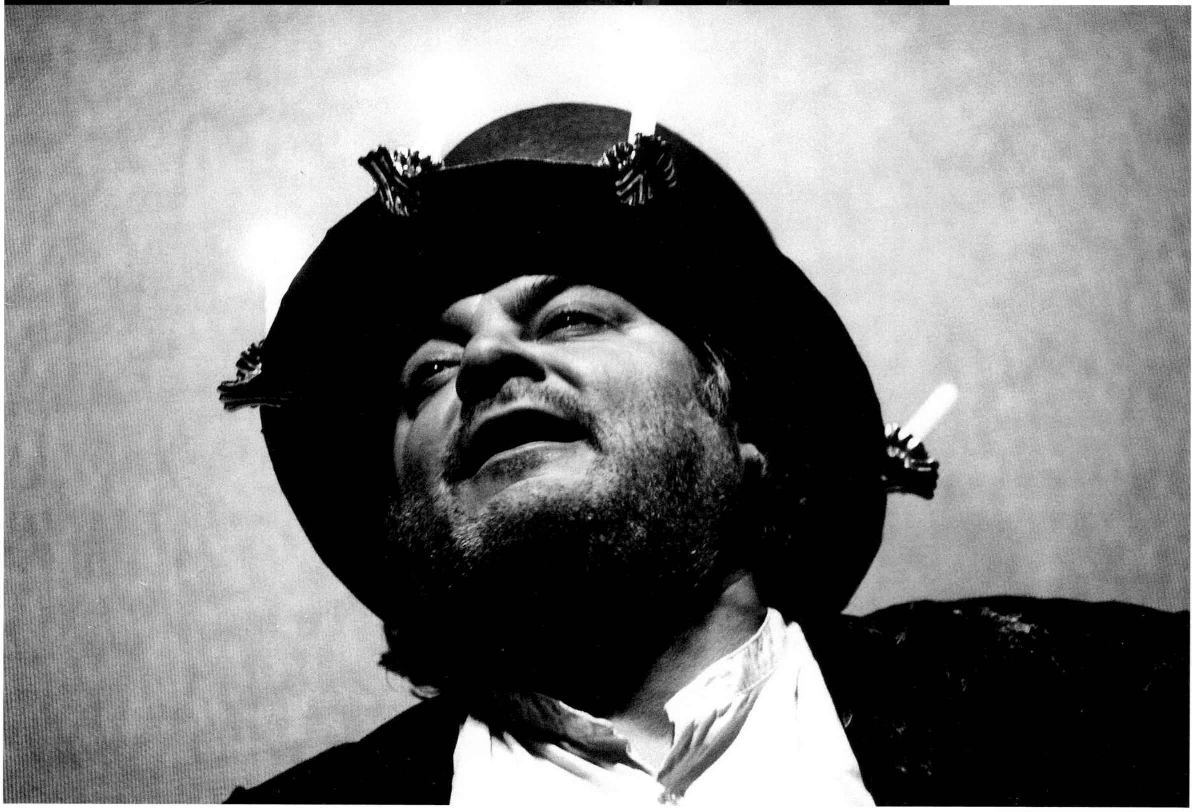

5b Mathias Gnädinger as Constable Walter Howald in the first *Tatort* film on Swiss TV, 1990
5c *Das Boot ist voll,* 1981. Written and directed by Markus Imhoof. Mathias Gnädinger with Tina Engel
6a Bruno Ganz on the poster for *The American Friend,* 1977, based on *Ripley's Game* by Patricia Highsmith. Director Wim Wenders **6b** Engagement at Schauspielhaus Zürich, 1969/70

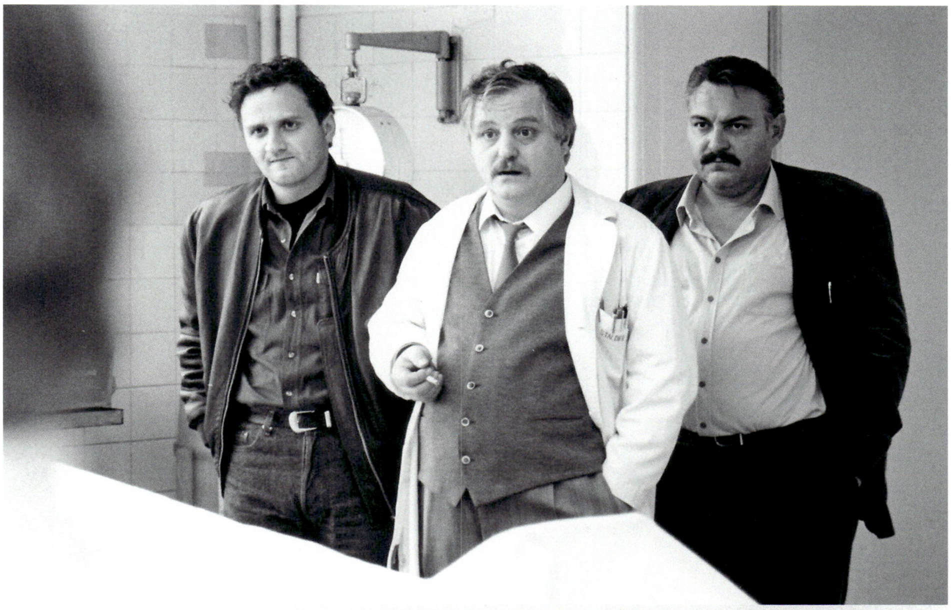

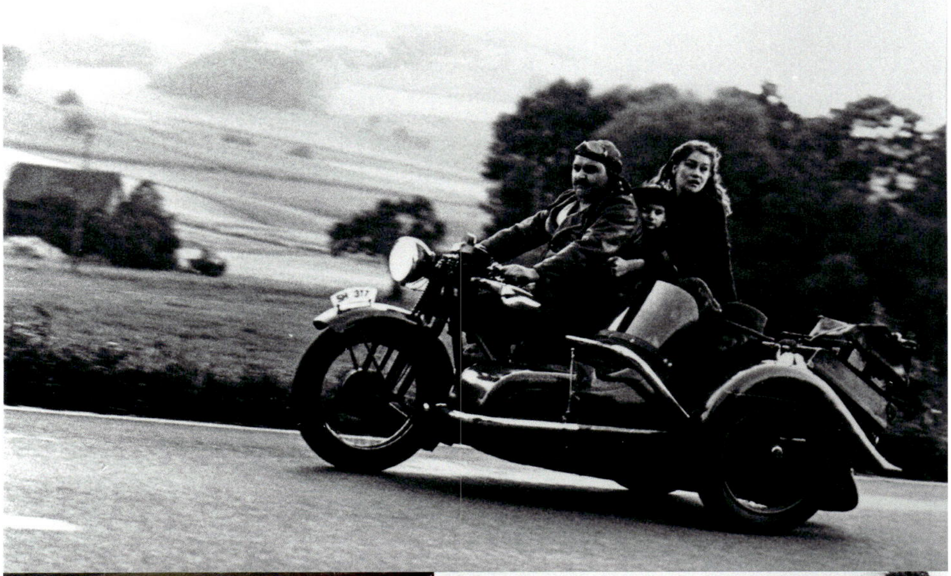

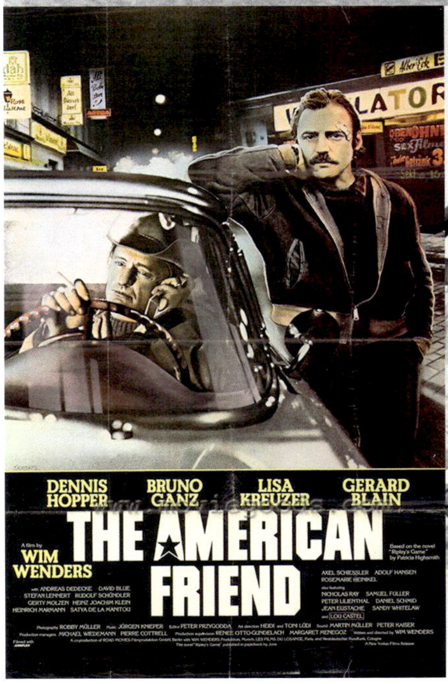

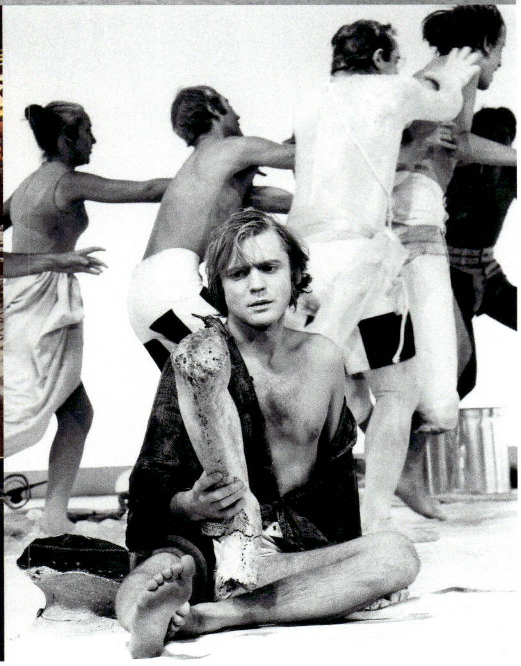

The abstractionists, the concrete artists, opposed the floral motifs, the tendrils, roses, and lilies that once adorned everyday products, combating the bombastic in general in art, in music, and in design with an honest and objective handling of the new forms of production. A new productive aesthetic, determined by the series, by the machine: lucid, smooth, and in keeping with the philosophical orientation and the demands of the times.

1
Ernst Keller (1891–1968)

He was and is the ultimate reference as a teacher for "objective design" graphic artists (Lohse, Hofmann, etc.) In his typographic posters he let the text predominate, bestowing on it the splendor of terse magnificence, and formed or rather cut words into the linoleum as impressive and independent poster scripts: he built stage settings for words. He is regarded as the renewing force of the Swiss poster: "A poster is not really any good until its subject is announced not just in the choice of motif, not just in the effective presentation of the written message, but also in its formal color scheme." Keller was the master of the text poster and, as founder of the first course of studies for graphic art, he exercised great influence on generations of graphic artists and was the real spiritual forerunner or even the founder of Swiss graphic art.

2
Hans Finsler (1891–1972)

For most of his life he was the hero of objective and architectural photography, or more properly: of New Photography, a term derived from New Objectivity in painting. With his constructivist approach he set objects dynamically within the picture frame in the form of diagonal compositions, e.g. silverware like fighter planes flying in formation. The future visions of modernist design thus found their appropriate photographs or "light images," the "language of pictures," as Finsler put it, or "the optical grammar of photography." But under the influence of concrete art his picture concepts became increasingly formalized and more geometric. His stupendous close-ups indulge the cult of materiality and objectivity and are elaborated in the truest sense of the word: exposed and developed to perfection in the laboratory. His architecture photography is, among other things, a photographic record of the Swiss National Exhibition of 1939 in Zurich.

From 1932–58 he directed the photography class. The list of his significant pupils—people like Bischof and Burri—forms part of the "world history of photography." Together with the typographer and designer Alfred Willimann he succeeded in making an important contribution to the visual communication of the ideals of modernism, by combining photography and the graphic arts at the School of Applied Arts.

3
Sophie Taeuber-Arp (1889–1943)

Sophie Taeuber-Arp was one of the earliest avant-garde artists, with classical modernism as the signum of her work. Although seen as a constructivist, she employed a broader artistic range: as a dancer she began appearing regularly in the Cabaret Voltaire in Zurich in 1916 and at other Dada events; as an artist she worked in the spectrum of stylization and strict, rhythmical geometry; as a designer and art instructor she designed textiles from 1916–29 at the School of Applied Arts; as an interior architect she, together with her husband, Hans Arp, and Theo van Doesburg, drafted the interior design of the halls of the Aubette movie theater and dance hall in Strasburg, one of the early great works of geometric-constructivist art. She also published trendsetting magazines, and as an inspired architect she was known for her home in Meudon near Paris; she was also a craftswoman renowned for her rugs and wall hangings. She used her puppets to create parodies of Dada sculptures, conceived from the basic design elements of the cone and sphere, etc.

She is regarded as a true precursor of concrete art. She died two weeks after the 1942–43 New Year's celebration under circumstances never fully explained—either in a traffic accident or by carbon monoxide poisoning—at the home of Max Bill in Höngg in Switzerland where she had sought refuge from Nazi persecution.

4
Alfred Willimann (1900–1957)

Willimann's legacy of graphic art and painting is small and barely known. Praise and enthusiasm for his teaching, on the other hand, is fulsome and for this he is well-remembered and honored. Above all his instruction in the photography course led to an unshakeable synthesis of photography and text and typography in the spirit of New Graphic Art. Finsler taught the use of the "machine" and Willimann the use of the "hand" and the "refining of good taste." Drafting text type and calligraphy were his domains and absolute perfection in presentation was mandatory. The advertising psychology department of the Zurich Psychotechnology Institute tested his stunning poster *Licht* (Light) and rated it at a very high 98 percent in terms of noticeability and memorability, but just 2 percent for legibility. Their devastating criticism: "That's how carefully prepared advertising falls flat!"

The preference for decoration became the characteristic trait of the vulgar, while social distinction was negotiated via asceticism.

Art concrete—also known as "cold art"—is concerned with the close association between visual structure or pattern and mathematics, a manifestation of the "mathematical mode of thought in the art of our time." The compositions of the Zurich concrete artists are assembled exclusively from basic geometric forms and "logical structures."

The fascination of this art lay in its systematic dimension. Designed programs. Elementary constructive units. Forms derived directly from formulae. The serial, the repertoire of combinatorial procedures: permutation, combination, variation are the elementary laws that generated art, music, and design.

He was a spiritual forerunner and guru of objective design **1**; his photographs are the quintessence of New Objectivity, and his technical ability as a photographer to "walk on eggshells" is legendary **2**; her artistic spectrum is universal, she is the forerunner of the concrete artists, an exponent of a highly subtle feminine aesthetic **3**; his drawings were executed in the service of good taste and fine distinctions **4**; a visionary communicator with the highest ethical objectives, he composed serial music with tremendous intensity and with international success **5**. His commitment to science as the foundation of his art was eminently political **6**; although he looms large in the annals of twentieth century design history, he can only be mentioned in lower case **7**; his grid-based approach to graphics, a typographic ordering principle of specifically Swiss provenance, was propagated globally **8**; he is a counterpart to the concrete painters, and endowed money with an exemplary new aesthetic luster **9**.

And yet this poster occupies one of the most prominent places of honor among the most beautiful products of Swiss printing of the last century; and to this day in urban areas the striking emblem of the Steiner construction company—drafted by Willimann sixty years ago—can be seen.

5

Klaus Huber (*1924)

If Klaus Huber is one of those few Swiss composers whose social conscience and political awareness have made them a role model for the younger generation, then not just on account of his settings of texts by Ernesto Cardenal, George Jackson, and Carolina Maria de Jesús. For what must also count among Huber's achievements as a composer is the way in which his countless large oratorios lent a new substance to the twelve-tone method of Anton Webern, whose successor he perceives himself to be.

At the Zurich Conservatory Huber studied violin with Stefi Geyer and then taught violin himself from 1949 to 1955, and also studied music theory and composition with Willy Burkhard—these formative years doubtlessly laid the foundation for the international acclaim he later received. This began with his reception at the 1959 Congress of the International Society of New Music in Rome. The countless pupils Huber taught in Lucerne, Basel, and Freiburg im Breisgau include such major contemporary composers as Brian Ferneyhough (of the New Complexity school of composition), Wolfgang Rihm, Ulrich Gasser (a member of the Zurich group of the composers, the Komponistensekretariat Zurich), and Hans Wüthrich.

6

Richard Paul Lohse (1902–1988)

"He was not only a painter and graphic artist who pursued radical constructive rigor with an overwhelmingly sensual sense of color, he was also a man who reflected on his art and society and was driven by a passionate commitment to social justice. In Lohse, the 'two avant-gardes' of the twentieth century coincided: the artistic and the political, which otherwise so often remained alien to one another," (*Lohse Lesen*, ed. Hans Heinz Holz, Zurich 2002). Lohse cannot be more accurately and subtly described.

Lohse was the most scientific among the "concretes": additive progression, group systematics, "objectivized" rhythm, serial structures, color intervals, color rotations, color quantity balance, serial image systems, combination methodology is the vocabulary used to identify his artistic constructs. Socially related motivation and unconditional radicalism are his legacy: "Flexible systems are appropriate democratic systems, unlimited structures the structural principle of the epoch, the formation of systems the mission." He was a convinced Marxist and based his painting on the foundation of materialist philosophy.

Lohse studied from 1918–22 at the Zurich School of Applied Arts and graduated as a commercial graphic artist for advertising. He played a decisive role in the development of the typographic grid and participated in the development of Swiss graphic arts of the 1950s. Numerous awards testify to Lohse's standing in the field of objective modernist graphic art, in his words: "industrial graphics."

7

max bill (1908–1994)

his name—radically spelled in lower case—is great and famous in the history of design, architecture, design theory and teaching, sculpture, and painting of the twentieth century. he is regarded as one of the main exponents of concrete art. doing him justice would require an "endless loop" (one of his main sculptural works), without beginning or end. he studied, taught, and published at and about the school of applied arts, on architecture, design, art. in his bitterly controversial *blaubuch* (blue book) (1967) on structural reform at the school of applied arts he called for a new type of designer whose work would not draw on emotions and instinct but rather be based on the function of the designer in society and on an undaunted belief in continuous technical progress. he called for the integration of the kind of school of applied arts of the past that was dedicated to "leveraging artistic craftsmanship" into a new kind of applied arts school. a new, visionary "institute for design" should be founded, but the feared consequences for then established faculty meant that his radical proposal for reorientation was nipped in the bud.

max bill studied at the school of applied arts from 1924–27 and continued his studies at the bauhaus in dessau. there he met with prominent international figures of constructivism: lászló moholy-nagy, oskar schlemmer, piet mondrian, josef albers. in 1951 he became the founding director of the world famous school of design in ulm whose school building he designed as "the standing

1 3
2
4

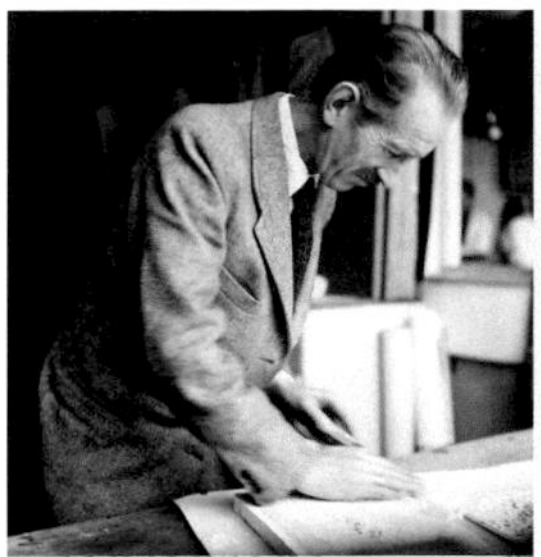
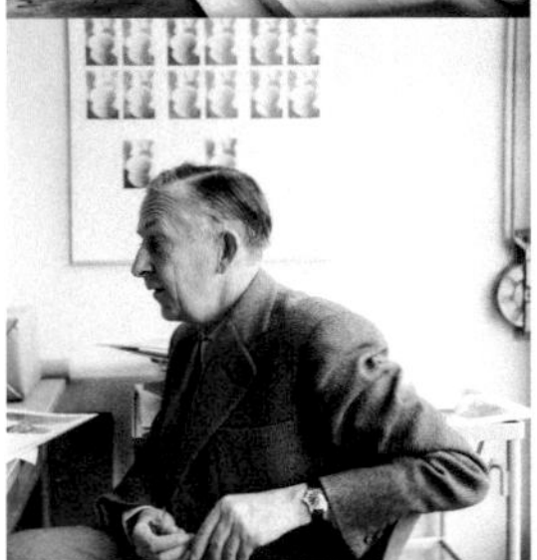
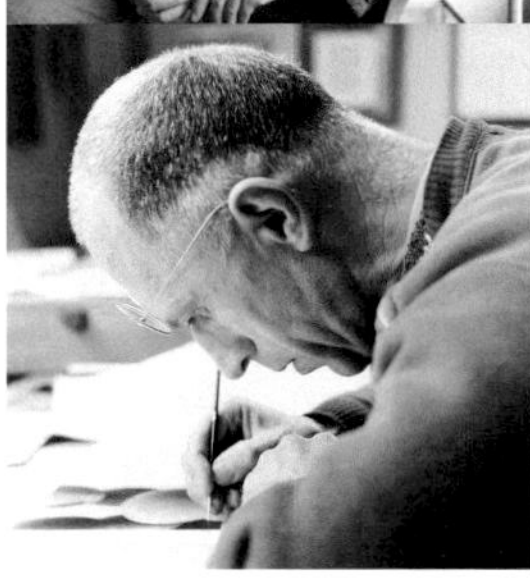
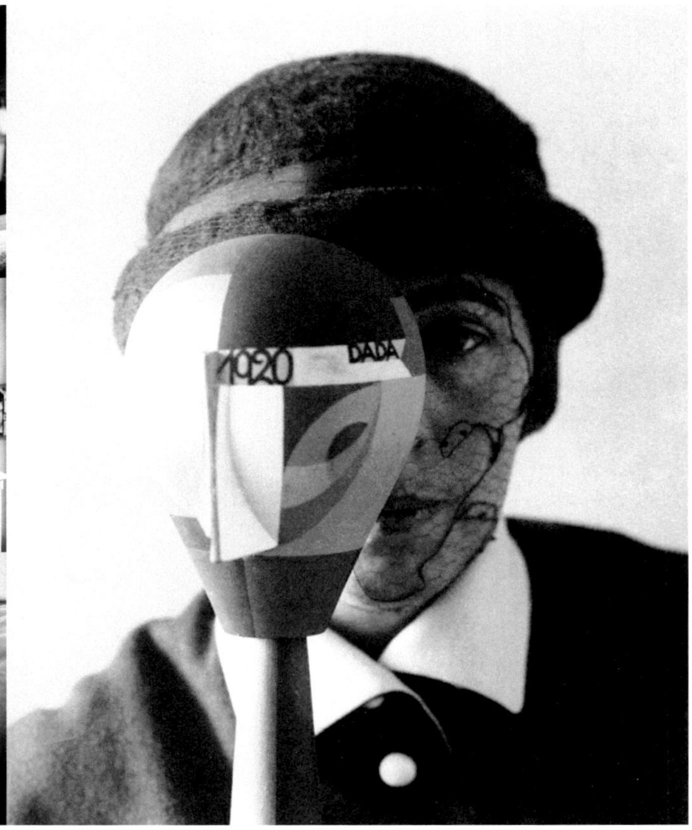

missionary outpost of modernism." he also designed the legendary "ulm stool." his main theoretical work is *die mathematische denkweise in der kunst unserer zeit* (the mathematical approach in art of our time; 1949), in which he called for a new art based on mathematics.

8

Josef Müller-Brockmann (1914–1996)

He is/was the leading figure of Swiss graphic art. With typical Swiss thoroughness he celebrated and implemented New Graphic Art: the clean, the objective, the calculable. His greatest legacy is his publication *Rastersysteme* (Grid Systems) in which, expanding on his course at the School of Applied Arts, he explicates the constructed grid as *the* ordering principle of typography and image. Some of his works have become firm features of our visual memory: the campaign posters *gegen Lärm* (anti-noise), *schützt das Kind* (protect the child), and more. These are visualizations and calls to action of the greatest effect and immediacy, using the media of expressive photography and appellative typography. His trend-setting posters of the 1950s and 1960s included his posters for the Tonhalle concert hall. These were thoroughly ridiculed by the daily newspapers of the time and denounced as "anti-audience," but now, in retrospect, they represent the most convincing synthesis of concrete design and a visual representation of New Music.

As a graphic designer, typographer, author, and teacher he was the leading theoretician and practitioner of Swiss typography and graphic arts. He represented and stood up for the ethical and aesthetic message delivered by New Graphic Art with uncompromising determination. He was absolutely convinced: "I have lived this conviction more or less purely." He taught at the School of Applied Arts from 1957–60; one of the first who also advocated cultural training. His goal was a well-rounded, broadly informed student. John Cage, for example, was one of the speakers he brought to the school. He was made Honorary Designer for Industry by the Royal Society of Arts London, was awarded the Gold Medal of the Canton of Zurich for cultural services, and received the Middleton Award of the American Center for Design in Chicago as well as the Design Prize of Switzerland. The influential design periodical *Print* rates him among the fifteen most important creative designers of the twentieth century.

9

Ernst Hiestand (*1935)

The radically new corporate identity for the ABM department store chain, packaging concepts and corporate design for companies doing business worldwide, design consultant to IBM, lecturer at the Ulm School of Design, director of the graphic art program at the School of Applied Arts, president of the Swiss Association of Graphic Artists, design consultant for the Swiss Federal Department of Foreign Affairs in Nicaragua: these are only the most important milestones in the career of Ernst Hiestand and his E+U Hiestand studio. The U refers to his wife, Ursula, with whom he founded the business. He is also the third "money maker" in a row to graduate from the School of Applied Arts in Zurich. His banknotes were the first discrete and limited series to be placed under the responsibility of a single designer. Their aesthetic and culturally autonomous representation of Switzerland gained international acclaim, both with respect to their content as well as their form. They became a trailblazer for the graphic design of banknotes and established a new "money aesthetics."

5 6 8
7
9

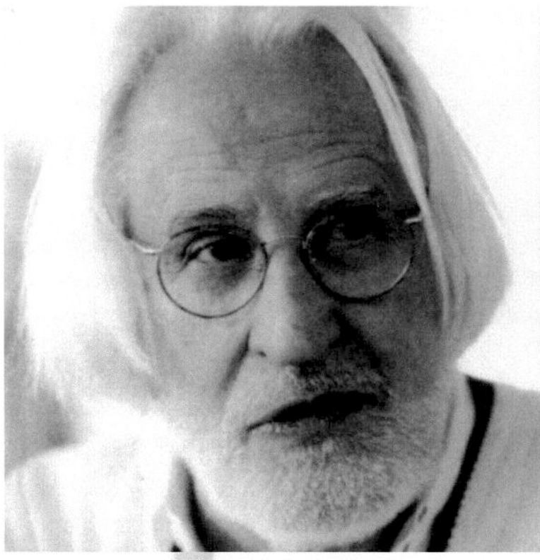

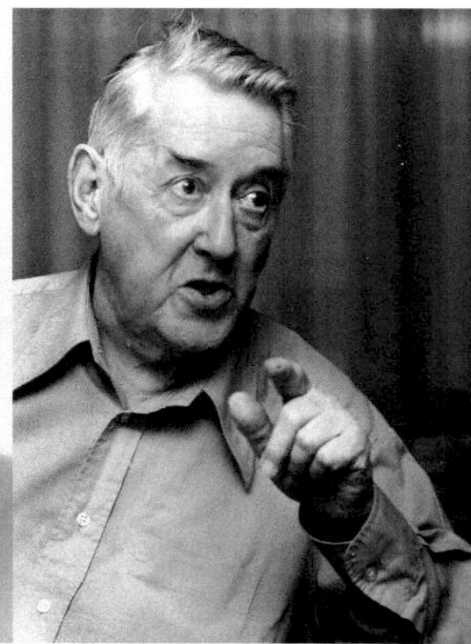

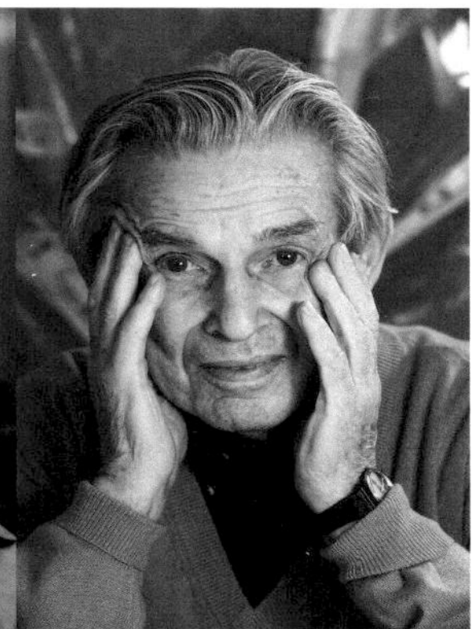

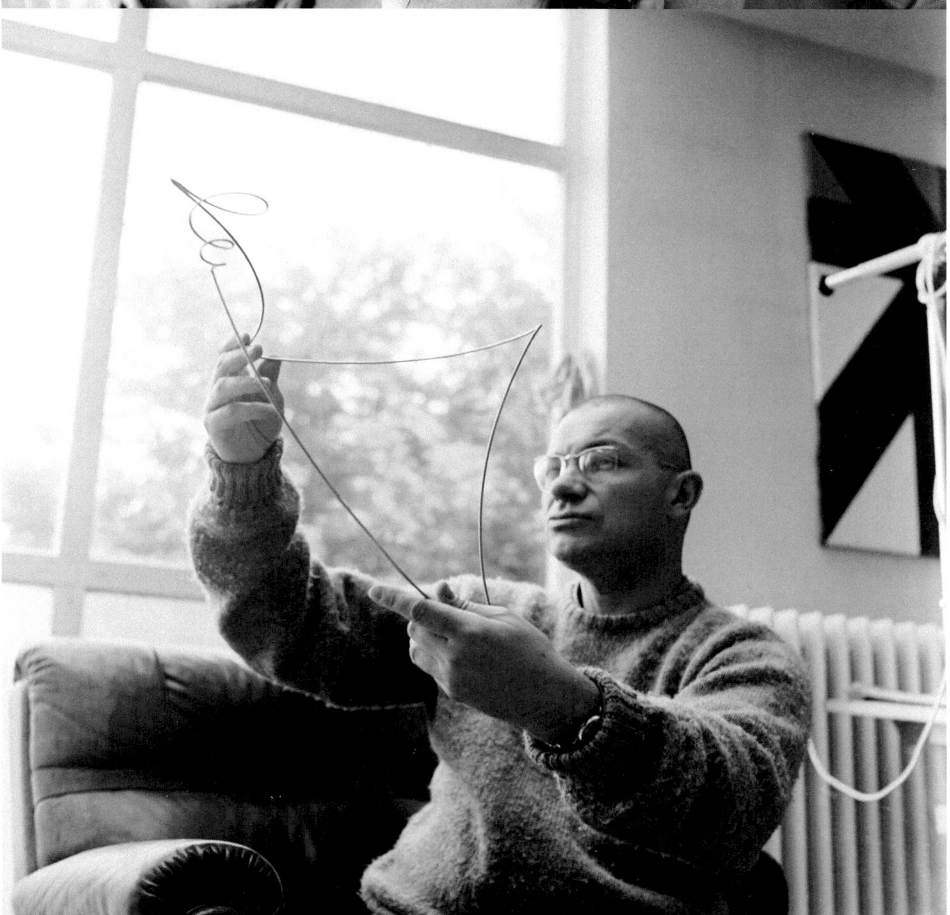

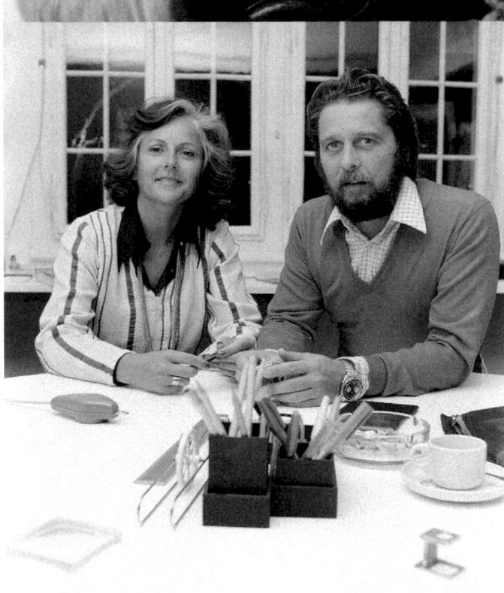

1a Ernst Keller, poster for Fein-Kaller & Co AG, Zurich, 1921

1b/c Campaign poster, 1933.—Sports event poster, 1968

2a Hans Finsler, "Kaech House on Herrliberg (Alfred Altherr, 1935)." Photo, 1936

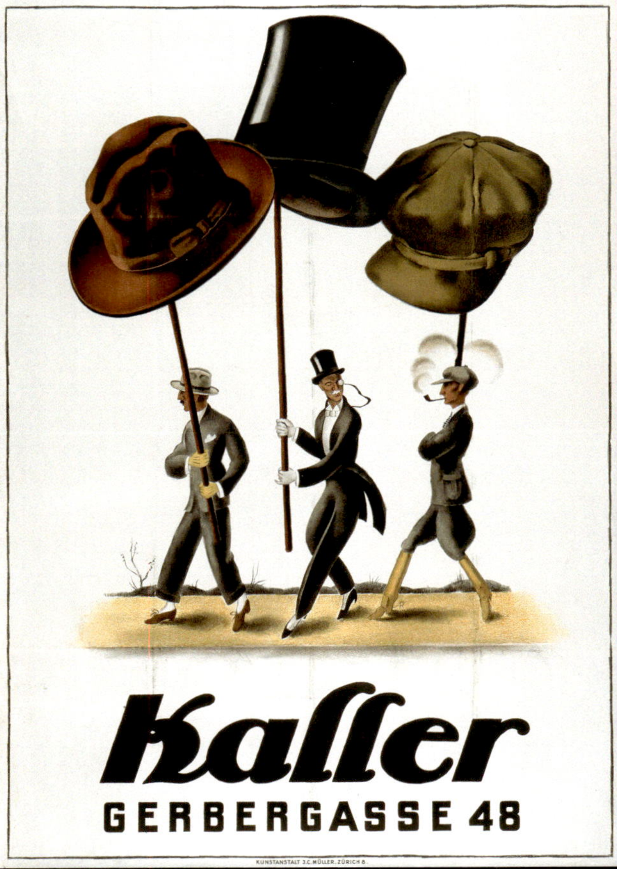

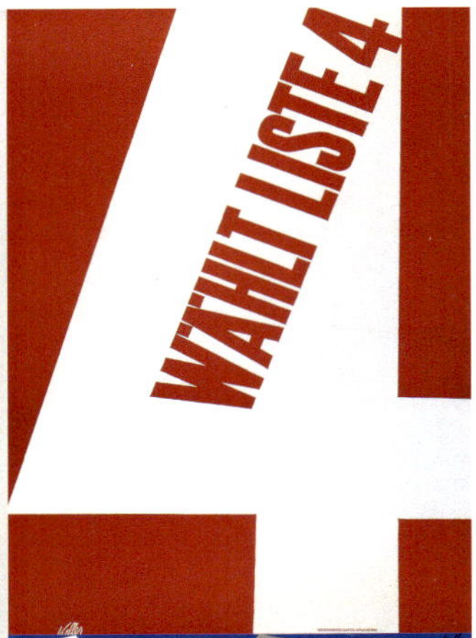

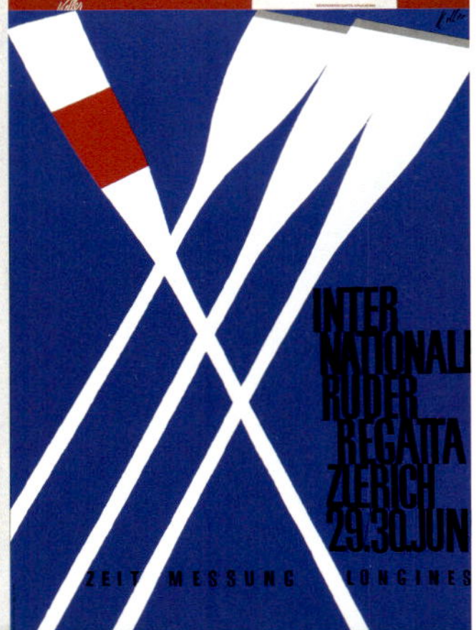

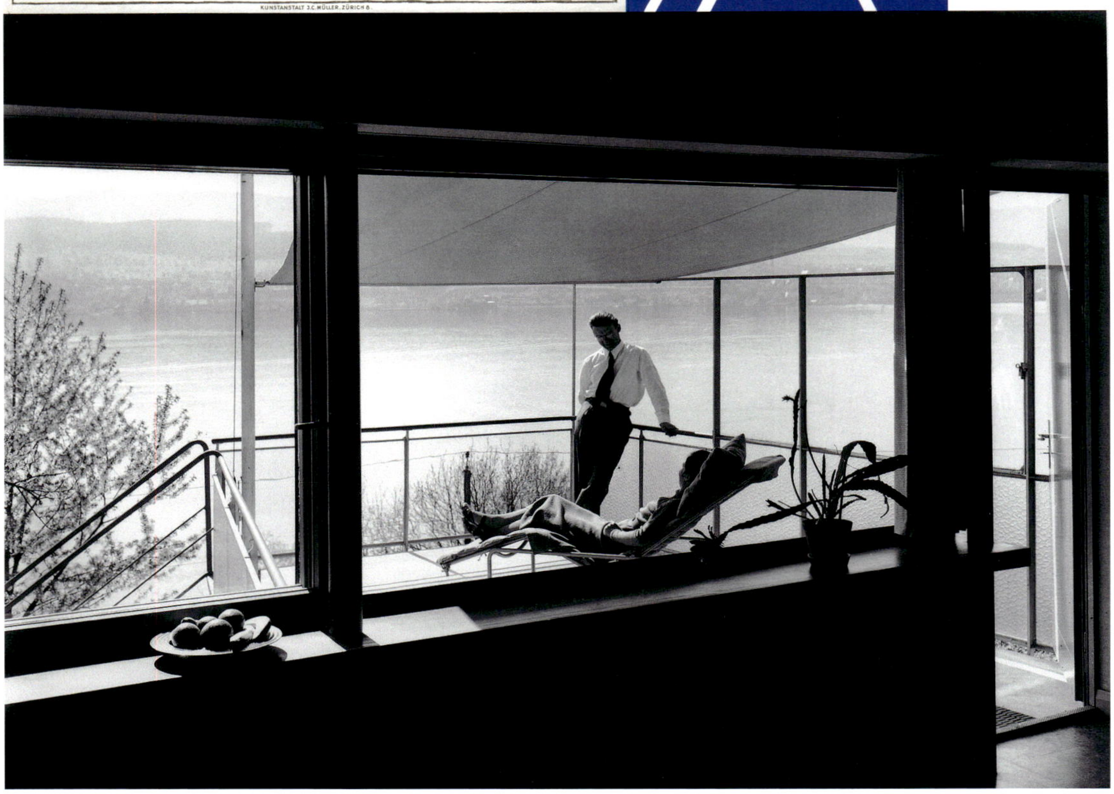

2b Teaching material; photos “Eggs in Mirror,” ca. 1929. Double page from *Reproduktionsverfahren,* edited by Hans Finsler and Alfred Willimann, layout by Alfred Willimann. Museum of Applied Arts and Design Zurich, 1951

3a Sophie Taeuber-Arp and her sister Erika, 1920/21

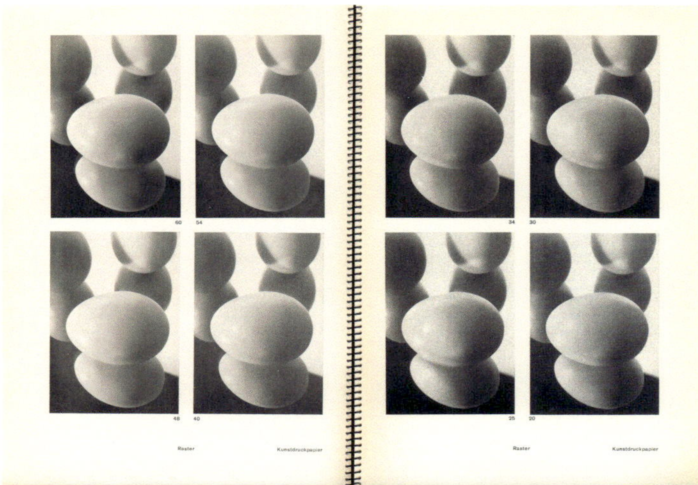

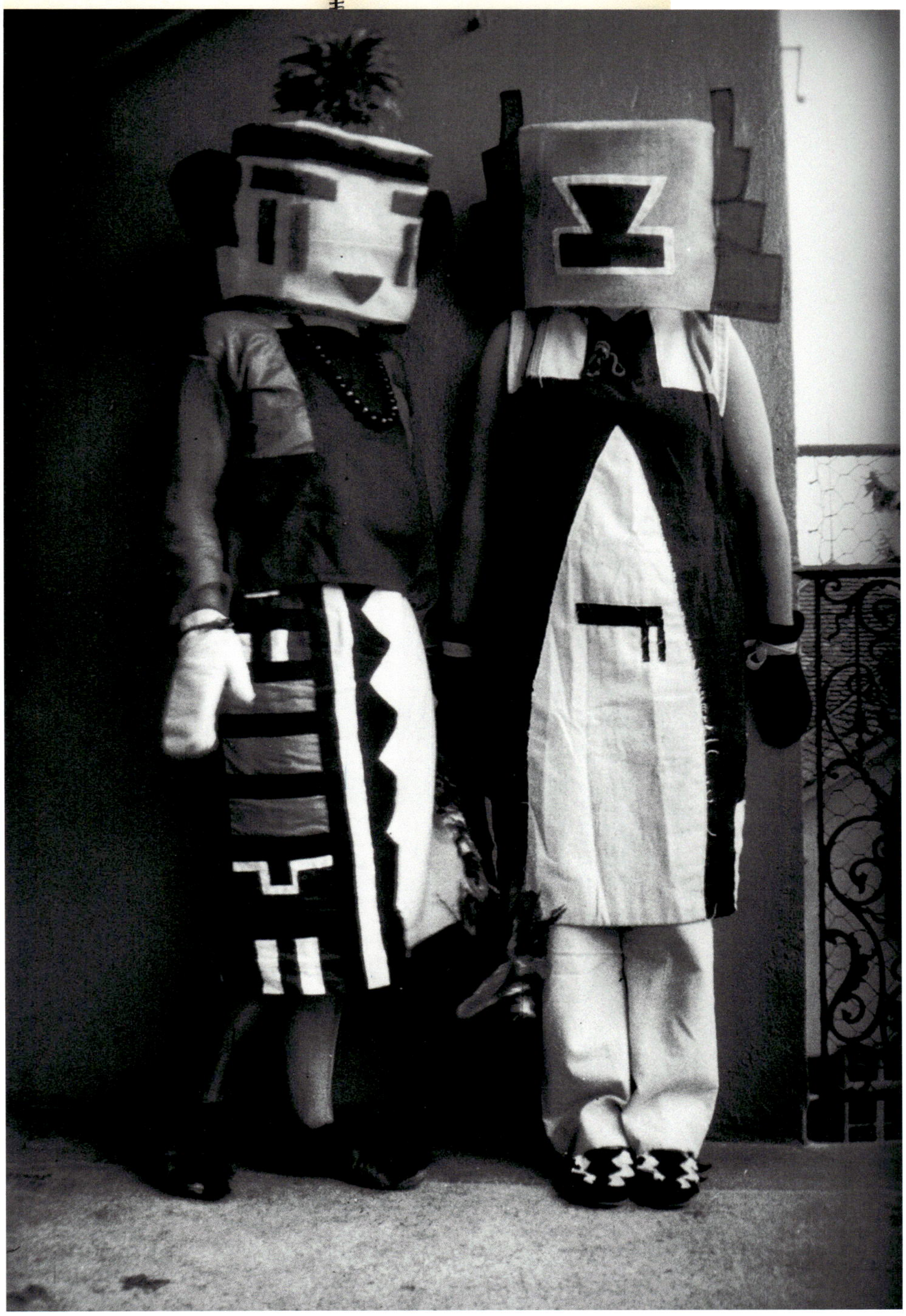

2c "Object Study (Form, Structure, Light) of Finsler's Last Egg." Serge Libiszewski, Willimann/Finsler photography class, ca. 1950

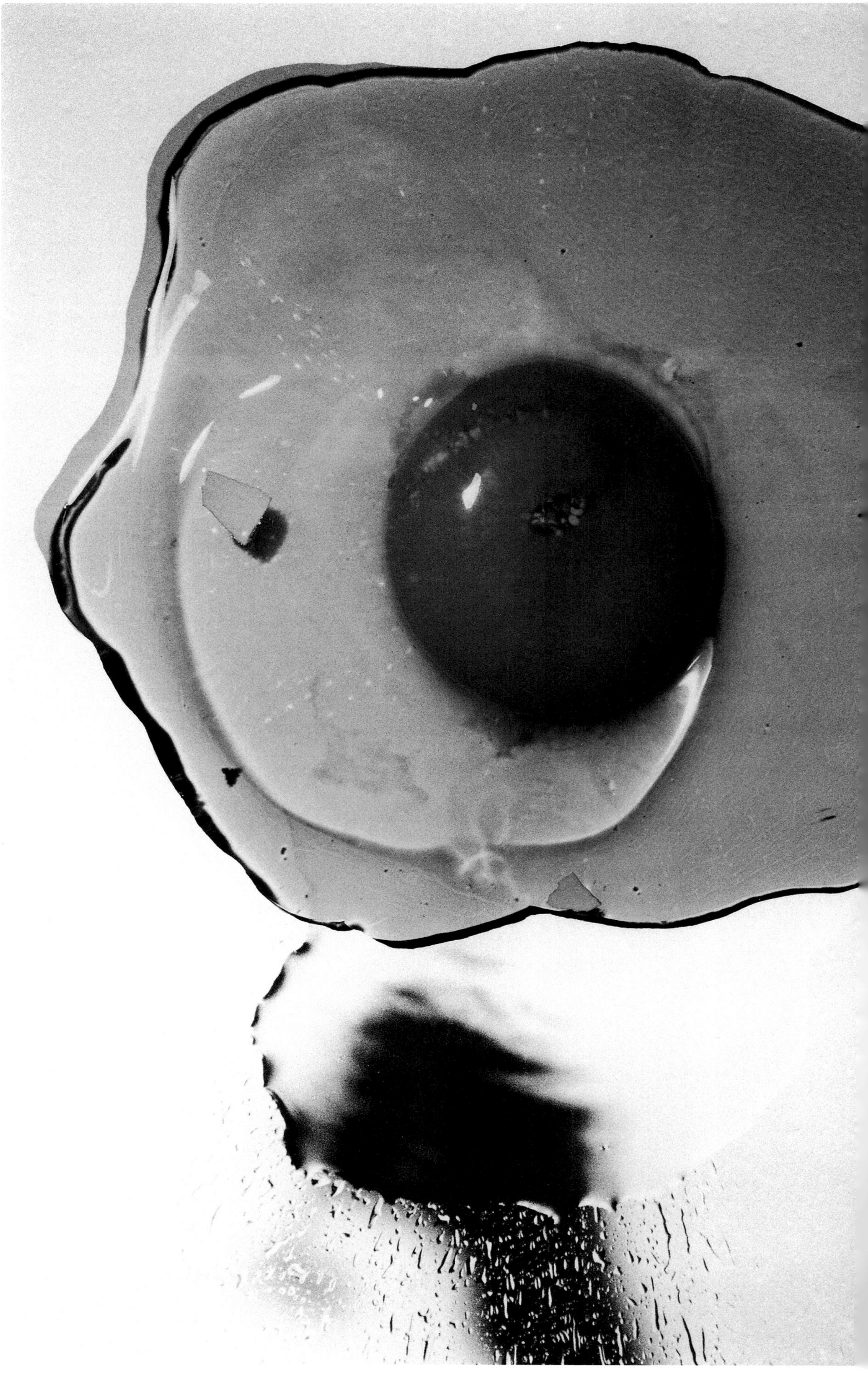

2d Hans Finsler's home and studio at the Neubühl Werkbund estate, Zurich Wollishofen, ca. 1935

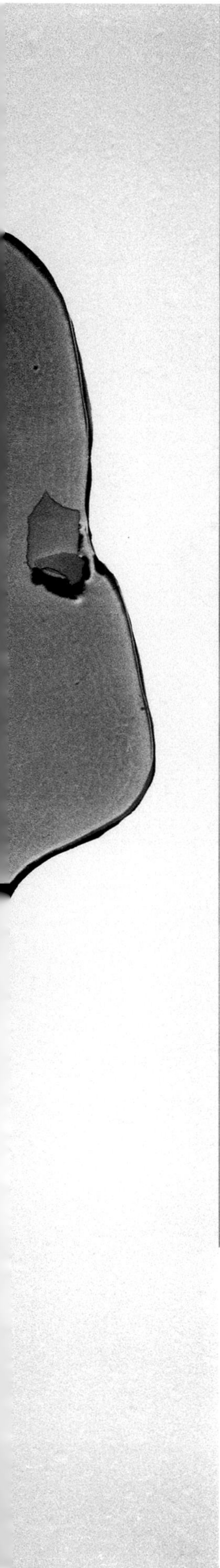

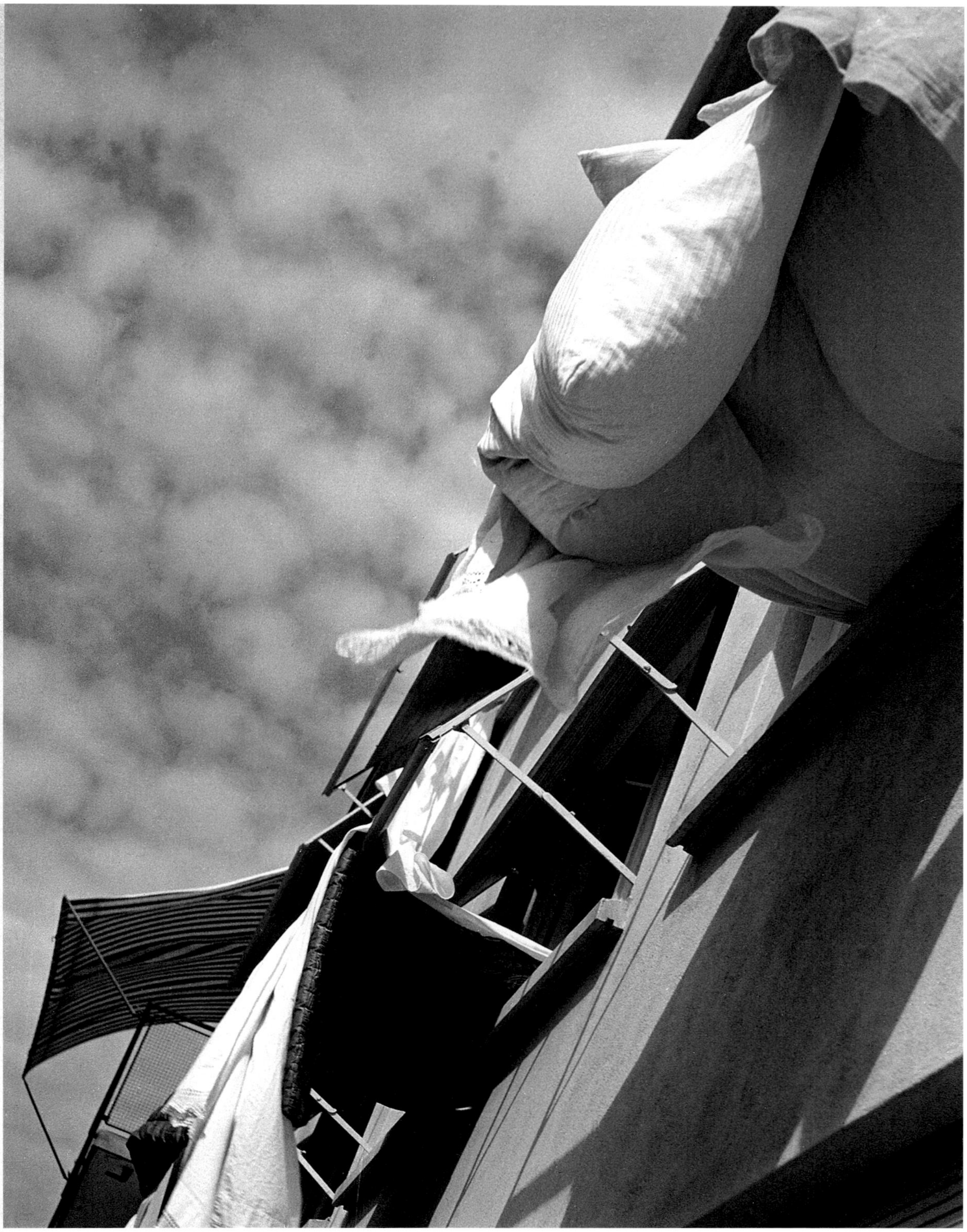

3b/c Sophie Taeuber-Arp, King Deramo and Bear. Puppets from the puppet show *König Hirsch*, 1918

4a/b Alfred Willimann, Farfalla Nera/The Black Moth. Playing cards, reverse.—Collage by Serge Libiszewski made during his trial period in the Willimann/Finsler photography class, 1948.

4c *Das Licht in Heim, Büro und Werkstatt.* Poster for the exhibition at the Museum of Applied Arts and Design Zurich, 1932

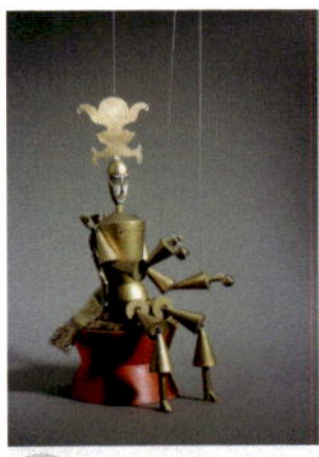

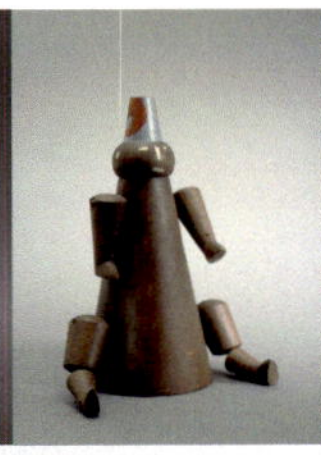

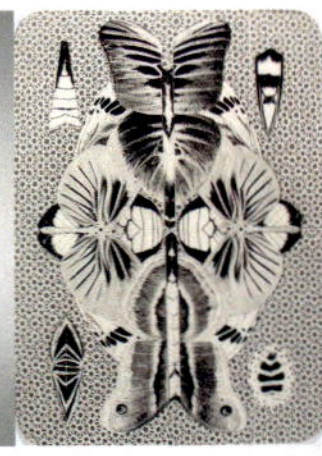

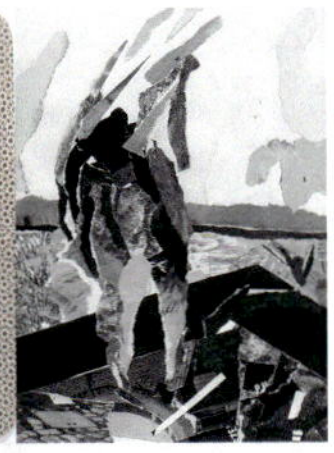

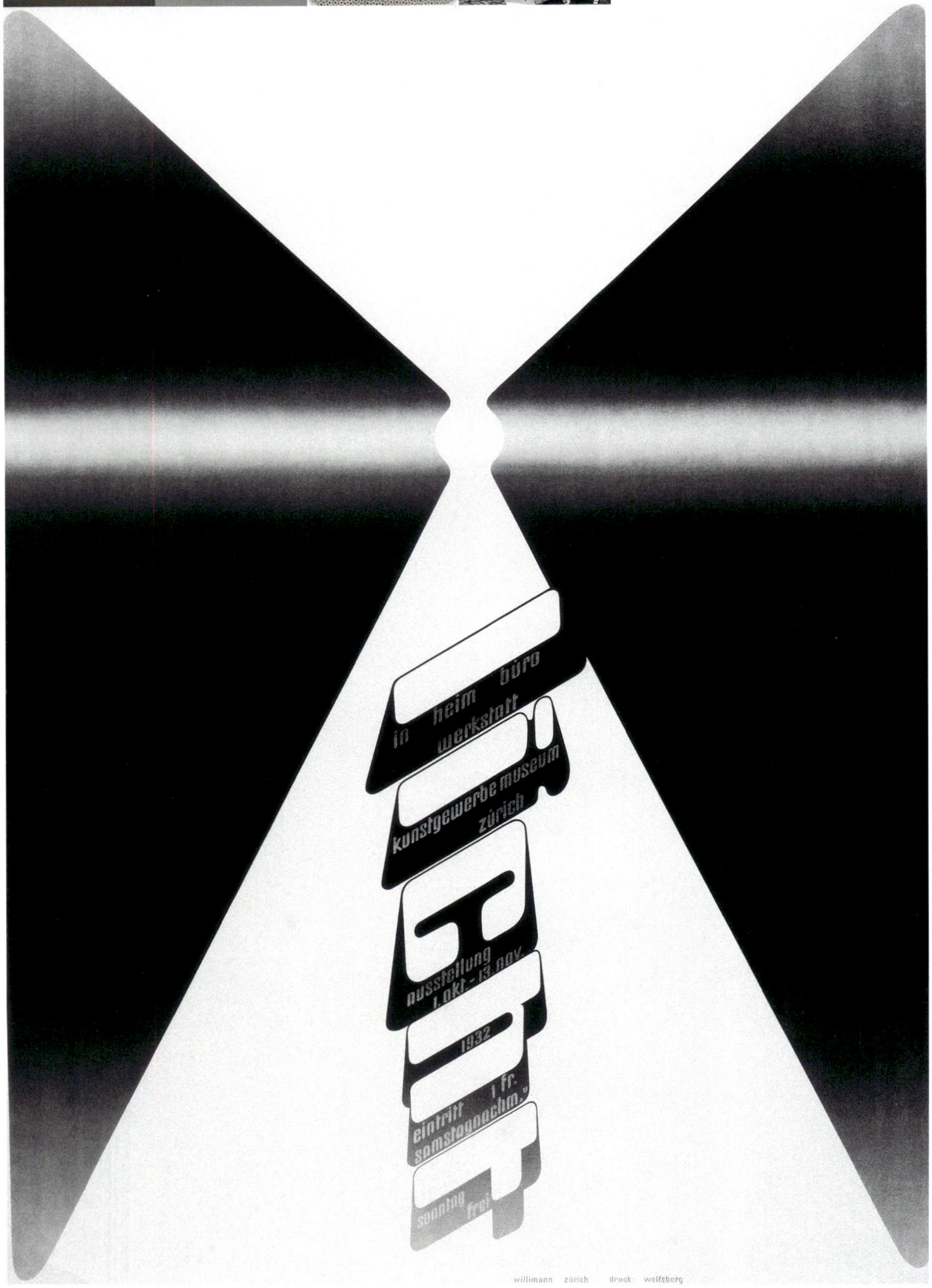

6a/b Flyer for Wohnbedarf AG, 1953. Design Richard Paul Lohse, photos Hans Finsler and Ernst Albrecht Heiniger

6c *Serielles Reihenthema in 18 Farben,* 1982. Oil on canvas

7a Max Bill at the Ulm School of Design with his (unrealized) model for a Venice Biennale pavilion, ca. 1960

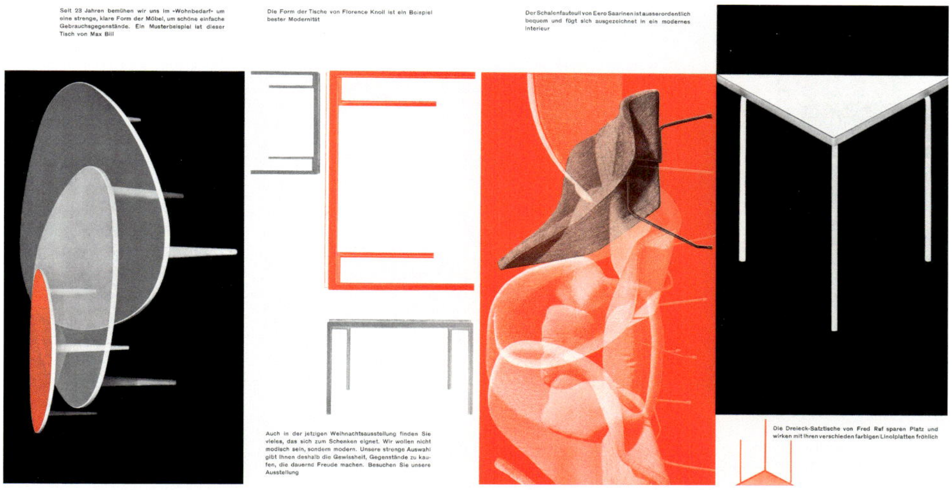

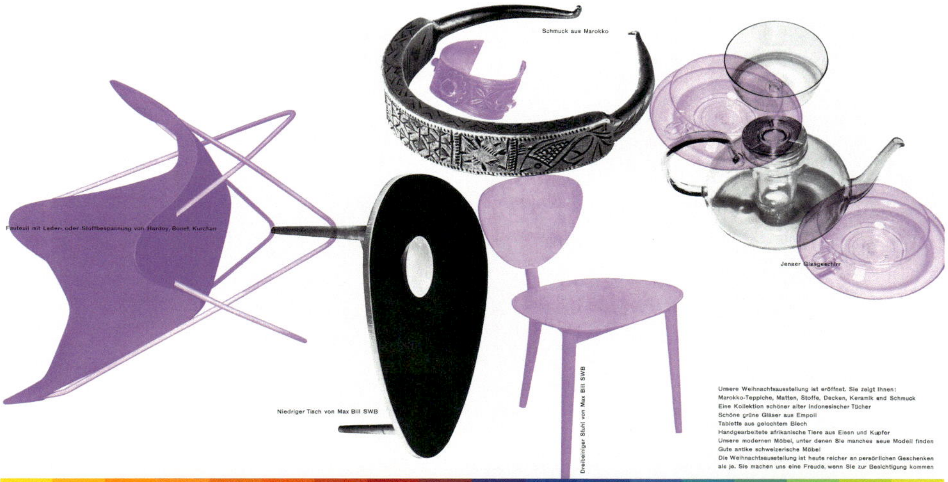

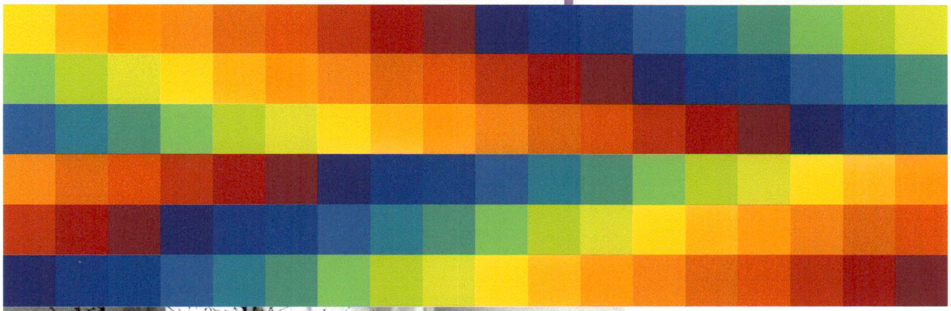

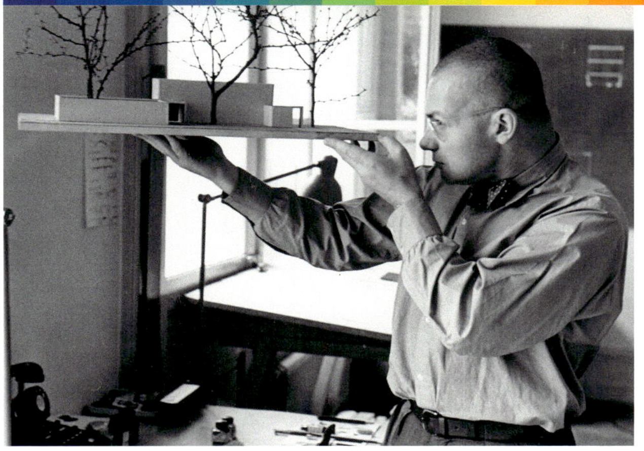

7b Max Bill, *Rhythmus im Raum*, 1947/48 **7c** *Kontinuität*. Installation of the sculpture at Züka Agricultural and Trade Fair, Zurich Enge, 1947

7d Design class at the School of Applied Arts. Photo by Ernst Scheidegger

7e Max Bill with plaster model, 1947 **8a** Josef Müller-Brockmann, exhibition poster, 1960

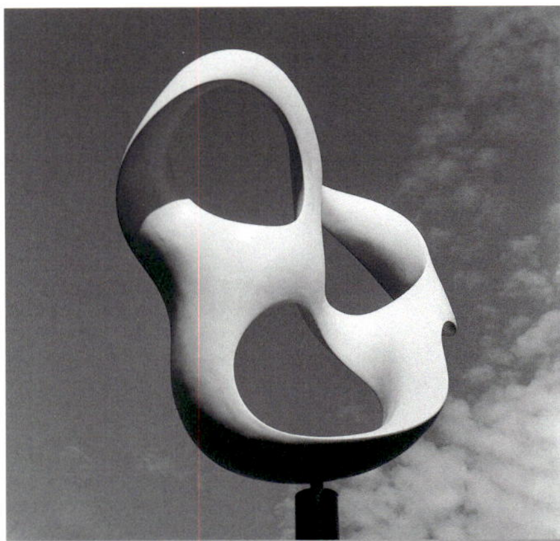

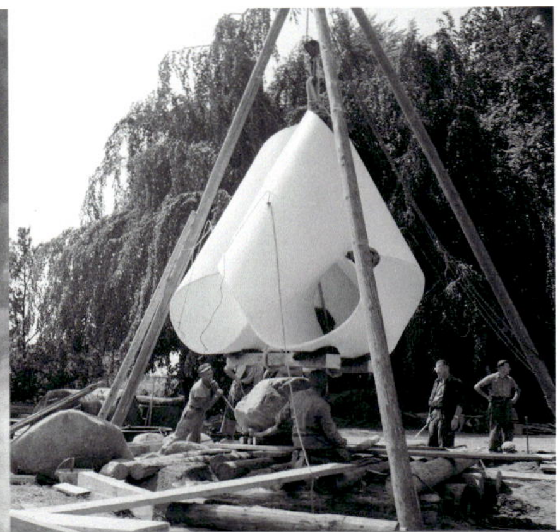

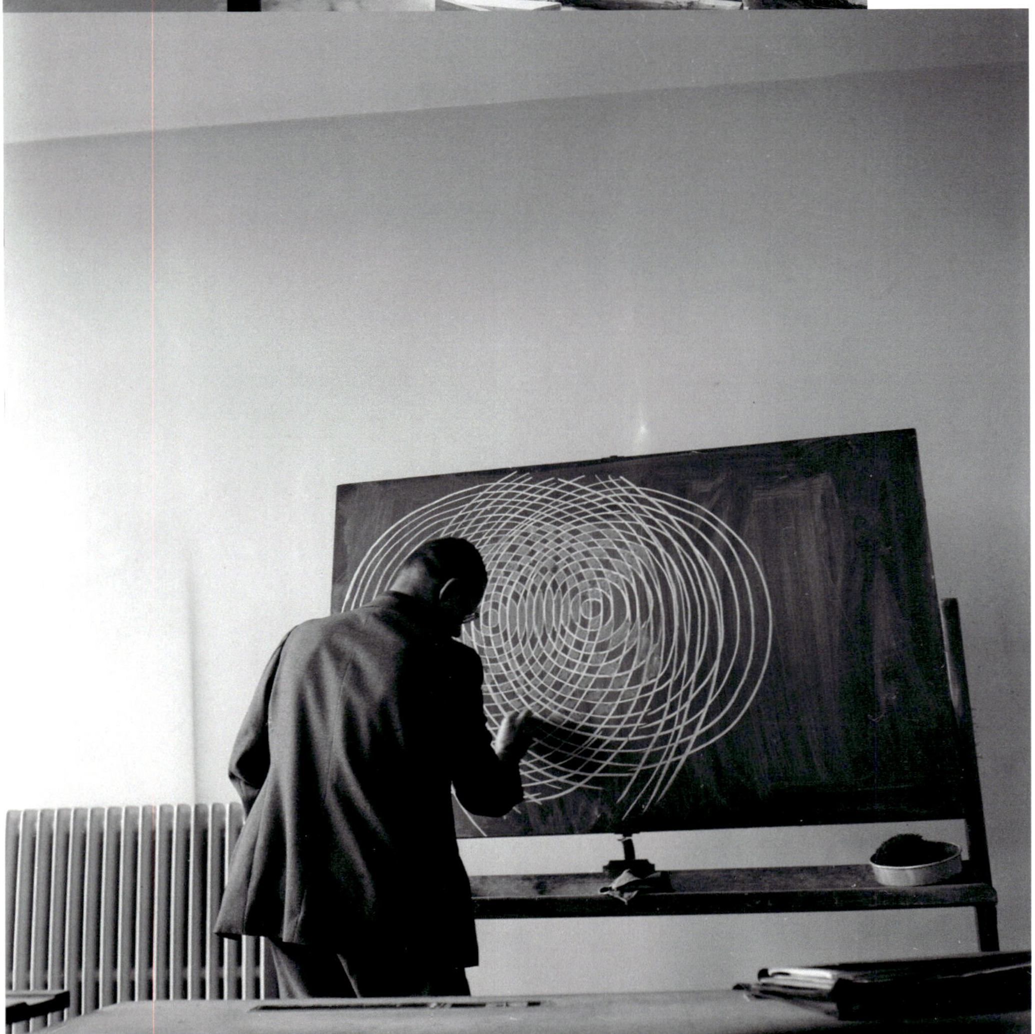

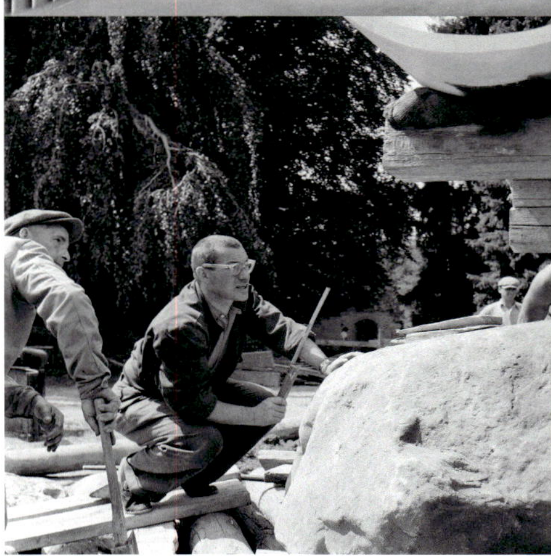

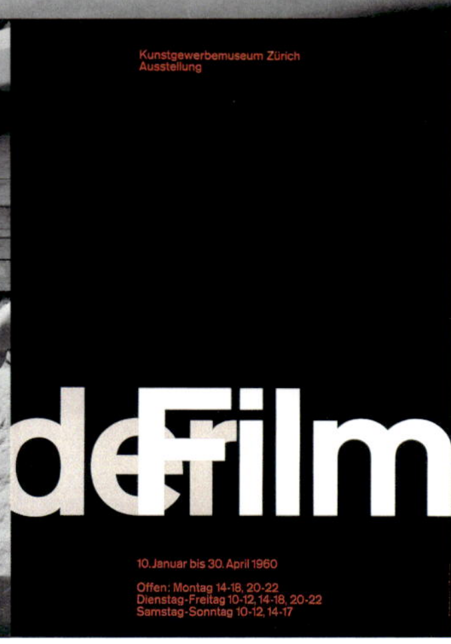

8b Josef Müller-Brockmann, flyer for Schindler AG's moving walkway. Atelier Müller-Brockmann, ca. 1962
8c Lettering for the vehicle fleet of CWS Apparate AG. Atelier Müller-Brockmann, ca. 1958
8d Concert poster for the Tonhalle-Gesellschaft Zurich. Atelier Müller-Brockmann, 1960

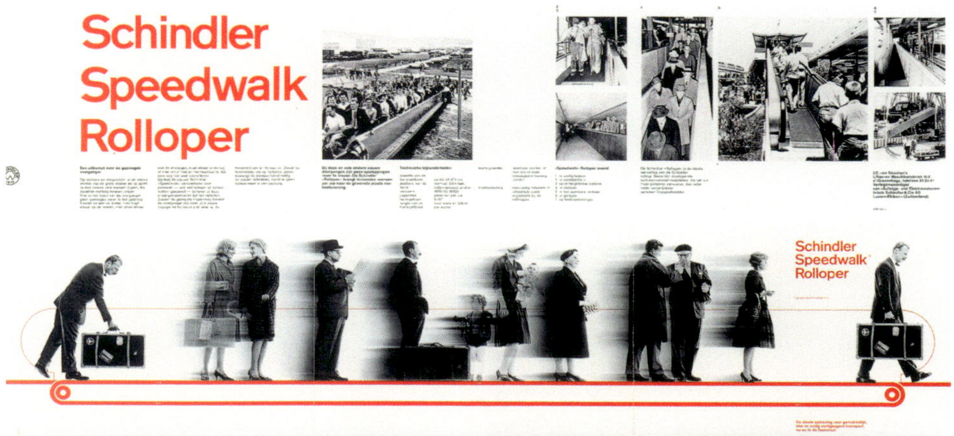

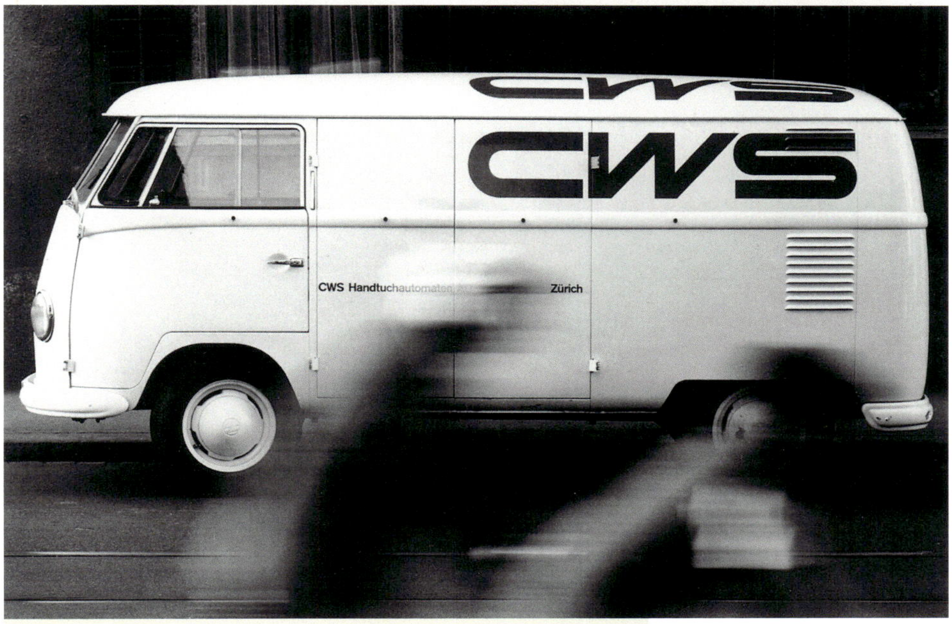

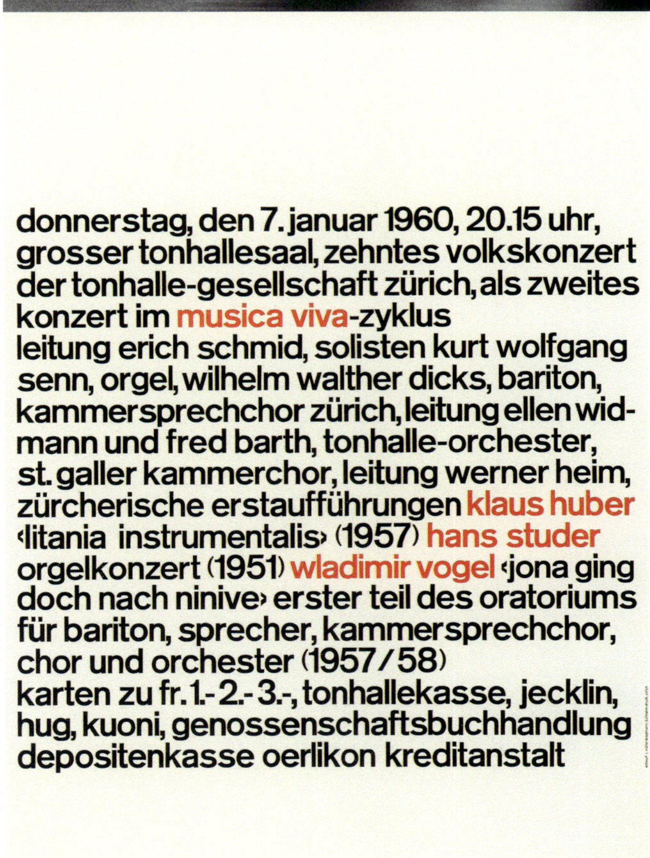

8e–g Josef Müller-Brockmann Concert posters, 1970–72 **8h** Poster series for *Neue Zürcher Zeitung*, no date
8i Exhibition poster, 1975 **8k** Poster design, no date (definitive version 1960)
8l/m Cover and lettering. Design concept for *Transatlantik* magazine. New Mag Verlag/Hans Magnus Enzensberger, 1980

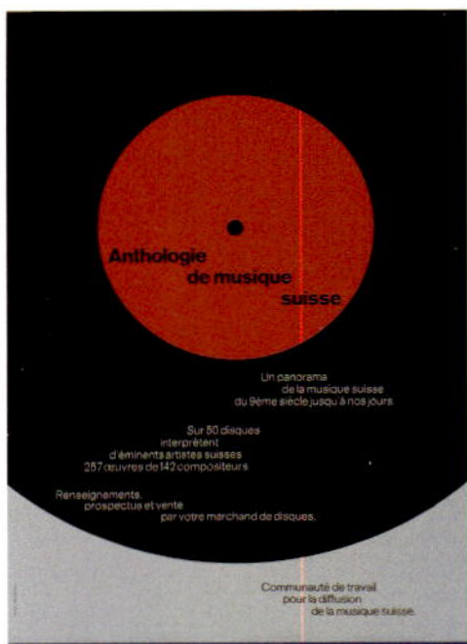

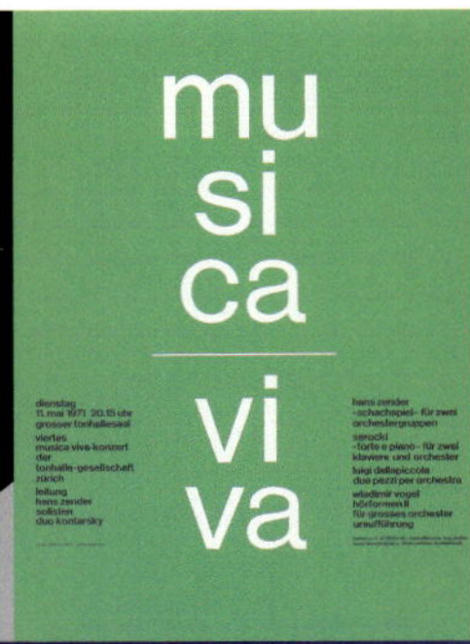

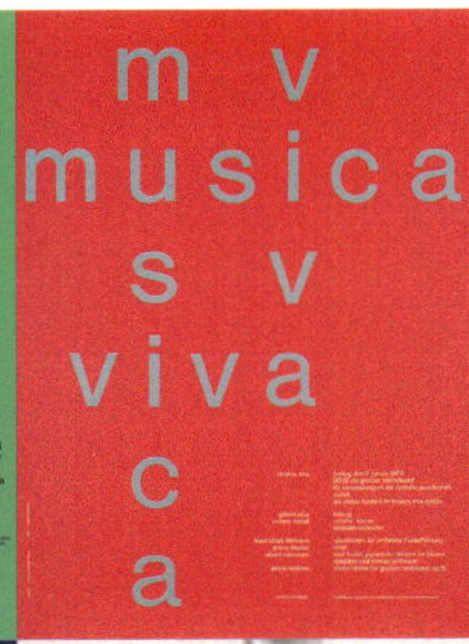

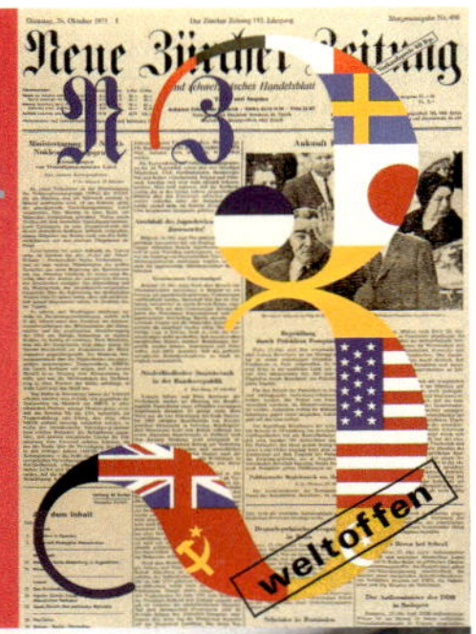

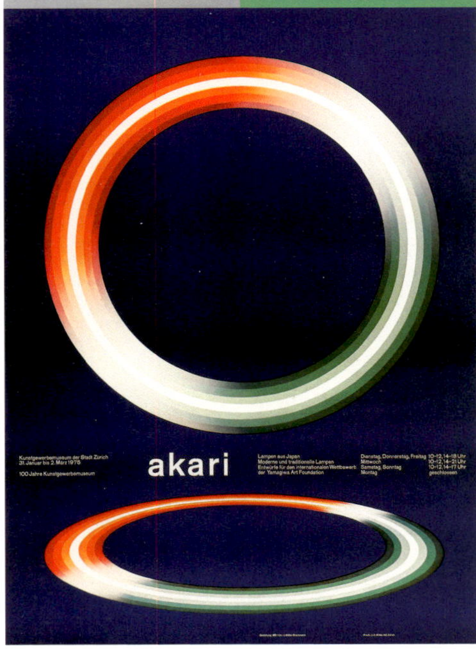

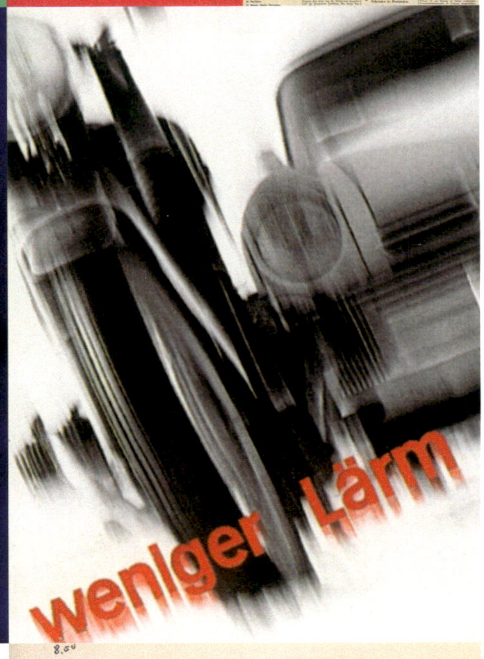

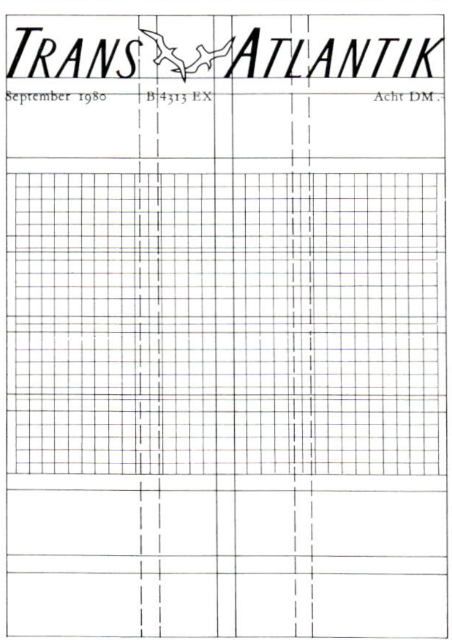

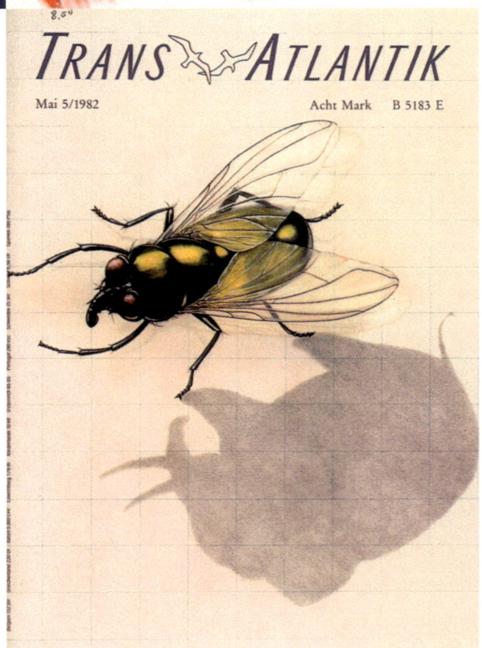

9a Ernst Hiestand, packaging series for Warenhaus ABM. E+U Hiestand, 1960

9b Publication on the ABM design philosophy, Zurich, 2005

9c/d E+U Hiestand, design for Swiss banknotes, sixth emission (1976–95)

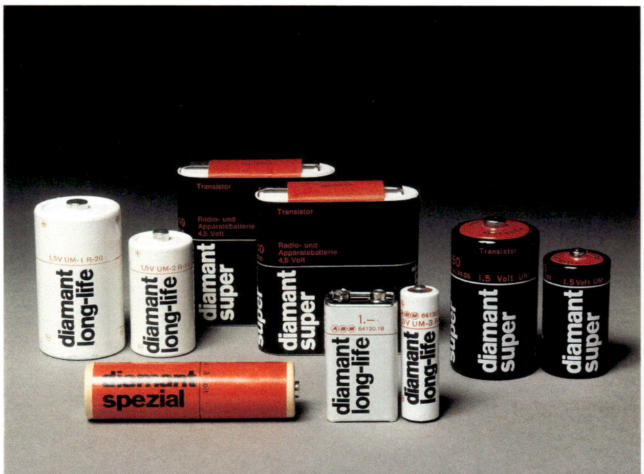

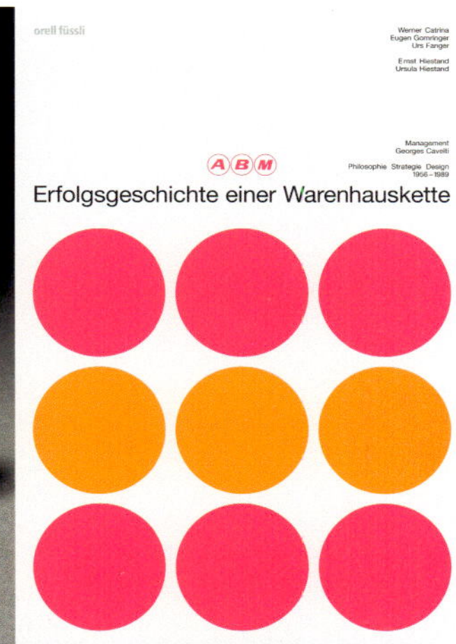

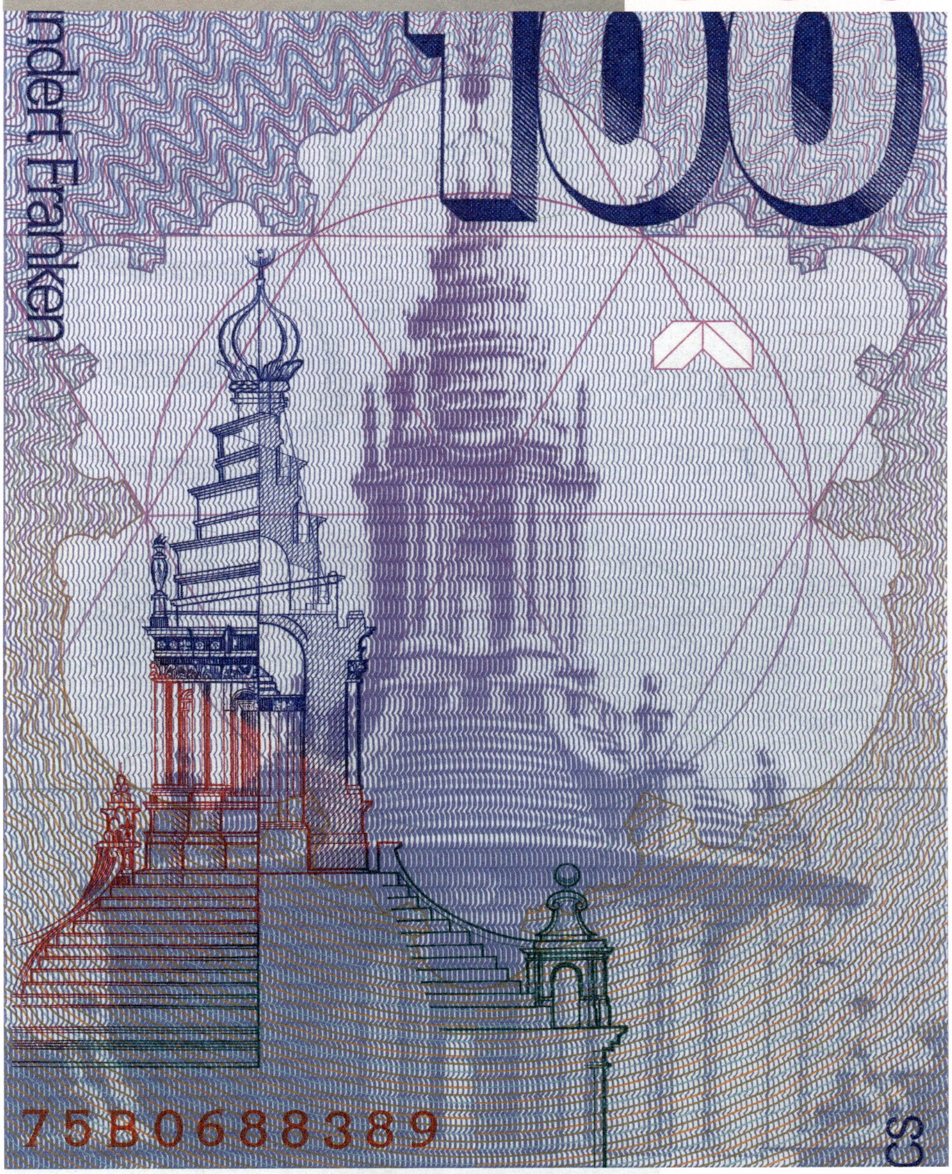

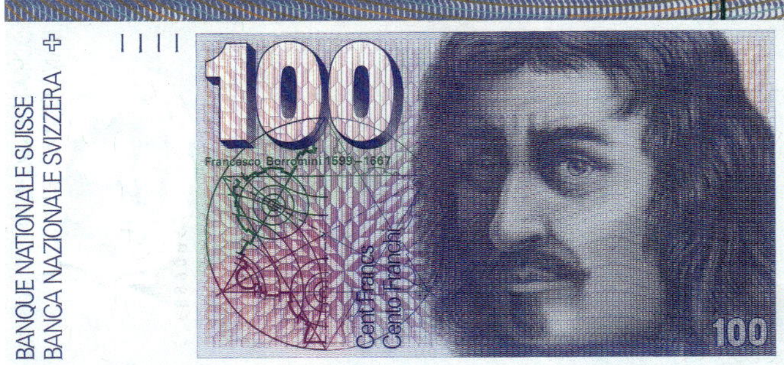

They are recognized, successful, they have made it—they constitute the elite in their profession, the "select few." *Arriver* means to "reach shore"; they have successfully completed their artistic odyssey and arrived on the island of Ithaca, that marvelously beautiful, enchanting place where sugar roses of every color bloom. They set standards for the reception of contemporary art and fix the value system that defines "above" and "below," the difference between trying and succeeding. They are the artists everyone knows or should know. They define the "state of the art" or the "state of the arts," and their success is pioneering—international stature is not out of the question.

His money has soul **1**; his singularity helped him become actor of the year **2**; his adroit unobtrusiveness sets him apart **3**; his publications are considered among the "most beautiful books" **4**; his interventions in urban space are milestones and guidelines **5**; with him all that glitters is gold **6**; his posters fetch high prices from collectors **7**; her vivid ornaments are more than a (house) facade **8**; she plays first violin—perfectly **9**; their sets are found on "the stages that make the world" **11**, **14**; his work is a great showpiece **10**; the Vienna Burgtheater is her true address **12**; his artistic stature is certified by *Documenta* in Kassel and the Biennale in Venice **13**, where her pictures, too, are shining lights in glossy paint **15**.

1

Jörg Zintzmeyer (*1947)

He is the "architect" of brands and images and their pictorial, functional, affective, associative manner of appearance and impact—succinct, systematic to the point of excess, and totally successful. "Design works!" is the terse motto by which Jörg Zintzmeyer propagates his design philosophy as today's most successful and highest profile Swiss designer in the field of corporate identity programs. The second motto, "design is commission," unconditionally distinguishes design from all its artistic blandishments. His banknote series for the Swiss National Bank (he is the fourth "money maker" from the School of Applied Arts in Zurich) can, however, be seen as an ironic turn. The montage, ornamental repetitions, differentiated coloring, and typographic overlays all produce a form of artistic expressiveness that transcends pure functionality, is seen as simply "beautiful," and reasserts the primacy of the aesthetic. His agency, Interbrand Zintzmeyer & Lux, maintains offices in twenty-two countries and its list of clients includes the likes of BMW, Deutsche Telekom, Deutsche Lufthansa, Dresdner Bank, Ericsson, Kraft Jacobs Suchard, and many others.

Jörg Zintzmeyer majored in graphic arts and completed the program of required instruction at the School of Applied Arts.

2

Ueli Jäggi (*1954)

Ueli Jäggi studied German and Romance languages and literature and history before cofounding the Kabarett Stirbelwurm in Basel in 1973 and, three years later, opening the first youth theatre in Switzerland. In 1979–80, he attended the Zurich Academy of Drama; after graduation, he was hired by the Theater der Jugend in Munich. In 1987–89, he worked at the Nuremberg Schauspielhaus, returning to Switzerland in 1990 and working there as an independent artist. His collaboration with Christoph Marthaler began in 1991 at the Theater Basel; since then, he has appeared in numerous Marthaler productions, especially at the Deutsches Schauspielhaus in Hamburg. In 2000–2004, Ueli Jäggi belonged to the ensemble of the Zurich Schauspielhaus. He received the German Audio Book Prize for best interpretation for *Bartleby der Schreiber* (Bartleby the Scrivener), as well as for Antonio Tabucchi's *Lissabonner Requiem* (Lisbon Requiem). He appeared in a number of television and film roles: in *Gegen Ende der Nacht* (Toward the End of the Night) by Oliver Storz; *Vollmond* (Full Moon) by Fredi M. Murer; *Der Onkel vom Meer* (The Uncle Who Came From the Sea) by Marie-Louise Bless; *Donna Leon: Commissario Brunetti* by Siggi Rothemund; *Tod durch Entlassung* (Death by Dismissal) by Christian Kohlund; *Tod einer Ärztin* (Death of a Doctor) by Markus Fischer; *Grounding: Das Ende der Swissair* (Grounding: The End of Swissair) by Michael Steiner; *Marmorera* by Markus Fischer; and also as detective superintendent Hunkeler in the audio books of Hansjörg Schneider. In 2001, Ueli Jäggi was chosen *by Theater heute* as actor of the year.

3

Hanspeter Müller-Drossaart (*1955)

Hanspeter Müller-Drossaart is omnipresent in the theater, in the cinema, and in various TV soaps. His most striking characteristic is his refined depiction of inconspicuousness. He knows how to transform himself like a chameleon: now the decent guy, now the arsonist, he is a true character actor. Born in Obwalden, he studied at the Zurich Academy of Drama, appeared in numerous theater productions and cinema movies at home and abroad, and has participated in more than ninety radio plays. Since the 2000 season, he has been a member of the ensemble of the Vienna Burgtheater, where he has worked with Andrea Breth, Peter Zadek, Dieter Giesing, Joachim Schlöhmer, Stephan Müller, and Johann Kresnik, and many others. In 2002, he switched to Christoph Marthaler's ensemble at the Zurich Schauspielhaus. Since summer 2004, he has been an inde-

1 3
2 4

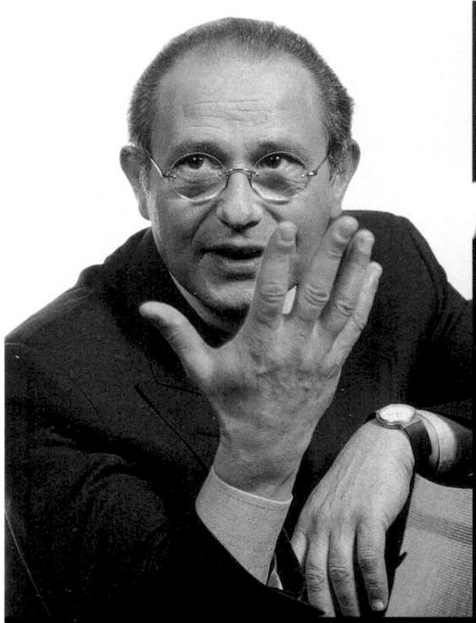

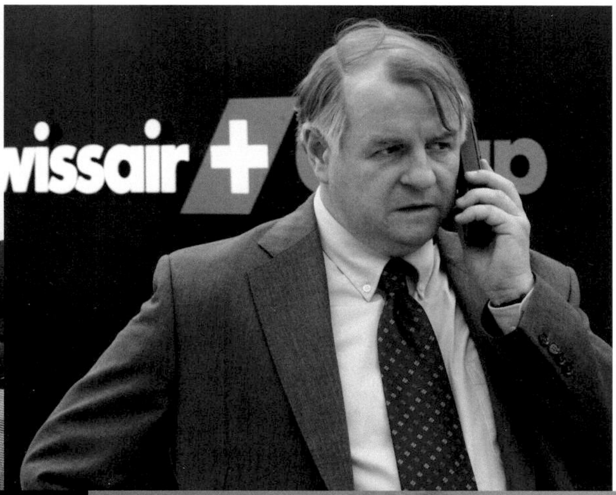

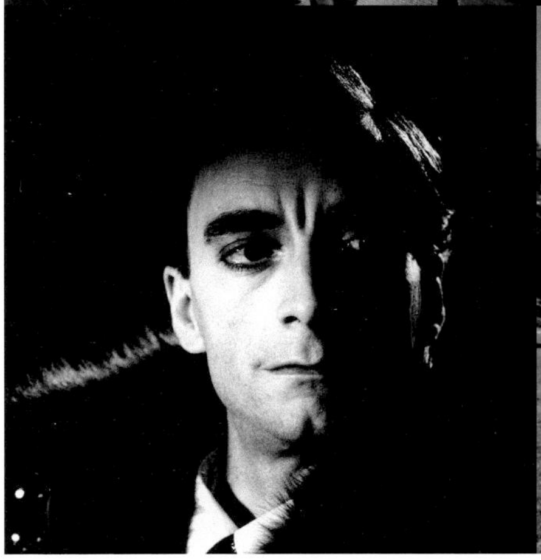

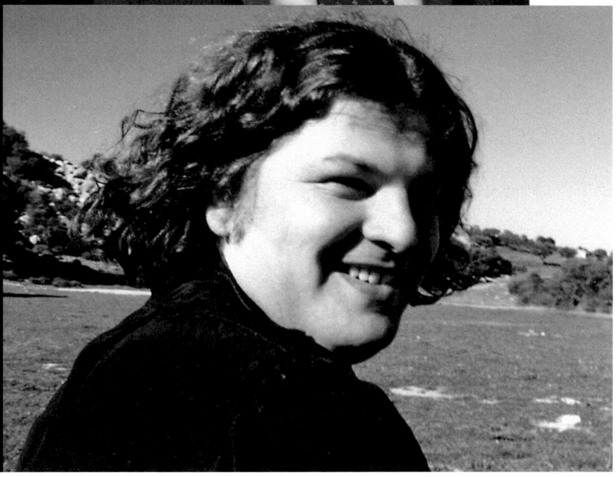

pendent actor, narrator, and instructor of stage acting at the Zurich School of Drama. Müller-Drossaart made a guest appearance at the Lucerne Theater in *Das Ende vom Anfang* (The End of the Beginning) in a production by Ueli Jäggi.

4

Lars Müller (*1955)

He really published only the "most beautiful books," at least from the point of view of designers, architects, and contemporary artists. He has taken home the prize for the most beautiful Swiss books awarded by the Art and Design Section of the Federal Office of Culture more times than anyone else. It was the passion of a book lover that led Lars Müller to edit his first book in 1983, *Die gute Form* (Good Form), by Peter Erni. The reprints of the Russian avant-garde that followed were aimed at combating memory loss —the whitewashing of history and visual memory in an overexcited present. His carefully designed editions mirror the state of our culture today, and with his program he demonstrates aesthetic satisfaction and designer fascination as well as sociopolitical involvement, particularly through publications like Walter Kälin's 2004 *Das Bild der Menschenrechte* (The Face of Human Rights). He has been known to give his publishing program the title "school of seeing."

Lars Müller graduated from vocational school as a draftsman and attended the required program of instruction at the School of Applied Arts. Already recognized even then as a dynamic personality—along with Rudi Baur, he organized ambitious seminars and was an early participant in the contemporary design debate.

5

Ruedi Baur (*1956)

Wikipedia calls him "today's Swiss star designer," who has built up an international profile with his unconventional and controversial design and visual concepts. His impact is primarily in France, particularly in Paris, where he has supervised projects like the colorful typeface and corporate identity for the Centre Pompidou, the Palais des Congrès in Paris, the Bibliothèque Nationale; in Switzerland, with the "plasticized guidance system" for the Swiss National Exposition, expo.02, and the hospital of the University of Bern; in Germany, with Cologne Airport; and in Canada, with the visual urban identity of Quebec. These projects demonstrate the global dimensions and influence of his work, which is steeped in his own tough style and political standpoint. Ruedi Baur also employs the tools of visual communication to fight against racism and human rights violations.

As director of the Design Institute at the School of Art and Design Zurich he supervises an important research program, has set up postgraduate courses and hammered out an exact description of the position of the designer in the context of urban development processes. From 1995–2004 Ruedi Baur was professor of Corporate Design at the Leipzig Academy of Visual Arts and was its president for two years. In 2002 he became president of the Alliance Graphique Internationale and in 2004 the School of Art and Design Zurich appointed him lecturer and director of its newly founded Design2context. In early 2007 the University of Quebec awarded him an honorary doctorate.

6

Christophe Graber (*1959)

Christophe Graber's jewelry creations oscillate between glitziness and a hint of gloom. They appear cultlike and do enjoy cult status among people who wear jewelry with independence and stylistic verve—and among people who give such items as gifts, including the greats of international show business and politics. His pieces are rendered unmistakable by their exclusive materials; the black of ebony, the white of matt gold, the green of jade contrast with rare precious stones, including spinels, rubies, and emeralds. Graber shapes the light reflections, luster, and color of these materials with a magic touch into glowing rings, armbands, earrings, and collars. In their eerily beautiful radiance, these reptiles, spiders,

7 6 8
9
5

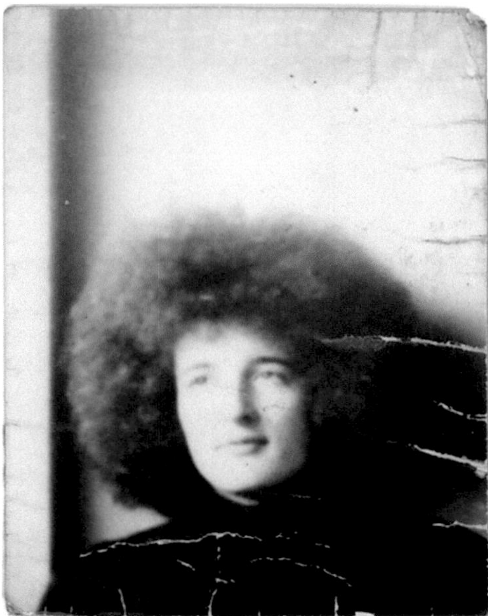
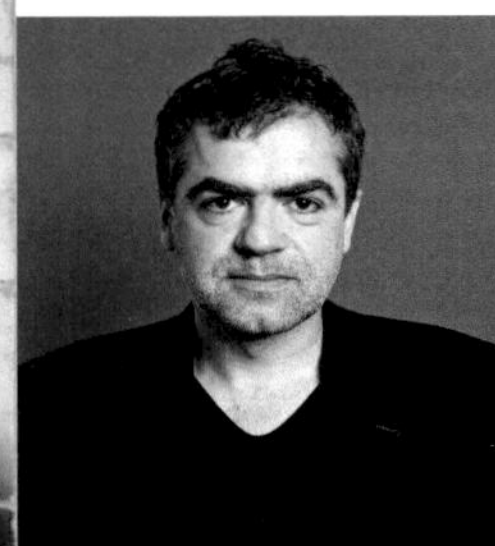
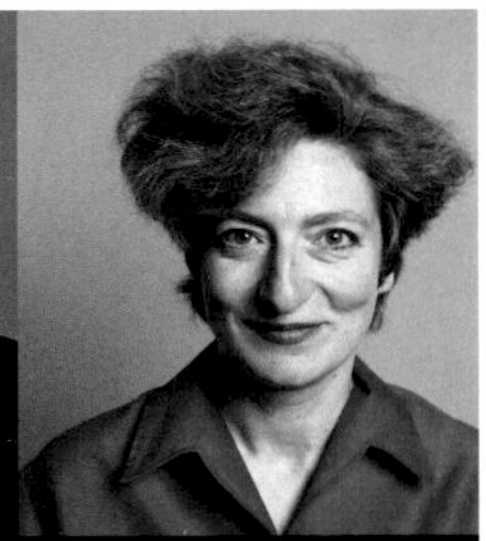
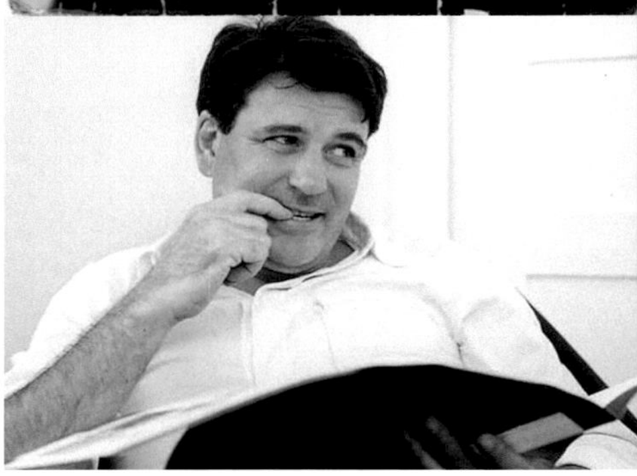
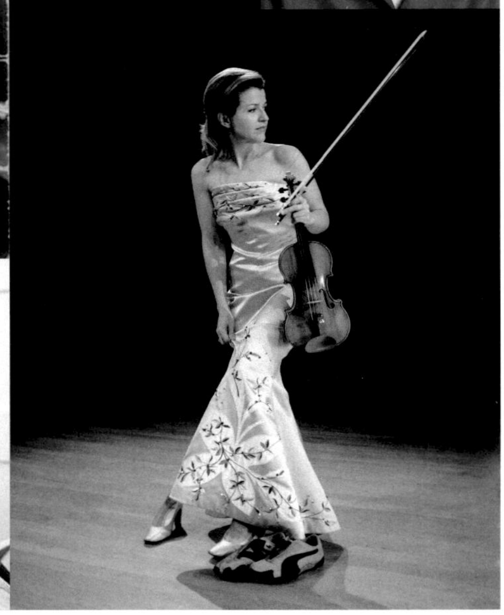

snakes, and beetles, cut into stone with engraving tools, become powerful emblems for their wearers. His masterpieces are displayed and sold in an exceptionally lovely atmosphere on Zurich's Fraumünsterstrasse.

Christophe Graber is a graduate of the program in jewelry and utensils of the Zurich School of Applied Arts.

7

Ralph Schraivogel (*1960)

His posters work toward obliterating the distinction between text and image: image becomes text and text becomes image, or, rather, seeing and reading become one, maintaining a precarious balance. The "pictorial climates" transmit the content and not, as is usually the case, the visual or verbal factual information. His posters are visual explorations of pictorial spaces and effects that work by means of the evocation of the novel and different. For more than twenty years they have always been good for optical surprises: perspectives tumbling into one another, typographic defamiliarization (illustrations), ornaments, complex overlays and superimpositions that challenge and fascinate the viewer over and over again.

His unconventional designs have won him a high level of international recognition as a designer of cultural posters. He attended the graphics program at the School of Applied Arts and as early as his diploma project strove for subtle and multiple interpenetration of photographic, graphic, and contextual positions.

8

Renée Levi (*1960)

Her preferred tool is the spray can; her favorite color, yellow-orange; her place of work, public space; her formal idiom, the ornament. The effect: oscillating, vibrating, delirious, overflowing. Here are sprayed patterns of movement, meandering networks, and mists that generate spaces of color, chromatic energetic fields of force, fluorescing spheres.

Renée Levi herself proclaims laconically: "A good picture is distinguished by its clarity—clear in form, clear in color, clear in space." The result is spatial intensities of effect whose magic is inescapable. Her laconic characterization stands in contrast to the effect of her image worlds, whose space-filling presence is capable of tipping "clarity" over into a state of colored trance.

Renée Levi is a graduate of the visual arts program.

9

Anne-Sophie Mutter (*1963)

Surely she needs no introduction—Anne-Sophie Mutter, born in Rheinfelden, has achieved everything a musician could dream of. And she laid the groundwork for this success, or so she herself has said, while a student at the Winterthur Conservatory: "If we are going to talk about those people who had a formative impact on my life, then we must be sure not to forget my wonderful teacher Aida Stucki," said Anne-Sophie Mutter in an interview with Ursula Nusser that was broadcast on Südwestrundfunk radio in May 2005. "Her influence on me was crucial and it was she who taught me to think for myself as well. A quality which is naturally especially important in teachers, but certainly not a matter of course." What Mutter says of Stucki can doubtless be said of countless teachers at today's Music Department and its predecessor institutions, and this philosophy will continue to be written large at the Zurich University of the Arts.

10

Bruno Cathomas (*1965)

In 1988, after growing up in Laax, this late bloomer simultaneously passed entrance exams at three different drama schools. Financial considerations made him decide for the Zurich Academy of Drama, where he received a training strongly oriented toward Stanislavski and Strassberg, and found instructors responsive to his budding acting ambitions. Frank Castorf hired him for the Volksbühne Berlin, and he remained in the ensemble until the end of 1997. After his experiences at the drama school these were the decisive years. Much was revised, as he passed through a second training period, so to speak, and got to know a stimulating theater: political, fast, risky,

12 10 13
15
14 11

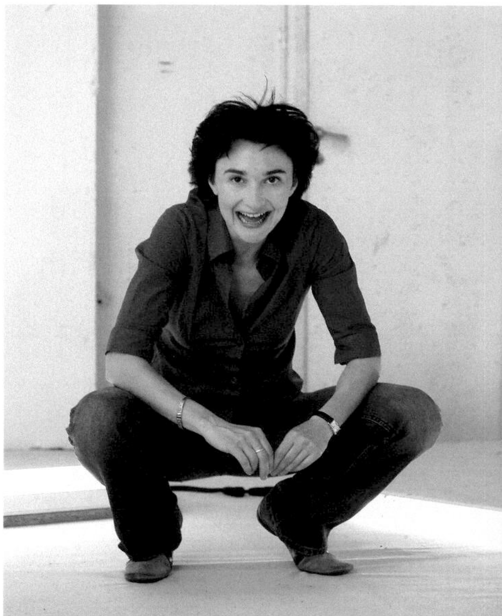
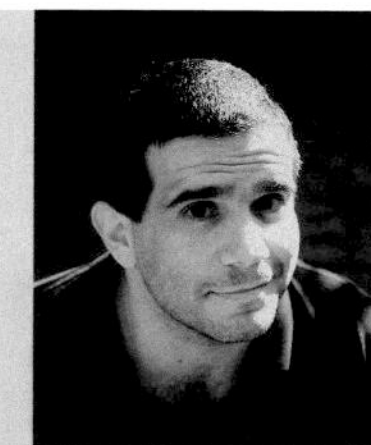
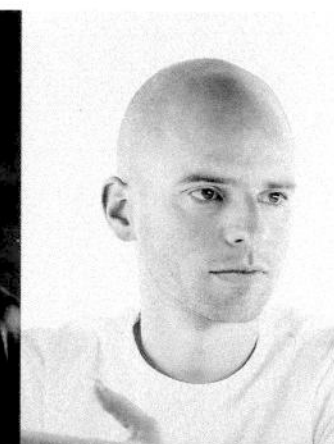
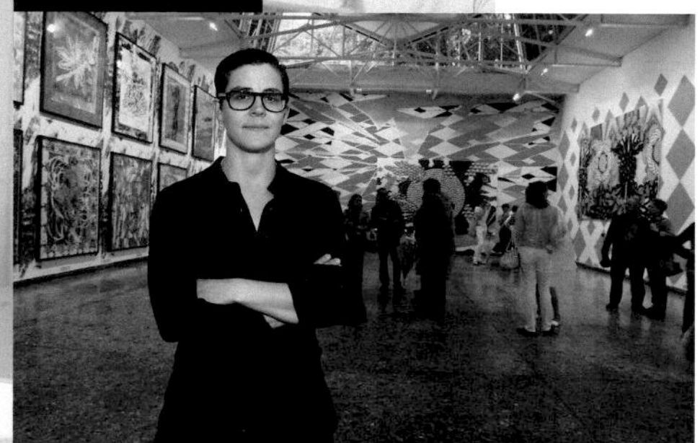
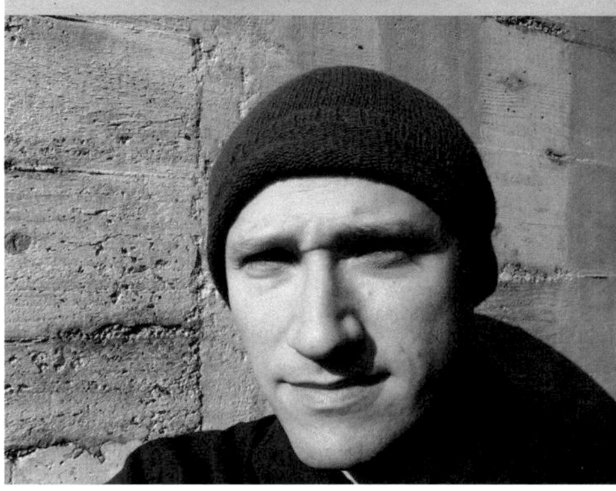
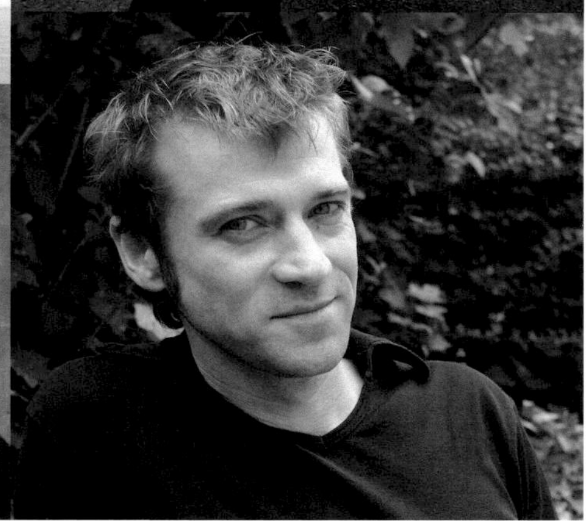

honest, often disturbing, often wounding, always provocative. Beginning in 1998, he worked as an independent actor in film and theater, among others at the Munich Kammerspiele, the Zurich Schauspielhaus (still remembered is his marvelous appearance in Marthaler's *Murx*), again at the Berlin Volksbühne, as well as at the Theater Basel. At the moment, his suitcases are in Berlin, and his main venue is the Schaubühne am Lehniner Platz.

11

Erich Sidler (*1965)

After his school-leaving exams in Lucerne, Sidler returned to Zurich, where he worked as a projectionist in a Zurich cinema, quickly losing interest in studies of art history. He studied directing at the Zurich Academy of Drama, and was hired as a directoral assistant by the Niedersächsisches Staatstheater, where he was soon able to stage his own productions. His dramatization and staging of Kleist's *Marquise von O.* received, among others, the Young Directors Prize of the German Academy of Fine Arts. He then went on to Theater Essen, Nationaltheater Mannheim, Maxim Gorki Theater Berlin, and finally to the Staatstheater Stuttgart, where he was house director. Since 2003, he has worked as an independent director at various theaters. His main interest is "new dramatism" and young authors.

In 2006, Sidler staged his first Swiss production at the Theater am Neumarkt Zurich, then at Theater Basel, and later gained a permanent position in Bern. Here, beginning in summer of 2007, he will begin shaping drama at the Stadttheater, and hence theater life in the federal capital—with "new dramatism."

12

Sylvie Rohrer (*1968)

Born in Bern, Sylvie Rohrer attended the Zurich Academy of Drama from 1988–91. She then worked for a short period at the Landesbühne Niedersachsen and the Zurich Schauspielhaus, before taking a position in Dortmund in 1992. In 1995 and 1996, she was named best young actress of the year by the magazine *Theater heute* for her appearance as Pegleg in *The Black Rider* in Dortmund, and afterwards for her Eglé in Marivaux's *Der Streit* (La Dispute) at the Thalia Theater in Hamburg, whose ensemble she belonged to from 1995–99. During this period, she worked with directors such as Jürgen Flimm, Martin Kusej, Sven-Eric Bechtolf, Wilfried Minks, and others, appearing in works from all epochs, from Sophocles and Shakespeare to Peter Handke and Tankred Dorst. In 1996, she received the Boy Gobert Prize.

Since 1999, Sylvie Rohrer has been employed by the Vienna Burgtheater. There, she has participated in many world premieres while also shaping the lead roles in works by Lessing, Rostand, Ödön von Horváth, Hofmannsthal, and Jon Fosse under directors including Martin Kusej, Thomas Langhoff, and Luc Bondy. She has made guest appearances at the Berliner Ensemble—*Mass für Mass* (Measure for Measure), *Schändung* (Desecration); and the Salzburg Festival—*King Arthur, Der Liederabend* (The Song Evening). She starred in a stage version of Arnold Schönberg's *Pierrot Lunaire,* produced by Hermann Beil, in Austria, Switzerland, Germany, and the USA. She has also participated in radio, television, and film productions.

13

Yves Netzhammer (*1970)

His computer-generated drawings, illustrations, and animations have become commonplace in European museums, galleries, and the arts sections of prestigious newspapers and magazines. They are obscure images and constellations of images with an unmistakable signature: terse, computer embellished, aestheticized, sterile, artificial. They are the de-definition of our real and factual reality: hallucinatory, divided images of figures, illusionist beings and spaces. Animals devouring themselves, absurd erotic constellations between man and beast, man and botanical nature, space and surface turned inside-out, confusion on subject and form. These images pose obscure riddles and lead straight as an arrow

1a Jörg Zintzmeyer, current, eighth Swiss banknote series (from 1995). Photo of Alberto Giacometti by Ernst Scheidegger

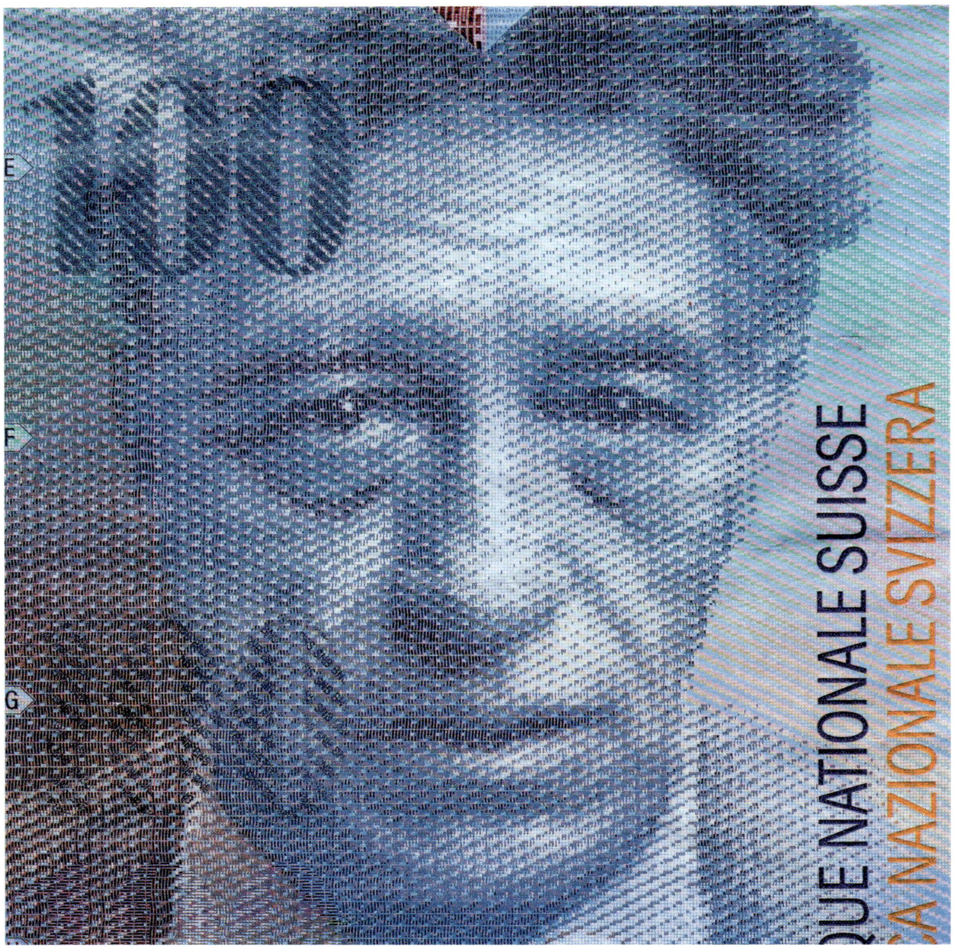

into madness. They suggest that they can be deciphered—but in vain, as they are designed so that meaning always fails. This fine balance between the normal and the abstruse, between absurdity and logic lends a crude double or "multiple meaning" to this art. In so doing the grotesque and tragic ascends to the level of the tragi-comic with its immanent laughter. Netzhammer represents Switzerland in 2007 at the Biennale in Venice.

Yves Netzhammer attended the continuing education course in visual design.

14

Samuel Schwarz (*1971)

Samuel Schwarz studied directing in 1995–98 at the former Zurich Academy of Drama. Immediately thereafter, he enjoyed the notable privilege of working with Benno Besson and Peter Palitzsch at the Zurich Schauspielhaus. In his free time, he founded the theater group 400asa (together with Lukas Bärfuss), whose very first production was a magnificent success. Shortages of funds prompted them to perform Horváth's *Italienische Nacht* (Italian Night) at a café table. This reduction to a minimum was of fundamental importance and was extremely successful. The production, which was played at many German theaters, opened up new perspectives. In 2001, with *Medeää* (Medea), based on Lars von Trier's film after Euripides, Schwarz began his intensive confrontation with cinematic and theatrical resources. Important projects since then have included his work with Filmbyen, the Danish film town; he also began his career as a solo director at municipal theaters. He has directed at the Theater Basel, the Maxim Gorki Theater, the Hamburg Schauspielhaus, the Bochum Schauspielhaus, the Theater St. Gallen, and the State Theater in Maribor, Slovenia. Last year, he founded Kamm(m)macher GmbH, which focuses on the development and analysis of screenplays and works for theater, and draws on dramatic techniques for this purpose.

15

Christine Streuli (*1975)

Trendy colors in conjunction with baroque ornamentation: an apt characterization of the paintings of Christine Streuli. Colorful works in enamel, her "installational painting," which fill the space, bursting the conventions of the panel picture, incorporating walls, ceilings and floors, all the way to the beholder's footprints. But there are also miniatures, which ask to be seen as precious objects. Streuli uses acrylic, enamel, oil, and stencils, paints, sprays, stamps, and mounts. Her signs, symbols, and signals, her paintings and overpaintings, suggest meanings which immediately slip out of reach, encodings of imagination and reality whose rational deciphering always founders.

Christine Streuli earned a degree from the visual arts program, spent the year 2002 at the International Studio and Curatorial Program (ISPN) in New York, was an artist in residence in Cairo, and represents Switzerland in 2007 at the Venice Biennale.

3a Hanspeter Müller-Drossaart (left) and Stefan Suske (right) in Friedrich Schiller's *Kabale und Liebe.* Stadttheater Bern, 2006

4a Lars Müller's book about Helvetica, the blue-collar worker and solo entertainer among typefaces

2a Ueli Jäggi on Christoph Marthaler's ensemble at Schauspielhaus Zurich

4b *Bild der Menschenrechte.* Edited by Walter Kälin. Lars Müller Publishers, Baden, 2004

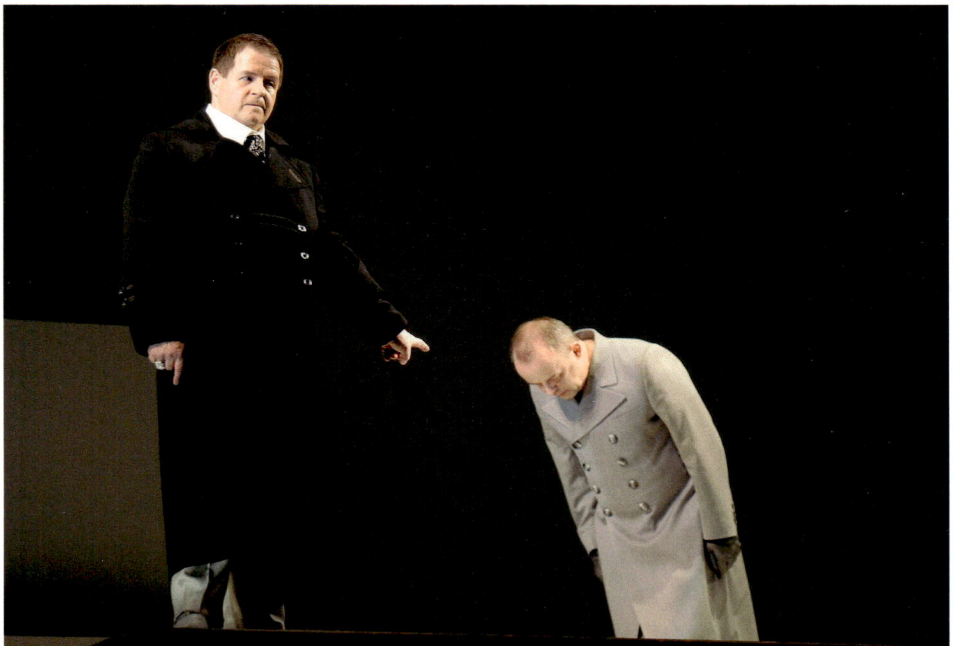

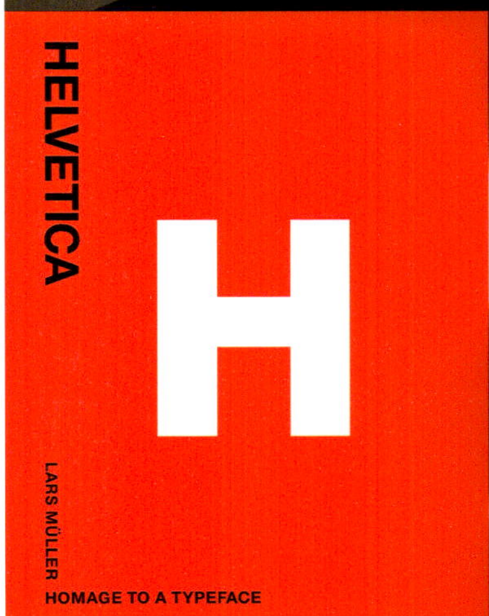

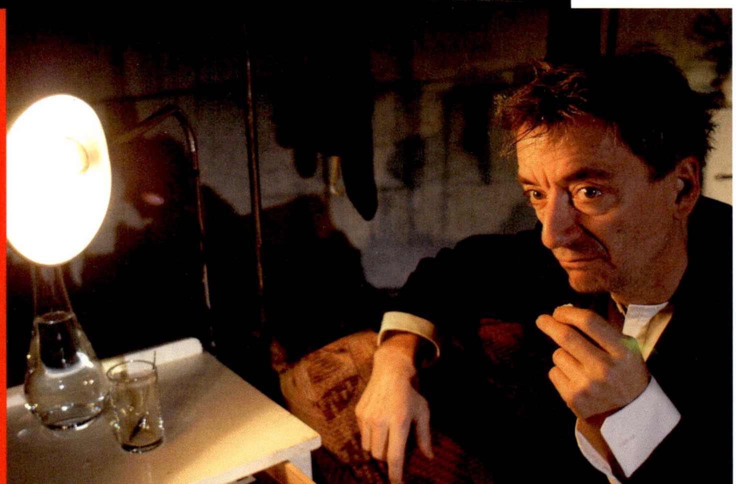

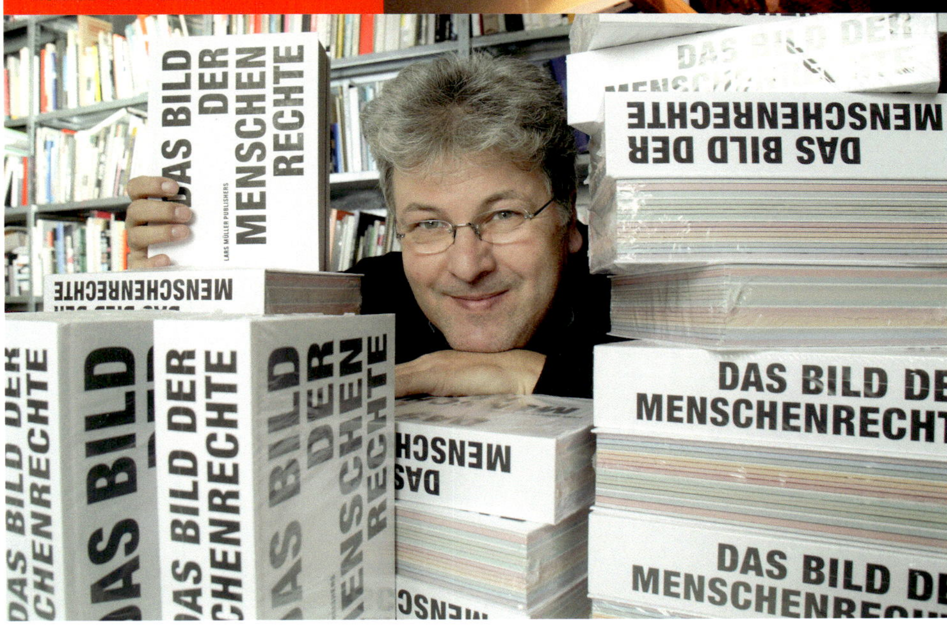

4c *Poster Collection 15.* Edited by Museum of Design Zurich. Lars Müller Publishers, 2007

5a/b Ruedi Baur, guidance system for Centre Pompidou, Paris

5c NORM. Dimitri Bruni & Manuel Krebs, commissioned by Ruedi Baur, Integral Paris, corporate typeface SimpleKoelnBonn

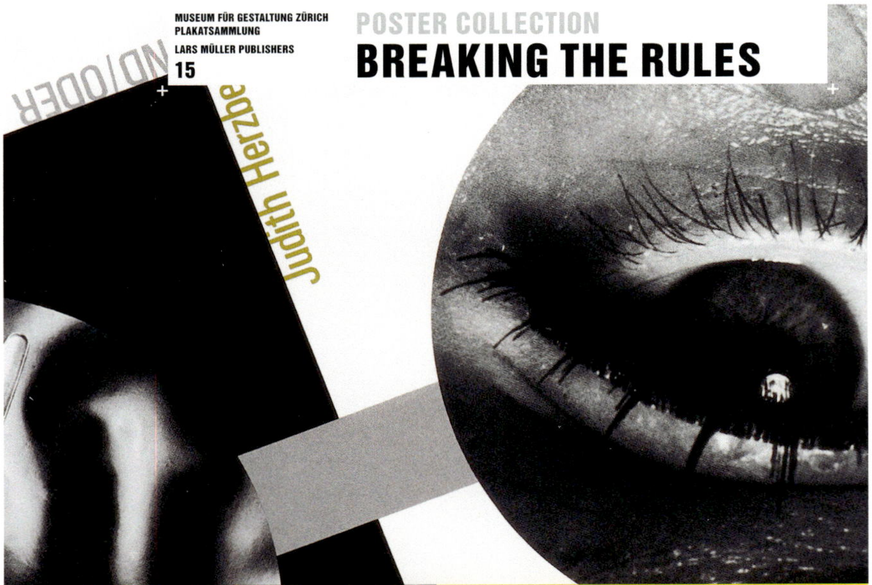

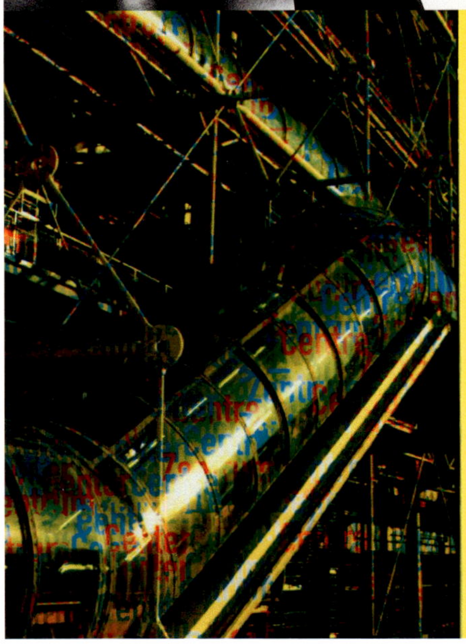

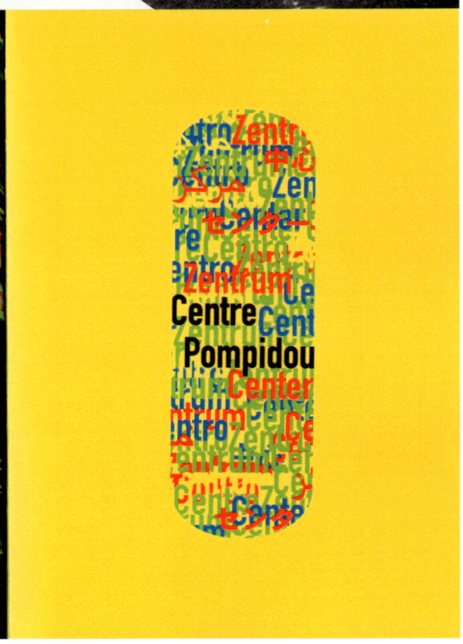

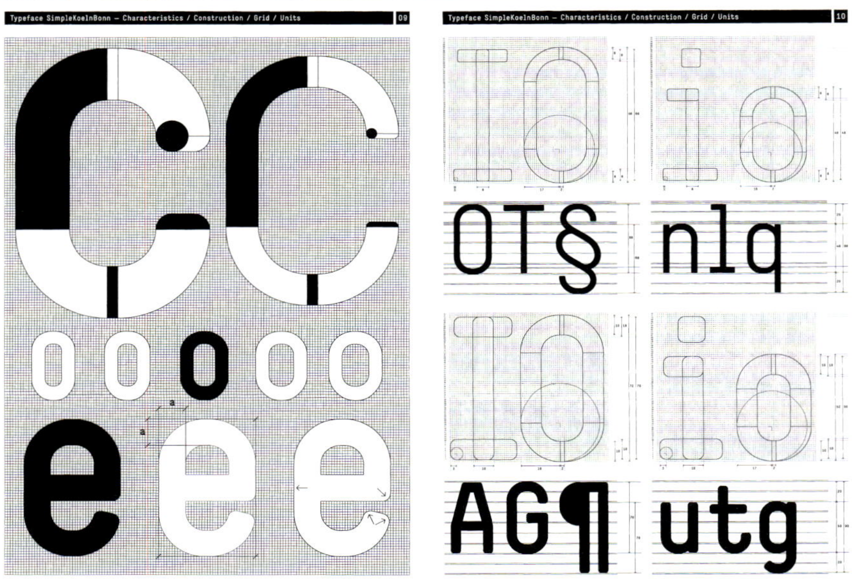

4d Lars Müller Publishers, *Freitag—Individual Recycled Freeway Bags*, 2004. Book announcement

5d Ruedi Baur, guidance system for the Swiss National Exposition expo.02

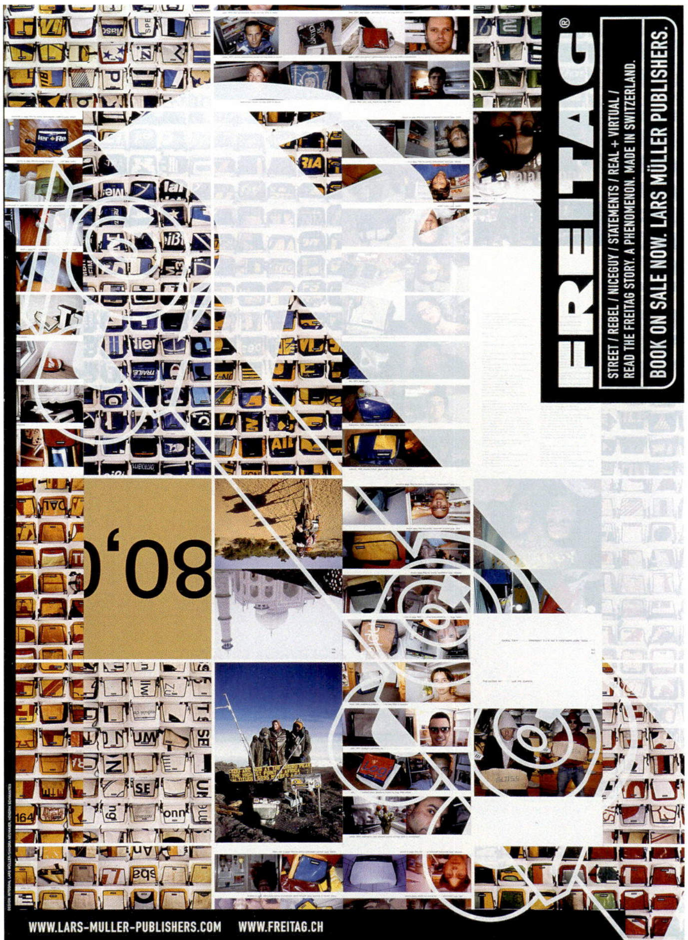

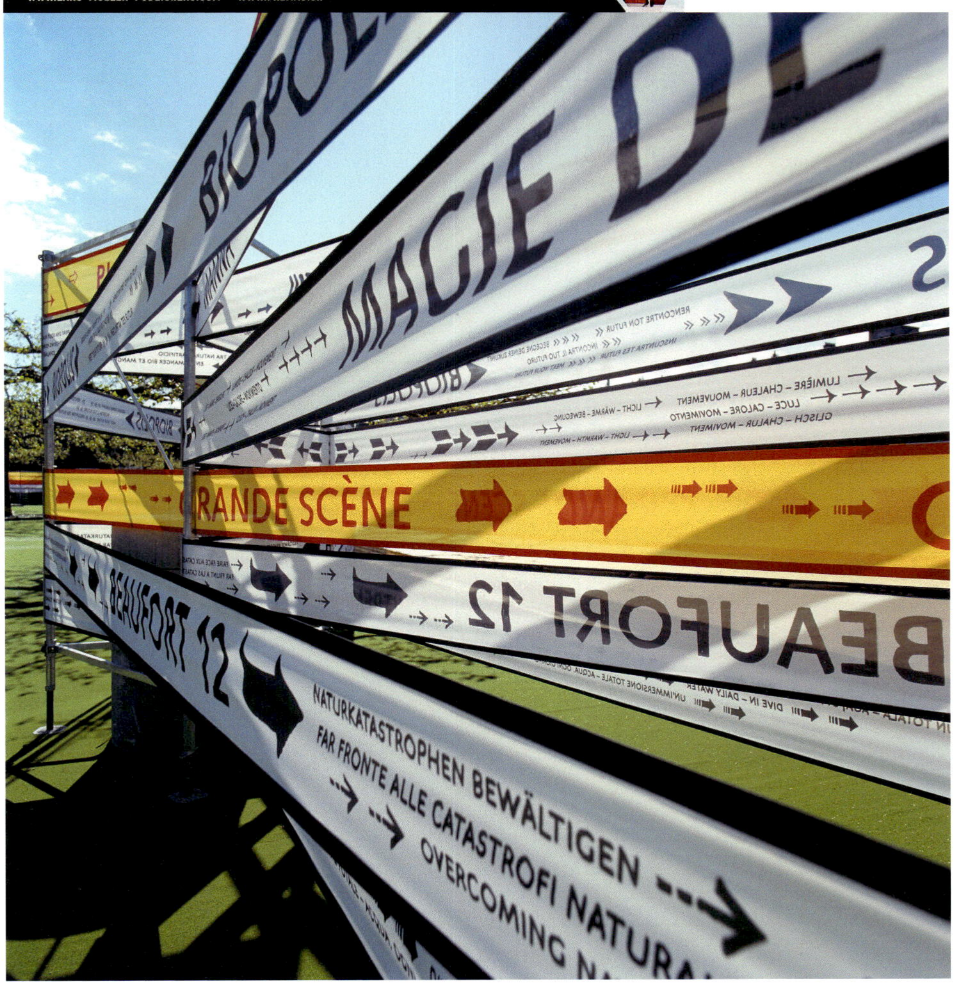

8a Renée Levi, *Orangen,* 2002. Acryl Fluo orange on alucore. Hochschulrektorenkonferenz and Studienstiftung des deutschen Volkes, Bonn

6a Christophe Graber Jewellry, *Imageportrait.* Design Karin Schiesser

6b–d Christophe Graber Jewellry

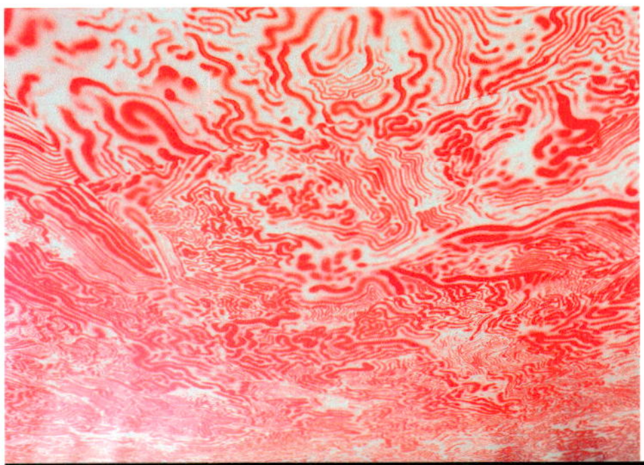

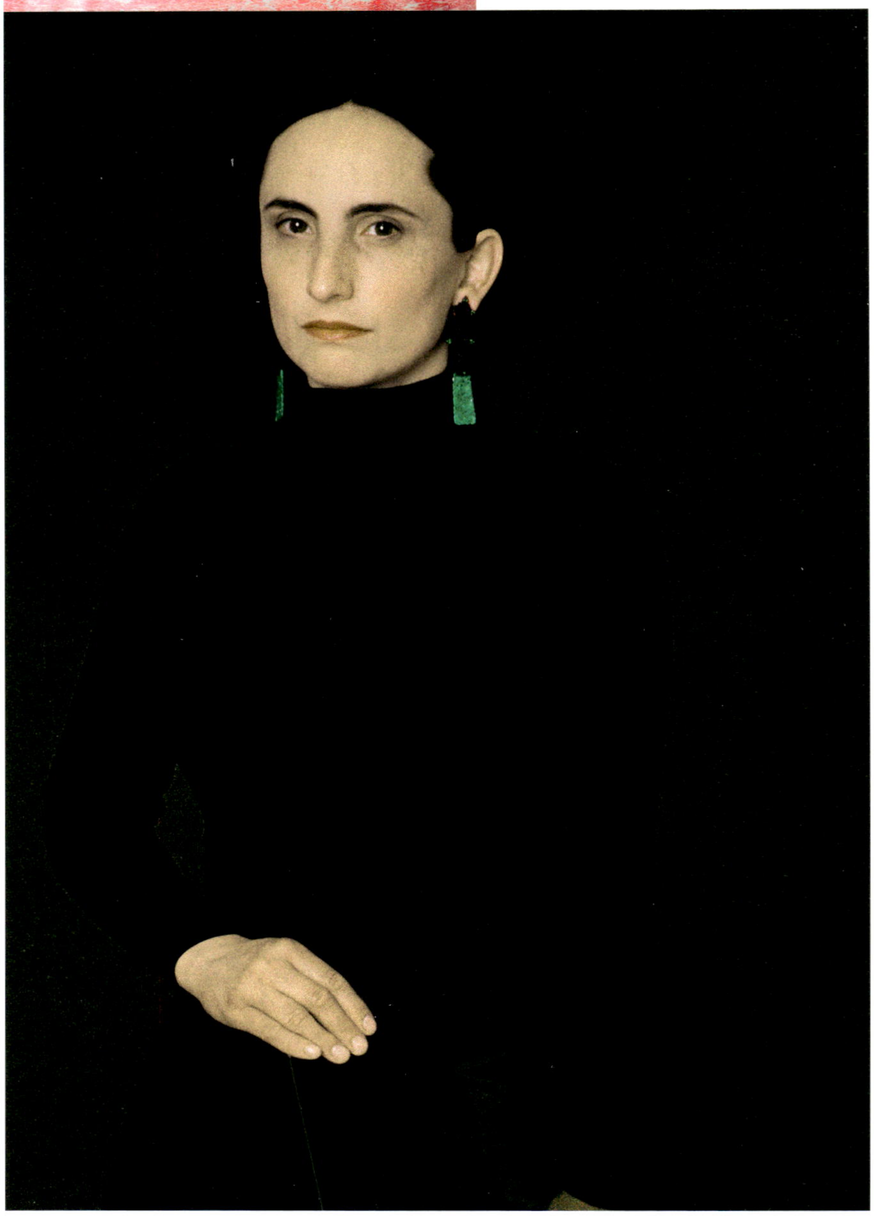

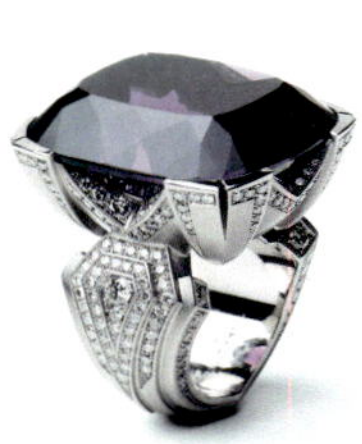

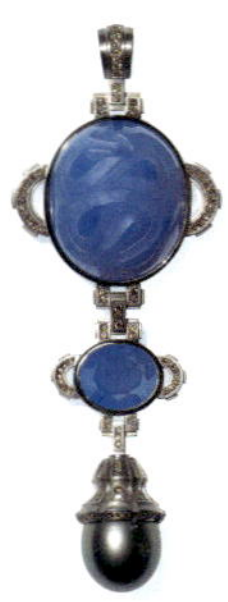

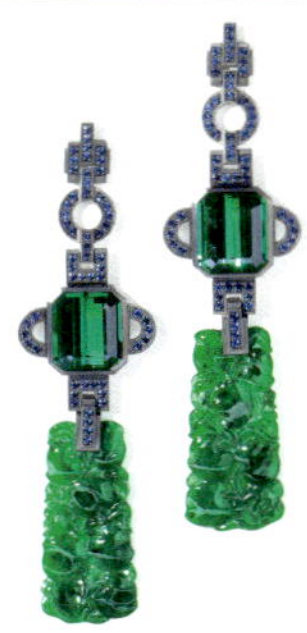

7a/b Ralph Schraivogel, posters for Filmpodium Zurich: *John Ford*, 1996; *Cinémafrica*, 1997. Screen prints

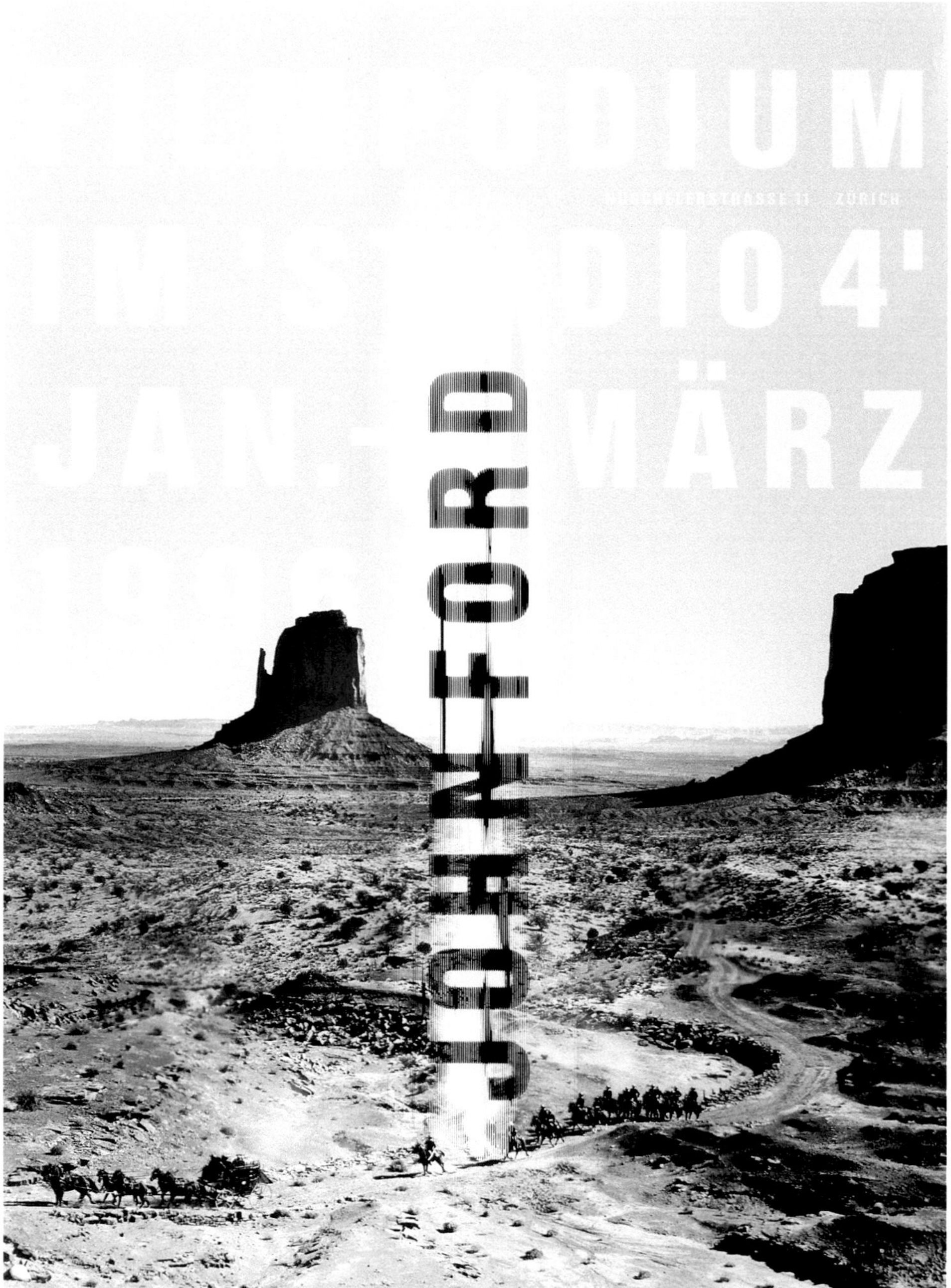

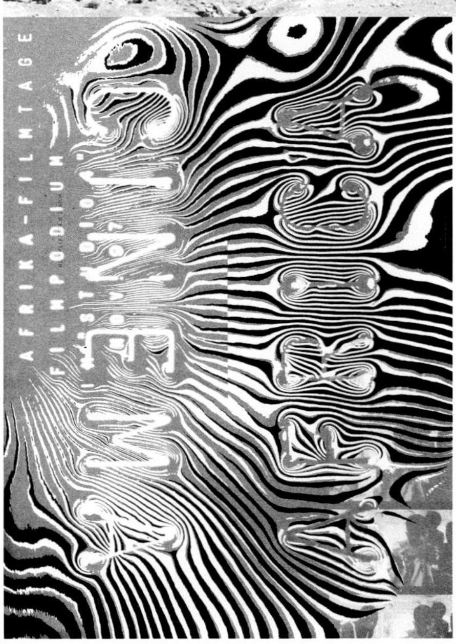

7c Ralph Schraivogel, poster for the exhibition *Gross und Klein* at the Museum of Design Zurich, 1997. Screen print

7d Poster for the International Jazz Festival Zurich, 1989

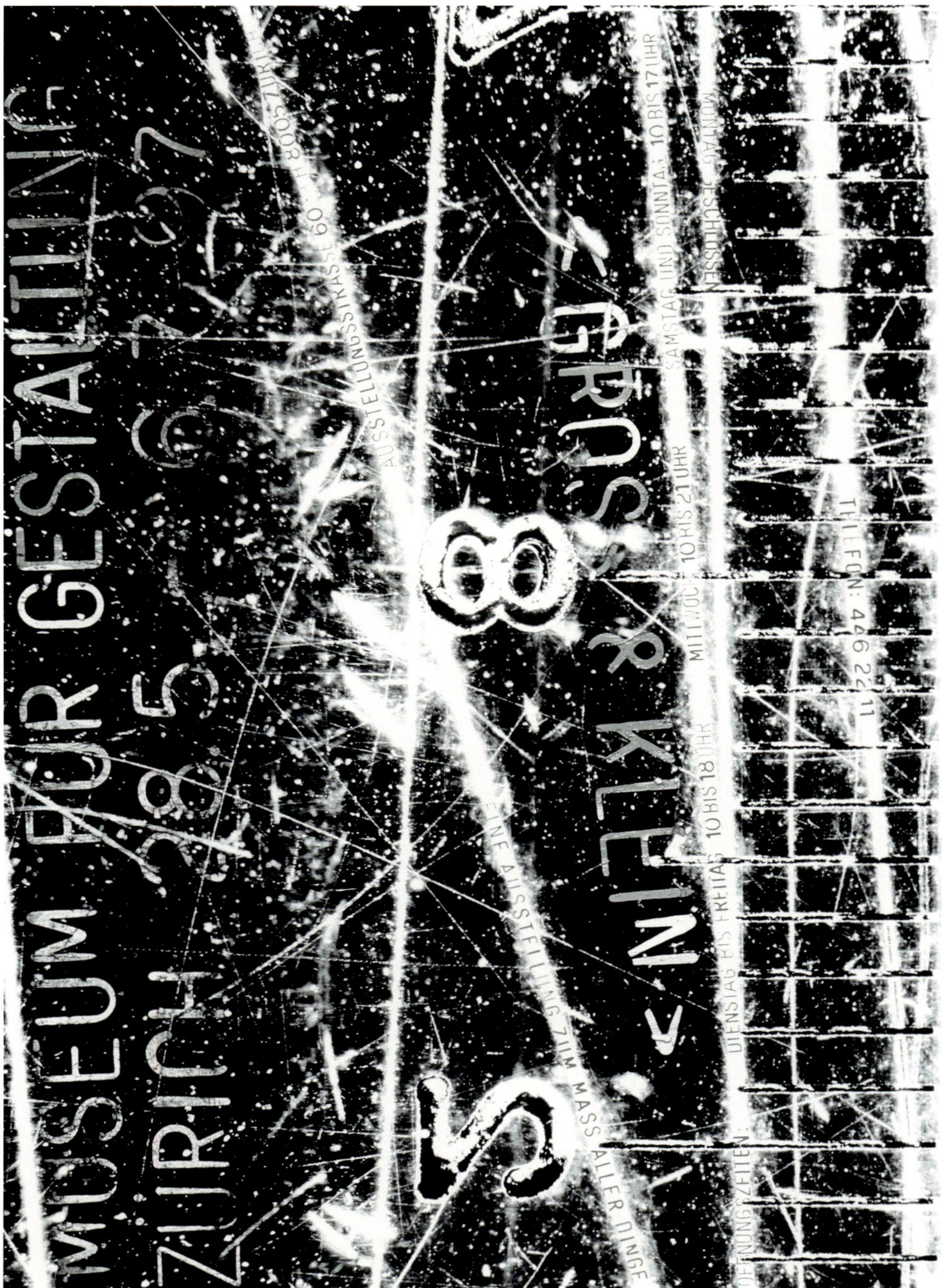

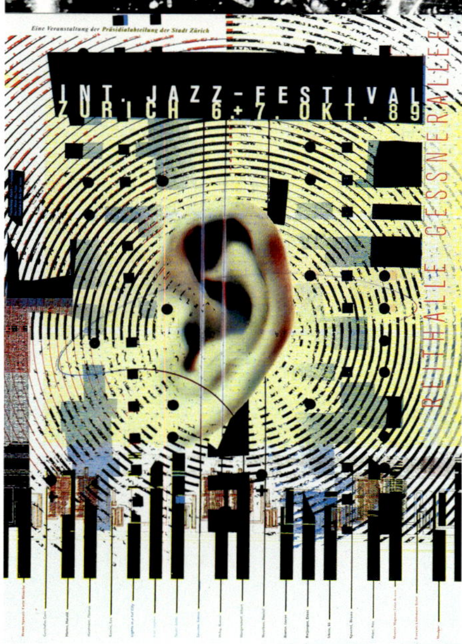

8a/c Renée Levi, *Regina*, 2000. Regina-Kägi-Hof Zurich Oerlikon, district heating station of the City of Zurich

8d *Kassiber*. Exhibition *Abstraktes Material*, Künstlerhaus Graz, 2005

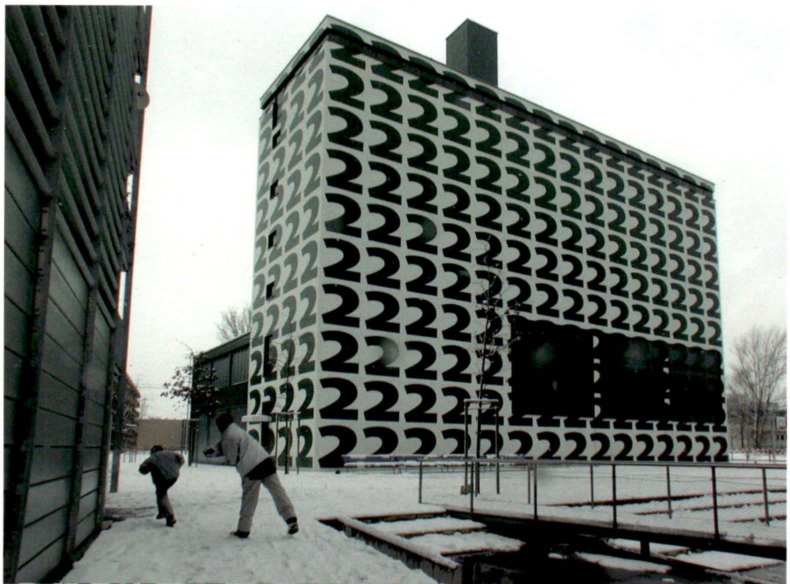

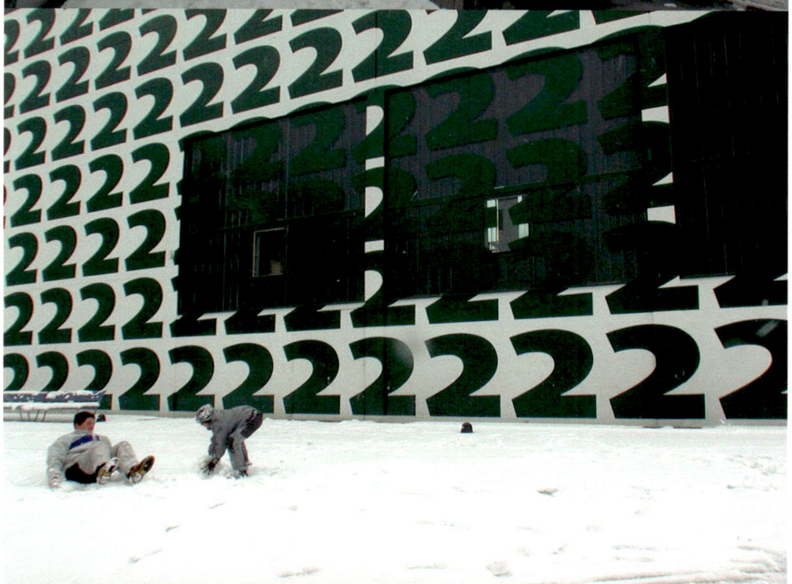

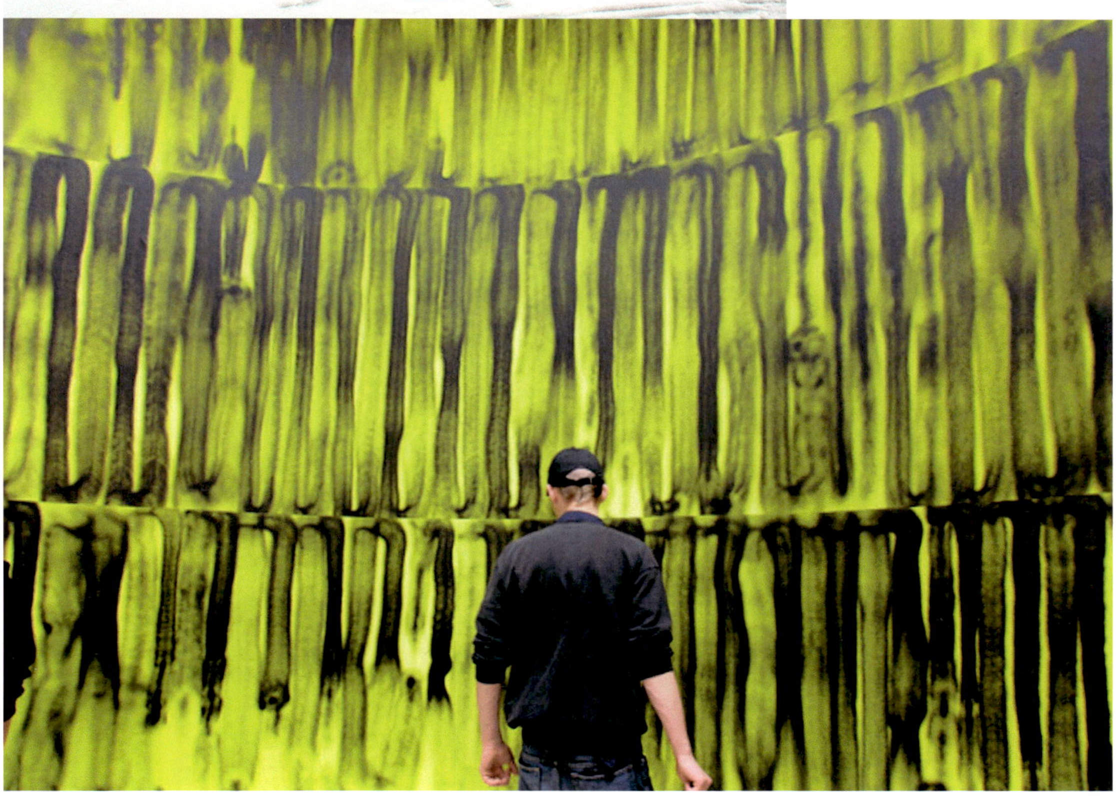

8e Renée Levi, *Untitled*, 2003. Acrylic white on Fluo orange

9a/b Anne-Sophie Mutter

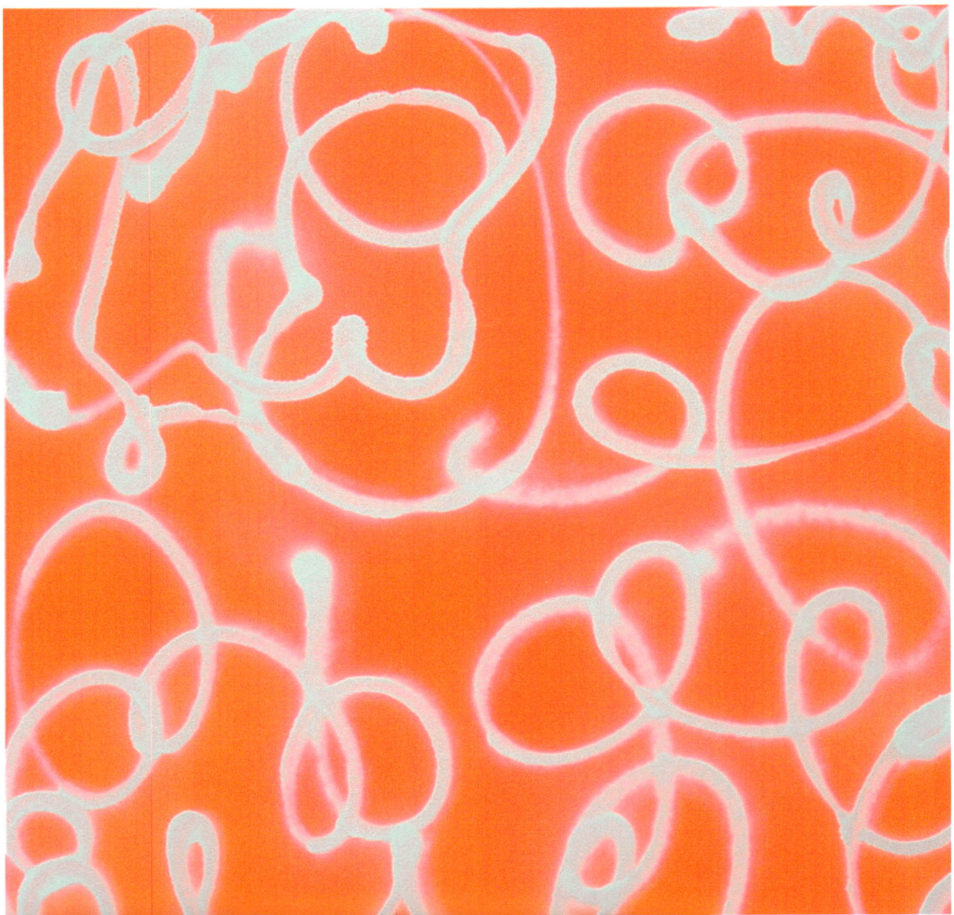

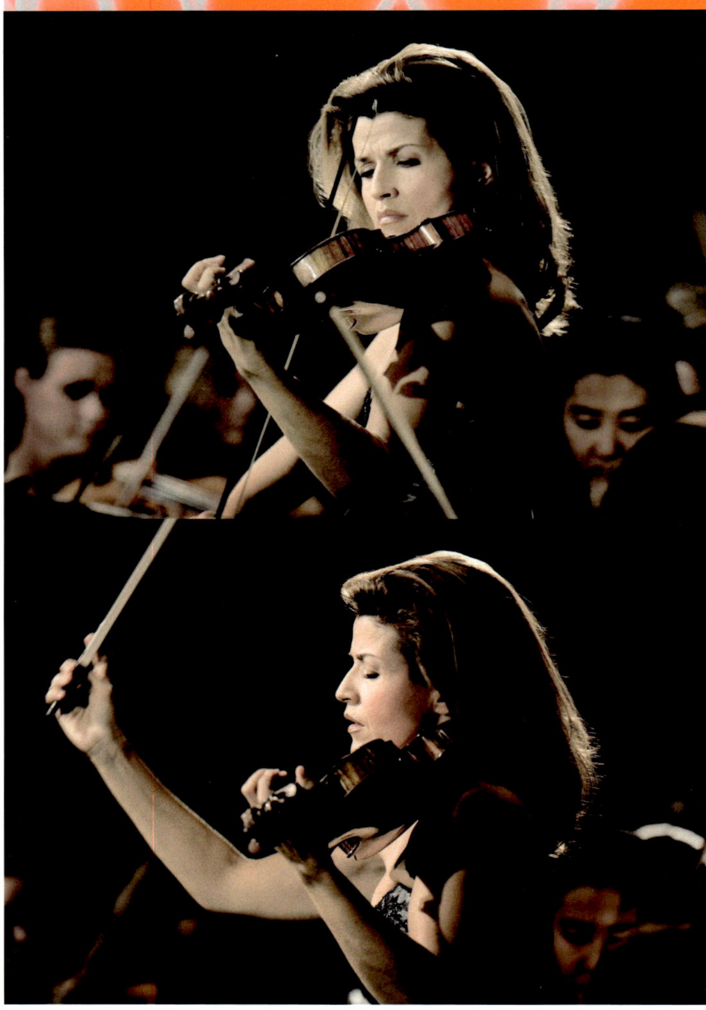

9c Anne-Sophie Mutter, Mozart Year 2006
10a Bruno Cathomas in *Gespenster*. Schaubühne Berlin, 2007

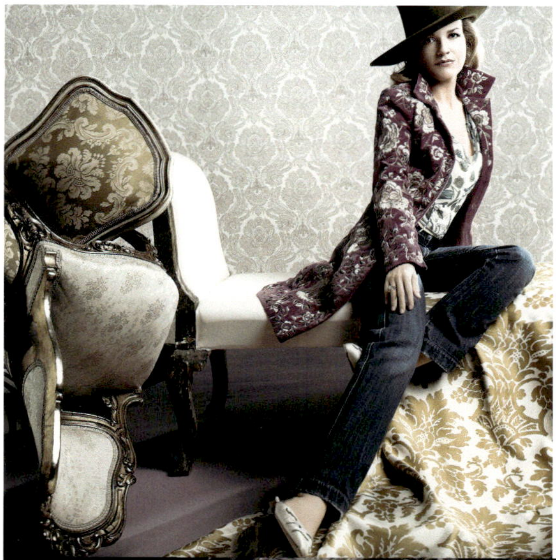

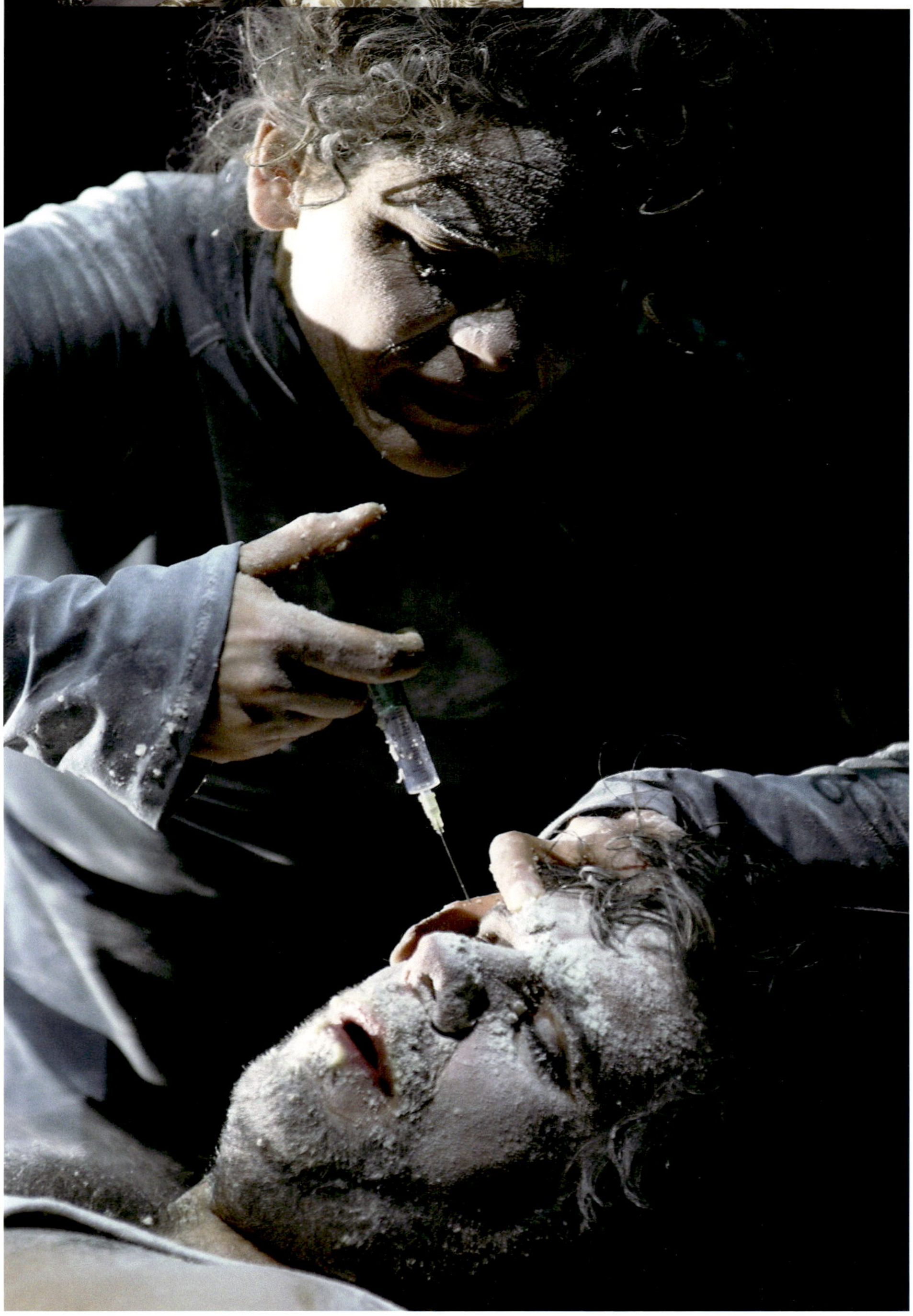

10b/c *Shoppen & Ficken*. Schaubühne Berlin, 2007. *Gespenster*. Schaubühne Berlin, 2007

11a *Vor Sonnenuntergang* directed by Erich Siedler, Schauspielhaus Basel, 2007

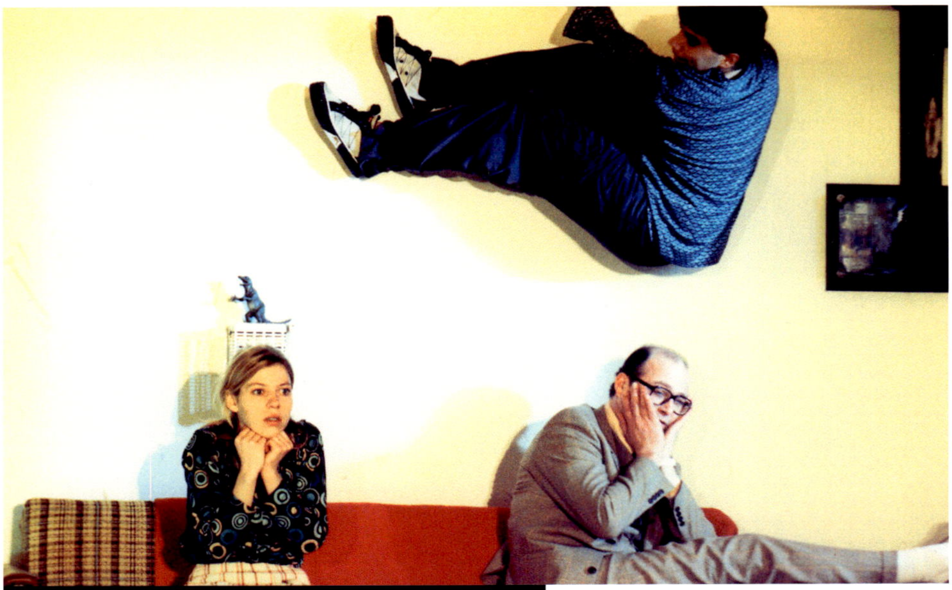

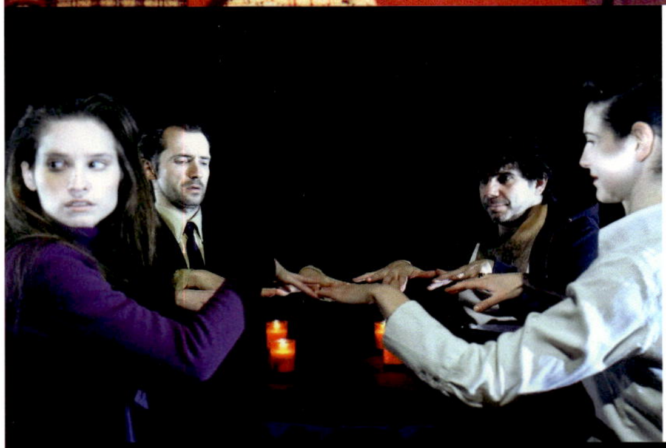

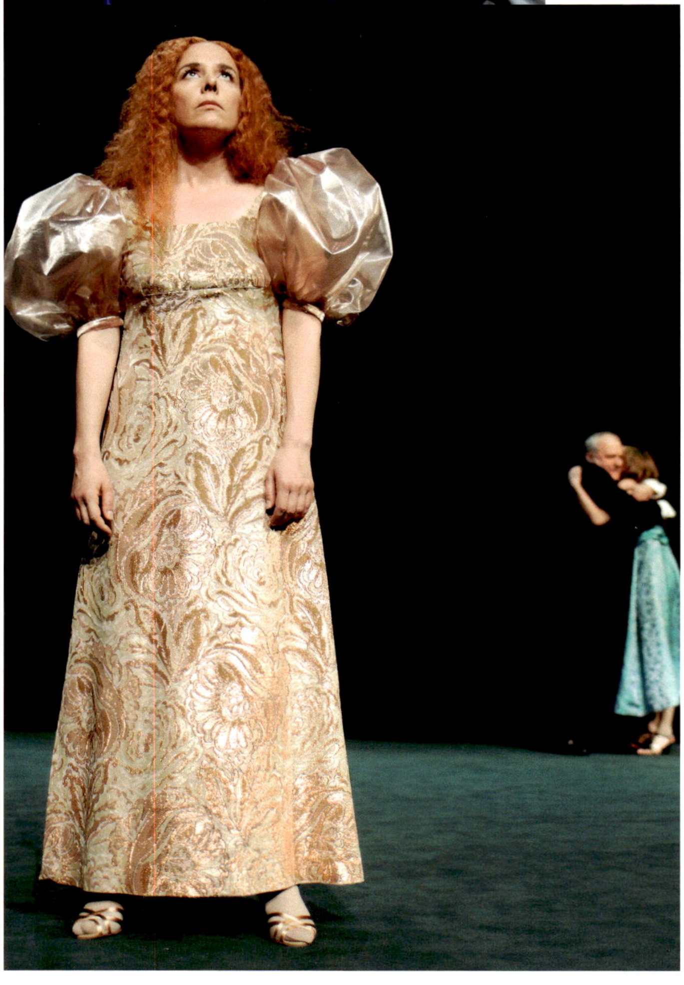

12a Silvie Rohrer in the title role in *Medea*. Burgtheater, 2006/07

12b As Marquise Duchamps in *Bérénice de Molière*. Burgtheater 2006/07

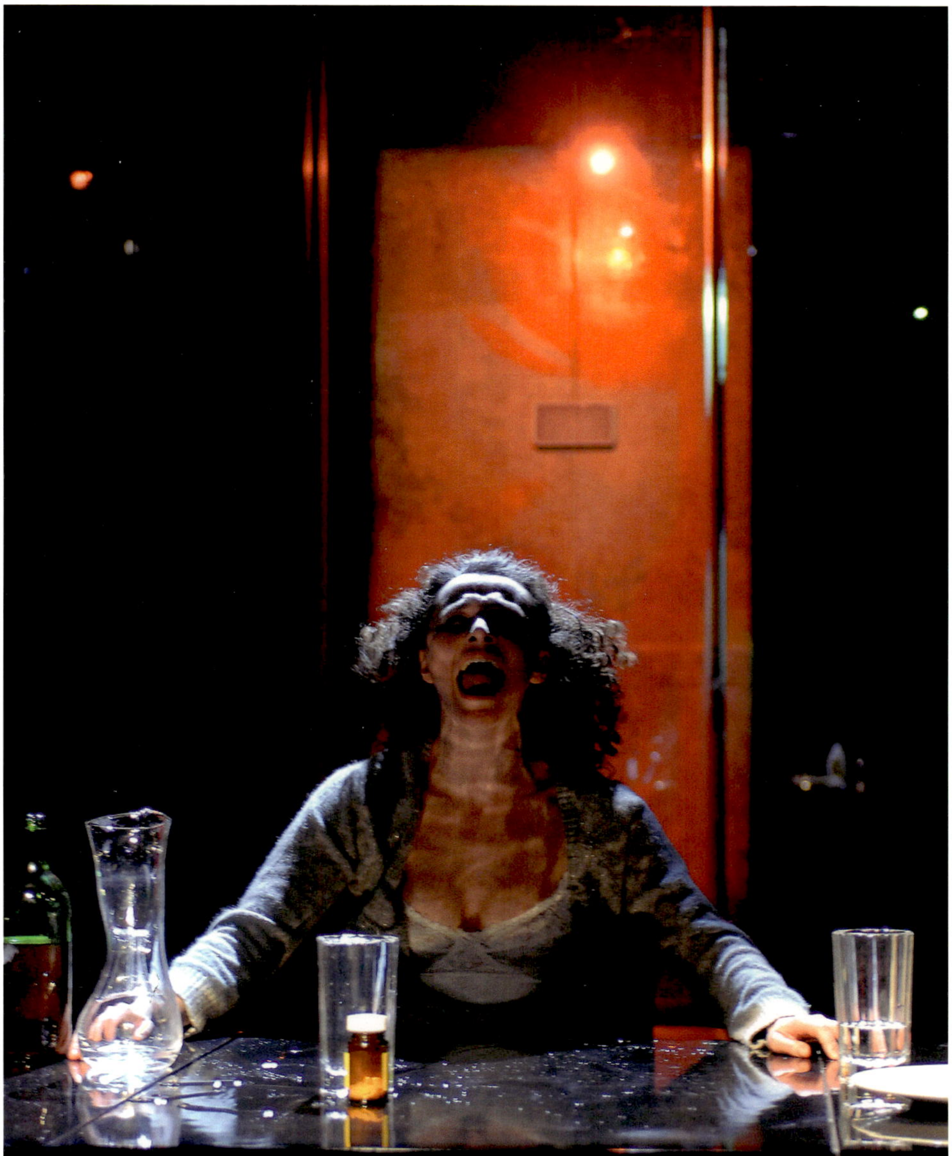

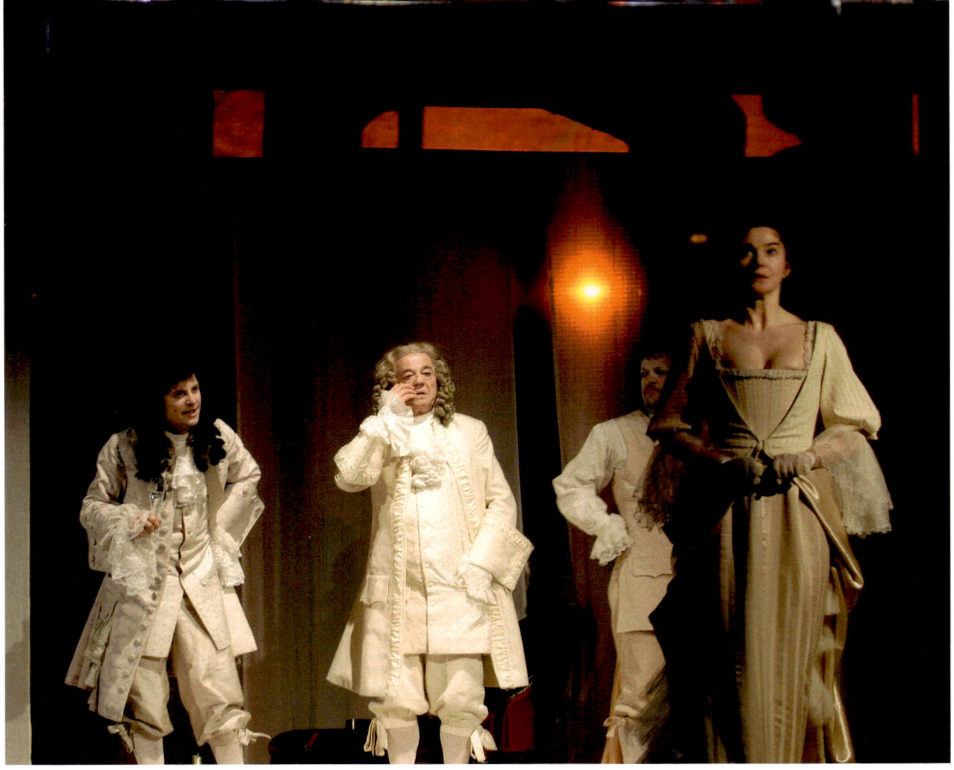

12c Silvie Rohrer as Marquise Duchamps in *Bérénice de Molière.* Burgtheater 2006/07

13a Yves Netzhammer, *Die umgekehrte Rüstung/The Reversed Armor.* DVD, 2002 (Photography Yves Netzhammer, sound Bjørn Melhus). Film still

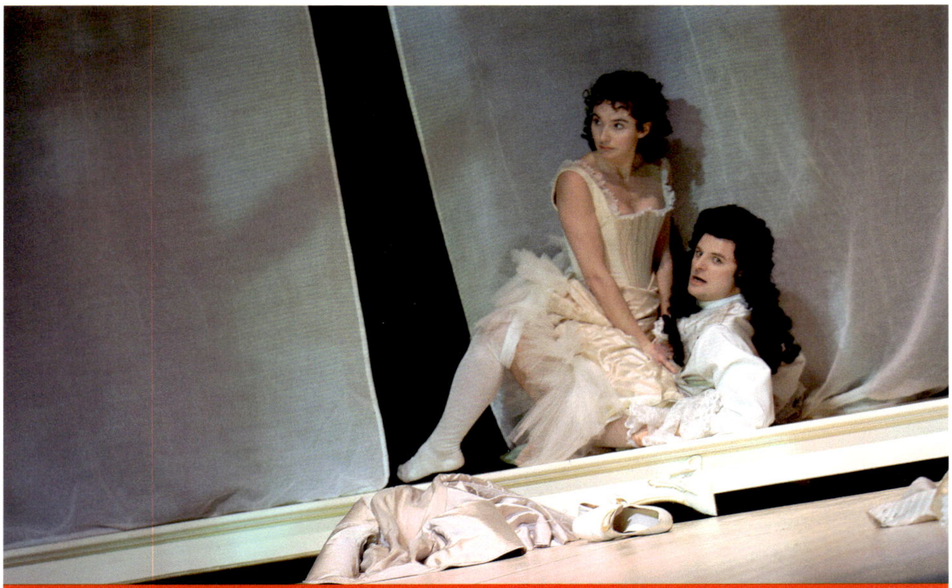

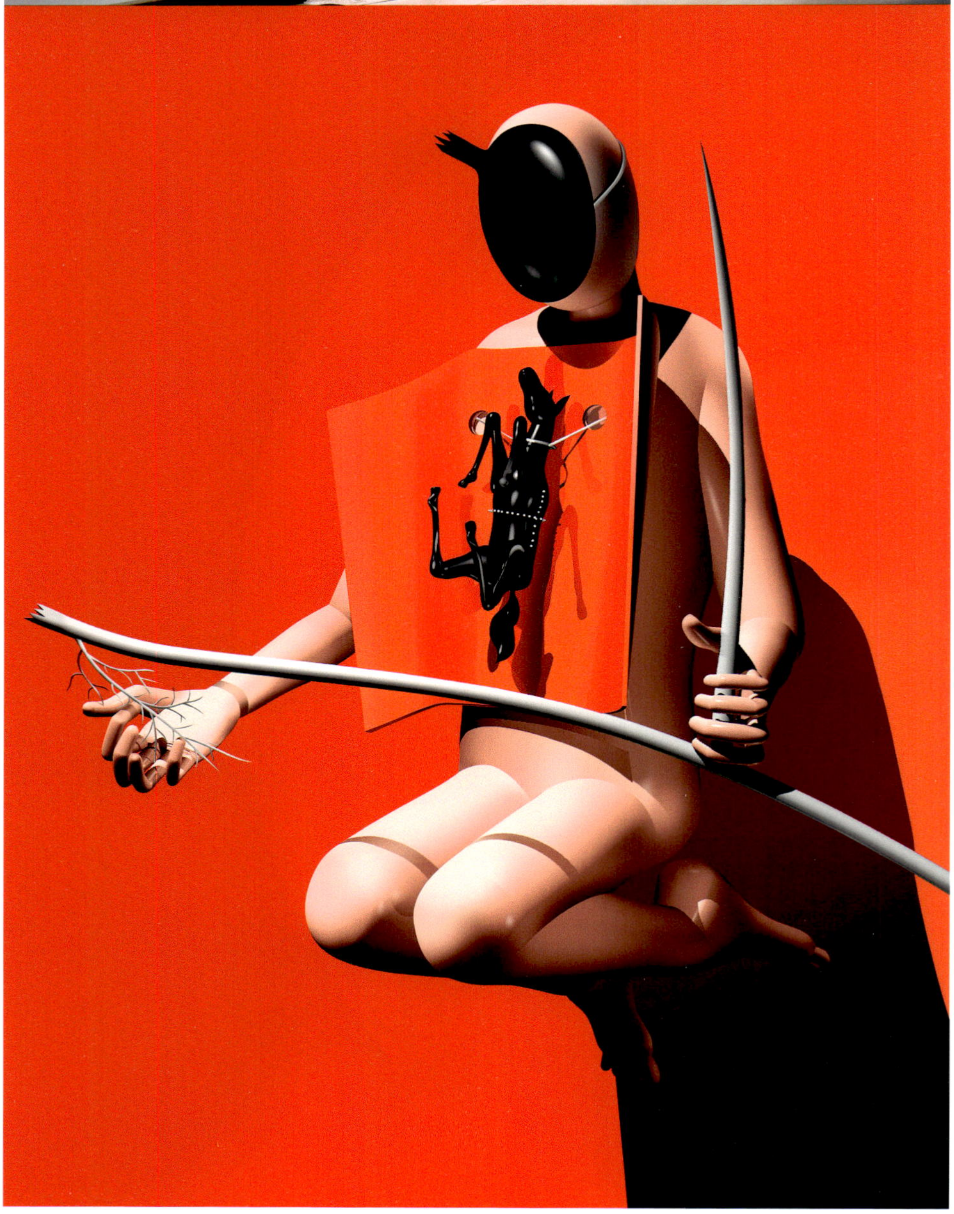

13b Yves Netzhammer, *Die Subjektivierung der Wiederholung*, Projekt B, *documenta XII*, Kassel, 2007. Film still

13c *Die Anordnungsweise zweier Gegenteile bei der Erzeugung ihres Berührungsmaximums/The arrangement of two opposites while their maximum contact is under generation*. DVD, 2005

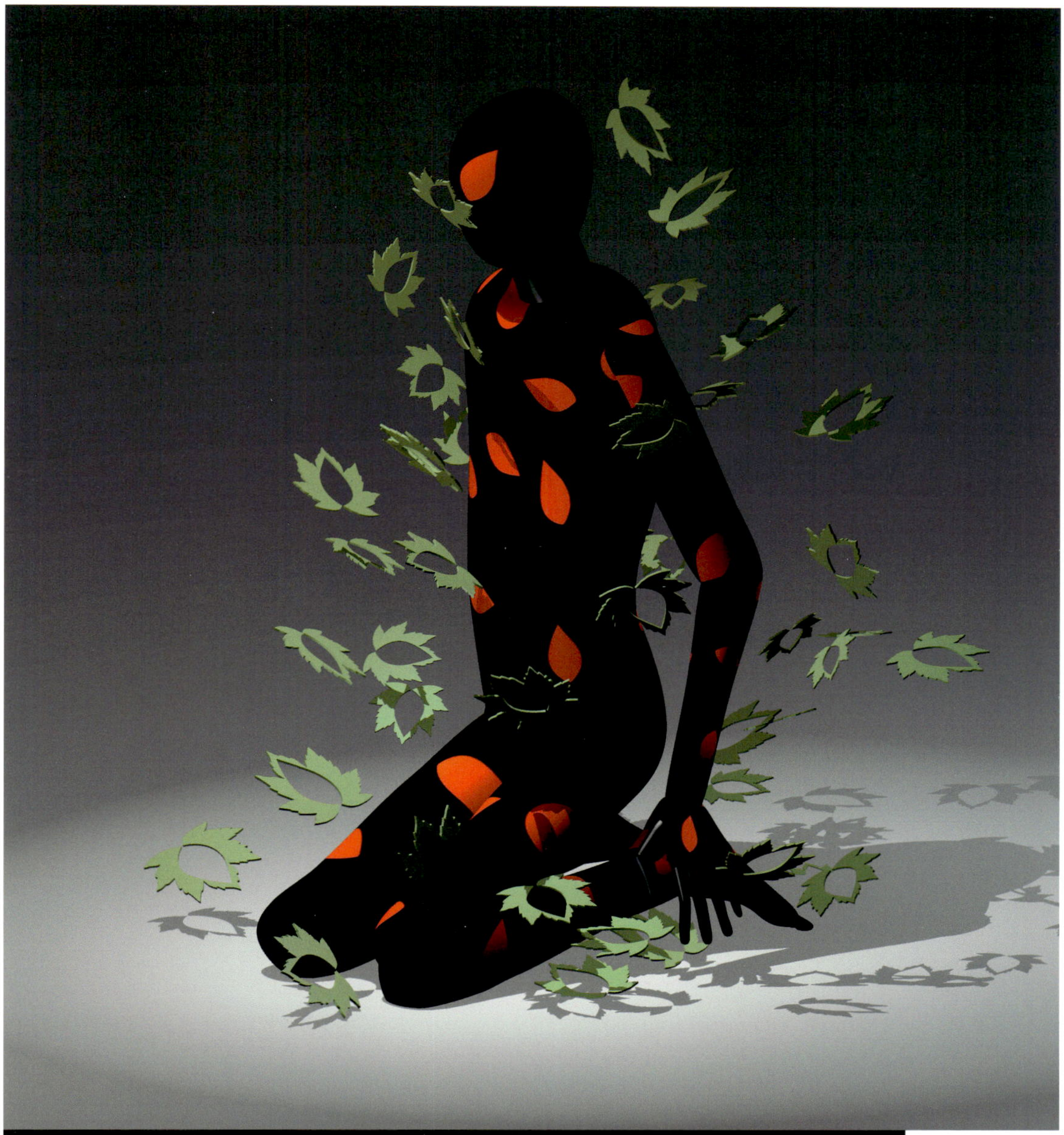

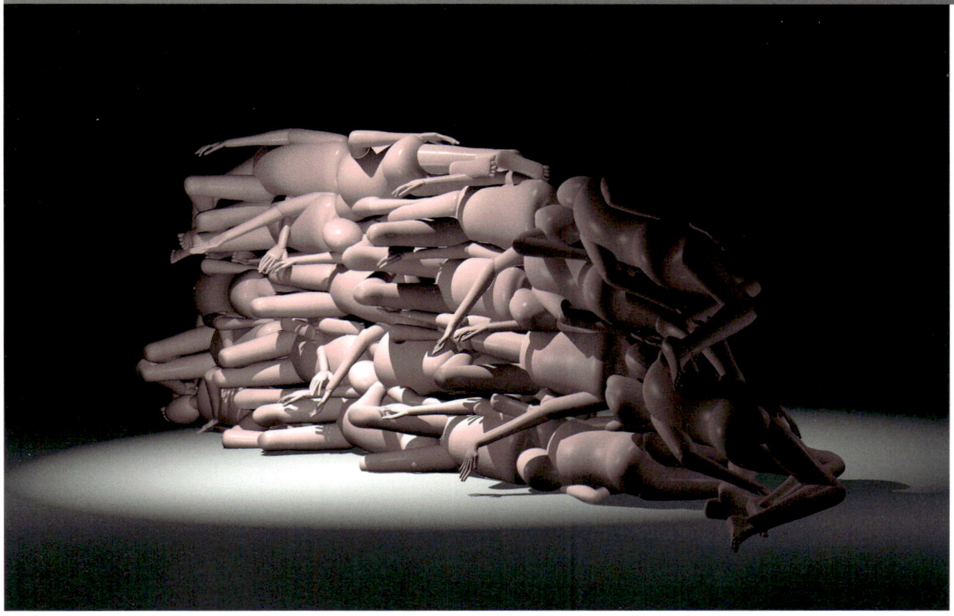

13d–f Yves Netzhammer, *Die Zeit bis eine Form entsteht, addiert mit der Zeit, bis die Form zerstört ist,* 2003. Film stills
13g *Die ungenauen Körper.* Video installation with balloon, 2006. Film still

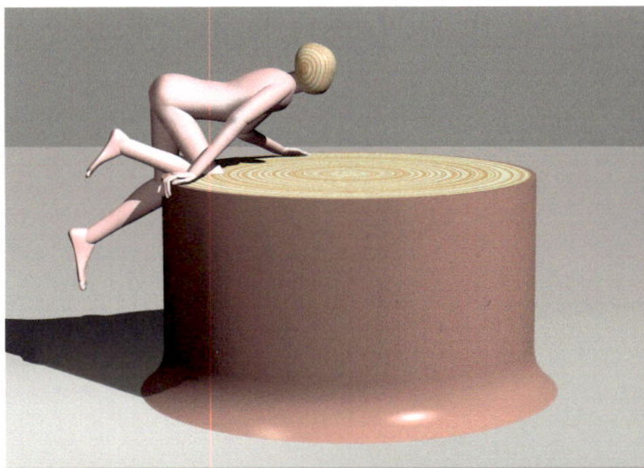

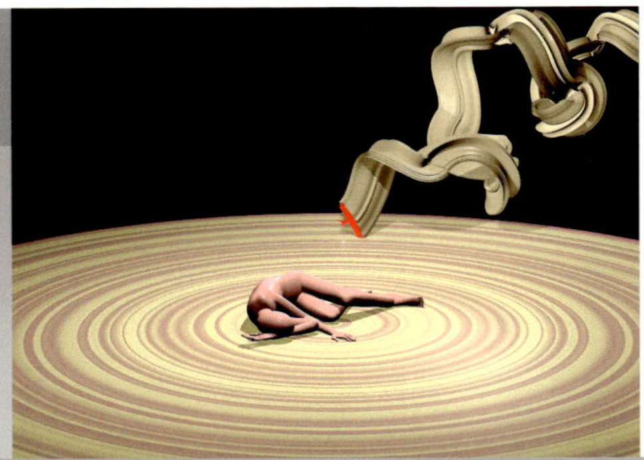

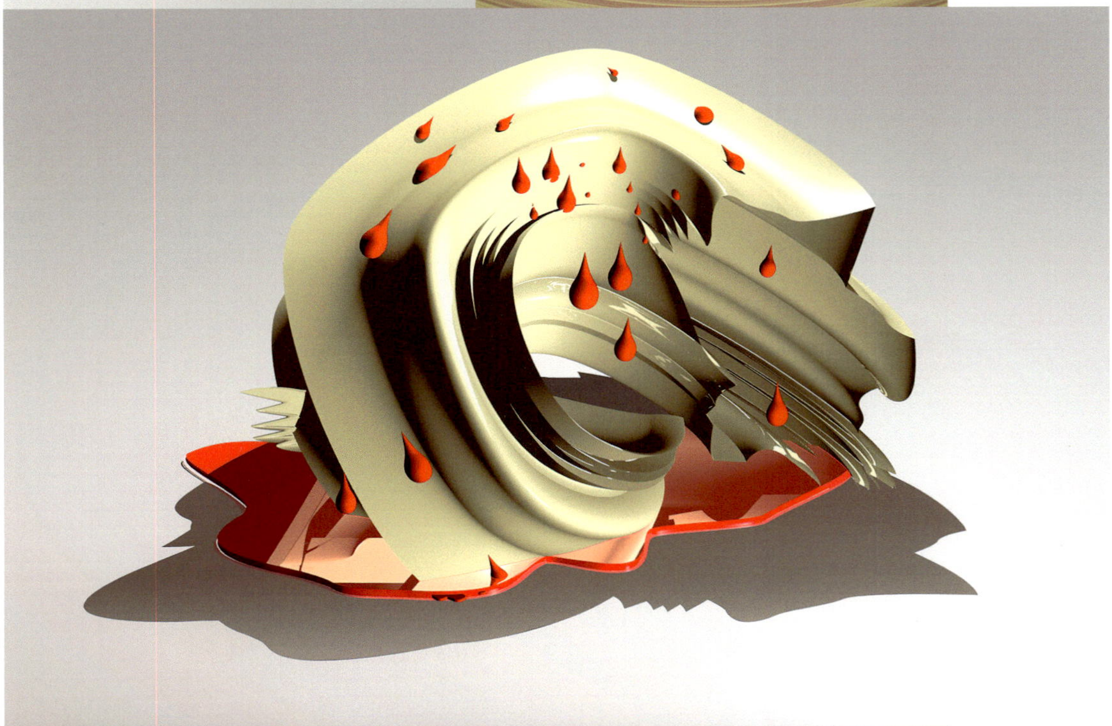

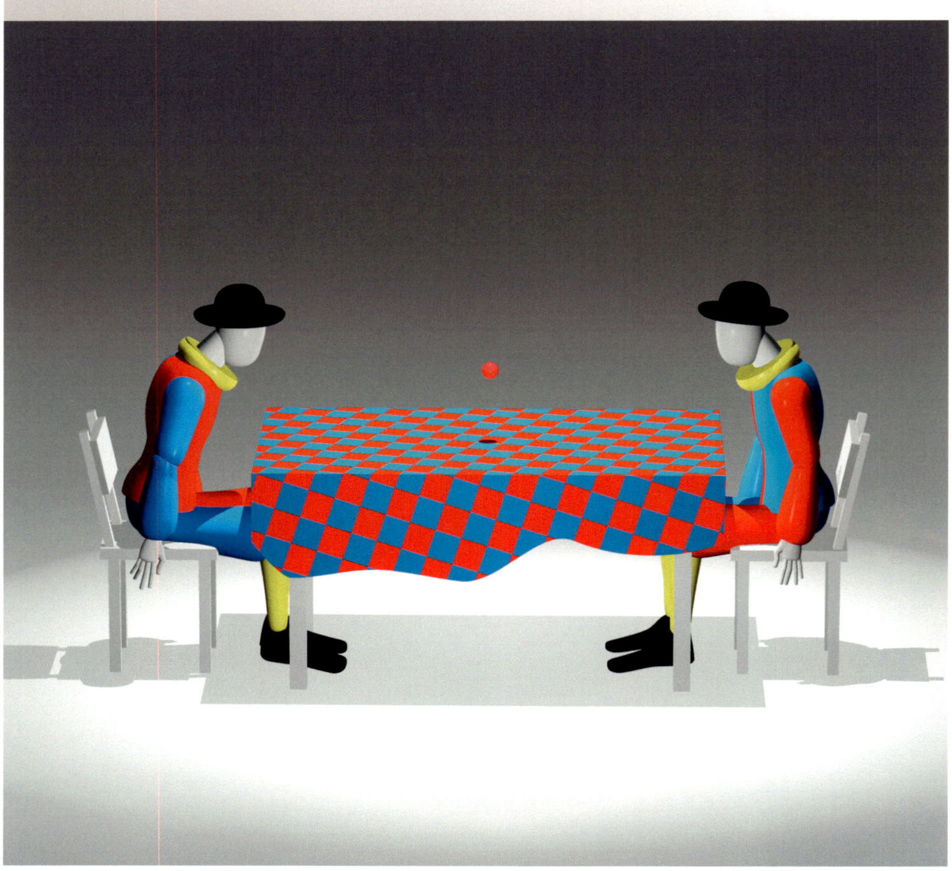

13h Yves Netzhammer, *Die Subjektivierung der Wiederholung*, Projekt A, Swiss Pavilion at the Venice Biennale, 2007. Film still

14a/b *Maria Stuart* directed by Samuel Schwarz, Theater am Neumarkt, Zurich, 2007

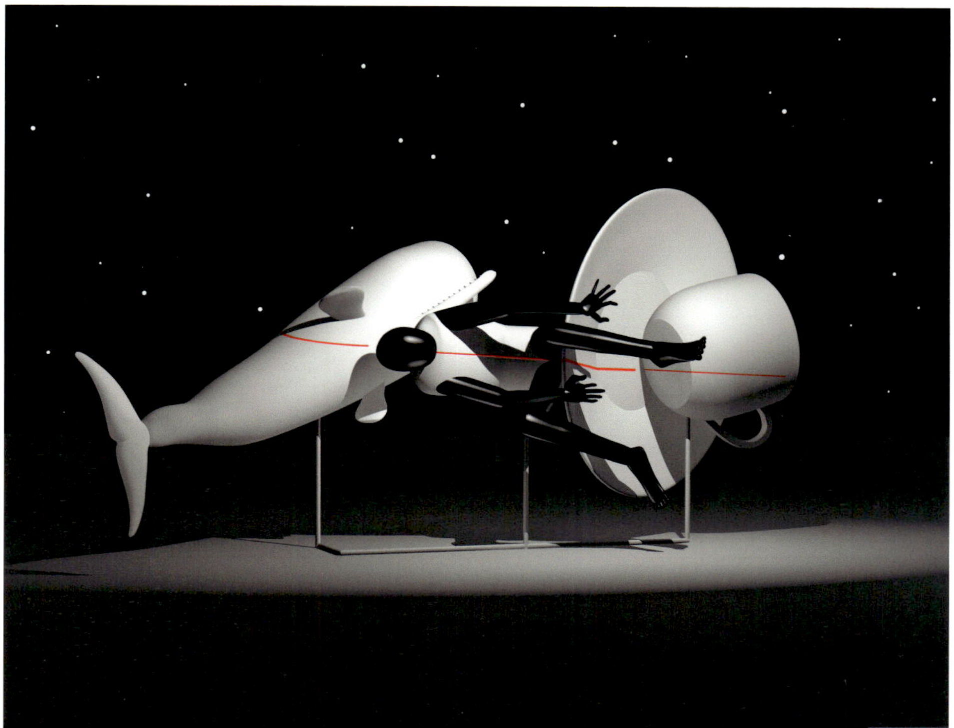

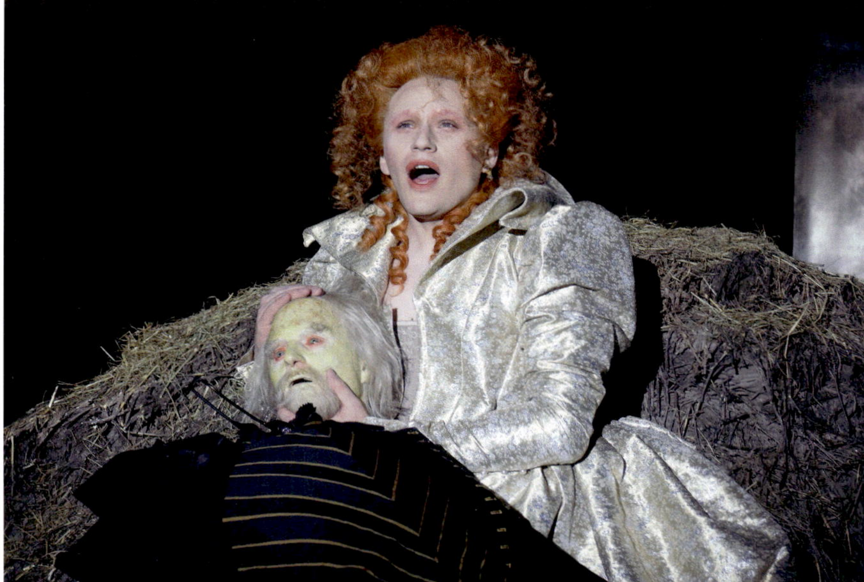

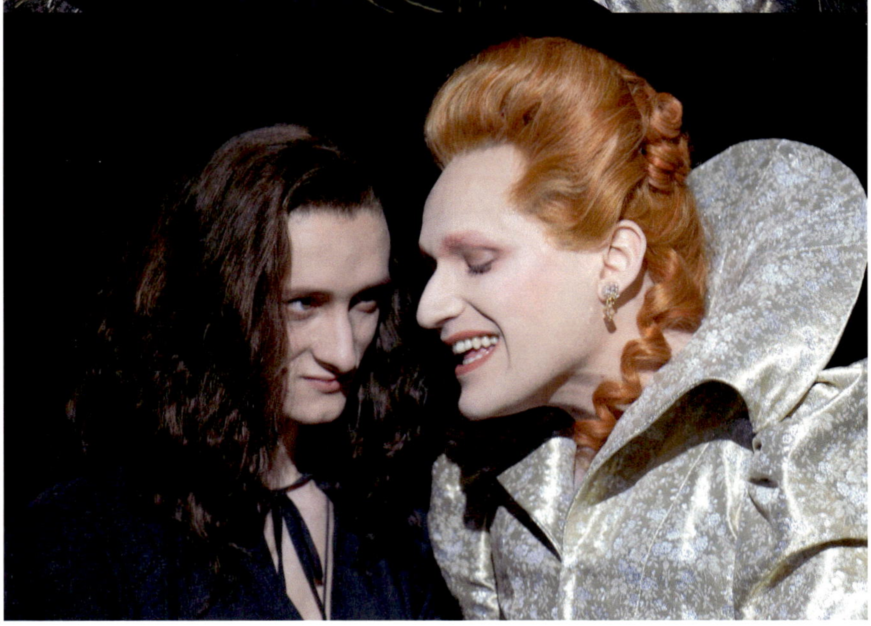

15a Christine Streuli, *bad mood,* 2006. Enamel paint on wood

15b *Ich lieb dich, ich lieb dich nicht...,* 2004. Acrylic and enamel paint on cotton

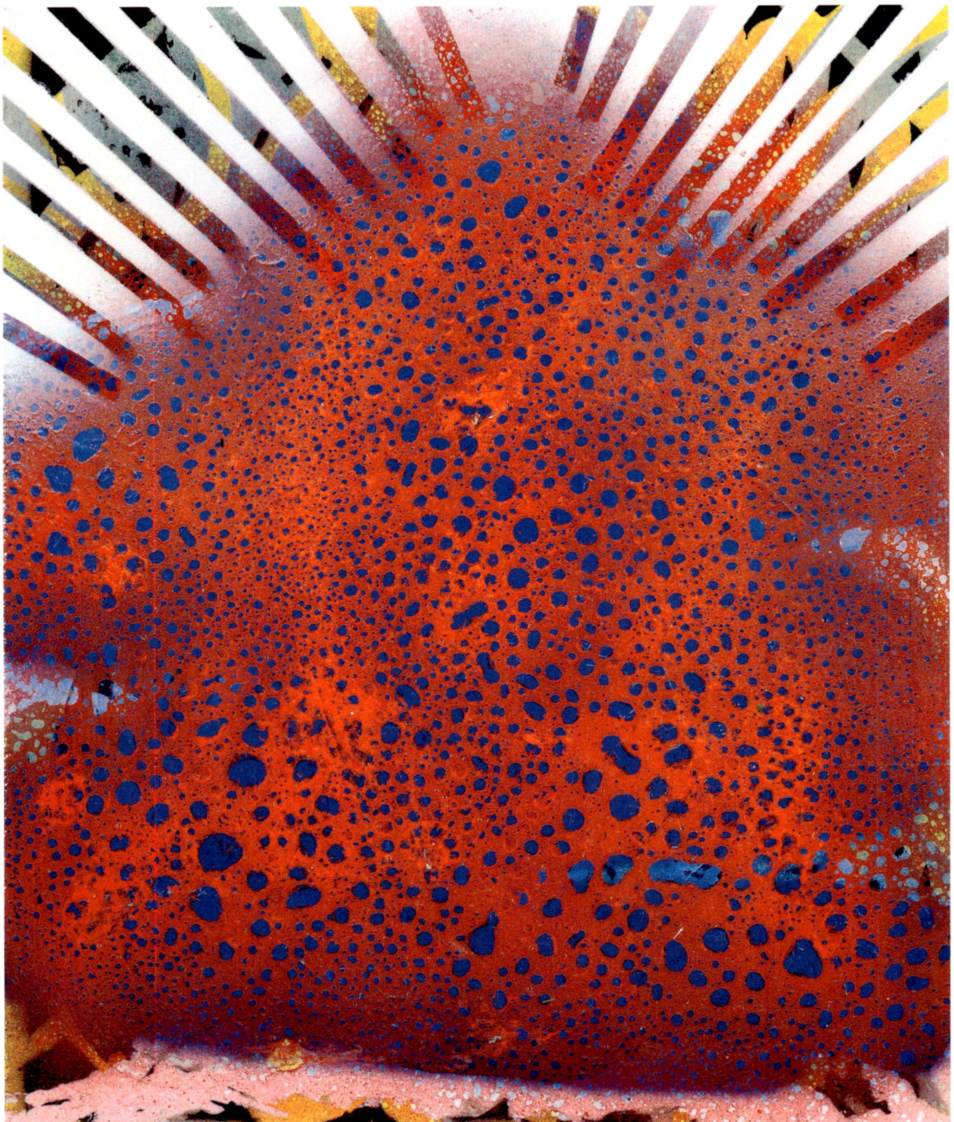

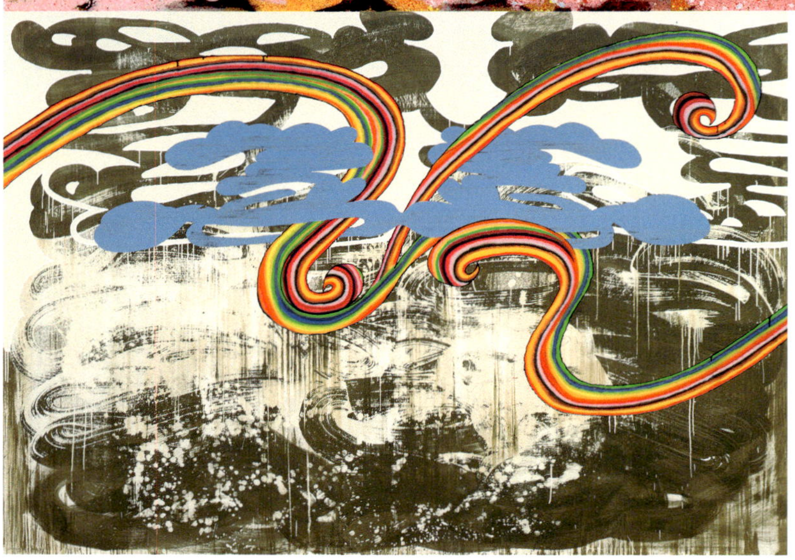

15c *ensemble ensemble*, 2005. Installation, Kunstraum Kreuzlingen, curated by Roman Kurzmeyer

15d *Groteskenvase mit Blumen*, 2004. Enamel paint on aluminum

15e *horizon takes me*, 2006. Acrylic and enamel paint on cotton

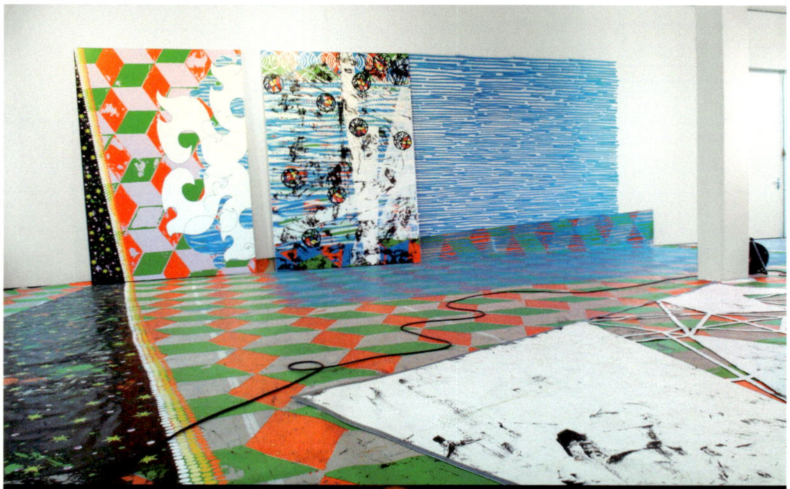

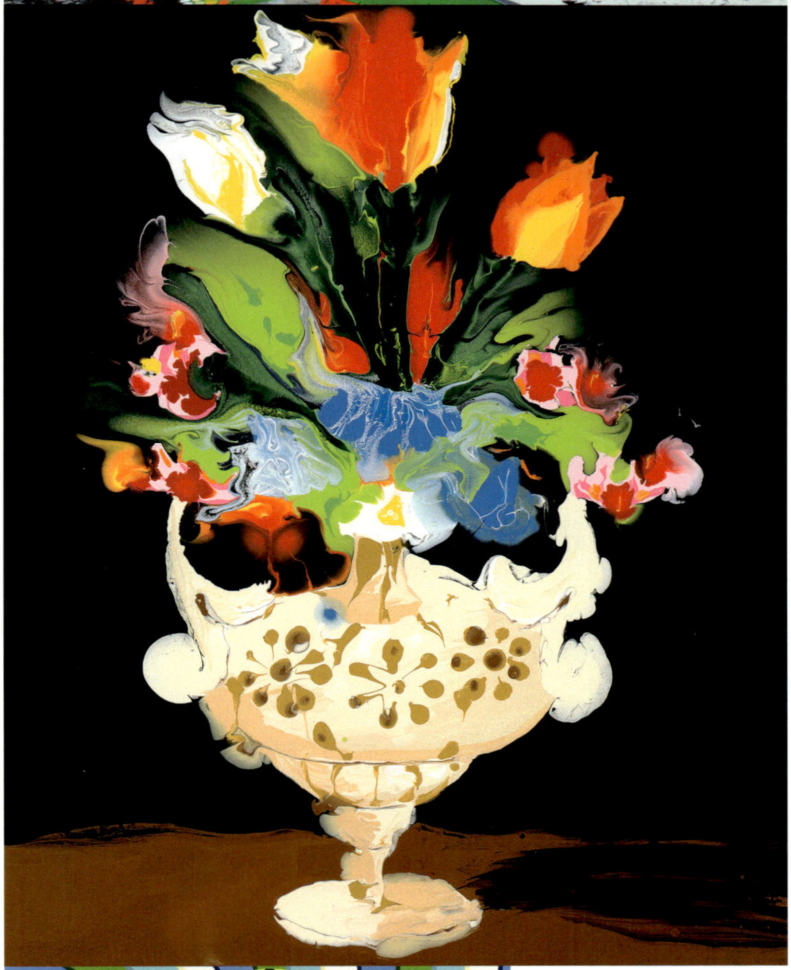

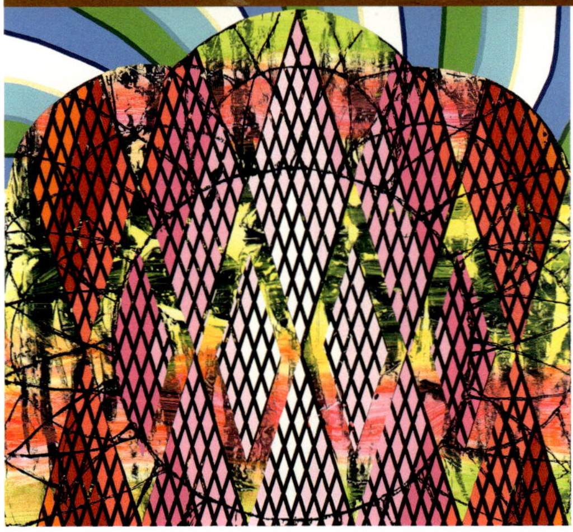

"Sharp equals true!" With this protest slogan, the students of the photography program revolted against the rigid demands for technical perfection issued by representatives of professional interests. They repudiated the hard, polished surfaces and standardized formulae of commercial photography, opposing them with the faded, the discolored, the anecdotally trivial, in low focus or poor coloring. To the present day, subjective artistic expression continues to enjoy a comeback, thanks to Nan Goldin: unretouched and successful.

Four walls and two children are the protagonists of her de-defined, anarchic, and highly poetic *Family Album* 1 his monstrosities alternate masterfully between the absurd, the comic, and the existential 3; her tableaux are "unlimited" in their strange and provocative ambivalence of beauty and defamiliarization 4; lately, he has been oscillating between photography and painting, an overstretched string, one that nonetheless seems only to heighten his expressive potential and artistic status 2.

1

Ruth Erdt (*1965)

She takes photographs, arranging mostly her family (*The Gang,* Verlag Lars Müller 2001) within the four walls of her own home in various combinations and guises: single mothers, beloveds, fathers, substitute fathers, lovers and, in the center her children Eva and Pablo; also friends and somehow those who just drop by. Gushes of blood, bouquets of tulips, toothpicks, moths, wild forest berries are stills that codefine the context and open up the associated spaces. Her work is a picture archive of the last twenty years, with hundreds of pictures that suggest the "family" in ever newer relationships and constellations. These are tableaux with ever new dramaturgies, chronologies, and leaps in time. They are clusters of pictures that render visible the corporeality, the embrace, but also the depths in these relationships, dirty tones, de-definings, the vague, and the distant.

The family album, or the ornament of her family, mirrors the family relationships of the present or that which remains of the image of a healthy family. It shows itself to be fragile, destructive, and at the same time highly poetic. The power and force of the photographs occasionally rises to the level of baroque allegories that recall the paintings of Caravaggio. There lies within them a great concentration and density and a medial directness in the sense of photography's explosive power.

2

Cat Tuong Nguyen (*1969)

At first it was bright, overexposed photographic portraits that drew away from the figurative and created their mysterious effect in abstract atmospheric realms. Cat Tuong Nguyen's diploma project was awarded the School of Art and Design promotional prize. He described his photographs of the time as "making the non-visible visible," thus exploring the outermost boundaries of photographic technique and expressive possibilities. In a subsequent thematic focus in Project 238, "Awareness of what Living in our Time Involves," he took photographs of clearly staged scenes, which created photographic allegories on complex contemporary issues such as the pressure to succeed, poverty, and homelessness. More recently, it has been exploding pastries, firecrackers, and small fires that leave their destructive mark on his photographs and thus add caustic potential to the usually controlled and cold medium of photography. At present, we see colliding airplanes, chain reaction car pileups, and other catastrophes as a combination of media images of victims and bystanders, and also pure expressive painting, completely divorced from photography.

His fleeting constructions are so obviously artificial that they mercifully distance themselves from reality —without, however, relieving the viewer of the burden of thought. One has the impression that no medium will satisfy Cat Tuong Nguyen's urge to burst the confines of the expressive possibilities of photography. All of this is created in the form of small-format experimental staging in the confines of his studio, and then transferred for presentation in large format.

3

Olaf Breuning (*1971)

Olaf Breuning takes great interest in the absurd and monstrous. His large scenes depict something alien, carnevalizations laden with meaning. These arrangements evoke stories, question the point of human existence, but ultimately remain "only" a review of the ridiculous. There are optical fouls and put-ons, presented dramatically and ready for the stage, and also always somewhat incomplete and contrived. His extras are human groups or herd animals, sometimes embellished, sometimes clownish, sometimes ugly; they suggest realities, a kind of non-existent hyperreality, as everyone knows.

1

4
3 2

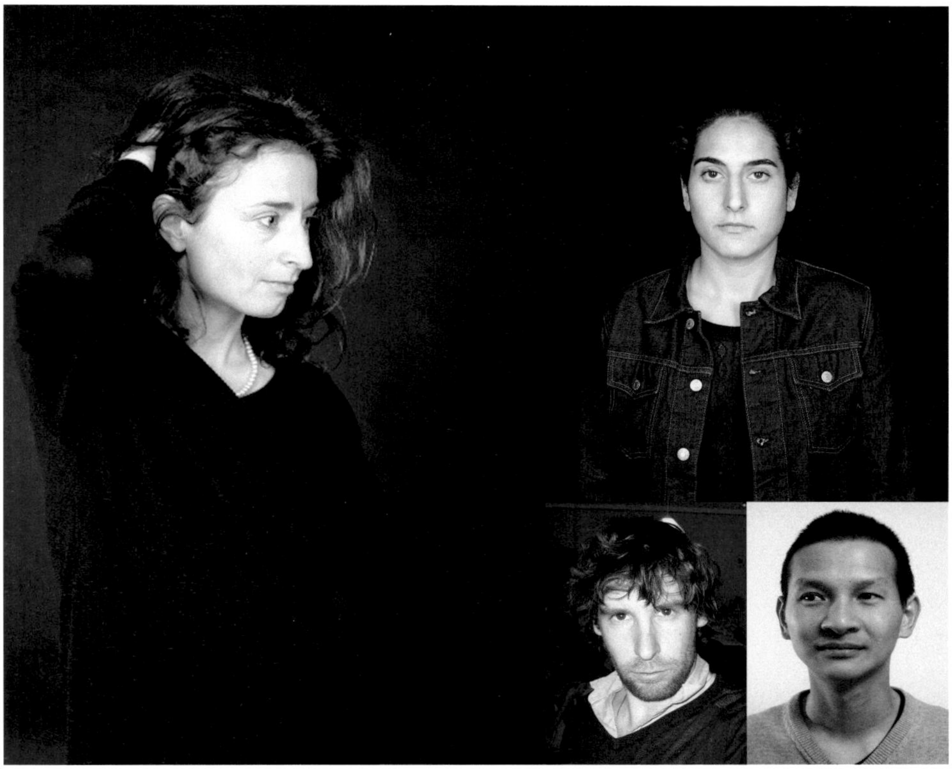

Breuning majored in photography and acquired international fame as a shooting star after he was exhibited by Beatrix Ruf in the Kunsthaus Glarus gallery. He "gilded" his cheerful relativities and disturbing paradoxes with the publication of the book *Ugly* (2001) at Hatje Cantz, richly illustrated and including responses from art critics.

4
Shirana Shahbazi (*1974)

In her diploma project, which attracted considerable attention, Shirana Shahbazi already concretized the cultural differences between Zurich, where she was studying, and Iran, where she was born. In a compelling and patchwork-like constellation of photographs of everyday Iranian life, bare landscapes, portraits, and photorealist paintings like those commissioned by the Iranian propaganda and advertising industries, she portrayed the foreign and unfamiliar—the distance of what is close by—as an aesthetic experience.

Despite its superficial precision and matter-of-factness, her photography evokes a multiple and ambiguous legibility, whereby the dialogue between the different pictures amounts to a way of dealing with the incommensurability of the subjects. The medial transformation of photography into realistic painting, of photography into carpet weaving, the installation of photography in combination with object worlds, the themes of landscape, portraiture, and still life are the "variable" manifestations and means of interpretation of her art. Accordingly, "variable interpretations" is one of her most frequently used expressions. She is in demand in international art where she appears prominently. She studied photography at the School of Art and Design Zurich.

1a–d Ruth Erdt, “The Gang: Eva,” 2000.—“Dogs,” 2000.—“Vic,” 2002.—“Thomas,” 1999

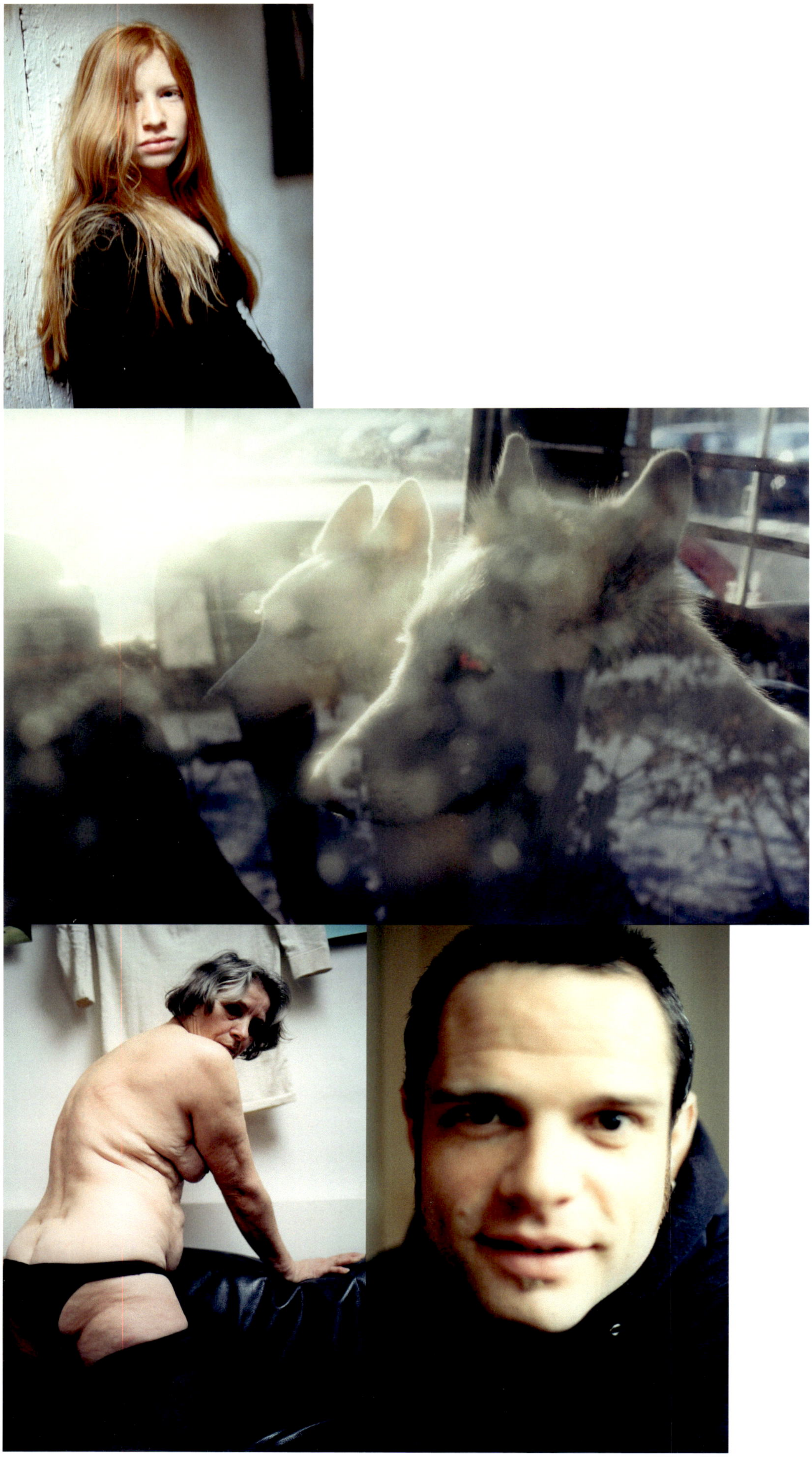

2a Cat Tuong Nguyen, “Untitled,” 2007
1e Ruth Erdt, “ The Gang: Serpent,” 2001
2b Cat Tuong Nguyen, “Kristallisation,” 2006

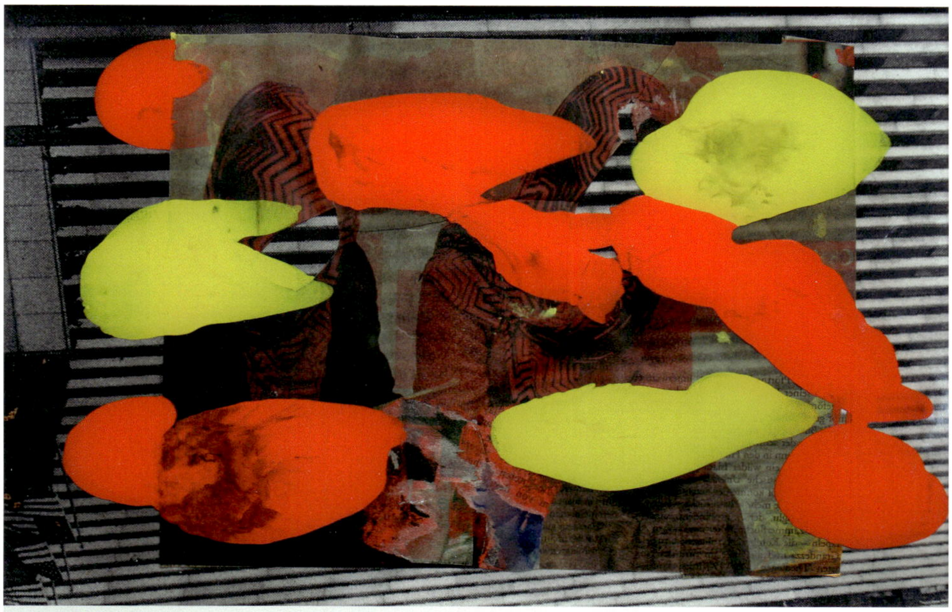

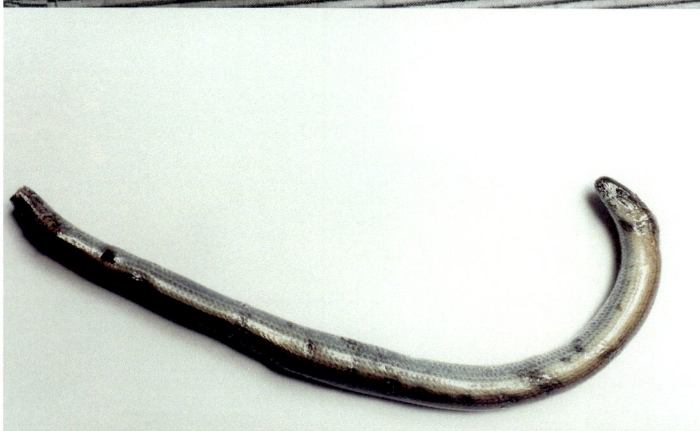

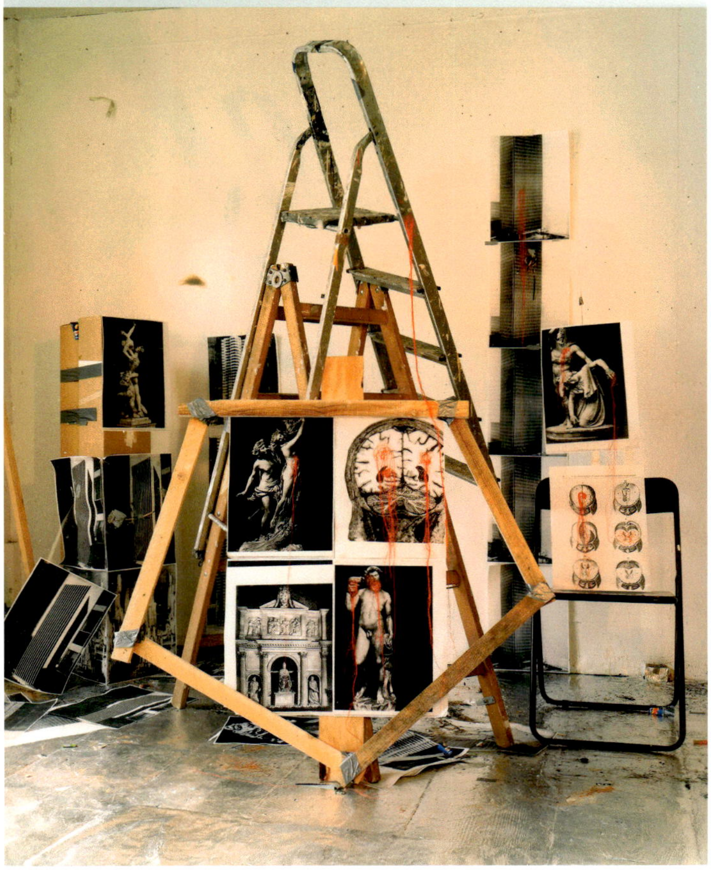

2c Cat Tuong Nguyen, "Antichamber III," 2005

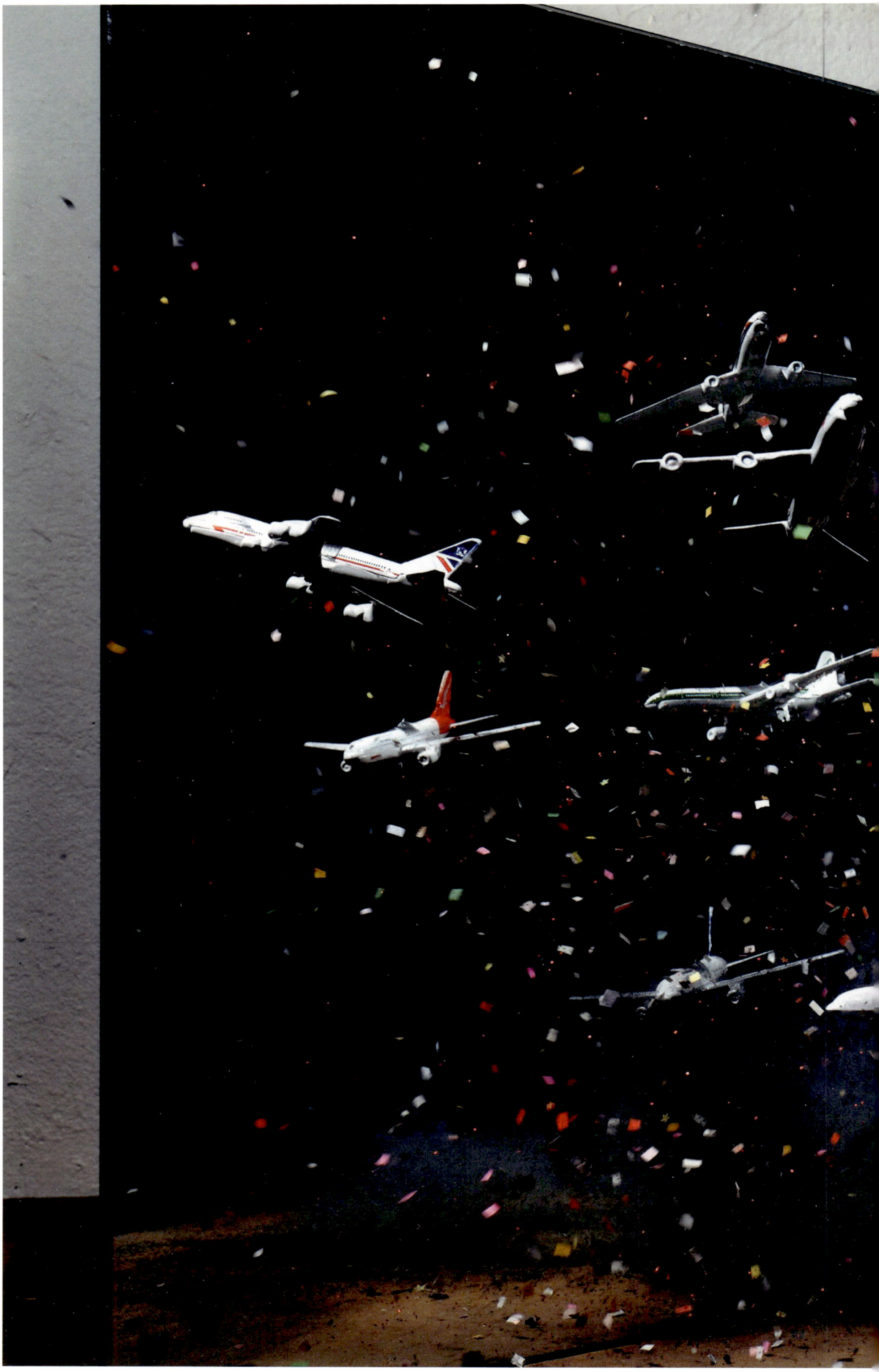

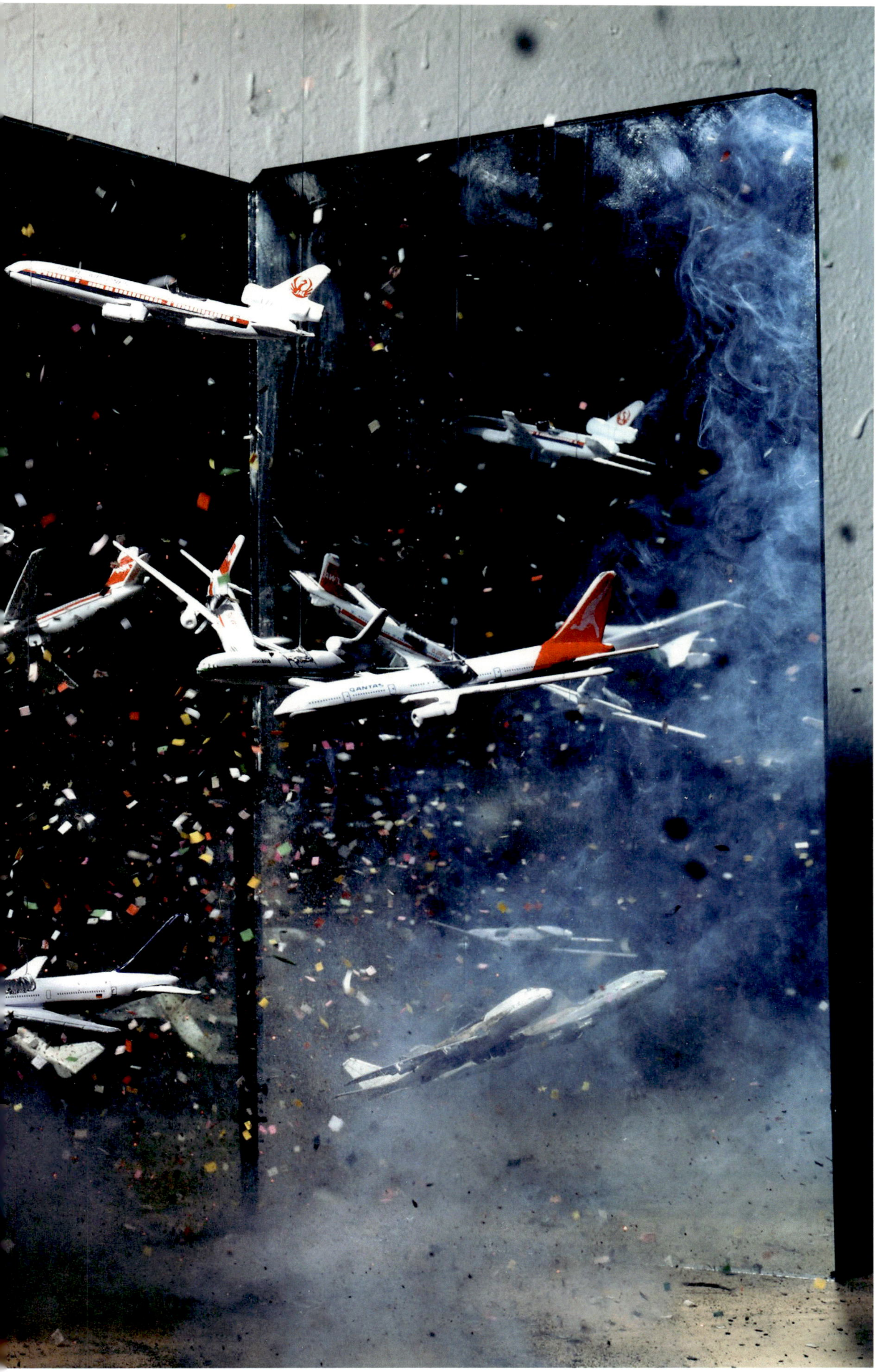

2d Cat Tuong Nguyen, "Brandung," 2006
2e "Homunculus," 2007
3a Olaf Breuning, "Easter Bunnies," 2004

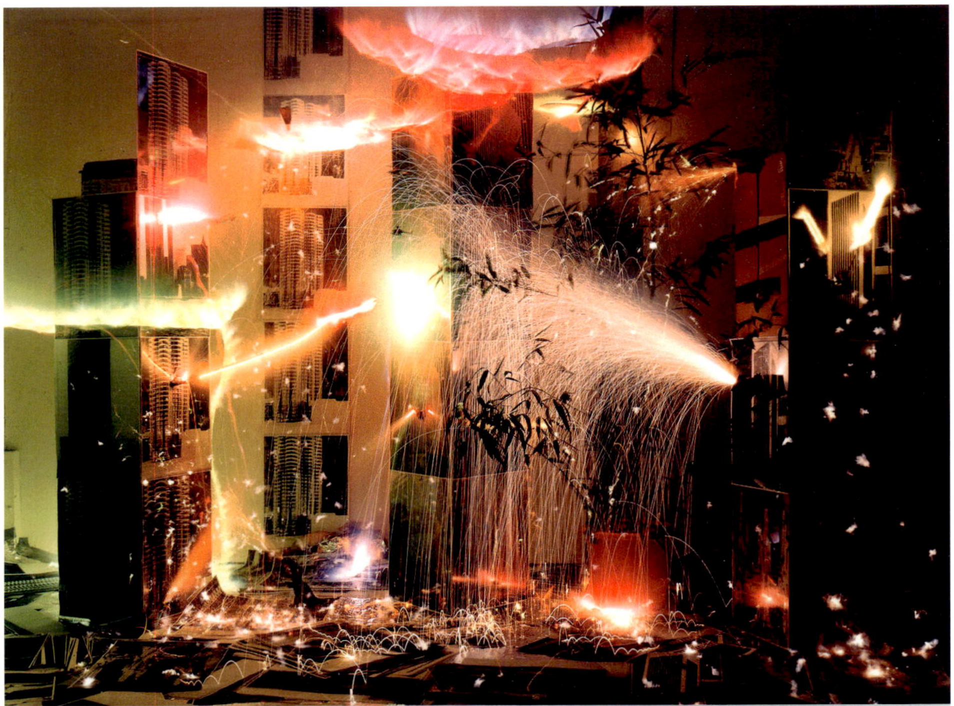

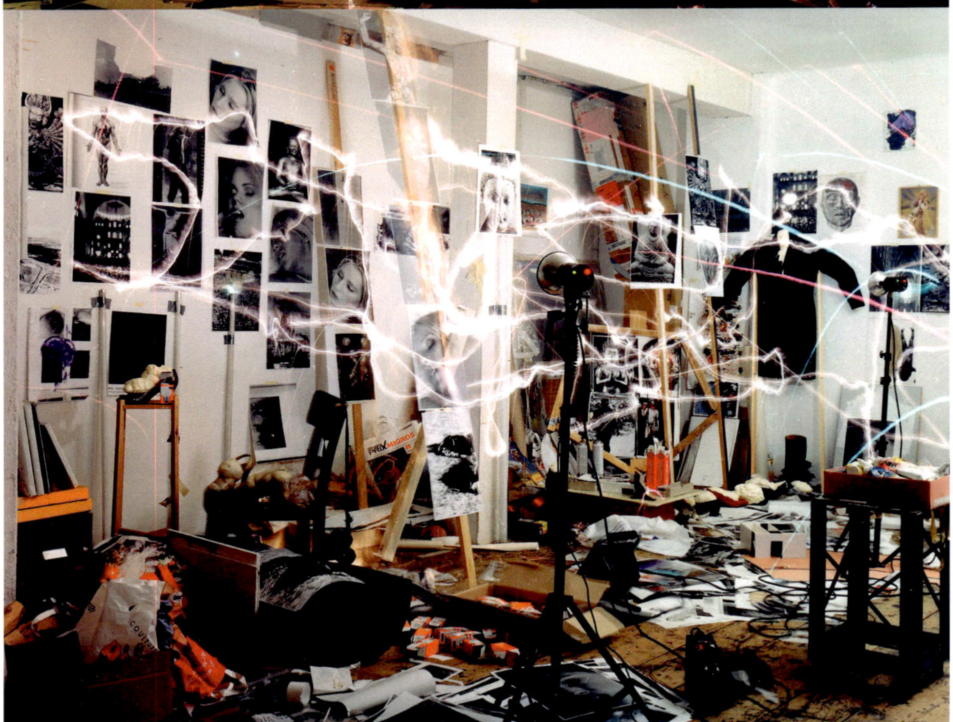

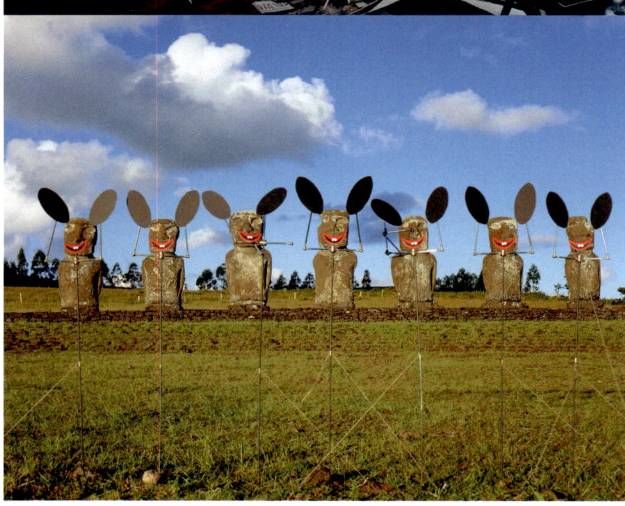

3b Olaf Breuning, “Can someone tell us why we are here?” 2006

3c “Cat,” 2002

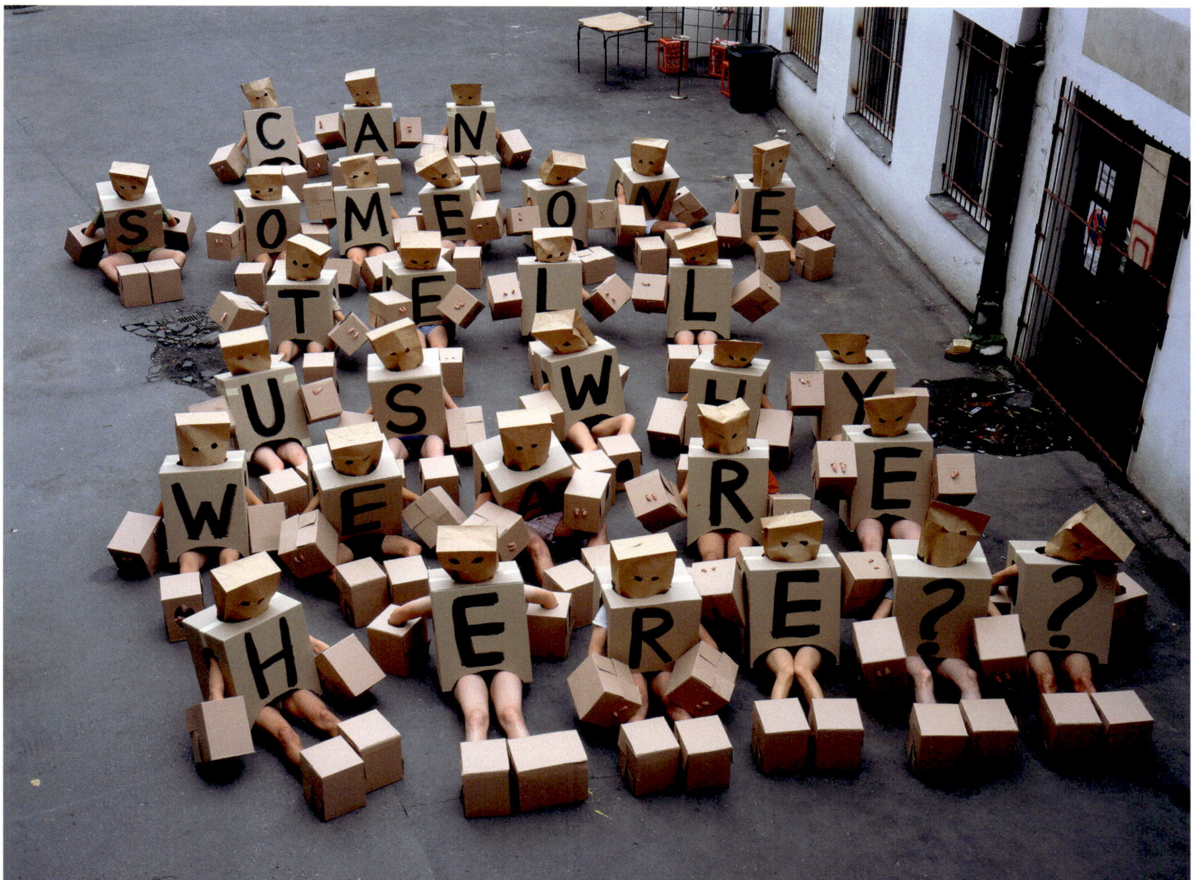

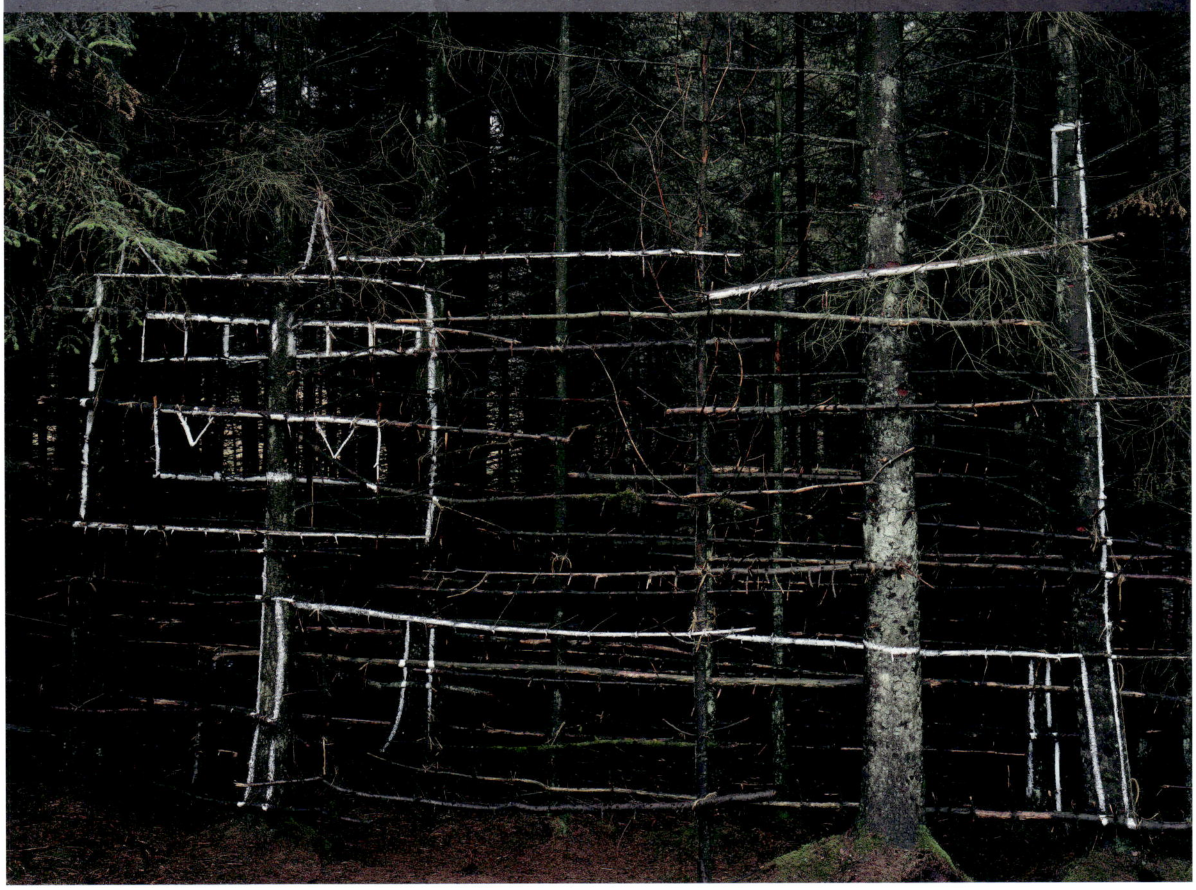

4a Shirana Shahbazi, “Tehran-03-2000”

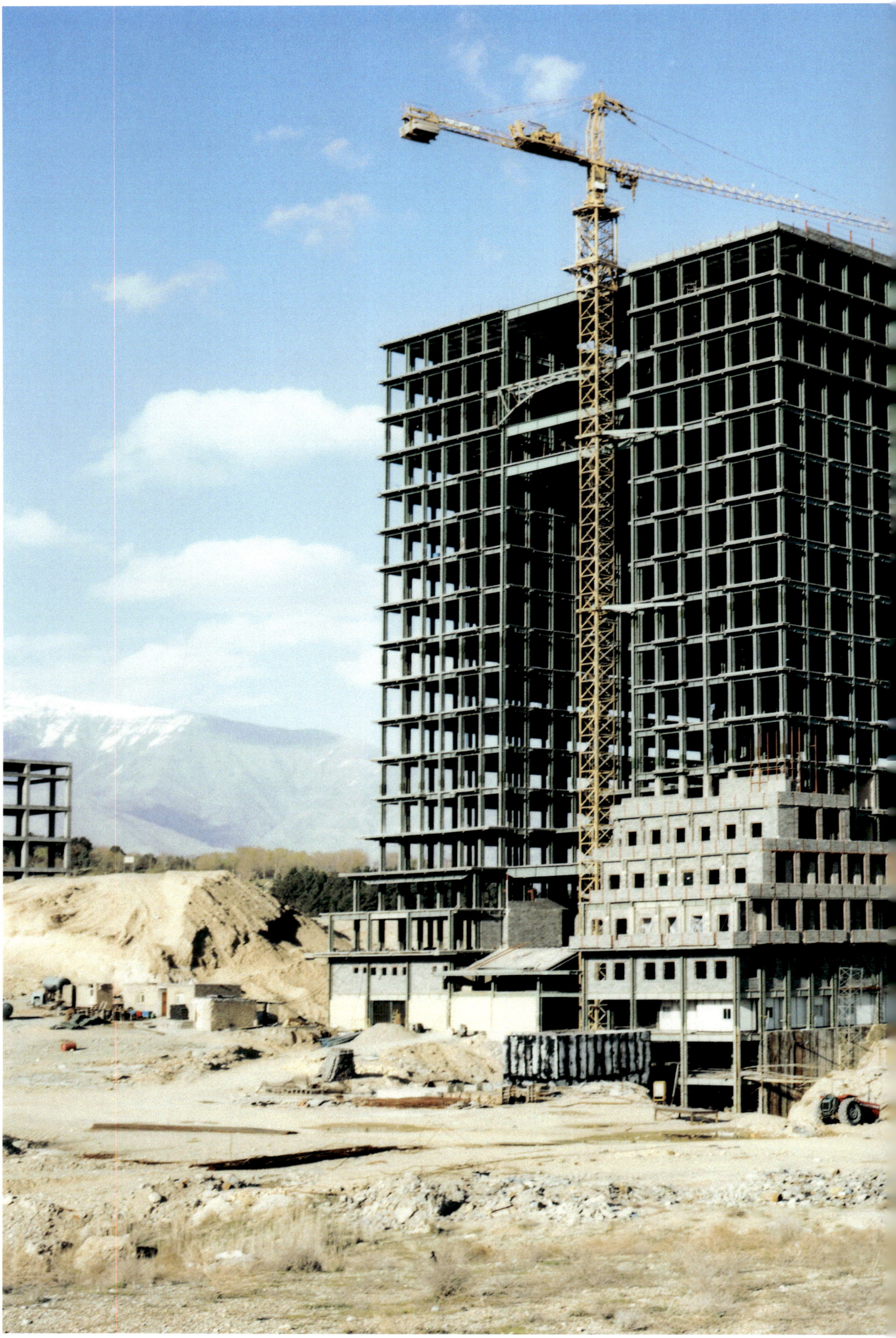

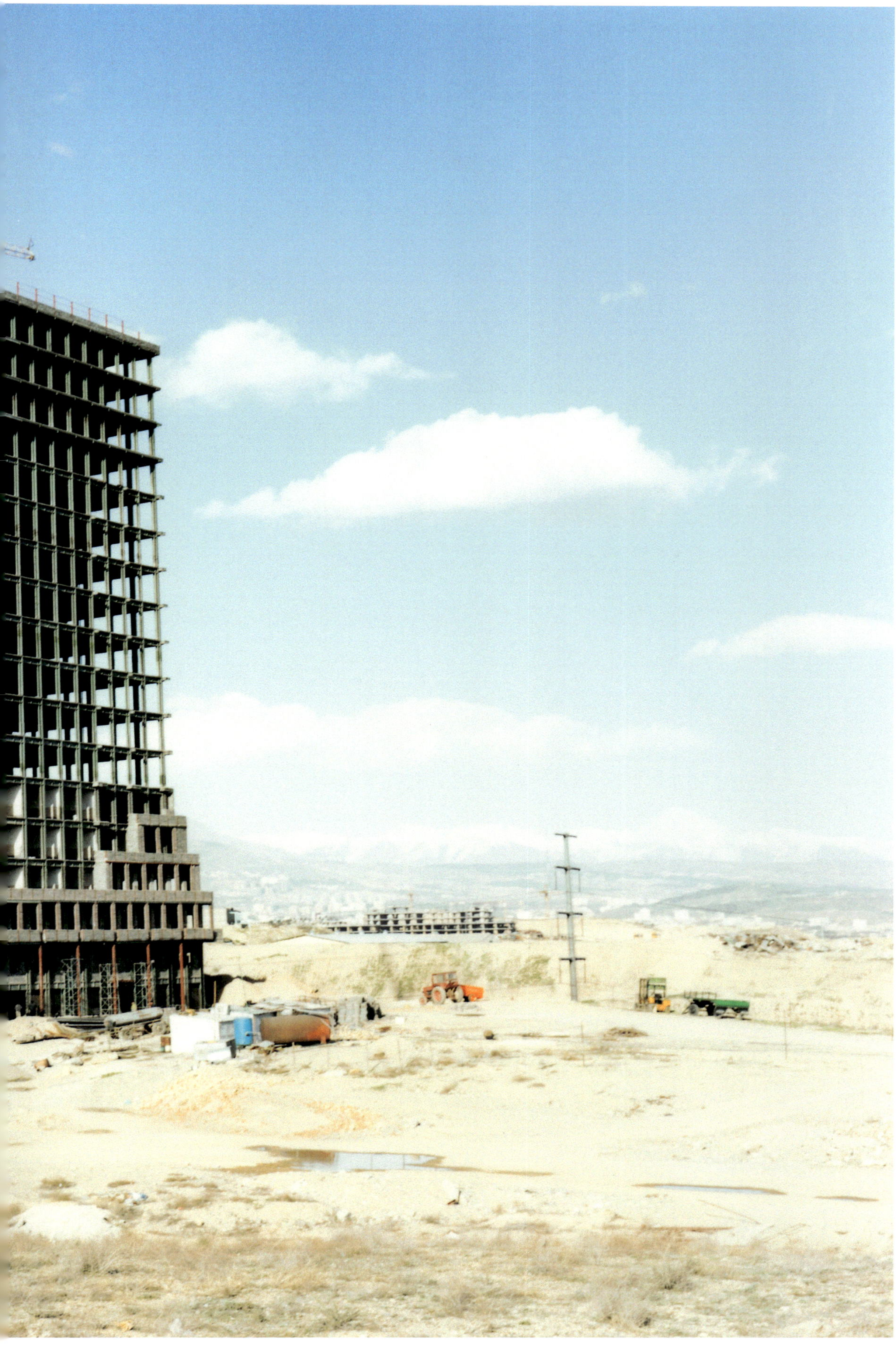

In the imaginary and actual reference works of contemporary art, they are the fixed entries. They have been accepted into the sources that guarantee "the quick and reliable overview"; the search engines spit out their names, ranks, and works; they are immortalized in the relevant dictionaries and encyclopedias. They are the summit from which the valleys and lowlands are visible.

He received an Oscar for his dark, extraterrestrial phantasmagorias **1**; she is the "art product" whose transformation explores loss of identity and the reinvention of the self **2**; he and his partner have ascended to the god-inhabited Olympus of art heaven **3**; he is the pendant to Manon in his shifting, shimmering, posturing celebration of his own personality, to the point of travesty **4**; she embodies a stringently conceptual, thought-provoking art **5**.

1

HR Giger (*1940)

The necrophiliac, morbid, extraterrestrial fantasy worlds of HR Giger are distant and near, from film to painting, to posters, furniture, clocks, interior decoration, and on to surreal spatial settings that finally get needled under the skin as tattoo motifs. These are eerie environments and creatures from an alien world and extraterrestrial beings such as his sphinx-like beauty from the film *Species*. As the creator of Ridley Scott's *Alien* (1979), he gained world fame and an Oscar for his set design and his creatures in the "biomechanical style," as he himself labels his artistic form of expression. *Alien 3* and *Poltergeist* were the other movie hits in his gloomy-magical aesthetic world. Giger's influence on popular culture has been immense and his work is thus viewed with corresponding suspicion by "real art."

In his museum, the 400-year-old castle of St-Germain in Gruyères, he created a bar as an erotic and macabre dream landscape, one of whose most remarkable features is an arched structure built using the "skeletal construction method" and whose enigmatic atmosphere is experienced as "black cathedrals." By "skeletal construction method" he means the formal language of the vertebrae and spinal column of the "bone man."

HR Giger attended the School of Applied Arts from 1962–65.

2

Manon (*1946)

After attending the School of Applied Arts and the Zurich Academy of Drama, in 1974 Manon designed her "salmon-colored boudoir," the first of her environments. She was later to use all the modern media in them, including, above all, herself and as many as sixty extras in various roles. She thus became one of the first and perhaps best known Swiss performance artists to employ an explicit form of photography as a way of staging herself in a work, and to bestow upon herself the title of both "director" and "art product." She stages her own living conditions and experiences and there is hardly an anthology of recent photography in which these images do not appear. Her predominant themes are corporeality, the erotic and transience, self-representation and identity. She undermines and infiltrates the feminine ideal of beauty using strategies of excess, reversal, or transformation to the verge of androgyny. Her works and those of Urs Lüthi are also seen under the term "transformers," as they seek to aesthetically address the transgression of the borders between the sexes or the transformation of the body and to strip away the taboos. Moving on from her works of rebellious, shrill protest in the 1970s, Manon has come to thematize the existential interfaces of life, taking recourse to archetypical metaphors and symbols—up to and including death.

3

David Weiss (*1946)

Actually the white (German: weiss) of a projection surface would suffice. It would be "populated" with his multitude of image and object realms that have assembled in our memory. The son of a Zurich priest, David Weiss is the Weiss of Fischli/Weiss. Who does not know them, the most important of their generation? Who does not know the video *Der Lauf der Dinge* (The Way Things Go) that enthralls us and won't let us go—over and over? Curiosity, a secret pleasure in viewing the precarious relationships of objects on the verge of catastrophe, losing balance and undergoing structural collapse—all trivial processes that allow existential hierarchies of values and perceptual certainties to fall to pieces. Sometimes presented as video, photography, rubberized plastic or installation, with fine poetry, as neo-Dada, do-it-yourself hardware store, or culinarily speaking: as sausage photography in the oriental rug decoration. Their art speaks volumes and here we're limited to 1,000 characters! You will have to substitute your own images and memories for what's been left unsaid.

2
1
3

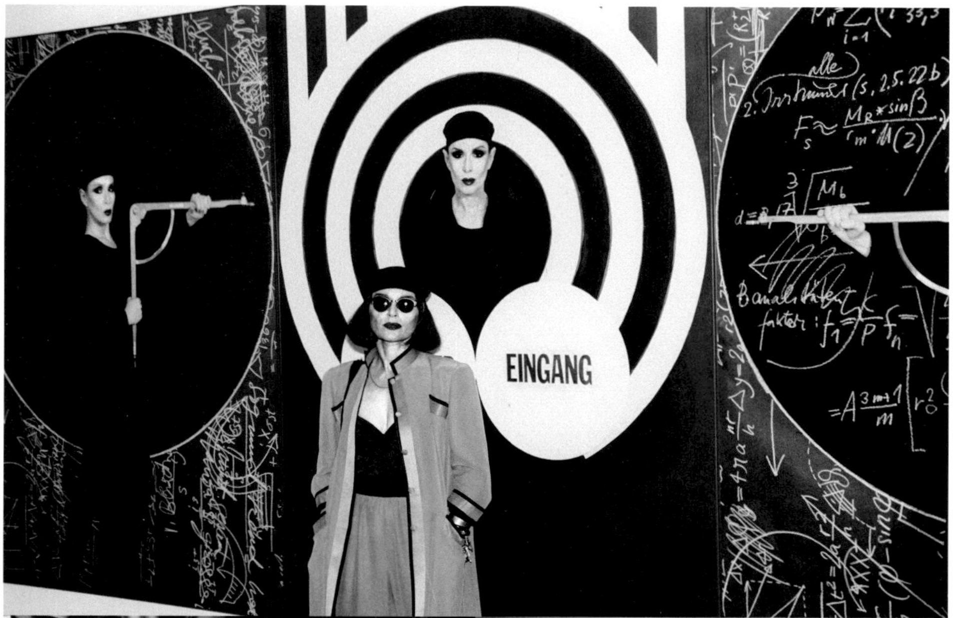

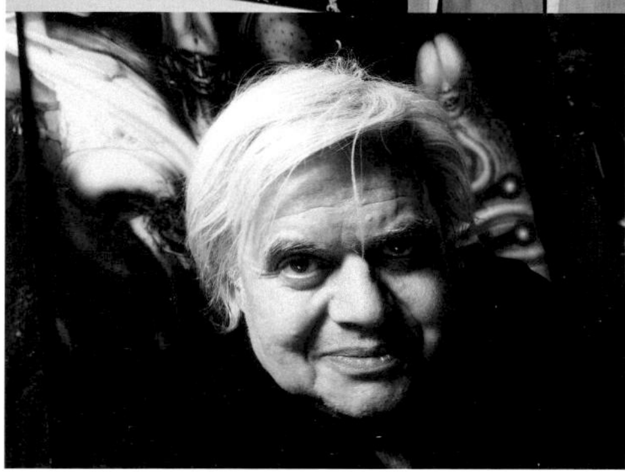

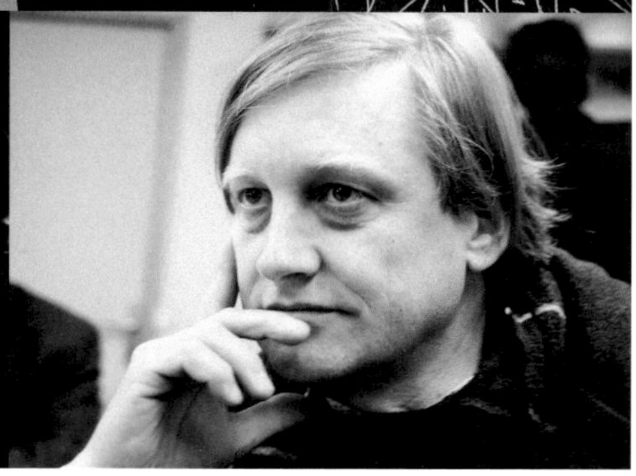

David Weiss graduated from the preliminary course at the School of Applied Arts in Zurich and studied sculpture for two more years at the School of Applied Arts in Basel.

4
Urs Lüthi (*1947)

His self-staging in stilted poses, suggestive costuming, and gender transformation is omnipresent in our imaginary museum of contemporary art. He is the convertible human sculpture, his own surrogate, photocopied in crass, unadorned realism. The clownish and the erotic are the two poles. However, his pictorial humor, like in a picture puzzle, threatens to quickly tip over into the earnest and existential. The question "who is Urs Lüthi?" can suddenly become a question concerning one's own identity. A catalogue entry by Cécile Dumont ends with the following statement: "It is said that there are ricochet artists who remain unrecognized as such because they always hit the bulls-eye. I think that Lüthi is one of them. And makes them."

He attended the School of Applied Arts in Zurich from 1963–64.

5
Maria Eichhorn (*1962)

She gets art involved with societal realities—very tricky. In Berlin she created a room with salty fog, creating the climate of the sea for harassed big city dwellers. Sometimes, as in her contribution to *documenta 11* in Kassel, which consisted of establishing a joint-stock corporation that would not allow any capital growth, she combines economic conditions of art and the art market with sociopolitical and communicative processes. In Bern she was involved with the concrete financial conditions and structures of a cultural institution: *Money at the Kunsthalle Bern.*

She leaves her conceptual art, installations, and objects open to interpretation. Viewers are left with the autonomy and freedom to choose whether they want to take a closer look or just react with indifference or fatigue. She delivers "only" the rooms of a particular event or a social construct with its concomitant heterogeneous viewing levels, thus provoking viewers to engage with it and with own thoughts and actions.

Maria Eichhorn studied at the Berlin University of the Arts and teaches conceptual art in the Department of Fine Art.

4

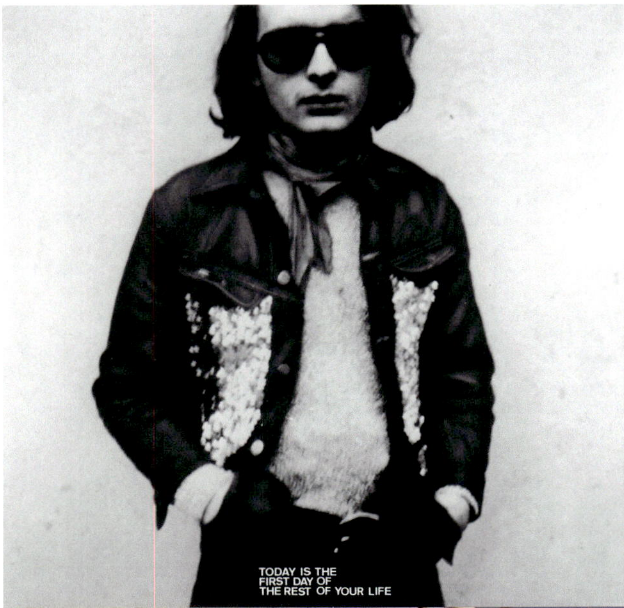

5

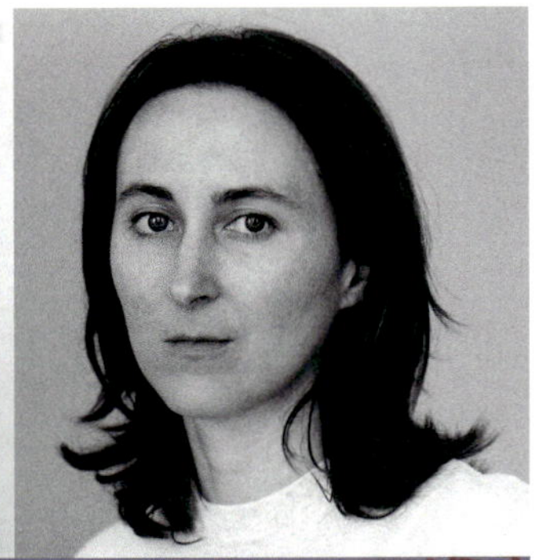

1a HR Giger, *Passage*, 1971. Acrylic, airbrush on wood

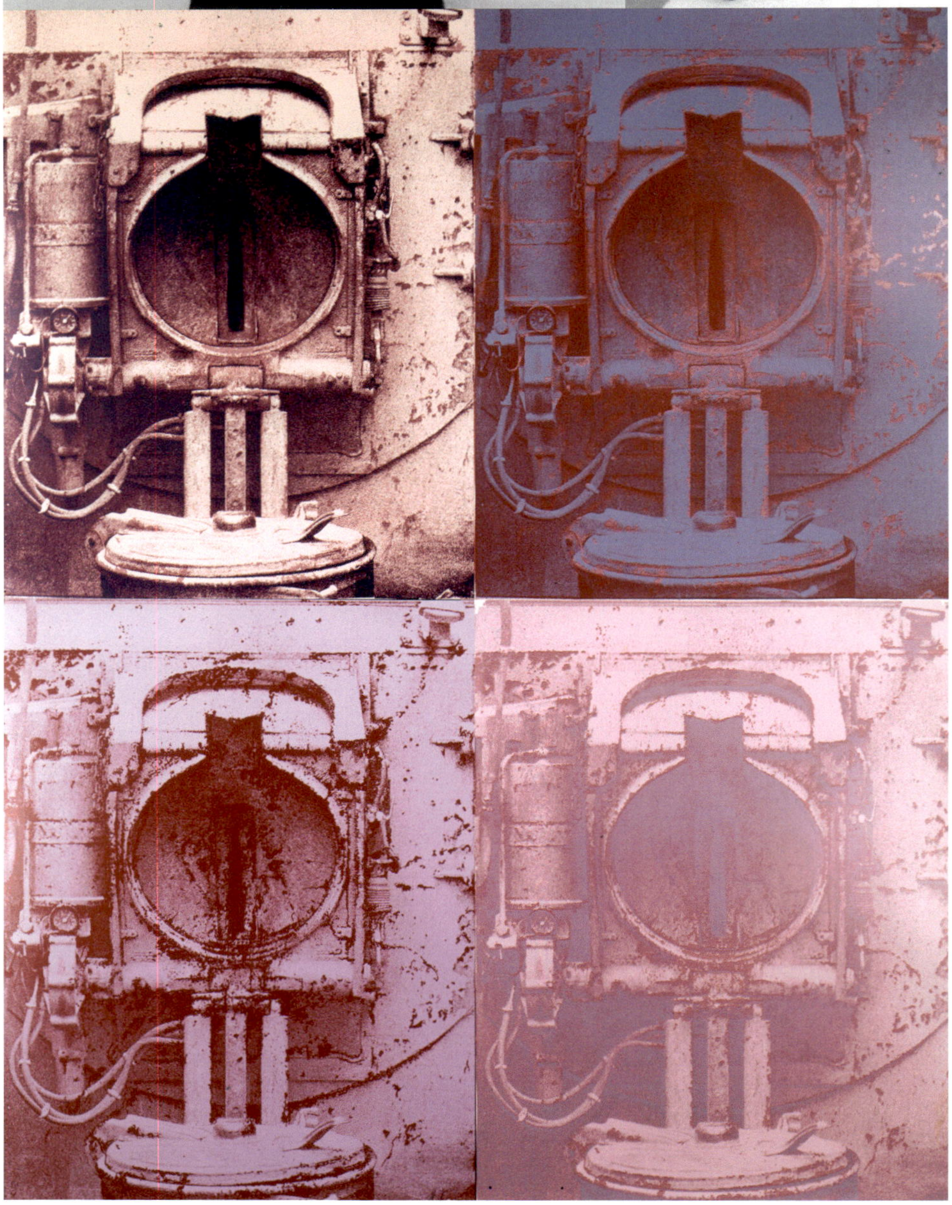

1b The bar at Museum HR Giger, Château St. Germain, Gruyères

1c *N.Y. City XXI: Subway,* 1981. Acrylic and ink on paper

2a–d Manon, from the series of black-and-white photos *36 Schlaflose Nächte,* 1979

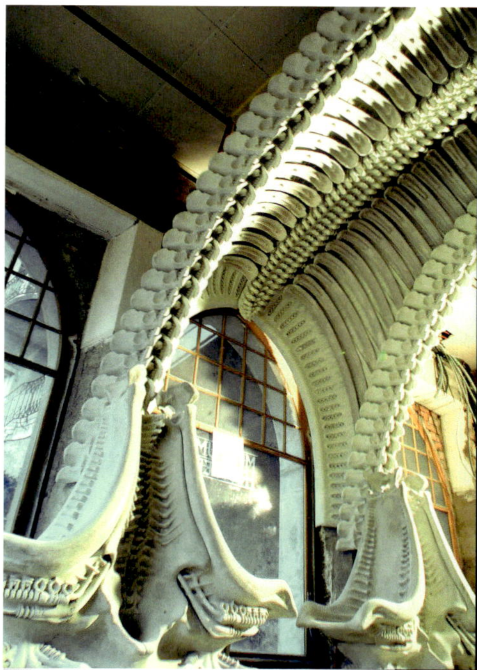

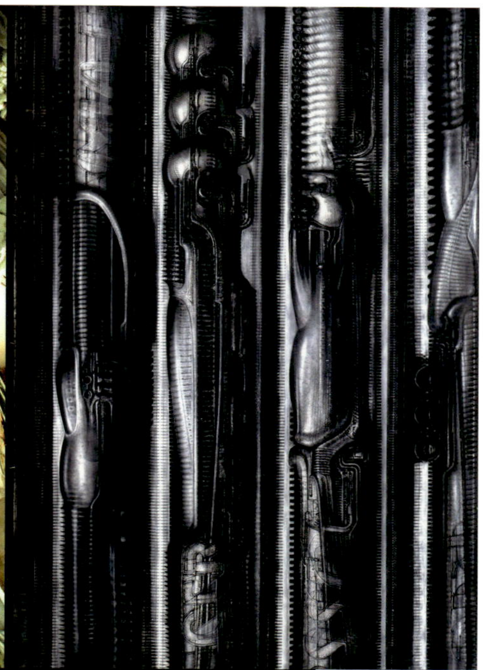

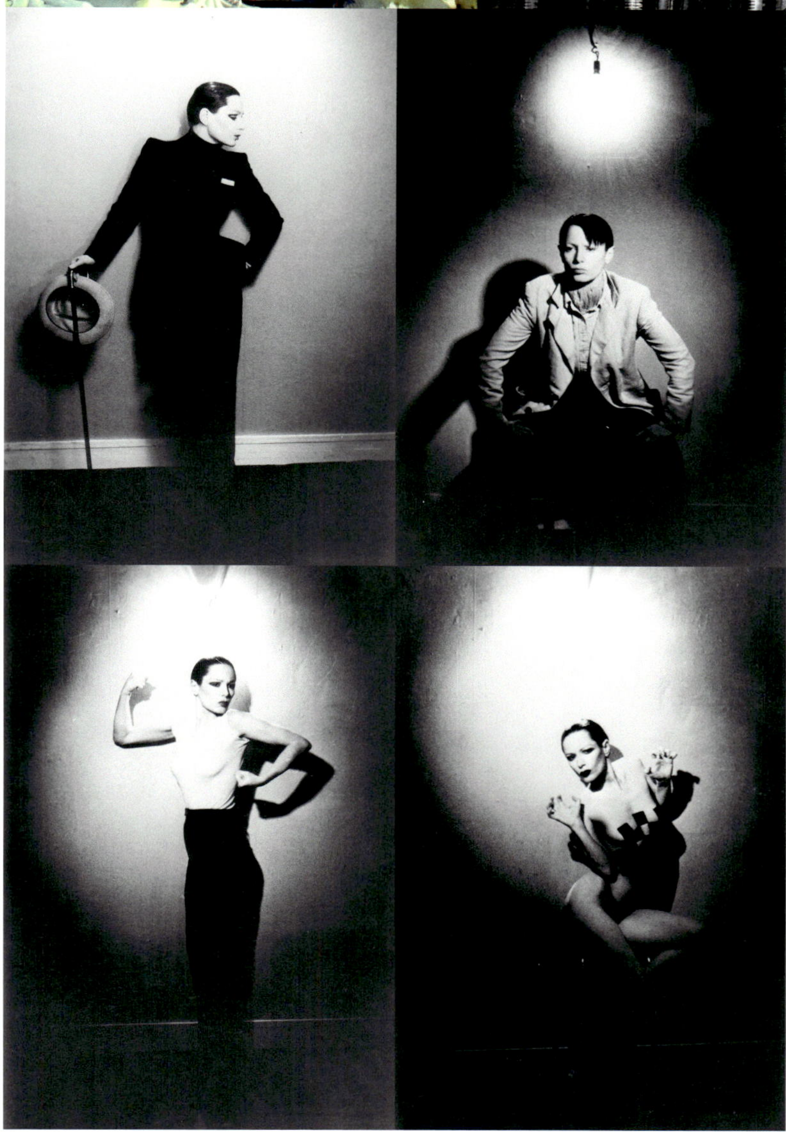

3a–h From *Sketches,* by David Weiss, Urs Lüthi, and Willy Spiller (photos). Eight-part portfolio. Edition Galerie Toni Gerber, Bern, 1970

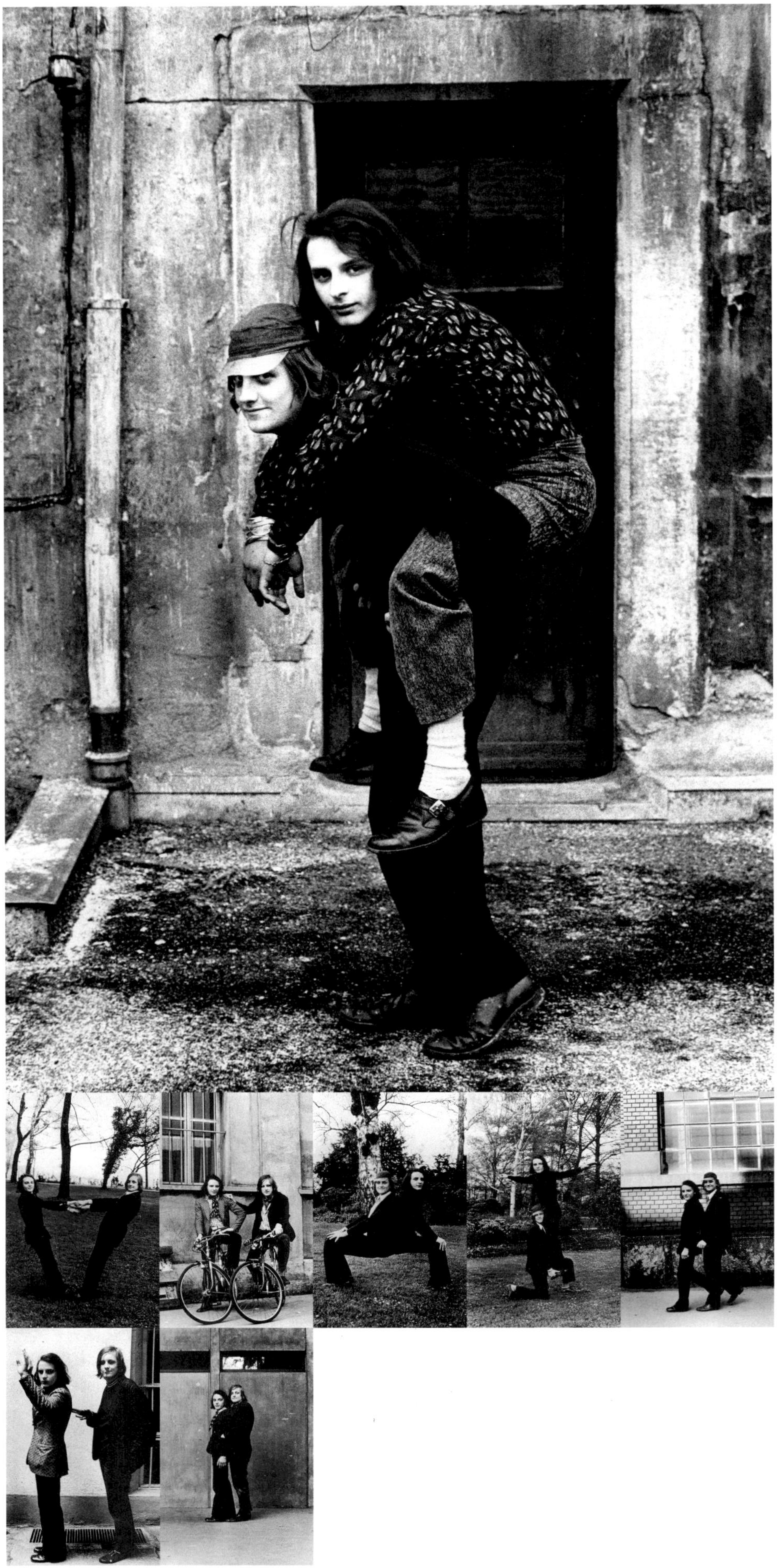

4a Urs Lüthi, *Superstars*, Kunsthalle Vienna, 2006

4b *Self Portrait*, 1976. Photo on canvas

5a Maria Eichhorn, *Nistkasten*, 2002. Handmade woodwork, printed card. Two parts

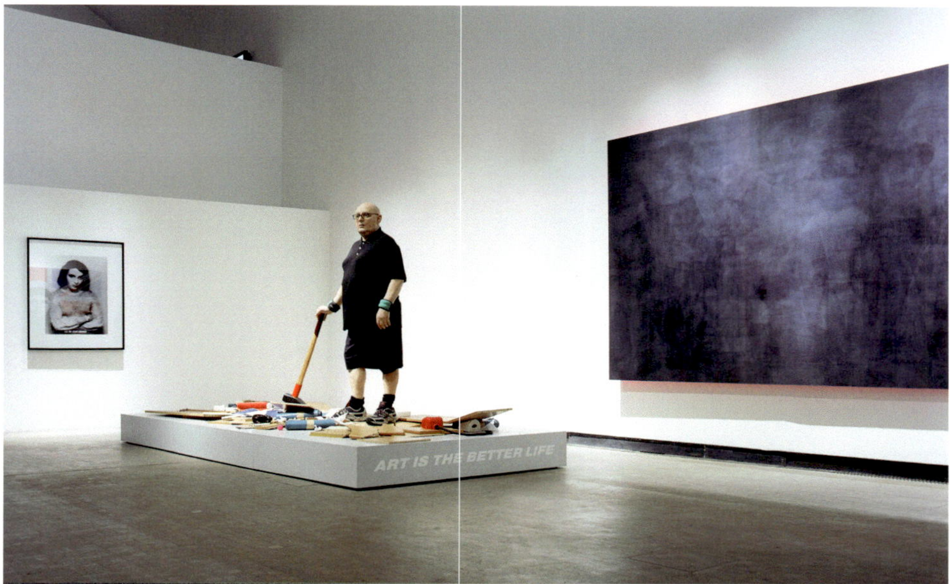

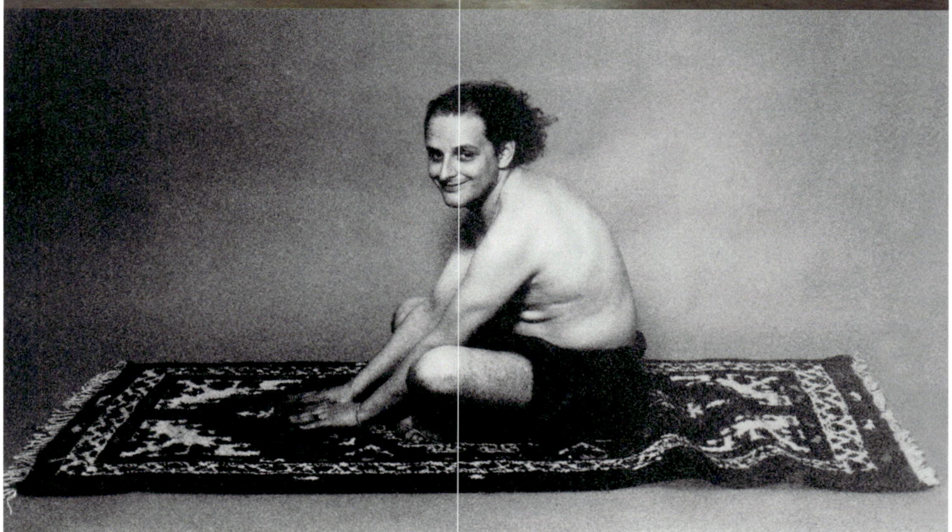

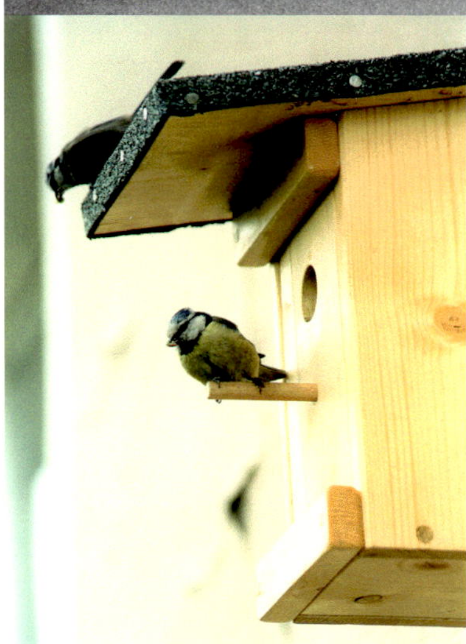

They learned the basics of their métier through calligraphy. They are the practitioners of the black art—every profession either directly or indirectly associated with the development of moving type and book printing. Here, "black" refers to the color of ink, and this particular "black art" is not to be confused with black magic. But magical, all the same, is the fact that despite the much ballyhooed "end of text," printed material continues to have such importance in our lives. From the Zurich type designers come the most frequently used—and frequently read—type fonts worldwide.

Globally, Helvetica occupies first place 1; his fonts are derivations of calligraphy and of the Grotesk family of fonts 2; he is the undisputed doyen of type development and his own fonts are Univers-al 3; his publications on text and typography are sources of exact knowledge 4; he is the anarchic typographer who has his text performed in the concert hall 5.

1
Max Miedinger (1910–1980)

Only his typeface is widely recognized, perhaps the most widely available Grotesk typeface, Helvetica, which in 2007 remains fifty years young, with no signs of aging. Also familiar is the "global bastard" that was cribbed from it, Arial, which has "unfortunately" achieved global diffusion through the monopolistic Windows operating system. In the Fontshop Ranking appearing in 2007, Helvetica ranked number one among "the 100 best typefaces of all times," and it is by a wide margin the most frequently used typeface ever. Helvetica embodies all of the formal criteria of Swiss graphic art: simplicity, clarity, utter reduction, and concentration to the essential. It manifests perfection in the absence of caprice: simple beauty and beautiful simplicity.

Alongside typesetting courses, Miedinger attended the obligatory lessons, courses, and electives at the Zurich School of Applied Arts, where he was taught by Walter Käch and Alfred Willimann.

2
Hans Eduard Meier (*1922)

After finishing school, Meier received training at a typesetter. He then attended courses at the Zurich School of Applied Arts. The art of calligraphy, which he learned from Alfred Willimann and Rudolf Käch, formed the basis of his later typeface conceptions. In 1950–86, he taught typeface, typography, and constructive drawing at the Zurich School of Art and Design. His bilingual teaching manual *Die Schriftentwicklung* (The Development of Type), edited by Erich Alb, was published there in 1994.

His internationally successful Syntax was produced in 1968–72, a typeface family marketed by the typefoundry Stempel in Frankfurt am Main. The development of Syntax was set off by a critique of existing Grotesk typefaces and an awareness of their formal inadequacies. As a calligrapher, he was accustomed to drawing letters with pen with the greatest precision, and he rejected the stiff, geometrical, and constructive typesetting forms of the 1950s and 1960s, the Grotesk typefaces such as Akzidenz-Grotesk, Haas-Grotesk (or Helvetica), and Mono-Grotesk. In the case of Syntax, Meier had recourse to the formal principles of Renaissance Antiqua. The result is a typeface with a distinctive character, inclined slightly to the right, whose round and diagonal strokes finish optically with right-angled termini.

3
Adrian Frutiger (*1928)

"On my first day at the School of Applied Arts, I presented myself to a fine lady, and expressed my desire to become a typeface designer. She informed me that two students had already completed the course: Hans Eduard Meier and Max Kämpf. She then wrote out my study plan: lettering with Alfred Willimann and calli graphy Saturday mornings with Walter Käch." So began the career of the doyen of twentieth-century Swiss typeface design, a man who pursued the development of his typefaces amply supplied with historical knowledge, consummate manual skill, and an extraordinary feel for formal beauty and fantasy.

Frutiger's sans serif Univers typeface represents perhaps the most important idea to be conceived and developed in the context of twentieth-century typography. The Univers typeface consists of a family of twenty-one different but interrelated and coordinated variants, a family that grew stroke by stroke to sixty-three in all. Finally, Frutiger came to be regarded as a classic modernist whose OCR-B (Optical Character Recognition), which he developed in 1968, came to be accepted as the world standard in 1973 by the computer industries of all of the industrialized countries. Altogether, Frutiger has created more than 170 typefaces.

Independently of printing procedures, design for Frutiger has always stood under one and the same premise: a typeface must affect the reader-friendly and efficient transport of content. For Frutiger, it is clear "that legibility and beauty are in close proximity, and that the typeface, in its reticence, should not be recognized as such by the reader, but instead only sensed intuitively. A good typeface is a tool, one that withdraws from the consciousness of the reader in order to serve exclusively the spirit of the author and the reader's comprehension."

1
2
3

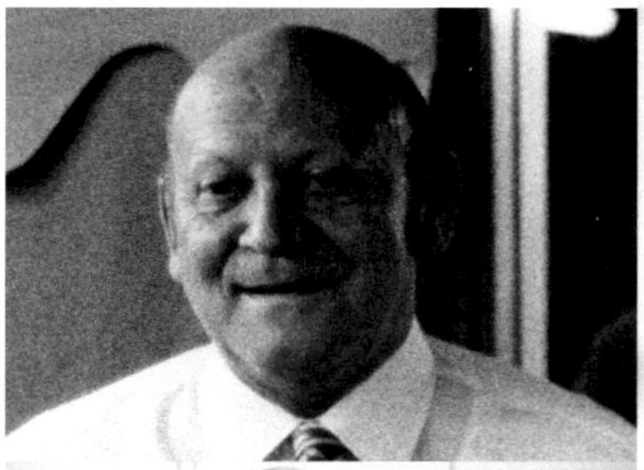

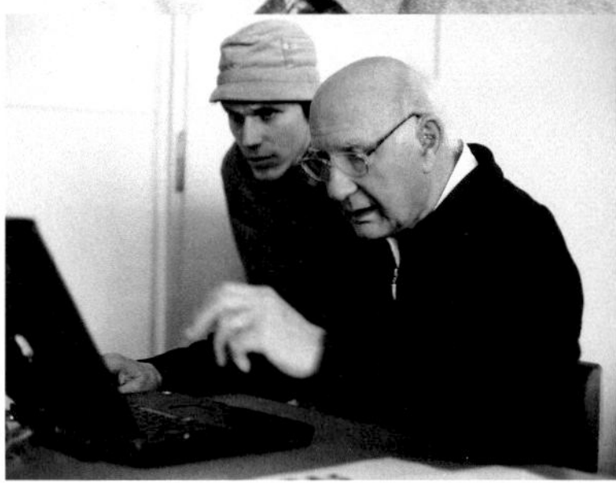

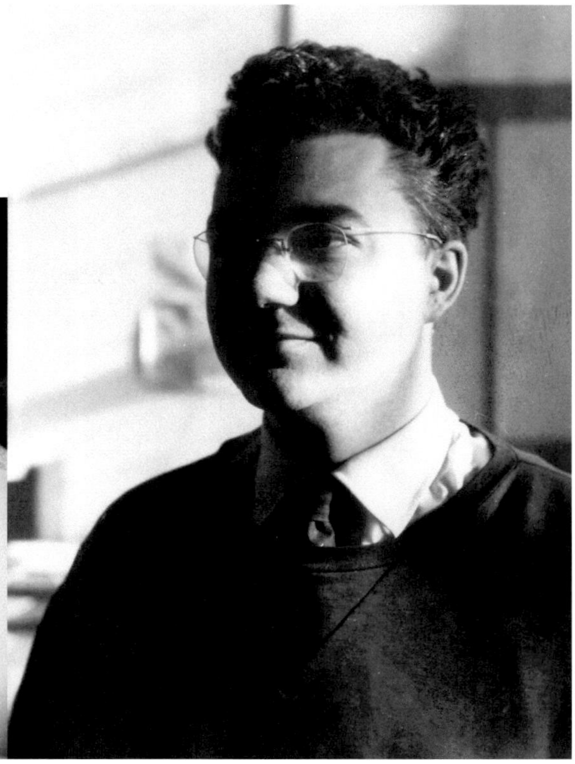

4
Hans Rudolf Bosshard (*1929)

Dressed in printer's black all the way to his salt-and-pepper closely cropped beard: so much for Bosshard's external appearance. The interventions and teachings of this typography instructor were razor-sharp. He conveyed the values of good printing in a series of publications in the fields of typography and design. Systematically and with exactitude, his texts organized and conveyed the entire spectrum of knowledge in typographical design. They have become standard teaching works in the field of typography, both indispensable and inspiring. Remarkably, Bosshard began by propagating the "corset of the grid," but his late work celebrates its dismantling.

Hans Rudolf Bosshard apprenticed in typography arts, and later taught typography and free design at the Zurich School of Applied Arts. He is a journalist, author, and book designer; among his publications are: *Die Demontage der Regel* (The Dismantling of the Rules; 1993); *Rastersysteme—Die Auflösung des Rasters* (Grid Systems: The Dissolution of the Grid); and *Typografie, Schrift, Lesbarkeit* (Typography, Text, Legibility; 1996).

5
Hans Rudolf Lutz (1939–1998)

Hans Rudolf Lutz was an anarchist of the black art: converging in him are the black of typography and the black of anarchy, realigned by punk and its aesthetic repertoire. His typographic experiments extend from constructive ornamentation using Univers, to figural typographic compositions (in the years around 1968, his typographic portraits of Karl Marx and Rosa Luxemburg circulated worldwide among comrades), to his revaluation of the mass media, and all the way to the cheekiness of his "style less" montages employing a typewriter and photocopier aesthetic.

He began his studies in typesetting: at that time, typesetting was regarded as the cultural and political avant-garde of the working class. He became a teacher of typography. He left the School of Applied Arts voluntarily in conjunction with the Scandal concerning the F+F (Form + Farbe = Form and Color class). Only in the late 1980s did he return as a guest instructor. In collaboration with Magda Vogel, head and lead singer of the cult band UnkownmiX, he brought the supercharging of music via typography and images to a crazy mix, staging a resistant synthesis of sound and image. According to contemporary critics, Vogel, with her guttural and melodious voice, unnerved and ingratiated listeners across three octaves, from the shrillest heights to the darkness abysses, with Lutz's projections adding evocative visual "sounds." His publications on typography and on the trashy global sign worlds of transport packaging, which he collected on wide-ranging travels, are found on the bookshelves of every advanced designer. With more subtlety, in contrast, he has also published the theatrical drawings of Hanny Fries.

4 5

1a Max Miedinger, Helvetica typeface, Letraset catalogue, 1987/88

1b The New Haas Grotesk (later Helvetica) in a dry-transfer lettering file, 1962

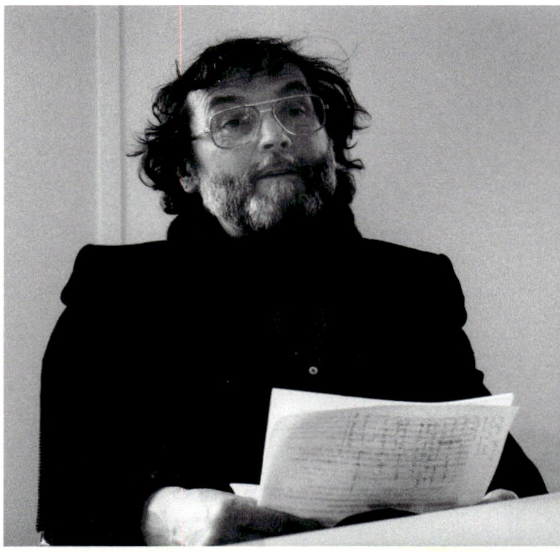

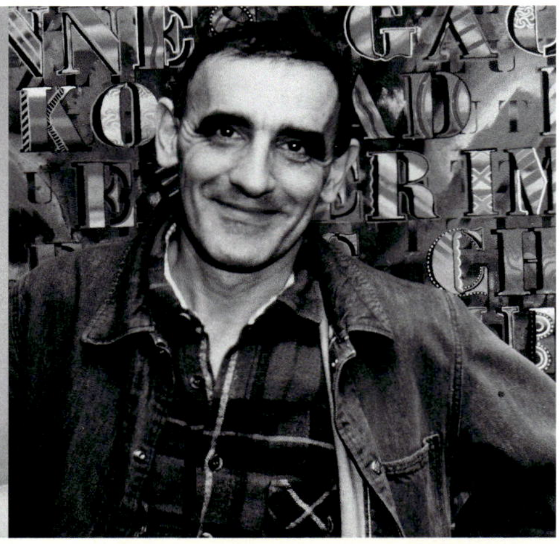

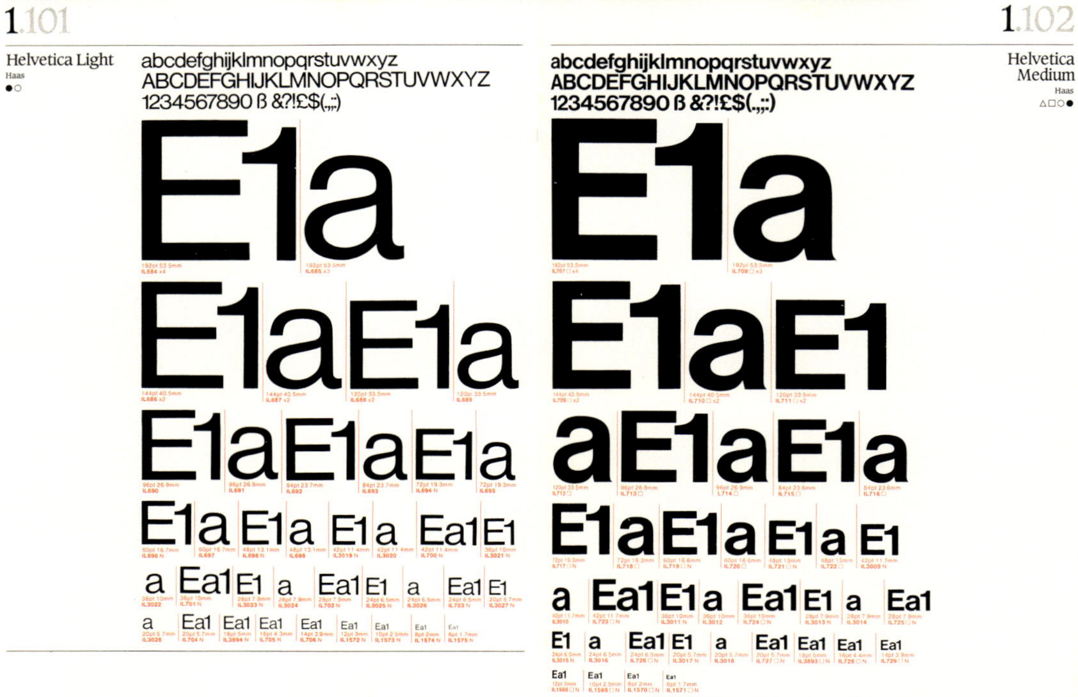

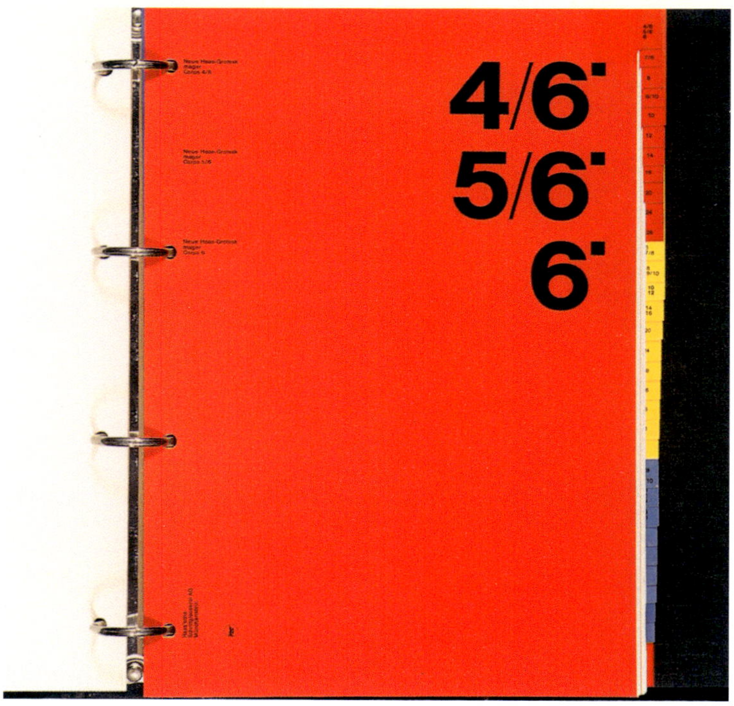

2a Hans Eduard Meier, Syntax lettering sample, dynamic development from the static Grotesk typefaces, 1968–72

2b Simplified new "basic lettering" for schools, 2006

2c Original Syntax drafts, 1965

2d Calligraphy class at the School of Applied Arts, no date

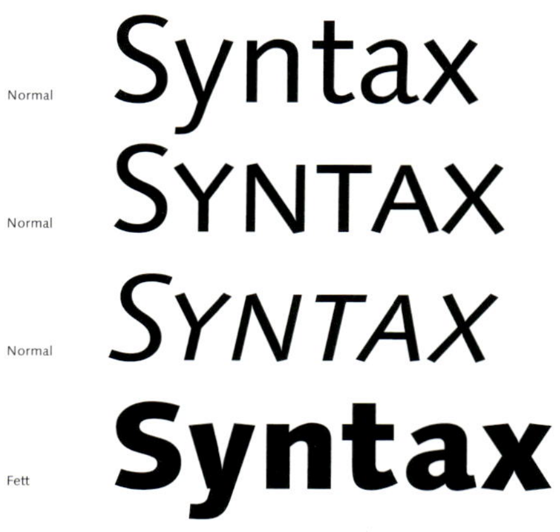

Weil mir die geometrisierten, „technisch" wirkenden Schriftformen der üblichen Grotesk nicht gefielen, begann ich um 1955 eine Schrift zu zeichnen, die zwar die Merkmale der Grotesk hatte, aber auf der Grundform der Renaissance-Antiqua basierte.

Durch das Studium der geschriebenen Schrift der Renaissance, welche als Vorlage für die ersten, sehr leserlichen Druckschriften diente, wurde mir bewusst, wie die Druckschrift unserer Zeit technisch und formalistisch geworden war. Sie eignet sich nicht als gut lesbare Mengenschrift. Dafür benutzte man die gut leserlichen Antiquaschriften früherer Jahrhunderte.

Sie wurde von 1968 bis 1972 bei der Schriftgiesserei D. Stempel in Frankfurt für den Handsatz und die Linotypesetzmaschine unter dem Namen Syntax hergestellt.

1986 erweiterte ich mit dem Fontographerprogramm die Syntax-Familie von ursprünglich fünf Schnitten auf fünfzehn: sechs aufrechte-, sechs kursive- und drei Kapitälchenschnitte mager, normal und halbfett.

Hans Ed. Meier, bei LinotypeLibrary

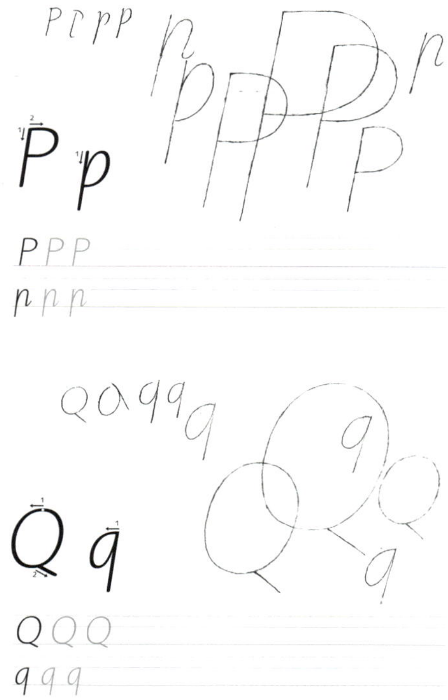

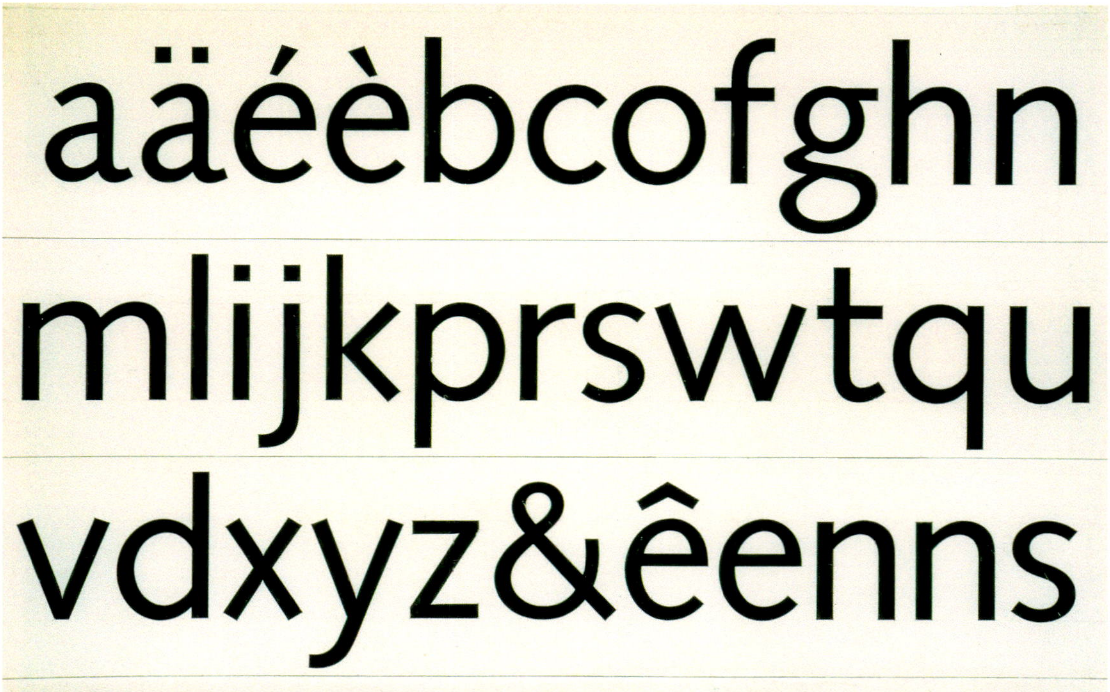

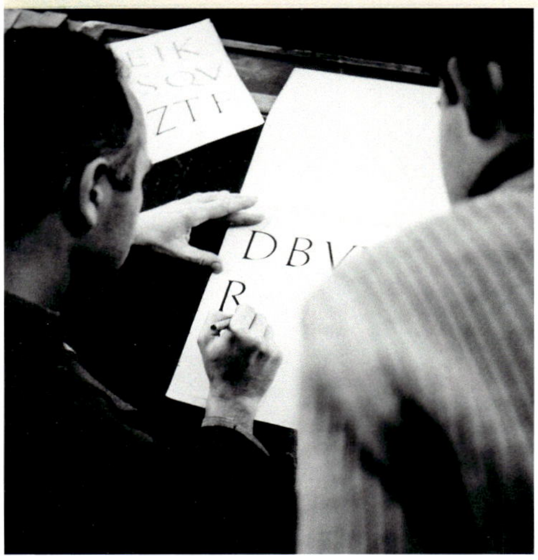

3a Adrian Frutiger, typeface development. Nine carved beechwood panels submitted in 1951 as degree project with Alfred Willimann/Walter Käch

3b/c Feature on Adrian Frutiger in *Tages-Anzeiger Magazin Zürich*, no. 25, 1988

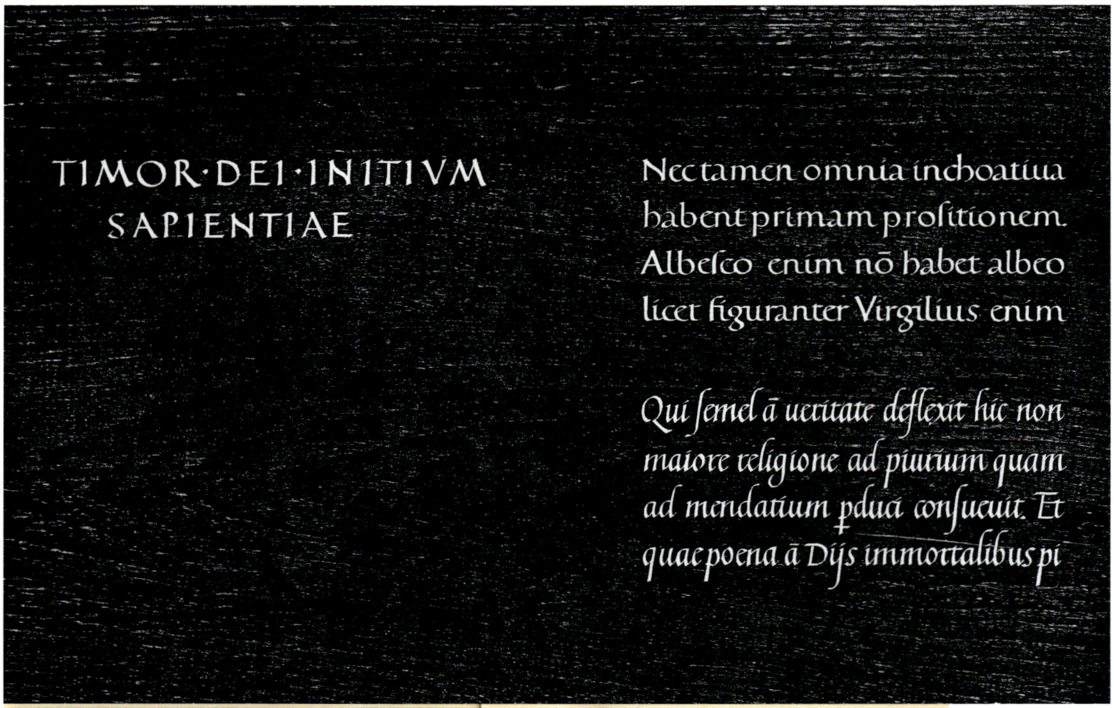

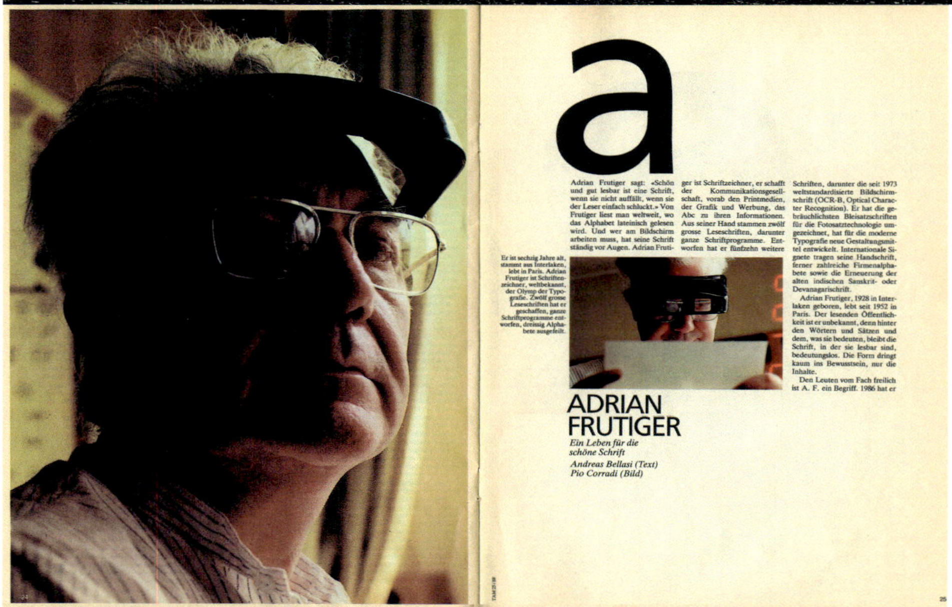

a

Adrian Frutiger sagt: «Schön und gut lesbar ist eine Schrift, wenn sie nicht auffällt, wenn sie der Leser einfach schluckt.» Von Frutiger liest man weltweit, wo das Alphabet lateinisch gelesen wird. Und wer am Bildschirm arbeiten muss, hat seine Schrift ständig vor Augen. Adrian Frutiger ist Schriftzeichner, er schafft der Kommunikationsgesellschaft, vorab den Printmedien, der Grafik und Werbung, das Abc zu ihren Informationen. Aus seiner Hand stammen zwölf grosse Leseschriften, darunter ganze Schriftprogramme. Entworfen hat er fünfzehn weitere Schriften, darunter die seit 1973 weltstandardisierte Bildschirmschrift (OCR-B, Optical Character Recognition). Er hat die gebräuchlichsten Bleisatzschriften für die Fotosatztechnologie umgezeichnet, hat für die moderne Typografie neue Gestaltungsmittel entwickelt. Internationale Signete tragen seine Handschrift, ferner zahlreiche Firmenalphabete sowie die Erneuerung der alten indischen Sanskrit- oder Devanagarischrift.

Adrian Frutiger, 1928 in Interlaken geboren, lebt seit 1952 in Paris. Der lesenden Öffentlichkeit ist er unbekannt, denn hinter den Wörtern und Sätzen und dem, was sie bedeuten, bleibt die Schrift, in der sie lesbar sind, bedeutungslos. Die Form dringt kaum ins Bewusstsein, nur die Inhalte.

Den Leuten vom Fach freilich ist A. F. ein Begriff. 1986 hat er

Er ist sechzig Jahre alt, stammt aus Interlaken, lebt in Paris. Adrian Frutiger ist Schriftenzeichner, weltbekannt, der Olymp der Typografie. Zwölf grosse Leseschriften hat er geschaffen, ganze Schriftprogramme entworfen, dreissig Alphabete ausgefeilt.

ADRIAN FRUTIGER

Ein Leben für die schöne Schrift

Andreas Bellasi (Text)
Pio Corradi (Bild)

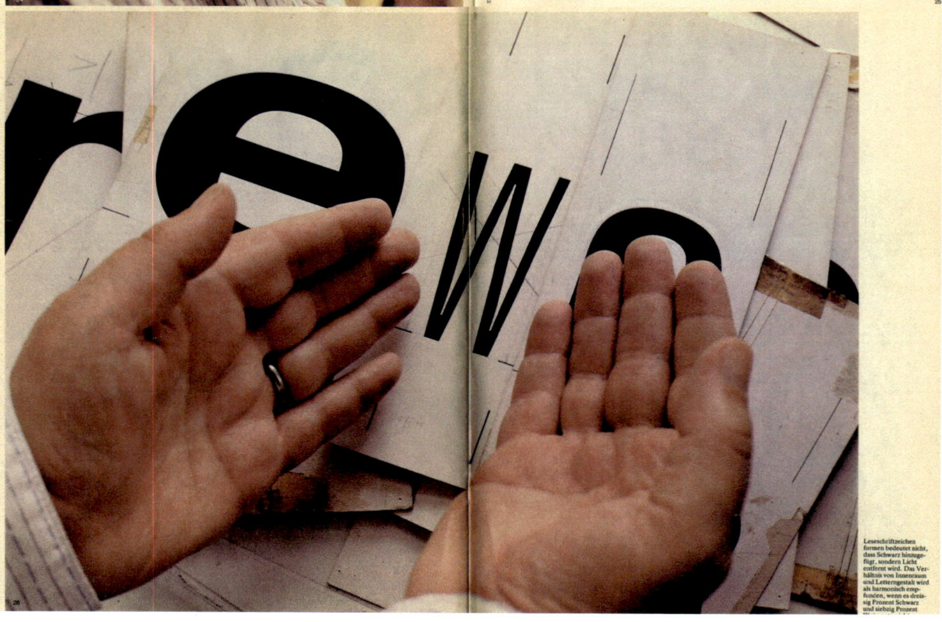

Leseschriftzeichen formen bedeutet nicht, dass Schwarz hinzugefügt, sondern Licht entfernt wird. Das Verhältnis von Innenraum und Letterngestalt wird als harmonisch empfunden, wenn es dreissig Prozent Schwarz und siebzig Prozent

3d Atelier Deberny & Peignot Paris, 1956. Ladislas Mandel shows Adrian Frutiger (left) the Bold Extended version of Univers while Lucette Girard cuts additional letters.

3e Adrian Frutiger with poster showing Univers, the most successful of his approx. thirty typefaces. No date

4a Hans Rudolf Bosshard, banned exhibition poster, 1978

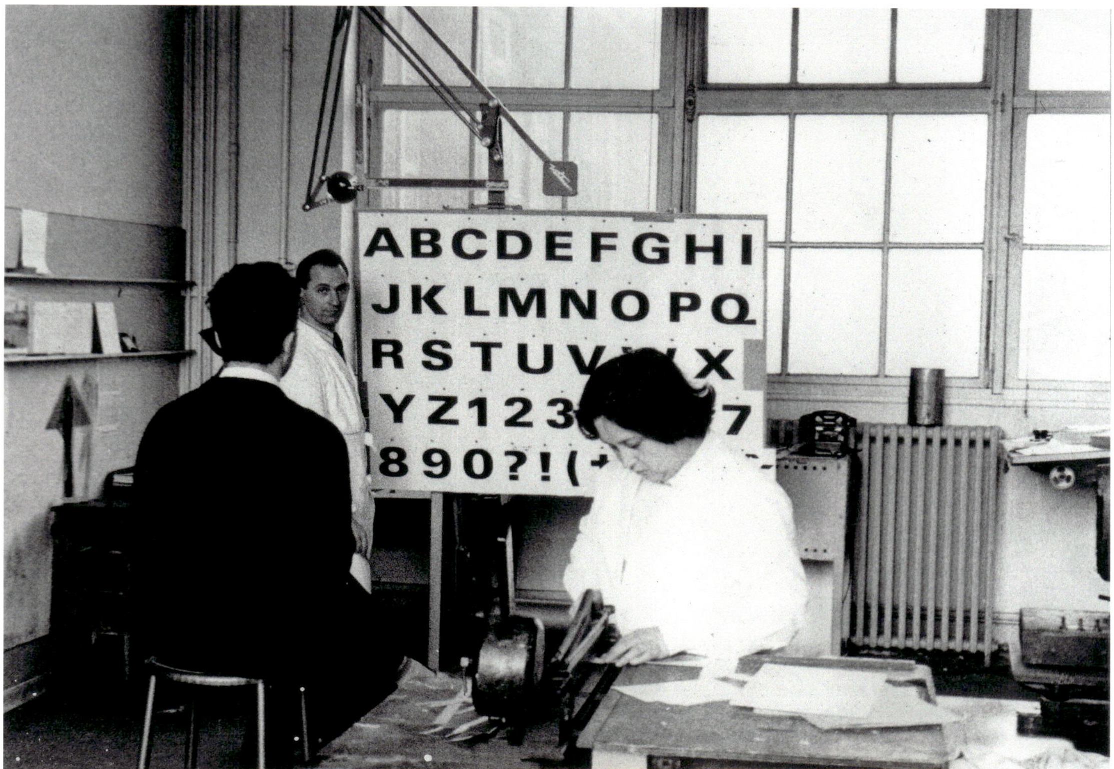

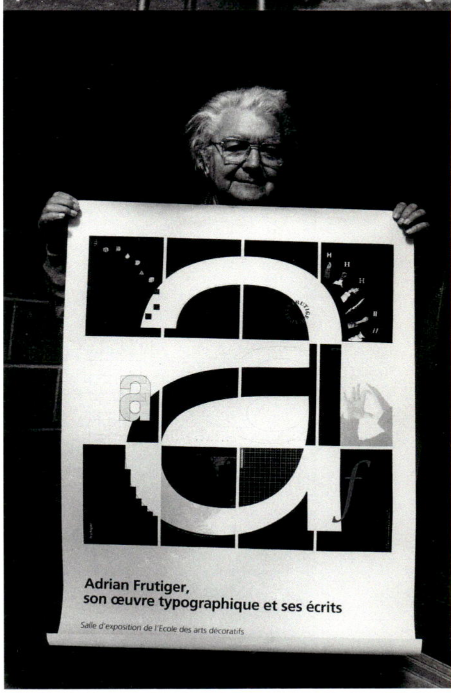

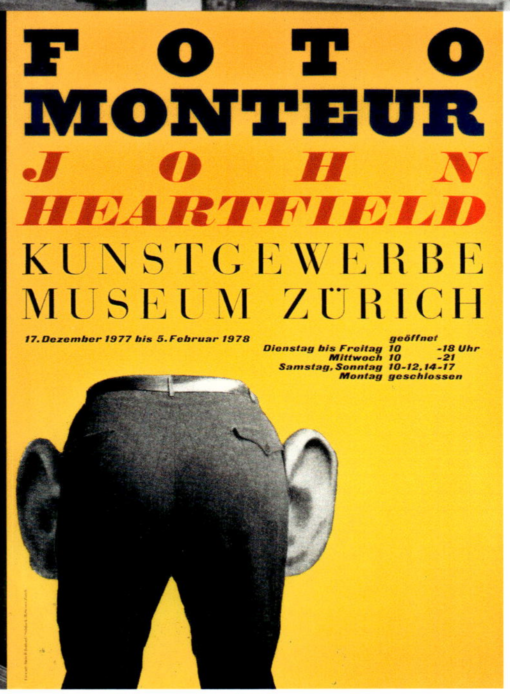

4b Hans Rudolf Bosshard, poster, 1990 **4c** Exhibition poster, 1990

5a Hans-Rudolf Lutz, visuals for the band UnknownmiX. Concert photo

5b/c *Today's Hieroglyphs: Imprints on Packaging for Transport.* Cover and detail by Hans-Rudolf Lutz, 1990

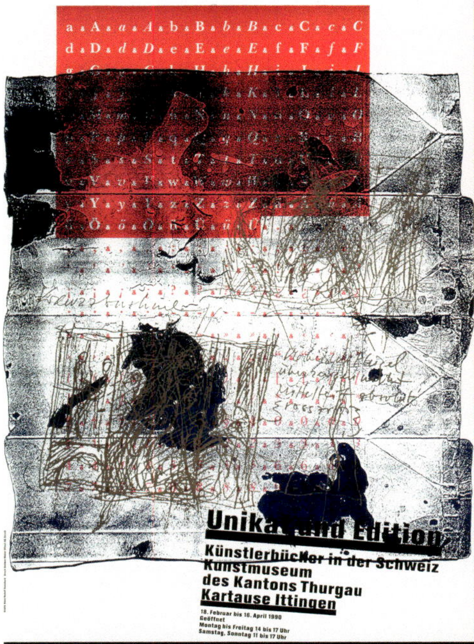

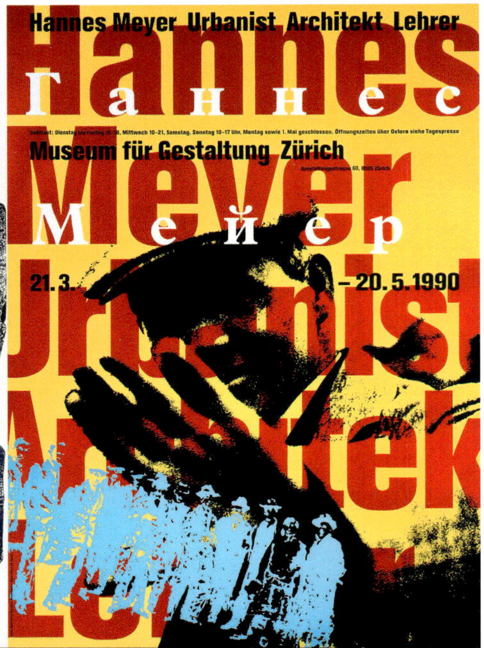

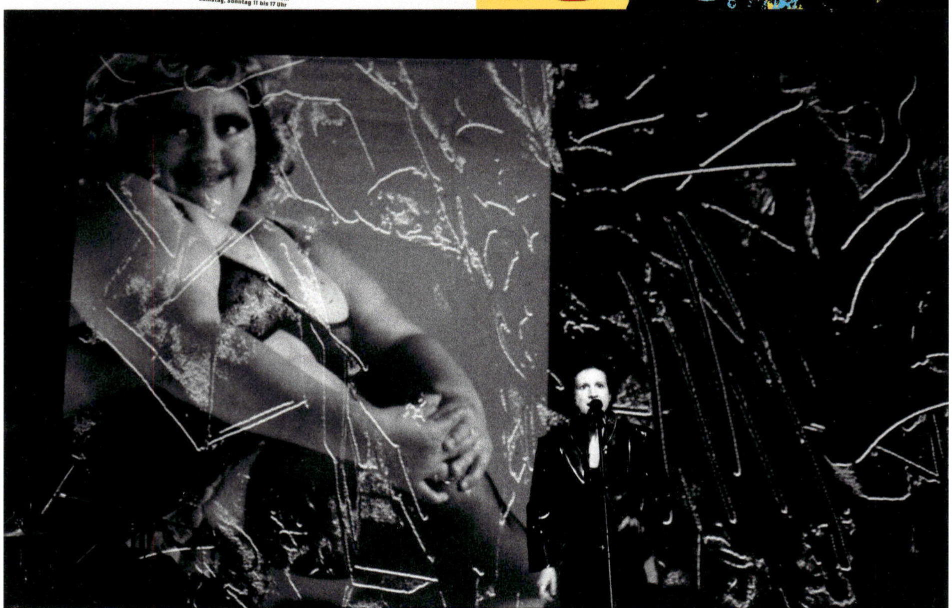

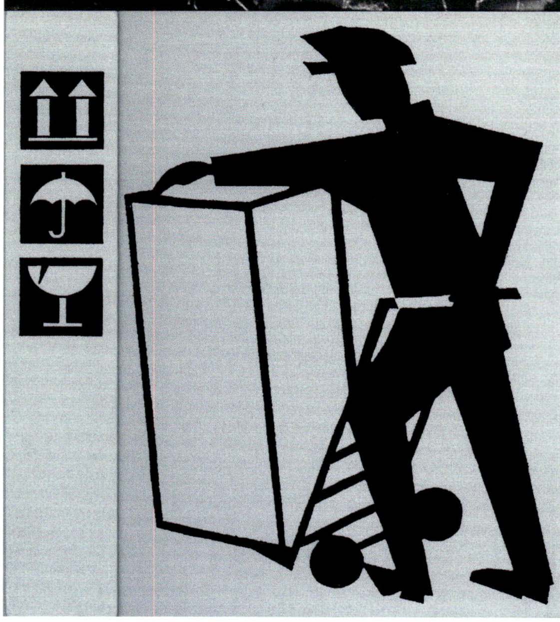

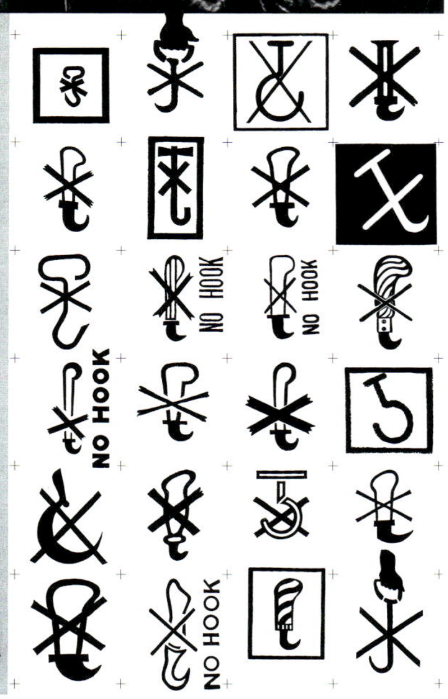

5d–g Publications from Verlag Hans-Rudolf Lutz. Covers

5h *Tribute to Lutz*, 1989. Poster by Tania Prill

5i *Typographische Monatsblätter*, May 1977. Title page

5k Rosa Luxemburg, “Über die russische Revolution.” Supplement to the trade union organ *Druck und Papier*, 1971

5l *Abc, Hommage/Mahnung an Muhamed Ali.* Poster, 1979

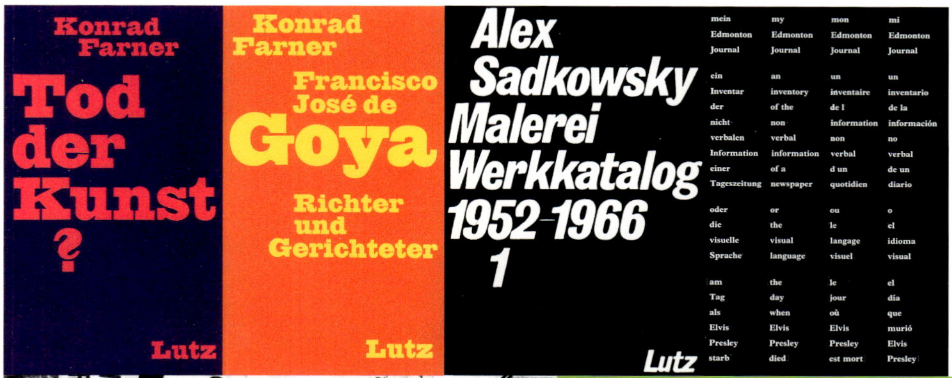

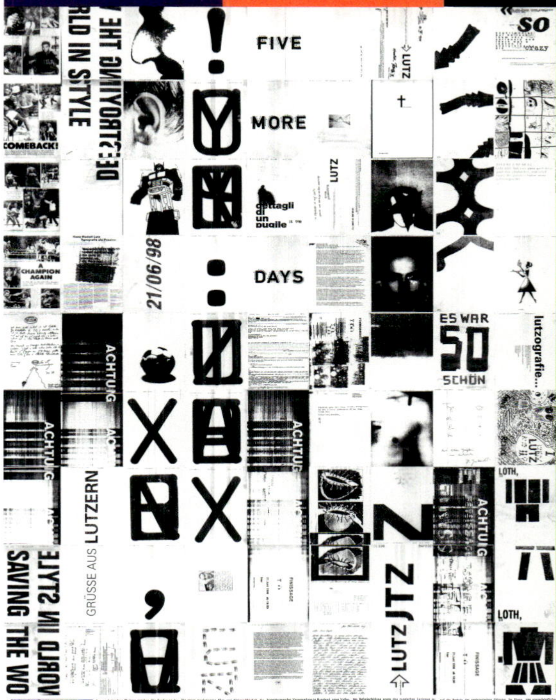

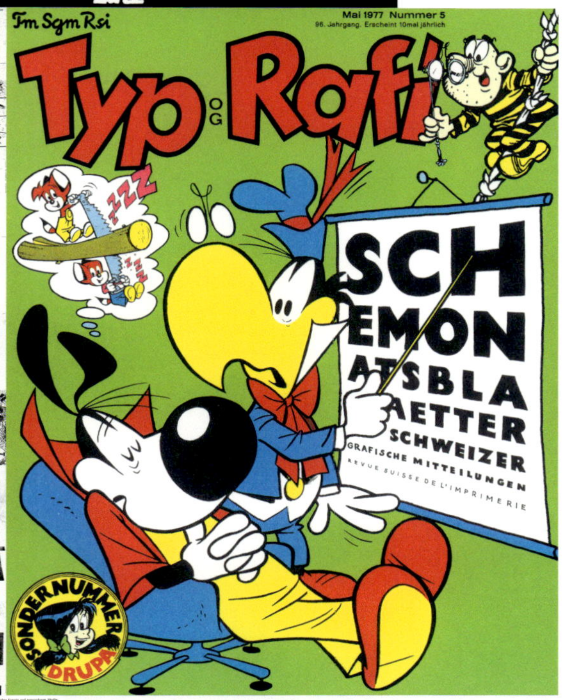

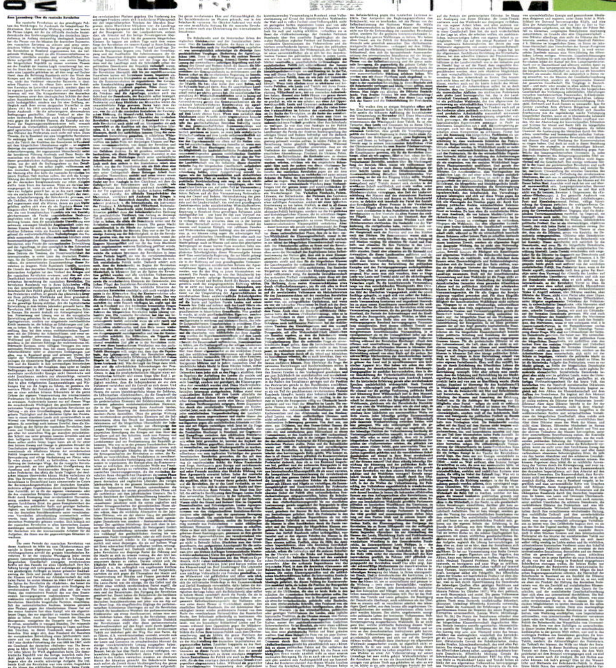

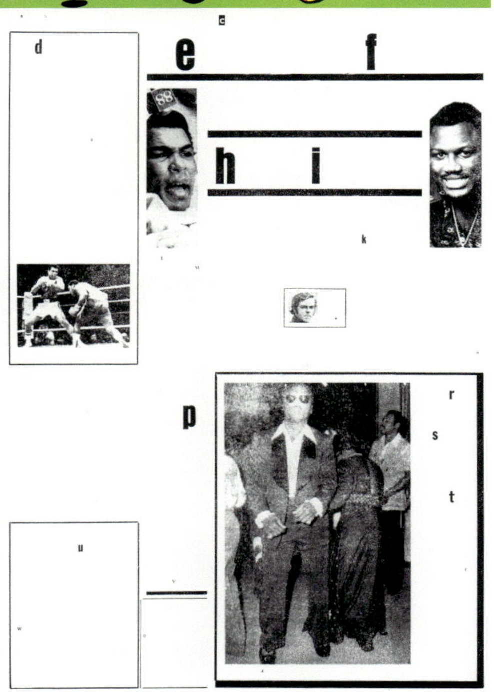

They investigate—whether practically or theoretically—the depths and recesses of cultural production in aesthetics, everyday life, the cultures of media and of the image, and the cultures of the senses. They generate theories and models of artistic and cultural practice, addressing social, political, technical, and economic frameworks, contributing to knowledge, articulating theses and models and elaborating transformations of artistic practice.

He was the art-theoretical mentor of the concrete artists, and he made object art respectable 1; his early postmodernist proclamations and his affinity for Pop Art and for cultural phenomena made him a thorn in the side of the "fundamentalists" of rigid modernism 2; his musicological impetus, his passion for research into and reflection on all aspects of music aesthetics, combined with his furious piano playing, was recognized by, among other distinctions, an honorary doctorate 3; his "interventions" fill volumes, and constitute a culture-theoretical memory of contemporary debates on aesthetics 4; with elaborate literary language, the *feu sacré* of his lectures and interventions, and his sheer verve, he presents his theory in signs and signals, combined with culture 5; his colossal theoretical and publishing productivity in advanced media philosophy and his reflections on the internal theoretical contents of the arts make him a cultural-philosophical expert of the highest order 6.

1

Willy Rotzler (1917–1994)

He was originally a student of Romance languages who, as an art historian and publicist, left his mark for decades on the public and scholarly perception of constructivism and concrete art. In his writings and interventions Rotzler always modestly retreated in a well-meaning way behind the concerns that he represented, namely dealing with pictorial works and artistic personalities. His prose is exemplary in its precision, objectivity, and consistency. The title of one of his works, *Aus dem Tag in die Zeit* (Out of the Day into Time; 1994), might well be his agenda. Among his other most important publications are the definitive *Werke and Schriften* (Works and Writings; 1972), which was hugely influential for the reception of the work of Johannes Itten, and *Konstruktive Konzepte. Eine Geschichte der Konstruktiven Kunst vom Kubismus to the Present* (Constructive Concepts: A History of Constructivist Art from Cubism to the Present; 1977). Among his most important actions were his intervention on behalf of the *Cube* by Sol Lewitt in Zurich of the 1980s. Willy Rotzler was curator of the Museum of Applied Arts and Design, lecturer at the University of Zurich, president and member of the Swiss Federal Art Commission and one of the first to publish on and teach new object art.

2

Alois Martin Müller (*1946)

Müller is director of the Academy of Art and Design at the University of Applied Sciences in Northwestern Switzerland, whose cultural scholarship and artistic profile he emphatically marks. He studied philosophy and art and architectural history and was academic assistant for Hermann Lübbe (philosophy and political philosophy) from 1986–90. In his many years of publishing activity (e.g. *Dialektik der Moderne*, Dialectics of Modernism; 1991), he continually addressed perspectives on modernism, both from inside and outside. His early contributions on the postmodern, in particular concerning the significance of religious structures in the secular, the compensatory religious and artistic elements in the liturgical and ritual, and notions of purity in classical modernism, were initially harshly opposed by modernist fundamentalists. History, however, has more than vindicated him.

Müller was the cultural editor of the *Tages-Anzeiger* newspaper, conservator and curator of important exhibitions in the Museum of Design in Zurich—including one on Daniel Libeskind, *Mehrwerte—Schweiz und Design; die 80er Jahre* (Added Value: Switzerland and Design; the 1980s) and coorganizer with Jörg Huber of *Interventionen*. Until his move to Basel he taught at various art schools and universities, particularly in the areas of design theory, art theory and literature, aesthetics and cultural philosophy.

3

Hermann Danuser (*1948)

Hermann Danuser of Frauenfeld has long been one of the German-speaking world's leading musicologists. He has been professor of historical musicology at the Humboldt University of Berlin since 1993 and before that held chairs in both Hanover and Freiburg im Breisgau. Danuser is also research coordinator at the Paul Sacher Foundation Basel, is a member of countless advisory boards and academies, has been a guest professor at some of the world's leading universities, and holds an honorary doctorate from the University of London.

It is worth remembering that Danuser's roots are not in musicology, but in music practice. He began his career as a student in the piano class of Sava Savoff, the erstwhile director of the Zurich Conservatory and Music School, and like Christoph Keller, actually worked as her assistant for a while. He completed his studies with a superb performance of Brahms's first piano concerto together with the Conservatory Orchestra at the Tonhalle Zurich. This was followed by an oboe teaching diploma and of course a degree in musicology at the University of Zurich. According to certain well informed sources, Danuser has taken up the piano again in Berlin and is said to be playing frequently again.

4

Jörg Huber (*1948)

His publications, exhibitions, and teaching are bound by one mindset and one approach. The mindset: alert, thirsty for knowledge, cosmopolitan; the approach: criticism—including a self-critical reflection on criticism, and not meant as the criticism that remains aloof but rather as taking positions. The career of this German studies expert and art historian has been determined at two institutions: first, the *Inventions* that he initiated from 1992–2005, from P as in perception of the present to C for conceits, from L as in Lyotard to S as

1 2
3 4

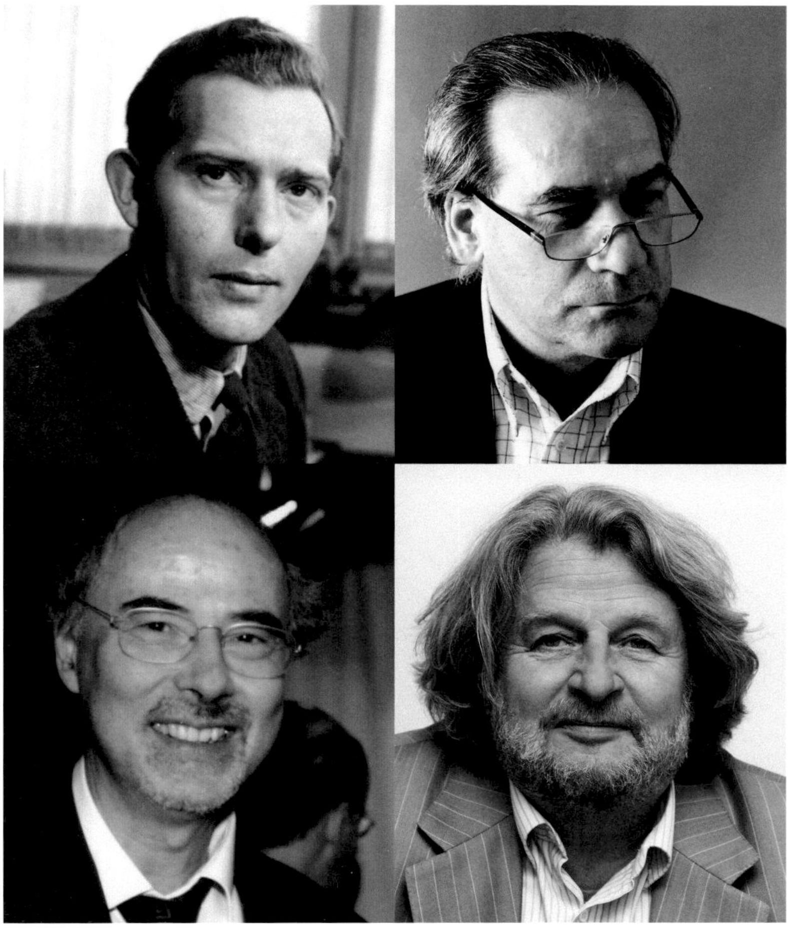

in Sloterdijk and V as in Venturi; the other was the Institute for Theory at the School of Art and Design with a likewise high level of productivity, performative events, research projects, and publications (e.g. the periodical *31* and the *TH:G* series). The issues he addresses in his own articles and essays include art, film, photography, and cultural theory. One of his special concerns is the image as a form of knowledge.

5
André Vladimir Heiz (*1951)

As a prominent bilingual author and semiotician he has a monopoly on pugnacious charm. One of his early and bold interventions was the essay written for Harald Szeemann entitled "Satz zum Gesamtkunstwerk" (A Sentence on the Total Work of Art; 1983). The titles of his literary works bear witness to his interests: *Sommersprossen: Liebeserklärung an die Ungleichzeitigkeiten der Sprache* (Freckles: A Declaration of Love to the Untimeliness of Language; 1995); *Liliane und Damian: Die ersten vierzehn Tage der Liebe* (Liliane and Damian: The First Fourteen Days of Love; 1997); likewise the exhibition in the Museum of Design: *Medium —eine Welt dazwischen* (Medium: A World In-Between; 1998), or the publication *Design—Ein Zwischenfall* (Design: An Incident; 2003). He has been a member of the jury of the Klagenfurt reading contest as a critic since 2007. As a publisher he is currently developing a paperback series at Swiss art universities concerning design principles entitled *Didaktika* and is highly praised as a lecturer who transcends the barriers of generations and culture.

6
Hans Ulrich Reck (*1953)

Philosopher, art and literature critic, journalist, and professor at the Cologne Academy of Media Arts, one of the most progressive, most brilliant media theoreticians and philosophers in German-speaking culture. He was lecturer of art history, architecture, and design theory, visual communication, semiotics, aesthetics, and media theory at the Higher School of Design Zurich. The theoretical concept of a suitable "art through media" and the "laboratory for medial strategies" has guided his work in Cologne. Along with Hartmut Böhme, Christina von Braun, Martin Burckhardt, Wolfgang Coy, and Friedrich Kittler, he is also a member of the program commission to set the direction to be taken by *Interface 5*, which was implemented in Hamburg under the title *Politik der Maschine* (Politics of the Machine). His publications such as *Singularität und Sittlichkeit. Die Kunst Aldo Walkers in bildrhetorischer und medienphilosophischer Perspektive* (Singularity and Morality: Aldo Walker's Art from the Perspective of the Rhetoric of the Image and Media Philosophy; 2004); *Kunst als Medientheorie. Vom Zeichen zur Handlung* (Art as Media Theory: From the Sign to Action; 2003); *Mythos Medienkunst* (The Myth of Media Art; 2002) fill bookshelves and are a treasure trove of contemporary media discourse.

6 5

1a Willy Rotzler on the road with Hans Finsler (left). Photo Serge Libiszewski

1b With Emil Landolt and Hans and Elena Fischli at the opening of *Family of Man* at the Museum of Design Zurich, 1958

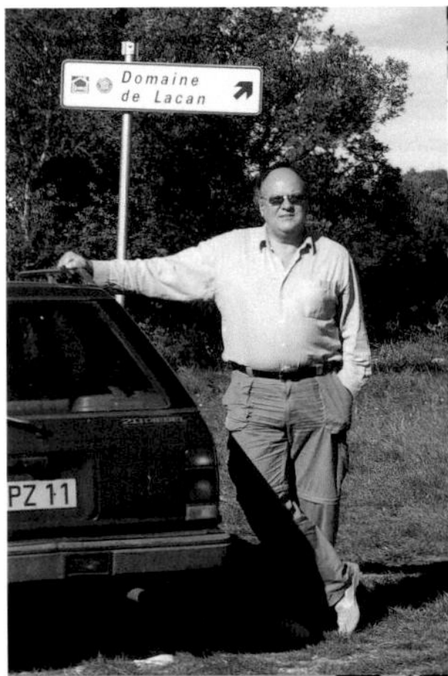

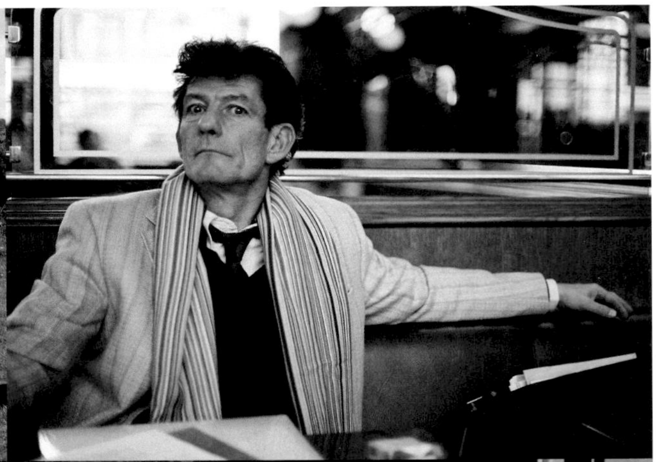

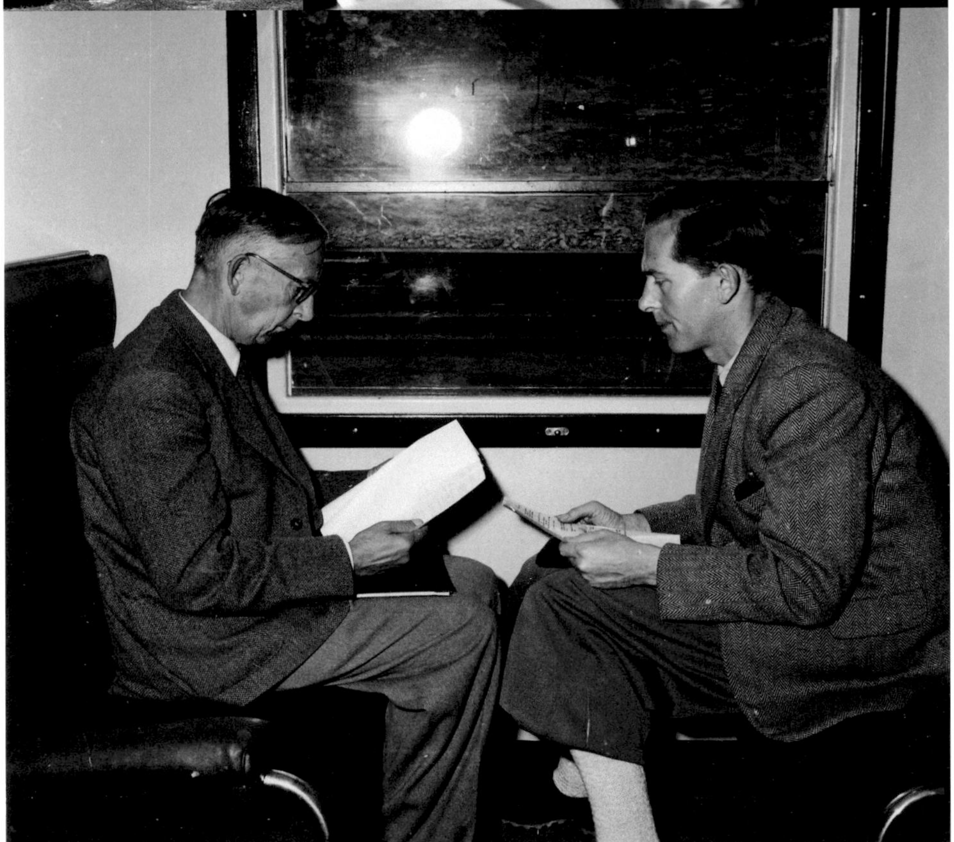

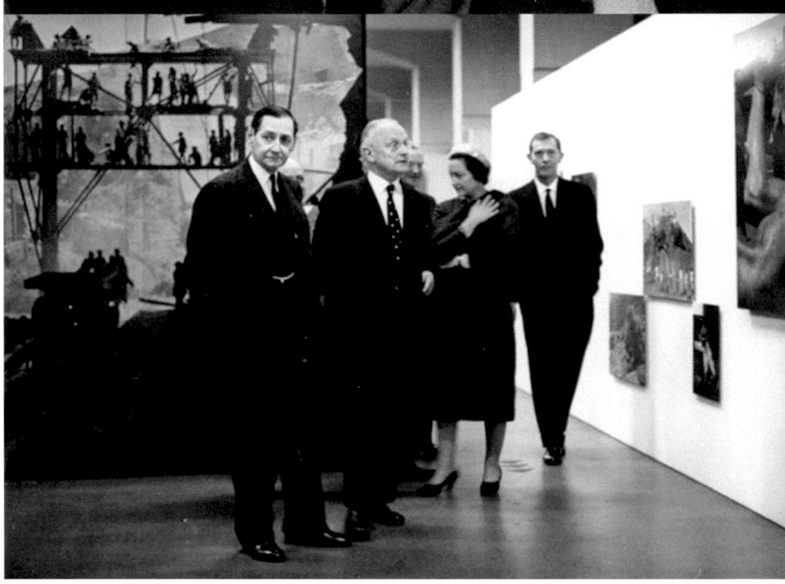

1c–f Reportage by Serge Libiszewski on „the activities of Herr Dr. Rotzler, academic assistant at the Museum of Applied Arts and Design." Degree project with Hans Finsler, March 1951

1g Photo from the exhibition *Finnisches Kunstgewerbe* at the Museum of Applied Arts and Design. Concept and organisation by Willy Rotzler, 1951

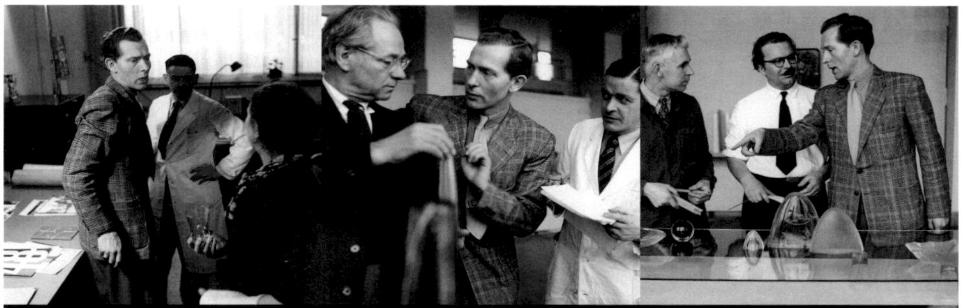

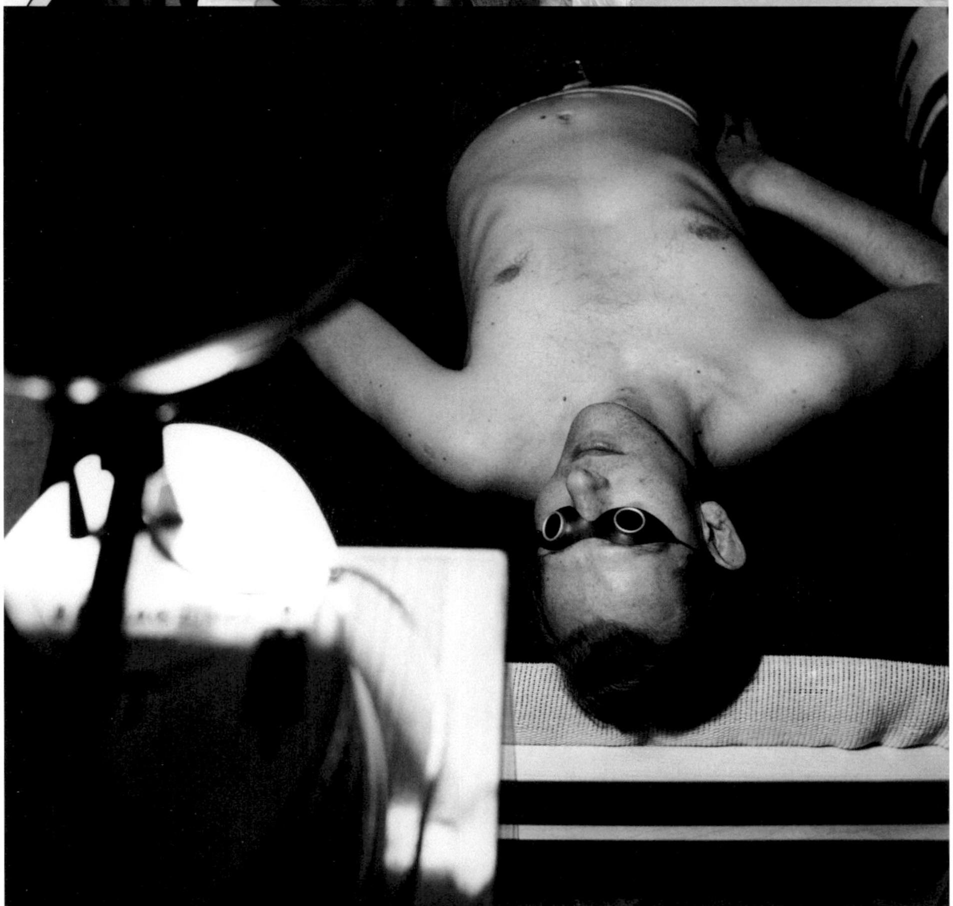

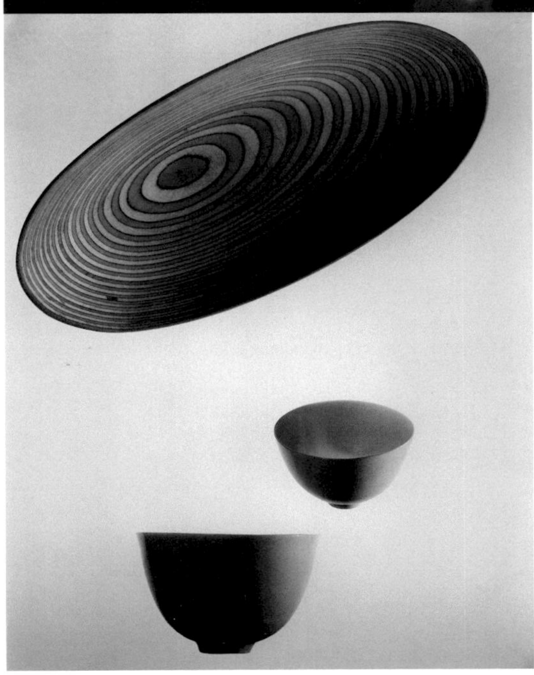

2a *Filmstills—Emotionen Made in Hollywood.* Project manager Alois Martin Müller, exhibition at the Museum of Design Zurich, 1992/93.

2b *Radix, Matrix—Daniel Libeskinds Architekturen.* Project manager Alois Martin Müller, poster design Cornel Windlin, 1994

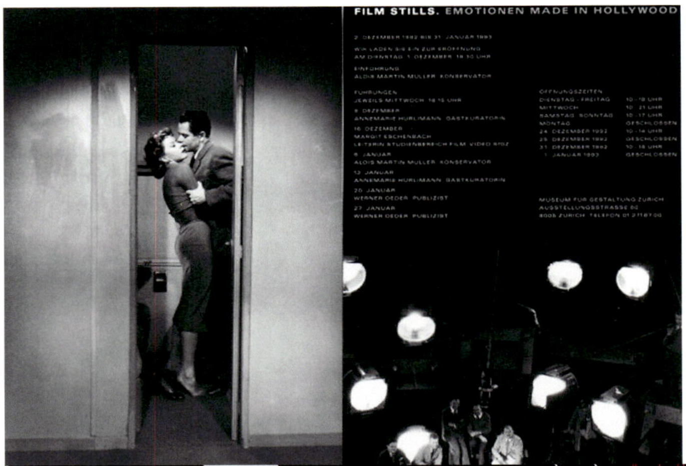

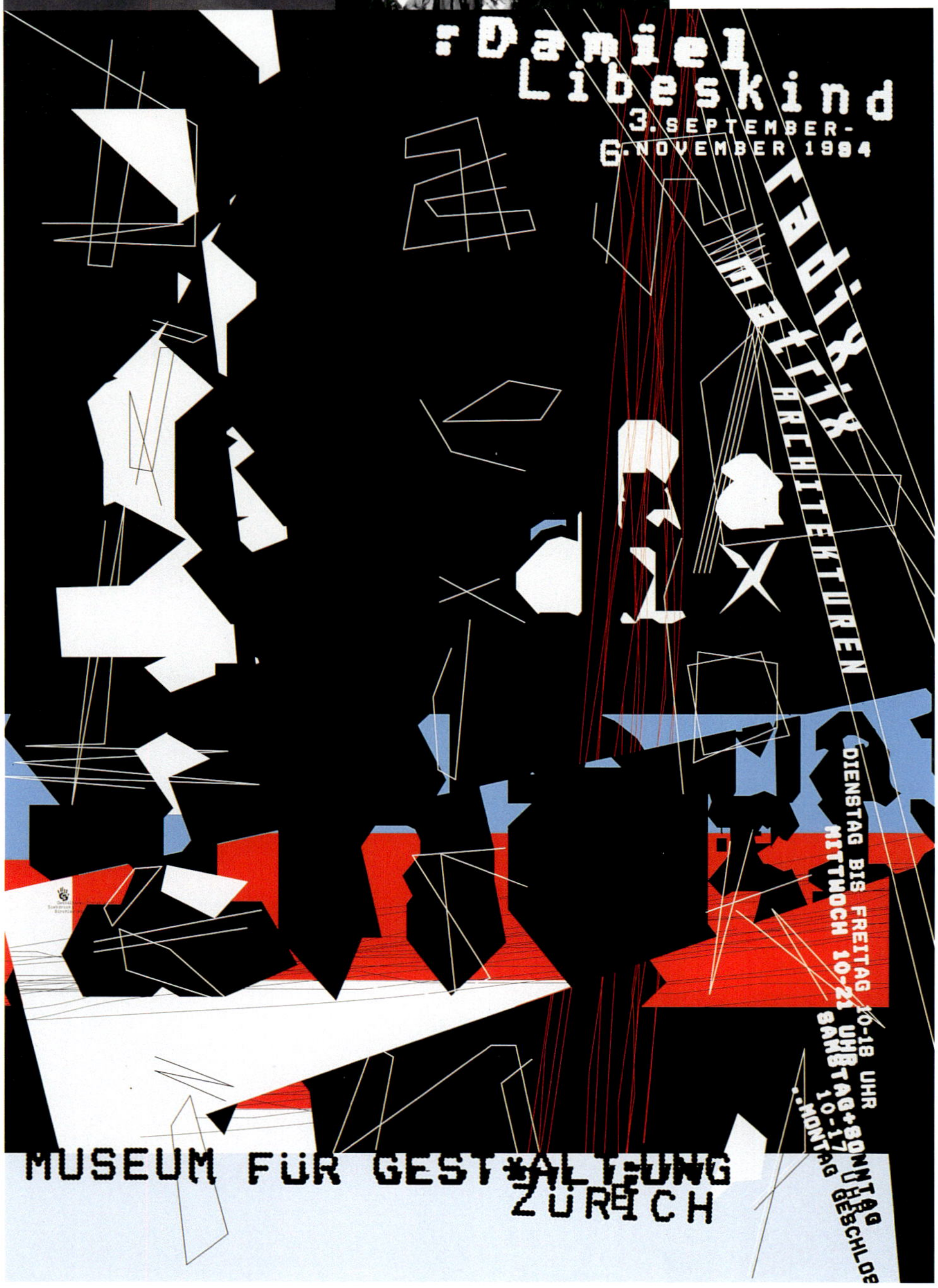

2c *Mehrwerte—Schweiz und Design: die 80er.* Concept Alois Martin Müller, poster Roli Fischbacher/Mihaly Varga, 1991

4a–d Jörg Huber, *Interventionen.* Series, 1991–2004

5a André Vladimir Heiz, *Es ist immer das Gleiche, aber nie dasselbe,* 2007

6a Book by Hans Ulrich Reck, 2004

6b Poster announcing a lecture, 1984

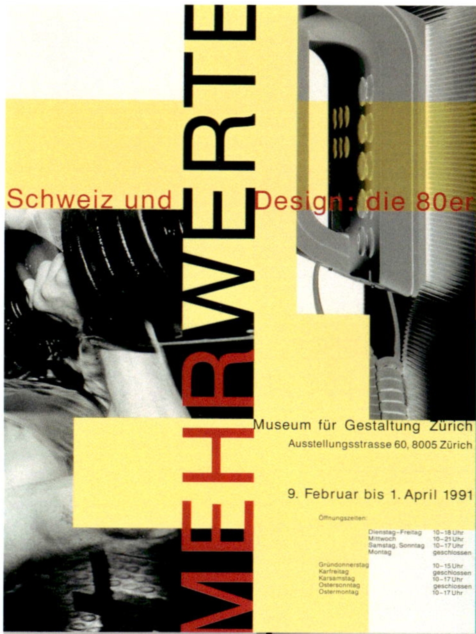

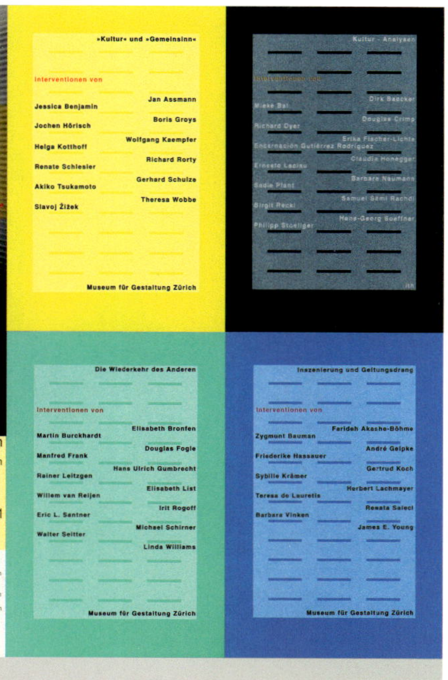

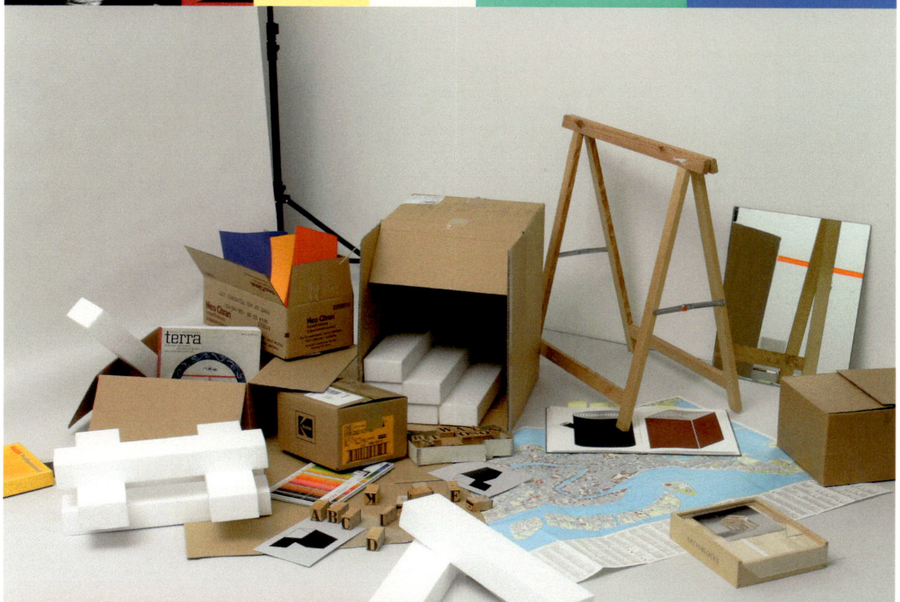

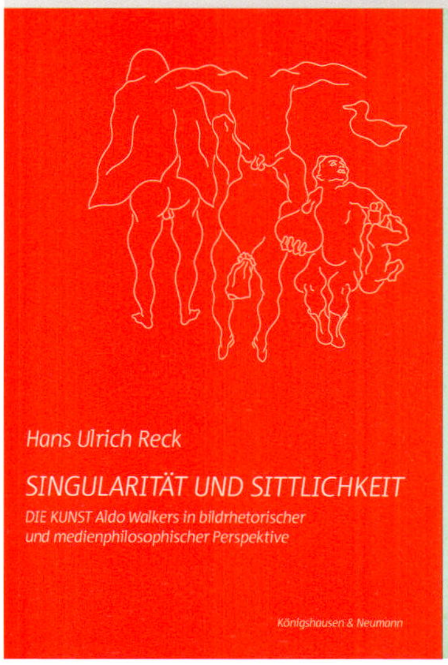

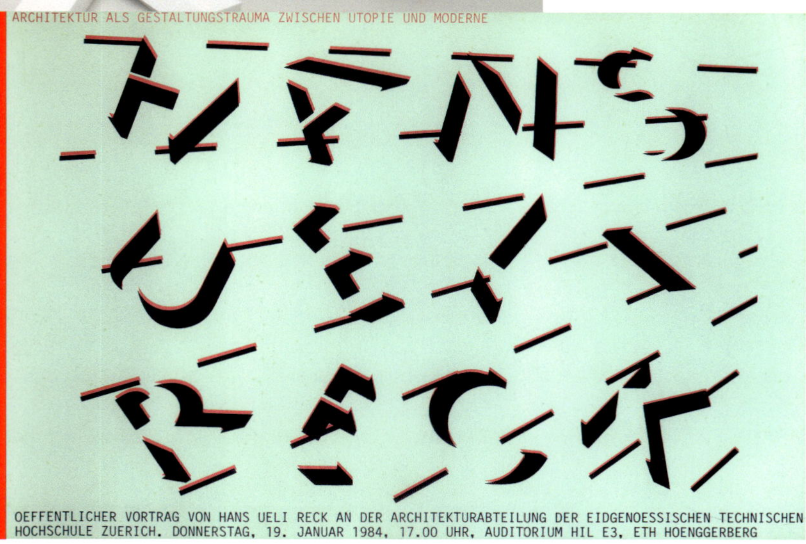

Even institutions like the Zurich University of the Arts, which are devoted to the present and to the future, have their pasts, which they cannot and should not cast off. And inevitably, these histories shape their futures.

Here are the predecessors, still present in memory, those who established the reputations of their institutions. They propagated new movements in art: revolutionary expressionist works, the avant-garde of the Bauhaus, the cultural seedlings of radical modernism, and classical and temperate modernism—and other styles that defy precise categorization. By means of inspired notations, they conveyed that which could not be spoken, deploying incisive artistic signatures with immediate individual attribution and recognizability.

His title of nobility is "master of colors" 1; he is seen as an important early abstractionist—and lyricist 2; this composer of lieder and opera, who was committed to moderate modernism, enjoys new currency today 3; his expressive and dynamic pictorial spaces are dizzying 4; his posters are among the most visually striking in Europe 5; his paintings in the style of New Objectivity remain standards for the painterly right up to the present 6; he permanently revolutionized church music during his brief lifetime 7; he and his art are the personification and embodiment of *peinture informelle* 8; she is the highly productive graphic chronicler of theater life in Zurich 9.

1
Augusto Giacometti (1877–1947)
He was one of the Giacomettis of the famous dynasty of painters from Bergell. He trained as a draftsmanship teacher at the first School of Applied Arts, which was then in Zurich Selnau in a building with old, poorly lit rooms and worn wooden staircases. However, he described the atmosphere and attitude of the school as somehow more elegant, more elevated, but also somehow tougher than life in his home town of Chur, and more "covetous" too: "The women students, to whom we always looked up with a certain awe—they wore white smocks." Giacometti expressed the upheavals of the time (art nouveau was entering the scene) as follows: "There was a kind of pride and energy in us, a premonition of spring, love, freedom, and joy. It was the birth of the art nouveau style."

Giacometti is considered one of the outstanding painters in the tradition of art nouveau and symbolism, a reformer of stained glass painting and an exponent of monumental mural painting, but he was also the designer of popular posters. He was one of the first artists of the twentieth century who conceded an almost total autonomy to the art of painting and who took the plunge into non-representational art. Subsequently, Giacometti became a great exponent of color. His tombstone recalls this aspect of his art, describing him as a "master of color."

2
Otto Meyer-Amden (1885–1933)
Otto Meyer-Amden is a master of the smallest format—small delicate pictures of incredible inner monumentality and density. His drawings in lead and colored pencil and his watercolors are outwardly wholly unspectacular, and yet of such outstanding quality that he belongs among the great Swiss painters. He is an early "abstracter" with consistent pictorial discipline, a lyric expressive voice. His pictures are imbued with religious symbolism found in numerous boarding school scenes, juvenile nudes, street scenes, and geometric designs. His works were shown at the first *documenta* and at *documenta III* in Kassel.

He completed a course of study in lithography and attended evening classes at the School of Applied Arts. In 1912 he received an invitation from the artists Willi Baumeister and Hermann Huber to go to Amden where they and other painters and sculptors had established themselves in an artist's colony. After they left, Meyer remained in Amden until 1928 and led a retiring and modest life in an old farmhouse. From 1933 onwards Otto Meyer-Amden taught technical drawing at the School of Applied Arts.

3
Othmar Schoeck (1886–1957)
Othmar Schoeck's ties to the Zurich Conservatory, or rather the Zurich School of Music, Drama and Dance, as the predecessor of today's Music Department was called, naturally go back to his studies there in the years 1904 to 1907, when he left for Leipzig in order to study under Max Reger. Yet even stronger than the loyalty he felt towards his alma mater was his romantic interest in one of the teachers there: "At last the lovely Stefi Geyer was there, playing wonderfully and enchanting me more than ever," as Schoeck wrote to his parents from Leipzig, describing the Hungarian violinist he must have first seen at one of her Zurich engagements and whom he would later meet among the faculty of the Zurich Conservatory.

Although Schoeck dedicated both his violin sonata of 1908 and the violin concerto he composed a short while later to Geyer, his main interest as a composer was not in instrumental music at all, but rather in vocal works. He composed more than 300 lieder as well as eight operas, one of which—his setting of Heinrich von Kleist's *Penthesilea*—has seen a number of performances in recent years.

Whereas *Penthesilea* was considered an avant-garde work when it premiered in Dresden in 1927, today's critics—who are showing renewed interest in Schoeck—tend to describe his oeuvre as "moderated modernism."

4
Otto Morach (1887–1973)
Morach taught at the School of Applied Arts from 1919–53 and became head of the Department of Decorative Painting there in 1930.

1 3
4 5

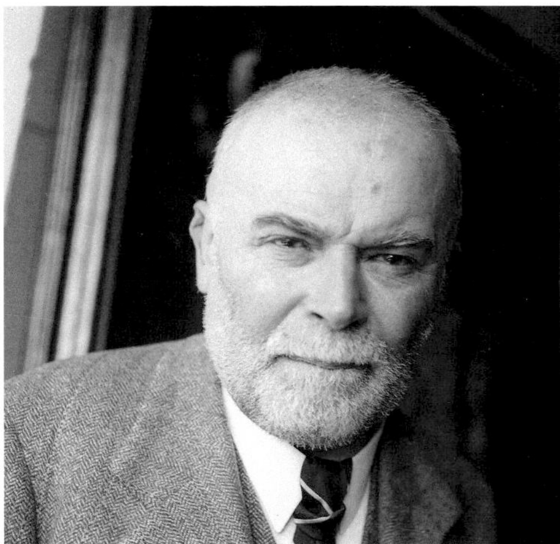

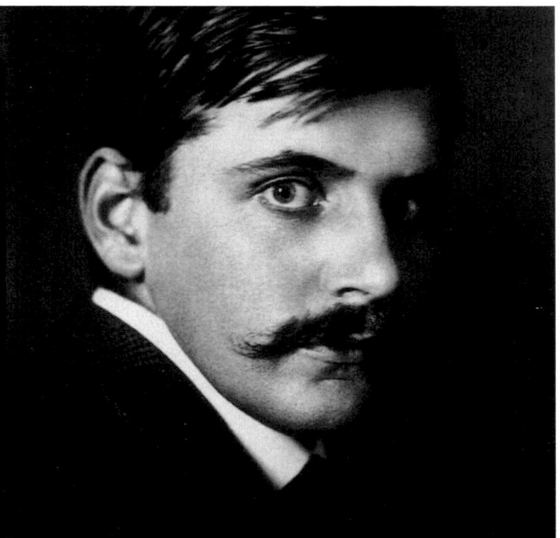

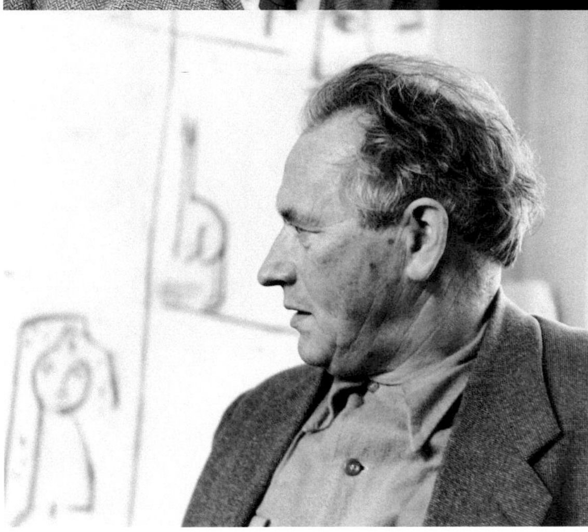

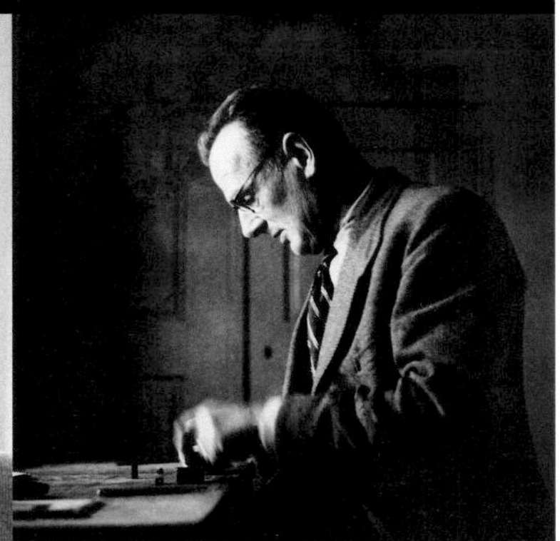

His stylistic modes were those of the then avant-garde, particularly cubism and futurism, and, later, his figurative world became marked by the impact of New Objectivity and surrealism. In his later work, he preferred dynamic pictorial spaces, images of human bodies and machines overlapping, the barren, things destroyed by violence; forest fires and ruins are among his later preferred subjects. He constructed, carved, and painted puppets for the puppet theater from cubes, cones, and cylinders, using the formal repertoire of shapes of the period to create mechanistically abstract human figures in a kind of cubist reshaping of the human form. Morach was also a successful poster designer. In their bold, dizzying perspectives and their large areas of coloration Morach's posters were far ahead of their time.

5
Otto Baumberger (1889–1961)

Otto Baumberger's artistic personality was torn between commercial art and high art. His passion was for the intellectual, the mystical, and the religious in the widest sense. In contrast, he described his celebrated poster designs—for which he gained an international reputation—as "incessant potboiler work" that he was obliged to do because he needed the money. As an artist, he combined a deeply rooted cultural pessimism with elitist aesthetic ideals: "The people, which is to say the masses, have no use for art and have never had any use for it in the past." This view set him apart from the progressive social utopias of the avant-garde of his time. Rejecting this avant-garde, he held that "any art which has something fundamental to offer to today's intellectual, materialistic, technology-oriented people must depict the miraculous." On the other hand, it is to Baumberger that we owe some of the icons of European functional poster art.

Baumberger attended both the compulsory courses and optional subjects at the School of Applied Arts. In 1916 he became an assistant teacher at the school. In 1931, he was given a post as associate professor for draftsmanship and design at the Swiss Federal Institute of Technology Zurich.

6
Max Gubler (1898–1973)

For his students, he was an exemplary role model and the epitome of a New Functionalist painter. His two older brothers, Eduard and Ernst, were artists too. He taught at the School of Applied Arts Zurich from 1939 to 1945. His art, which began as dark-toned expressionist works harking back to cubist forms, developed into a style of painting with gentle, light-flooded landscapes and allegories with a starkly reduced range of colors. Gubler's wall painting in the stairwell of the new School of Applied Arts (1935)—a work commissioned by the architect Karl Egender—initiated an entire generation of teachers into Gubler's idea of art.

The painting fell into disfavor when plans were made to express the modernity and up-to-date thrust of the museum and the school in the entrance area of the building. The historicist aura of the painting became a thorn in the flesh of those who followed the *zeitgeist*. However, those in favor of the painting defended it as though its removal were a sacrilege. The empty wall bears witness to the winners of this internal cultural conflict between the innovators and the preservers.

7
Willy Burkhard (1900–1955)

Although he lived to be only fifty-five, Willy Burkhard was without a doubt one of the most distinguished composers of twentieth-century Switzerland. After studying in Leipzig, Munich, and Paris, and gaining some experience as a teacher in Bern, Burkhard came to the Zurich Conservatory as a teacher of theory and composition in 1942. He was to prove a pioneer as both teacher and artist alike and is widely credited with having initiated a renaissance of church music in Switzerland. His pupils include such important personalities as Klaus Huber, Ernst Widmer, Rudolf Kelterborn, Giuseppe Englert, and many others.

8
Hans Falk (1918–2002)

Hans Falk has left a rich life's work in the form of paintings, posters, and graphic art that made him one of the most important Swiss artists of

6 8
9 7

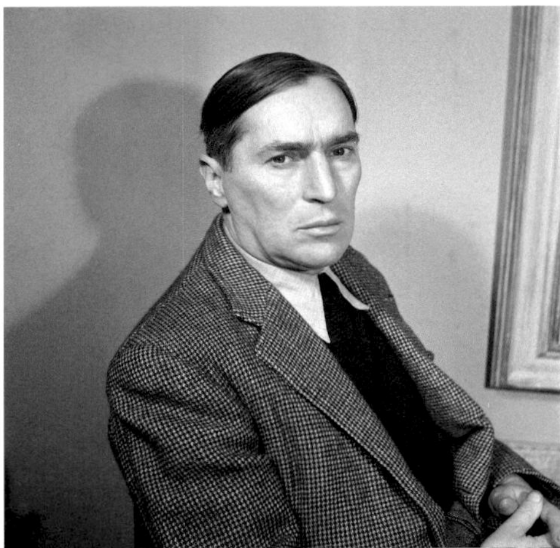
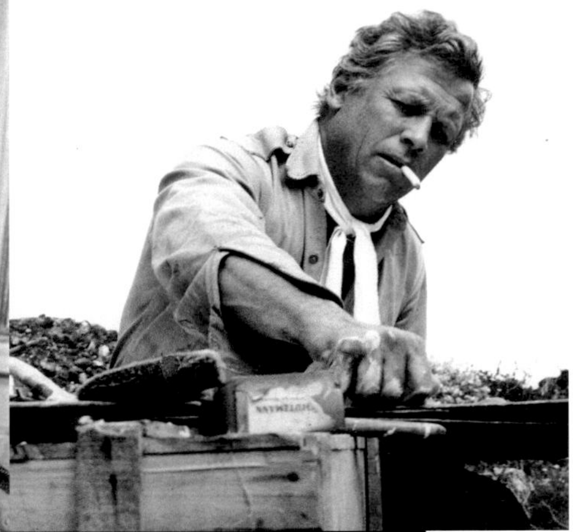
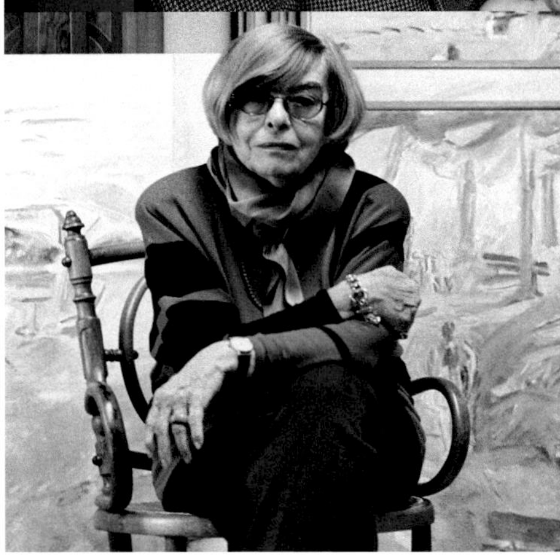
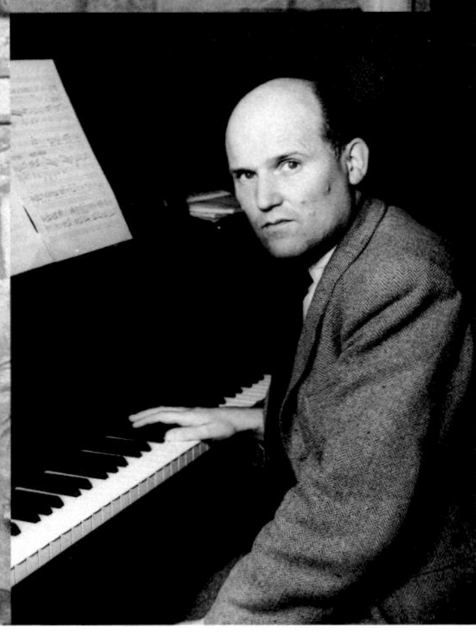

the twentieth century. His circus paintings are particularly memorable, and reproductions of them can be found in living rooms everywhere. He is the most important exponent of an art known as *peinture informelle.* Falk studied under Max Gubler and Walter Roshardt from 1942–43 and he taught at the School of Applied Arts from 1950–55. He created innumerable posters and as a poster artist placed himself above all at the service of social aid organizations and politics. His most prominent public appearance came in the form of the abstract and expressive posters he created for Expo 64. A footnote to his career is his friendship with Werner Bischof with whom he shared a studio in the 1940s.

9

Hanny Fries (*1918)

In 1981 Hanny Fries received the art prize of the city of Zurich for an oeuvre that had extended and branched out over decades—Hanny Fries's work can be seen as the memory of the city of Zurich in the media of painting and drawing just on the basis of the remarkable number of theater drawings from the Zurich Schauspielhaus. These theater drawings are a "chronicle of Zurich theater life compressed into graphite," and everyone in the theater—Frisch, Dürrenmatt, Stein, Düggelin, Besson, Muschg—knew her and appreciated her as an insider. Her artistic rendering of theater life was a hallmark of the culture sections of Zurich newspapers—condensed views of events in the theater that photography simply could not match. Fries is also a *femme de letters*, well-read and remarkably well informed on all matters pertaining to the stage. To the present day Fries the obsessive drawer still fills stacks of paper and hundreds of sketch books. She sketches her subjects on trips, fixing what she later transfers to her canvas as a painter: common and everyday places like railroad stations, construction sites that she constantly overpaints using her smudging technique and that she distills into lucid, spherical worlds. As a gifted portraitist she has immortalized innumerable citizens of Zurich and prominent Swiss cultural and political figures.

1a/b Poster design by Augusto Giacometti: exhibition poster, 1928; brewery ad, 1923
1c *Der Ausbruch des Aetna*, 1928. Pastel on paper
1d/e *Rote und weisse Nelken*. Still life, 1925.—*Weisse Pfingstrosen*, 1940. Oil on canvas

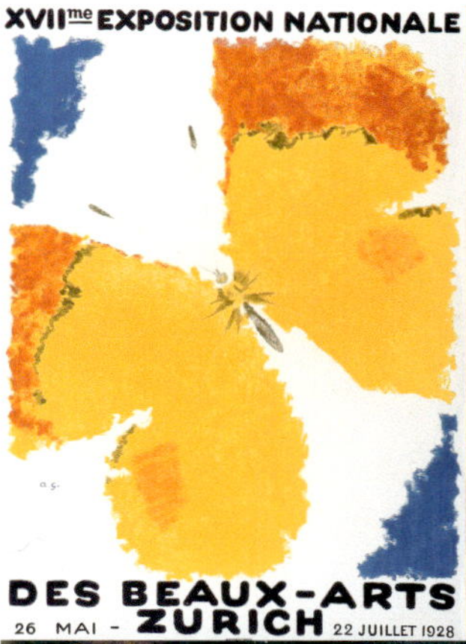

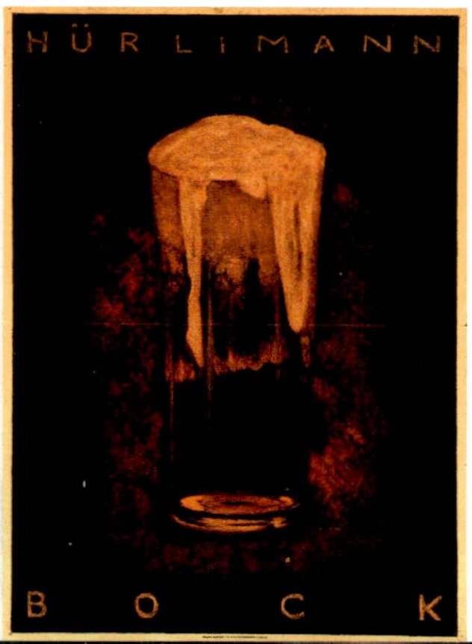

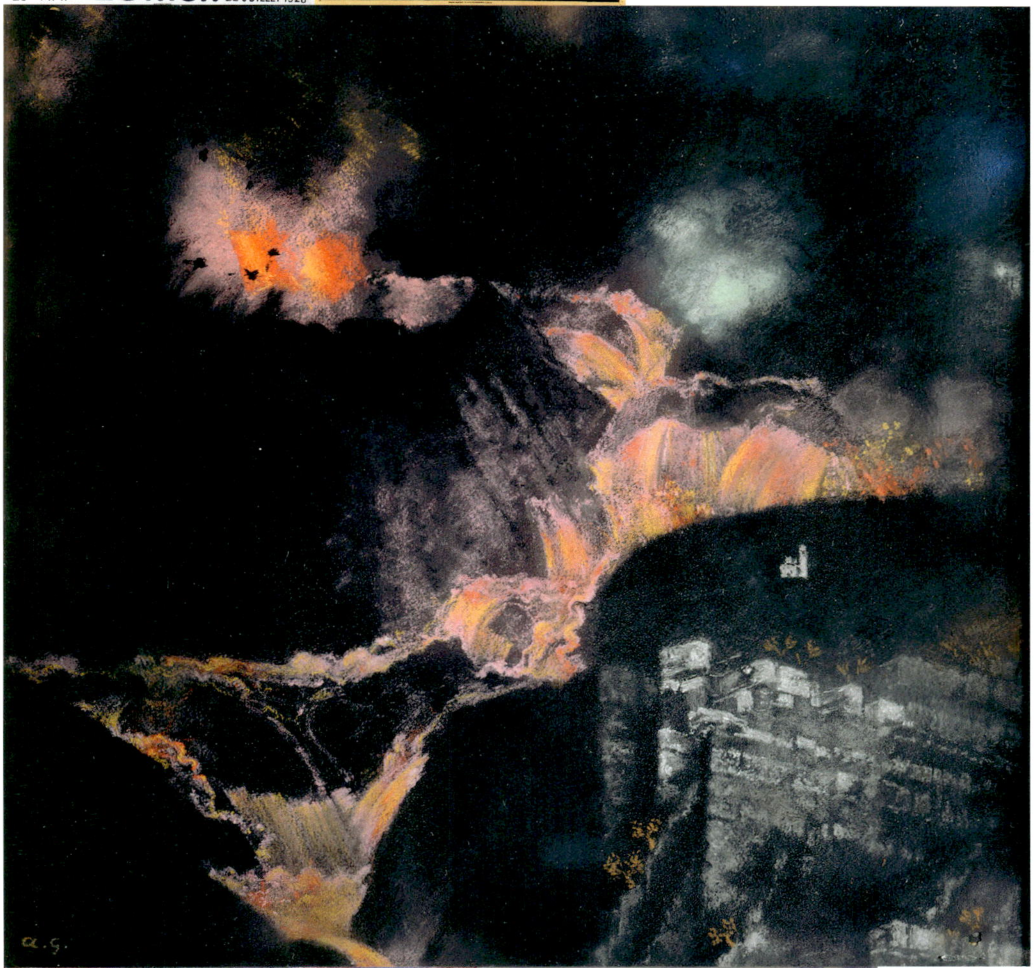

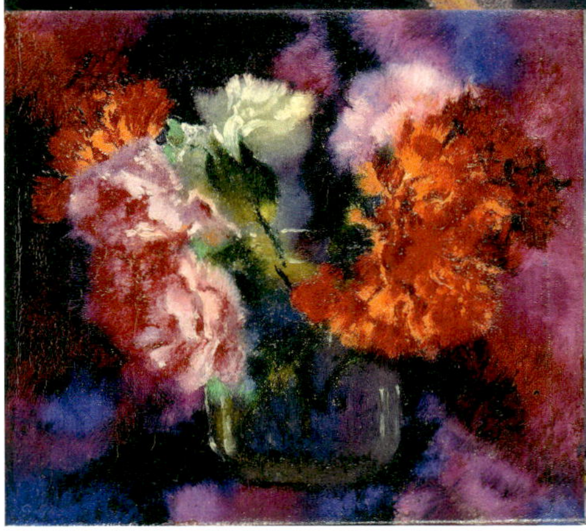

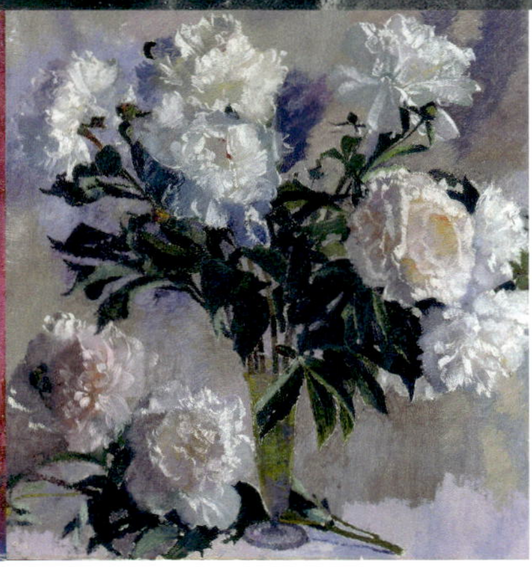

2a Otto Meyer-Amden, *Gesamtkomposition II.* Oil on canvas, ca. 1922

2b *Nude Study,* no date. Drawing

3a Othmar Schoeck, “Nachruf.” Lied based on a poem by Joseph von Eichendorff. Autograph op. 20, no.14, ca. 1915

4a Otto Morach, *Die Bergwerke von Estaque,* ca. 1927. Oil on canvas

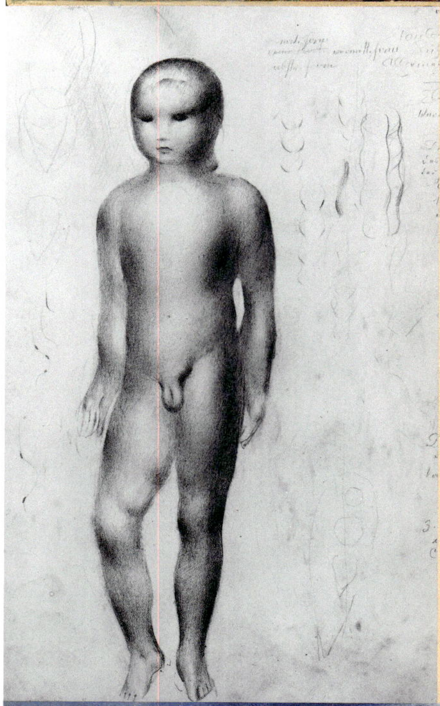

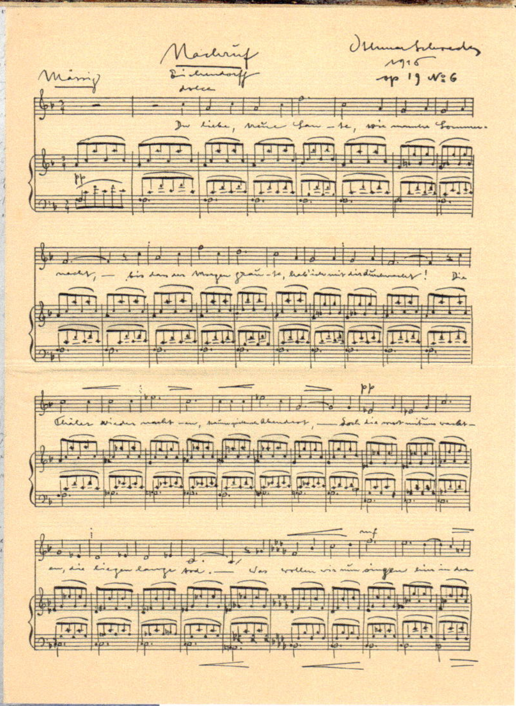

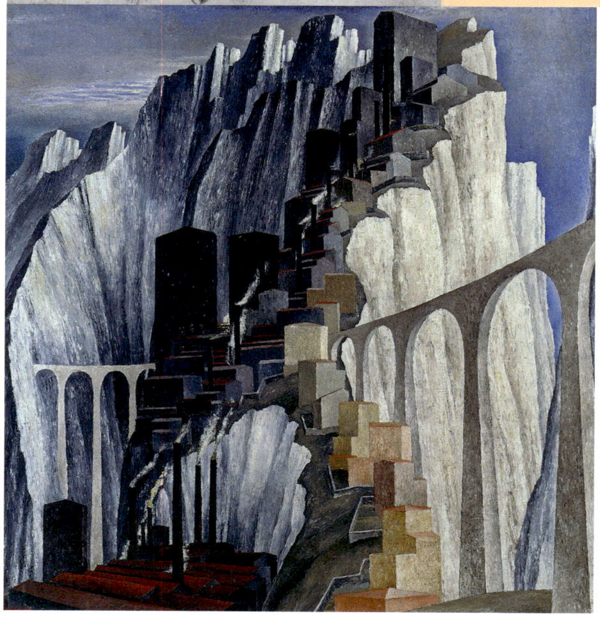

4b Poster for A. Welti-Furrer AG, Zurich

4c *Sterben im Krieg*, 1915, Oil on canvas

5a/b Posters by Otto Baumberger, Zurich, 1932/37

5c *Die Entstehung der Eidgenossenschaft.* Mural at Landi 39, Zurich, 1939

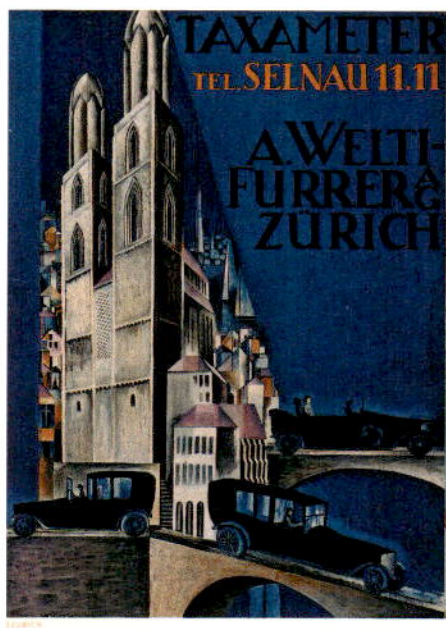

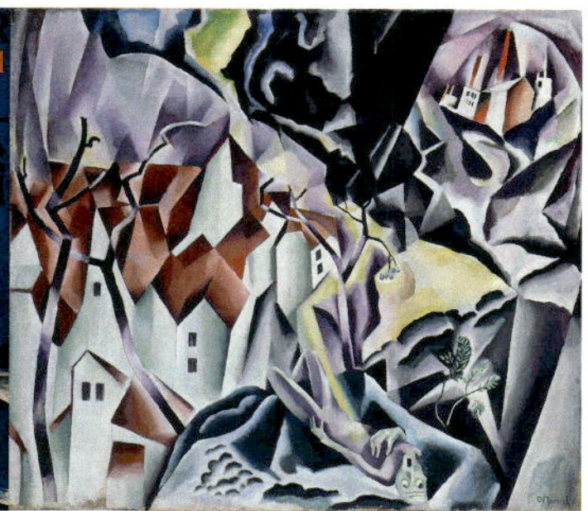

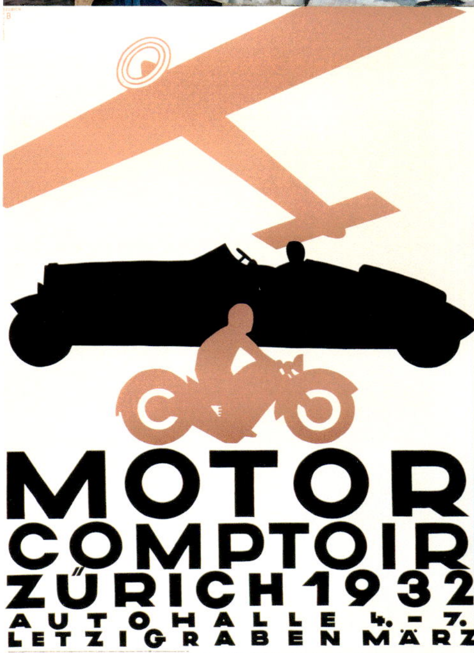

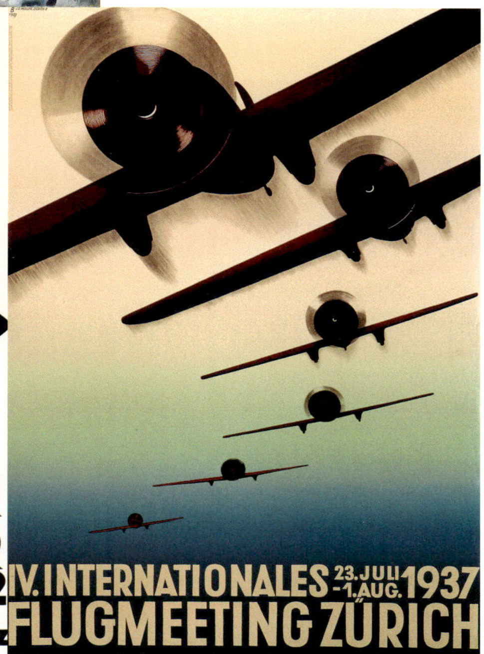

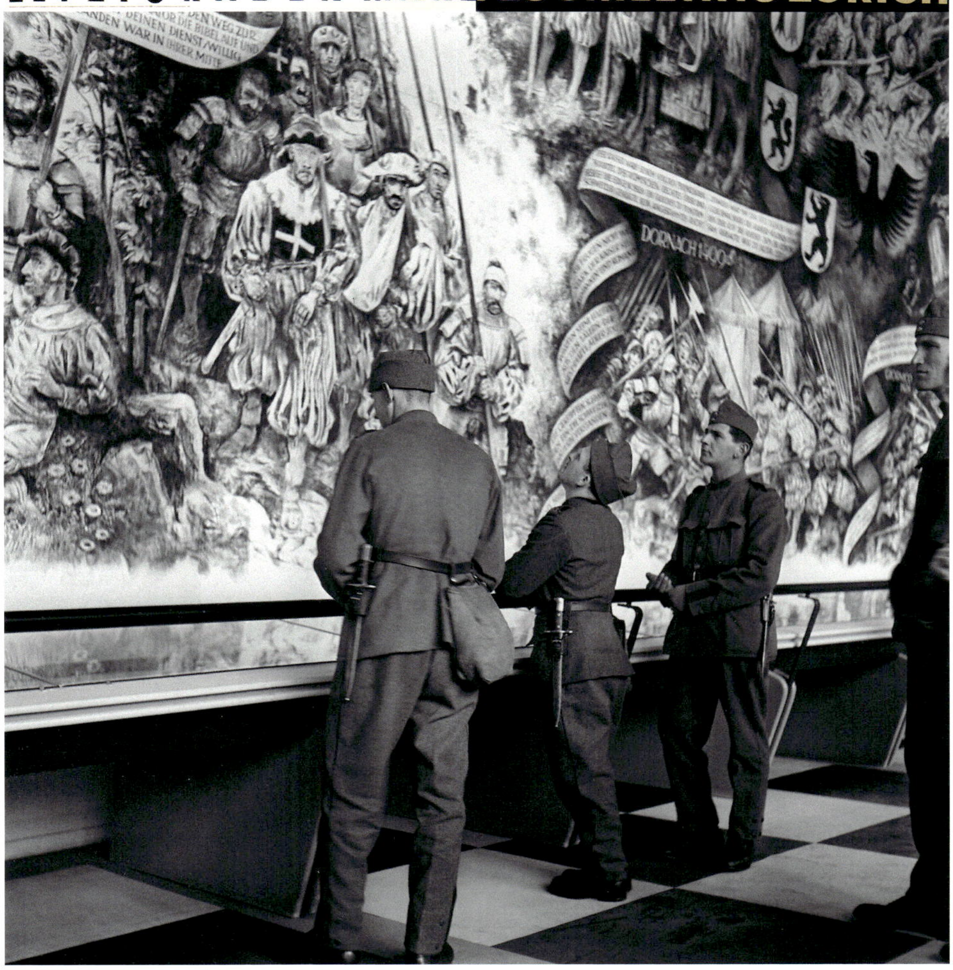

6a Max Gubler in his studio, no date **6b** *Bildnis der Mutter*, 1938. Oil on canvas
6c *Badende (Zürich Letten)*. Mural commissioned for the staircase of the new Zurich School of Applied Arts, realized in 1935

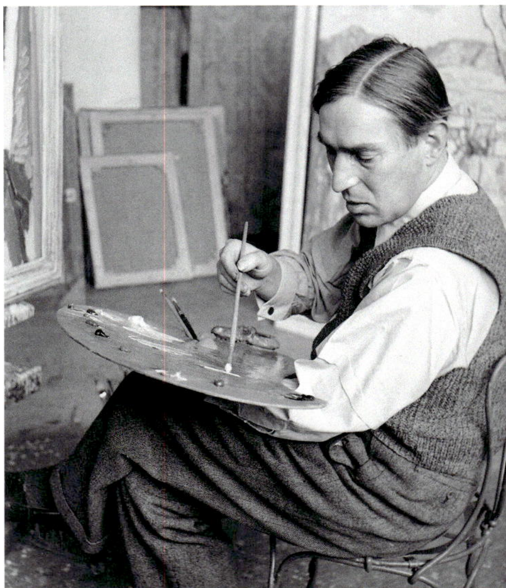

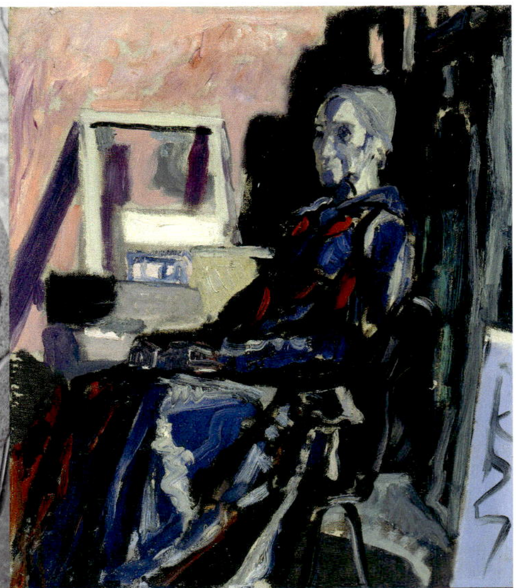

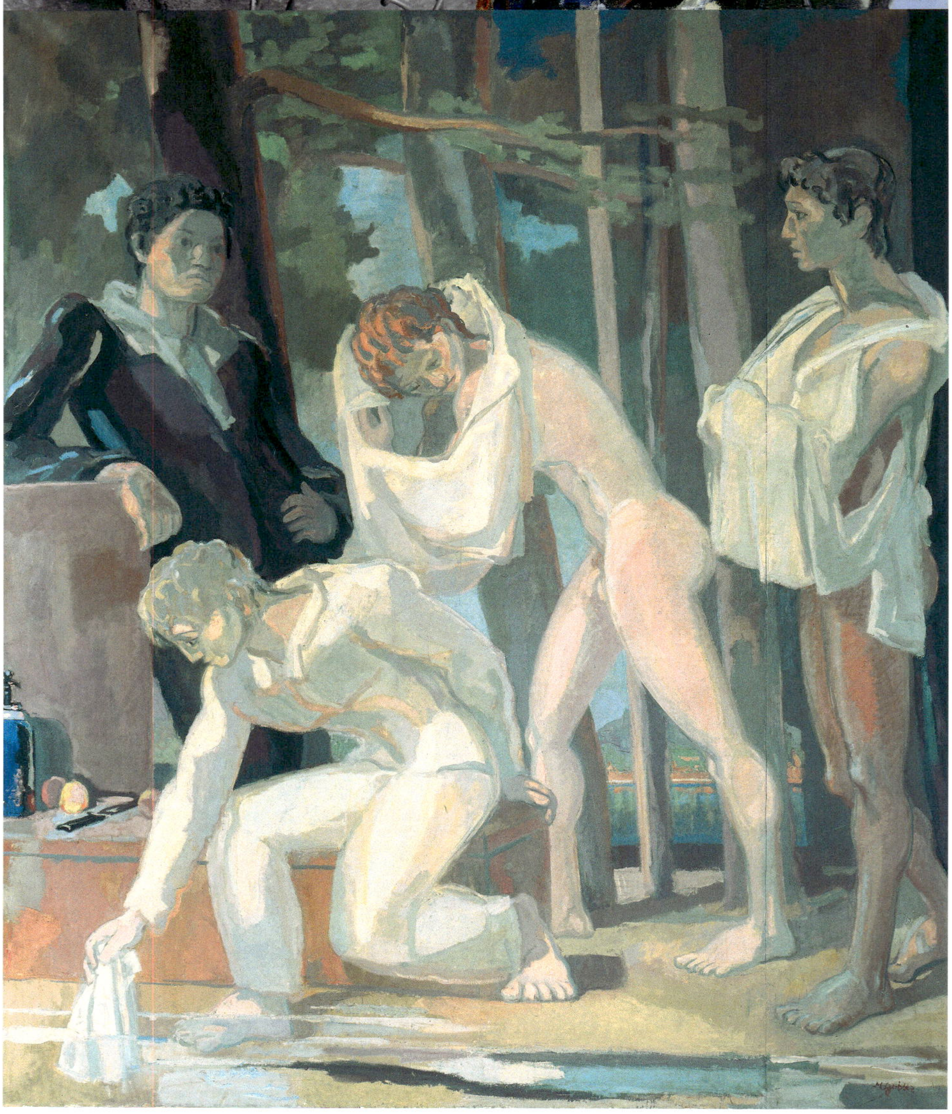

8a Hans Falk, *Stromboli,* Art informel, 1961. Oil on canvas

8b Hans Falk draws on musicals and performances, using material from the media in large-format pictures. London 1969–73

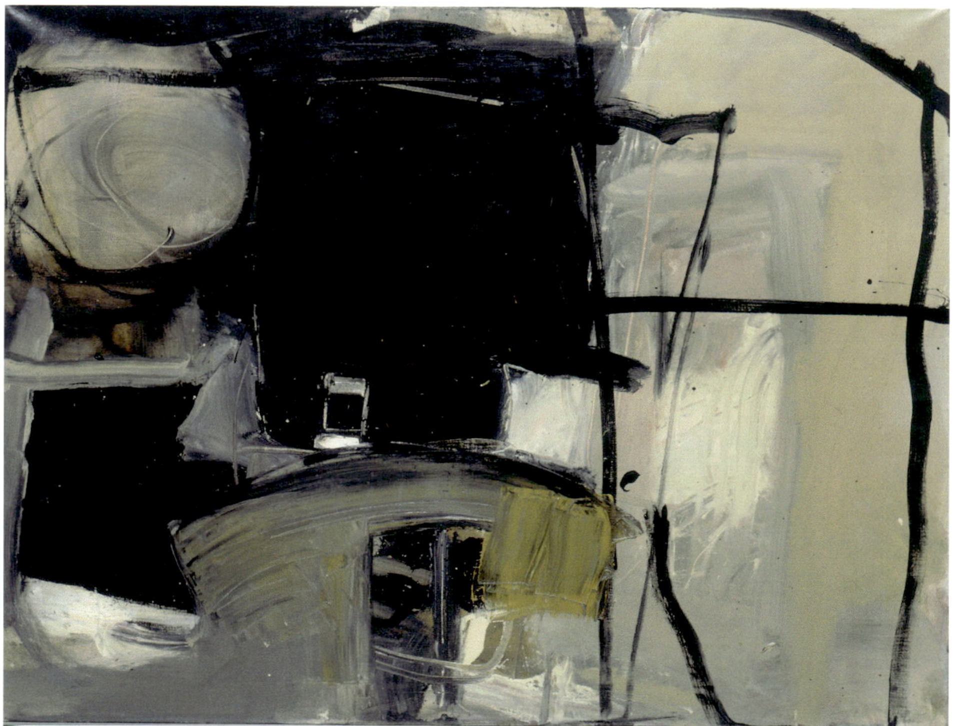

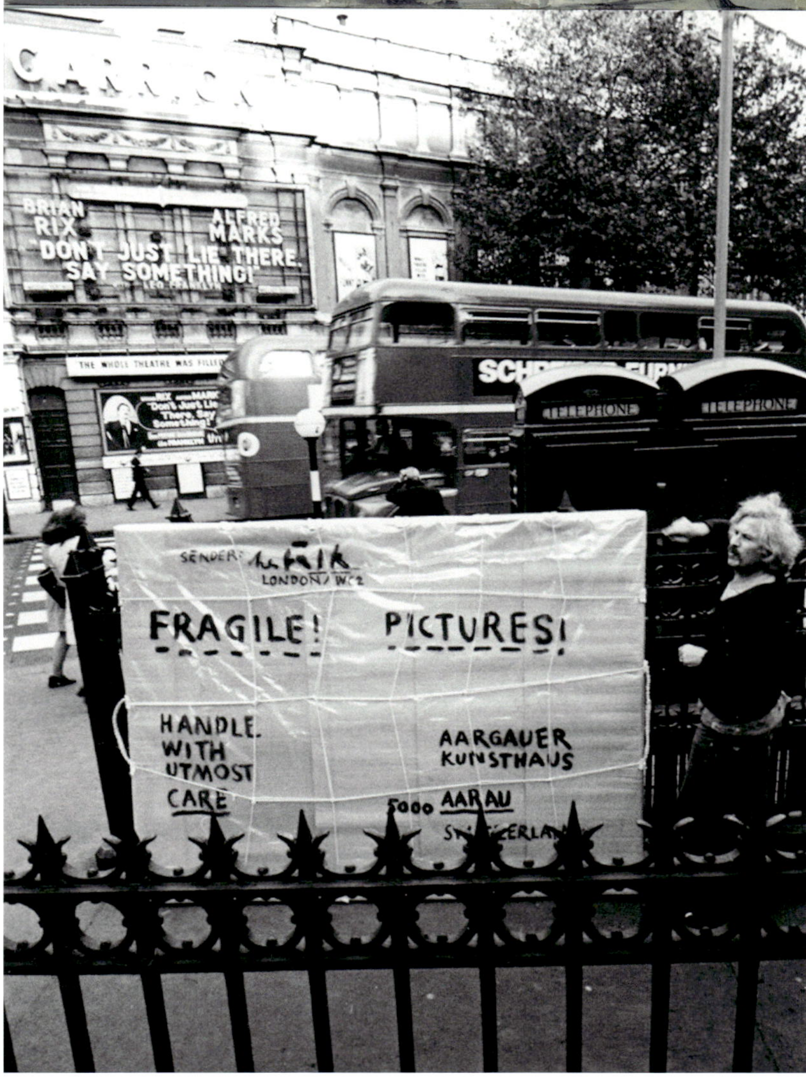

8c–i Hans Falk's controversial poster series for the Swiss National Exposition, Lausanne 1964

9a Hanny Fries, "Performance of Dürrenmatt's play *Die Frist,*" 1977. Drawing from the exhibition and catalogue *Dürrenmatt am Schauspielhaus Zürich: Theaterzeichnungen 1954–1983,* Stadthaus Zürich, 2007

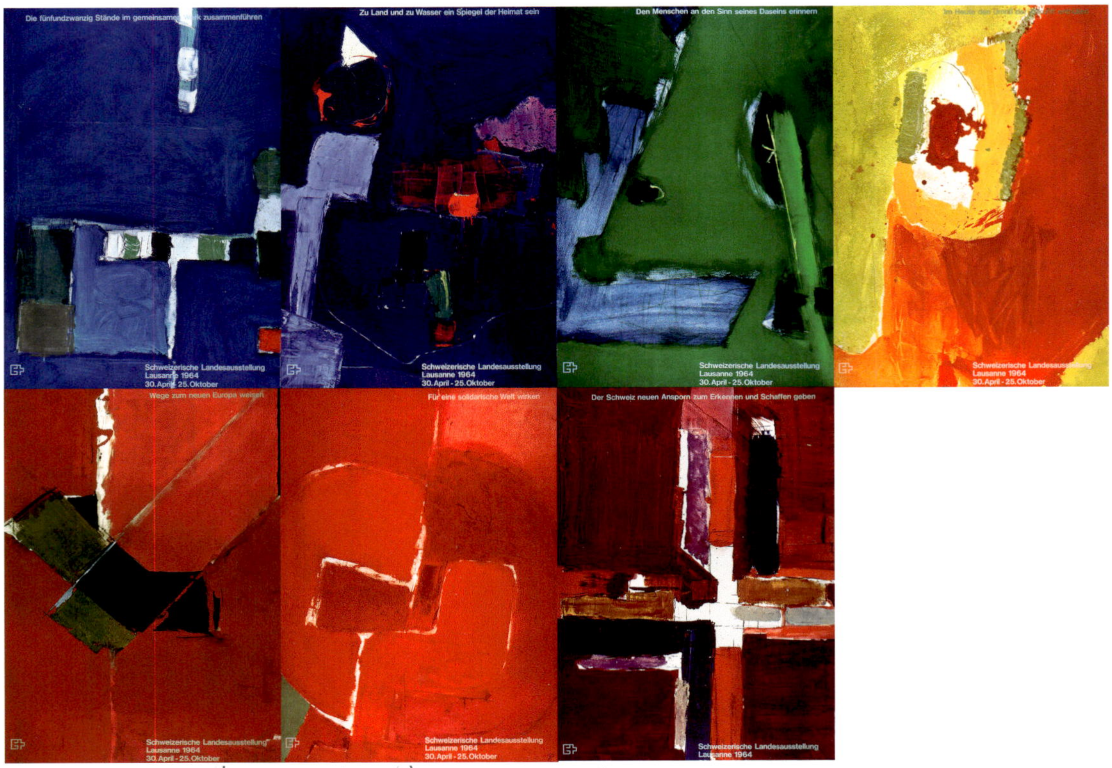

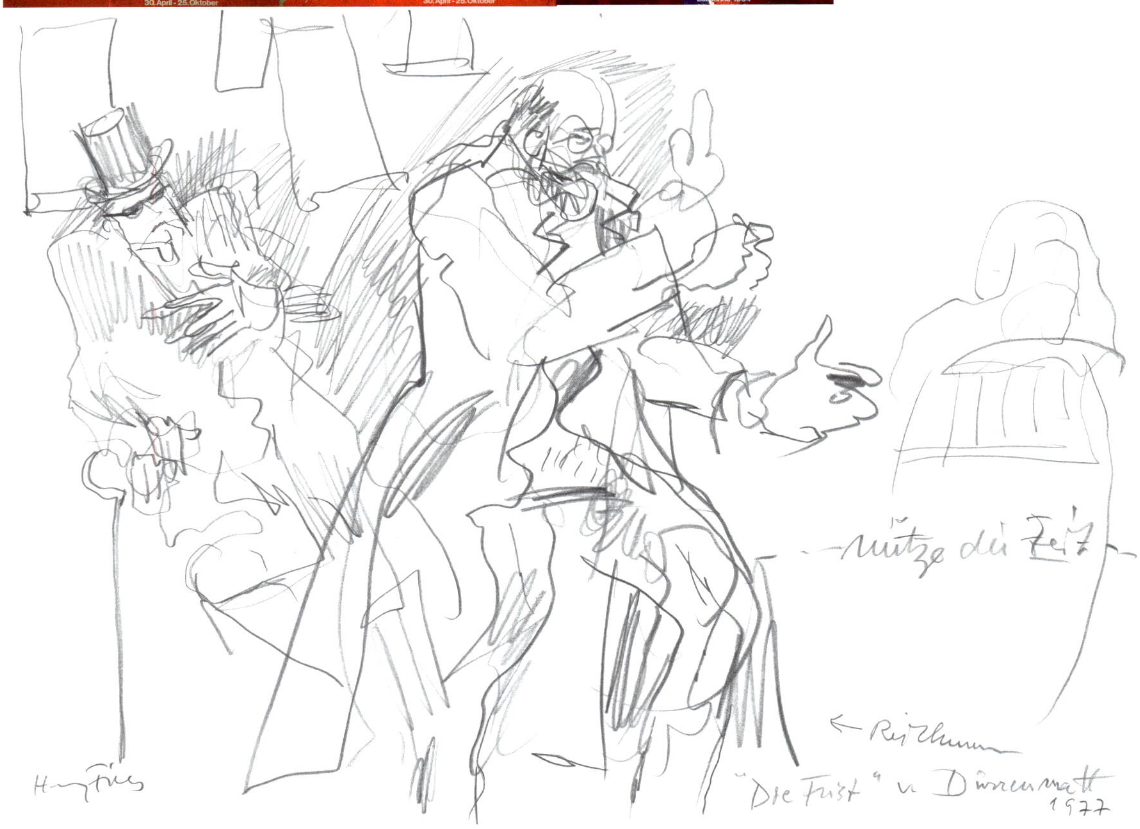

9b *Bahnstation Zürich Wipkingen*, 1997/98. Oil on canvas
9c Hanny Fries in her studio in Zurich, 1998 **9d** "Dürrenmatt at Rehearsals for *Der Mittmacher*," 1973
9e "Dürrenmatt and Press Photographers (Rehearsals for *Der Mittmacher*)"

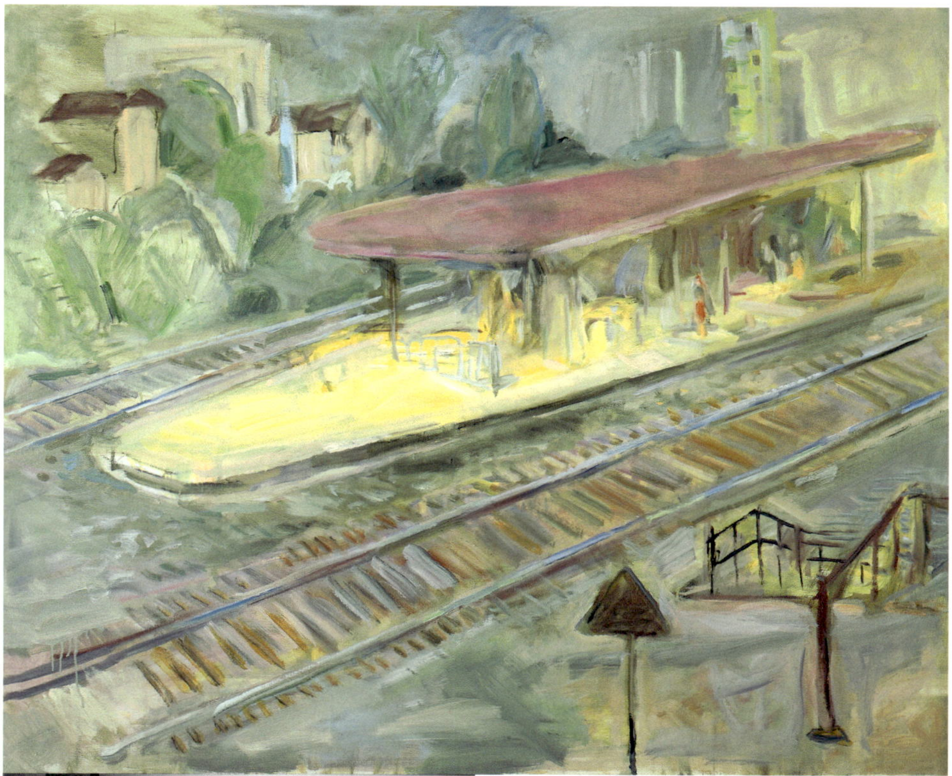

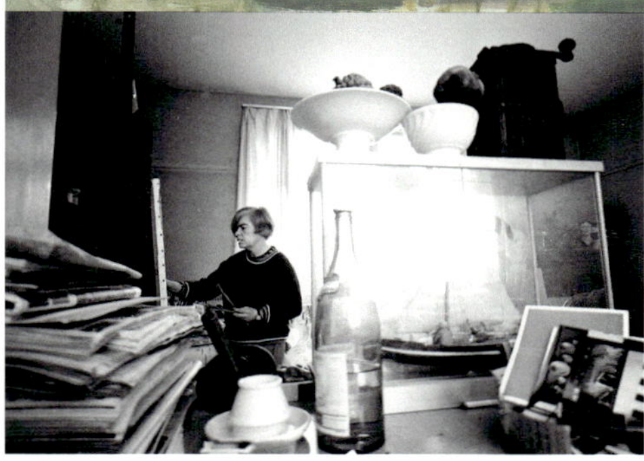

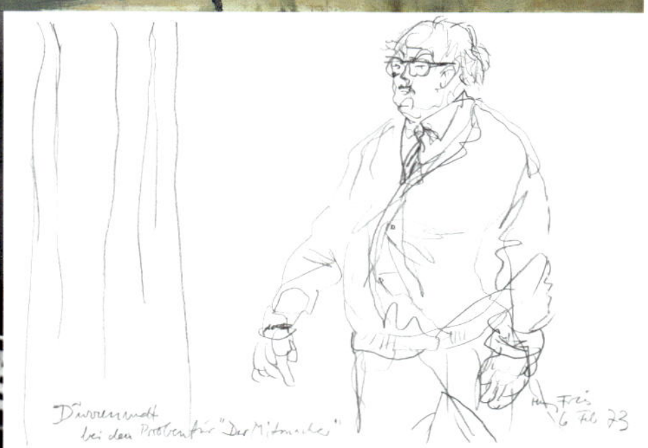

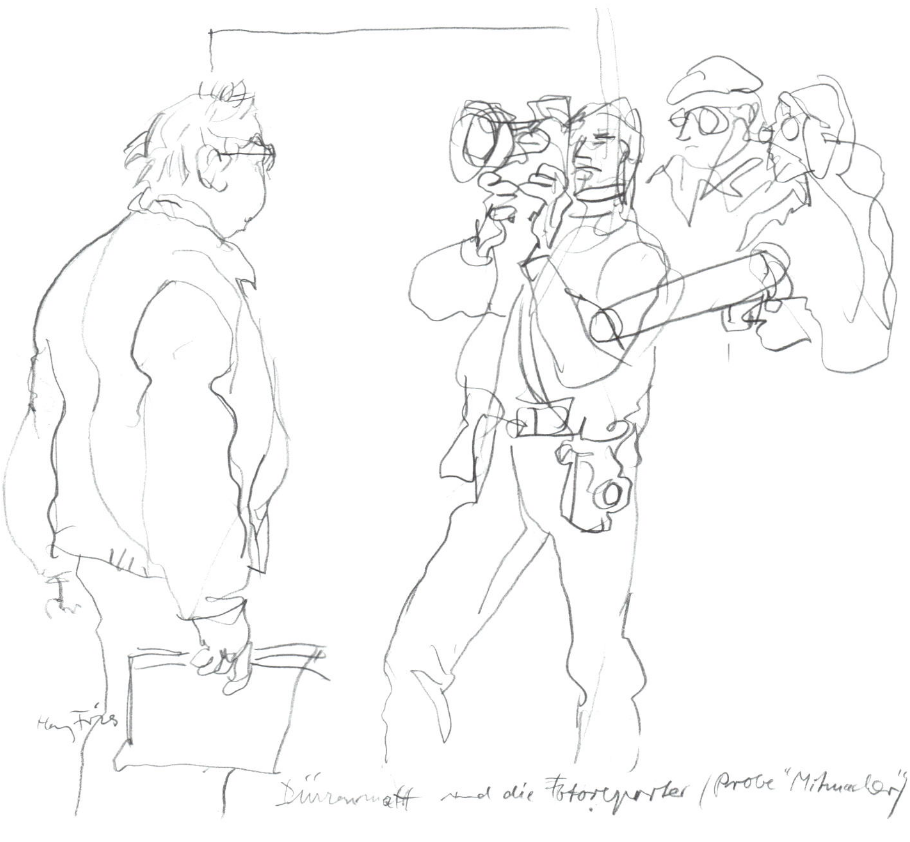

They command the luxury liners, freighters, tankers, ferries, icebreakers, banana boats, and slaughterhouse ships. They hire their own crews —often no strangers to mutiny and ship-boarding—and are responsible for the passengers as well as for the stowaways, the safety of the cargo, and navigation. Metaphorically speaking, institutions of art education are like these colossi of the sea, and their command is a titanic responsibility. The waters are often turbulent, filled with the crashing waves of corporations, pirates, trade unions, and guilds, of political factions and cultural cabals. Their ultimate mission is to hold course for Arcadia—in the ambivalence of nostalgia and utopia.

He was the supporting founder of the first School of Music, with Johannes Brahms and Gottfried Keller as his godfathers 1; he was the inspired Atlas who bore on his shoulders both the Vocational School and the School of Applied Arts in Zurich 4; he was the embodiment of the Werkbund ideal, who broke through the rigidity of pseudo-academicism 2; his stature as master conductor was praised by none other than Gustav Mahler 3; she was the speech trainer who drove the dialect out of Swiss actresses and actors 5; he was the mystical guru of color and form master of the Bauhaus foundation course 6; he dealt the death blow to the "pseudo-academy" 7; he acted his way to directing modern theater education 9; he directed and played out cultural policy from the competing metropolis of Winterthur 8; he transformed and reformed the School of Applied Arts into the upper echelons of education 10; he was the actor who played in crisis and turned the Academy of Drama into an institution of higher learning 12; he was the singer who in-toned the first chord of the arts academies in Zurich 13, his gift of eloquence moved bureaucratic mountains 11.

1
Friedrich Hegar (1841–1927)

Friedrich Hegar was a friend of Johannes Brahms and moved in the same circles as the writer Gottfried Keller. In 1865, he conducted a performance of Schumann's piano concerto in A minor with Brahms at the piano, followed by the latter's D major Serenade. Indeed, he was "virtually unrivalled" as a conductor of Brahms—or so one contemporary later said of him. Keller may well have been present at the aforementioned concert, for in a letter to Hegar, he had promised "to visit the Hall of Tones as often as possible as long as you are in charge there." By the time Hegar returned to Switzerland after studying in Leipzig and launching his career as a conductor in Warsaw, he was one of the most popular and sought-after composers and guest conductors of the age. His appointment as conductor of both the Tonhalle Orchestra and the Mixed Choir of Zurich—a position he held for nearly forty years—gave him considerable sway over the musical life of that city so that when, in 1876, his native Basel tried to lure him away again, he agreed to stay on in Zurich only on condition that he be allowed to found a music school, of which he then became principal. The year 1876 can therefore be regarded as the year that saw the birth of the School of Music that now forms the Music Department of the Zurich University of the Arts.

2
Julius de Praetere (1879–1947)

He is one of the most important actors in the post-1900 reform of applied arts, as the commemorative volume of the Deutscher Werkbund of 1907 demonstrated. Together with illustrious figures like Peter Behrens and Josef Hoffmann, he was a member of its managing board. Dedication to purely artistic tendencies was banned. The motto then was: "Art should be taken to the people, to the workshops, to the industries." For the museum it meant this incontrovertible solution: "Commercial exhibitions should ensure that only those items are displayed that are valid as models in every respect: the technical, the artistic, and the economic. In order to carry out this principle, exhibition work must be closely monitored and its direction must be placed in the hands of a far-sighted, artistic personality with a high degree of technical expertise." For the schools: "Instead of the pseudo-academic stagnation of a school of ornamentation and decoration, the craftsmanship of the student should be developed and his technical ability placed in the service of beautiful forms."

The native Belgian, craftsman, painter, art historian, and art teacher was chosen from thirty-six candidates for president in 1905. He became one of the founding reorganizers of what was then the School of Applied Arts. In 1912 de Preatere resigned as president.

3
Volkmar Andreae (1879–1962)

He almost succeeded Gustav Mahler as conductor of the New York Philharmonic, but in the end decided to stay in Zurich. Born in Bern in 1879, Volkmar Andreae was a student of Fritz Brun at the Cologne Conservatory and began his career in Munich before taking over from Friedrich Hegar as conductor of Zurich's Tonhalle Orchestra—a post he was retain for the next forty years—in 1906. As conductor of the Zurich Students' Choral Society he was at the same time administrative director at the university, where he also gave lectures and from which he received an honorary doctorate. This also made him the obvious choice when it came to finding a successor for Carl Attendorfer as head of the Zurich Conservatory in 1914. Here too, Andreae proved to be remarkably constant, devoting no fewer than twenty-five years of his life to teaching conducting and composing at the Conservatory.

What made Andreae's career so crucial to Switzerland's musical development in the 1920s and 1930s was his commitment to contemporary music in general and to the works of his friend, Othmar Schoeck, in particular. Indeed, he can be credited with having spread Schoeck's fame not just in his capacity as conductor of the Tonhalle Orchestra, but also as president of the Swiss Composers Association from 1920 to 1925, and

1 2 3
5 4

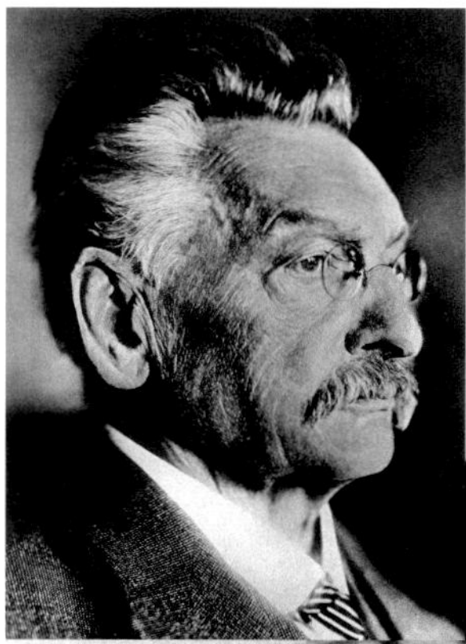
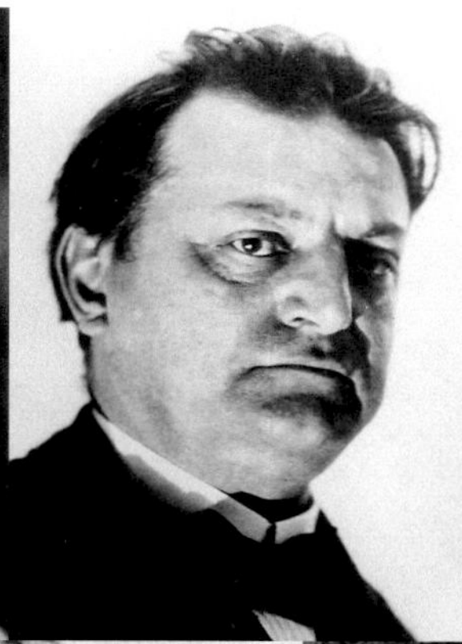
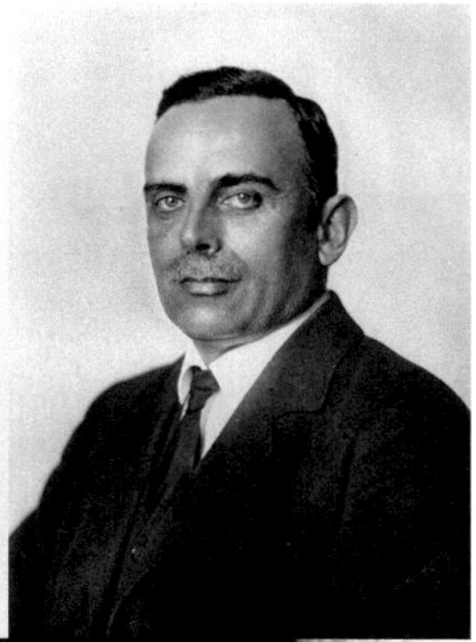
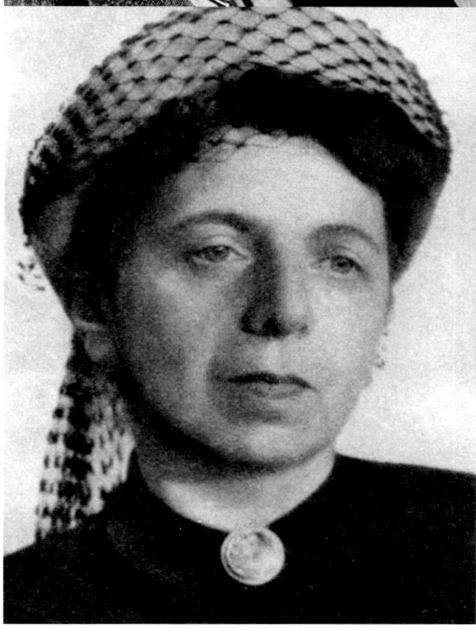
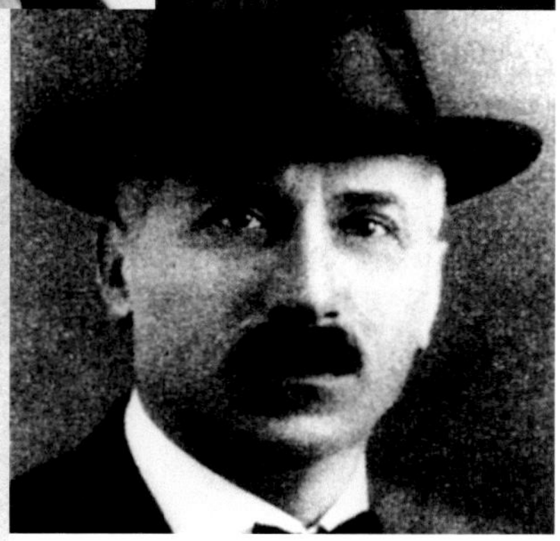

as guest conductor of such world-class ensembles as the Berlin and Vienna Philharmonics.

4
Alfred Altherr sen. (1875–1945)

When simultaneous overlapping courses at the School of Applied Art and the Vocational School made their merger a certainty, de Praetere resigned and Alfred Altherr became the sole director of both schools and the Museum of Applied Arts. His own work was based on interior architecture and interior design in a moderate modernist style, which sought to unify historical and contemporary stylistic elements. It was an aesthetics of manifold styles that marked his impact as director. He pushed for collaboration between the school and the museum; founded, among other things, the Vocational School of Interior Design under Wilhelm Kienzle and also the School for Embroidery with the craftswoman and painter Sophie Taeuber-Arp. His primary concern was to create the artistically shaped prototype for industrial production. Under his direction the Swiss Werkbund was founded within the Museum of Applied Arts in 1913 and he became its first chairman. Its goal was to ennoble commercial work by collaborating with art, industry, and craftsmanship through education, enlightenment, and taking a stand on artistic and practical economic issues.

Altherr was president from 1912–1938.

5
Paulina Treichler

In 1937 the singing teacher Paulina Treichler founded the first Swiss drama school, the Zurich Stage Studio. It all began at her home, a romantic little house in Krautgartenstrasse, also known as “Hundskehre” —“the dog’s place.” With four paying pupils and a five-person board she began the training program that eventually evolved into the Academy of Drama and ultimately into the School of Drama. Despite criticism that it was irresponsible to train young actors who might not find employment, Treichler was determined to continue with her bold project, and she soon managed to engage a large number of reputed stage artists as teachers, including Erwin Kalser, Mathilde Danegger, Wolfgang Heinz, and Ernst Ginsberg, who, like Treichler herself, were prepared to work for very modest fees. It was fortunate for her that there were many excellent stage artists living in exile in Switzerland at the time who needed to make ends meet.

At the beginning she gave most of the elocution lessons and voice training herself, sometimes assisted by her sister, the dancer Bella Reine, who would come to Zurich from Paris for a week at a time to teach actors how to move expressively, how to carry themselves, and how to mime. It is ironic that the principal —who is described as a little woman with an unfashionable haircut and a foreign accent—was the person responsible for teaching elocution. Given that her Swiss pupils spoke Swiss dialect this was a particularly important part of the training, though rather hampered by their teacher’s Russian intonation. It is alleged that she managed to rid a highly regarded character actor of the “lump in his throat” by the end of the first lesson. Her apparently inexhaustible reserves of energy enabled her to overcome every obstacle, until finally, weakened by serious illness, she handed over the keys to the first Swiss drama school to Felix Rellstab.

6
Johannes Itten (1888–1967)

The most important legacy of this pathfinder and teacher was his theoretical work *Kunst der Farbe* (The Art of Color), which appeared in many languages and saw many new editions. In it, he categorizes the effect of color and the visible forms it takes—the seven color contrasts. In this “expressive theory of color” Itten classifies color and form.

Itten worked at the Bauhaus from 1919–23 as the form master in the metal workshop and was highly influential on the newly established preliminary course, which aimed at getting a picture of the abilities of the students, freeing their minds from prejudice and giving them independent experience with the basic properties of composition, color, materials, and tools. Itten was

6 7
8 9

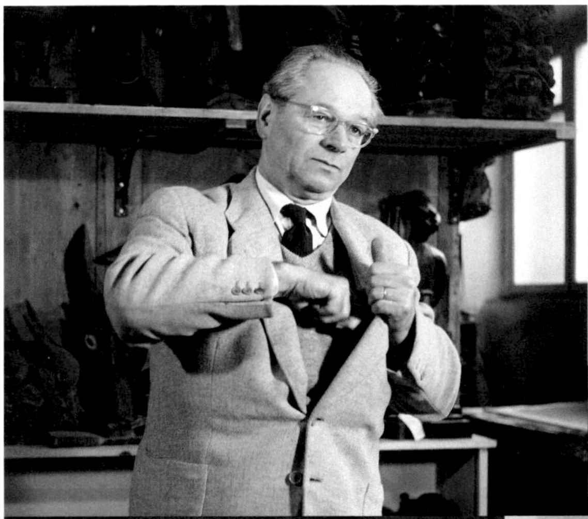

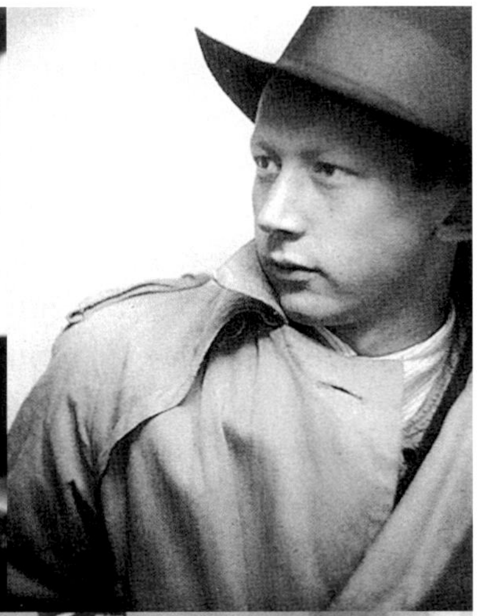

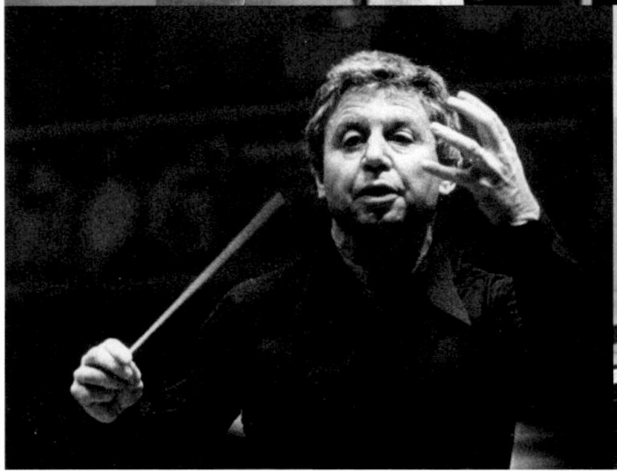

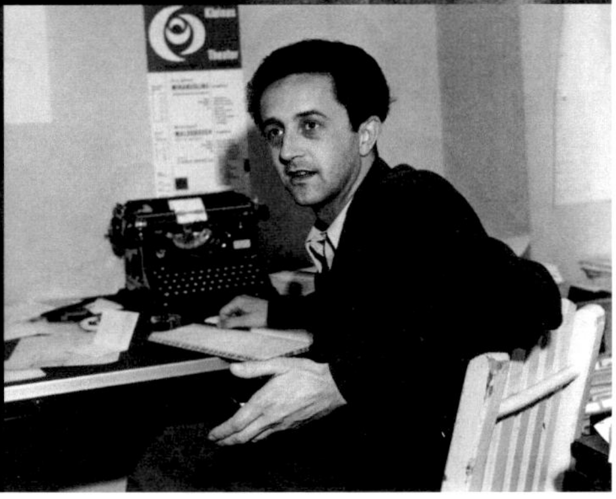

also a founder of color type theory (with its unmistakable esoteric features), which played a key role in the theory of fashion. According to this theory everyone has a skin undertone that is determined at birth and remains unchanged throughout life. Itten's painting is classified as concrete art.

From 1938–54 Itten was director at the School of Applied Arts and from 1943–60 he was director of the Zurich College of Textiles. From 1949–56 he taught at the Rietberg Museum in Zurich. The Technical University of Darmstadt awarded him an honorary doctorate and in 1966 he represented Switzerland at the 33rd Biennale in Venice.

7
Hans Fischli (1909–1989)

The concise resume is: studied to be a construction draftsman; studied at the Bauhaus in Dessau with Josef Albers, Wassily Kandinsky, Oskar Schlemmer; friend of Max Bill; drafted plans for factories and simple residential dwellings for workers and employees; later also single family homes and villas; coinitiator and builder of the Pestalozzi children's village in Trogen; 1954–61 director of the School of Applied Arts and the Museum of Applied Arts.

These aesthetic, educational, and sociopolitical components imbued his life and his work. "Applied artistic handiwork and pseudo-academia will have no place within this school." That was his dictatorial way of proclaiming his goals as director. Under his aegis, there was a particular emphasis on "industrial form" with a tough course of discipline and with objectivity at its core: rigor, emphasis on function, formally simple, technical solutions were the aesthetic results! Worn down by resistance to his methods and the day-to-day conflicts of school life, he decided in 1960 to become an independent artist—certainly no misfortune given his great artistic qualities.

das Eineck (the One-angle) and *das Zweieck* (the Two-angle) as he paradoxically and playfully titled one of his works, might be taken as a kind of oblique reference to the paradoxes and grotesque in the work of his son, Peter Fischli.

8
Willi Gohl (*1925)

Willi Gohl headed the Winterthur Music School and Conservatory for more than a quarter of a century. Gohl is a pianist and conductor who has worked all over the world, together with Brenton Langbein, Ottavio Corti Raphaele Altwegg, and other instrumentalists from the Chamber Musicians of Zurich. He gained international acclaim above all as a choral conductor, and Gohl and his wife, the singer Verena Gohl, were the 1981 winners of the Winterthur Culture Prize. Known far beyond the bounds of Winterthur, Gohl is a patron of the arts and a dedicated policymaker who has played an important role in the musical life of his country over many years.

Gohl's own popular choral arrangements are especially noteworthy and have had a lasting impact—such as those in the renowned *Grosses Liederbuch,* illustrated by Tomi Ungerer—and he has worked untiringly to make singing a regular and popular feature of Switzerland's cultural calendar. As president of the Swiss Music Council—to mention but one of the many offices he holds—he has also had some success in ensuring that Switzerland's policies on education, arts, and culture take greater account of the interests and needs of its musicians. The career of many a famous Swiss musician would have been unthinkable without Gohl in the role of teacher, colleague, or mentor. At the time of writing, Gohl was settling into a senior citizens home, as always with the support and care of his wife. Many of the Gohls' own children are now active musicians in their own right—among them Franziska Gohl of the Music Department at the Zurich University of the Arts.

9
Felix Rellstab (*1924)

In 1960, Felix Rellstab assumed directorship of the former Stage Studio and developed it from its modest beginnings into the Zurich Academy of Drama, the largest theater school in Switzerland. Soon after taking up studies in the natural sciences, he found himself drawn to the theater. He received training

10 11 12
13

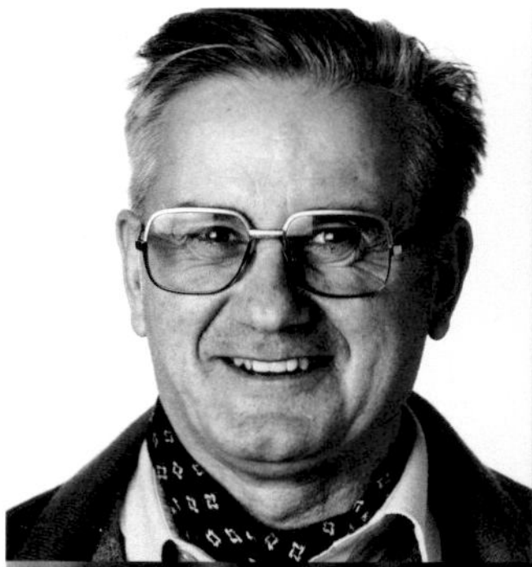
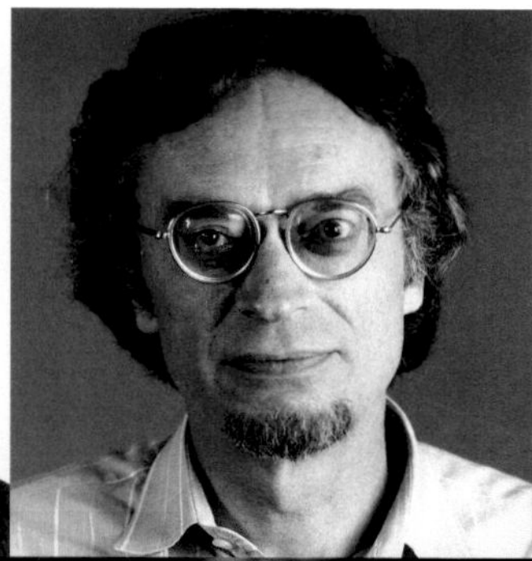
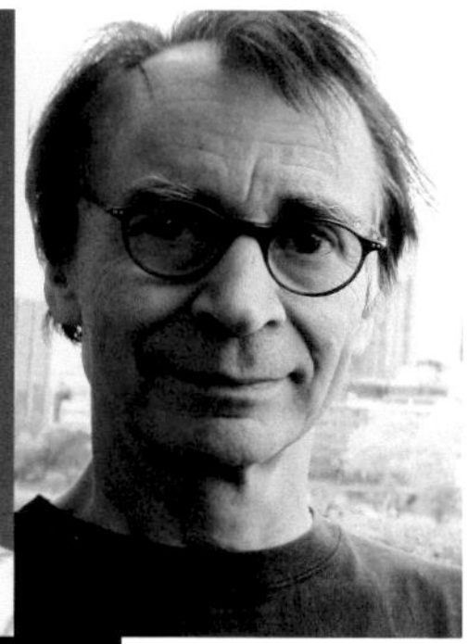
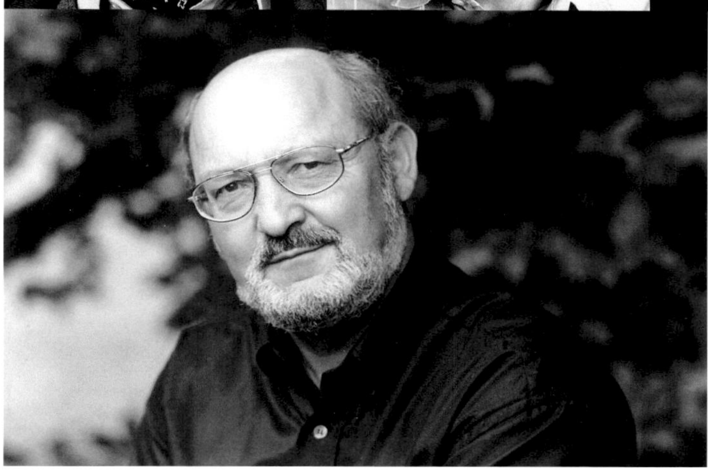

as an actor and director, and made his first appearance at the Zurich Schauspielhaus. His encounters with Therese Giehse, Wolfgang Heinz, Erwin Kalser, and Leonhard Steckel were decisive. He engaged in wide-ranging activities as an actor, author, and festival director, and as the artistic director of the Kleines Theater in Zurich. In the mid-1950s, he returned to Zurich University in order to study philosophy, psychology, and therapeutic pedagogy. In the 1970s, he initiated the course for directors and theater instructors, as well as the Theater im Schulhaus, predecessor of the junges.theater.zürich. He was coeditor of the magazine *Spektrum*, and cofounder and first director of the Theater am Neumarkt. In 1992, he was honored for his considerable services with the Cultural Prize of the City of Zurich. At the center of all of these undertakings is the acting individual, the actual bearer of culture. He attempted constantly to make a broader public aware that the theater is more than a useless luxury, and is instead necessary to the lives of individual and society alike, because it illuminates our lives and the state of the world in a unique way. Many graduates of the Zurich Academy of Drama owe a debt to his commitment, and have since gone on to become important protagonists in contemporary theater.

10
Hansjörg Budliger (*1925)

The qualified primary teacher and legal scholar with a dissertation began as a vocational school instructor for the general education of apprentices. In 1970 he became interim deputy chairman of the School of Applied Arts, and in 1971 he became chairman for special missions of the school and museum, 1973 interim director, and from 1975–90 its president. He was the troubleshooter who was supposed—and able—to restore order and discipline.

The final decision to choose him as president was bitterly contested by the professional design associations who wanted a dual presidency with one administrative and one artistic director. They claimed that the latter would provide the great vision and the overdue reforms. Budliger gave the lie to all the Cassandras. He became a great force of renewal and a politically skilled institutional director. In 1986 he used the hard-won status of a higher school of design to lay the foundation for the future School of Art and Design. His membership in the canton council certainly contributed to his ability to build bipartisan trust. His creative power and his commitment to the institution was proverbial, enormous, and highly visible, especially when at 6 a.m. his Maserati could already be seen parked at the main entrance and could frequently be heard roaring through the industrial quarter well after midnight. He supervised the establishment and management of the vocational middle schools, the management of schools *and* museums, directed the centennial jubilee of the museum in 1975 and that of the School of Applied Arts in 1978. The reforms he himself instigated were exemplary: the film program, the continuing education program in visual design, the art program, the establishment of Departments of Visual Communication and Design, the inauguration of a program of general education in design theory that ended with the establishment of the theory pool, etc., etc.

Budliger was uncompromising in the implementation of his goals, promoted disciplined work, was reliable, and competently and selflessly administered his portfolio of responsibilities. He was a highly respected model for others, and on the occasion of his farewell the frank admiration for his services and the many friendships that linked and continue to link him to this institution were more than apparent.

11
Rudolf Schilling (*1940)

His "addresses to the nation," as he calls his annual speeches, have always been surprising, astute, and intellectually stimulating; with a predilection for targeting the mental states and sensitivities of those working at the school with his mischievous, spot-on formulations—and respect. He thought the students were the greatest. He loved them. His limitless enthusiasm for their ideas and work was unique.

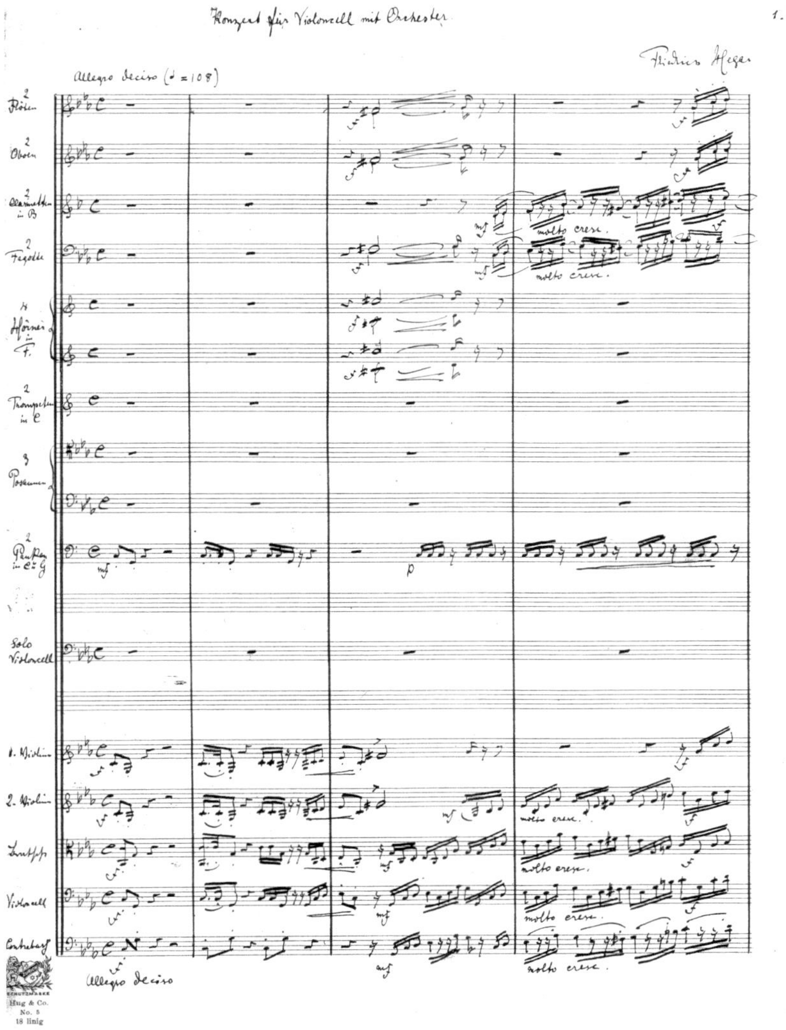

1a Friedrich Hegar, *Concerto for Cello and Orchestra.* Autograph

One of his favorite experiences was collaborating with a group of film students on the subject of Paris suburbs: the preparations, the study trips to Paris, the documentary film that resulted, the exhibition at the Museum of Design.

The educated, contemplative, and retiring intellectual Rudolf Schilling could mutate into an archaic warrior if it involved realizing some goal that was important to him. Then the man with the gift of empathy and the beautiful turn of phrase became unyielding, obstinate, and unpleasant. He argued, fought, and negotiated until even the most stubborn opponent capitulated.

Rudolf Schilling's greatest service was his implementation of the conversion of the higher Swiss design schools into schools of applied arts, a step which at the beginning of the 1990s was still a long way off. It was due to his persistence that this goal was achieved before the end of the millennium. In this sense he is an important trailblazer for Swiss applied arts schools, to include the School of Applied Arts in Zurich. From 1990–2000 he was president of the School of Design.

12
Peter Danzeisen (*1941)

Peter Danzeisen succeeded Felix Rellstab at the Zurich Academy of Drama, became the first director of the Zurich School of Music, Drama and Dance, and retired in mid-2006. Back then, in 1990, he had already enjoyed a long, successful career as an actor on various renowned German stages, and was among others a member of the directorship of schauspielfrankfurt.

After a few years, he was able to exchange the theatrical, dilapidated Jugendstil villa "Egli" am Pfauen for spacious premises on the culture island between Sihl and Schanzengraben. This concentration of facilities on a single location made him the envy of drama school heads all over Europe. His principal qualities are professionalism, indifference to considerations of prestige, trust in his colleagues and in instructors and students, whose own initiative he has always encouraged and supported. One example shows the mark Danzeisen has made on Gessnerallee: the idea for the Theater an der Sihl, which he transformed from a theater for children and young people into a permanent practice area and research laboratory for the drama school. This offered students unique opportunities to work during their training with experienced actors and major directors, and finally to appear in public—a much-imitated model that enjoyed prestige internationally. Danzeisen's achievements are powered by his passionate and visionary spirit, and his devotion to Swiss theater. He has always remained an actor and stage artist, and always enjoyed ironically demolishing the obstacles of the educational bureaucracy, and insisting on fantasy and play as essential aspects of the development of an art academy. In him, the Zurich University of the Arts had an inspired architect.

13
Fritz Näf (*1943)

The singer and choirmaster Fritz Näf was born in a wine-growing region near Zurich. After heading the Music School and Conservatory for fourteen years, he presided over the merger of the School of Music and the School of Theater and Dance in the year 2000. As a member of Mike Piquet's ensemble Ricercare, Näf has become a keen advocate of historical performance practices. As a singer, he has collaborated closely with such famous ensembles as the Dresdner Kreuzchor and the Schola Cantorum Basiliensis, of which his own Basler Madrigalisten is an spin-off. Näf has also worked a great deal with the Swiss Chamber Choir and in 2000 he was appointed its artistic director.

As president of the School of Music, Drama and Dance, Näf held the first talks with the president of the School of Art and Design, at which the possibility of founding a university of all the arts was discussed—an initiative which, obviously under somewhat different circumstances, then led to the founding of the Zurich University of the Arts.

3a *Briefe an Volkmar Andreae: Ein halbes Jahrhundert Zürcher Musikleben* 1902–1959. Atlantis Musikbuch-Verlag, Zurich, 1986

2a Jules de Praetere, poster for A. Welti-Furrer AG, 1915

4a *Raumkunst — Ausstellung des Schweizerischen Werkbundes*, 1918. Exhibition concept and organization by Alfred Altherr

4b Sales exhibition of the Zurich section of the Swiss Werkbund at the Museum of Design Zurich,1930

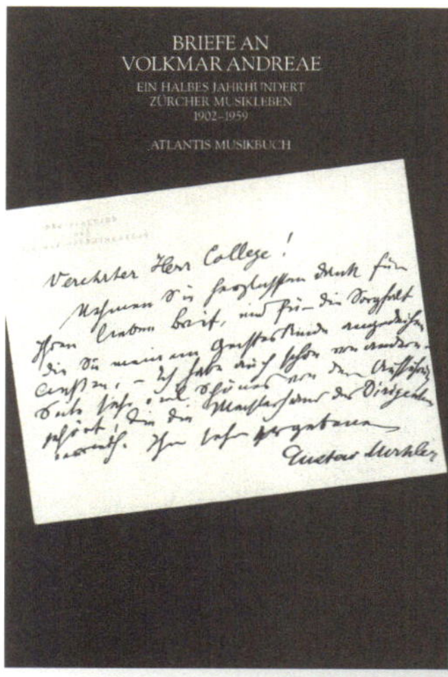

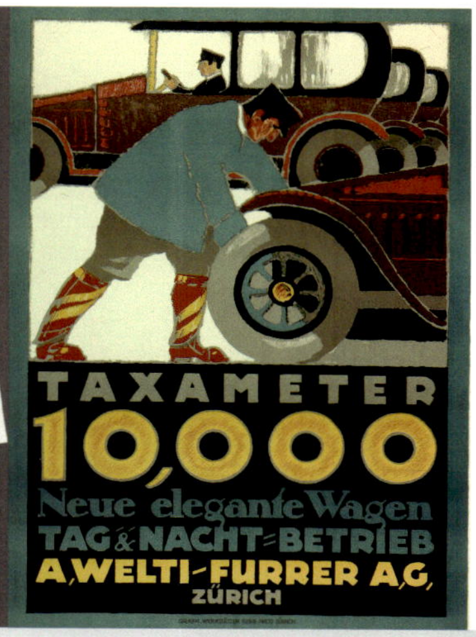

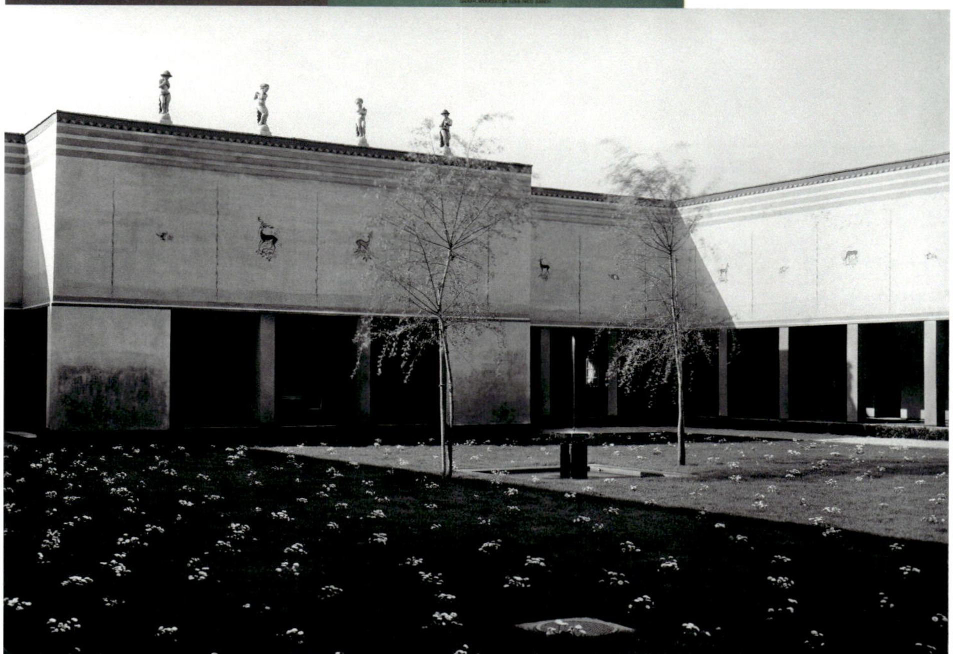

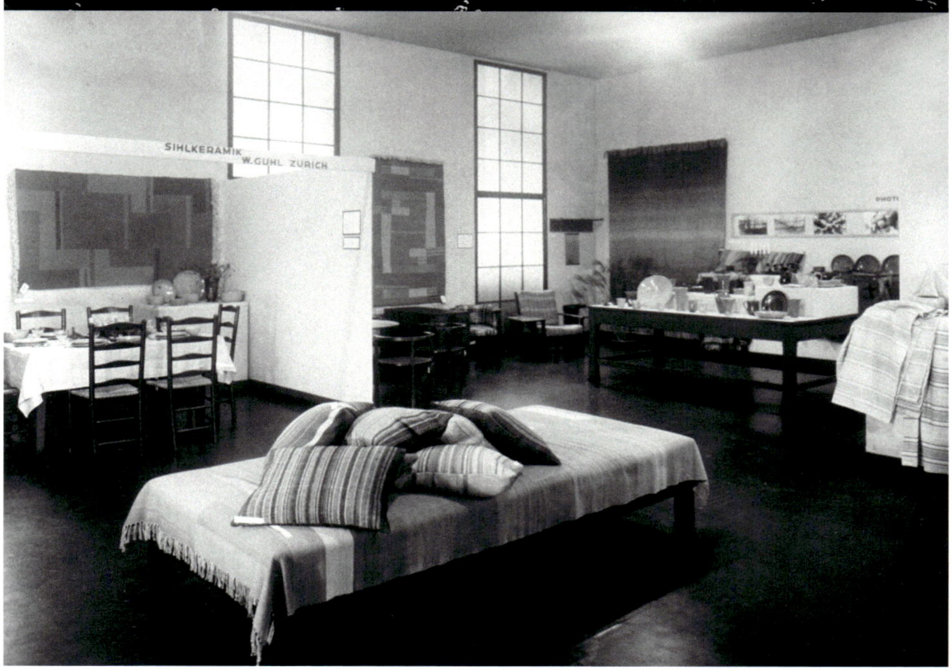

6a Johannes Itten, form master and founder of the preliminary course at Bauhaus Weimar, 1919–23

6b *Begegnung*, 1916. Oil painting

7a Hans Fischli, Schlehstud Studio and House, Obermeilen, 1933

6c *Der Bachsänger*, 1916. Oil painting depicting oratorio singer Helge Lindberg

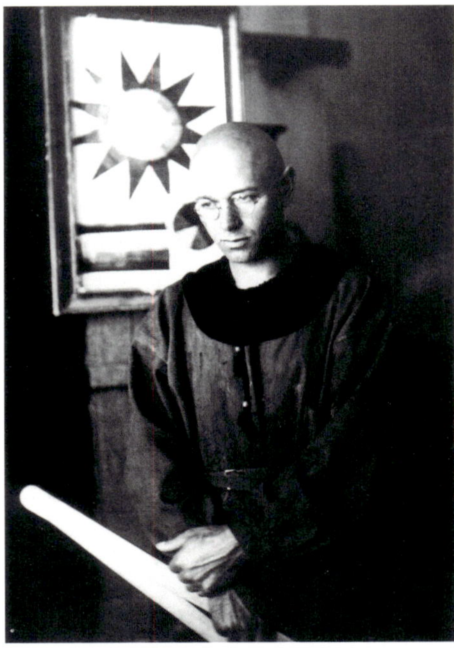

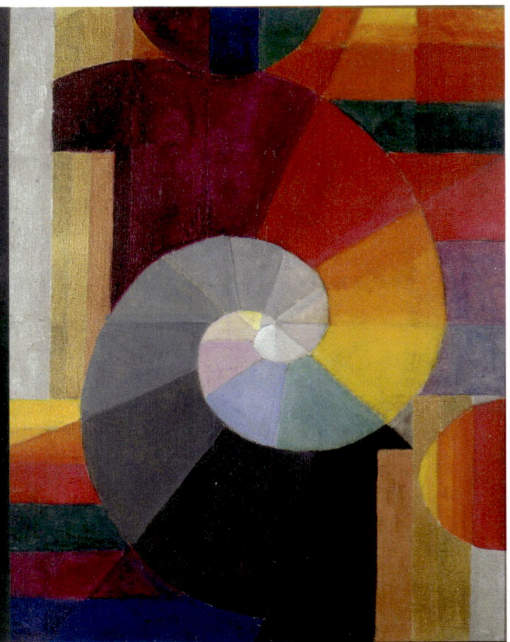

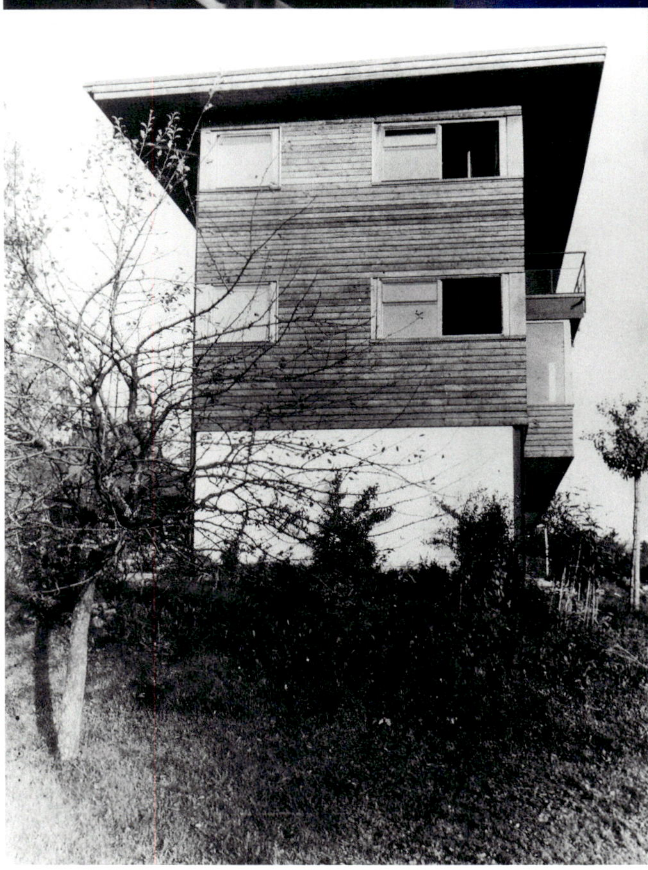

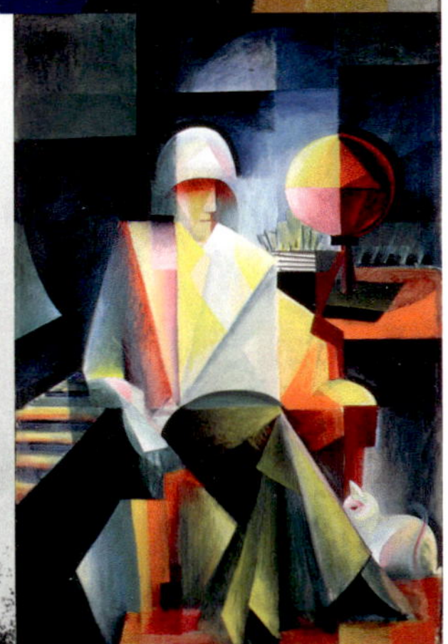

7b Hans Fischli (left), Willy Rotzler, and Max Fröhlich at the opening of *The Family of Man* at the Museum of Design Zurich, 1958

7c *Blaue Wand.* Four sections, Schlehstud House, Obermeilen, ca. 1953/54

7d *Lauschen auf die Stimme im Innern der Dinge.* Sculpture in front of Schlehstud House. Photo 1982

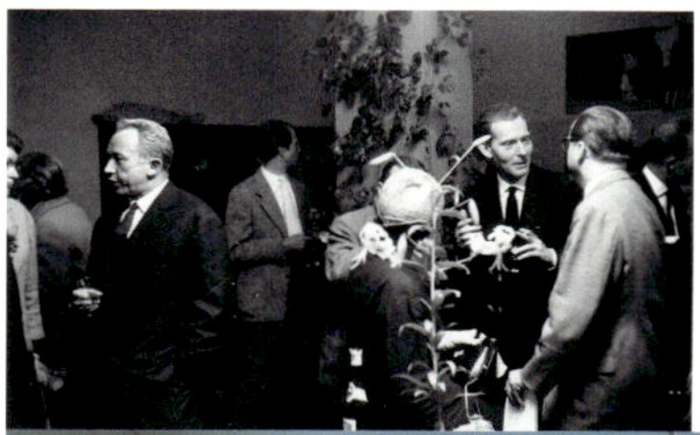

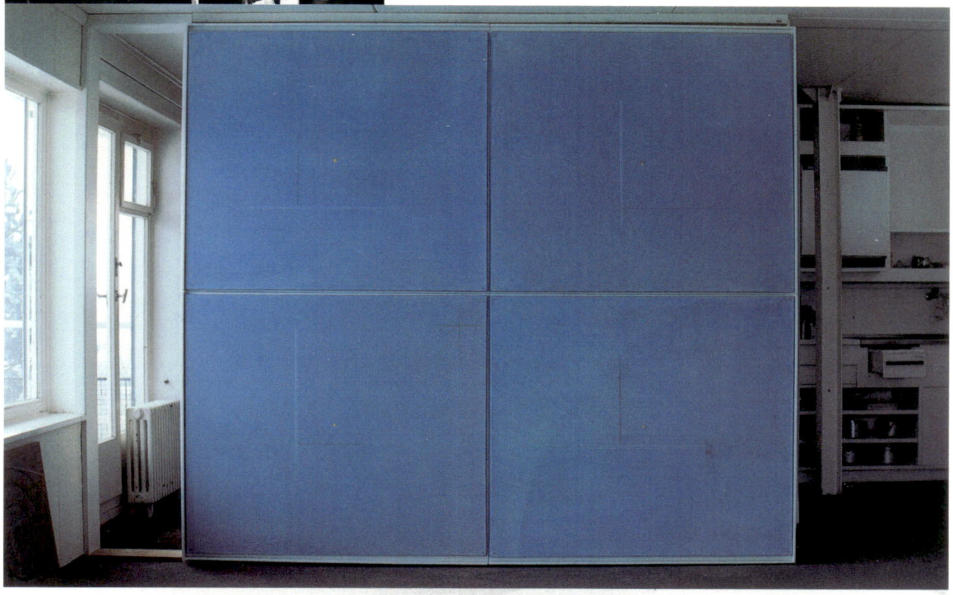

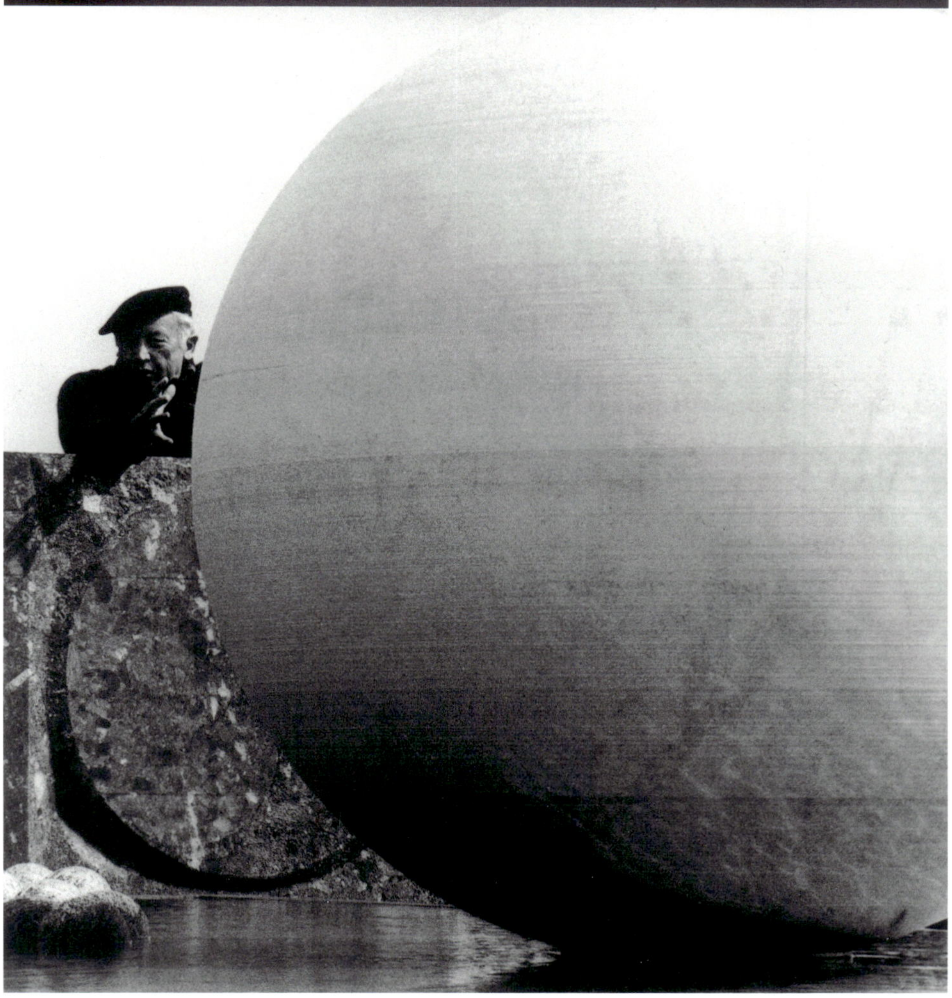

8a Willi Gohl, Songbook. Diogenes Verlag, 1978

9a Textbook by Felix Rellstab. Verlag Stutz+Co. AG, Wädenswil, 1992

10a Course introduction for the Drawing and Images Class at the Zurich School of Art and Design under head Hansjörg Budliger

10b Hansjörg Budliger, no date

11a Rudolf Schilling, 1986

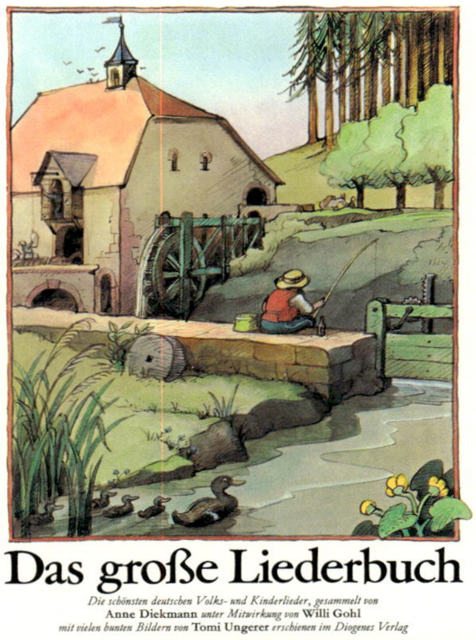

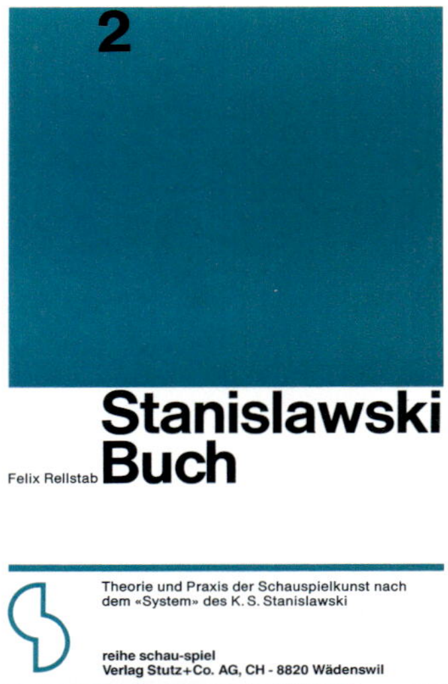

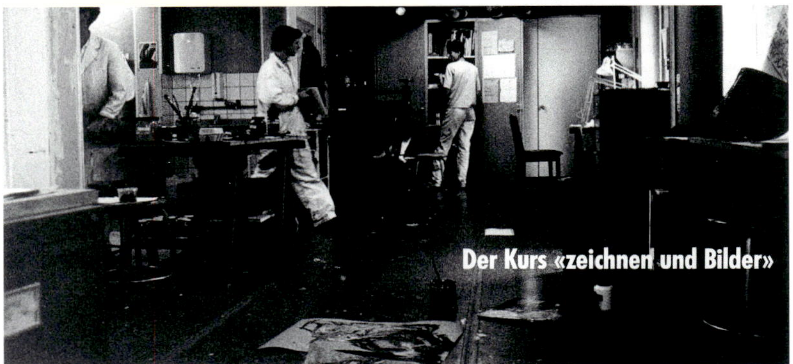

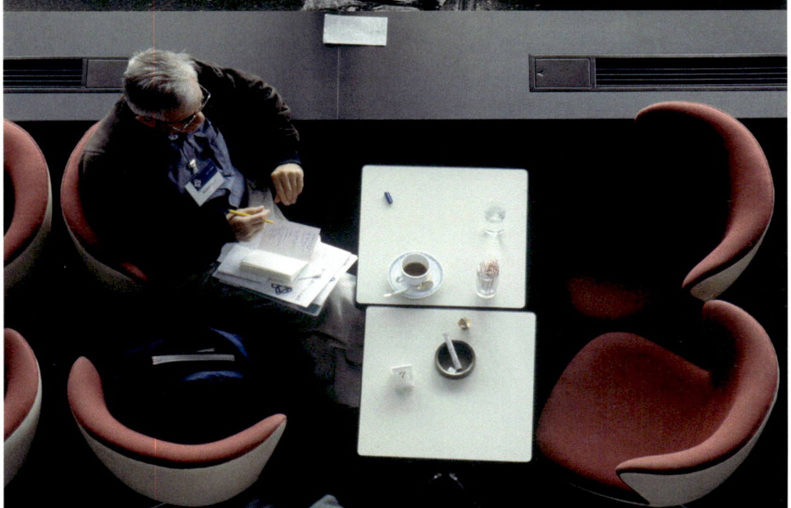

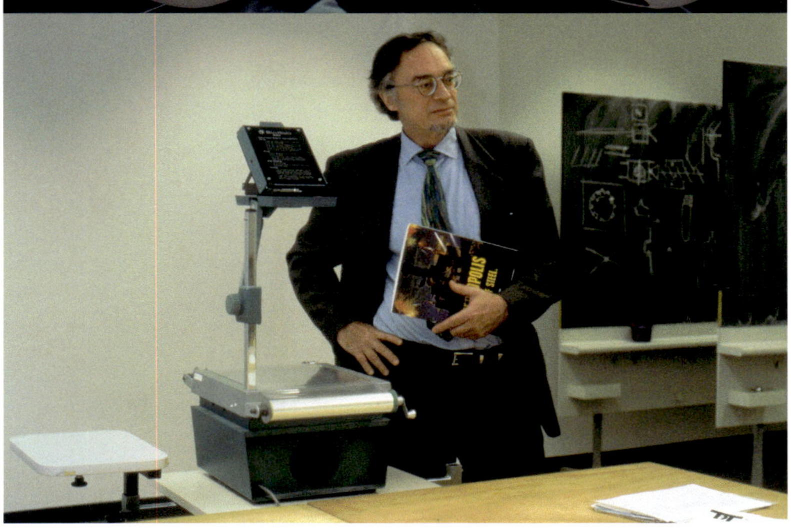

12a Peter Danzeisen (right) with Lukas Ammann and Ruedi Walter in *Der eingebildete Kranke,* 1983
12b Design for a new building for the School of Music, Drama and Dance in the stables of Zurich's Alte Kaserne, 1987
13a Fritz Näf at the piano
13b Concert at the Kiev Philharmonic, Ukraine, 2002. Conductor Fritz Näf

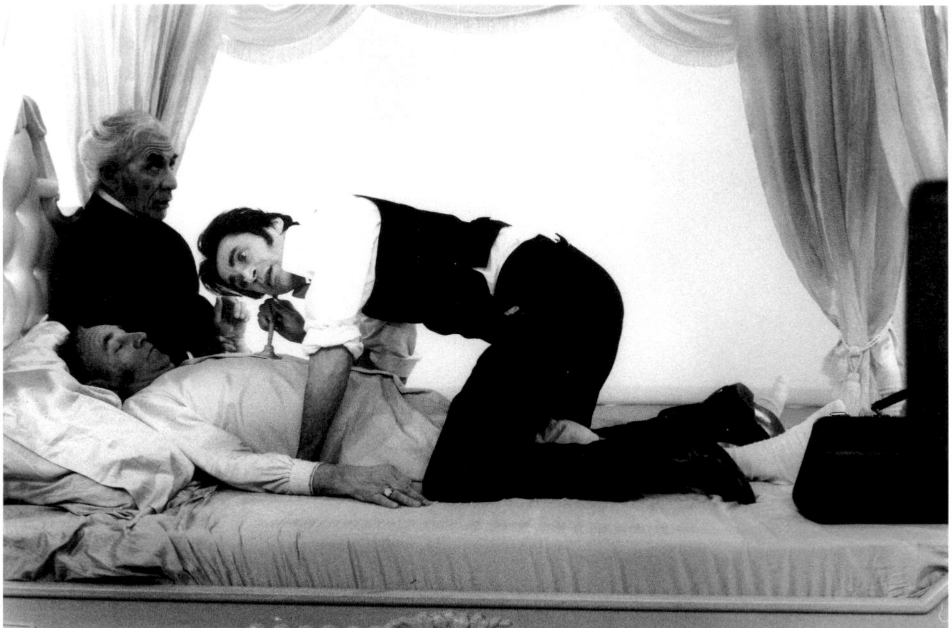

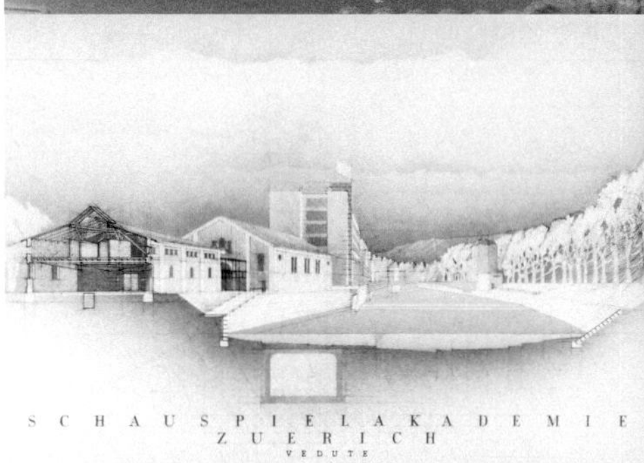

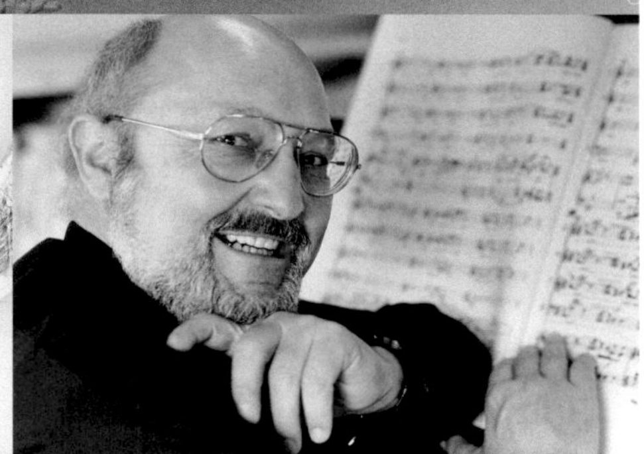

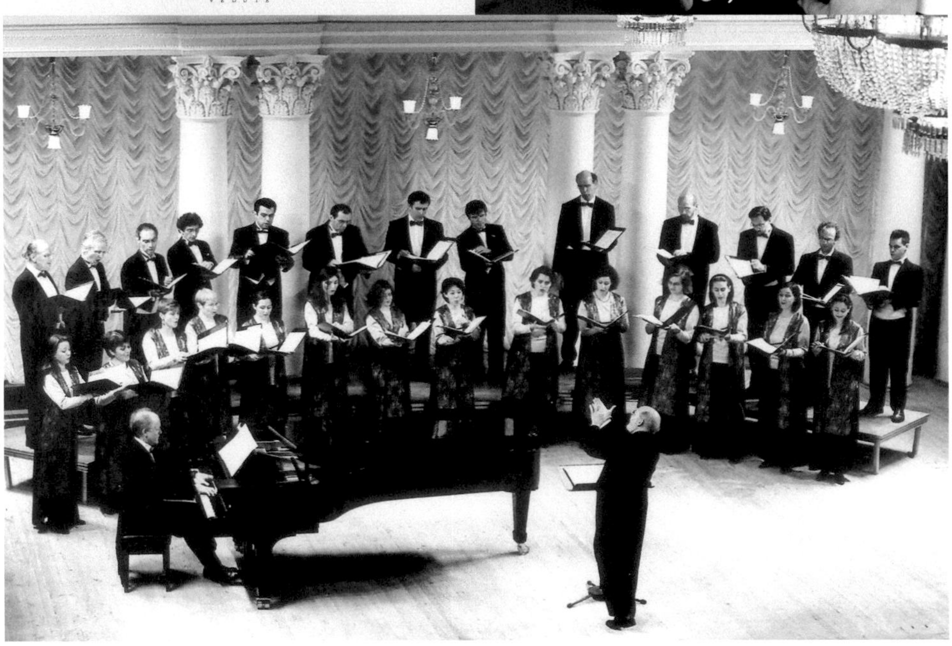

In his series of letters *On the Aesthetic Education of Man*, Friedrich Schiller radically claimed: "There is no other way to make a reasonable being out of a sensuous man than by making him first aesthetic." In his work on education, Gottfried Semper fulminated against the extinction of the organs of artistic receptivity, calling for the universal and popular teaching of taste.

Aesthetic education and formation throughout the entire complexity of aesthetic production is their métier. They convey stupendous artistic skill, the refinement of taste and expression, contemporary culture, national independence, creating identity and cultural dynamism in cities and regions; they are the middlemen and -women vis à vis the formation of artistic endowments.

Through music, she gave expression to her sparkling, magical personality 1; she influenced an entire era of music pedagogy 2; her passion for the violin was infectious, and she was responsible for transforming a highly gifted *wunderkind* into the world's top female star violinist 3; she communicated the syntax of ballet (balance, taut and relaxed limbs, the *pas de deux*), forming character by means of dance 4; he heard the grass growing 5; she is a musical authority par excellence, learning piano with celebrated teachers and becoming a great teacher herself 6; he publishes his own magazine—*Hochparterre*—conveying a grand overview of design from the canton of Graubünden 7; his initiatives and enterprises in inspired and attractive cultural management are in demand beyond his gigantic national exhibitions 8; his house is an inspired exposure of contemporary photography 9.

1

Stefi Geyer (1888–1956)

"She was the daughter of Josef Geyer, a police doctor in Budapest who was himself an amateur violinist. When three-year-old Stefike asked to have an instrument of her own, she astounded everyone by playing wonderfully, without ever having practiced and certainly without ever having been taught." The anecdotes and legends surrounding the person of Stefi Geyer are legion. This naturally has to do with her extraordinary musicality and exceptional gifts as a violinist, although her charismatic personality must also have had a role to play. Othmar Schoeck, Béla Bartók, and Willy Burkhard all wrote concertos for her, and the emotions that flowed into their works—at least in the case of the first two men—were certainly not just of a musical nature. Geyer's first husband fell victim to the terrible Spanish flu pandemic immediately after World War I, and Geyer remarried in 1920 and accompanied her new husband, the Swiss composer Walter Schulthess, when he returned to Zurich. There, she was able to continue her international solo career and as concertmistress of the Collegium Musicum, which she and Paul Sacher founded, succeeded in winning the hearts and minds of the Zurich concert-going public too. The master classes she gave at the Zurich Conservatory between 1934 and 1953 were to have a lasting impact on an entire generation of violinists.

2

Mimi Scheiblauer (1891–1968)

That rhythm is now widely used both in music therapy and in teaching generally is thanks in no small part to Mimi Scheiblauer, who began teaching at the Zurich Conservatory in 1912 and gave her first rhythm lessons to mentally handicapped, sight- and hearing-impaired children and young people in 1922. Once a student of Jacques Dalcroze, Scheiblauer not only pioneered a new understanding of the relationship between music and movement, but thanks to her wide ranging activities became a highly influential personality for an entire generation of music teachers. From 1926 onwards, she taught at the Conservatory's newly founded Department of Music Education and Rhythm and later in children's homes, special schools, and nursery schools as well. She worked at the Zurich Opera House from 1930 to 1944 and in 1942 founded a publishing house called Sämann-Verlag. She remained on the editorial board of the periodical *Lobpreisung der Musik—Blätter für Musikerziehung* right up to the end of her most eventful and influential life in 1968.

3

Aida Stucki (*1921)

Her most famous pupil was Anne-Sophie Mutter. And that scarcely an interview goes by in which Mutter does not express her indebtedness to her erstwhile teacher at the Winterthur Conservatory and the woman who actually "discovered" her is clear proof of Aida Stucki's caliber as a teacher. Dozens of those musicians who define today's classical music scene would no doubt confirm this. Stucki herself was a pupil of Stefi Geyer in Zurich and Carl Flesch in Lucerne. The career that followed included both numerous solo engagements as well as concerts in chamber ensembles, such as those she gave with the pianists Christoph Lieske, Clara Haskil, and Walter Frey and as a member of the Piraccini-Stucki String Quartet, founded in the late 1950s, in which her husband Giuseppe Piraccini played first violin. Stucki began her teaching career in Winterthur in 1948, and in 1992 was put in charge of Winterthur's first violin master class, a post she retained right up to her retirement three years later.

4

Anne Woolliams (1926–1999)

Anne Woolliams was an all-rounder, living, shaping, and teaching dance, and yet never committing herself to one particular style or method. After being introduced to dance by a pupil of Mary Wigman, she underwent a broad classical training and danced in London and with Kurt Jooss's Folkwang Ballet before starting to teach in Essen. In 1963 she followed John Cranko to Stuttgart as ballet mistress and was a key figure in creating the "Stuttgart ballet miracle" and in establishing the school associated with it. As an internationally recognized teacher she did pioneering work first in Australia, then in Zurich from 1987 onwards. Until 1990 she was the first director of the Swiss Professional Ballet School (SBBS) and put all her energy into establishing it as the first fully recognized subsidized training institution for

1

2

3

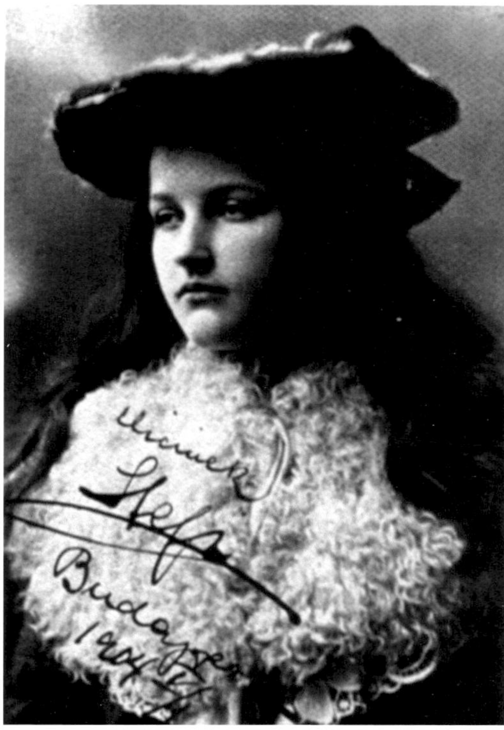

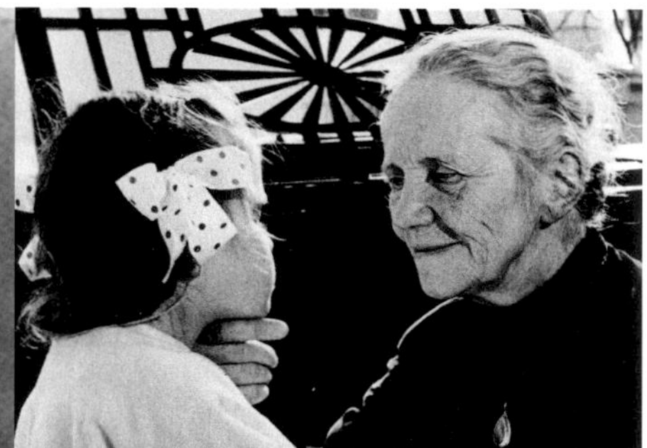

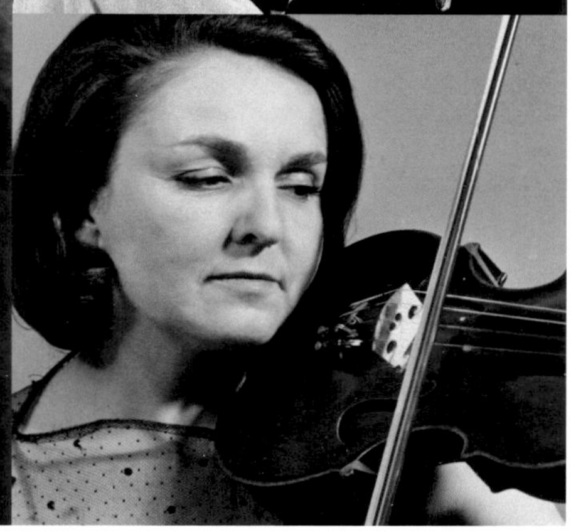

professional dancers in Switzerland. She had a gift for discovering and nurturing the creative talents of young dancers and helping them to blossom. She was never interested in producing pure virtuosos, but rather taught her pupils to become independent-minded, highly expressive artists, and in general she saw dance as a means of personal development.

5

Hans Wüthrich (*1937)

Hans Wüthrich studied composition with Klaus Huber at the Zurich Conservatory, while also writing a PhD in literature, philosophy, and musicology—awarded to him in 1973. This explains how he came to spend fourteen years teaching phonetics and phonemics at the universities of Zurich and Basel before becoming a lecturer in music theory, analysis, and aural training at what was then still the Zurich-Winterthur School of Music in 1985. Wüthrich is especially interested in those areas in which music and theater overlap—an interest which has manifested itself both in his compositions and his founding of the ensemble "mixt media basel."

6

Erna Ronca (*1943)

The pianist and piano teacher Erna Ronca undoubtedly ranks among the most influential personalities in today's Music Department. One reason for this is the fact that she has been teaching there for thirty-five years, while another is the fact that she has always done far more than "just" teach. Her versatility and competence owe much to the training she received from the famous piano teachers Hubert Harry und Louis Hiltbrand in Switzerland, and Gerald Moore, Erik Werba, and Dorothy Taubman abroad. Ronca's first teaching assignments were at the University of Michigan and for a ghetto project in East Harlem.

Her work in Zurich involves giving piano lessons at all levels, right up to professional further training, and also doing pioneering work in music education—which is at the same time her core expertise. Ronca was also the first head of the General Department—the former Conservatory—sat on the research committee of the School of Music, Drama and Dance, and has been extremely generous in her support of the Circle of Friends. She is known to the concert-going public not only as a pianist, but also as an expert on various boards and commissions, as a concert manager and as the author of a history of the piano called *Fis, Schätzchen* (F Sharp, Deary).

7

Köbi Gantenbein (*1946)

For decades Gantenbein has been the catalyst of "Swiss culture and design"—roguish, humorous, competently equipped with the gift of eloquence. He is dedicated to work on and within networks, to fight for cultural political issues, and he also offers his services as a writer and a public speaker on nearly anything that concerns the architecture, design, urban and social planning of Switzerland, and especially the canton of Graubünden. For years this trained sociologist has been the (im)pulse and breath of that "organ" that he and Benedikt Loderer founded and that he runs with greater or lesser commercial cunning (as he puts it): the design periodical *Hochparterre*. His accomplishments of special note include a considerable number of exhibitions, particularly on the subject of Swiss design, his highly influential presence in the Industrial Design Department of the School of Art and Design, whose director he has been, and the promotion of "bands of hundreds" of creative people in Switzerland. Gantenbein is a many-facetted figure who drapes himself in text (and he is always reinventing his "clothes").

8

Martin Heller (*1952)

He studied art education and then did a second university major in art history, ethnology, and anthropology. From one career move to the next Martin Heller has refined his contemporary profile as a "cultural intellectual" with a high degree of managerial competence; his profound and reliable discourse, his degree of networking, and the adeptness with which he deals with the media and politics make him unique in this country. His resume: from 1989 director of the Museum of Design with many memorable exhibitions and associated publications; 1996–97 visiting professor at the Center for Art and Media Karlsruhe; 1999–2003 artistic director of the Swiss National Exposition expo.02; since then Europe-wide cultural entrepreneur and consultant and acclaimed author and exhibition

4

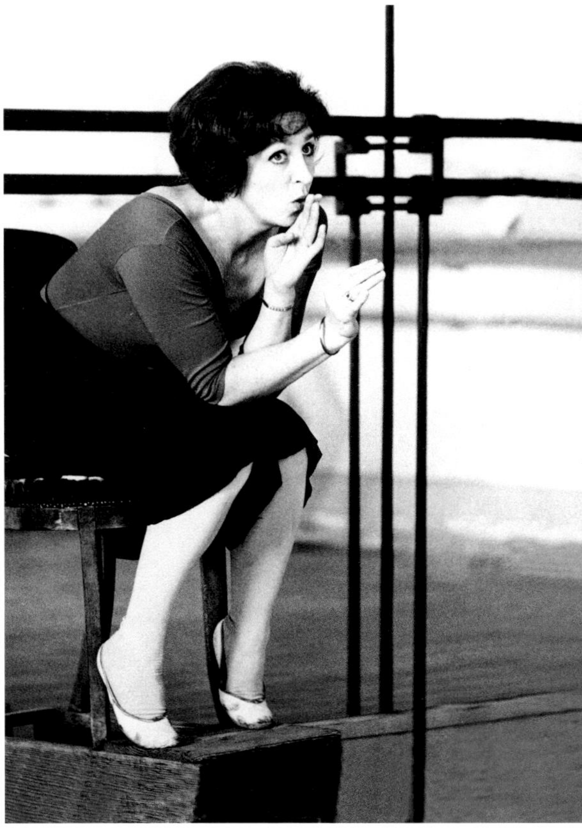

5

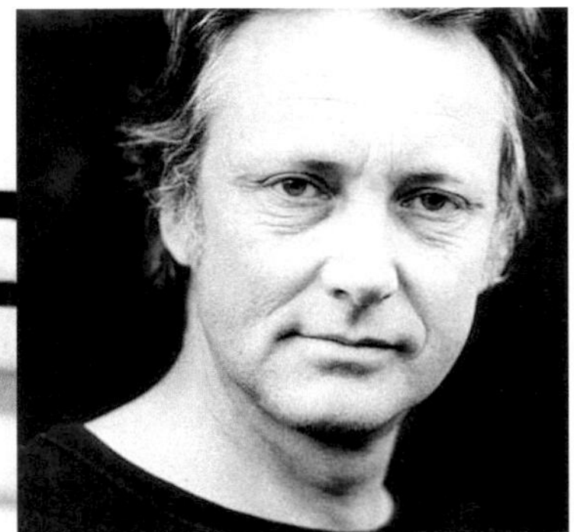

6

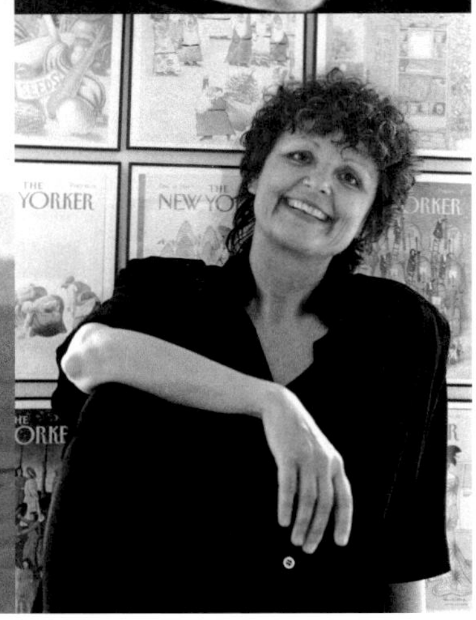

organizer (Heller Enterprises). One of his credos: "Hand full of pictures. Read what's in front of your eyes. And understand what the pictures say. Set something going with this: in the arts, on the ground, a special case—anything at all. That is my pleasure and daily business. That's where my 'enterprises' come from. They become hyperactive spaceships, headquarters turned nomadic, base camps of obsession. This orbital dance began with that heart's blood which flows everywhere and will not stop until the chambers are empty, the skin is dry, the eyes exhausted. That's the way it is. That's the way I want it. So I can touch and change the world with what touches and nourishes me: my hand full of pictures."

9

Urs Stahel (*1953)

He is the initiating, inspired, knowledgeable, and dynamic promoter of photography as a cultural phenomenon in a manifold variety of thematic and exhibition contexts. Since 1993 he has been the first director and managing curator of the Winterthur Photo Museum which has achieved its current stature and international importance through the large number of exhibitions he organized: *Stranger than Paradise* (1994); *Weltenblicke* (World Views; 1997); *Die Lager* (The Camps; 2001); *The Last Picture Show* (2004); as well as numerous shows devoted to single photographers.

Stahel majored in German studies, history, and philosophy. Until the Photo Museum was founded in Winterthur he was active as editor and art critic, lecturer for photo and art history at the Higher School of Design in Zurich, as well as an organizer of exhibitions, including the epochal show *Wichtige Bilder* (Important Pictures; 1990) that he put together with Martin Heller at the Museum of Design.

7
8
9

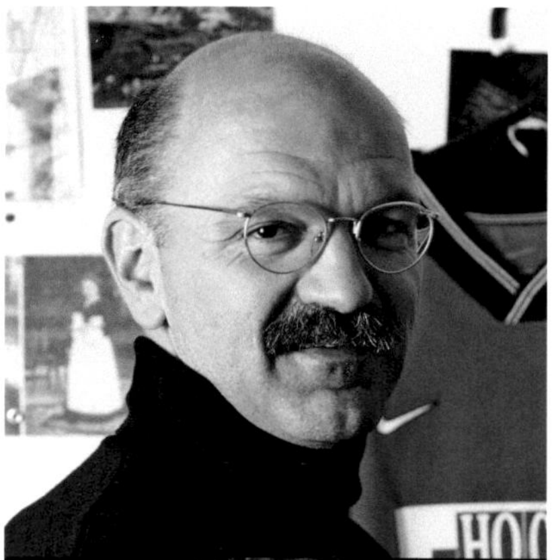

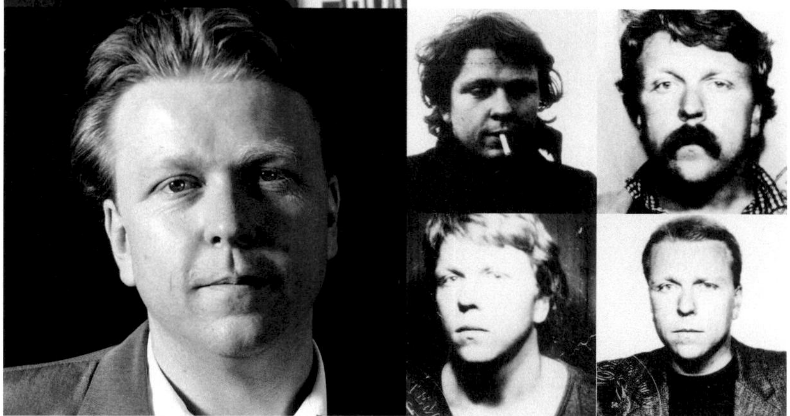

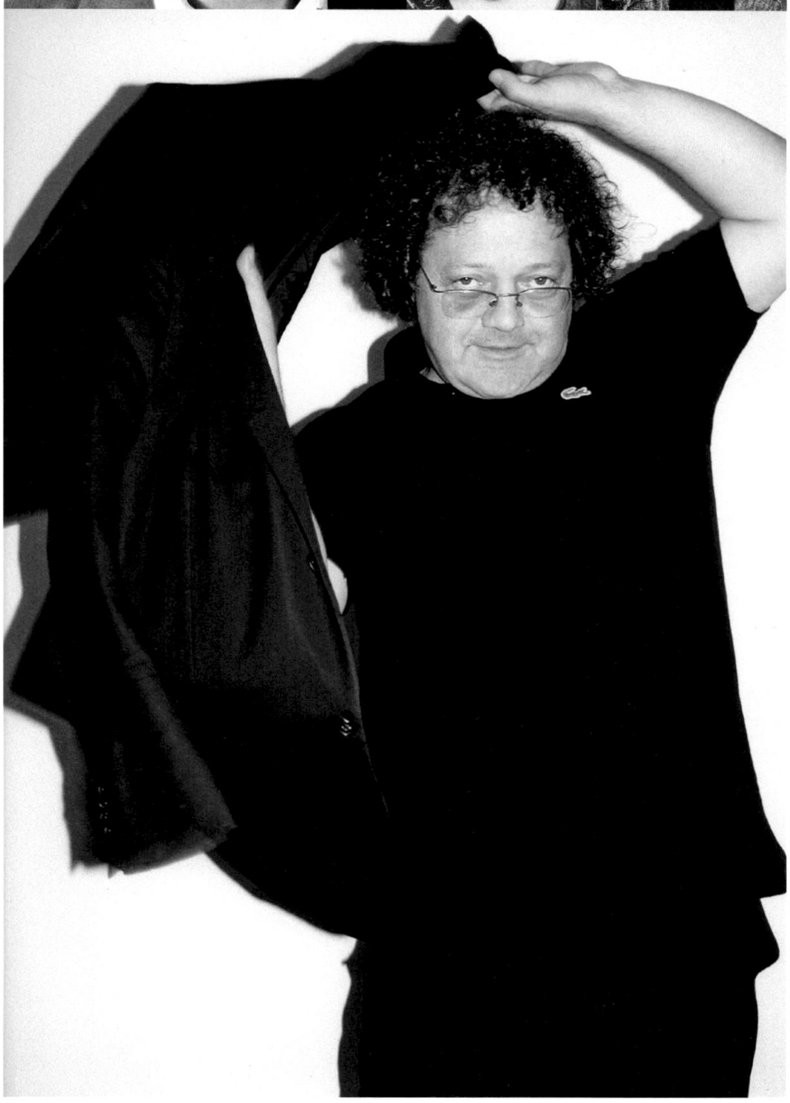

2a Mimi Scheiblauer in *Ursula oder das unwerte Leben*, 1966. Documentary by Reni Mertens and Walter Marti

4a Anne Woolliams with her ballet class, 1971

7a Cover of the January/February 2006 edition of the design periodical *Hochparterre* edited by Köbi Gantenbein

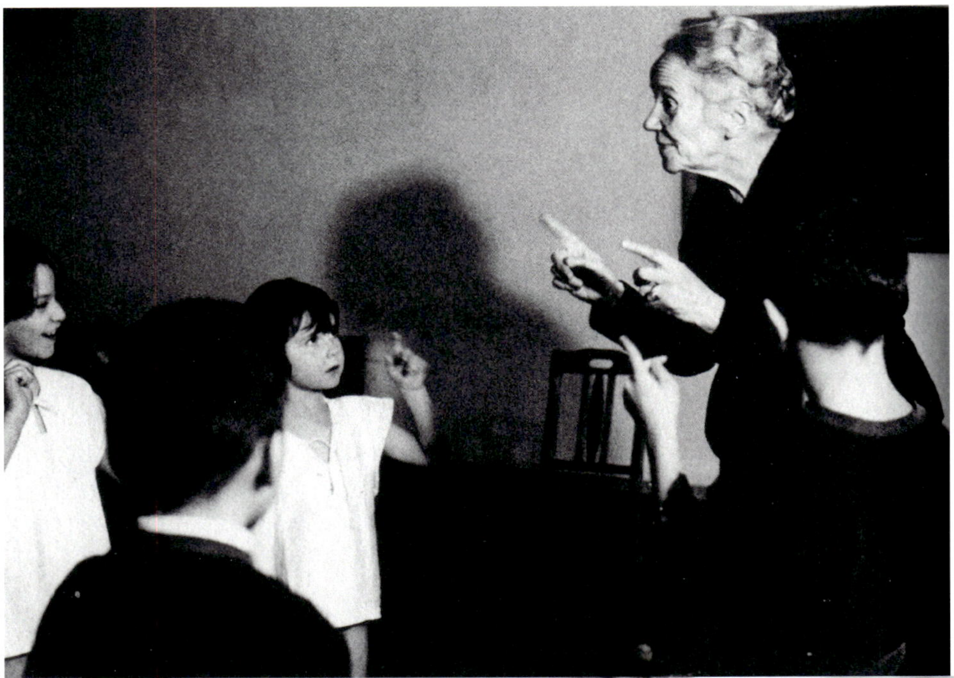

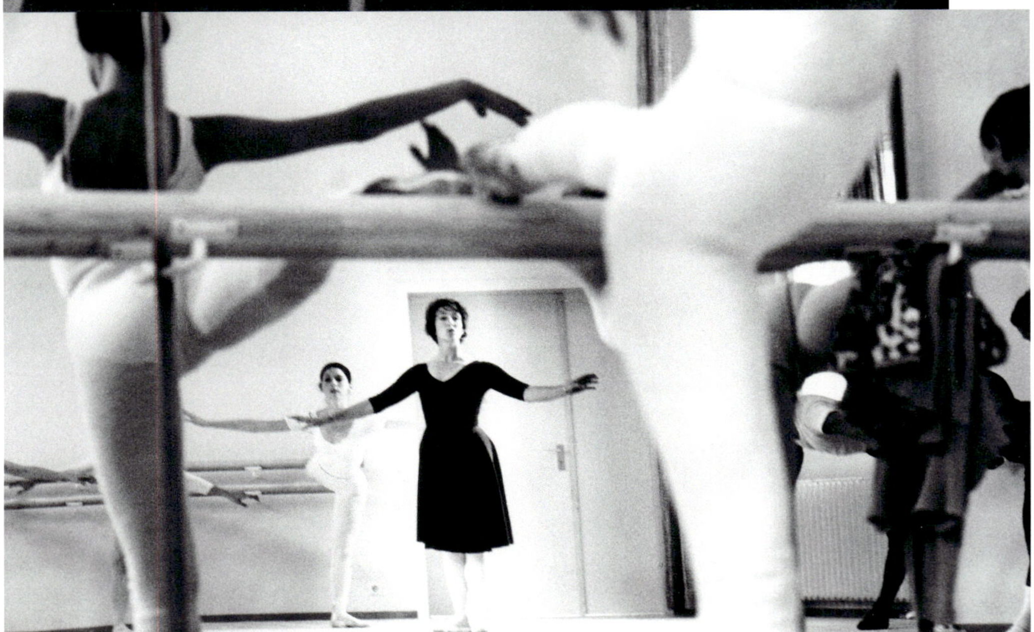

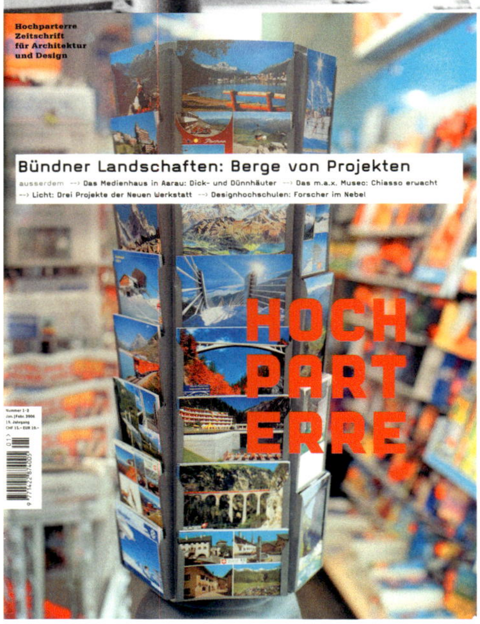

8a *Die Klasse.* Exhibition of works by students of the photography class at the Museum of Design Zurich, 1996. Project head Martin Heller, poster Cornel Windlin **8b** School of Art and Design lecture series, 2007
8c *Medium—Eine Welt dazwischen,* 1998. Exhibition at the Museum of Design Zurich. Project managers Martin Heller/André V. Heiz

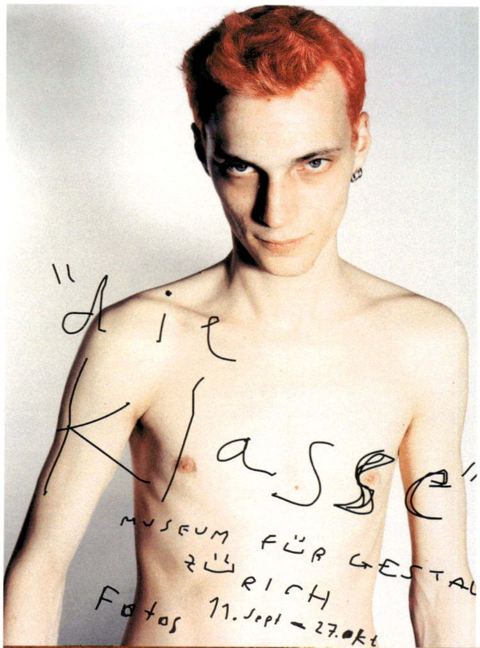

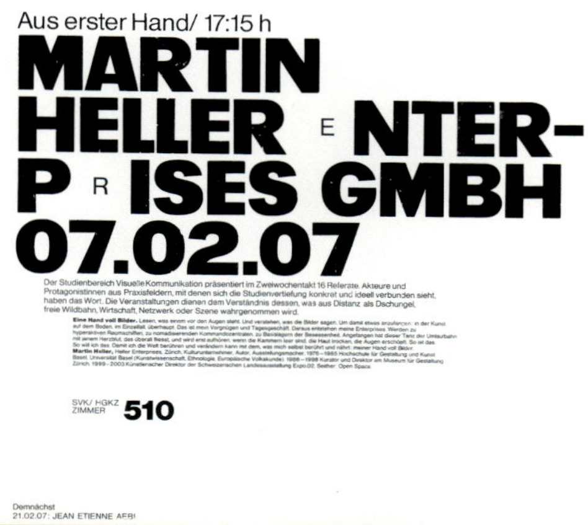

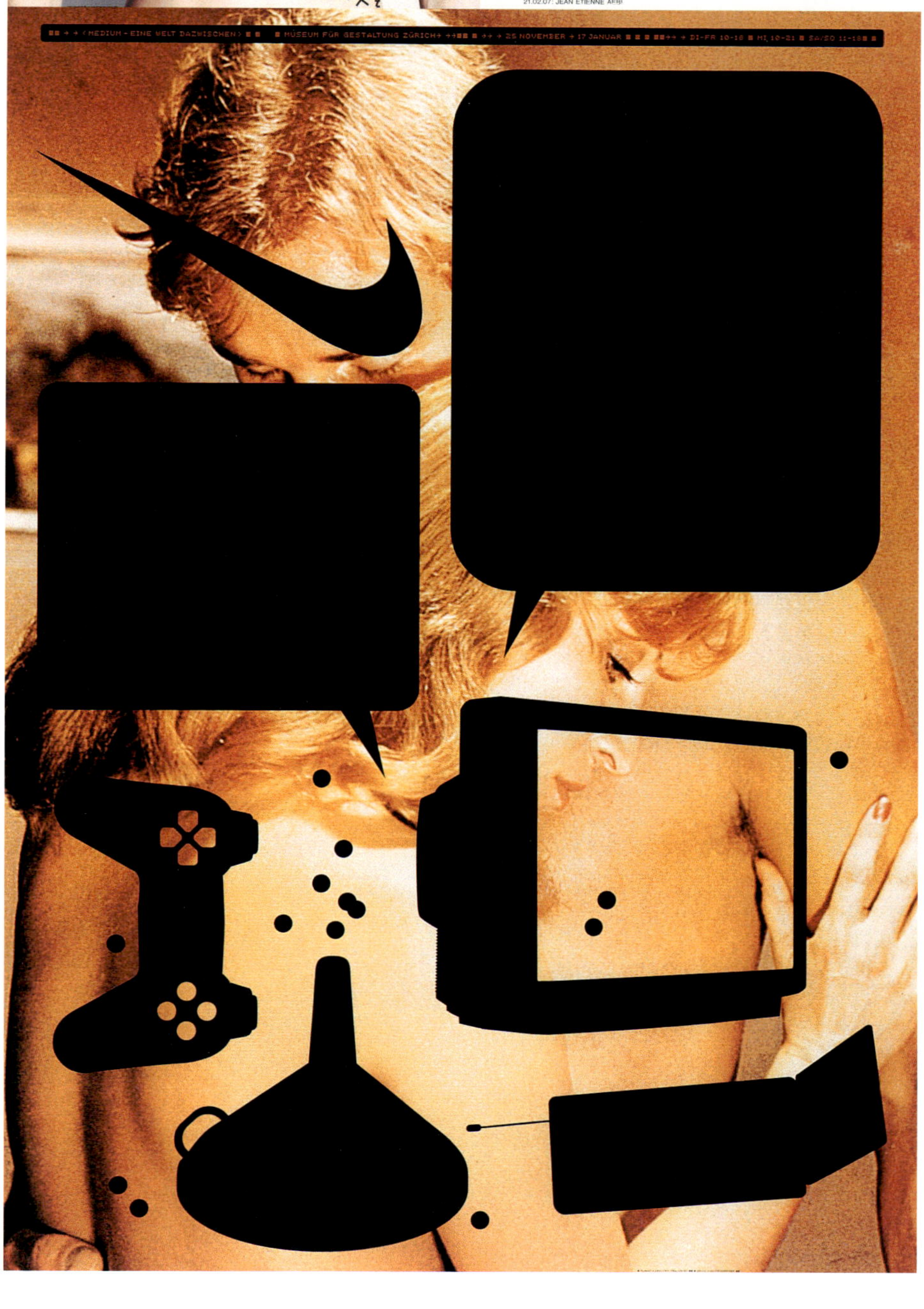

8d Poster and invitation for the exhibition *Zeitreise*. Museum of Design Zurich, 1993. Design Cornel Windlin, Photo Istvan Balogh

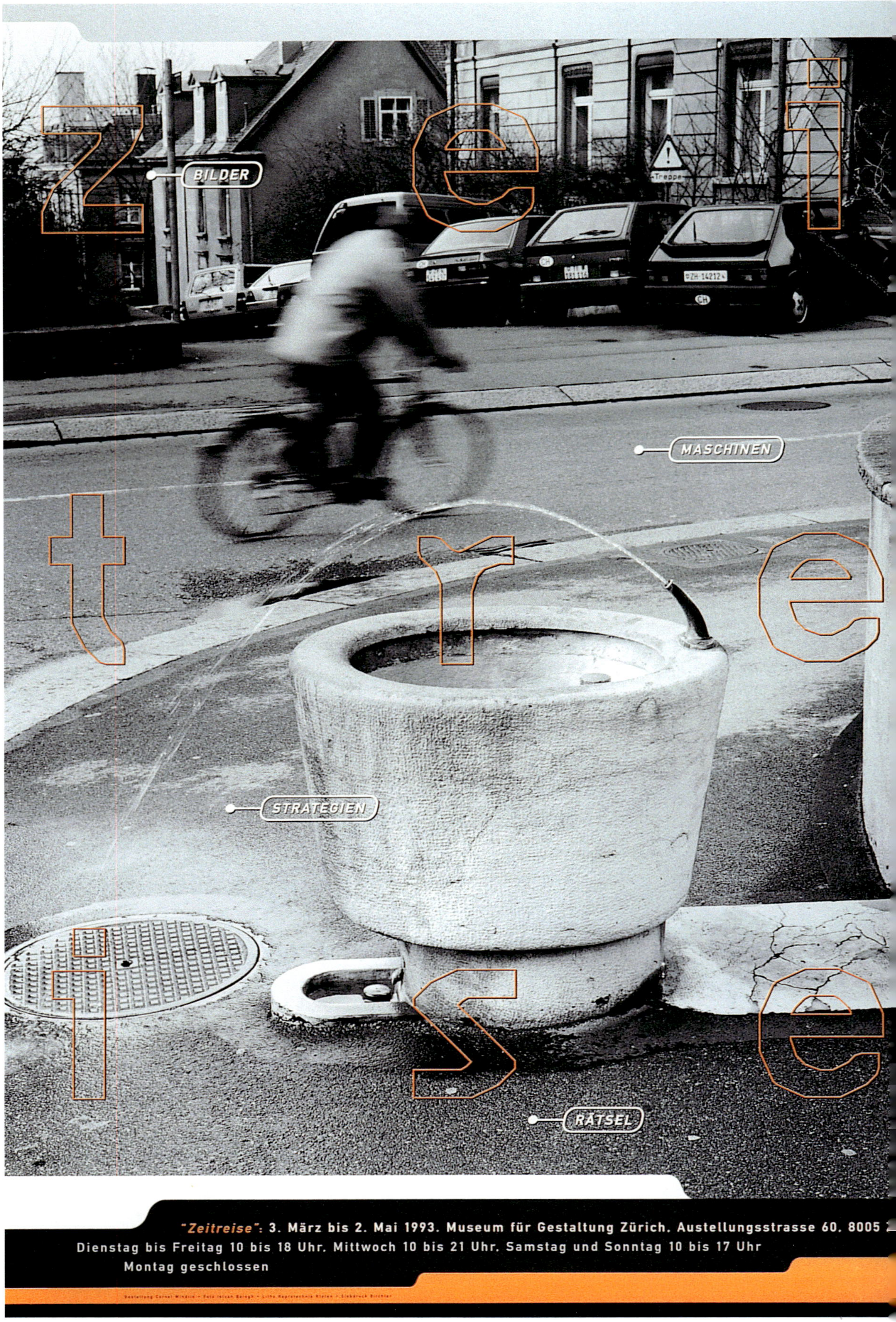

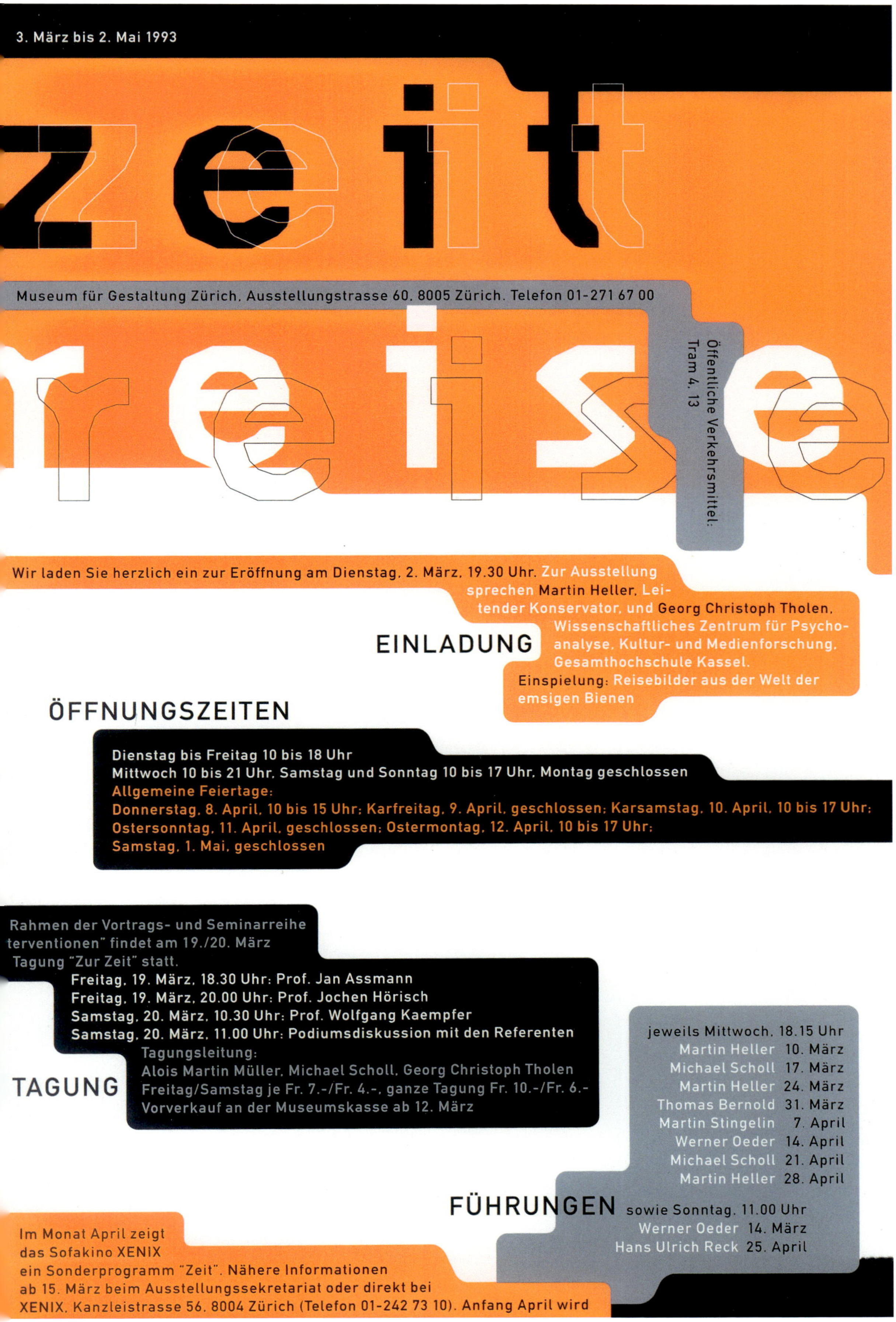
3. März bis 2. Mai 1993
zeit
Museum für Gestaltung Zürich, Ausstellungstrasse 60, 8005 Zürich, Telefon 01-271 67 00
reise
Öffentliche Verkehrsmittel: Tram 4, 13
Wir laden Sie herzlich ein zur Eröffnung am Dienstag, 2. März, 19.30 Uhr. Zur Ausstellung sprechen Martin Heller, Leitender Konservator, und Georg Christoph Tholen, Wissenschaftliches Zentrum für Psychoanalyse, Kultur- und Medienforschung, Gesamthochschule Kassel.
Einspielung: Reisebilder aus der Welt der emsigen Bienen
EINLADUNG
ÖFFNUNGSZEITEN
Dienstag bis Freitag 10 bis 18 Uhr
Mittwoch 10 bis 21 Uhr, Samstag und Sonntag 10 bis 17 Uhr, Montag geschlossen
Allgemeine Feiertage:
Donnerstag, 8. April, 10 bis 15 Uhr; Karfreitag, 9. April, geschlossen; Karsamstag, 10. April, 10 bis 17 Uhr;
Ostersonntag, 11. April, geschlossen; Ostermontag, 12. April, 10 bis 17 Uhr;
Samstag, 1. Mai, geschlossen
Rahmen der Vortrags- und Seminarreihe
terventionen" findet am 19./20. März
Tagung "Zur Zeit" statt.
Freitag, 19. März, 18.30 Uhr: Prof. Jan Assmann
Freitag, 19. März, 20.00 Uhr: Prof. Jochen Hörisch
Samstag, 20. März, 10.30 Uhr: Prof. Wolfgang Kaempfer
Samstag, 20. März, 11.00 Uhr: Podiumsdiskussion mit den Referenten
Tagungsleitung:
Alois Martin Müller, Michael Scholl, Georg Christoph Tholen
Freitag/Samstag je Fr. 7.-/Fr. 4.-, ganze Tagung Fr. 10.-/Fr. 6.-
Vorverkauf an der Museumskasse ab 12. März
TAGUNG
jeweils Mittwoch, 18.15 Uhr
Martin Heller 10. März
Michael Scholl 17. März
Martin Heller 24. März
Thomas Bernold 31. März
Martin Stingelin 7. April
Werner Oeder 14. April
Michael Scholl 21. April
Martin Heller 28. April
FÜHRUNGEN sowie Sonntag, 11.00 Uhr
Werner Oeder 14. März
Hans Ulrich Reck 25. April
Im Monat April zeigt
das Sofakino XENIX
ein Sonderprogramm "Zeit". Nähere Informationen
ab 15. März beim Ausstellungssekretariat oder direkt bei
XENIX, Kanzleistrasse 56, 8004 Zürich (Telefon 01-242 73 10). Anfang April wird

8e *Herzblut: Populäre Gestaltung aus der Schweiz*, 1987. Exhibition at the Museum of Design Zurich. Concept Martin Heller/Walter Keller, poster Hans-Rudolf Lutz

8f *Letten It Be: Eine Stadt und ihr Problem*, 1995. Exhibition at the Museum of Design Zurich. Concept Martin Heller/Claude Lichtenstein, poster Daniel Volkart

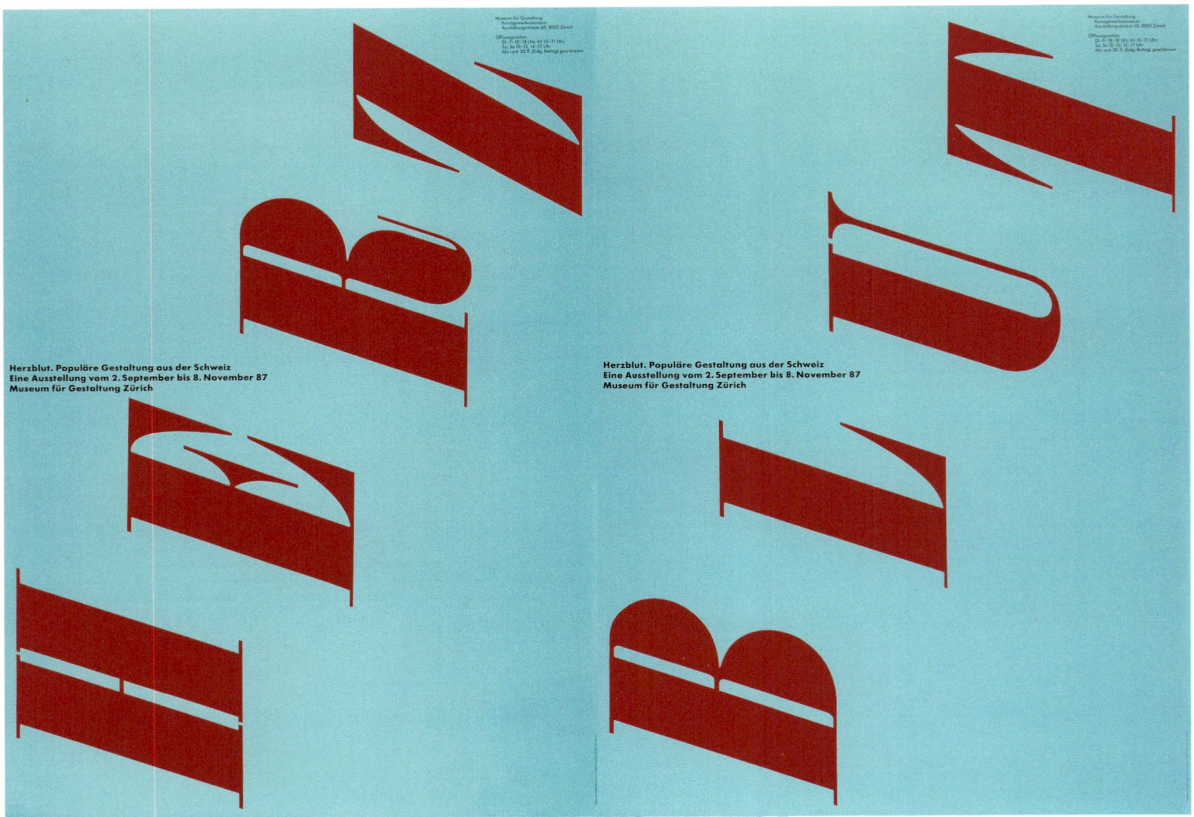

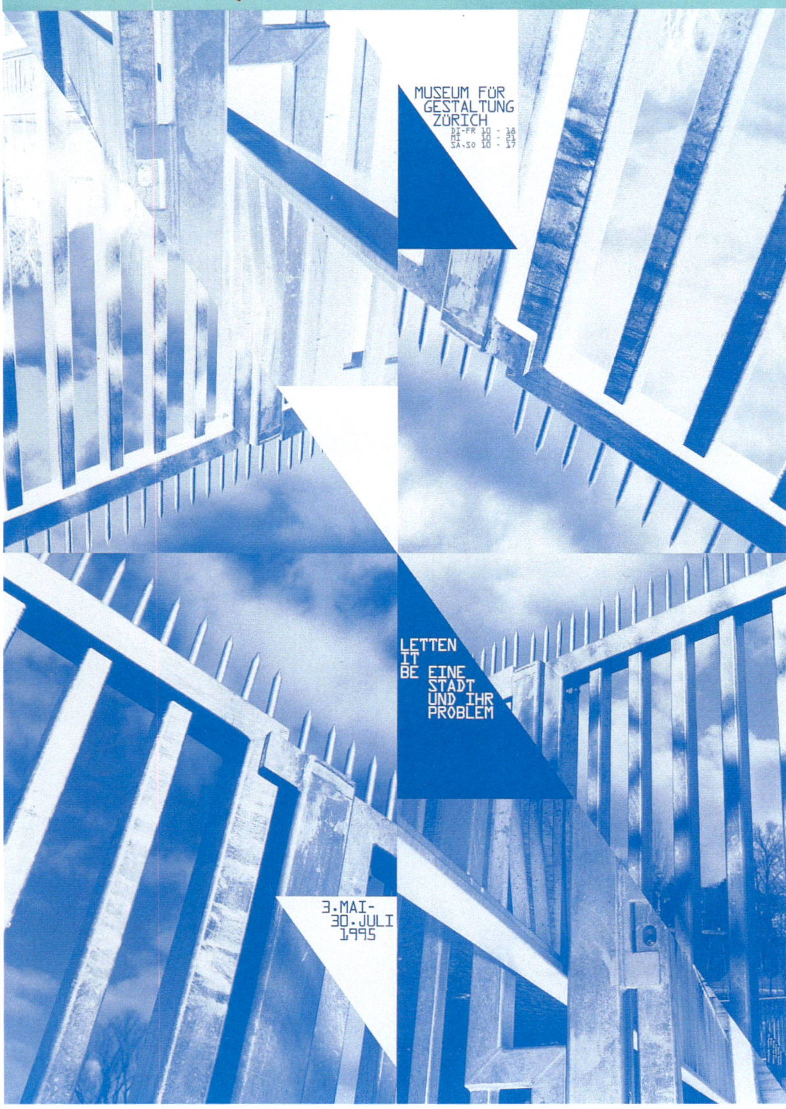

8g–i *Im Angesicht des Todes: Fotografien aus Kambodscha,* 1995. Project manager Martin Heller, poster Cornel Windlin.—*Wissenschaftliches Zeichnen,* 1990. Exhibition at the Museum of Design Zurich. Project manager Martin Heller, poster Polly Bertram/Daniel Volkart.—*Hoffnung und Widerstand,* 1998. Exhibition at the Museum of Design Zurich. Project manager Martin Heller, poster Cornel Windlin

9a *Industrie Bild,* 1994. Exhibition catalogue, cover detail. Fotomuseum Winterthur, curator Urs Stahel

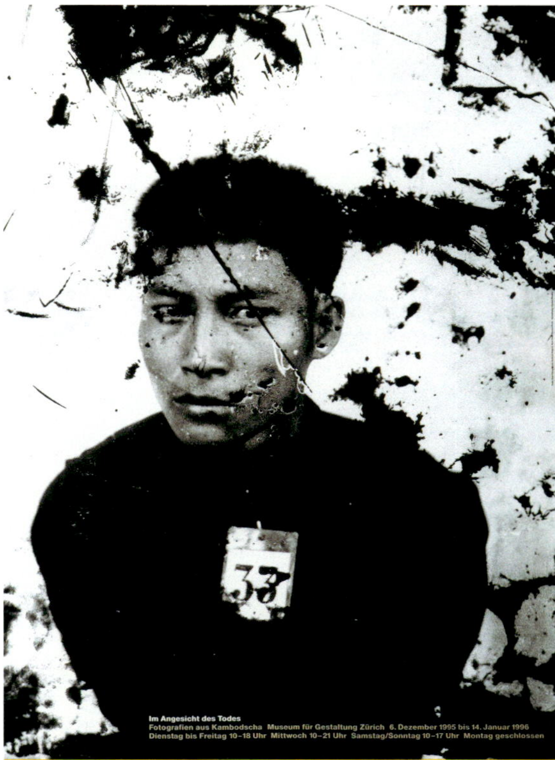

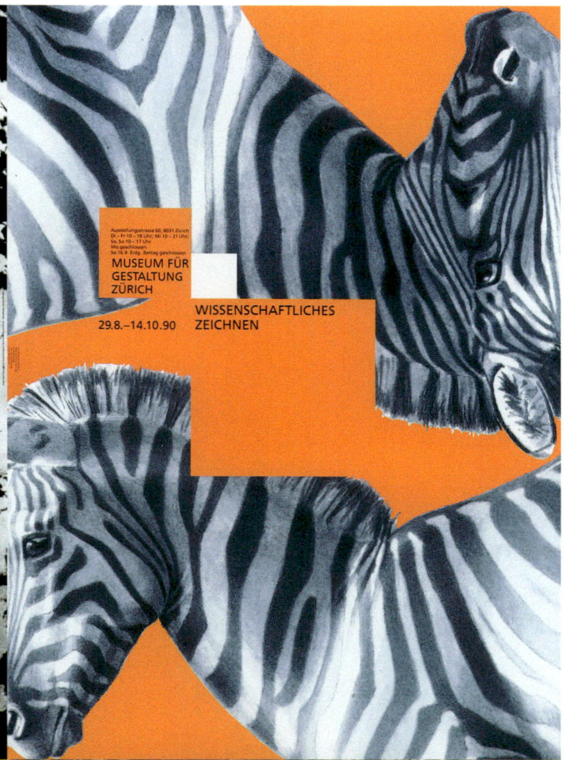

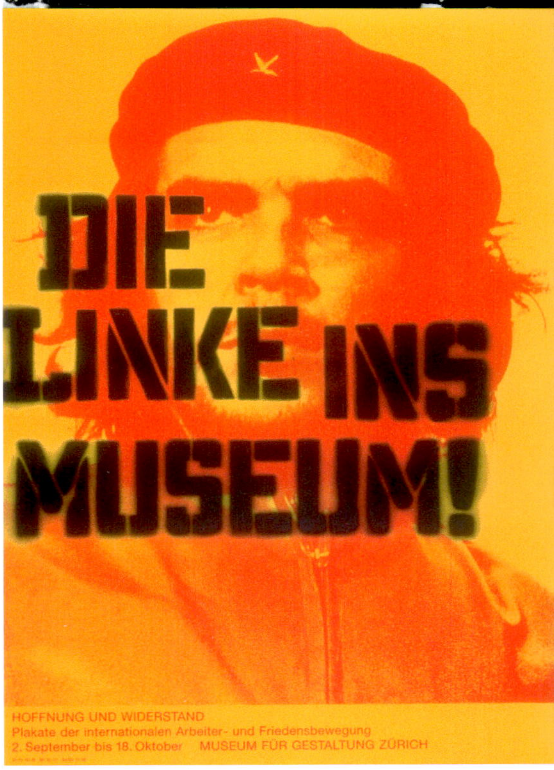

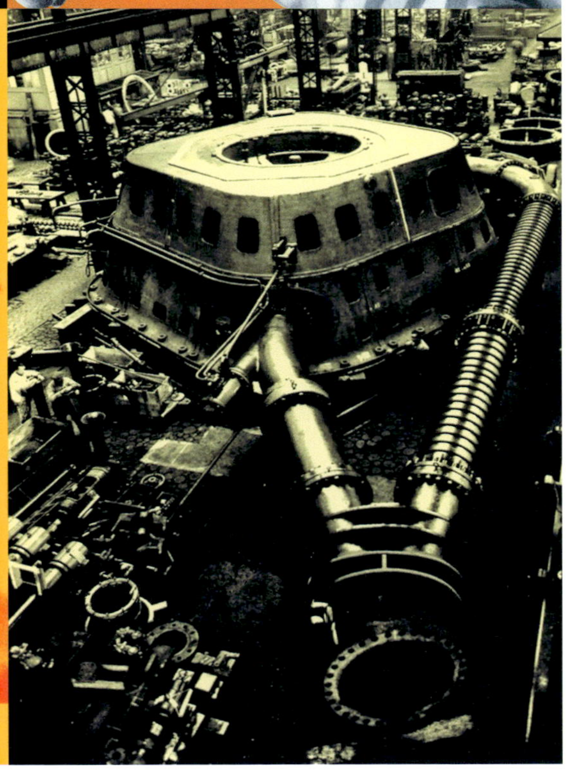

9b–e Invitation cards for exhibitions at Fotomuseum Winterthur. Curator Urs Stahel, design Jean Robert & Käti Durrer, Trix Wetter, Hanna Koller

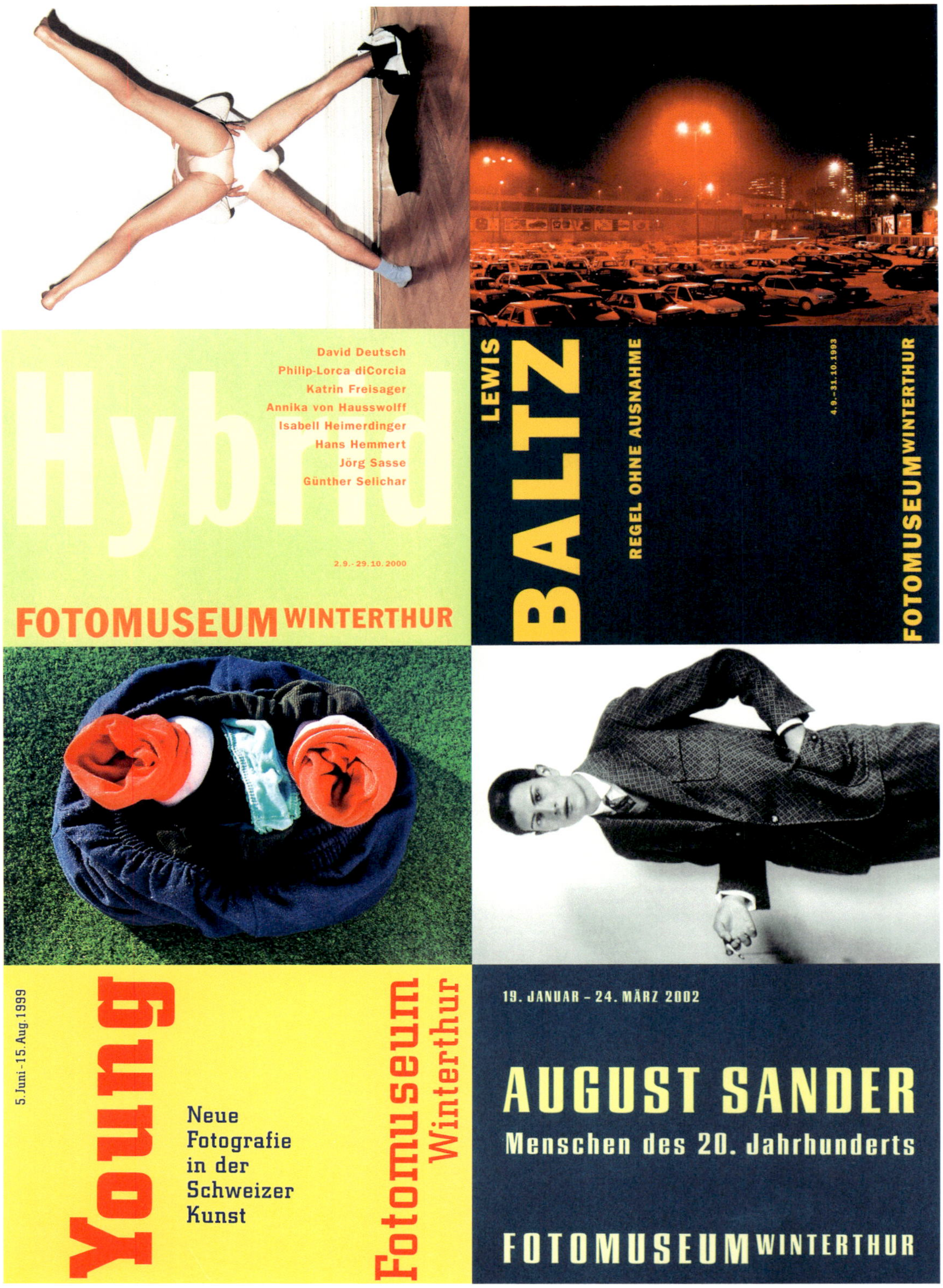

9f/g Invitation cards for exhibitions at Fotomuseum Winterthur. Curator Urs Stahel, design Jean Robert & Käti Durrer, Trix Wetter, Hanna Koller

9h *Wichtige Bilder,* 1990. Exhibition at the Museum of Design Zurich. Concept Martin Heller/Urs Stahel, poster Jean Robert & Käti Durrer, Zurich

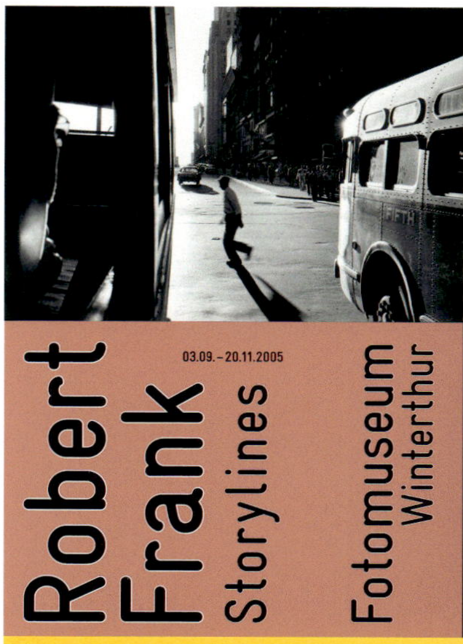

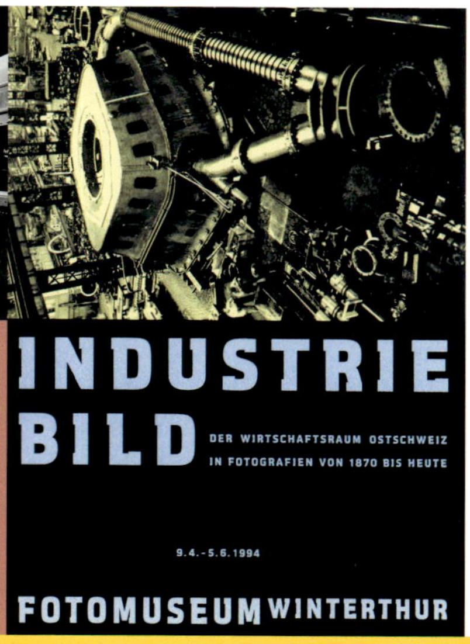

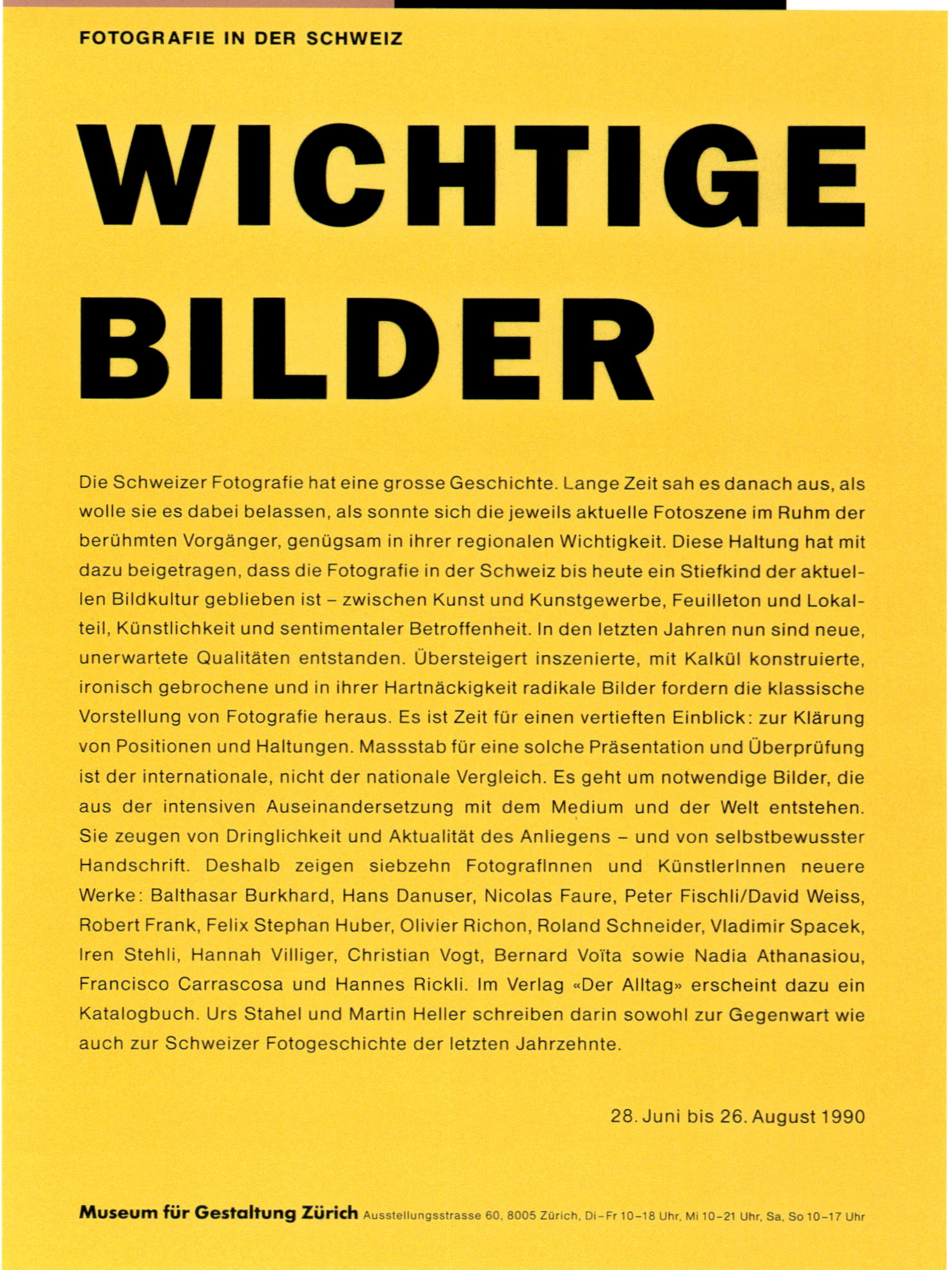

Acknowledgments

This collage of text and images has been put together by many different authors. To all of them we extend our heartfelt thanks for the commitment and the unflagging effort they put into giving this immense project such opulent form.

The musical past and present and its protagonists were intoned by the euphonious pens of Michael Eidenbenz, Daniel Fueter, Patrick Müller, and Hans-Peter Schwarz, while the film classics were cast and credited by Thomas Schärer; Ruedi Widmer worked out the portraits of our thinkers and critics; and Ursula Pellaton outlined the light-footed lives of our dancers. The dramatis personae were illuminated by Peter Danzeisen, Petra Fischer, Christoph Kuhn, Ralph Müller, Anton Rey, Lukas Schmocker, and Hartmut Wickert, with special thanks to Christoph Kuhn for harmonious casting of characters. Many portraits from art and design were written by Urs Fanger. We would also like to thank Janine Schiller, who relentlessly rounded up the texts, subjected them to meticulous editing, and suggested many sensible alterations.

For the Visual Worlds we would like first and foremost to thank Claudia Hürlimann, who showed great commitment in finding ever-new sources of material and navigated the flood of images with great skill; we are equally grateful to Kurt Eckert, whose vast store of visual memories supplied us with ever fresh images; Daniela Huser, who took on the visual aspects of the acoustic arts; Rilli Scanzi and Guido Krummenacher, who generously opened up their archives; Ursula Rey, who enriched the dramatic view; Ursula Pellaton and Thomas Schärer, who illustrated dance and film; Claudia Götz, to whom we owe the technical perfection of the scanned material; Regula Bearth and Betti Fleck, who edited the photographic material. Further valuable contributions came from Bettina Richter (Poster Collection), Barbara Junod (Graphic Design Collection), Regula Blass (Swiss Institute for Art Research, SIK), Martin Dreier (Swiss Theater Collection), and Sandra Floreano. We would also like to thank the many people who cannot be named here who assisted us with this publication, in particular all the artists we portrayed and who generously provided documentation.

Credits

p. 159, fig. 1: Werner Bischof in the Zurich School of Applied Arts, 1933, photo: Luzzi Herzog-Wolgensinger, Fotostiftung Schweiz;
fig. 2: © Martin Stollenwerk/remote.ch

p. 160, fig. 4: Photo: Micha Auer;
fig. 5: Courtesy Walter Binder;
fig. 6: Media and Information Center ZHdK (Photo: 1952, Photographer unknown)
fig. 8: Photo studio, © ZHdK

p. 161, fig. 7: Photo: Stephan Vanfletere;
figs. 1a/b: © Werner Bischof/Magnum Photos

p. 162, figs. 1c–f: © Werner Bischof/Magnum Photos

p. 163, figs. 2a/b: Photo: Ernst Scheidegger, © Neue Zürcher Zeitung, 2007

p. 164, fig. 2c: Fotostiftung Schweiz; © Neue Zürcher Zeitung, 2007;
figs. 3a–d: Photo: René Groebli

p. 165, figs. 3e/f: Photo: René Groebli

p. 166, figs. 4a–c: © Peter Knapp, Collection M.+M. Auer;
fig. 5a: Archive Walter Binder, Zurich

p. 167, fig. 5b: Archive Walter Binder, Zurich;
figs. 5c–e: Photo: Walter Binder

pp. 168–172, figs. 6a–f: Photo: René Burri, © Magnum Photos (fig. 6e: © Text: The Sunday Times Magazine/NI Syndication Universitätsbibliothek Frankfurt am Main)

p. 172, fig. 7a: Photo: Therese Frare, ZHdK, Museum of Design Zurich, Poster Collection
figs. 7b/c: Photo: Oliviero Toscani, Archive Oliviero Toscani,

p. 173, figs. 8a/b: Photo: Daniel Schwartz

p. 175, fig. 1: Media and Information Center ZHdK, 1948;
fig. 2: Media and Information Center ZHdK, 1960;
fig. 4: Photo: Betty Fleck;
fig. 5: Photo studio, © ZHdK

p. 176, figs. 1a/b: Media and Information Center ZHdK;
figs. 1c/d: ZHdK, Museum of Design Zurich, Design Collection

p. 177, figs. 1e/f: ZHdK, Museum of Design Zurich, Design Collection;
fig. 1g: Photo: Werner Nefflen, Media and Information Center ZHdK;
fig. 1h: ZHdK, Museum of Design Zurich, Poster Collection

pp. 178/179, figs. 2a–g: from: Museum of Design Zurich, *Willy Guhl—Gestalter und Lehrer.* Schweizer Design-Pioniere 2 (Zurich, 1985)

p. 180, fig. 2h: ZHdK, Museum of Design Zurich, Poster Collection;
fig. 3a: Photo: Niklaus Spoerri

p. 181, figs. 3b–d: Courtesy Franco Clivio

p. 182, figs. 4a/b: Courtesy Sonnhild Kestler;
fig. 5a: Alfredo Häberli, *Design Live: Shirana Shahbazi, Walter Pfeiffer u.a. inszenieren Alfredo Häberli* (Basel: Birkhäuser Verlag, 2006)

p. 183, figs. 5b/d: Alfredo Häberli, *Design Live: Shirana Shahbazi, Walter Pfeiffer u.a. inszenieren Alfredo Häberli* (Basel: Birkhäuser Verlag, 2006), photo: Walter Pfeiffer;
fig. 5c: © I & I Fotografie, Zurich

p. 185, fig. 1: Photo: Leonard Zubler;
fig. 2: Photo: Birgit Hupfeld;
fig. 3: Photo: Lena Mayr/framtidsbild

p. 186, fig. 4: Photo: Franca Pedrazzeti;
fig. 6: stimmreise.ch

p. 187, fig. 8: Photo: Sascha Kletzsch;
fig. 9: Photo: Efren Hernández Arias;
fig. 10: © RDB/SI/Willy Spiller;
fig. 1a: Photo: Leonard Zubler

p. 188, fig. 2a: © Dschoint Ventschr Filmproduktion AG;
figs. 3a–c: Photo: SAT1/Flynn Schürle;
fig. 4a: Photo: Franca Pedrazzeti

p. 189, figs. 4b/c: Photo: Franca Pedrazzeti;
fig. 7a: Photo: Hans Jörg Michel, Mannheim

p. 190, fig. 8a: Photo: Wilfried Hösl;
fig. 9a: Photo: Efren Hernández Arias

p. 191, figs. 10a–c: Photo: Judith Schlosser

p. 193, fig. 1: © RDB/ATP, 1960;
fig. 2: Photo: R. Brandt, 1953;
fig. 4: Photo: Giorgio Wolfensberger, 1968

p. 194, fig. 5: © Klopfenstein.net, 2006;
fig. 6: Photo: Dominique Meienberg;
fig. 7: © RDB/Gary Kammerhuber

p. 195, fig. 8: © RDB/Christian Lanz;
fig. 9: Dschoint Ventschr Filmproduktion AG;
fig. 10: © RDB/SI/Hervé Le Cunff;
fig. 1a: © RDB/Präsens-Film

p. 196, fig. 1b: © RDB/Präsens-Film;
figs. 2a–c: © Jacqueline Veuve

p. 197, fig. 2d: © Jacqueline Veuve;
fig. 3a: Filmcoopi Zurich;
fig. 3b: Bernhard Lang AG;
fig. 3c: ZHdK, Museum of Design Zurich, Poster Collection

p. 198, fig. 4a: © RDB/Christian Lanz;
fig. 4b: www.markus-imhoof.ch;
fig. 4c: © RDB/SI/Willy Spiller

p. 199, figs. 5a–c: © Klopfenstein.net, 2006

p. 200, figs. 6a/b: Fontana Film;
fig. 6c: Triluna Film AG

p. 201, figs. 7a–d: Vega Film, Zurich

p. 202, figs. 8a/b: Max Music & Vision;
fig. 9a: Dschoint Ventschr Filmproduktion AG

p. 203, figs. 9b/c and 10a: Dschoint Ventschr Filmproduktion AG

p. 206, fig. 1: Photo: Isabelle Wettstein, 1983, courtesy Doris Stauffer;
fig. 2: Photo: Christian Känzig

p. 207, fig. 5: Photo: Regula Bearth, © ZHdK;
fig. 6: Photo: Zeljko Dejan Gataric;
fig. 7: Photo studio, © ZHdK
p. 208, fig. 8: RDB/Reuters/ Jack Dabaghian;
fig. 9: Photo studio, © ZHdK;
fig. 12: Photo: Marc Wetli
p. 209, fig. 11: Photo: Schnittholz;
fig. 13: Photo: Isabel Truniger;
fig. 14: © Urs Fischer;
fig. 15: Photo: Wilfried Hösl, TAKT 6
p. 210, fig. 1a: Mattmüller + Stauffer, F+F, photo Doris Stauffer, Christian Guy;
fig. 1b: André Thomkins, *Gesammelte Anagramme* (Zurich: Seedorn Verlag, 1987)
p. 211, fig. 2a: Aargauer Kunsthaus, © Daniela Walker;
fig. 2b: Kunstmuseum Luzern, collection, © Daniela Walker;
fig. 2c: Roman Kurzmeyer, *Kunst überfordern, Aldo Walker (1938–2000): Geschichte und Lektüre seiner Kunst* (Zurich: Edition Fink, 2006)
p. 212, figs. 4a/c: © Berndt Höppner, 2002
p. 213, figs. 5a–c: © Ruedi Wyss, ZHdK, Museum of Design Zurich, Poster Collection
p. 214, fig. 7a: Courtesy Daniele Buetti;
fig. 8a: Courtesy Arnt & Partner, Berlin;
fig. 8b: Photo: Urs Fanger
p. 215, fig. 8c: Courtesy Arnt & Partner, Berlin;
figs. 9a/b: © chalet5 Zurich
pp. 216/217, figs. 9c/d: © chalet5 Zurich
p. 218, fig. 10b: Photo: Daniel Suter, © Martin Woodtli;
fig. 10c: ZHdK, Museum of Design Zurich, Poster Collection
p. 219, fig. 10d/e: ZHdK, Museum of Design Zurich, Poster Collection;
fig. 11a: Courtesy Galerie Brigitte Weiss;
figs. 11b/c: Courtesy Maes & Matthys Gallery, Antwerp
p. 220, fig. 11d: Photo: Sabine Gebhart Fink;
fig. 12a: © Wehrli & Müller Fotografen
p. 221, figs. 13a–c: Photo: Noë Flum
pp. 222/223, fig. 14a: Photo: A. Burger, © Urs Fischer, 2004
p. 224, fig. 14b: Collezione Giancarlo e Sandra Bonollo, © Urs Fischer, 2004;
fig. 14c: Sammlung Ringier, Zurich, Sadie Coles HQ, London, © Urs Fischer, 2004;
fig. 15a: Photo: Wilfried Hösl
p. 225, fig. 14d/e: Sammlung Ringier, Zurich, © 2004 Urs Fischer;
fig. 15b: Photo: Wilfried Hösl
p. 227, fig. 1: ZHdK, Museum of Design Zurich, Poster Collection;
figs. 2 and 4: Photo: Ernst Scheidegger, © Neue Zürcher Zeitung, 2007;
fig. 3: Photo: Livio Piatti, remote.ch;
p. 229, fig. 8: Photo: Monika Matta, 1990
p. 230, fig. 12: Photo: Bernhard Fuchs, Theater Ticino;
fig. 14: Photo: Lenka Reichelt;
fig. 16: Photo: Anne Steudler
p. 231, figs. 1a–e: © Schweizerische Nationalbank;
fig. 1f: Photo: Jakob Tuggener, 1943, ZHdK, Museum of Design Zurich, Graphic Design Collection;
fig. 1g: ZHdK, Museum of Design Zurich, Poster Collection
p. 232, figs. 2a/b: Photo: SIK, Zurich;
fig. 3a: ZHdK, Museum of Design Zurich, Poster Collection;
figs. 3b–e: Deutscher Taschenbuch Verlag dtv
p. 233, figs. 5a–m: Courtesy K. Domenic Geissbühler
p. 234, fig. 8a: Courtesy Kathrin Graf;
figs. 9a–e: Courtesy Cornelia Hesse-Honegger
p. 235, figs. 11a–e: Photo: Hans Knuchel
p. 236, fig. 11f: Courtesy Hans Knuchel
p. 237, fig. 11h: © blelb;
fig. 12a: Photo: Bernhard Fuchs;
fig. 12b: Bernhard Lang AG
p. 238, fig. 13a: © RDB/Sobli/Clara Tuma;
figs. 14a/b: Photo: Bernhard Fuchs
p. 239, fig. 15a: Photo: Daniel Rihs; figs. 16a/b: Photo: Anne Steudler
p. 241, fig. 1: Continental (Ellen Widmann as a revolutionary with Heinrich George in *Sturmflut*, Volksbühne Berlin, no date);
fig. 2 and 3: Photo: Leonard Zubler;
fig. 4: © RDB, 2001
p. 242, fig. 5: Photo: Daniel Gendre;
fig. 6: © Cinémathèque Suisse, Lausanne;
fig. 2a: © RDB/Eric Bachmann
p. 243, fig. 3a: Studio illustration Campo News;
figs. 3b–d: Photo: ZDF
fig. 4a: © RDB/Sobli/Bruno Torricelli
p. 244, fig. 4b: © RDB/Präsens-Film;
fig. 5a: Photo: Leonard Zubler
p. 245, fig. 5b: © SF;
fig. 5c: © Markus Imhoof, www.markus-imhoof.ch;
fig. 6a: © Cinémathèque Suisse, Lausanne;
fig. 6b: Photo: Leonard Zubler
p. 248, fig. 1: Media and Information Center ZHdK, 1944;
fig. 2: Photo: Serge Libiszewski, 1951, Media and Information Center ZHdK;
fig. 3: Stiftung Hans Arp und Sophie Taeuber-Arp e.V., Rolandseck (photo: Paris, 1931);
fig. 4: Photo: Ernst Hahn, 1951, Media and Information Center ZHdK
p. 249, fig. 6: © Keystone;
fig. 7: Photo: Ernst Scheidegger, © Neue Zürcher Zeitung, 2007
fig. 8: © RDB/SI/Hervé Le Cunff;
fig. 9: © RDB/Blick/Bruno Torricelli
p. 250, figs. 1a–c: ZHdK, Museum of Design Zurich, Poster Collection;
fig. 2a: Photo: Hans Finsler, © Stiftung Moritzburg Halle
p. 251, fig. 2b: Photo: Hans Finsler, Media and Information Center ZHdK;
fig. 3a: Stiftung Hans Arp und Sophie Taeuber-Arp e.V., Rolandseck
p. 252, fig. 2c: Photo: Serge Libiszewski, ca. 1950, Media and Information Center ZHdK
p. 253, fig. 2d: Photo: Hans Finsler, © Stiftung Moritzburg Halle
p. 254, figs. 3b/c: Photo: Marlen Perez, Museum of Design Zurich, Applied Arts Collection;
fig. 4a: Media and Information Center ZHdK;
fig. 4b: Photo: Serge Libiszewski, ca. 1948, Media and Information Center ZHdK;
fig. 4c: ZHdK, Museum of Design Zurich, Poster Collection
p. 255, fig. 6a/b: ZHdK, Museum of Design Zurich, Graphic Design Collection;
fig. 6c: © Richard Paul Lohse Foundation;
fig. 7a: Photo: Ernst Scheidegger, © Neue Zürcher Zeitung, 2007
p. 256, fig. 7b: © Keystone/Photopress-Archiv, 1999;
figs. 7c/d/e: Photo: Ernst Scheidegger, © Neue Zürcher Zeitung, 2007;
fig. 8a: Media and Information Center ZHdK
pp. 257–258, figs. 8b–d and f–m: *Josef Müller-Brockmann, Gestalter* (Baden: Lars Müller Publishers, 1994)
p. 258, fig. 8e: ZHdK, Museum of Design Zurich, Poster Collection
p. 259, fig. 9a: E+U Hiestand;
fig. 9b: E+U Hiestand, © Orell Füssli;
figs. 9c/d: © Schweizerische Nationalbank
p. 261, fig. 1: Courtesy Jörg Zintzmeyer, Brand Consulting;
figs. 2 and 3: © SF;
fig. 4: Courtesy Lars Müller
p. 262, fig. 5: Courtesy Ruedi Baur; figs. 6 and 8: Photo: Photo studio, © ZHdK;
fig. 7: Courtesy Ralph Schraivogel, 1975;
fig. 9: Photo: Harald Hoffmann/ DG
p. 263, fig. 11: Photo: Stephan Rappo;
fig. 12: Photo: Reinhard Werner, Burgtheater;
fig. 13: Photo: Noë Flum;
fig. 14: Photo: Heiko Brunk;
fig. 15: © RDB/SI/Kurt Reichenbach
p. 264, fig. 1a: © Schweizerische Nationalbank
p. 265, fig. 2a: Photo: Leonard Zubler;
fig. 3a: © Keystone/Philipp Zinniker;
fig. 4a: © Lars Müller Publishers, Baden;
fig. 4b: © RDB/SI/Kurt Reichenbach
p. 266, fig. 4c: © Lars Müller Publishers, Baden;
figs. 5a/b: Courtesy Ruedi Baur;
fig. 5c: Edited and published by NORM, Dimitri Bruni & Manuel Krebs, © NORM, Zurich 2004
p. 267, fig. 4d: ZHdK, Museum of Design Zurich, Poster Collection, © Intergral Lars Müller GmbH, Baden;
fig. 5d: Courtesy Ruedi Baur
p. 268, fig. 6a: Courtesy Christophe Graber, image design/editing: Karin Schiesser, original photo: Katharina Lütscher;
figs. 6b–d: Courtesy Christophe Graber;
fig. 8a: © Renée Levi
p. 269/270, figs. 7a–d: ZHdK, Museum of Design Zurich, Poster Collection
p. 271, figs. 8b–d: © Renée Levi
p. 272, fig. 8e: © Renée Levi;
figs. 9a/b: Photo: Harald Hoffmann/DG
p. 273, fig. 9c: Photo: Tina Tahir/Shotview photographers/DG; fig. 10a: Photo: Arno Declair, Schaubühne Berlin
p. 274, fig. 10b: Photo: Gerlind Klemens, Schaubühne Berlin;
fig. 10c: Photo: Matthias Horn, Schaubühne Berlin;
fig. 11a: Photo: Judith Schlosser
p. 275, fig. 12a: Photo: Georg Soulek, Burgtheater;
fig. 12b: Photo: Reinhard Werner, Burgtheater
p. 276, fig. 12c: Photo: Reinhard Werner, Burgtheater;
fig. 13a: Courtesy Galerie Anita Beckers, Frankfurt
pp. 277–279, figs. 13b–h: Courtesy Galerie Anita Beckers, Frankfurt
p. 279, figs. 14a/b: Photo: Marion Nitsch
p. 280, fig. 15a: Private collection, Berlin, photo: David Aebi, Burgdorf;
fig. 15b: Courtesy Galerie Monica De Cardenas, Milan, photo: Andreas Ilg, Zurich
p. 281, fig. 15d: Kunsthaus Zurich, Vereinigung Zürcher Kunstfreunde, Gruppe Junge Kunst, photo: Heinrich Helfenstein, Zurich;
fig. 15e: Courtesy Galerie Monica De Cardenas, Milan, photo: Andreas Ilg, Zurich;
p. 283, fig. 4: Photo: P. Fantys
p. 284, figs. 1a/b/d: *The Gang* (Baden: Lars Müller Publishers, 2001), photo: Ruth Erdt;
fig. 1c: Photo: Ruth Erdt
p. 285, fig. 1e: Photo: Ruth Erdt;
figs. 2a/b: Photo: Cat Tuong Nguyen
pp. 286–288, figs. 2c–e: Photo: Cat Tuong Nguyen
fig. 3a: Photo: Olaf Breuning

p. 289, figs. 3b/c: Photo: Olaf Breuning
p. 290/291, fig. 4a: Photo: Shirana Shahbazi
p. 293, fig. 1: © RDB/Sobli/Sabine Wunderlin;
fig. 2: © Keystone/Niklaus Stauss;
fig. 3: © RDB/Vera Isler Leiner
p. 294, fig. 4: *Today is the first day of your life,* 1972, in: *Urs Lüthi,* exh. cat. Museum Folkwang (Essen, 1978), © Urs Lüthi;
fig. 1a: © HR Giger
p. 295, fig. 1b: © Wolfgang Holz;
fig. 1c: © HR Giger;
figs. 2a–d: Photo: SIK, Zurich
p. 296, figs. 3a–h: Photo: Willy Spiller
p. 297, fig. 4a: Photo Kunsthalle Vienna, courtesy Galerie Lelong;
fig. 4b: *Urs Lüthi,* exh. cat. Museum Folkwang (Essen, 1978), © Urs Lüthi;
fig. 5a: Photo: Jens Ziehe, courtesy Galerie Barbara Weiss
p. 299, fig. 1: Courtesy Pierre Miedinger, Gary Hustwit (from: *Helvetica,* 2007, documentary film by Gary Hustwit);
fig. 2: Photo: Rudolf Barmettler, 2002;
fig. 3: Photo: Albert Boton, 1956
p. 300, fig. 4: Archive Hans Rudolf Bosshard;
fig. 5: Courtesy Tania Prill;
fig. 1a: Archive Claudia Klein;
fig. 1b: *Josef Müller-Brockmann, Gestalter* (Baden: Lars Müller Publishers, 1994), courtesy Lars Müller
p. 301, figs. 2a/b/d: Courtesy Hans Eduard Meier;
figs. 2c: Photo: Rudolf Barmettler
p. 302, fig. 3a: Media and Information Center ZHdK;
figs. 3b/c: Photo: Pio Corradi, text: Andreas Bellasi, © Tages-Anzeiger Zürich
p. 303, fig. 3d: Photo: Albert Boton;
fig. 3e: Courtesy Linotype GmbH, Bad Homburg;
fig. 4a: Archive Hans Rudolf Bosshard
p. 304, fig. 4b: Archive Hans Rudolf Bosshard;
fig. 4c: ZHdK, Museum of Design Zurich, Poster Collection;
fig. 5a: Courtesy Magda Vogel;
figs. 5b/c: © Verlag Hans-Rudolf Lutz, Zurich
p. 305, figs. 5d–g: © Verlag Hans-Rudolf Lutz, Zurich;
figs. 5h/k/l: Courtesy Tania Prill;
fig. 5i: © Comedia-Verlag;
p. 307, fig. 1: Media and Information Center ZHdK;
fig. 4: Photo: Regula Bearth, © ZHdK, 2007
p. 308, fig. 5: Photo: Geoffrey Cottenceau;
fig. 6: Courtesy Hans Ulrich Reck, 2006;
fig. 1a: Media and Information Center ZHdK;
fig. 1b: Photo: Walter Studer, Media and Information Center ZHdK
p. 309, figs. 1c–g: Photo: Serge Libiszewski, Media and Information Center ZHdK
p. 310, figs. 2a/b: ZHdK, Museum of Design Zurich, Plakatsammlung
p. 311, fig. 2c: Photo: Thomas Kern;
figs. 4a–d: Media and Information Center ZHdK, Institut für Theorie der Gestaltung und Kunst, ith;
fig. 5a: Photo: Geoffrey Cottenceau, © André Vladimir Heiz;
fig. 6a: Königshausen & Neumann, Würzburg;
fig. 6b: ZHdK, Museum of Design Zurich, Poster Collection, Design Rudolf Barmettler and Kurt Eckert
p. 313, fig. 1: © RDB/ATP;
figs. 4 and 5: Media and Information Center ZHdK;
p. 314, fig. 6: © RDB/ATP;
fig. 7: © RDB;
fig. 8: Photo: Jürg Bay, Stromboli, ca. 1967;
fig. 9: © Keystone/Martin Ruetschi
p. 315, figs. 1a/b: ZHdK, Museum of Design Zurich, Poster Collection;
figs. 1c–e: SIK, Zurich, © Nachlass Augusto Giacometti
p. 316, figs. 2a/b: SIK, Zurich;
fig. 3a: STASZ, Depos. 17, Gemeinderat Ingenbohl/Schoeck Manuskripte;
fig. 4a: SIK, Zurich
p. 317, fig. 4b: ZHdK, Museum of Design Zurich, Poster Collection;
fig. 4c: SIK, Zurich;
figs. 5a/b: ZHdK, Museum of Design Zurich, Poster Collection;
fig. 5c: © Keystone/Photopress-Archiv
p. 318, fig. 6a: Media and Information Center ZHdK;
figs. 6b/c: SIK, Zurich
p. 319, fig. 8a: Courtesy Cornelia Falk;
fig. 8b: Photo: Georg Stärk, Foto Grafik, Aargauer Kunsthaus
p. 320, figs. 8c–i: Schweizerische Nationalbibliothek/NB, Bern;
fig. 9a: © Benno Blumenstein, Zurich
p. 321, figs. 9b/d/e: © Benno Blumenstein, Zurich;
fig. 9c: Photo: Rob Gnant
p. 323, figs. 2 and 4: Media and Information Center ZHdK;
fig. 5: Annabelle, 1954
p. 324, fig. 6: Media and Information Center ZHdK;
fig. 7: Photo ca. 1930;
fig. 8: Photo: Ursula Markus;
fig. 9: Photo: Edi Baur, Archives of the City of Zurich
p. 325, figs. 10 and 11: Media and Information Center ZHdK;
p. 326, fig. 1a: Archives of the Zurich School of Music, Drama and Dance/ZHdK
p. 327, fig. 2a: ZHdK, Museum of Design Zurich, Poster Collection;
fig. 3a: Atlantis Musikbuch-Verlag, Zurich;
fig. 4a: Photo: E. Linck, Media and Information Center ZHdK;
fig. 4b: Media and Information Center ZHdK
p. 328, figs. 6b/c: SIK, Zurich;
fig. 7a: *Hans Fischli — Architekt, Maler, Bildhauer (1909–1989),* ed. by Karl Jost (Zurich: gta-Verlag, 1992), Photo: Heiri Steiner
p. 329, fig. 7b: Photo: René Burri, Media and Information Center ZHdK;
figs. 7c/d: *Hans Fischli, 1909–1989* (Lions Club Meilen, 1990), courtesy Abbot Daniel Schönbächler, Disentis Monastery
p. 330, fig. 8a: Diogenes Verlag AG;
fig. 9a: Felix Rellstab, *Stanislawski-Buch: Theorie und Praxis der Schauspielkunst nach dem «System» des K.S. Stanislawski* (Wädenswil, Verlag Stutz+Co. AG, 1992);
figs. 10a/b: Media and Information Center ZHdK;
fig. 11a: Photo: Regula Bearth, © ZHdK, Media and Information Center ZHdK
p. 331, fig. 12a: © RDB/Sobli/Sasha Portmann;
fig. 12b: Archiv HMT;
fig. 13a: Photo: Ursula Markus;
fig. 13b: Photo: Lukas Näf
p. 333, fig. 2: *Ursula oder das unwerte Leben,* 1966, documentary film by Reni Mertens and Walter Marti, distributed by Langjahr Film GmbH
p. 334, fig. 4: Photo: Gundel Kilian;
fig. 5: Photo: Claire Niggli;
fig. 6: Photo: Yvonne Böhler
p. 335, fig. 7: © Keystone/Mirjam Wanner;
fig. 8: Photo studio, © ZHdK, (left). Portraits Martin Heller 1976–88 from: *Imitationen: Von der Lust am Falschen,* exh. cat. Museum of Design Zurich (Zurich: Verlag Stroemfeld Roter Stern, 1989) (right);
fig. 9: Photo: Dan Cermak
p.336, fig. 2a: Distributed by Langjahr Film GmbH;
fig. 4a: Photo: Gundel Kilian;
fig. 7a: © Hochparterre
p. 337, fig. 8a: ZHdK, Museum of Design Zurich, Poster Collection;
fig. 8b: Archive Kurt Eckert;
fig. 8c: ZHdK, Museum of Design Zurich, Poster Collection;
p. 338, fig. 8d: Media and Information Center ZHdK
pp. 340/341, figs. 8e–i: ZHdK, Museum of Design Zurich, Poster Collection (fig. 8g: Tuoi Sieng Photo Archive Project, New York/Phnom Penh, US/KH Z [participant institutions]; fig. 8i: Bruno Margadant Collection, St. Gallen [on the occasion of its integration into the Poster Collection of ZHdK, Museum of Design Zurich, in 1998]);
fig. 9a: © Fotomuseum Winterthur
S. 342/343, fig. 9b–g: © Fotomuseum Winterthur
p. 343, fig. 9h: ZHdK, Museum of Design Zurich, Poster Collection

Thanks

to all persons and institutions involved in the project for their collaboration and generous help with loans, digital data, documentary material, and helpful hints, owing to which we were able to realize this complex image research despite the time constraints. Special thanks go to all those not mentioned specifically, in particular, the artists we have portrayed, their relatives, friends, collaborators, and executors. We would also like to thank the institutions—theaters, museums, collections, galleries, libraries, film distributors and companies, publishers, graphic design and printing firms—and photographers for their support.

Zurich University of the Arts ZHdK

President's Office, Giuliana Casaulta, Christine Domkowski
Photography Studio, Regula Bearth, Betty Fleck
Media and Information Center MIZ, Jan Melissen, Rilli Scanzi, Guido Krummenacher
Department of Music, Daniela Huser
Department of Performing Arts and Film, Ursula Rey (theater), Sabine Albrecht (Zurich Academy of Dance, taZ), Laura Zimmermann (film)
Project Manager "Cinémémoire, an Oral History of Swiss Film," Thomas Schärer

ZHdK, Museum of Design Zurich:

Edition Museum für Gestaltung Zürich, Christina Reble
Museum of Design Zurich, Miriam Ruesch
Museum Bellerive, Jacqueline Greenspan, Tanja Trampe
Poster Collection, Susanne Giezendanner, Alessia Contin
Design Collection, Norbert Wild, Liana Bähler
Graphic Design Collection, Barbara Junod
Applied Arts Collection
Photographer for the Collections: Franz Xaver Jaggy

Others

Sandra Floreano, Kopfsturm, Zurich
Leonard Zubler, photographer at Schauspielhaus Zürich
Claudia Götz, Visualisation, Schneisingen
Walter Binder, Zurich

Cultural Institutions

Aargauer Kunsthaus, Aarau
Cinémathèque Suisse, Lausanne
Deutsches Filminstitut DIF e.V., Frankfurt am Main
Diogenes Verlag AG, Zurich
Fotostiftung Schweiz, Winterthur, Rosa Schamal
Kunsthaus Luzern
Kunsthaus Zurich, press office and collection
Othmar Schoeck-Gesellschaft OSG, Jasmin Blättler, Beat Foellmi
Richard Paul Lohse-Stiftung, Zurich, Johanna Lohse
M.+M. Auer Collections, Geneva
Swiss National Library NB, Federal Cultural Office BAK, Bern
Swiss Theater Collection, Bern, Prof. Dr. Martin Dreier
Swiss Institute for Art Research SIK, Zurich, Regula Blass, Elisabeth Senn
Schweizerisches Sozialarchiv, Zurich, Stefan Länzlinger
Stiftung Hans Arp und Sophie Taeuber-Arp e.V., Rolandswerth, Germany
Stiftung Moritzburg, Halle, Germany
Zentralbibliothek Zurich, music section

Galleries

Galerie Anita Beckers, Frankfurt; Galerie Barbara Weiss, Berlin; Galerie Eva Presenhuber AG, Zurich; Galerie Lelong, Zurich

Theaters

Bavarian State Opera; Burgtheater Vienna; Theater am Neumarkt, Zurich; Theater Basel; Schaubühne Berlin

Film

Bernhard Lang AG; Dschoint Ventschr Filmproduktion; Filmcoopi Zurich; Fontana Film; Max Music & Vision; Triluna Film AG; Vega Film, Zurich

Publishers, Archives, Companies

Edition Fink, Georg Rutishauser
Egli Kunz & Partner AG, EKP, Bruno Casutt
Hug Musikverlage, Zurich, Dr. Anna Katharina D'Uscio
Hürlimann Medien AG
Institute for Cultural Exchange, Tübingen, Germany, Caroline von Canitz
Integral Lars Müller GmbH, Baden, Esther Schütz
K. Kieser Verlag, Munich, Germany
Lars Müller Publishers, Baden
Neue Zürcher Zeitung NZZ, archive and publishing house
Paranoia City, Zurich bookshop, Thomas Geiger
Swiss National Bank SNB, Bern
ProLitteris, Virginia Suter
Weiersmüller Bosshard Grüninger WBG, Zurich

Photo Agencies

Ringier Bilddokumentation RDB; Keystone; Remotephoto.com GmbH, Zurich; Magnum Photos, Paris

A Universe of Arts. Fragmer
selections from concerts, films,
media art are brought together
multiple facets, aspects, and me
be found at the Zurich Universit
Visual Worlds with vivid acousti

from shows and productions,
ys, dance, performance and
DVD and CD to present the
al forms of expression of art to
f the Arts, complementing the
nd performative impressions.

DVD

Art (Media Art)

Fabian Vögeli *Lavaterzimmer* (Lavater Room)
Sven König *sCrAmBlEd?HaCkZ!*
Oliver Marty *Alpsegen, zum Ritornell* (Swiss Alpine Prayer as a Ritornello)
Valentina Vuksic *Harddisko*
Daniel Schibli *See, Berg, Pilz, Fluss...* (Lake, Mountain, Mushroom, River)
Marc Lee *TV-BOT*
Andre Gwerder *I Happen to Know This for a Fact*
Judith Albert *Übergang & Untergang* (Transition & Sunset)
Andalus Liniger *Freedom for Money*

Theater

Jo-Anna Hamann *Auf der grossen Strasse* (On the Big Street)
David Bösch *Frühlings Erwachen* (Spring Awakening)
Christoph Mörikofer *Schellen-Ursli und Flurina*
Marcelo Diaz & Matthias Lehmann *Pausen-Rehe & Platz-Hirsche* (Sissies & Bullies)

Dance

Marius Petipa Dance of the four little swans from the ballet *Swan Lake*
Leo Mujic *Lakes Eleven*
Birgit Scherzer *Erdbeeri Mareili* (Strawberry Mary)
Marius Petipa Prince Desiré's variation from the ballet *The Sleeping Beauty*

Film

Bettina Oberli *Klara und Alfred*
Andrea Staka *Hotel Beograd*
Thomas Ott *Sjeki Vatcsh!*
Claudia Lorenz *Hoi Maya*

Music

José Lopez Montes "GEST..." for ambisonic tape and video projection

Interaction & Game Design

Daniel Lüthi & Christian Iten *Tangent* Goldener Hase
Daniel Lutz *Polygon Chase*
Dominik Haug *Silent Hill*
Renzo Thönen *Rewrap*

CD

1 **22'41" Othmar Schoeck** (1886–1957) Suite from the opera *Penthesilea,* Op. 39 (arrangement: Andreas Delfs, 1991) © Bärenreiter-Verlag Orchestras of the Zurich School of Music, Drama and Dance and the Conservatoire de Musique de Genève Conductor: Andreas Delfs

2 **9'36" Juhee Chung** (b. 1973) In Biel for ambisonic tape Commissioned by IMEB, created in 2007 in the studios of IMEB and HMT

3 **9'08" Oliver Messiaen** (1908–1992) "Antienne de la Conversation intérieure (Dieu présent en nous...)" from *Trois petites liturgies de la Présence divine* (1944) © Editions Durand Oleksiy Stukalenko, piano; Jacques Tchamkerten, Ondes Martenot Orchestra, percussion ensemble, and vocal ensemble of the Zurich School of Music, Drama and Dance Conductor: Karl Scheuber

4 **6'07" Jürg Lindenberg** (b. 1975) *Herbsthauch* for ambisonic tape

5 **3'43" Witold Lutosławski** (1913–1994) *Sacher Variation* for solo cello © Chester Music and Novello & Co. Moritz Müllenbach, cello

6 **5'38" Autum Leaves (Joseph Kosma)** Marianne Racine, voice; Christian Rösli, piano

7 **6'35" Joiku** Christian Röver, guitar and loops; Rätus Flisch, double bass and loops; Enzo Zirilli, drums and percussion

8 **4'42" Autum Leaves (Joseph Kosma)** Adrian Frey, piano; Daniel Schenker, trumpet; Philippe Mall, tenor saxophone; Christoph Merki, alto saxophone; Heinrich Baumgartner, baritone saxophone; Martin Lehner, trombone; Felix Utzinger, guitar; Hans Peter Künzle, double bass; Tony Renold, percussion

9 **4'53" Improvisation über die traditionelle chinesische Melodie «Blumentanz»** Yang Jing, guzheng; Anders Miolin, guitar

Sound mixer: Sound mixing department of HMT (Silvan Gretener, Tobias Stritt, Ueli Würth), live recording in the Tonhalle Zurich, February 2007 (1); Sound mixing department HMT (Samuel Groner, Ueli Würth), live recording in the Stadkirche Winterthur, May 2006 (3); Samuel Groner, March 2007 (5); Lasse Nipkow, August 2005 (6, 8), September 2006 (9), Robbo Vigo, March/October 2006 (7) Mastering: Ravi Vaid

Super Audio CD: Tracks 1–4 can be played in surround sound on an SACD player. All tracks can be played in conventional CD players.